The next day, I went
store in Hammond, Hal
Music, and told Hal I had
thing they would not be
Boy, were they impressed
they saw Les and me! To
have a copy of the photo i
studio lobby. Directors,
producers, and actors
about Les' early guitar
sometimes they'll
"...who's the kid?" in th

TOP: Th
Suns on their RCA
Tour in Osaka,
Japan, in De

GUiTAR people

By Willie G. Moseley
Foreword by Mark Farner

Guitar People
By Willie G. Moseley

Vintage Guitar® Books
An imprint of Vintage Guitar, Inc., P.O. Box 7301, Bismarck, ND 58507, (701) 255-1197, Fax (701) 255-0250, publishers of Vintage Guitar® magazine and Vintage Guitar® on the World Wide Web at http://www.vintage guitar.com.

ISBN 1-884883-06-0

Front Cover photography: Ted Nugent - Eddie Malluk, Neal Schon - Neil Zlozower, Steve Howe - James Steinfeldt, Billy F Gibbons photo by Danny Clinch courtesy of Lone Wolf Management Company, B.B. King - Guy Z. Kline.

Back photography: Lemmy - Eddie Malluk, Briefcase - Bill Ingalls, Jr.

Cover Concept and Design: Doug Yellow Bird, Vintage Guitar, Inc.

Printed in the United States of America

For **Fred Sanford, Sally Patterson,** and
Bobby Locklier

In Appreciation for the Motivation

and

In Memory of Randy California

Not Just a "Guitar Hero," but a Real-Life Hero as Well

Foreword

Mark Farner

First, let me tell you what an honor it is to have been asked to write the Foreword for Willie Moseley's *Guitar People* book. It is my privilege to accomodate brother Willie with pride in my heart, because of the nature of our friendship.

When my manager, Bobby Roberts, first contacted me through our

Nashville office about an interview for *Vintage Guitar* magazine, I had no idea what kind of rag it was, nor had I even heard of its existence before then. When I consented to do the article, I was given the name of writer "Willie Moseley." I had these wild thoughts and a vivid image of what ol' Willie looked like, and the kind of interview it was gonna be. I thought he'd end up being one of those know-it-all, cocky guitar magazine writers with his own opinion and interpretation for every question he'd be asking me.

Way wrong! After I talked with Willie for the first time, I knew he was the genuine ar-

ticle; a good ol' Southern boy with music in his heart and all the right questions in his mind (Since my mother and all her kin are from Leachville, Arkansas, I've got a special place in my heart for southern folks anyway).

I had so much fun with Willie doing the *VG* article (which turned out to be a two-parter) that he and I have become friends; we hit it off like foxhole buddies, and have kept in touch ever since. Moreover, he wrote the text for an article in *VG Classics*, Vintage Guitar Inc.'s full-color quarterly, that showcased almost all of the guitars I've used over the years; everything from that old Messenger with the taped-up f-hole to the Peavey instruments I've been endorsing since the early '80s.

For the record, Grand Funk is called "the People's Band," because of the nature and topics of the songs I wrote in the early days. It was the Vietnam era, and a lot of things needed to be said, so I took the opportunity to speak for my brothers and sisters, and to speak to them as well. There were songs like "People Let's Stop The War," songs about crooked politicians, the ecology, the greed of man and the fall of freedom.

And Willie Moseley is a "people person" to the gills as well, considering the number of players he's interviewed. It seems he can have a decent conversation with anyone who happens to play a guitar. So as the lead guitarist of "the People's Band," I consider my friend and brother Willie to be "the People's guitar writer." Read on and see if you don't like him as well as I do.

Mark Farner

Grand Funk Railroad

Table of Contents

Spencer Davis

TOP: *Del Casher on tour with The Three Suns in Osaka, Japan, December 1959.*

LEFT: *John Kay with his Rickenbacker 381JK Limited Edition.*

intro

I think it was sometime in 1993 when I told Michael Wright: "You take the instruments, and I'll take the people."

That remark didn't represent any kind of attitude-copping on my part; rather, it was my perspective on how things were rapidly evolving concerning the growth of *Vintage Guitar*, and how Wright and I figured into the mix. Michael Wright's "The Dif-

ferent Strummer" column and his other research articles are, in my opinion, absolutely indispensable as the interest in classic fretted instruments (domestic and foreign) continues to increase. Whether it's an unusual series like Gibson's oddball creations in the '70s, a budget brand like Kay, or a bizarre imported line like those Davoli/Wandre guitars, Wright does his homework before presenting his informative and readable essays, and his willingness to do a lot of digging is appreciated by his readers, including yours truly.

That's because I'd rather talk to people instead of rummaging through old catalogs and shipping records. Obviously, Wright talks to many individuals when he does his research, but another popular facet in *Vintage Guitar* each month are the interviews. I'm not the only one who does 'em, but over the years I've more or less settled into doing a couple of Q & A sessions for each issue, and another gratifying phe-

nomenon that seems to have evolved (in addition to *VG*'s growth) is the fact that nowadays, P.R. firms that handle players that might fit the format of *Vintage Guitar* are contacting the magazine about arranging interviews for their clients. Time was, it was the other way around.

VG still tries to maintain a format that is quite flexible when it comes to potential interviewees, and personally, I try to adhere to a policy with a mandate that any player who only plays an Ibanez guitar with a Floyd Rose idiot stick on it probably won't fit into the guidelines *Vintage Guitar* tends to follow. As further proof that this policy is valid, let me point out at this juncture that one recent survey of the *VG* readership indicated that our average reader is forty-three years old (READ: "Aging Boomer").

So since over 90 percent of this sequel is composed of interviews and profiles, it's going to be called *Guitar People* instead of something like *Stellas & Stratocasters 2*. The *original* working title for this tome was *More Stellas, Fewer Stratocasters*, on accounta some cynics might have figured that the export of classic American guitars might have reduced the vintage guitar market to the working title (check out George Gruhn's interview for some detailed rumination about the world-wide interest in old stringed instruments).

But no new essays concerning the state of the international vintage guitar market from the viewpoint of this average consumer are proffered this time around; suffice to say that there's now a guitar show held almost every weekend somewhere in the United States, and sometimes as many as three are being staged on the same weekend! The love of stringed instruments and the music those instruments make still beckons folks from all walks of life to gaze, fondle, buy, sell and trade at dozens of guitar shows each year (*Vintage Guitar* even runs advertisements for shows that are staged overseas).

Two anecdotes from guitar shows I've attended in the last few years *do* need to be told, so this place is as good as any: First, ex-

Willie G. Moseley has been a feature writter and colmnist for Vintage Guitar® *magazine since 1989. He resides in central Alabama with his wife Gail and their daughter Elizabeth. This is his fourth book. Photo by Gail Moseley.*

Motorhead drummer Phil "Philthy Animal" Taylor was spotted at one of the California shows that was being staged at the Fairplex in Pomona by Texas Guitar Shows, Inc., the largest guitar show promoter in the world (*Vintage Guitar* co-sponsors their shows). I walked up to Taylor, and in my best pseudo-Limey accent, inquired: "'Ere! Wotsa drummah dewing at a guitah shew?" To which the spikey-haired percussionist responded by surveying the venue and growling: "Right; ya got anything I can hit???"

The other incident involved the most bizarre and brilliant marketing innovation I've ever seen at a guitar show. A company named Hazard Ware has been selling unusual "historical" t-shirts and posters for some time; they take old photos and superimpose instruments on them to where it looks like the persons are playing 'em. One example shows "the Axis Trio" (Hitler, Tojo, and Mussolini) rockin' out on guitar, bass and drums, but the company's most popular offering is called "Killer Vintage;" it's the photograph of Lee Harvey Oswald being shot by Jack Ruby. In Hazard Ware's offering, Oswald's now gripping a microphone (it almost looks like he's crooning), Ruby's charging in with a left-handed 1959 Fender Stratocaster, and the Dallas Police Dept. officer, James Leavelle (in the light-colored suit and hat) brandishes a 1960 Gibson ES-335; his guitar strap is made from one of those "POLICE LINE DO NOT CROSS" tapes.

The point is, at one Texas show, Hazard Ware had James Leavelle (now retired) signing autographs at their booth. Unreal...

The other ten percent of this anthology consists of several guitar-oriented columns, and hopefully most of 'em exemplify why vintage fretted instruments are such fascinating cultural icons. I've done some other guitar-oriented "Executive Rock" columns over the last several years as well, but the others were commentaries about the *business* side of the "old guitar phenomenon." I think these seven essays reflect the fascination of a singular enthusiast, so maybe other enthusiasts will be able to identify with some of the opinions (and some of the enthusiasm as well).

Some "fine tuning": Another *VG* writer had interviewed pickup mogul Seymour Duncan some time back, but being as how he's another enthusiastic guitar lover and a friend (not to mention the fact that he's wound some terrific pickups for some of my personal instruments), I've opted to include a tour article I wrote about his facility. Seymour walked up to the *Vintage Guitar* booth at a 1992 guitar show in Texas and announced

that he wanted to write for the magazine, and his column is one of the more popular features in *VG* each month.

The essay which includes a profile of blues guitarist Kris Wiley ("Regarding the 'Blues Guitar Gender Gap'") is in first person instead of third person, so it's obvious that it was an "Executive Rock" column as well, and its location in the Table of Contents is where Wiley's surname would be in the alphabetical order of the interview and profile section.

Co-credit for the Bob Crooks interview goes to Steve "The Surfin' Librarian" Soest.

As was the case with *Stellas & Stratocasters*, articles and columns are presented as they were printed in *Vintage Guitar*. Updated information (if known and pertinent) follows each essay.

And this intro also gives me the opportunity to update a few things that have occurred since *Stellas & Stratocasters* was published: Among the interviewees in that first anthology, Forrest White died in late 1994 (see "In Memory of the Organization Man" herein), and Ted Turner left Wishbone Ash for a second time early that same year. Another interviewee (who shall remain nameless) assumed "whereabouts unknown" status under somewhat dubious circumstances ('Nuff said; that's as detailed as I'm gonna get).

The Mosrite factory in Arkansas closed, and Loretta Moseley moved back to Jonas Ridge, North Carolina; as of this writing she's getting guitars made on a very limited basis there.

On the flip side, Jerry Jones Guitars of Nashville is still in a back order situation. Jones's retro-Masonite creations are still so popular that it takes about four months to get one, according to the founder. Jones did apply the maple neck with truss rod to Jerry Jones instruments (eliminating the Neptune brand name in the process); the tunable Neptune bridge is available on Jerry Jones instruments as an option.

My love and thanks go out again to Gail and Elizabeth, and my appreciation is extended once again to Cleo, Alan and the Vintage Guitar staff, and to Bill Ingalls, Jr.

Another positive omen that the interest in "guitar people" will be ongoing in *Vintage Guitar* is the fact that interviews that had already been recorded when this intro was sent to the publisher included conversations with Ritchie Blackmore, all of the members of the Ventures, Martin Barre, Charlie Daniels, Eldon Shamblin, John Fogerty, Stephen Stills, and Bo Diddley, among others.

But in the meantime, I hope you enjoy this assemblage.

—W.G.M.

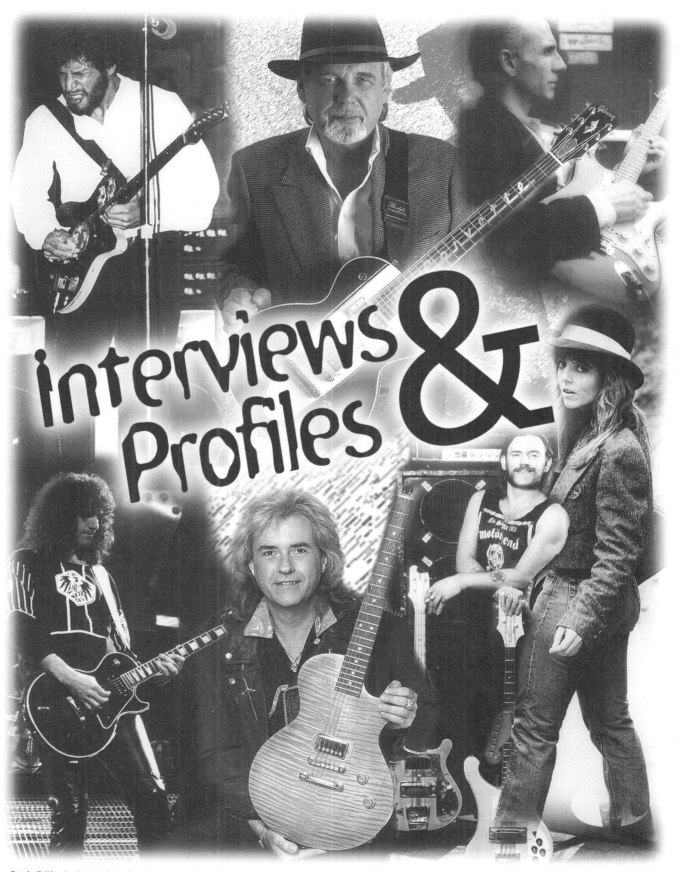

interviews & Profiles

Randy California photo by Brian Record, courtesy of Bruce Pates. Duane Eddy photo by Miki Slingsby, London, England. Larry Carlton courtesy of Larry Carlton. Debbie Davies photo by Cari Pike. Lemmy photo courtesy of Rickenbacker International Corp. Howard Leese photo courtesy of Howard Leese. Bruce Kulick photo courtesy of Bruce Kulick.

R.C. "Dick" Allen

Guitar History in the Golden State

Dick Allen may not be a household name among vintage guitar enthusiasts, but he's been involved in the California guitar and music scene for decades. Mr. Allen not only plays and collects instruments, he builds them as well. Among his more notable clients (and friends) were players such as Merle Travis and Joe Maphis; he also knew Paul Bigsby and other builders in the early days of the California electric guitar industry. Recently Mr. Allen sat down to reminisce about his years of experience in the fretted instrument scene in Southern California. Allen was interviewed at a Pomona guitar show, where he had brought three classic instruments for display at the *Vintage Guitar* booth, and our first comment concerned one of those instruments:

VG: I'm a bit embarrassed to admit this, but I didn't realize that the 1948 Bigsby solidbody you've brought to a couple of shows is in Tom Wheeler's *American Guitars*, in the Bigsby chapter. I happened to thumb through it for the first time in months the other day, and I did a double take when I saw your instrument.

DA: The Martin with the Bigsby neck on it that I brought to this show is in there as well. The book also has my Epiphone Triumph, my early Mosrite, and my Rickenbacker Ken Roberts model. I had some instruments on display at a Los Angeles guitar show back in the late

Seventies, and Tom Wheeler was there taking pictures. He took a photo of my Bigsby and some others but they didn't turn out, so I took some photos and sent them to him. The Bigsby guitar won the prize at that show as the most historically-important instrument.

VG: What about your personal reasons for wanting to play guitar?

DA: I got polio in 1948; I was just laying there with my leg in a cast, and I started trying to play my mother's ukelele. The high school had a jazz band which had a couple of guitar players; one of them was about to graduate, so I got him to show me a couple of chords. The next year I took his place. The guitars I used back then were a Gibson Century model that someone had put a pickup on, and a Gibson L-50.

We called that kind of music "jazz," but it was really "swing"; Benny Goodman, Glenn Miller-type stuff. "Western Swing" soon came around, and I got to play rhythm guitar with Jimmy Bryant at Sunday afternoon jam sessions at clubs in El Monte; I did that a *lot*.

VG: Did you enjoy playing those types of music more than other styles?

DA: Well, I'd been listening to country music since the mid-Forties. Western Swing and Country overlapped a lot, of course. I think the best Western Swing music came from this coast.

VG: So what got you interested in *building* guitars?

DA: Around 1950, I saw a picture of Merle Travis holding his Bigsby guitar; the photo was

TOP: *Mid-Seventies Dick Allen with Merle Travis's Gibson Super 400.*

LEFT: *1957: Dick Allen (right) with his mentor, Merle Travis (2nd from right) in a restaurant following a performance.*

RIGHT: *Merle Travis onstage with Dick Allen's Gretsch Country Club; that's Joe Maphis on the left.*

in a Hank Thompson songbook. I really liked the looks of it, so I built a crude copy. Then in 1952 I bought the Bigsby that I still own, but Merle's Bigsby was what inspired me to become a builder.

VG: Details concerning your own Bigsby guitar?

DA: It belonged to a player named George Grohs; he'd built Paul Bigsby's shop in exchange for the guitar. Grohs was the one who designed the peghead of this guitar. Originally, Merle's peghead was different; the scroll on it went the other way. He got Bigsby to change it like this one, which was the second one made; Merle's was the first. Neither guitar had a cutaway originally, either.

You see, I had Merle's guitar off and on for a couple of years; I'd borrow it, and at one time he was thinking about burning it because he was so upset about Fender. I got it and gave it to Joe Maphis to be sure nothing happened to it. Merle was having health problems and was in pretty bad shape. Later on, Merle was glad we took care of the guitar, but while I had it I studied it real close. If you ever get to see the case for Merle's guitar, you'll see that the case looks like it's a couple of inches too long, and that was because the original peghead scroll was different. But my guitar fits the case perfectly.

After I bought George Grohs's Bigsby in 1952, I got Paul Bigsby to make it just like Merle's, which meant that my Bigsby got a cutaway, an armrest, a pickup ring, and a bridge like Merle's instrument.

VG: Did you ever play with Merle Travis and Joe Maphis?

DA: Not in public; I'd go over to Merle's house and we'd show each other new chords. I did repair work for him as well.

VG: The peghead story you just related is another facet of the Bigsby-Travis-Fender solidbody guitar design controversy.

DA: I know, but that story has been around so long that I don't think it will ever be resolved, and since Merle and Leo are both deceased, I don't think it needs to be stirred up any more than it already has been.

VG: When did you get the Stromberg you brought to the show today?

DA: Actually, I bought that guitar in 1952, just before I bought the Bigsby. The rhythm player for Roy Lanham & the Whipporwills, a guy named Gene Monback, had a Stromberg, and I thought that was the prettiest guitar I'd ever seen. One day I went into a music store in downtown Los Angeles, and they showed me a Stromberg they'd just gotten in on trade; Oscar Moore had traded it in on an electric L-5, and I bought it the same day. I walked out with it for $250. It's a nineteen-inch wide "400," I think it was made in 1946. As far as volume goes, the Stromberg "barks" (laughs); you can hear it clearly as far away as fifty to a hundred feet. One time I was comparing it to a D'Angelico Excel, and the Excel "died" after about ten feet. But the Stromberg will stand right up and "bite" you! (chuckles)

VG: Was the Stromberg the first instrument you ever bought for yourself?

DA: No, I did buy the L-50 I mentioned previously, when I was playing in that high school jazz band. I got it new; I got my grandmother to co-sign for it.

VG: You showed me a photo of Travis and Maphis playing onstage together, and

TOP: *Friends in the Fifties: Chet Atkins and Dick Allen.*

MIDDLE: *R.C. Allen at the Vintage Guitar booth at a Pomona Guitar Show. He owns the three instruments on display behind him.*

LEFT: *Two current examples of R.C. Allen's archtop electrics, with different finishes, pickups, and hardware.*

RIGHT: *A guitar made by Dick Allen for Merle Travis graces the cover of the thumbpicker's Strictly Guitar album*

3

Travis is using a Gretsch guitar with "Dick Allen" on the fretboard.

DA: That's a Country Club; a friend of mine named Gary Lambert had one made with his name on it, so I got one made as well. I also ordered it with chrome parts instead of gold. I got it around 1956.

I took the guitar down to "Town Hall Party" where Merle was playing, and he looked at it in the case and asked to try it out. Someone happened to have a camera, so I got them to take a photo of Merle playing my Gretsch. Joe Maphis was playing a Super 400 with a Bigsby pickguard on it.

VG: What other instruments have you owned over the years?

DA: Two L-12s, and I still have one of them; an L-10, several herringbone D-28s, several Gretsches, including a nice Synchromatic that I brought to the last Pomona show. I have another Stromberg, a G-1 that's in sad shape. At the present time I have about two hundred guitars and banjos; a lot of the banjos date from the 1800s.

VG: Have you always lived in the Southern California area? How about "day jobs" you might have had?

DA: I was born in Alhambra and I live in El Monte; I've always lived in the area. I worked sixteen years as a warehouseman for a wholesale paper company; I left there in '67 and went into full-time guitar work for a while. Then I did the service work for C. Bruno for a couple of years; after that I did service work for Pacific Music for four years; I worked on their Guild, Goya and Alvarez guitars; they were a wholesaler/distributor. Around 1972 I went into building guitars full-time, and I've been doing it ever since.

VG: What about the types of guitars you've built over the years?

DA: In the Sixties I probably built over a hundred electric guitars and around two hundred banjos; I also built some electric mandolins and a few Martin-style guitars.

VG: Which reminds me: How did you acquire that third instrument you brought to the show, the Martin with the Bigsby neck?

DA: That belonged to Zeke Clements, who wrote a lot of Eddy Arnold's early songs; his name's on the inside of the guitar. His brother brought it over to my place one day and told me he had Zeke's Martin for sale. I wasn't too interested until he opened the case. This was around 1974 or '75.

VG: What's the story of how and why the Bigsby neck was installed on it?

DA: Zeke had that neck put on the guitar when it was brand new; around '48 or '49. A lot of people were having that done back then; there's maybe a hundred Bigsby necks on different guitars; players liked the look and feel of Paul Bigsby's neck, and I think it improved the sound of Zeke's Martin. The Bigsby neck is more rigid, and it gives the Martin a smoother sound. Paul also made fancy pickguards for people with their names in them.

VG: Back to your own instruments; were the ones you made in the Sixties solidbodies?

DA: They were semi-hollow, sort of like some Rickenbackers. They looked like a big-bodied guitar but they had a flat top and back. Most of them had f-holes and were 1 to 2 inches thick.

VG: The first guitar of yours I ever saw was the one made for Tommy Walden; it had definite Bigsby and Mosrite influences, in my opinion. It was a "Mystery Guitar" one month in *Vintage Guitar*.

DA: That was a semi-hollow model with no f-holes. I originally made that guitar for myself; I loaned to a guy and he broke the peghead off. When I got it back, it just sat around for years. Jess Walden, Tommy's brother, had me make it up for Tommy; that was the last I ever knew about it until I found out Mike Whisenant in Alabama had it; Mike is really proud of that guitar!

VG: What about other body styles you've made?

DA: I've made about a dozen solidbodies, but I prefer making hollowbodies and semi-hollow styles. Over the last couple of years I've begun concentrating on making "jazz box"-style archtops. I finally got the molds for the tops and backs; I'd bought some tops and backs from Gretsch at one point and made a couple of instruments using those. I'm not doing carved top guitars yet, but I'm thinking about it.

VG: What distinguishes your guitars?

DA: They have the same headstock profile I've been using since the late Fifties; that shape is on the guitar I built for Merle. I took a bit of inspiration from a D'Angelico headstock. The bodies of my guitars are similar to a Gretsch 6120 as far as shape and depth. I offer a lot of options to a customer; hardware color, fretboard inlay, finish, and control layout. Pickups are humbuckers or P-90s. The f-holes on my gui-

TOP: A former VG "Mystery Guitar", made by R.C. Allen (Currently owned by Mike Whisenant of Lacey's Springs, AL).

tars are somewhat different.

VG: The recent archtops you've made have one master volume knob and a master tone knob, even if they have two pickups. Is that a standard feature?

DA: I'll put separate volume and tone controls for each pickup on a guitar if a customer wants, but I've always liked the control layout on a Telecaster; it was really simple, and besides, Merle taught me to play an electric guitar "wide open"; he said: "Control it at the amplifier." By the way, I also own a couple of Merle's amplifiers. I have the Standel he used to own; it was the second one made, and I have a 1939 Gibson amp of his; it's a fliptop piggyback type.

VG: You're still at this after several decades. As a veteran builder and player from California, even if you're not a household name, what do you think of the current interest in old guitars and handcrafted instruments?

DA: I think it's great; there are a lot of fine young builders all over the country these days, and that's encouraging as far as the future goes.

I'd like to note that I have had a few heroes in the music business: Paul Bigsby, about whom there hasn't been enough written; John Dopyera, who taught me a lot about repair work. Then there's Bob Crooks of Standel, who came up with a better amplifier, and Hartley Peavey; what more can be said about him.

A few guys in this area have known me all along; folks like Eddie Dean and Jerry Wallace, but even though I'm not a famous builder, I enjoy what I'm doing. I'm not making a lot of money but I'm having a lot of fun!

Conversing with someone like Dick Allen makes one wonder how many other builders with that much experience who are still making quality instruments are around; not just in California, but all over the country. If each of them has stories such as the ones Dick Allen has told, a collection of such recollections would make a fascinating anthology! Mr. Allen is a bit humble about his own instruments; they're well-made and attractive. Persons interested in R.C. Allen guitars should contact the veteran luthier at:

2801 New Deal Ave.
El Monte, CA 91733
(818) 442-8806.

Dave Amato

Speedwagon Six-stringer

Joining an established rock act like REO Speedwagon might be the dream of many a *Vintage Guitar* reader, but such was exactly what occurred for guitarist Dave Amato in 1989. Amato has had experience with other major acts as well, and his love of guitars has taken him to Texas and California guitar shows. He currently resides in the L.A. area.

When *Vintage Guitar* talked with the personable player, REO Speedwagon was in the process of recording a new album. "We've got five songs down," Amato enthused, "and we're now putting background vocals on them." It was apparent that Amato relished the opportunity to talk about his love of fretted instruments:

TOP: *Dave at VG's World Headquarters with Publisher Al's 1961 Gibson Les Paul Jr., (which he really, really wanted to take home).*

RIGHT: *Dave and his favorites: form left a '52 all gold Les Paul, '55 red Fender Strat, '57 Les Paul TV model, '58 black Fender Strat, '58 tan Fender Strat, '59 triple pickup Black Beauty Les Paul, '59 Fender Esquire, '63 Black Fender Strat, '64 white Fender Strat, and a '64 Sea Foam Fender Strat. On the back line: three early '70s Vox AC 30s, three late '60s Marshall Plexi Heads, and six late '60s Marshall Basket Weave cabinets. Photo by Pat Amato.*

VG: I might be putting the cart before the horse, but it's my perception that you show up at a guitar show every chance you get.

DA: Always! (chuckles) I know a lot of dealers, and it's great to see them all in one place. I love old Strats and Les Pauls, and the "atmosphere" at shows makes them a lot of fun. I really look forward to them; I try to go to Dallas in the Spring and Arlington in the Fall; I've been to California shows as well.

VG: What kind of a collection do you have?

DA: I have a '55 Strat, two '58s, a couple of '63s that are refins, a '59 Esquire, a '59 triple-pickup Les Paul Custom, a '57 TV model Les Paul, and a '52 all-gold with a trapeze tailpiece, and a bunch of others. I'm pretty much of a Gibson and Fender guy; I've also got some old Marshall and Vox amps.

VG: Are you originally from California? What about your "pre-REO" bands?

DA: I'm originally from Boston; I've been out here for fifteen years, but people still ask me where I'm from, so I must have a kind of "East Coast twang." (laughs)

I was playing in local bands; I would open for bands like Aerosmith; they're great guys. I wasn't really getting anywhere, so I moved to L.A. in 1980. I played with Black Oak Arkansas for a while; it didn't last very long. The wife of Jonathan Cain from Journey had a band up in San Francisco; they were on RCA. Jim Pierce and I were the guitar players; he's a great player and does a lot of session work. Then I did sessions with LaToya Jackson; I did background vocals for David Lee Roth, Rick Springfield and Motley Crue. I joined Ted Nugent in 1985 as his lead singer and guitarist; I was with him for about three years. I did *Little Miss Dangerous*, and *If You Can't Lick 'Em, Lick 'Em.*

VG: What about the evolution of your instruments over the years?

DA: The first guitar I had was a Harmony hollowbody. Early on, I lucked out and found a couple of Fifties Les Paul TV models, but I didn't know what I had back then, and I sold them to get a brand new Stratocaster. I vowed that I'd get another TV model one day, and I picked up that '57 one a couple of years ago. I loaned it to Brad Whitford, who was in town for a photo session; it's on the inside sleeve of [Aerosmith's] *Get A Grip*. It seems like I've gone back and forth between Les Pauls and Stratocasters; now I have both; probably

about a dozen of each.

VG: Did you do anything between Nugent and REO?

DA: I commuted to Australia and played on a lot of Jimmy Barnes records. I was doing that while Ted was off on one of his hunting trips in the winter; he wasn't supposed to tour until spring, and I wanted to keep working. I had a contract with Jimmy to do several dates, and Nugent unexpectedly got a call to open for KISS. I couldn't get out of my Australia commitment, so Ted went back to using Derek St. Holmes, who'd been with him before. After that I played live gigs with Cher for about two years; I didn't do any records with her.

VG: Were you in her video that was filmed on that battleship?

DA: No, I joined right after that. Those weren't really musicians; they were actors, except for her son. Then I joined REO Speedwagon in '89.

VG: How did that come about?

DA: A friend of mine told me about the auditions; I wasn't really a fan but I thought I'd give it a shot. We got together and played some songs at Kevin Cronin's house, then we played some basketball for a while (chuckles), then we played some more music. After about four or five hours they asked me to join the band. They didn't really want to put out a "cattle call" for auditions; it was word-of-mouth that put us together.

VG: Did anybody else even audition?

DA: I don't think so.

VG: You replaced Gary Richrath, who'd been in the band about eighteen years. Is the lineup of the band still the same as it had been for such a long time?

DA: Brian Hitt came in as the drummer at the same time I joined. Neal Doughty is still on keyboards, there's Bruce Hall on bass, and Kevin. 1996 will make twenty-five years for the band.

VG: What was the reaction of long time REO fans who might've been used to Richrath and his sunburst Les Pauls?

DA: Well, they asked "where's Gary" for a while, but that was only for the first couple of years. I've never met Gary, and would really like to meet him. I respect the stuff he did; he wrote great songs.

VG: The obvious follow-up question would be to ask how you play on "classic" REO songs.

DA: On songs like "Keep On Lovin' You" there's a solo that I play basically note-for-note, because that's what the audience expects. It would be stupid of me not to play it like the record; I'd be cutting my own throat. People know such songs so well, they know the *solos* in them too, so I try not to change things very much.

There are songs like Bruce Hall's "Back on the Road," however, which are classic REO Speedwagon songs, but the solos aren't that memorable. I can do my own thing on songs like those and "spruce them up."

I'll say this about Gary's use of a Les Paul: When I joined the band I was using Les Pauls *and* Strats. Some of those songs where there's a lot of bending didn't work at all on a Strat; it was pretty interesting to learn that I couldn't force a Strat on some of the "Les Paul songs." (chuckles)

VG: I Have you done any off-shoot projects since joining REO?

DA: Richie Sambora from Bon Jovi did a solo project in 1991, and I played in his band. He's a great player and a good friend.

VG: A profile of you appeared in *Fender Frontline*.

DA: I'm a Fender endorser; they're treating me great.

VG: The band is still touring quite a bit, right?

DA: We've toured about six or seven months each year since I've been in the band. It's pretty much been domestic tours, but we want to get this album out so we can go to Europe and Australia to support it.

VG: What's the concept, or perhaps I should say "style," of the upcoming album?

DA: We want to keep the old REO "feel," but we're also going for an up-to-date, Nineties sound with some classic REO ballads in the mix. We're touring an awful lot this year; hopefully we'll finish it by the end of the year. The goal is to have it done by Christmas.

VG: Any instruments you're still seeking?

DA: I'd still like to have some Fifties Strats; I love their V-necks and their sound.

Some persons might opine that Dave Amato had some big shoes to fill as the lead guitarist for REO Speedwagon, but the amiable musician is looking ahead, not back. His enthusiasm for his band's music and his stereotypical vintage guitar mania are the marks of a respectable player.

The Summer of 1996 saw a release of a new REO album, Building the Bridge, and the band toured with Foreigner and Peter Frampton.

TOP: *The current R.E.O. Speedwagon lineup: Kevin Cronin, Neal Doughty, Bruce Hall, Bryan Hitt, and Dave Amato. Photo by Breeze Munson.*

Mark Andes

Son of Straight Arrow

There probably aren't too many fathers of rock stars who've had a song written about them, but such is exactly the case with veteran actor Keith Andes. His son Mark has been the bass player with such bands as Spirit, Jo Jo Gunne, and Heart, and is now backing up Dan Fogelberg on tour.

Mark Andes has been in the public eye since the late Sixties, when Spirit's loping "Mechanical World" first began to be heard on what was then termed "underground radio" by some listeners. When *Vintage Guitar* talked with Andes, he was preparing to go back out on the road with Fogelberg, but we started his interview by inquiring about his youth:

Circa 1970: Mark Andes onstage with Spirit in Salt Lake City. (From a photo by Brian Record, courtesy of Bruce Pates.)

VG: Is it fair to say that you grew up in a show business family?

MA: Definitely; my father was an "up-and-coming leading man" in the late Forties and the Fifties. He had his own television show called "This Man Dawson"; he also went on to act in series such as the original "Star Trek" and movies such as ...*And Justice For All*.

VG: I always thought Keith Andes had such a distinctive, resonant voice.

MA: That's why I think a lot of his best work was done onstage, in plays like *Man of La Mancha*. His voice could really be "featured" in that kind of format.

VG: Regarding the Spirit tune "Straight Arrow," which was written about your father; was that the name of some character he played on TV?

MA: (chuckles) My father was a disciplinarian; that's where the title comes from. Jay Ferguson, whom I've known since the seventh grade, wrote that song as kind of a good-natured

lampoon; there was a "Dudley Do-Right mentality" about it. (laughs)

But growing up within a show business family had some unique things going for it; my brother Matt and I got to go to Europe for a year while my dad was working over there, and people like Rod Steiger would visit our house. Dad worked with people like Marilyn Monroe and Robert Ryan. I went to school with Roy Rogers' kids.

VG: As far you ending up in the entertainment business yourself, how and why do you move towards music instead of acting?

MA: My father was against Matt and I pursuing any theatrical stuff; he wanted us to go to college and get a commendable career; we got into music, which is just as bad and just as unpredictable as acting! (laughs) There have been some times in my adult life where I've pursued acting a bit, but those were when the musical career was in a lull for me, like the time between Firefall and Heart. And I discovered that as far as music goes, I picked the right path in entertainment; I didn't have any hidden acting talent.

One of the first songs I ever heard that got to me was Johnny Horton's "The Battle of New Orleans"; it was a "gimmick" song, but I fell for it. I liked the groove with the snare drum cadence. Then when surf music came around with players like Dick Dale, I figured I could play that kind of instrumental music, so by the time I was twelve or thirteen my brother and I were playing surf instrumentals on acoustic guitars; one of them was an old "The Gibson" that we had in our family. Then my grandfather got us a couple of Epiphone solidbodies in a cherry finish with a single pickup. That was sort of a "green light"; the elders realized we'd put a lot of energy into playing those acoustics, so they helped us out; by 1964 we had a high school band called the Marksmen.

I knew Jay by then, and we'd decided that we might want to do something musically. He went off to UCLA, and when I got out of high school I was asked to join Canned Heat. Their producer at the time was Barry Hansen, who is Dr. Demento; he asked me to join.

VG: There was a surf band called Dave Marks & the Marksmen; any connection?

MA: No; we were the Standells for a while, but another group with *that* name got pretty big;

we were constantly changing our name. (chuckles)

VG: You started on guitar; when did you switch to bass?

MA: During the high school band time; the bass player left and I switched over out of necessity. I was able to borrow a friend's Jazz bass and Bassman amp, so I was lucky to have an initial experience with that instrument using good equipment; I think that's one reason I've always loved the instrument; I still play guitar and write on guitar, but I never went back to it as a performance instrument.

The first bass I got for myself was a '63 or '64 Precision; I put a '57 Precision neck on it when I was in Spirit, and that's the instrument I used for years; I still have it. Originally it was a three-tone sunburst; at one point I stripped the finish off of it, then sometime later I got a guy in Nashville to put a two-tone finish on it, and I put a gold anodized pickguard on it as well; so these days it looks pretty much like a '57.

VG: So how did Spirit form?

MA: While Jay was going to UCLA, he and I actually played with Randy Wolfe, who became Randy California later, and Randy's step-dad, Ed Cassidy; we were called the Red Roosters. We played places like the Ash Grove a lot. When that group broke up, Randy and Cass moved to New York; I was just barely eighteen but Barry got me into Canned Heat. The other players were Henry Vestine, Bob Hite, Al Wilson, and Frank Cook; other than me that was their original lineup. We played a lot of great gigs, and right about the time Randy and Cass came back from New York, Canned Heat was about to sign with Liberty Records. Jay and I had been talking again about putting a band together with Randy; when we looked up Randy, he and Cass were playing with John Locke and an upright bass player, doing a jazz gig. Jay and I thought it was interesting, so after talking with them we decided to form a band, and I left Canned Heat; Larry Taylor took my place.

VG: Wasn't Spirit one of the first bands that signed with Lou Adler on Ode Records?

MA: We were the second signing; Scott MacKenzie, who sang the song about San Francisco — "wear some flowers in your hair" — was the first artist. Jay and I had originally wanted a band with Randy to be a kick-ass rock and roll group, and Spirit was capable of doing that, but we also got into this esoteric concept of bringing a lot of influences together; the jazz experiences of Randy, Cass and John were one facet. At that point, the record companies were very supportive; they didn't require singles and such. The whole nature of airplay, radio and concerts was so different back then. Now it's so "corporate," even on the independent label level. In a way, independents still allow some creativity, though, but these days with the major labels and MTV figuring into the business, it's really hard to "bust out".

VG: It seemed like you had a chance to do more bass solos back then, on songs like the extended "Elijah" on the first album, "Dark-Eyed Woman," "1984" and "Animal Zoo".

MA: Those were all done on my P-Bass with a pick. On "Elijah" I think I was using a Fender Dual Showman amplifier; around the same time I got into using Acoustic 360s. "Elijah" isn't on the *Time Circle* anthology that came out a while back; there's another CD anthology that has some things like demos

and such; it's called *Chronicles* and "Elijah" may be on there. I *do* know that the first Spirit album isn't available as a CD itself, and that would be a good one to have on Compact Disc.

There's another song you didn't mention called "Silky Sam"; at the end of that there's a weird sounding part on the bass. Lou was listening to the playback and discovered I'd blown out the microphone in front of my amp; it was distorted but it worked; it sounded real crunchy.

VG: Why was "1984" only released as a single? It didn't show up on an album until the greatest hits anthology.

MA: I'm not really sure, but one reason may have been because we were trying to have a hit record; we always felt like we had to struggle to get our material heard. It was also released at a time when things had slowed down a bit. It had been a bit ironic that the first hit we had was "Mechanical World," and it busted out of Florida. We would have loved to have had more hit records.

VG: Do you recall any best or worst gigs?

MA: I remember playing the Newport Pop Festival with Hendrix; there was also a New Year's Eve gig we did once at a theatre-in-the-round which was close to Topanga where we lived. There were some magical concerts we did back in those days.

There was one gig many years later that might have been a combination of "best" and "worst" (chuckles); I was playing in Firefall, and we opened for a Spirit reunion; I was playing in both bands! I invited Neil Young onstage to jam with Firefall, but when I called him back out from the wings to jam with Spirit, Randy flipped out and shoved him offstage. (laughs)

VG: You and Ferguson departed to form Jo Jo Gunne after Spirit's *Twelve Dreams of Dr. Sardonicus*. Comment?

MA: Things were pretty nuts; some people were going through changes, and the dynamics of the group were very strained. Jay and I talked about doing something that would be an unpretentious rock band, and by the time he and I left, we knew we were going to form a band with my brother on slide and Curly Smith on drums. While we had been in Spirit, a lot of the stuff that had been really "liberating" at one time seemed to get "confining" or "restrictive" later on; Jo Jo Gunne was sort of a reaction to that; we wanted to have more freedom and wanted to rock more.

The headquarters for the band was my guest house. We had a powerful beginning; we worked with Tom Dowd on the first album. But the vibe between Jay, my brother and me sort of deteriorated, and I left. I was very hurt and discouraged, and I was burnt out on the whole L.A. scene; I moved to Colorado. While I was there I ran into Rick Roberts, who'd taken Gram Parsons' place in the Flying Burrito Brothers. He said he was putting a band together there in Colorado, and was I interested? I said sure, and that turned into Firefall. Boulder was rocking in the Seventies more than a lot of people realized; Joe Walsh and Stephen Stills were there; it was awesome and a lot of fun.

VG: But the stereotypical image Firefall conjured up was that of a mellow country-rock band. Wasn't the first hit "Just Remember I Love You"? That's pretty laid back.

MA: (chuckles) It was worse than that, it was "You Are The Woman." I think Firefall was a better band and rocked harder than we ever captured on record; our hits were sugary, syrupy **** (laughs) Not exactly my favorite stuff, but in retrospect I can see how going from Canned Heat to Spirit to Jo Jo Gunne to Firefall gave me a wonderful perspective that I ended up using in Heart. I was on five albums with Firefall; still used the P-Bass.

Heart and Firefall did a lot of shows together; we went to Japan in 1979. We had a good relationship and the same manager at one point. I left Firefall, and one day while I was rehearsing at a rehearsal studio in the Valley, I saw Howard Leese's gear there, so I left him a note telling him that I'd left Firefall and that I was back in L.A.

I was struggling, playing bar gigs at night and trying to do sessions. It wasn't an easy time. Howard called me about a month after I'd left him the note, inviting me to audition for Heart if I was interested. I told him I thought it would work; and everyone else in the band thought so too, so I joined in 1982. I played in Heart for ten years, until 1992; I did five albums with them. The circumstances under which I left really sort of hurt, especially since I thought I was always a person who had a "group-oriented" attitude, but I do think it was probably a good decision to part ways.

VG: What's happened since then?

MA: I worked with Stevie Nicks; I went on one tour with her. After that there was actually an attempted Jo Jo Gunne reunion; Curly Smith called me up and noted that it was the twentieth anniversary of when that band had formed; Steve Lukather took us into the studio and we recorded a lot of new material, but it didn't go anywhere.

Then Curly, my brother and I got a new project called Little Brother going with a couple of other guys. It sounded great; sort of like a cross between the Eagles and Little Feat. We spent about a year trying to make that work, and there were some dark personal experiences that happened during that time. My brother lost his wife, and I lost my girlfriend in a car wreck. Obviously, it has a very trying time for more than one person in the band.

Robert McEntee, who was one of the other players in Little Brother, had also been with Dan Fogelberg for several years, and he got me hooked up with Dan. The Fogelberg band now consists of Joe Vitali, who's a veteran drummer that's played with Joe Walsh and Crosby, Stills & Nash, Alan Fitzgerald from Night Ranger on keyboards, and

Robert and me. Things have been quite tumultuous over the last couple of years, so I'm glad to have this opportunity.

VG: I'm sort of playing devil's advocate here by noting that Dan Fogelberg doesn't have a reputation for "rockin' out"; you've alluded to your experiences in "kick-ass" rock and roll bands.

MA: Actually, this whole tour has been billed as sort of a "semi-acoustic" concept; he leans more on his acoustic-type songs, but the band does a great electric set.

VG: What about tour instruments?

MA: I'm using a Modulus Graphite five-string bass; I really like that low B string. I use a Marshall stack; my rack is powered with two eight-hundred watt Crown amps and a James Demeter preamp; I don't use any effects. I'm also taking a reissue Fender P-Bass as a backup.

VG: Do you collect?

MA: I'm not a big collector; I like to play any instrument that I happen to have around. I have a beautiful '61 "stack knob" Jazz Bass, and a '57 Les Paul Goldtop that Howard Leese traded me. I also have a Martin D-21 that was made in 1965, and a Guild acoustic bass; there's my old P-Bass, the reissue I just mentioned, and a fretless P-Bass; a Warwick Thumb five and a Thumb fretless, a Modulus fretted five-string and fretless five-string. I have a gold reissue Strat from Fender's Custom Shop that's gorgeous, plus a reissue of a '59 Les Paul Sunburst. That's my "arsenal," but I use them all for recording; I don't have guitars and basses that I don't play.

VG: Do you anticipate that the Fogelberg gig will go on for some time?

MA: I think it's a good association; the whole bands connects in a big way. Depending on his goals and plans, I can see this continuing and being mutually beneficial.

I know that I've been at sort of a crossroads in my own life; I'd like to find a niche where I can play music in clubs and at small concerts; hopefully there'd be a record deal as well. I'm grateful that the opportunity to play with the Fogelberg band came along when it did; anytime you can go out on the road, playing music that's worthwhile and fun, it's an honor and a privilege.

The opinion of this writer is that the last comments made by Mark Andes weren't done in a "light-hearted" manner. Considering the experiences of the veteran bass player, his attitude about his past and present situations have given him a keen perspective on his future plans; here's hoping that what lies ahead for Mark Andes will be "in the plus column" of his musical career.

Paul Barrére

The Feats Affect a Feminine Facet, Etc.

The eclectic music of Little Feat has been a staple of discriminating rock music fans for a quarter-century, even though the band had broken up around the time of the death of one of its founders, singer/songwriter/slide-guitarist Lowell George, in 1979. Regrouping in the late Eighties, a revitalized Little Feat began recording and touring once again, with former Pure Prairie League singer Craig Fuller handling the bulk of lead vocals.

But this "Phase Two" version of the band was also to have its share of unfortunate occurrences. Fuller left the band in 1993, and the next year artist Neon Park, who'd provided all of the artwork for Little Feat's albums except the first one, died. Despite such discouraging events, the band opted to continue their efforts, shifting gears slightly with the addition of a female lead singer.

Guitarist Paul Barrére has been through the good times and the bad times during his tenure with Little Feat (both "phases"). The band was on the road in support of its first album featuring new vocalist Shaun Murphy, *Ain't Had Enough Fun*, when we conversed with Barrére; it might be a bit surprising to some readers to discover that for all of the unique influences that meld into Little Feat's music, Barrére was "born and raised in the heart of Hollywood":

VG: You weren't a founder of Little Feat, were you?

PB: No, I joined in 1972; they'd just released *Sailin' Shoes*, and they'd done one tour, which was ill-fated. When they got back, Roy Estrada, the original bassist, quit the band. He'd been in the Mothers with Lowell, and Billy Payne had been sending tapes to Bizarre/Straight, Frank Zappa's label, trying to get a job. Lowell heard them, and he and Billy got together and wrote a bunch of songs. They got signed by Warner Brothers, and got Richie Hayward to play drums; he'd been in a band with Lowell earlier, and was then in the Fraternity of Man, of "Don't Bogart That Joint" fame. Then they auditioned about fourteen bass players, of which I was one; I was playing in a garage band in Laurel Canyon; the name of the band is not fit for print, (chuckles) but this *was* the Sixties! Lowell brought me a Precision; I'd never played bass before. When I

auditioned, Billy put a sheet of note paper in front of me with a chart on it that nobody could read except Billy; it was for an instrumental called "Nubile Virgin Slaves." It was a combination of jazz and rock, and had about four key changes and five different time changes, and I told them I thought they needed a *real* bass player.

So while I didn't get that spot, I got to know the band members, and I got Billy and Richie to come to some jams, and they discovered that I *could* play guitar, even though I couldn't play bass. So they ended up hiring me a second guitarist, to free up Lowell to play lead and sing. I joined when Roy Estrada left; they added Kenny Gradney on bass and Sam Clayton, and we went on to record *Dixie Chicken*; things stayed the same until Lowell died in 1979.

VG: What kind of guitars were you playing before you joined Little Feat?

PB: My parents made me take piano lessons from age six to eleven, at which point I asked for an instrument that I could take to my room, the park, the beach, whatever. I picked up a three-quarter Gibson at a party once, and at the time Jimmy Reed was real hot. His stuff is probably the easiest kind of blues to play; the progressions are very simple. I talked my folks into getting me one of those three-quarter Gibsons when I was thirteen.

I found a guitar teacher in the "beatnik" area of Los Angeles; this was the "pre-hippie" era, and she was more into folk music than blues. I took some lessons from her; learned about six chords, then she took off to the Newport Folk Festival in Rhode Island and never came back. But she talked me into trading my Gibson in for a folk guitar made by a builder named Alvarez. So now I was playing folk music and blues, and

Paul Barrére back on track with a revitalized Little Feat in 1988.

I'd been indoctrinated into rock and roll since I was ten; I had an older brother who was listening to Elvis, Jerry Lee Lewis and Little Richard. In fact, the first record I ever bought was a 78 of Little Richard's "Tutti Fruitti."

When I turned fourteen I started a garage band with two friends. I got my folks to take me to Betnum's music store in Hollywood, and they bought me an incredible '57 Gibson ES-175, which I still have. It had been painted orange, but later on I had it refinished back to a sunburst. I also borrowed our drummer's Stratocaster, which his father had given him. We'd play covers of songs by the Stones, Them, the Animals, and the Yardbirds, and some traditional blues; I'd heard a record of Mississippi John Hurt, which is why I started to play slide guitar; that folk guitar teacher had played it for me. Like a lot of players, I found out that the British bands were doing songs by Muddy Waters and John Lee Hooker, so I started looking for records by the original artists as well.

VG: You and Lowell George both played slide; what kind of "interplay" was involved? Didn't George use a metal socket?

PB: I was playing slide a lot more in the band I was in when Little Feat asked me to join them; Lowell was *such* an accomplished slide player. I used to use a glass slide, but I kept breaking them on mike stands, and Lowell put a Sears & Roebuck Craftsman wrench on me. He was using an 11/16 size, but that was a little big for me, so I went down to a 5/8. I still use one of those; they're great. They don't break, but if they do, you get a new one for free! (laughs) We recorded one song, "Down the Road," where we both played slide; I wound up playing rhythm and straight leads more than slide.

By the time I joined Little Feat, I had bought a 1969 Stratocaster; I still have it and still play it. Around 1973 I got a walnut-finished Stratocaster; I still have that one too. Both of those guitars have been reworked a dozen times. I use them for my slide playing; one in an open A tuning and one in open G. They still go on the road

with me, and I've got a newer Strat Plus that I use for straight guitar.

VG: When I saw the band on "The Tonight Show" a while back, you were playing a black Strat with a large headstock and a lot of wear on its forearm bevel.

PB: That's the '69. The guitar fell over once and got a ding, and I would occasionally have to scrape at the finish where the ding had spread and cause the finish to peel up.

VG: Is it possible to describe the type of music purveyed by Little Feat back then as well as now?

PB: One of the things that attracted me to Little Feat was the idea of Lowell and Billy that it should be diverse; we didn't want to play one type of music or be part of the "pop culture." I think the simplest way to put it is that we play "American music"; anything that has its roots in America, whether it's country, jazz, rock & roll, blues, rhythm & blues; *not* the kind of music you see on the R & B charts in *Billboard* these days. *Now* we're into Cajun music, and Lowell had started bringing in Third World music before he died; "Fat Man in the Bathtub" had sort of a Spanish feel.

VG: What other bands did you get compared to back then?

PB: We got branded as a Southern band; we were lumped in with the Allman Brothers, Skynyrd and Wet Willie. People thought we were from the South. We do songs in that vein, like "Dixie Chicken" or "Let It Roll," but there's so much more; Lowell wrote songs like "Willin'," "Long Distance Love" and "Truck Stop Girl," which were a little more sophisticated.

VG: Were you ever compared to the Band?

PB: A couple of times; to me that's an honor. *Big Pink* is probably one of the classic albums of all time. The Band was always a group that

TOP: *Little Feat today: (front) Paul Barrére, Shaun Murphy; (middle) Ken Gradney, Fred Tackett; (back) Richie Hayward, Sam Clayton, and Bill Payne. Photo: Dennis Keeley.*

RIGHT: *Philadelphia, 1994: Barrére works out onstage with the latest incarnation of Little Feat. Photo courtesy of Paul Barrére.*

portrayed images in its music, as opposed to the "Ooo-weee, ooo-weee, baby" kind of crap, and it was the same for Little Feat. We always wanted to tell a story, and it's a shame that there weren't videos back when Lowell was alive; we could have done some great ones based on some of his songs' storylines.

VG: Any favorite albums from the first era?

PB: There were eight albums from that time; the ninth was *Hoy Hoy*, which was a tribute to Lowell and our fans. As for favorites, I loved *Sailin' Shoes*, even though I didn't play on it. *Dixie Chicken* was exciting because it was really my introduction to recording, and *Waiting for Columbus* is probably the benchmark; it's our bestselling record even today.

VG: Some of the album titles have been beyond my comprehension; *Waiting for Columbus* and *Hoy Hoy* are examples.

PB: The painting by Neon Park that showed the tomato in the hammock was called "Waiting for Columbus," because when Columbus discovered America, he also discovered the hammock and the tomato. Neither had been known about in Europe, and the hammock changed the way sailors slept on boats. So that painting is a bit of a history lesson.

Hoy Hoy is Spanish for "Today Today." There was a Hispanic movie theatre from where we used to rehearse in Los Angeles; its marquee had "Hoy Hoy" on it, with the name of the movie that was showing. It's also printed on the license plate of the car that's on the cover of *Feats Don't Fail Me Now*. Some people think it's from the old growl that Howlin' Wolf used to do.

VG: Is it fair to say that the band went into an extended hiatus following George's death?

PB: Actually, we had already broken up while we were recording *Down on the Farm*, and that wasn't the first time it had happened, either. The band had been in constant turmoil; we were constantly bickering because some of us were constantly loaded, but I've been clean and sober for over ten years now. The problems that arose from that lifestyle got out of control; there was no focus and direction.

However, during the first two weeks that Lowell was out on the road supporting his solo album, he was calling up all of the band members, saying he was going to patch things up with Billy, and that we were going to get back together and tour again, but he passed away while he was on that tour. It was a big shock to us, and we didn't have enough faith in ourselves to continue on like the Allman Brothers did af-

ter Duane passed away, because Lowell had been the member of the band who had been focal point. It wasn't until seven years later when we got together for an impromptu jam session that we realized there was still something there that was worthwhile.

VG: You didn't stay completely inactive in the interim; I know for example that you sang on a T. Lavitz album. What else kept you busy?

PB: I did two solo records that were released on Mirage, a subsidiary of Atlantic/Atco. I was in a band with T. Lavitz, Catfish Hodge, and Freebo, who was Bonnie Raitt's bass player, and Larry Zack on drums; he'd been with Savage Grace out of Detroit and had played with Jackson Browne. That band was called the Bluesbusters, and we did two records on a small label out of Atlanta called Landslide.

VG: How did the Little Feat reunion jam session come about?

PB: Alley Rehearsal Studios, where Little Feat had always rehearsed, had remodeled their main room, and we got together at their request to "christen" it. They had even put up a bronze plaque dedicated to the memory of Lowell George. Everyone had been working with other artists, but Billy and I had kept up with each other; he was concerned about me because I'd started to get close to the way Lowell wound up, but by the time of the jam session I'd been sober for over a year. We got together and had a ball, and we did it again a couple of months later. Then Billy asked me what I thought about putting the band back together with another singer and another guitarist; he said we shouldn't do it unless we honestly felt like what we were doing was in every way, shape and form as good as what we had done in the past, if not better. Billy went out on tour with Bob Seger, and Fred Tackett, who had played on Little Feat records and had written songs with

1977: Paul Barrére and Lowell George onstage during the "phase one" Little Feat days. Photo: Nancy Goldfarb.

us back in the Seventies, was the guitarist on that tour. Billy called me up and asked what I thought about Fred as the other guitarist; I thought it was great. Fred and I had done dozens of sessions together, and had compatible styles.

We were still wondering who we were going to get as a vocalist; I couldn't hit the high notes that Lowell did. Out of the blue, Craig Fuller called Billy on some publishing matters about some songs that they had written together; he'd sung in Pure Prairie League and the Kaz-Fuller Band, which was the last band to tour with Little Feat before Lowell died. He sounded good, and we spent the rest of '86 and most of '87 writing songs for *Let It Roll*, which was a good record; it was strong and did well.

We did two more records, then Craig told us he couldn't take the "road life" anymore. We were sitting around writing songs, wondering what we were going to do, and we got Shaun Murphy to sing backup on some demos; she'd sung background vocals for us before, and she'd sung with Seger and Eric Clapton. She did things on *Let It Roll*, *Representing the Mambo* and *Shake Me Up* that made the hair stand up on our arms and the backs of our necks! So she was at my house doing the same things for these demos, and we decided to *really* throw a curve ball into the mix and asked her to join the band. Fortunately, she said yes, and she said she'd do any of our songs but "Fat Man in the Bathtub" and "Rocket in My Pocket," for obvious reasons! (laughs) We started writing songs for her to sing, and went into the studio to record *Ain't Had Enough Fun* thinking that a lot of these songs were "performance-oriented," so we decided to record them live in the studio.

VG: Is that the first time you've done that?

PB: It really is; I did one electric guitar solo overdub on that record.

VG: When the band regrouped, music videos had come into their own as an entertainment option; the one Little Feat did for "Rad Gumbo" was funny. What do you think about videos as a facet of popular music?

PB: I think they've made some careers for some bands that wouldn't have gotten to Step One with their music, but I know videos are important. We've done six or seven; we can't seem to get through whatever the agendas of MTV or VH-1 are to get a big push with our videos. We did videos for "Hate to Lose Your Lovin'," "Let It Roll" and a *great* one for "Texas Twister," which the censors at Warner Brothers objected to because of the gunshots, helicopters, and police in it, so we cut it down and made it into a piece of pabulum... We did one for "Things Happen" down in New Orleans; the Memphis Horns were on that song. We tried to get that song to cross over to C.H.R. [Contemporary Hit Radio]; in fact, the people who were promoting it would take it into C.H.R. stations and not tell the station personnel who the band was. The programmers liked the song but wouldn't play it when they found out it was Little Feat. I don't know if we're too artistic for our own good or if we just don't play ball.

VG: But hasn't the band always had a core of supporters that kept you going, almost like Little Feat was, and may still be, a "cult" band, for lack of a better term?

PB: Absolutely. But I need to point out that we *have* topped some charts, like the one that used to be called A.O.R. There's all kinds of charts out there now; too many of 'em. But the charts that seem to *mean* something are the Adult Contemporary and C.H.R. ones, and we've never been able to bust into that area.

But think of all the years Bonnie Raitt spent in anonymity before she hooked up with Don Was, and got across into the public eye. People finally recognize her for the great artist that she is. Little Feat has sort of been "bubbling" in that same category; not only do our core of fans keep us going, but the band grew in popularity due to Classics radio during the years after Lowell died. All of the years I was doing my solo records and the Bluesbusters gig, I was getting great royalties from Little Feat records. When they started putting them out on CDs, that showed how popular the band still was.

And Shaun adds not only a new dimension to the band, but a lot of energy as well; she's got a great stage presence, which I think comes from her background in musicals. She was in one of the touring companies of *Hair* with Meat Loaf; she did a record with him called *Stoney & Meat Loaf*.

VG: Do you collect?

PB: I'm not a collector, but I've got a few instruments besides my old Strats and my ES-175. I have a '72 Martin acoustic that I use on demos, and an old Danelectro short-neck bass; you can't beat something like that! (chuckles) They just *honk*. I have two new Dobros and an old Hound Dog dobro that I bought new in '72 to play on *Dixie Chicken*; it was stolen two years later in Washington D.C., but when Little Feat was touring in support of the *Let It Roll* album, it got returned to me.

When Leo Fender started the Music Man company, he sponsored Little Feat for about three or four years, and I had three or four of his guitars and probably a half dozen amps. Some time afterwards, I sold the guitars when I was touring in Japan with Nicolette Larson.

VG: What's ahead?

PB: Another live album; we'll go out for a couple of weeks to record it after we get back from Europe. We're planning on recording at the Fillmore in San Francisco, and in Portland, where our records have sold real well, for some reason. There's a theatre there which has impeccable sound; Bonnie Raitt recorded her live album there. We'll try to get the live album out next year, but right now we're working real hard to get this album across.

VG: My perception is that you've toured more extensively in support of *Ain't Had Enough Fun* than you may have for other "Phase Two" albums.

PB: Absolutely; we really believe in this one. We're playing a lot of clubs so we can get that intimate feel with an audience; we're promoting *the band* as well as *the record*. If you come to see the band live, we guarantee you'll walk out with a smile on your face.

Despite collective and personal hardships, Little Feat continues to delight listeners with their "American music," and *Ain't Had Enough Fun* is a confident statement concerning the band's musicianship and direction.

Dick Burke

Over Three and a Half Decades Behind the Scenes at Rickenbacker

Dick Burke isn't a man of many words, but many people who build guitars don't seem to be too talkative. Rather, such peoples' "eloquence" seems to be in the products they make, whether such individuals are solitary luthiers laboring in a tiny shop or participants in the research, development, and manufacturing of instruments for a major company.

Burke fits into the latter category; he's been with Rickenbacker for over 35 years. Originally from Chattanooga, Tennessee, he doesn't play guitar, but has worked his way up through the Santa Ana, California, manufacturer to his current title of Production Manager.

The affable-yet-soft-spoken Burke was working in Chicago for B.F. Goodrich, and migrated to the Golden State in search of a climate more suitable for a Southern-born individual.

"A friend of mine, Darryl Heird, and I came out together," he said. "Darryl's father worked for Rickenbacker and that's how I got a job. Darryl worked here for a short time; later he went to work for Paul Barth in the '60s. I went to work here in May 1958."

Manufacturing experience wasn't an asset of Dick Burke's, but a fondness for woodworking was.

"I was real good in shop in school," he states. There were only about six employees "in the back" when Burke went to work at the facility (which at that time was still located in Los Angeles). Among the individuals already working there was legendary designer Roger Rossmeisl, with whom Burke began a close working relationship; he corroborates other folks' assertions concerning Rossmeisl's importance in designing many of the "classic" Rickenbacker body styles: "Those were basically Roger's designs," he says, "and on some of the earliest ones I cut them down; they were too fat."

Roger Rossmeisl went to work for Fender following his tenure with Rickenbacker; he designed Fender's first acoustic series of guitars, and according to Burke, attempted to get his former Rickenbacker associate to go to work at Fender as well, but Burke declined. "I was

happy here at Rickenbacker with the way Mr. Hall was treating me," he says, exhibiting a loyalty to his employer but at the same time giv-

ing credit to the appropriate person; "I guess I owe almost all my guitar design ability to Roger," says Burke.

Following Rossmeisl's departure in 1962, Burke had even more involvement in Rickenbacker body styles. "The original 360 was double-bound," he says, "and Mr. Hall wanted something rounded on a guitar like that; something "softer" and more comfortable. We came up with a new style pretty quickly; the Rickenbacker 360 that's bound only on the back came out around 1964."

The Rickenbacker 400 was reworked by Burke into the instrument that ultimately became known as the 620. "The fingerboard on the 400 was basically right on the body, and Mr. Hall wanted something that was like the 360, with the fingerboard up about three-fourths of an inch."

Burke is quite proud of the quality level Rickenbacker instruments have attained. He is in a unique position, as he was involved with many of the *original* instruments that are now being reissued as part of Rickenbacker's Vintage series, and he feels the quality of the reissues is actually better than the quality of the

Photo by john P. Quarterman

originals. "We've had people on the job doing inspections for as long as 10 or 12 years," he states, "and that makes a big difference."

In his current position as Production Manager, Dick Burke oversees the construction of instruments, from their beginnings as raw lumber to their completion as high-quality guitars and basses. He doesn't purchase wood products, "but if it comes in and I find it's no good, it gets sent back."

He also currently works on developing "signature" instruments with musicians with whom the company works, such as Roger McGuinn, Pete Townshend, etc. "Chris Squire wanted his fretboard to be wider than a normal 4001," said Burke with a laugh. "He had probably the biggest hands I've ever seen!"

There are other facets of Rickenbacker's history of which Dick Burke is proud; he cited such events as his involvement in the redesign of their truss rod, and the receipt of the Presidential "E" Award for export percentages in the late 1980s. He enjoys his job and is dedicated to his company, which in many respects seems to be a rare occurrence among many workers these days. He looks back at the memorable accomplishments of his company since he went to work for Rickenbacker in 1958, and he looks forward to more exciting developments in the future.

Makes ya wonder how many more folks like Dick Burke work for *other* guitar manufacturers, doesn't it???

Jon Butcher

Land of the Midnight Sun, California Sun

...with a side trip to Boston as well. Such represents the sojourn of guitarist Jon Butcher in his musical ventures. He's released many albums, first with the Jon Butcher Axis, then as a solo artist; a recent project has been his participation in a band called Barefoot Servants (the moniker was culled from "All Along the Watchtower," a Bob Dylan song popularized by Jimi Hendrix).

When Butcher recently conversed with *Vintage Guitar* about his musical history as well as his love for guitars (particularly Strats), a question about his home state was irresistable (he's now part of the L.A. music scene):

VG: You've probably heard this pun before, but Alaska ain't exactly a hotbed of rock guitarists. How'd you end up hailing from there?

JB: My dad worked for the government; like a lot of other kids at the Air Force base, I got interested in folk guitar; I was listening to whatever the radio station in Fairbanks played, but you have to remember that in Alaska, some things are about five or ten years behind the times (chuckles), so I grew up listening to folk singers like Joan Baez and Pete Seeger.

And I was as much of a "victim" of the Beatles' invasion as anybody. I saw them on "The Ed Sullivan Show," then I saw *A Hard Day's Night* at the base theatre, and I said: "That's for me!" That had to have happened to who knows how many kids back then.

VG: I wonder how many Silvertone/ Danelectro guitars with the amp built into the case were sold because of that one phenomenon.

JB: Hundreds of thousands, I would think. I had one of those; who *didn't?* When I got it, I thought it was the coolest thing ever. Open up the case, and there you are, ready to rock. I wish I had it now.

VG: What about your bands back then?

JB: To be honest, I wasn't in that many bands. Like a lot of the other musicians, I was too shy to meet girls, and a band was the way to get a date. My dad was originally from the East Coast, and after I graduated from high school, I went to Boston to go to college. Those people who are familiar with the Jon

Butcher Axis probably think of me as being from Boston. I ended up playing around the area; I happened to be the local guy that everyone was talking about around the time the J. Geils Band went out on their *Freeze Frame* tour; it was their biggest album. Peter Wolf had heard me, and somehow I got the gig to open for the Geils band on that tour. I hadn't even started making records; I'd been playing nightclubs, and the first gig on the *Freeze Frame* tour was at Cobo Hall in Detroit. I was amazed!

VG: The fact that the word "Axis" was tagged onto your name, *plus* your heritage, *plus* the fact that you were sporting a white Stratocaster on the "Life Takes A Life" video should have meant that you could've expected comparisons to Jimi Hendrix.

JB: The fact is, I didn't name the band; it was named by a "peripheral" guy who used to help us move equipment. At the time, I didn't have any idea it might have certain repercussions; I just thought it sounded cool. When my first album came out on Polygram and I started doing interviews, some people wanted to know if it "bothered" me being compared to Jimi Hendrix. I thought that might happen; given the times, there wasn't any way such an association wasn't going to be made. Initially, I thought it might actually be negative, but it didn't work out that way. Gradually, as people got exposed to my music, it became obvious to listeners that I'd been influenced by Hendrix along with *everybody else* in my generation of guitar players; white, black or any other

Photo : Henry Diltz

color. It took four or five national tours to make folks aware that it wasn't a Hendrix clone band like Randy Hanson's Machine Gun.

VG: For what my opinion's worth, back then I thought you looked more like [Thin Lizzy bassist] Phil Lynott.

JB: (chuckles) Yeah; I met Phil once. They were on tour; I think this was a few months before he passed away. My roommate knew him, and he ended up over at our apartment. We talked for a while, and at the time I didn't have an appreciation for his caliber of musicianship, but afterwards I realized that it had been a lucky opportunity.

VG: What about your progression through certain models of guitars, after your Silvertone amp-in-the-case model?

JB: I've had everything. I've had just about every model of Gibson made, and *I like Strats.* I like the way they feel to me, and I like the fact that you have to work a little bit harder to make them produce. I've had SGs, Les Paul Customs, and others, and I've always gone back to the Fender Strat.

VG: A couple of other brands you've been seen playing are Kramer and Robin.

JB: Those were good guitars; we were getting endorsements because of the high visibility that came from the Geils tour and the *Pyromania* tour I did with Def Leppard. But even though I might have been on big tours, I wasn't making big money, so to be able to use a decent guitar on the road was really great.

VG: When and why was the "Axis" term dropped?

JB: When it wasn't relevant anymore. The band had made all the inroads it was going to

make, and I was moving in another direction musically. The Axis did two albums on Polygram and two on Capitol; the rest of the albums I did for Capitol were solo albums.

VG: Was any live material ever released by the Axis *or* from your solo period?

JB: No, but I can't tell you how many live bootleg albums I've come across; it's mind-boggling. I was in Tokyo, and a kid had a bootleg that didn't even have English on its cover.

VG: *Pictures from the Front*, from your solo period, has a more "somber" or "ominous" feel to it; some of the songs like "Beating Drum" and "Division Street" have some socio-political commentary in their lyrics.

JB: You know, if I could re-write history, I'd have done that differently, and I'll tell you why: I found out that what really matters to people are albums that just talk about basic, simple topics. Breaking up with your wife is more fundamental to people instead of talking about South Africa. I realized when I did subsequent albums that socio-political topics may have been my mindset at the time I did *Pictures from the Front*, but I'm more interested in talking about getting through the day or how hard it is to be a good enough musician to avoid all the clichés some people try to lay on me.

VG: A while back, you got into another "band" effort, and this one didn't have your name in the name of the group, which was Barefoot Servants.

JB: Best thing I ever did! There was some discussion that something like "featuring Jon Butcher" might be part of the hype, but I was adamantly against it. I had really turned a lot of pages by then, and I wanted to make good music and be part of a group effort.

VG: I think I also read that you'd "bagged" your effects rack when Barefoot Servants got going.

JB: Yeah, I had the monster effects rack along with everybody else, but the best thing a musician can do is to re-invent himself. I just got a couple of good amps to go with a couple of good guitars that I had. I toured with Peavey Classic series amps, they held up and they sounded good.

VG: What about your primary utility guitar?

JB: For the most part, it's between two guitars; I have a '63 OlympicWhite Strat that's really nice, and a guitar that got put together from parts. It's a Mighty Mite neck, some other brand of body, and a Seymour Duncan "JB" model pickup by the bridge. It's beat to ****, and it's my favorite guitar; it's got the sound. I wouldn't sell it for $10,000. It's well-used; it's been on almost every tour I've done. Fender also made me a prototype white '61 re-issue Strat that I use as well.

I've got about twenty-five instruments; I bring everything to the studio. I take four guitars on tour.

VG: The photo of you on the Barefoot Servants cover shows you playing a resonator guitar, and some dobro-like tones could be heard on some of the songs.

JB: That's a National, and there's plenty of it on there. I played a tri-cone, too. It gets back to re-inventing yourself. I've always been in love with the blues; all of my music has had that base, and this band has paid more attention to it.

VG: What else have you been up to lately?

JB: I've started a production company that's called Axis, Too. I learned a lot from Leland [Sklar] about having a labor of love like Barefoot Servants, which is not a money-maker at this point, and wearing *other* hats; doing other projects. Leland's well-known as a session guy; I'm not as well-known in those circles as he is, so I started this company where I'm available to do projects as a guitarist and singer. So far we're having great success.

I also recently finished recording a blues album for Shrapnel; the tracks we did are amazing. There's a couple of slide boogies on there that'll blow minds; we used a G-tuning and D-tuning, and we're doing a lot of acoustic dobro, too. Ben Schultz from Barefoot Servants is a collaborator on this album, too; we're sharing some songwriting, and he's taking some slide solos as well. We're using an assortment of vintage guitars and amps and some Marshall plexi-amps. The album will be released in Europe first, and it's the best guitar playing I've ever done.

VG: Let me get cynical at this point and ask how much you use a Floyd Rose on it, since it's a blues album?

JB: (chuckles) No Floyd Rose, but I might have used a whang bar one time on the album, because it got in the way of my hand. It's a

blues album in the sense that when I listen to Stevie Ray I think of the blues; it's not a Mississippi Fred McDowell album.

The bass player on the album is named Saul McCartney, believe it or not, and the drummer is Buck Smith.

The album turned out so well, we're going to do a tour to support it. This is probably the only release I'll have out in '95, even though we've started another Barefoot Servants album. We're looking for management for both projects as well as a bass player and drummer for the Shrapnel album tour; any interested parties can get in touch with me at my business phone number, (818) 759-4062.

VG: I think your solicitation for management and touring musicians represents a first for an interviewee in this magazine.

JB: It can happen! A lot of people who read your magazine are into the same kind of blues music that I'm into. I've made a lot of connections in this business, and a lot of friends as well. It's important as a guitarist to keep working, and I can play a note or two!

Jon Butcher's enthusiam indicates that he's dedicated to his craft, which includes exploring the facets of what his guitar-playing abilities can offer him as a working musician. He is indeed living his own words about a musician re-inventing himself, and that he's making such an effort is another admirable facet of his career. Stay tuned for further developments.

Since the interview with Jon Butcher was published, he's gotten more into work with television music, including a promo clip for the Fox Network's Fall 1996 season.

Photo : Ann Elliott

Randy California

In the Spirit of Things

Of the guitar heroes that many *Vintage Guitar* readers recall and admire (considering the demographics of this publication), Spirit's Randy California is probably on many guitar enthusiasts' lists of favorite players, due to his unique tone (purveyed with a cheapo Danelectro/Silvertone instrument), and Spirit's innovative music, which almost defied categorization.

Spirit's auspicious and eclectic debut album was released in 1968, and the eerie and fascinating howl of Randy California's Silvertone probably turned the head of many an aspiring guitarist. The magnificent harmony leads on "Uncle Jack" and "Mechanical World," and the mysterious, melodic instrumental called "Taurus" are only small portions of a tour-de-force guitar performance (there's been an ongoing controversy for decades as to what extent Led Zeppelin "borrowed" a few lines from "Taurus" for the introduction to "Stairway to Heaven"). Not surprisingly, a lot of *VG*'s inquiries during our interview with Mr. California addressed some of the sounds heard on that self-titled album from the late '60s.

But long-time Spirit fans had a reason to celebrate in 1995. An all-new live album, *Spirit Live at La Paloma*, was released on the C.R.E.W. label. The band now consists of California on lead vocals and guitar, Ed Cassidy on drums and vocals, and Scott Monahan on vocals, keyboards, and keyboard bass. Original Spirit drummer Cassidy is Randy California's stepfather, and may well be the world's oldest rock musician; his date of birth is May 4, 1923.

When *Vintage Guitar* conversed with Randy California, Spirit had just completed a tour, and California had other projects in the works. An excellent two-disc CD anthology called *Time Circle* had been released in the early Nineties, and the extensive liner notes contained therein told the Spirit story in an admirable manner. Accordingly, some of our questions were concerning details that guitar lovers might want to know (such was also the case with *VG*'s interview with Duane Eddy in our June 1995 issue), and the first inquiry was an example of such:

VG: Liner notes and photos in the *Time Circle* anthology booklet confirmed two rumors that I'd heard for years, concerning you being related to Ed Cassidy as well as your use of a Danelectro/Silvertone guitar. Readers will want to know what else was involved in how you got that unique tone back then.

RC: In addition to the Silvertone, I used a Boss-Tone fuzz-tone; the kind that plugs into a guitar, and a DeArmond amplifier with a twelve-inch speaker. I wouldn't mind having another amp like that one; so if any of your readers know where I could get one, put them in touch with me.

Another thing I did was to put a piece of the thickest unwound guitar string I could find across the wood part of the Silvertone's bridge; that helped its sound as well. I think the string gauge was .020 or .022. That Silvertone was my first electric guitar, I modified it a lot but kept it a long time out of loyalty.

VG: What about the sitar on "Girl in Your Eye" on the first album?

RC: That was a real Indian sitar that I played; it belonged to Brian Berry, who was Jan Berry's brother; Jan of Jan and Dean.

VG: Jay Ferguson got most of the writing credit for the songs on the first album; what about the harmonic guitar leads on songs like "Uncle Jack" and "Mechanical World"? One would presume you wrote those parts; they preceded recordings by the

TOP (this page and next): *Circa 1970: Randy California onstage in Salt Lake City with his fabled Danelectro/ Silvertone (photographs by Brian Record, courtesy of Bruce Pates).*

Allman Brothers and Wishbone Ash. What inspired you to do such parts?

RC: Somebody had the idea *way before* we did our first album to do harmony guitar leads; it was probably Barry Hansen, who was better known as Dr. Demento. He produced our first recordings. The whole band contributed to songs that one member might have originally written. I worked out guitar parts and other things; for example, I wrote the middle part of "Mechanical World"; the short fast section.

Barry Hansen lived in the same house we did; he had a big record collection, including a lot of 78s. We still keep in touch; a few weeks ago we played in Glendale along with the Strawberry Alarm Clock and Big Brother & the Holding Company, and he was the M.C.; he's a great entertainer. Most of what he produced can be found on another Spirit anthology called *Chronicles*.

VG: Comments about some of the other guitars you've played in your career? I've seen you playing a plexiglas Ampeg/Dan Armstrong, for example.

RC: I played that guitar on *The Twelve Dreams of Dr. Sardonicus*. I knew Dan Armstrong; I'd met him in New York. He actually used my idea with the unwound string on the bridge of his guitars, replacing such with actual fret wire on the wood part. I got that guitar because it had a super-long neck and I could get up high on it. I also used an SG; its long neck appealed to me as well.

My current guitar is a Charvel Strat-type that was made by Jackson, when Charvel was still a domes-

tic-made name.

VG: What about the acoustic guitars that have been on some of your recordings? In particular, I'm thinking about "Taurus" on the first album and the introduction to the new live album.

RC: That was a Martin 000-18 on "Taurus"; the guitar on the *La Paloma* album is an older Yamaha that I've had for some time.

VG: Did you play slide guitar? An example might be "Nothin' to Hide"; I might have thought that was the Ampeg/Dan Armstrong.

RC: That was an old Fender lap steel that I bought in a pawn shop. One interesting thing about that song was that the "build-up" at the end of "Nothin' to Hide" was done note-by-note on *two separate tracks* that "ping-pong" from speaker to speaker.

VG: Mark Andes told me that the band used Acoustic amplifiers because they got an endorsement deal. Weren't those solid state?

RC: They were, but I ran through a tube model Echoplex as a preamp.

VG: What about the siren effect on songs like "Dark-Eyed Woman"?

RC: That was a WEM Copycat machine; it's like an Echoplex with a single tape loop and eight heads, I think. The tape was only a foot in length. I'd start a note and would turn up the volume to where I'd get some feedback; the machine didn't have a ON-OFF switch for its motor, so I rigged one up. By switching the motor off but having the electronics still on, you'd hear the tape literally slowing down; that's how that descending, siren sound was done. WEM Copycats were made in England.

VG: Did you ever use a Theremin?

RC: I sure did! At one point I actually put it into my Silvertone; I had a separate switch for it so I was able to play it onstage. That was in the *real* early days! I think Led Zeppelin got the idea about using one from us when we were in England; that's what I was told later.

VG: Are there any recordings that feature you using a Theremin?

RC: I don't think so; I used it live before we really got into recording.

VG: As far as Spirit anthologies go, what's the difference between *Time Circle* and *Chronicles*?

RC: *Time Circle* contains material from our first

four albums as well as some unreleased recordings, including some songs we did for the soundtrack of a movie called *The Model Shop*. *Chronicles* features some of our earliest recordings and alternative versions of songs, including "Elijah." I think that version on *Chronicles* is much better; it's over twelve minutes long, and we really get off on our solos. I don't think of the songs on *Chronicles* as "demos"; they were probably considered demos because they weren't released on a major label until just recently. It was *raw* Spirit, and the energy was there. Twenty-five years later you can listen to our earlier albums and note how the drums were buried in the background of the mix. It gave us a tweaky sound sometimes, and we were a *rock* band; people were surprised at how much energy we had when we went on the road. We were much more "powerful" than some of our early albums indicate, which is why I prefer a lot of the songs on *Chronicles*.

VG: By the time the *Spirit of '84* album came out, videos were a factor in the music business, and a performance video for "I Got A Line On You" not only featured a reunion of the entire original band, but some guest artists as well.

RC: There was Alan Gratzer and Neal Doughty from REO Speedwagon, Jeff Baxter, Joe Lala, Gary Myrick, and Mark's brother Matt Andes from Jo Jo Gunne, among others.

VG: What was the difference between Spirit and Kaptain Kopter & the Fabulous Twirly Birds, another group you played with at one point?

RC: Kaptain Kopter was supposed to be more of a power trio idea, inspired by Jimi Hendrix. Noel Redding was the bass player, but because of contractual reasons he had be called "Clit McTorius" on the recording credits.

VG: The liner notes in *Time Circle* noted your playing experience in New York with Hendrix, but they didn't explain why he named you Randy California.

RC: There was another guy in the Blue Flames who was also named Randy, and he was from Texas; he became Randy Texas and I became Randy California.

VG: After you returned to California and Hendrix went to England, did you keep up with each other?

RC: Not in the strict sense; we weren't writing letters to each other. But when he came out to the Monterey Pop Festival, he came down to L.A., and he sent a limousine to pick me up to take me to a party. I ran into him at the Atlanta Pop Festival, the Seattle Pop Festival, and a Lake Chatsworth performance. We'd hook up if he was anywhere near me, whenever I got the chance to do so.

VG: Did you see him at the Isle of Wight festival?

RC: Our name was on the poster, but we didn't play there; I don't know how that happened. We were *supposed* to play at Woodstock but that didn't work out either; the manager thought it was more important for us to go around the country on a radio tour.

VG: You had a chance to peruse the interview *Vintage Guitar* did with Mark Andes; any comments?

RC: Well, I guess your readers will probably want to know my version of the Neil Young incident. (chuckles) I really get into my performance when I'm onstage, and I wasn't told that Neil was coming back on. An unfortunate occurrence, and I'm sorry. I have the utmost respect for Neil Young's music.

VG: Concerning the current incarnation of the band, it's a trio with no bass player. Are any of the bass parts in your performances sequenced?

RC: Absolutely not. Some of my favorite songs on the *La Paloma* album are the jams, and there was no way we could have done any sequencing on those kind of songs.

VG: Other than the live album, what else have you been doing recently as far as musical efforts?

RC: A while back I played with John Locke, Matt Andes, and his daughter Rachel at Topanga Canyon, which is where it all started back in the Sixties. That went so well, we went into the studio; we're working on an album called *Blues From The Soul*. The vocal harmony sounds great; we're really excited about it.

I also went down to Johnny Sandlin's studio in Decatur, Alabama, and played on two songs for Gregg Allman's new album; I think they're in the process of mixing it. The first night I got there Gregg and I stayed up 'til two in the morning, playing some old acoustic blues songs; he's a good player.

VG: Any chance we'll ever see another reunion of the original five members of Spirit?

RC: Well, I'm open to it. We all grew up together; if we ever wanted to make some music together again I think it would be a wonderful experience.

VG: If someone asked you to name the definitive Spirit song and album, what would you select?

RC: (laughs) That's real tough.

VG: Okay, what about your personal favorites?

RC: Probably "Fresh Garbage," "Nothin' to Hide," "Mr. Skin," some of the new stuff like "La Paloma Jam," because jamming is what got us off *now and then*. "Elijah" was always fun to do because we always ended our set with it; we would all jam on it, just like we do with "La Paloma Jam" today.

And *Sardonicus* seems to be the album that everybody remembers more than any other. What was *your* favorite song on that album?

VG: Uh, maybe "When I Touch You," because it was somewhat, um, "heavier" than some other Spirit material, and right or wrong, I was into sort of a "heavy music" phase then.

RC: Like I said, we were a *rock* band!

Spirit Live at La Paloma features commendable versions of classic Spirit songs, as well as new material (including the aforementioned jams). Randy California is still evoking unique tones from his guitar after decades of experience, and Spirit's new live album avers such.

Randy California signed autographs at the Vintage Guitar *booth during the Winter Nationals Guitar Show at Santa Monica in January, 1996.*

Spirit's new album, California Blues, *was released in late 1996.*

In January of 1997, Randy California was swimming in the surf in Hawaii with his eleven-year-old son, when they were caught in an undertow. Randy managed to get his son to safety, but was swept out to sea himself.

His body was never found.

Larry Carlton
"Larry on the Left..."

The instrumental surf music fad of the early Sixties might seem like an unusual starting point for a guitarist who went on to become a highly respected session musician and solo artist, and such wasn't the case for Larry Carlton either; he'd started playing *before* surf music came into vogue. Nevertheless, many *Vintage Guitar* readers may recall that Carlton spent some time as a guitarist for Eddie and the Showmen, one of the preeminent South Bay surf bands (see *Surfin' Guitars* by Robert Dalley; the chapter about female guitarist Kathy Marshall shows her being backed by the incarnation of the Showmen that included Larry Carlton).

In a recent conversation with *VG*, a relaxed Larry Carlton recalled his decades of playing in studios on a myriad of hit records, as well as his membership in the Crusaders for several years. A recent collaboration album with Lee Ritenour was also discussed; we talked with Carlton two days after we'd interviewed Ritenour, and the subtitle of Carlton's interview notes where his guitar appears in the mix on the *Larry & Lee* album (same goes for the subtitle of Ritenour's interview, and that's why each begins on a left and right page of *VG*).

Some years ago, the guitar world was rocked with the news that Larry Carlton had been shot in the throat by an intruder at his residence. He's in fine shape these days, yet our first question was about any aftereffects of that unfortunate incident:

VG: How are you feeling these days?

LC: I'm completely back; as good as can be expected. As you probably know, I only have the use of one vocal cord, but I can talk, so I'm tickled pink.

VG: Let me read what another *Vintage Guitar* interviewee told me about his recollection of you during the surf days; I'd asked about players that had gone on to fame in other musical genres. We talked about guitarists like Jim Messina, and how the Crossfires had become the Turtles, and he also said: "Another 'tidbit' involved Larry Carlton, who was this upstart kid from Lomita. Around '63 we became aware of him in Eddie and the Showmen because he could play rings around all of us! He was more jazz-oriented, and it was obvious he was going

someplace."

That was from Paul Johnson of the Bel-Airs.

LC: Well, obviously those are very nice observations. In '63, I was fifteen years old, and I had already been playing in supper clubs with older musicians; in the ninth grade when I was fourteen I was working three nights a week at a nightclub that served food. I was playing pop music and some standards, and that gig ended because the leader of the band got drafted. So I joined Eddie & the Showmen as the third guitar player, even though they didn't need another guitar player. It really wasn't because I had a "passion" for surf music; I'd been playing other kinds of music before then.

VG: What about your "pre-surf" playing experiences and instruments?

LC: The story that I've been told by my parents is that I was fascinated with an old acoustic guitar that was at my grandmother's house; I was four years old and wouldn't leave it alone, but I was too small to hold it correctly. So they waited until I was six, when I could physically hold a guitar, then they found a teacher and I started taking lessons. And I've never put it down; that's all I've ever done! (chuckles) My mom had played as a teenager back in Oklahoma, and her father played fiddle, so there had been some family influences as well.

I don't know what kind of guitar that old acoustic was; it didn't have a label on it. I still have the body. My first electric was a Fifties Broadcaster, I'd been taking lessons for about six months, and it was obvious that I was *very* interested in playing guitar, so we bought a Broadcaster. I don't remember how long I kept that guitar; maybe a year or a year and a half, then I upgraded to a Tele. Then I just went through the Fenders over those next years; I ended up with a Strat, then a Jazzmaster; whatever the new and "hot" model was. I traded in to trade up. I wish I had all those old guitars!

VG: What sort of music were you interested in playing as your ability developed?

LC: Country music was very big on TV in the late Fifties; I watched Joe Maphis, Jimmy Bryant, and Larry Collins on "Town Hall Party." Also, Elvis Presley and the rock and roll era were starting. By the time I was eight, I was trying to learn solos from pop records. I got sort of an agent who took me around to local talent shows, and at age ten I ended up performing on weekends as a "special guest" with Spade Cooley's big Swing band. I had a lot of exposure playing pop music and country music prior to going into supper clubs.

VG: Well, is it fair to say that you may have been considered a child prodigy back then?

LC: I think so, although I never thought about it *then*. Now that I look back, the amount of attention I was getting from people that had a lot to do with guitars and music had a *lot* to do with my "acceleration," because they were right there for me and would give me some great input.

VG: Was Eddie & the Showmen the only surf band you played in?

LC: Yes, but I recorded with the Challengers, which was Richard Delvy's band. He was active in producing, and when I was sixteen, he was doing an album of "cover tunes in a surf mode", and he called me to do the session, but he also had the top studio players in Los Angeles at the time playing on it; Hal Blaine, Joe Osborne, Larry Knechtel. He had me come in because I could read, but I still sounded like a kid. (chuckles) As I looked back, I knew exactly what he was thinking; he didn't want to call Howard Roberts for the part; Howard would have been too "slick."

VG: I was going to ask if you went from surf bands straight to session work, but the Delvy session story sounds "transitional."

LC: It was part of it, but I also ended up form-

ing my own trio; I played in local clubs. I also need to note that when I was fourteen I got into studying jazz. I got real excited about Joe Pass, Wes Montgomery, Barney Kessel, Tony Mottola, Johnny Smith; I just couldn't get enough of it. I played pop songs and standards in clubs, but was concentrating on learning jazz.

VG: Comments about your first session?

LC: Well, I did my very first session when I was about twelve. It came about by chance, with that manager that I talked about earlier. I'd played someplace, and Tommy Rettig, who was the original Jeff on the "Lassie" TV show, had been there. Tommy was into music, and I ended up at his house one weekend; he wanted to cut a demo in his garage for these four singers. Three months later I heard the tune on the radio; the song was "Oh What A Night" by the Tokens, so I played on my first hit song when I was twelve, and it happened to be my first session.

VG: "Favorite" or "most memorable" session?

LC: (pauses) I really don't have one, because there are a number of them that were milestones in my career.

VG: What about the "hardest" or "worst" session?

LC: (another pause) Well, the hardest session *type* I've had to do involved a couple of film calls, where the reading was very, very difficult. I remember Tommy Tedesco and/or Dennis Budimir would have been on those dates playing the first chair, and I would have been playing the second chair. There would be a ten-minute union break every hour, and those guys would be having coffee and donuts, and I'd still be looking at the music we were going to have to play the next hour, and it was *scary;* I was on the edge of my seat! (laughs)

VG: Are there any recordings you're on where one might not have expected to hear Larry Carlton?

LC: There's a number of them; the Hager Twins, David Cassidy & the Partridge Family, others.

VG: You noted that you went through Fender models of guitars, but at one point you were being referred to as "Mr. 335" by guitar enthusiasts. How and why did you get involved with that Gibson model?

LC: At around age sixteen I started using an ES-175 in my club gigs for the bulk of my playing, but I also had a solidbody of some kind for some of the pop stuff. Then in late 1969 I started getting calls for a lot of sessions, and I

As the liner notes in Carlton's On Solid Ground *state: "This album was almost killed by a gunshot..." Though most of the tracks had been cut before the shooting, most hadn't been titled, and a few still needed to be completed.*

wanted to find a guitar that was as versatile as my playing was, so I wouldn't have to carry three or four guitars to all of those sessions. It just made sense. I played a 335, and thought: "Well, I can get a country sound on the back pickup, and kind of a jazz sound on the front pickup, so I bought one. Its versatility was the reason I chose it, because I was getting calls for all kinds of music. I was the first guitar player on the L.A. recording scene to use an ES-335.

VG: What about your association with the Crusaders?

LC: In 1971 I got called for a session for Donovan, the English singer. Joe Sample, the keyboard player for the Crusaders, had also been called. He was playing acoustic piano while I was plugging in my instruments, and I joined in; there was an *instant* musical connection. Two days later I got a call from the office of the Crusaders asking me to record five sessions the next week, and five the week after that. It was a great musical marriage; I was with the Crusaders from 1971 to early 1977; we did thirteen albums.

VG: Was your decision to pursue a solo career the reason you left the Crusaders?

LC: It wasn't, and most people think it was. When my tenure with the Crusaders ended, I also felt like I was burned out on doing sessions. I'd had over six years of doing over five hundred sessions a year. My heart wasn't in it anymore; I could have continued doing sessions but something in me told me I didn't want to be there. So I put the word out that I wasn't doing sessions; I wanted to try my hand at producing. I had arranged a number of hit records in the Seventies, so I produced a few albums, but I also played in a local jazz club one night a week, just for fun.

And that's how my solo career came about; some record company came in one night and heard me playing. They were already aware of me, and they said: "Don't you want to make a record?"

VG: Of the solo albums you've done, is there one that's your favorite?

LC: Two come to mind: The first Warner Brothers album, which was simply called *Larry Carlton*, set the standard for "the Larry Carlton sound in a solo situation." On this record I really stretched out, and it really opened a lot of folks' ears to the way I would play for four or five minutes on each tune, instead of the way I played at sessions. As I listen to it years later, I realize that nobody had played like that on solo records, so I'm proud of that one.

Then in 1986, I did my first acoustic guitar album called *Alone But Never Alone*. It's just good easy-listening music.

VG: *On Solid Ground* starts off with a cover of Steely Dan's "Josie," and you played on the original. The kickoff sounds *exactly* like the same setup, including guitar, amp, strings, EQ, whatever. I'm not opining that it's a "clone," but is that what you were going for?

LC: Yeah; I played on "Josie" for Steely Dan, but I *didn't* play the solo on that particular track, which is why I chose that tune to cover. I didn't want to pick a tune where I'd played the original solo, because it would have been too familiar to everybody.

VG: That album was also the first one you released following the shooting incident. For what my opinion's worth, that album, and even the *title* of it, sounded somewhat "confident" and/or "assertive." Was that the intent?

LC: I think it's interesting, Willie, because all of the tracks had been cut *prior* to the shooting, but most of them hadn't been titled, and I had three or four of those tunes that I hadn't finished the guitar parts on yet. So after the shooting and after I healed, I went in and finished the album, but my attitude towards the titles and the last overdubs was obviously "after the fact," and it's one of those records that is very reflective of that time in my life, even though the tunes had been written and recorded for the most part before the shooting.

VG: Did most of your fans and/or the critics feel like it was an "assertive" album, even if they might not have known the recording details you just imparted?

LC: Yeah, I think so. I did a show at the Universal Amphitheater as kind of a "comeback" in December of '88, after I healed. I had a bunch of my friends there, including Michael McDonald, Michael Franks, David Pack, Kirk Whalen; it was a big show and a real celebration. I played the blues that night, as I normally do in performance, and I was told by close friends that they had never heard me play that aggressively in all the years they'd heard me play. And that wasn't something that I *consciously* did; there was just a change inside that came out through my music.

VG: You've played with guitarists like B.B. King before, haven't you?

LC: I have; B.B. was a special guest on an album I did in '84 called *Friends*. I've done other shows and sat in with him as well. Some time ago, I got a call to play on a musical special in Canada; I don't even remember the show. I was the guest host and B.B. was my guest. That was the first time I got to sit on a stool next to him and ask him *all those questions* that guitarists would want to ask. (chuckles) I asked him things like: "B.B., do you think you're the first guy who ever played (CARLTON SCAT-SINGS A BLUES LICK)?", and he said: "Yeah, I think I am." It was really fun; he's a wonderful guy.

VG: I know this isn't a viable business venture anymore, but I *do* need to inquire about the Larry Carlton signature guitar that Valley Arts made.

LC: I was going for tone first; Mike McGuire and I have been together for years, and he knows I like a smooth, aggressive sound; thick but not muddy. I joked with Mike once that I don't practice; I don't pick up a guitar until it's time to go play. I asked him to build a guitar with a scaled-down body and neck, so when I picked it up it would "play like a race car"; if I played something real "physical" my chops would be down. So he made the neck *very* slim, and the body was about Tele-sized but contoured to my body type.

VG: McGuire now works at Gibson; you still work with him, don't you?

LC: Mike just finished the first prototype of the new Larry Carlton guitar last summer, and it's *killer*. It won't come out until the NAMM show early next year. On this one, Michael and I included a lot of the stuff we'd talked about over the last twenty years; I played the prototype in concert for a few days, and the engineer who was mixing for us said it was the best sounding guitar onstage. Mike really nailed it this time!

VG: Another Nashville connection is Steve Wariner; I heard you've worked with him as well.

LC: I co-wrote the "Who's The Boss" theme song with Robert Craft, and the show ran in the Top Five for five years. The first version had Larry Norman, who wrote "Rhinestone Cowboy," singing; the producers asked me to cut a new version for another season, and I said I'd like to change singers, and I called Steve Wariner, who sang on the new version. Steve is one of a lot of *strong* players out of Nashville, and he has a new instrumental album coming out; he sent me an ADAT so I could overdub and play on one of the tunes, so I did that during one of the tour breaks last summer. I haven't heard the final stuff yet.

VG: Some of the questions I'm going to ask about the collaboration with Lee Ritenour may get a bit redundant for some of the magazine's readers, since I interviewed Ritenour a couple of days ago. I opined to him that the *Larry & Lee* album doesn't sound like a "showdown"/"look-what-I-can-do" type of recording; it's really more of what I would call a true collaboration.

LC: I agree. What excited me about the opportunity to work with another guitar player like Lee was that I could work with someone who could understand things like the little "guitar orchestra" sounds I like to write, but I don't do that on my own albums because I can't reproduce it live, and the "texture" is very important. So on at least three of my tunes, I voiced everything; there are times where I'm playing three notes and Lee's playing three notes, and it becomes a little "cluster" that really tickled my ear; I really enjoyed the opportunity to do that on this project.

VG: I didn't ask Ritenour how the tour to support the album went.

LC: Phenomenal, because our fans had wanted to see us together for so many years. I'm sure Lee told about both of us getting fan mail forever, wanting to know if we'd ever play together. When the tour finally happened, we'd look out into the audience, and there would be big grins everywhere! (laughs) It was a great experience.

VG: Think you'll ever do it again?

LC: I do; in another five years or so; although I really don't know how long, it would nice to come out with a *Larry & Lee 2* and do it again.

VG: There's a '63 Stratocaster cited in your instrument list-

ing in the *Larry & Lee* credits; is it the same one you're seen playing behind Kathy Marshall in the *Surfin' Guitars* book?

LC: No; unfortunately I got rid of all those guitars as I upgraded. Five or six years ago I got into the Strat again. Actually, I hadn't played the 335 in a good six to eight years prior to this project with Lee, and I think I only used it on one cut. For the last two and a half years I've been playing a '57 Goldtop with PAFs.

VG: You thanked Jesus in the liner notes on *Larry & Lee*; one reader wanted to know if you might have had a born-again experience following the shooting.

LC: I was brought up in a home that went to church, but in my late teenage years and early adulthood, I was completely neglectful of that. I had a born-again experience in 1983. When I came to know Jesus, it changed my whole life.

VG: Then I guess it's safe to opine that it helped get you *through* the trauma of the shooting.

LC: It did, and it's an ongoing experience that I'm faithful to, and that I'm thankful for. Both of my kids were saved and baptized last year, which was beautiful.

VG: What's ahead, now that the collaboration with Ritenour has wound down?

LC: Musically, I don't have anything specific in mind; I know I'll be back in the studio sometime between now and the Spring of 1996. The passion I have for the blues keeps surfacing, and it's getting stronger. I want to continue to play very emotional music, but with a blues base to it. I'm going to have to find a way to incorporate all of that into my next project; music that's still melodic but as close to down-home as I can get without offending anybody.

And I know what I *don't* want to do as well. The last thing I want to do is to put out another album of what I call "happy jazz." To me, the contemporary jazz music that's out now is so watered-down it's becoming elevator music, and that's fine because people need music to listen to. But it's not my lot in life to play music "in the background"; music that goes unnoticed and doesn't have any emotional impact. I'm a *player.*

Anybody wanna debate Mr. Carlton's closing remarks? Larry Carlton is not only a *survivor,* he's an *enduring and important player,* and *Larry & Lee* is simply another facet of his abilities and efforts. If he plans on getting more blues-based in his future solo efforts, such recordings will probably be eagerly anticipated by his fans. Count this writer in among such individuals.

Brian Carman
Two More Sides of the Chantays

One of the most recognized sounds in electric guitar history (as well as surf music history) is the reverb-soaked, double-picked glissando that introduces the smash instrumental "Pipeline" by the Chantays. The two guitarists on that tune were Bob Spickard and Brian Carman, and *Vintage Guitar* recently had the opportunity to converse with both players about their experiences with the early Sixties surf music craze, as well as their musical efforts since that time. The Chantays are still an active band, even though both guitarists are now grandfathers!

Brian Carman now plays bass for the Chantays, but was originally their other guitarist. While he departed from the group at one time, he's been back on board for a good while, and at the time of our conversation was employed in the guitar-manufacturing industry as Rickenbacker's Director of Manufacturing. We conversed with Carman in his office at Rickenbacker's Santa Ana facility about his experiences with guitars; not only playing them, but building them as well:

VG: I may be putting the cart before the horse, but what does your current title at Rickenbacker involve?

BC: I'm in charge of production and purchasing. A lot of what I'm having to concentrate on these days involves lumber, considering changes in the market. Sometimes I have to search out exotic woods, such as the African vermilion we used on the Chris Squire bass, or bird's eye maple if we do a run of 381s. The bird's eye in particular is getting harder to find.

VG: Are you originally from California? What about your earliest musical experiences?

BC: I was born right here in Santa Ana; we moved to Colorado for a few years when I was in elementary school. While we were there I had the good fortune to learn flute from a world-famous band director; he'd even played at one of Eisenhower's Inaugurations. He was a real taskmaster, but he got my head straight about such instruments. When we moved back to California, I began playing other instruments like sax; woodwinds. Then around the eighth grade I fell in love with guitar music. So in my "formative years" I had a lot of extensive, formal music training; when I was twelve I was playing in a dance band that played all over the county. But I found guitar to be more "expressive," as I think

a lot of people did (chuckles), plus I loved rock and roll.

VG: What players and/or songs turned you towards guitar?

BC: I loved rockabilly; Eddie Cochran and Buddy Holly are the obvious players to note. Then around 1960, the very first inklings of surf music began to be heard; Dick Dale was the main player that got my attention. I'll have to say, though, that my brother Steve was my "guiding light"; he was in the Rhythm Rock-

ers, and to this day they're the best band I've ever heard. They were about three years older than those of us in the Chantays, and were much better musicians, yet we were the ones who ended up with the bigger amount of success, as so often happens. Steve played sax, by the way, not guitar.

VG: Did the Chantays start out with the idea of becoming a surf band?

BC: Well, we went in that direction pretty quickly; surf music became quite dominant back then. I do, however, remember us experimenting with sax players, trying out some of the Fireballs' stuff, which I *loved*. We weren't really hearing surf music that much on the radio when we got going; there were the live performances of Dick Dale at the Rendezvous, and the Rhythm Rockers were an R & B band. They switched to surf later, as a one-time experiment. Chuck Spencer of the Rhythm Rockers got a reverb unit, and I heard Dick Dale's reverb, so that appealed to me.

When we wrote "Pipeline," it wasn't written as a surf song. It was originally called "Liberty's Whip," and it just had a unique sound. I guess I'd have to say that we were one of the forerunners of surf music, because a *lot* of people started playing surf music after they heard "Pipeline."

VG: Are you saying that a "gizmo," the reverb unit, had more to do with the band's style rather than instrumentation?

BC: Definitely! There was a lot more creativity

Left to Right: Bob Welch, Brian Carman, Warren Waters, Bob Spickard and Rob Marshall in the band than we may have been given credit for, but we would experiment with unique sounds as well.

VG: I've got to admit that the first time I heard "Pipeline," I visualized something sort of "industrial," and the double-picked signature glissando represented oil gurgling through a pipeline, rather than a tubular surf wave.

BC: (chuckles) A lot of people thought that! Surfers were the only ones who knew about that term as applied to surfing. The title was actually changed from "Liberty's Whip" while we were in the studio.

VG: What about your progression of guitars back then?

BC: My first guitar was an acoustic that my parents got by trading in my flute; the first electric was an Airline from Montgomery Ward; I think it was made by Kay. It's the guitar I used on "Pipeline"; a lot of people think I used a Stratocaster on that song. Of course, I got a Stratocaster later; that's really about all I used.

VG: I saw an early photo of the band onstage in Robert Dalley's book. Considering the length of most of the players' pants, it looked like you guys were expecting a flood, and the reverb units were on the floor!

BC: (laughs) Well, that was the look back then, as far as fashion. The reverb units were placed on the floor on purpose, so we could get that *"KKSSSSSH!"* crash anytime we needed it. Listen close to the intro to "Pipeline"; that sound is heard before the slide. Whenever we played, we'd position the reverb units so they wouldn't cause any problems during normal playing, but we *would* kick them at certain times for effect. I'm sure there were times where the stage was so shaky we had to place them elsewhere, but we used them to our advantage.

I've got to tell this story on Bobby (Spickard): he and I got our reverb units at the same time, and our first gig using them was at a local high school. We were really excited; Bobby was apparently so jazzed he forgot to unlock his reverb spring! All night long he thought he'd gotten a bum unit! (laughs) Boy, was he upset! It sounds like a little thing now, but back then it was traumatic; we'd waited so long to get those things.

VG: Who came up with the aforementioned double-picked glissando?

BC: I did. It started out as just a slur on the bottom; almost a Duane Eddy-type lick over and over again, then I added the slide part to it.

VG: According to Dalley's book, you didn't make that trip to Japan where Spickard says the band was treated like the Beatles in terms of adulation.

BC: That was in 1965; I was still in the band but didn't go overseas because I'd just started at Rickenbacker. I'd gotten married in 1963, and wanted to get into a job that had some responsibility. Other than being a musician, that was really the first job I had, other than odd jobs before I got married. The first two years I was married we weren't making tremendous money, yet we were getting by, but I was gone too much.

There were also managerial problems, record company problems, so I figured I'd better go to work during the day.

VG: Stereotypically, Rickenbacker wasn't considered a surf guitar.

BC: I wasn't even familiar with the brand! The bass player had

quit the Chantays before I did, and he worked at Rickenbacker for a short time; I heard about the company from him. My first job here was in Assembly, putting parts on instruments. After that I was a Check-Out Musician; ultimately I was in charge of the instruments from the paint room until they went out the door. They really didn't have job titles as such back there then.

VG: When Dalley's chapter on the Chantays was written, it stated that you were at that time employed at Music Man.

BC: I left Rickenbacker in 1974 and returned in 1984. I worked in the amplifier division at Music Man; I had the opportunity to go to the guitar division with that company but stayed in the amplifier division because it was a change of pace and there weren't as many headaches. I worked very closely with Babe Simoni, who'd been at Fender for a long time; I think he went to work with them in 1952, when he was a kid.

Forrest White had been at Music Man, of course, and I worked under Forrest when I came back to work here. Basically he was in the position that I now have.

VG: What about your musical ventures after you left the Chantays?

BC: I formed a duo with a friend of mine named Steve Crawford he'd been in a surf band as well. We started writing songs and cut about twenty sides in Downey at the same studio where "Pipeline" was recorded. I'm prouder of those songs than anything else I've ever done. I got back together with Bob Spickard around 1973; I don't think he ever stopped playing. We gradually built things back up to where now the Chantays are a four, five, or six-member group, depending on the job. Three of the members are original. When Bob and I regrouped, we didn't want to be known as the Chantays; we were called Catalina. Then we realized using "Chantays" would be more profitable! (chuckles)

VG: What basses do you use live these days?

BC: A Rick 4003 and a Music Man Sting Ray, which is one of the first ones that was made.

VG: You seem to be pretty content with both your "day job" as well as your current musical venture.

BC: I'm very proud of what we're accomplishing; the quality control here is phenomenal. As for the band, the main reason I'm playing these days is for the friendships. Whenever we get together, the laughter starts almost immediately, and we haven't rehearsed in ten or twelve years! Well....maybe we've rehearsed a half-dozen times in that time. We really don't see each other socially, but it's a tremendous outlet for all of us. Considering how I enjoy my job so much and I enjoy the band so much, maybe I really do have the best of both worlds!

If Brian Carman isn't in an enviable position among musicians, then find someone who is. There's a look of pride on his countenance when he discusses his past and present musical accomplishments, just as there's a look of pride when he talks about the products he helps create. It just doesn't get much better than that, does it?

Brian Carman has advised Vintage Guitar *that since this interview was conducted, he is no longer employed with Rickenbacker International Corporation.*

Del Casher

Of Wah-Wahs, Ecco-fonics, and the West Coast Studio Scene

...and other earlier gizmos as well. Del Casher (nee Del "Kacher," the reasons for the name change are forthcoming) has been a fixture in Los Angeles-area studios for decades, and he was a pioneering player in the use of more than one device for musicians (particularly guitar players).

Some of them, such as the Ecco-Fonic, are now considered antiques compared to modern equipment, but Casher is still on the cutting edge of technology. He's a big advocate of MIDI, but he still loves his old guitars, as well.

Casher has seen a lot of changes in the L.A. music scene since he migrated to the Left Coast after attending the University of Pittsburgh on a music scholarship (he's originally from Hammond, Indiana). He recently sat down with *Vintage Guitar* to discuss his years of experience. Among the items we were able to peruse prior to our on-the-record conversation was the cover of a 1961 issue of Fender's *Fretts* magazine, where "Del Kacher" is brandishing a Fender Jazzmaster with a larger-style pickguard, so we started off with an inquiry about his name change:

VG: Apparently you had some success as "Del Kacher." When did you change your name?

DC: I went through school known as Del Kacher, but when I came to California, there was some confusion about the pronunciation and spelling. Some people didn't think I was in the union book, and I missed out on some musical projects because of that. When I got into the

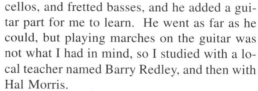

film industry about 10 or 15 years ago, I thought it represented a good time to make a change, and it worked.

VG: Didn't your "musical upbringing" involve more of a "formal education" as opposed to "the school of hard knocks?" Do you have a degree in music?

DC: My education was in Liberal Arts, but my father was my first music teacher. He was an arranger and composer for string music, so I had a very thorough reading and orchestration background. He'd orchestrate works like "The William Tell Overture" for mandolins, mandolas, fretted cellos, and fretted basses, and he added a guitar part for me to learn. He went as far as he could, but playing marches on the guitar was not what I had in mind, so I studied with a local teacher named Barry Redley, and then with Hal Morris.

Later, I studied sightreading using the guitar, with a fine clarinet teacher. It really took some convincing for him to give me lessons; he thought it was crazy for a guitarist to study classical clarinet books!

Guitar was not a lead instrument in those days, but I knew that George Barnes was working with the NBC Orchestra and could read as well on guitar as any symphony player could. George was the sort of player I wanted to be like, and later in my career I had to learn to play *exactly* like him when I joined the Three Suns.

VG: Does your interest in the application of technology to music also date from your childhood?

DC: I'm not exactly sure how it evolved. I think my fascination with science began when I started doing experiments with my chemistry

TOP: *Del Casher today. Photo: Preston L. Gratiot*

LEFT: *Del, age 16, at home with the guitar he customized with his own hand-made parts. All photos courtesy Del Casher*

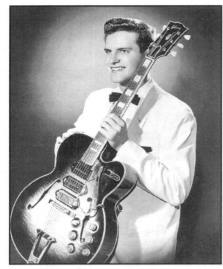

set when I was about 10 years old; I'd build miniature rockets, using powdered magnesium and potassium nitrate. My next love was electronics. I had a cousin who had a radio shop, and the weekends I spent there convinced me that I wanted to get into electronics and science; I was about 11 or 12.

Then at 13, I heard Les Paul, and my life changed. I'd known who he was because of my brother's extensive record collection, which included his early releases. But suddenly, I heard what he was really doing with his guitar and electronics, and I was hooked. His recordings were magic!

I felt like the guitar was the future of music. By the time I entered high school, I was the number one guitarist, and was playing professionally with local dance bands and groups. I'd learned how to read charts for Glenn Miller tunes, and I was always the youngest in the band.

VG: What kind of instruments were you using?

DC: I built my own electric guitar. I bought a used blond acoustic archtop, got some guitar pickups, and wired and installed them, just like Les Paul's guitar. My cousin told me about potentiometers, so I cut a hole in the back of the guitar and wired it internally. A friend's dad had a metal shop, so we built a mechanical tremolo for that guitar.

These days, it's not unusual for a young musician to have an electronic engineering degree *and* to also be a great guitarist, but back then, musicians were sometimes considered

"weirdos" (chuckles). Also, people didn't really seem to know what the guitar really was; it's hard to believe that today. I had to stand my ground because I believed in the future of the guitar.

VG: I understand you had your own radio show at a fairly early age.

DC: I'd practiced really hard, and I landed my radio show on WJOB in Hammond, at 16. I had to pre-record my background rhythm guitar tapes with added harmonies, and of course, the famous speeded-up guitars just like Les Paul. I could only go up to three or four generations before the noise buildup, so I'd get as much of the rhythm parts down as I could and would play the guitar melody live. I used Magnecord PT-6 machines; they got the job done. The shows worked out so well that the program director, Earl Vioux, recommended me to produce radio commercials for some department stores in Chicago. I called the musicians' union in Hammond to get a singer for those commercials; her name was Eleanor Ford. What a trip! My modified guitar with multiple recordings, and a gal named Ford! It was a valuable experience.

VG: Did you finally get to meet Les Paul in person?

DC: Yes I did. I used to go to the Lyon and Healy music store in Chicago, and the man who ran the guitar department, Bob Dayton, was a dear friend of Les Paul's, and had played in Les' trio at one time. I told Bob that I would do *anything* to meet Les Paul; he smiled and wrote a note on the back of his business card, gave it to me, and told me to go to

TOP: *Del in 1956, displaying his Gibson ES-5 during his time with the University of Pittsburgh "Tamburitzans."*

MIDDLE: *Ecco-Fonic brochure, which promotes Del performing with the Three Suns at the Ambassador Hotel.*

LEFT: *Del and Les Paul in the Chicago Theater dressing room playing Les' first gold top, modified with vibrola and his custom pickups – photo taken by Mary Ford, August 1953.*

RIGHT: *May 1993, Del accompanies Les Paul at the Gene Autry Museum in Los Angeles during Les Paul Day.*

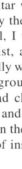

the Chicago Theater, where Les Paul and Mary Ford were appearing. I got to meet them backstage, and they took me to their dressing room where Les had his gold prototype guitar. I still haven't gotten over it; Les Paul and Mary Ford were bigger than life!

Les was so gracious to me; he let me play his prototype guitar. Mary Ford asked me if I'd like to have a picture taken with Les, and I told her that I didn't have a camera. She took out a Polaroid camera, which was a new idea at the time, and took a picture of Les and me playing his guitar.

Going home on the South Shore train that night, I guarded that picture like I was carrying ten million dollars (laughs)! And of course I made five negatives from that photo and put them in a vault.

The next day, I went to my favorite music store in Hammond, Hal Morris Music, and told Hal I had something they would not believe. Boy, were they impressed when they saw Les and me! Today, I have a copy of the photo in my studio lobby. Directors, film producers, and actors ask about Les' early guitar, and sometimes they'll ask "who's the kid?" in the picture (chuckles).

VG: Did you keep in contact with Les Paul and/or ever meet up with him again?

DC: Later, when I moved to California, Zeke Manners brought Les to my home recording studio in Hollywood. Les and I have since remained very dear friends throughout the years. I appeared with him on Les Paul Day in Los Angeles in 1993 at the Gene Autry Museum, along with Jeff Baxter on bass.

VG: Details about your college experiences?

DC: Well, I studied *everything that I would never need in the music business* (chuckles); subjects like Geology and Russian. But I met some wonderful musicians like Joe Negri and Johnny Rector; they

helped me understand the guitar, and that helped me immensely. For my scholarship, I was required to perform concerts with an ethnic college group called The Pittsburgh Tamburitzans. A tamburitza is a European stringed instrument that originates from Serbia and Croatia. Pittsburgh has a lot of ethnic folks from many lands, so our show was comprised of Italian, Slavic, Polish, Bosnian, Macedonian and Slovenian music. I was the first to play an electric guitar in such a group, and I did a lot of orchestra modifications that enhanced their traditional sound. The college kids in the group loved it.

During our summer concerts, I convinced our music director, Matt Gouze, that in addition to the ethnic music, we ought to do an "Americanski Guitar Boogie-Woogie and Jazz" part of the program. He agreed that it was a good idea, and it became the highlight of our concerts from then on. We even did Elvis Presley tunes which would later prepare me for the recording scene in Hollywood, since rock was taking over, bigtime. I had fun with those college performances, but during that time my heart was always in the complexity of recording, overdubbing, and getting a "quality" sound from my guitar.

VG: Did you feel like you had to come to L.A. if you were going to become a successful professional musician?

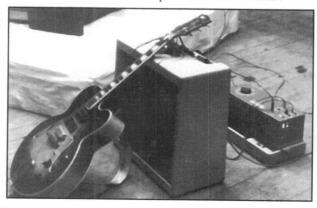

TOP: *The Three Suns on their RCA Tour in Osaka, Japan, in December 1959.*

MIDDLE: *Del on the front cover of a 1960 Fretts magazine with a Fender Jazzmaster.*

LEFT: *Del's Ecco-Fonic, Bandmaster amp, and ES-5 in Tokyo.*

RIGHT: *Del holding the original Vox Wah-Wah pedal he used for Vox promo records and his first film scores. Photo: Preston L. Gratiot.*

DC: I felt like I had a choice between L.A. and New York, and since I was from the Chicago area, I thought I'd rather come to where there was some sunshine. My brother was already out in L.A., playing for society parties, film producers, etc., and he helped me get some jobs. I also knocked on a lot of doors, but nothing happened.

Then one night I went to the world-famous Coconut Grove and saw The Three Suns perform; they were on RCA Records. They seemed to be having trouble with their new guitarist, so I told Artie Dunn, who was the band's organist and leader, that I thought I was the guy for their group. They invited me to audition the next day, and I was hired on the spot.

The many concerts I played as a featured soloist during the Pittsburgh college days taught me stage presence, how to relate to the audience, and how to get the biggest applause. That training paid off when I got this job.

VG: Tell me about your experiences with that band.

DC: Well, during that time I met up with E.S. Tubin, who owned a company called Ecco-Fonic. He needed someone with a high profile to use this new invention on live performances, and I was the guy now playing at the world-famous Coconut Grove with the famous Three Suns. The Ecco-Fonic was a portable box with a recording circuit and a tape cartridge; you could adjust your echo delay with the movable playback head that could be moved closer or farther from the record head. During performances I would reach back to the unit behind my Fender Bandmaster amp and get delays that were so long the audiences thought they were

hearing five guitars out of my one (chuckles). I also performed on all of the Ecco-Fonic demonstration records that helped sell the unit; Joe Maphis and I played together on those demos and performed at NAMM shows. Don Randall, from Fender, began to distribute a modified solidstate version of the Ecco-Fonic designed by Russ Allee, under the able guidance of Bob Marks from the Automata Corporation. Fender had me produce and perform on the Fender Ecco-Fonic 45 RPM record; it was used to promote the sales to guitar players.

The Ecco-Fonic was important in my situation with the Three Suns. Their sound was comprised of accordian, Hammond B-3, and electric guitar. At the time, they had the number one album in Japan, and after the Grove, we played the Tropicana Hotel in Las Vegas, then went on to Japan via a Japan Air Lines DC-6B. Twenty six hours one way! When we arrived at the Tokyo Airport, I saw about 2,000 people waiting at the arrival area, and when I asked why, I found out they were waiting for the Three Suns!

VG: What was it like playing for Japanese audiences?

DC: They were wonderful; very polite and attentive, but enthusiastic, too. We were one of the first American music groups to perform for the civilian audiences in Japan. Prior to that, only military entertainment had toured Japan.

We required a Hammond B-3 organ to follow us throughout our multi-city tour of Japan. A very thin, good-looking young man owned what seemed to be the only B-3 in Japan, and he accompanied it wherever we performed, from Hokkaido to Kyushu. During our performances he was always taking pictures of my guitar, my Ecco-Fonic, and me. He, as well as the audiences, were very amazed when I would do the "five guitars" sound with only two fingers moving; I would always place my Ecco-Fonic behind my new Fender Bandmaster amp, and after every concert in every city, Japanese musicians would offer to buy my amp for almost any price I asked! Later it hit me: *they thought the amp was making the multiple-note sounds.*

But the young man with the B-3 knew very

TOP: *Bill Page and his Vox Ampliphonic Band, which featured Del on guitar.*

MIDDLE: *The Ecco-Fonic Demo record*

well what was going on with the amp. His name is Ikutaro Kakehashi, and he's now the Chairman of the Roland Corporation. He has become a very good friend through the years, and in the '70s he invited me to introduce the first Roland GR-500 guitar synthesizer to Japan. I have always considered him a great genius of our time, with vision beyond imagination.

VG: What kind of guitar were you playing on the Japanese tour with the Three Suns?

DC: A Gibson ES-5 Switchmaster, and I'm indebted to Mr. Julius Bellson for it. He was kind and generous, and he took a personal interest in me when I was in high school. My father and I would visit the Gibson factory in Kalamazoo, and I already had an ES-350 with a cutaway. Mr. Bellson would ask Ward Arbanus and his staff to adjust the guitar, because I asked for a very low   action.

During one visit, Mr. Bellson had an ES-5 Switchmaster sitting in his office. He said it had some holes drilled in the wrong places, and asked if I was interested in it. My dad and I "gulped," because we knew a guitar like that would cost a fortune, and it was more money than we could ever afford....with or without wrong holes (chuckles)!

Mr. Bellson said he couldn't give it to me, but would sell it to me for $75 as a courtesy. It was his way of showing us that Gibson wanted me to do well, and how they were supportive of young people. I have fond memories of that experience; of Mr. Bellson and Gibson.

With that ES-5, I figured I might as well continue the experimenting process, so I put in passive high and low-pass filters, which gave it more flexibility and more sounds. I changed the center pickup to get a brighter sound, and made a clear plastic pickguard to make it more special.

VG: Back in the '50s, you were also seen playing other guitars, like a Gretsch Duo-Jet.

DC: I loved my Gretsch, and was pictured with it on the Ecco-Fonic brochure, but Artie Dunn felt that "those funny-looking solidbody small guitars" weren't professional-looking. You have to remember bandleaders in those days. They just didn't understand.

VG: What kind of work did you do in the L.A. area when the Three Suns returned from Japan?

DC: I played on Gene Autry's "Melody Ranch" TV show every week, and used my Gibson L-4 modified electric sprucetop. After several shows, I went down to visit the Fender guitar company, and met Leo Fender. He was so gracious; if you played country music, Leo would give up his whole day and do anything for you. He gave me a Telecaster, but made me promise that I'd play it or I'd have to give it back. I loved the guitar and *did* play it, but I went back about a month later and told him the guitar that really excited me was the Stratocaster; I had some upcoming Motown record dates. I told him I wanted one with a maple neck, and that I wanted the front pickup to be brighter-sounding. He took a Stratocaster apart in front of me, and rewound the front coil five or six times until I was satisfied. I still cherish that Stratocaster, and am honored to own a guitar that Leo himself modified, while I watched.

I met Bill Carson back then, along with Stan Compton and Don Randall, head of Fender

TOP: *Del during a Fender workshop, at Finder Music Store, San Diego, using his pre-recorded rhythm and bass backup tapes during performances.*

MIDDLE: *Ad from the* Los Angeles Free Press *for a 1966 concert featuring Frank Zappa and the Mothers of Invention.*

BELOW: *Del with Elvis at Paramount Pictures during filming of* Roustabout.

Sales. They were all wonderful to me. I also have a Jazzmaster, and I played a Jaguar in a Jerry Lewis film.

I built my first garage studio in 1963; guitar playing was an obsession, but so was recording on my own professional equipment. I bought two Ampex 351 stereo decks, and a Telefunken U-47 tube microphone; today I still consider that microphone to be a collector's item. I would produce demo songs, recording my guitar rhythm parts first, just like I did at WJOB, but with the Ampex recorders I could do a lot more generations than I could with the old Magnecords.

In 1964, I appeared with Elvis Presley in his movie *Roustabout*. One day on the set at Paramount Pictures, Elvis' buddy, Red West, came up to me and said "Elvis really likes your guitar playing and wants to get together in your garage studio when he finishes this picture, to try out some new tunes with you. Del, you've got to keep this very quiet because it could be a problem if people started coming in."

After the film was done, Elvis went on tour and it never happened, but Red would come in and sing on tracks I made for Elvis to hear, and Elvis eventually did record one of the tunes that Red and I thought would be good for him. Red sang just like Elvis, and I still have the tape.

VG: Also among the material I was able to peruse prior to this interview was a photostat of a poster for a Mothers of Invention concert.

DC: Frank Zappa was from Cucamonga; he came by one day, said he'd heard about me, and said he wanted to record something for a singer who had a song about a Russian cosmonaut who was lost in space (chuckles). I used to get these strange requests all the time, and Frank's request was no different. In those days he wasn't a guitar player, so he asked me to play guitar and bass, laying down tracks using the Ecco-Fonic to get the spacey sounds, while he played on a snare drum I had in the studio. I think this was one of the first recordings Frank did when

TOP: *Del with Jimmy Durante at Vox.*

MIDDLE: *Del on a morning television show in Tokyo, with Japanese rock band Godeigo, presenting the new Roland GR-500 guitar synth. This was the first time Japanese audiences heard the instrument. Photo courtesy of Mr. Kakehashi, Roland Corp.*

RIGHT: *Del playing Bob Hope's show on which Del served as conductor.*

he arrived in L.A. He was very pleasant, and he looked as weird as the sounds we created, but boy, was he talented! When he played the drum, I knew something great was going on, and we enjoyed that session so much he asked me to join his new group. I politely declined because my studio schedule was beginning to happen. Later, he formed the Mothers of Invention, and he asked me to play at several of his concerts while he and his manager, Herb Cohen, were getting a record deal together; it was an interesting experience. Frank employed me to perform with him on the David Susskind TV show featuring a "Freak Out" concert. I met with Frank a few years ago and he mentioned this show to me; I'm still trying to find a copy of it.

To me, Frank was one of the most exciting musicians I've known, because he went beyond being a musician. When I first met him, he said he was interested in playing guitar, and asked me what was the most expensive guitar, and I

told him that the most expensive one was a Gibson ES-5, like the one I had, so he went out and bought one.

He invited me to his home one evening, and instead of putting on a bunch of records and saying "listen to these," he showed me his 8mm home movies. He was fascinated with film, and he proved that his talent was much more in-depth than just with music.

He also asked me to play one of his early concerts at U.C. Santa Barbara. During the concert, the smoke machine freaked out everybody, which is what he wanted. My wife was in the audience, and was terrified! She expressed some feelings about that on the way home from Santa Barbara to Los Angeles, which is about 120 miles. I *did* play the Whiskey A-Go-Go on Sunset Strip with Frank.... without telling my wife where I was that night. We had a ball; we alternated sets with a kid named Lowell George and his band, Little Feat. Playing with Frank in his early days was great.

VG: Other Los Angeles musicians of note with whom you've worked?

DC: At that time, I was doing a lot of record dates in addition to operating my new studio in Hollywood in 1967. Tommy Tedesco used to call me to play on a lot of his sessions. He became a good friend and was sort of like my mentor. He showed me how to do things right for recording sessions, and hired me on many of the *Fifty Guitars of Tommy Garrett* albums. I worked a lot with Carol Kaye, a fabulous Fender bass player, and Hal Blaine, the most recorded drummer of all time. I'd perform on the Gene Autry TV show, then go to a record date, and I'd finish the evening with Frank Zappa. Sort of an A-to-Z music schedule (chuckles).

VG: In the mid '60s you became involved with another "gizmo" that was new at the time – the wah-wah pedal.

DC: I was always looking for a new sound for the guitar. I got a call from the Thomas Organ Company, which owned Vox Guitars; they said they had a new pedal they wanted me to try. I told them I didn't think I was interested, but they insisted. I was given the prototype wah-wah pedal by Stan Cutler, Vox's engineer, and the minute I plugged my guitar in, I

said "this is brilliant! It had a very narrow band, so the "cut" for the midrange of the guitar was extreme. Stan told me to take it home and play it for a few days. I called him back the very next morning and told him I couldn't give it back

(laughs). So they hired me to make a promotional recording using the pedal.

I said to myself "someone is going to become very famous with this pedal," but I didn't know what musical style it would be. I overdubbed my bass and three guitars with drums, using the wah-wah with some original blues, jazz, rock, country, and even sitar tunes; I recorded in my garage studio. This was 1967, and no one could imagine what Jimi Hendrix would later do with the wah-wah.

The record was pressed on a piece of plastic-

coated orange cardboard that was played at 45 RPM. It says "New from Vox, the Wah-Wah Sound, Recorded in Hollywood, California, U.S.A., February 1967." Since it was on cardboard, I didn't think much of the pressing, and I also didn't think I'd be talking about it 29 years later! I was paid $500, but I didn't insist on being credited as the guitarist on the record, as I had for Ecco-Fonic records. But that's me on it, and I have the master tapes and that rare cardboard record. I was later retained by Vox, and I demonstrated the wah-wah for James Brown, Jimmy Durante, and just about anybody else who walked in at Vox. I also appeared at the 1968 NAMM show in Chicago.

During a wah-wah press conference at the Century Plaza Hotel in L.A., TV stations were filming me jamming with the wah-wah, and a guy introduced himself and told me he wanted me to play on his film scores. His name was Vic Mizzy; he was the composer for "Green Acres," "The Addams Family," and other shows. Vic and I became great friends; he hired me as the first musician to use the wah-wah pedal on films. The first movie soundtracks I used the wah-wah on were *The Shakiest Gun in the West* and *The Ghost and Mr. Chicken*. I have a photo of Vic conducting and me with the prototype wah-wah on the recording stage of MGM, we're playing on the Tony Curtis movie *Don't Make Waves*. Vic became a very big wah-wah fan, using this sound on practically everything he did from then on.

TOP: *Promotional material, featuring Del, for the Vox wah-wah pedal.*

LEFT: *Del at the MGM scoring stage, using the Vox wah-wah pedal with Vic Mizzy's film score for the Tony Curtis film* Don't Make Waves.

Del's California Digital Post studio, in the media district of Burbank, California. Digital Post is a complete in-house package sound facility featuring a spacious mixing stage, a large ADR stage, complete Foley stage, and digital workstations for dialogue and sound effects editing.

Even Tommy Tedesco had to buy one, since he also did a lot of work for Vic.

VG: Were you involved with any other innovative products from Thomas/Vox back then?

DC: Yes, I produced and played on a Vox album with Bill Page, who led the Vox Ampliphonic Orchestra. Bill had just left the Lawrence Welk TV show, and was in charge of promoting the wah-wah pedal for use in big bands. We used wah-wah for saxophones, trumpets, clarinets, bass clarinets, and even a wah-wah bassoon, along with my wah-wah guitar. We recorded tunes by the Beatles, old standards, originals, and just about anything we thought would get a listener's attention. I still have the records and photos of this orchestra. It was really unique, because the music stands were triangular amplified speakers that said "Vox" on the front, and each one had its own built-in wah-wah pedal.

One day, Joe Banaran, Vox's President, asked me what they should call this version of the wah-wah pedal, because they planned on promoting it to big band players. I remembered hearing "Sugar Blues" by Clyde McCoy when I was a kid; he used a mute on his trumpet to get a "talking" sound, so I told Joe to call it the Clyde McCoy wah-wah, and that's exactly what he did.

VG: Were you ever a Fender endorser?

DC: Yes, when I came to California, Fender's *Fretts* magazine did a feature article on me with a cover photo. Through the years, Fender has always been great to me. Dan Smith has been a good friend, and Mike Caroff, a brilliant writer who's with Fender's *Frontline* magazine, wrote a very nice article about me a few years ago, about my transition into recording post-production sound for the film industry.

VG: You alluded earlier to hooking back up with Mr. Kakehashi in the mid-'70s, when they were developing their guitar synthesizer.

DC: Mr. Kakehashi has vision, patience, and passion for the guitar, and for anything else he does. He wanted to see the guitar become the "equivalent" to what the keyboard synthesizer could do, and he contacted me in 1976, when he learned I was in Los Angeles and I had a recording studio. We discussed his new ideas for Roland's GR-500 guitar synthesizer, and he asked me what model of guitar was most popular with players. I said "either a Fender Strat or a Les Paul," so they made the GR-500 in a Les Paul shape. He brought his new prototype to my studio; Bill Botrell was my engineer then, and we recorded this guitar on my 16-track, overdubbing all of the different voices the GR-500 could possibly make, then we mixed it down.

It sounded like 30 players on the tape! Mr. Kakehashi and I were amazed and very pleased. He took the tape to a trade show in Germany and played it for Bruce Bolen, who was then with Gibson. He was astounded; he didn't think a guitar could do what the GR-500 was doing.

When we got a final model we both liked, Mr. Kakehashi brought me to Japan to introduce the GR-500 to Japan's press; I also made public appearances on TV. Then we introduced it at the 1977 NAMM summer show in Atlanta. Mr. Kakehashi was most generous; he treated my wife and me like royalty during our trip to Japan.

VG: Any other devices with which you've been associated?

DC: Yes, the Foster Freaky. A friend of mine, Don Foster, built a gadget that made a swishing, phasing sound, like the guitar was coming over a short wave radio. At that time there were no phasers or flangers in the recording industry, unless you got the effect by using two tape recorders; that's were the word "flanging" comes from. Flanges are the metal reels on professional tape recorders that can be taken apart. The cool thing about this gadget was that I could "flange" or "swish" by rotating a knob.

About that time, in 1971, NBC in Los Angeles asked me to come up with a new sound for their closing theme for "NBC News Center 4," just before the Johnny Carson show. The Foster Freaky had the perfect sound for this project. I used my Vox Ultra-Sonic wah-wah guitar with distortion, and my Fender Telecaster for the lead guitar, through a modified GE tube phono preamp for guitar equalization.

It was an immediate smash hit; everyone thought it was some kind of new synthesizer. The TV audience demanded to know where they could buy this record, but there wasn't any record; I had only recorded what they asked: 30 seconds of a closing theme. Tom Brokaw and Tom Snyder, then part of the NBC News team in L.A., often commented at the end of the news how much they and their viewers liked this theme. An NBC executive called me one day and said that I had to make a record, because requests were coming in every day. So I edited the original version, extended it to two minutes, and added a violin section. It was flattering to have a major network ask me to make a record to sell to their *news audience!* The theme played from May 1971 through 1986, and was the longest-running theme NBC has ever had. But nobody has ever heard of the Foster Freaky or knew it was me playing that theme except for ASCAP, which paid me my royalties every month all those years!

VG: Tell me about some of the work you've done with famous performers.

DC: Dick Stabile, the orchestra director for the Coconut Grove, would call me whenever a new artist appearing needed guitar for their arrangements. This required very astute reading of charts, and Dick was very comfortable with my work. I worked with Eddy Arnold, Connie Francis, Bobby Vinton, Julie London, Bobby Troup, Buddy Rogers, Bob Hope, Peggy Lee, Buddy Ebsen, Donald O'Connor, Danny Thomas, and many others.

I recorded with Burt Bacharach and Gene Page, who was the arranger/conductor for a lot of the Motown hits. I also recorded with the Ray Conniff Orchestra, Sonny and Cher, and Phil Spector and his "wall of sound" efforts. I produced several albums by the Billy Vaughn Orchestra for JVC, using Bill Bottrell as my engineer. Bill recently received the producer Grammy Award for Sheryl Crow, and he was Michael Jackson and Madonna's engineer. He started his career with me, and I'm very proud of him. I appeared as guest solo artist on the Lawrence Welk TV show when Buddy Merrill left for the service.

VG: What about your work on movie soundtracks?

DC: I recorded the balalaika and tamburitza for Warren Beatty's film *Love Affair*, with Annette Benning. He liked what I did, so he put me in the movie. Earlier, I did the Matt Helm films with Dean Martin, *The Patsy* with Jerry Lewis, *Roustabout* with Elvis, *My Girl* for Columbia-Sony Pictures, and others.

Recently, I composed and performed the soundtrack score on a new film, using my MIDI guitar as the entire orchestra. All of the sounds are samples, using French horns, bassoons, brass, vibes, strings, and tymp. The sound is very sensitive, different and very real because everything is phrased from the guitar, just as I had envisioned 20 years ago.

VG: At the first Santa Monica guitar show, you renewed a friendship with R.C. Allen, who had some instruments on display at our booth.

DC: Dick was one of the first people I met when I came to California. He's a very talented luthier, and he introduced me to a lot of people. He built me a great plectrum banjo; it sounds terrific. He also makes great guitars; Dick is one of the best in everything he does.

VG: How many different fretted instruments do you play?

DC: I have about 45 instruments, and many of them are guitars with modified electronics, tunings, altered bridges, and hand-wound pickups. I also play bouzouki, tamburitza, oud, balalaika, electric mandolin, 12-string mando-guitar, plectrum and 5-string banjo, tenor and baritone uke, and a modified Gretsch electric 12-string guitar.

VG: What do you think is the most-often-heard example of your playing over the years?

DC: Probably the early wah-wah soundtracks for "Green Acres" and "Chico and the Man," and of course the "NBC News Center 4" theme.

VG: Over the decades, what do you think was your toughest assignment?

DC: I think the *toughest, but most lucrative,* was when I was musical director for "The New Zoo Revue," a syndicated children's show that ran for four years in the early '70s. Each show had three songs, which meant 15 songs had to be written, then arranged by me, and recorded each Wednesday for use on shows that began the next Monday. It wasn't difficult, but it was probably the most stressful, because after writing the arrangements, I would have to call the players in, conduct and play guitar on the sessions, then I'd stay over to mix down the tracks for the singers to overdub during the next few days. It was like producing an album a week!

VG: On the flip side, what about the best assignment, or the one that was the most fun?

DC: I think playing those concerts with Frank Zappa was the most fun, because as a studio player I was constantly being told "play it this way," "don't play this," or "you're playing too loud," so I was confined. But Frank would turn to me onstage and say "take 20 choruses." When I'd get to the twentieth one, with the audience cheering wildly, he'd say "take five more." I felt like I had the freedom to go on forever.

VG: Looking to the future, you're a big proponent of MIDI guitar.

DC: Ever since Mr. Kakehashi came to me with his first synthesizer guitar, I've known that the guitar as an orchestra was no longer a dream, but a reality that he helped make come true. So many times, on my TV productions or albums, I needed to play the piano, or needed to overdub a clarinet or trombone. Now I can phrase what I hear in my head without having to explain it. All I have to do is play it. I think the only limit to the MIDI digital musical world now is one's imagination and playing ability.

VG: But some of the old guitars still sound good.

DC: You bet! I recently recorded my trio in my new post-production facility in Burbank, using my Stromberg and my Fender/D'Aquisto acoustic. Al Vescovo had his fabulous old Gibson L-7, and Fernando Cortez was on bass. We recorded "one-takes," with no overdubs, all to digital tape. If we made a mistake, we stopped and got a good take straight through. It's a satisfying sound that no synthesizer can create. That's why I never use guitar samples on my film scores. I will always use the real guitar.

Readers may have noticed Del Casher's answers are usually quite meticulous, which is probably how he also approaches his studio work. Casher has had more unique experiences in his musical career than most players, but he's certainly not the type to rest on his laurels. He's still pursuing the latest musical innovations, from where he began with Ecco-Fonic to today's MIDI, to further his knowledge and abilities. That's an admirable legacy.

Paul Chandler's
Accessory Adventures (and Guitar Adventures As Well)

Situated between San Francisco and Silicon Valley, Chandler Industries of Burlingame, California is probably a familiar name to many *Vintage Guitar* readers. Company literature states: "For fourteen years we have built our reputation by providing quality guitar components, innovative electronics and great customer service. All Chandler products have their roots firmly in the Golden Era of American Guitars, offering classic style with an emphasis on tone."

Vintage Guitar recently toured the Chandler facilities, and came away with the distinct impression that the company is indeed living up to the statement in its catalog. But prior to our tour, we sat down with President and founder Paul Chandler to discuss his company's history as one of the leaders in the guitar accessory market, as well as the firm's more recent ventures with original-style guitars that have a "retro-vibe" look:

VG: Are you originally from the Bay Area?

PC: I was from southern California; my father got transferred to Oklahoma in the late Sixties and I really got into music while I lived there. I moved to San Francisco when I wanted to do something in the guitar business; there's more financial activity and more venture capital; there's a stock market exchange there. It's easier to get a factory going in this area than it would be in Oklahoma.

I've always enjoyed playing in bands, and I still do on weekends. I'd been repairing and trading instruments since the mid-Seventies, and I left the insurance business in 1980 to do this full time, although I'd been doing it for years in the evenings and on weekends.

VG: Was your first facility in San Francisco?

PC: Yes, it started out in a one-room apartment (chuckles). I expanded to a larger place, then in 1981 we went into an old two-story house in the Richmond district; it was a nice area with great neighbors, but they didn't appreciate the routers going at eleven o'clock at night (laughs)! I had a total of four locations in San Francisco, then in the summer of '92 we moved down here to Burlingame; we're about twenty minutes south of the city.

VG: Even when you were doing this part-time, were you more oriented towards parts or guitars?

PC: Accessories. I made my first pickguards in the Seventies, when I was working in music stores in Oklahoma; I started a template collection then. You might think: "Pickguards; big deal," but I really like making them. There are so many variations we can do; we have about seven hundred different patterns to choose from. I got into other guitar parts, but pickguards were what got me interested. After that we started doing necks and bodies. In 1984 I began importing necks and bodies from Japan that were built to my design specifications. Eventually we brought the neck

and body business in-house; I couldn't monitor how well my designs were being manufactured overseas.

VG: What was unique about your designs?

PC: I have a vintage guitar collection, and I was going for certain shapes. The neck I've always liked is the one on an SG Junior, and I put that carve on Strat and Tele-type necks, plus I made a few refinements. I think the imported Chandler products were some of the best that were coming out of Japan back then. But the currency changes over the last eight years or so meant that we were getting more standardized products; factories couldn't economically figure our specialized products into their production schedules. I felt like we were going to lose control of the situation, so I really "beefed up" our efforts here about four or five years ago.

VG: Were you still located in San Francisco?

PC: Right; things got so busy I had to look at moving again, but the politics of San Francisco aren't really oriented towards manufacturers, so I began to look elsewhere. I actually went to Austin, Texas to check things out; I've got family there.

You see, we were having to do things like share bandsaws for pickguards and guitar bodies; I'd been farming out my painting, but the guy couldn't keep up. So we knew we had to make a big move, and I found that I could make a move down here for around the same it would have cost to relocate to Austin, plus I could maintain all of my business connections; legal, accounting, etc. The last facility we had in San Francisco was five thousand square feet; this plant is thirteen thousand, five hundred. Once you have roots in an area, it's hard to uproot yourself, so I think we're going to be here for a long time.

VG: What comes out of this factory?

PC: Pickguards, guitars, and bodies and necks, for the most part. We have a place down in Silicon Valley that does devices, and pickup winds are done by a high-tech company in Nebraska.

VG: One of the first things you marketed that got my attention was the reissue of the Danelectro "lipstick tube" pickup.

PC: Ours was the first replacement lipstick tube pickup on the market. I've concentrated on the winding, the magnets, and the wire when I've developed pickups. The Nebraska company has sophisticated machinery that does precise windings; we can market a P-90 or a Tele-type pickup that won't squeal. When you're playing a gig, there are so many things a player needs to concentrate on, you don't need the distraction of a guitar whistling.

VG: The pickups on a Sea Foam Green "555" I saw in your upstairs area looked "Firebird-ish."

PC: They *sound* very Firebird-ish as well. They have two Alnico V magnets inside the coils; we put a lot of work into that design. That guitar is for Steve Miller; he played it at the NAMM show and bought it right there. All we had to do was put heavier gauge strings on it; he likes .011s. I put one of our "Tone X" units in it as well.

One of the benefits of being in the parts business is you can design instruments that can be hot-rodded or modified, and that's what we did with the 555; there's a channel under the pickguard where all types of pickup configurations can be installed. A guy ordered one yesterday with P-90s on it instead of mini-humbuckers; no problem.

VG: When and why did you opt to get into more original-looking instruments in addition to traditional styles?

PC: Around '92; I've still got a lot of other original designs that I want to do, but for a small company it's hard to do everything all at once. One step at a time.

I ultimately decided that there was no real future for me in selling Fender-style bodies and necks, even though we'd done real well with them. Fender's items are trademarked, and part of the legal aspect of the guitar business is that you don't sell assembled guitars with Fender trademarks on them. It's not "user friendly" selling guitar parts; it can be difficult fitting a body from one company to a neck from another company, for example.

We designed the "555" first, which has some inspiration from early Les Paul Juniors and Specials as well as some Rickenbacker models, plus it has the mini-humbuckers we were discussing earlier. From there we went onto the "Austin Special," which has lipstick tube pickups, then our latest model, the "Telepathic"; it's selling very, very well.

VG: Comments about some of your endorsers?

PC: Joe Satriani was a local guy; we met in a bar back in 1980 when I first moved here. I ended up taking some guitar lessons from him; he got me going on the use of echo.

Eric Johnson has been using our stuff since around Day One; he's always been a great customer and has given us a lot of support. Danny Gatton, an alternative band called Redd Kross....

VG: A previous *Vintage Guitar* interviewee, Marshall Crenshaw, was singing the praises of your company's digital echo as well as some of your other products.

PC: The digital echo's a great unit; it's been made overseas but we're getting ready to switch it to domestic production. I use one when I play; in fact I can't stand to hear my guitar without it on! Even if it's just a little bit in the background, it makes a big difference .

VG: You've got a fairly diverse list of endorsers.

PC: We've never really pursued relationships with heavy metal players. I just don't think that what we're doing product-wise is very interesting to players in that genre. Now, we do a lot of work for Billy Sheehan and Paul Gilbert of Mr. Big, but they're not really metalheads.

What we do is for guys who grew up playing Harmony guitars, and who can understand why you'd want a guitar with lipstick tube pickups and pearl binding. We pay a lot of attention to the *details* on a guitar; not just its looks, but its sound as well. You can buy an imported Telecaster copy for around two hundred dollars, or you can buy a guitar that looks somewhat similar for around three thousand that was made by Tom Anderson. They may both play music, but the difference is in the details, and that's what drives this company.

VG: Back to that "Tone X" accessory that you were talking about a few minutes ago. As I understand it, the device turns a tone pot into sort of a miniature wah-wah. How does it differ from something like the Alembic "Q" switch?

PC: I'm not that familiar with the "Q" switch; both units are similar in that they have a sweep, but the inductor on ours is exactly like the inductor on a 1968 Vox chrome-top wah-wah. The heart of the sound on any wah-wah-type product is the inductor, and the mass-produced units that are on the market now are using cheap, imported components. That's like making $1,000 guitars with a $5 pickup. The inductor we use costs a lot, but it sounds right and it doesn't feed back. It's a great little rock and roll booster. When I play gigs, I really like to get a certain sound, and it's hard to get it below "2" on the amplifier volume control. I use a fifty-watt amp, and when I have to turn down, the Tone X helps me get a good, punchy solo tone at a low volume. It's great to help me "articulate" some of my playing, too.

VG: What kind of music do you play on weekends?

PC: "Retro-electro;" bad cover songs from the Sixties and Seventies (chuckles). We just put a groove down and go from song to song to song; forty-five minute medleys, and as it approaches one o'clock in the morning, the medleys get longer and wilder. Last weekend, we started one such medley with "Red House," then went into " Mony Mony," then "Keep Your Hands to Yourself," then "Love Lies Bleeding" by Elton John, then "Stop Breaking Down" by the Rolling Stones. This is all non-stop, and it keeps drifting back and forth into previous songs.

I'm a Seventies guitar player, and for me, the whole idea of what I'm doing can be summed up by listening to the guitar solo at the end of a song called "Sway" by the Rolling Stones, on the *Sticky Fingers* album. That solo lays down the law for my electric guitar playing (chuckles). That's what my band does, and that's what we sound like. I think Mick Taylor's the man.

VG: Final comments?

PC: The root of everything we do is being a "retro"-oriented company. Everything this organization does will reflect that, from the plating on pickguard screws that we sell to the finest finished instruments we make. The whole aesthetic is based on what Leo Fender and Ted McCarty were doing in the Fifties and Sixties. Almost everyone who works here is a guitar player, and as such, employees have a lot of input into the designs of our products.

Think about what happened to the motorcycle business in this country. We lost it all to the imported products, with the exception of Harley-Davidson. God bless those guys! They hung tough through the bad times and came out on top; they're now one of the Fortune 500 companies. The same thing almost happened to the guitar business, but thanks to a lot of hard working people, not just in this company, of course, but all over the country, I think we're in the process of taking the guitar business back to a position of respect as well. What I'm interested in doing in my own small way of contributing is carrying on the heritage that got me interested in guitars in the first place. *That's* why I do lipstick pickups and pearl pickguards.

CRAIG CHAQUICO
Beyond the Starship

If you're a fan of New Age and "light jazz" guitar music, you're probably familiar with the Pat Metheny Group's earlier albums on the ECM label, as well as more recent recordings by such artists as Max Lasser and Special EFX. If you like that kind of playing, you'll probably enjoy a new release on the Higher Octave label entitled *Acoustic Highway*.

And a listener would probably quite surprised to discover that the guitarist who made this album is none other than Craig Chaquico of Jefferson Starship/Starship fame.

Chaquico's expressive lead guitar was a staple of the Starship sound for over a decade and a half. After numerous personnel changes and legal controversies, Chaquico opted to end his association with the Starship (which in some persons' opinions might have been existing in name only; details to follow) and strike out in more than one new musical direction. *Vintage Guitar* recently conversed at length with the amiable guitarist; Chaquico is not only an established and talented player, he also has some enviable vintage instruments, and he's an accomplished artist as well.

VG: Are you originally from California? Did the area where you grew up have any effect on your playing and/or musical aspirations?

CC: I grew up on a farm in Elverta, California, which is outside Sacramento. It seems like guitars went with farms, just like cattle, horses, sheep and wranglers. After a couple of years of accordion lessons—

VG (interrupting): Wait a minute. Is your heritage Italian?

CC: No, Portugese. Why? The accordion lessons?

VG: This isn't the first time accordions have been mentioned by an interviewee as a childhood instrument. A couple of years ago Jeff Carlisi of .38 Special told me that his first instrument was an accordion, and I interrupted him as well; I told him that I didn't believe in stereotyping, but I assumed he was of Italian heritage. He said he was, and added that he had an espresso dispenser built onto the accordion.

CC: (laughs) Persons of Portugese heritage also

took accordion lessons! Jeff's one of the nicest guys that I know in this business, and he's a hell of a guitar player, too! Some of the best times I ever had when I was with Starship were when we toured with .38 Special. Those guys were Southern gentlemen and a lot of fun; I used to talk some of the members of their crew into riding in the Starship bus just so I could ride in the .38 Special bus. I gave Jeff two original nickel-plated P.A.F. pickup covers for a guitar he had; if I remember correctly he'd put some original P.A.F.s in a Les Paul of his, but he needed covers; I think I gave these covers to him for his birthday.

VG: What about your earliest instruments and influences?

CC: Well, my earliest influence was a female wrangler named Bonnie; she played a four-string tenor guitar; you don't see those instruments much anymore. I'd listen to her play folk songs like "Old Stewball." Not too long after that I got my first record, which was Quicksilver Messenger Service's first album. That *totally* turned my head around.

VG: I would think Cippolina's fingerpicking would *definitely* sound different from folks songs!

CC: Not just the fingerpicking, but that SG sound of his as well as his use of the Bigsby vibrato. That album changed my life; after that I started listening to Hendrix, Cream, Zeppelin, Floyd. Ironically, I ended up not only with original Quicksilver member David Freiberg in Starship, but the band that plays live in support of the *Acoustic Highway* album has Mario Cippolina, John's brother from Huey Lewis & the News, playing bass.

I started pestering my parents for an electric guitar when I was about twelve, then I was in a car accident. I broke my arm, my thumb, my wrist and my leg in two places. I had a cerebral concussion and was in a coma for three days. When I woke up, the first thing I did was ask for a guitar again (chuckles). My doctor thought it would be good therapy, even though I could only reach the high E string. These days I start my set with a song called "Elizabeth's Song"; she's the doctor who encouraged me back then. Twenty-six years later I've come full circle since I'm concentrating on acoustic guitar again, and the first place I played these new instrumental songs was the hospital where I was a patient so long ago.

VG: What about your earliest electrics, once you

Photo courtesy of High Octave Music/Engel Entertainment

were able to play?

CC: A lot of my friends had electrics before I did and I'd borrow them. One guy had a St. George with three pickups and a tremelo bar; it even had a hole in the body that was a "handle." I guess that made it a primitive version of the Steve Vai guitar! (laughs) I'd do things like mow this guy's yard so I could borrow that St. George.

Now *my* first guitar was a Winston; it was a copy of a Vox "teardrop" style, and I still have it. I had posters of my guitar heroes all over the wall in my room, but my parents really supported me and bought me my first equipment. They'd been musicians as well, but ultimately got "responsible" jobs. After all these years I've looked back and realized my real heroes were my parents.

My dad bought me an SG/Les Paul, and that was my first "important" guitar. I played it on Grace Slick's solo album when I was sixteen. Once I got going with Jefferson Starship, I went to see Norm Harris when I got my first big check (chuckles). I bought a '57 Goldtop Les Paul, which I used on all the earlier Jefferson Starship albums. It was a rare one because it didn't have a maple top; its construction was all mahogany so it had kind of a different sound. One time back then a blind guy I met told me: "You're the guy who plays a Les Paul that sounds like a Strat"; his hearing was that acute. I also bought a Firebird from Norm, a '57 Strat with a maple neck, and others.

VG: Were you a collector before you joined Jefferson Starship?

CC: No, because I couldn't afford to buy guitars. Now, I was *aware* of the desirability of old guitars; Norm would always tell me to check out certain instruments but I couldn't afford them. Maybe it's fair to say I became a collector *immediately* after I got that first check! (chuckles) I wasn't even twenty-one years old, and I also bought myself a sports car and a house.

VG: Do you still have that house?

CC: I still have the house. I was nineteen when I joined Starship, but I didn't become a "full-fledged member" until the *Red Octopus* album went multi-platinum. Up until that time I didn't make as much money as other members, but their management probably decided to sign me up before someone else did.

My house was actually "decorated" with guitars! (chuckles) The night stand next to my bed was a vintage tweed amp with a flag draped over it. The whole house was empty; I had no idea how long I'd be there because I didn't know how long the band would go on. I was only there a couple of months out of the year because of touring; I had a mattress, a TV, a lava lamp and a lot

of guitars and amps, and that was it. Each Christmas, instead of putting up a tree I'd set one of my guitars on a stand and put Christmas lights on it! (laughs)

VG: Pete Sears and David Freiberg both played bass in Starship; each one played on specific songs. Didn't that make things somewhat awkward?

CC: Not as much as a lot of people might think. You see, Pete and David would each play *piano* on songs they'd written, and the other guy would play bass. Not only that, but their styles were different. David was more of a funk/"in-the-pocket" player, while Pete had more "flash."

VG: Your setup at one point included a lot of old Bassman amps.

CC: Jorma Kaukonen's brother Peter played for a short time with Starship, and he told me to turn the Presence on those old Bassman amps all the way up, the Treble and Volume all the way up, and the Bass all the way down. He also showed me how to play with my teeth and behind my back; all that Hendrix **** (chuckles). I think his *Black Kangaroo* solo album shows a definite Hendrix influence. Peter played bass with Starship on the first tour, but never recorded with us. He taught me so much about old guitars; when we were in New York we went to all of the guitar shops. I watched him buy guitars like an Explorer, a Flying V and a Firebird.

I had several "mentors" in my early days with Starship. Peter taught me about instruments and how to get a killer tone, Johnny Barbata taught me about health food and vitamins; I've been a vegetarian for a lot of my life. Grace was a musical mentor as well.

VG: The reason I asked you if you still had the house a bit earlier was because I believe that most if not all of your vintage guitars were destroyed in that German concert riot in 1980.

CC: The ones that I toured with were, but those happened to be my favorite pieces as well. I lost two '57 Goldtops, a '59 sunburst Les Paul, a Firebird, and all my Bassman amps. I went back to the scene of the riot the next day and there was nothing left but ashes. All that was left of the Bassman amps were the metal corner pieces.

After that I decided I needed to find a line of

Photo: Jay Blakesberg courtesy High Octave Music/ Engel Entertainment modern guitars that played and sounded like vintage guitars. I endorsed B.C. Rich for a while; they were pretty cool, and I liked the fact that they were hand-made in California. I could go to the factory and pick out the ones I liked. Then I found out about Carvin, which is also hand-made in California. I went down to the factory in Escondido, and told them I wanted something that felt and sounded like a vintage Les Paul; fat neck and big, fat frets. They ended up making me some V-220s; although they don't look like Les Pauls, the set-up, feel and sound is in my opinion like a Les Paul. I'm still endorsing Carvin.

VG: Seems like the stock finishes on the V-220 were either white or black but I think I saw you playing one on a video that had a natural finish with a lot of flame maple on the body.

CC: Yeah; I still have that guitar. It reminds me of my '59 Sunburst that got destroyed.

VG: I'm aware of the platinum sales awards and the Grammy nomination, but I understand the band had an Oscar nomination as well.

CC: That was for Best Song; the tune in question was "Nothing's Gonna Stop Us Now" from the movie *Mannequin*. That was the best movie since *Gone With The Wind*; that's my opinion and I'm stickin' to it! (laughs) We actually played on the awards show; that was really exciting. If I remember correctly, we received a Golden Globe nomination as well for the same song.

VG: Does Starship exist as a band anymore?

CC: As such, it doesn't; I'm the only one who was on every album, every video and every real tour. Now there's two bands that are using the Starship name; each band has one guy who was in the band, but neither person is me (chuckles). Go figure...

VG: Around the same time the last Starship album came out, the Jefferson Airplane reunion album was released. Do you happen to know which one charted higher?

CC: I'd have to think it was ours, since we had a Top Five single called "It's Not Enough" on that last album. I don't think any Airplane reunion songs ever made the charts. Right after "It's Not Enough" did well, the band sort of broke up; we never did follow up with another single release but we did do a greatest hits compilation.

VG: And currently you have *two* musical projects, the afore-mentioned instrumental acoustic group and a rock band called Big Bad Wolf.

CC: Right. Big Bad Wolf played at the Cabo Wabo as part of the live Van Halen broadcast in the summer of 1992. We've done a lot of playing around the Bay Area. Big Bad Wolf really reflects how I wish Starship had been when I was doing a lot of the songwriting; I always went in a melodic, guitar-oriented direction. Right before I left Starship, the only ones left were Mickey Thomas and me; all my favorite players were gone: Pete, David, Grace. The band's management wanted us to record with L.A. studio musicians and call the results a Starship album, and they wanted to hire other musicians to go on a so-called Starship tour. I told them: "While you're hiring, get a lead guitarist, 'cause I'm not going to put up with this bull****." (chuckles) I got into the acoustic venture and Big Bad Wolf almost immediately afterwards.

VG: You've got to admit that most music fans wouldn't ex-pect an album like *Acoustic Highway* from a player with your kind of experience.

CC: No question. I started playing acoustic guitar again on a regular basis for my wife when she was pregnant. She got preg-nant right after I left Starship; funny how that works out! (chuck-les). When my son Kyle was born, I'd play for him; the music would soothe him and calm him. Then began making tapes of such music for him. Someone heard those tapes and suggested I send them to a New Age label, and it developed from there. I think if someone listens to it, they'll see that I still drew a lot from the likes of Zeppelin and Floyd; at least from some of their quieter stuff.

VG: The intro to the third song, "Gypsy Nights," sounds a bit like the intro to "Stairway to Heaven," in my opinion.

CC: It does a little; "Stairway to Heaven" always reminded me of something like a Renaissance Faire or maybe "knights in shining armor." I was trying to get that kind of feel in "Gypsy Nights."

VG: I still heard some electric guitars on a couple of songs.

CC: Those are Carvins; I hope you noticed that the electric guitar solos are exactly where such solos would be in a vocal song. The acoustic guitar is "singing the melody" instead of a voice.

VG: What acoustic instruments did you use on *Acoustic High-way*?

CC: A Washburn acoustic-electric. Even though I've got some great old Martins and Guilds, I always had trouble getting the right sound for recording with them; expensive studios and ex-pensive mikes still left me frustrated. Washburns have got a great pre-amp in them that immediately eliminates all of that kind of hassle; they're great guitars. I don't have to worry about where I'm sitting or how the mike is set.

VG: Do you still have any vintage instruments? Are you still collecting?

CC: I've only kept the old guitars that I use; I got rid of all of the ones that I was simply holding on to and not playing. I've even loaned some guitars to some of my friends in my neighbor-hood; at least I know where the instruments are, and I know they're being played.

VG: Sounds like you're excited about your new musical di-rection.

CC: You bet! This is something that has turned out better than I ever would have thought. I still like playing with Big Bad Wolf, but the *Acoustic Highway* album was a radical change for me, and I'm really proud of how it sounds.

Craig Chaquico practically grew up in a world-famous rock band. Now that obligations such as parenthood have come into his life, he's shifted gears and headed in a new musical direction with the *Acoustic Highway* album, but he still looks forward to rockin' out with Big Bad Wolf as well. His experiences have helped him to develop a mature attitude, and that's a commend-able trait for a musician.

Chaquico's next two albums were titled Acoustic Planet *and* A Thousand Pictures. *Like* Acoustic Highway, *they charted high on* Billboard*'s N.A.C. chart.*

Bob Crooks
CALIFORNIA "FIRSTS"

Included with the many "firsts" concerning Bob Crooks and the history of California amplifier technology is the fact that this is the first interview the Standel founder has ever done with a guitar-oriented publication. For all of his innovations in the guitar amplifier field, and considering the well-known artists who used Standel amps in the Fifties and Sixties, Crooks' name is not as well known in the annals of fretted instrument and amplifier history as some other builders, but knowledgeable vintage enthusiasts are probably familiar with the Standel name, as it has been seen on powerful amplifiers, and guitars as well.

When *Vintage Guitar* talked with Mr. Crooks, he stated he is now retired, but keeps busy. He goes into BBE Sound "about four days a week," and is still working on some innovative products (more about those later). Mr. Crooks' tales of the "glory days" of the California guitar and amplifier industry made for another fascinating perspective on those memorable times.

VG: What kind of electronics training did you have that made you want to build amplifiers?

BC: Well, I could go way back to when I got out of high school in Loveland, Colorado. I thought I wanted to be a musician; I played rhythm guitar and did the vocals and some arranging in a band back in the Thirties. We had anywhere from six to fourteen players, depending on the job. It appeared to be a glamorous life, but as we went around playing dances, I realized that to be a successful musician didn't so much depend on your talent, it depended on your determination and luck, so I looked around for something else.

I got interested in electronics and took several

correspondence courses. Ultimately I worked for Lockheed; I was the engineer in charge of their Electronics Standards Lab. I supervised all of the technicians in the service and calibration of all of Lockheed's electronic test equipment.

VG: Was this during World War II?

BC: No, it was after; during the war, I was in Communications with the tank destroyers down in Fort Hood, Texas.

I still liked the guitar and music, and didn't want to get away from it completely. I had a shop in my garage where I would fix radios on evenings and weekends for extra money. I also built a Ham radio station.

The opportunity to get into the music business came from a friend who also knew Paul Bigsby. He told me Bigsby was building steel guitars like mad in his back yard, and that Bigsby wanted someone to build him an amplifier, so I went down and met Paul; he was quite a man. He advanced me fifty bucks. I thought, "This is what I want to do for a living!" (chuckles)

It sounded so easy. I thought that if I could play a recording of guitar music over an amplifier and it sounded okay, it was going to work. I bought an old turntable and a Les Paul recording of "Lover"; I trimmed up the amp until the record sounded good, then I called Paul to come over to my house in Temple City with one of his steel guitars. When he plugged it in, it was the worst sound I've ever heard. I was embarrassed, and Paul took a "back to the drawing board" attitude, but he left the guitar with me to use as a test instrument. I finally got what I thought was a good sound.

Have you ever seen any of those old Thirties radios that have round tops?

VG: Like Atwater-Kents and Philcos?

BC: Yes; Paul built a cabinet shaped like those. The knobs were at the bottom, and he laminated the wood in strips going over the top; he spent a lot of time on it and did a heck of a job. I asked him why he'd gone to so much trouble, and he noted that other amps were cube-shaped and had cigarette burns all over them; he said, "They can't lay a cigarette on this cabinet!" (laughs)

TOP: *Bob Crooks in 1994 with his personal Standel guitar, made by Harptone. It's a model 910S with gold hardware, DeArmond pickups, and a master volume control on the cutaway horn.*

LEFT: *1968: (left to right) Frank Garlock (Standel Public Relations), Wes Montgomery, Bob Crooks.*

TOP: *A Classic Photo of Classic Players: Joe Maphis and Barbara Mandrell demonstrating Standel equipment at a Chicago show*

MIDDLE: *A 1969 Standel model MC II amplifier head sits atop a rare "Artist 30" powered speaker cabinet with two 15" JBL speakers in it.*

LEFT: *The prototype amplifier built by Bob Crooks, circa 1950.*

RIGHT: *Two Fifties Standel amplifiers built by Bob Crooks in his garage.*

We took it around to clubs for musicians to try; Paul Bigsby already knew most of them, so he's the reason I got to meet the players. We went around for a couple of weeks, but didn't impress anyone, so Paul changed his mind about wanting an amp.

I didn't want to forget about making amps, though; I was really interested by then. I got Paul to loan me an amplifier that he used to test pickups; he liked the way it sounded. That amp had a circuit that was in the back of an RCA tube manual. I didn't want to copy another amp, I wanted something that was new and different, something that was mine. I finally figured out that the reason a record and a guitar pickup sounded different through an amp was because in a recording studio, the engineer was controlling the frequency response and adjusting levels, picking out what he wanted to be on the record. So I figured I had to do that with my amplifier, so by fooling around with different equalization ideas, I came up with a fixed circuit that gave me a "notch" or "dip" in the middle, right around 350 cycles. I figured out that you have to control the midrange, and amplify the harmonics. I suppressed the midrange, and put bass and treble controls on the amp so you could move the "ends" up and down. The sound I had been looking for was there.

VG: What else was unique about that amp?

BC: Several things, at least to my knowledge no other amp on the market at that time, which was around 1952, had the following features:

1. I had bass and treble tone controls. Other amps at that time had a single control that

would adjust the treble frequencies.

2. I think it was the first constant current tube amp at that time.

3. I used open weave Hi-Fi Grille cloth, which doesn't sound like much, but try using a flocked wire grille which was common at that time and see what your amp sounds like.

4. One of the more important features was using a fifteen-inch JBL model D-130 speaker.

VG: Did this amp have a Thirties radio cabinet as well?

BC: (chuckles) No, I had a standard case upholstered in Naugahyde. I gave the customers a choice of several colors with an engraved plate with their name on it.

VG: Did you take the new amp out to the clubs again?

BC: Actually, I built several prototypes after Paul and I separated. I would take them into the country music clubs in L. A. without much success. I decided to try some of the leading musicians that were playing in the Los Angeles area, like Speedy West, Merle Travis, and Joe Maphis. They were at least kind enough to plug into the amp and in a nice way let me know that it wasn't what they were looking for.

When I finally developed the sound I wanted, I decided to try it out on a young steel player named Jim Corwin whom I met through Paul Bigsby. Jim was playing with a band at a country music club called The Blue Room in Pomona.

I wanted to check the amp under normal playing conditions on the band stand. When Jim began to play, I knew I had a winner and before the night was over, Jim wanted to buy one.

The next two nights I went back to Speedy

West, who was playing with Cliffie Stone and went to Merle Travis and Joe Maphis that were playing on the "Town Hall Party" show, and received the same positive results. Dickie Stubbs, who played steel on the "Town Hall Party" show also ordered an amp. Suddenly I had orders for four amps. I also had several dealers asking for a franchise.

VG: Do you still have that amp?

BC: No, I'm sorry to say, when the company went out of business many years later, I gave the amp to one of my salesmen. I should have kept it.

VG: Had you envisioned your amplifier as being utilized primarily by steel players or electric Spanish-type guitar players?

BC: As it turned out, the amp performed very well with almost any stringed instrument.

VG: It's interesting that your first sales were to "big name" entertainers

BC: That is the only way you can get into an industry that is already controlled by established companies unless you want to get into a price "dog fight" with the cheapy stuff and I not only wasn't interested in that kind of a business, I also didn't have the financial means. So I took custom orders and built them one at a time for several years.

Irby Mandrell, Barbara Mandrell's father, was my first salesman and did a fine job for a few years. Barbara was eleven years old at the time, a natural entertainer. She played several instruments including a four neck steel guitar and demonstrated our equipment at The National Music Show in Chicago.

Bill Lanzendorf, the West Coast rep for Gretsch guitars, called me one day. He had seen some of my amps and offered to buy stock in the company and represent the West Coast sales, but he stated that I had to go into the business full time, which I did. This was in 1960. Shortly after that, I received a call from a salesman in St. Louis named Al Simpkins who had also seen some of my amps and wanted to represent the Eastern sales and all of Europe. Al was on a first name basis with every major music dealer in this country and Europe, and from that time on the company began to grow rapidly.

VG: Where did the Standel name come from?

BC: When I was repairing radios, my business in the garage was called Standard Electronics. "Standel" is a combination of the beginnings of those two words.

VG: Those years when you went into business full-time had to be both scary and exciting.

BC: Yes, it was. When I started full time, my wife, Dolores, came into the business and took care of the accounting and organized the front office functions. I was attempting to develop a more complete line of equipment and learn how to manage a rapidly expanding business. The only thing that saved us was the fact that I was too stupid to know it was impossible.

VG: Another "first" I've heard about was solidstate amps. Did you make any "hybrid" amps that had tube and solid state components before you went into solid state exclusively?

BC: I began to work with semi-conductors in 1961. I built a solid state tape echo that worked reasonably well, but was very crude. I then began to work with solid state pre-amplifiers and tone circuits and finally developed a hybrid amplifier, and by 1963 or early '64 I had a high-powered solid state amp.

VG: What about two-piece amplifiers?

BC: In late 1956 or early '57 I decided to add

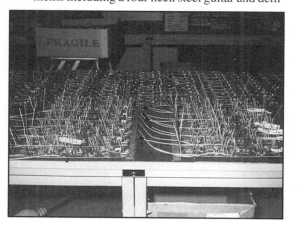

TOP: *Merle Travis with his Standel amp, 1953.*

MIDDLE: *This 1961 gospel album by Joe Maphis has a Standel amplifier, a primitive "Ecco-Fonic" device, and Maphis' Mosrite double-neck guitar on its cover.*

LEFT: *Circuit boards at the Standel factory during the Sixties.*

a bass amplifier to my amp line. I built a closed back reflex cabinet for a 12" speaker. The speaker cabinet was so large that it wasn't practical to include the amplifier, so I put the amplifier in a separate cabinet that sat on top of the speaker cabinet. At that time, the amp was all tubes. It turned out to be a real winner.

VG: Was yet another "first" front-mounted controls? What inspired that?

BC: When country music started in California with the Foreman Phillips Barn Dance, the musicians positioned the amps in front of them, so the dial on the back of the amp made sense. Later, they began to put the amps behind them on a chair or against the wall which made the rear dial very awkward, so I moved the dial to the front.

VG: What artists played Standel amps? Any interesting anecdotes?

BC: There were too many to list here, and many of them I can't remember. Some of the rock bands were the Jefferson Airplane, the Lovin' Spoonful, the Grass Roots, the Nitty Gritty Dirt Band, and Kaleidoscope; there were many others. Someone stated that Hendrix was using Standels at one of his concerts in Los Angeles; however, I cannot verify that.

Some of the country players were Merle Travis, Joe Maphis, Chet Atkins, Hank Thompson, Noel Boggs, Speedy West, Ralph Mooney, Buddy Emmons, Barbara Mandrell, Larry Collins, and Marian Hall. I think Chet Atkins still uses an old original Standel in the studio; I believe it's one that I made for Hank Thompson. Paul Yandell, who's played with Chet for many years, collects and restores old Standels.

There were many more. You mentioned anecdotes and one in particular comes to mind. A guitar player named Shorty Bacon and his brother had a band in L. A. Shorty had a Standel with a 15" speaker. He was at the factory one day and mentioned that his amplifier would lose power sometimes when he was playing. This happened in some of the older clubs with bad electrical wiring, so I told Shorty I would get him a regulator. I got him an adjustable regulator with a meter on it so you could set the voltage from zero to about 200 volts. I told him to set it for 120 volts on the meter.

Dolores and Bob Crooks at a NAMM banquet in Chicago, circa 1965. Mr. Crooks is the man closest to the camera, Mrs. Crooks is the blond woman at the far right.

About two weeks later, Shorty brought his amp in with a big hole burned in the grille cloth and speaker cone. I asked him what in the world happened to his amp. He looked a little sheepish and said, "Well, the other night I was adjusting the regulator and I found out that if you set the knob clear up, the amp got real loud. It played for about five minutes and caught on fire and before I could turn it off, it burned up the speaker and the grill cloth," Needless to say, Shorty didn't do that any more.

VG: What about jazz artists?

BC: The only way I could keep track of the Jazz players was through the warranty cards. The only one I was acquainted with was Wes Montgomery, who came out to the Coast twice a year. When he was out here, he would stop by the factory to have his amp checked. Ike Turner also came by the factory once in awhile.

VG: I've got to ask this: Were your amps played by a band called the Standells, which had some hit songs in the mid-Sixties?

BC: No, they played Fenders, but I understand that at one time a band called the Fendermen was playing Standels (chuckles)!

VG: Do you feel like talking about the reasons your company went out of business?

BC: I don't mind, that was a long time ago; twenty-two years to be exact. I was moving too fast with the product development. Instead of keeping a few hybrid amps in production, I would commit my total production to solid state systems, and for several years the reliability was excellent. In 1970, I suddenly had massive field failures. The so-called reputable company I was buying from had their power transistors manufactured in Mexico with worn-out tooling and bad welds, which made it almost impossible to detect with standard quality control procedures. Within a few months the Standel quality reputation disappeared. Actually, I cannot blame the failure entirely on transistors; it was also a management error. I finally sold the company to CMI in Chicago and went to work for them for two years.

VG: There were some Standel brand guitars, some of which were built by some famous builders.

BC: After several unsuccessful attempts to develop a line of Standel guitars, the Harptone Company in New Jersey contacted two of my salesmen with an offer to build a line of Standel guitars. Harptone hired Sam Koontz and some other guitar makers to build a fine line of guitars for me. Unfortunately, this was about the time that I began having amp problems, and I had to terminate the association with Harptone.

VG: You stated earlier that you stayed with the Gibson parent company for two years.

BC: I designed the SG line of amplifiers for CMI. It was a hybrid amp that sold very well, but CMI decided to move everything to the Moog factory in the East. After that I went to work for Barcus & Berry in Long Beach who manufactured acoustic instrument pickups.

While I was with Barcus & Berry, I began to investigate the difference in the sound of transistor and tube amplifiers. I had been interested in this from the time I built my first transistor amp. Also, an article by Russell Hamm in the *Audio Engineering Society Journal* made it even more interesting. Mr. Hamm stated that one of the areas where tube circuits made an audible difference in sound quality was where there was an "electrical mechanical interface." In a musical instrument amplifier, this is the connection between the power amplifier and the speaker. After a considerable amount of experimenting, I built a unit that anticipates the speaker errors and modifies the signal going into the amplifiers. It doesn't correct all of the problems, but it does improve the performance of the audio systems. We call it the Sonic Maximizer.

Investors were interested in the unit and formed a new company to build and market it. The company is called BBE Sound Corporation, and I have been working there since its inception. The unit is sold all over the world, and with John McLaren in charge, the operation has done very well. Although I am retired now, I still go into the Lab four days a week. At the present time I am experimenting with some new Standel amplifiers.

VG: Do they have the Sonic Maximizer unit in them? Do they sound like tube amps?

BC: The Sonic Maximizer isn't necessary if you have a fixed amplifier speaker combination. As far as a tube sound is concerned, there are many tube sounds. The basic characteristics that everyone talks about are transient response and harmonic content. Tube amps with moderate feedback will produce a non-symmetrical wave shape which produces even harmonic distortion. "Even" harmonics will enhance the sound, while "odd" harmonics degrade the sound. The tube amp is also more sensitive to load changes than the transistor amp. This characteristic alone produces a much better transient response, but to make a long story short it is a very complex problem. I can only state that although my new amplifiers may not duplicate a so-called "tube sound," they perform considerably better than a conventional transistor amplifier and generally I think the sound quality is very competitive.

VG: How does it feel trying to still be "competitive" with a sound that's extremely popular today, even though the technology is fifty years old? Is it frustrating?

BC: (chuckles) Well, I am not trying to be competitive. I am just filling my time with some interesting projects that I wasn't able to finish when I was operating Standel.

It seems too bad that the amplifier industry was not able to develop the solid state technology into a more acceptable product which is forcing the musician to pay ridiculous prices for obsolete equipment.

VG: Your "forward, not backward" attitude reminds me of some of the philosophy of Hartley Peavey, who I interviewed some months ago. The "cutting edge" of Peavey's technology, and perhaps the most controversial to many of our readers, is probably his use of computers to build guitar components.

BC: I am certainly not qualified to comment on some one else's company, however, I might say that Mr. Peavey did what I tried to do and did it very well. The constant growth of his company is obviously due to progressive thinking and excellent management. It is a prime example of the possibilities in our free enterprise system.

VG: You've still got some projects in the works that ought to keep you busy for some time.

BC: Well, I will always find something interesting to do and I am so thankful that I have been able to make a living doing something I enjoy.

VG: Any last anecdotes we ought to hear?

BC: At the present time I can think of two. Many of them I have forgotten.

I was at Capitol Records one night when Hank Thompson was recording. He had a big band at that time, two steel guitars and three violins. They were having trouble with the violin section on one of the songs. They played it over several times and the violins didn't sound right. After a lot of discussion and checking the music, one of the violin players said, "Hey, Hank, I think I have found the problem. I have been playing the fly specks." After everyone had a good laugh, they played it again and sure enough it sounded OK.

Another incident that might be of interest happened at the trade show one year. The display room in the hotel had an air conditioner mounted in the window. When we put our drapes up we had to leave a space for it. We then lined the amplifiers up on each side of the window. One day one of our major dealers came in. He was a very serious business man who didn't have time for idle conversation, but he always placed very nice orders. He started down the amplifier line with his order pad asking the price of each model. Halfway down the line, he pointed at the air conditioner and said, "How much is that one?" I didn't want to embarrass him and possibly lose the order. At first I thought I would add some comic relief and say "That is a cool one sir, but it belongs to the hotel," but then I thought when in doubt tell the truth. So I said "that is the air conditioner." Without any hesitation he said, "Well, so it is," and went on down the line. We all heaved a sigh of relief when he handed us a nice order and left.

Hopefully this first interview with Bob Crooks has enlightened *VG* readers, and has given them reason to ponder what Mr. Crooks' place should be in the history of California amplifier technology. His recollections made for a fascinating conversation, and his perspective on innovations in sound amplification is as commendable in the Nineties as it should have been decades ago, in this writer's opinion.

Crooks advised in mid-1996 that he was planning on introducing a limited run of Standel amplifiers later that year.

Warren Cuccurullo's
Thanks to Frank Ain't No "Big Hair" Album

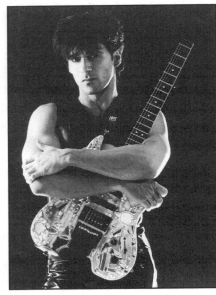

Considering the most famous bands with which guitarist Warren Cuccurullo has been associated, Missing Persons and Duran Duran, many readers might expect a solo album from him to be a similar exercise in the dance/pop/New Wave/glam/whatever mode. But Cuccurullo's *Thanks to Frank*, released in March of 1996, is a live-in-the-studio instrumental guitarfest that showcases the Brooklyn-born fretmeister's numerous chops (the title cut was recorded in concert *prior* to the studio sessions, details later).

And as might be expected, the album title is a toast to the late Frank Zappa, with whom Warren Cuccurullo got his first dose of major musical experience on a European tour, as well as the *Joe's Garage* album. In a recent transAtlantic phone conversation, Cuccurullo discussed his playing and recording history, speaking from his home studio in England, where Duran Duran records:

VG: Is it fair to say you're an expatriate? My perception is that a lot of English stars were leaving Great Britain due to the tax rates, and your situation seems to be reversed.

WC: The rates are the same in the U.S. and England these days. I also live in Rio De Janiero.

VG: That's a long way from growing up in Brooklyn, musically and otherwise.

WC: I played in a lot of garage bands, did a lot of things like church dances. The first guitar I got was a gift from my godfather; it was a Japanese guitar that was a decent beginner's instrument, sort of Strat-shaped. I had an Ampeg Reverb-O-Rocket II amp with tremolo and reverb. I played rhythm guitar for a while, then I started a band with a friend of mine; he had a fuzz box and a wah-wah. He'd do things like kneel down in front of his amp, getting it to feed back. I thought: "That looks like fun," (chuckles) so I started getting into stomp

boxes; I'd buy whatever came out.

The next guitar I got was a Hagstrom semi-hollow; it was a nice step up and it had really low action, but the pickups weren't that great. By that time I was really more "tone-oriented," and a guy in our neighborhood was a great blues player who had a 335, so I decided I had to get one. Eventually, I got a walnut-colored one in 1972, and I still have it. When I got the 335, I was using an old pre-CBS Deluxe Reverb and a Foxx Tone Machine and a MuTron III, and I'd do things like kick the amplifier so the reverb would make "explosion" noises (laughs). I had wahs-wahs and phasers; *a lot* of things on the floor!

I tried to stay "adventurous" in my music; I went from the Beatles and the Stones and Top 40 stuff like the Monkees and Motown, into blues. Johnny Winter was playing *very fast* stuff, as opposed to Clapton, although some of the Cream jams were intricate. But, Winter had a *blazing* style, and Alvin Lee in the *Woodstock* movie blew me away. And after that, I got into Frank's playing; I heard "Willie the Pimp" and thought it was a great song. I was also listening to Deep Purple and Zeppelin, but Frank's guitar playing was a bit more left-of-center. I liked the way he used a wah-wah; some of his music had an Eastern-type of feel. I really got into his stuff, plus guitarists like McLaughlin and horn players like Coltrane and Miles Davis.

VG: How did you end up joining Zappa's band?

WC: By 1973, I was a *die-hard* fan; I thought

TOP: *Warren Cuccurullo with a customized Steinberger guitar. All photos courtesy Imago.*

RIGHT:
Cuccurullo tunes one of his custom-made Tom Mates Acoustics.

the guitar playing on *Overnight Sensation* was *beyond* ridiculous. When he would tour, which was usually in the Fall, I'd go to as many shows as I could. Eventually, I became friends with his sound man, Davie Moire, who introduced me to Frank on Halloween of 1976. I also met the drummer, Terry Bozzio, and the bass player, Patrick O' Hearn. I got to hang out whenever they came to the East Coast. Frank would encourage me to stick around after shows; we'd go to dinner or clubs. He would observe things closely, because he was thinking he might be able to get a song out of the experience! The more people he had around him, the better.

I'd play some of the tapes of my guitar playing for him, and he thought it was great. I went to see him on New Year's Eve in L.A., and he invited me up to his house after the show. He wanted to play me some music he'd done for his movie, *Baby Snakes*. I knew he had *vaults* of stuff he hadn't put out. While I was there he gave me a sitar that was sitting in the corner of the room. It was beautiful, and I was scared it would be in 20 pieces by the time I got back to New York!

The next tour started in Florida, and I went down there and hung out with him. I told him a story about this "she-male" I'd met in the revolving doors at the Empire State Building (laughs), then he made me tell the story *onstage* while he conducted the band doing "incidental music" behind me! That was Halloween of 1978 in New York, and in a way that was my audition, even though I wasn't playing a guitar!

A few weeks after that we went out to dinner with William Burroughs and Allen Ginsberg, the great writers, and Frank introduced me to Ginsberg, calling me "a guitar player." That was the *first time* anybody ever referred to me as a guitar player; it felt great. Three weeks later, Frank called me and wanted me to audition for a European tour. I flew to L.A. the next day, and I got the job.

VG: So when you were with Zappa, you were on one studio album and more than one live album, right?

WC: Yeah; *Joe's Garage* was a triple album; 17 tracks. We recorded all three Hammersmith-Odeon shows on that tour, and we did some guitar duo stuff in his basement that was on *Shut Up and Play Yer Guitar*. There was live stuff from the Hammersmith shows on *Tinseltown Rebellion, You Can't Do That Onstage Anymore*, and another volume of *Shut Up and Play Yer Guitar*.

VG: What guitars did you use then?

WC: A '63 Strat that belonged to the bass player, Arthur Barrow, and my 335; I ran through Marshalls. I had a Big Muff along, too.

VG: Some months ago we profiled Mike Keneally, who was the lead guitarist on Zappa's final tour. Ever hear any of his material?

WC: Yeah. Mike's a great composer and an excellent player. He's a nice guy and a great all-around musician.

VG: Did you go straight from Zappa's band to forming your own band with Bozzio and O'Hearn?

WC: At the time, Terry was in a band called U.K., with John Wetton and Eddie Jobson. Patrick was doing something *completely* different; I think he was working in a wine factory. After we finished *Joe's Garage*, I had a few months off; I was hanging out with Terry and his wife Dale, and everybody always thought we were a band because we looked sort of New Wave or post-Punk, so we decided to write some songs. We did some rough demos of about eleven songs, so we went for a record deal. I had to make a decision, because one of Frank's people called around then, telling me it was time to start rehearsals for the next tour. I brought those tapes to Frank's, and he showed me a Devo album. They had been real hot, but weren't too much in demand by then; he told me that he liked what he heard, and that what I was wanting to do would be real hard, but he gave me his blessing, and offered his help.

A few weeks later, Terry, Dale and I went to Frank's to let him hear some updated material, and he offered us the use of his new home studio while he was on tour, if we could get producer Ken Scott to work with his technician, David Gray, to get the "bugs" out of his studio. Ken loved the tapes, and we made what became our EP. We put it out ourselves, and sold about 12,000 copies; we got airplay on about 70 stations. It got a buzz going. In L.A., we sold out a 3,000-seat gig; all of the record companies came to hear us, and Capitol signed us the next day.

Patrick had played on the original demos, but he didn't join until after we'd gotten the

Cuccurullo with the redoubtable Frank Zappa "wah wah guitar"; that's Warren's ES-335 in the background.

record deal.

VG: You referred to the New Wave term a bit earlier; is that the vibe Missing Persons was going for?

WC: (chuckles) Right; a lot of makeup, a lot of hairspray, a lot of eighth-notes, and odd-time signatures!

VG: What kind of instruments did you use for recording and touring with Missing Persons?

WC: I used the 335 on the EP. The "fee" Frank paid me for those guitar duo sessions was a guitar that was made out of a Vox wah-wah pedal; it looks like a stick, and it's totally neck-heavy! I decided to use it at all of our live gigs. Then I started building all of my own guitars. I liked the wah-wah guitar, but I wanted something that was slightly bigger and made out of wood so it wouldn't be neck-heavy. I copied the neck off of my 335, and the body looked like an early Steinberger, except it had a slight cutaway. That design had a lot of electronics in it; there were two 9-volt batteries needed. Performance Guitar in Los Angeles built it.

VG: The band played the US Festival; what was that like?

WC: Pretty amazing. That was the most people we ever played for. In fact, I think that was the most people that most of the bands had played for! We played on the third day, with David Bowie; we went on after U2. It was run really smooth; everything worked.

VG: Is it fair to say that you went straight into your association with Duran Duran when Missing Persons split?

WC: Pretty much; we had the same business managers and were on the same label. Andy Taylor heard that we'd broken up, and he needed a rhythm section, and he asked Terry and Patrick to help hire out with some stuff he was doing. I was sitting in my apartment with nothing do, and I knew Duran Duran was making an album, so I called them, even though their guitar player was playing with my old band! So I called them up and sent them a tape. Two weeks later, one of their production guys called me and asked me to come to New York, because Andy wasn't going to come back.

VG: Sounds almost like two lead guitarists trading places.

WC: In a way, but I needed some work, and I thought my kind of playing would really suit their kind of music, and would take their music to another space. I went to New York and worked with Nile Rodgers, then they invited me to come on the road with them. I started out more or less as sort of a sideman, but in '89 I signed on as a full partner in the band.

VG: And now you've got your first solo project, *Thanks to Frank*, completed.

WC: It's just my way of thanking him for letting me have a chance to make a career in music. It's not a "tribute" album of covers. I had the songs, and I knew who I wanted to play on the album; I knew I wanted Vinnie Colaiuta to play drums; he was in Frank's band when I was. I had a bass player here in England named Nick Beggs lined up, and I wanted another bass player that I knew about for years named Pino Palladino. They're both monster bass players. Nick plays Chapman Stick as well.

I'd performed the songs live at the Stone Pony in Asbury Park, New Jersey; my brother played drums that night and Nick played bass. I figured that if we could do things that well on one night, I'd like to get the best players in the world and do live-in-the-

studio versions in 32 hours; I had two 16-hour sessions booked. Vinnie plays with Sting now, and those were the two days that he had off (laughs)! I knew it was doable, and we got it done. It was beyond magic.

VG: What guitars did you use on the recording?

WC: One electric, a Steinberger GL-4 the Strat-shaped model. My friend, Andrew Logan, is a sculptor, and he's done up all of my Steinbergers with things like jewels and broken mirror glass. The one I used for *Thanks to Frank* has Duncan pickups in it. As for amps, I used a Bob Bradshaw 3-channel preamp and a Mesa Boogie amp; I use Marshall power now.

VG: "Hey Zawinul" has a tabla player on it, and an acoustic guitar as well. It's probably the most eclectic track.

WC: I use acoustic guitars built by a fine British builder Tom Mates. I have a 12-string, and 6-strings in different body sizes. He's really inspried by the old Martin and Gibson models.

That track really had a Weather Report kind of vibe; I had Pino playing the lead melody, and I was playing the lead melody, and I was playing a rhythmic figure on one of Tom's guitars. The end of the song is almost like "Hey Ravi," (chuckles) because I go into a full raga kind of thing.

VG: The title cut is the only live track from the Stone Pony that appears on the album; it starts off as kind of a 2-chord meditation then goes into some raucous riffing, then back to the lower volume pattern.

WC: When I heard the recording from the Stone Pony, I knew I had to make an album, but I didn't want to touch "Thanks to Frank," because it sounded exactly like it should have. It could have been a little bit better, quality-wise, but I didn't want to alter it at all. I used a Mesa Boogie Tremoverb on the live recording; it *screams*.

VG: Any other projects you've got in the works?

WC: I've been compiling ambient guitar music for something called *Machine Language*; I've had it in the works for years. I've done some solo material and I've worked with Shankar, the violinist with Shakti: he now plays with Peter Gabriel. The first volume will only have guitar on it, but it was all done live to 2-track.

VG: Have you got any other guitars you'd like to note?

WC: I have a Ken Parker Fly that I really love. I think it's the best guitar ever made for switching from acoustic to electric in the middle of a song. It's a great-sounding rock guitar as well! I got rid of most of the old stuff I had. I still have a Gibson Chet Atkins steel-string solidbody, and a Chet Atkins-type guitar that's shaped like a Tele; John Carruthers built that one. He makes those big fretless basses, as well.

VG: It sounds like you're quite satisfied with how *Thanks to Frank* turned out; what about your future with Duran Duran?

WC: We've got a new album called *Medazzaland* coming out this Spring, so I'll be concentrating on working with the band again, but I really do get excited about *Thanks to Frank* as well.

Warren Cuccurullo's fretboard prowess is obvious when one listens to *Thanks to Frank*, and it was a commendable move on the guitarist's part to honor his musical mentor with such an album. Cuccurullo is wearing more than one musical "hat," and he's wearin' 'em well.

Debbie Davies
Lady Sings the Blues

...and plays 'em on the guitar as well. We ain't talkin' tokenism, but *Vintage Guitar*'s recent conversation with blues guitarist Debbie Davies represents the magazine's first in-depth interview with a female player. Just as there seems to be a dearth of women guitar players in all genres of music, there also seems to be a dearth of female blues interpreters these days. We discussed such with Davies during our session, as well as her experience with artists such as the late Albert Collins, while Ms. Davies was taking a break from extensive touring in support of her most recent album, *Loose Tonight*, on the Blind Pig label:

VG: I understand you came from a musical family.

DD: Well, my mom had a teaching credential in music, and she had been a classical pianist; she was giving professional recitals by the time she was sixteen. My dad was a professional studio singer for radio and television; his show, "Hit Parade," started in Chicago, and when it moved to Los Angeles to go onto television, he moved with it, so he got in on the ground floor of early television. He also played a lot of instruments at the "dabbling"

level; he read music and did a lot of sessions, and he eventually became a vocal arranger. My parents were really into the music of their era like Big Band, Swing, and Jazz; I grew up hearing a lot of it, but as far as my own generation goes, I was listening to rock and roll; I was into the British blues/rock thing before I got hip to *real* blues. I always sang in the chorus in school, too, so I had a love for a lot of kinds of music.

VG: As for the British blues players that you listened to, who did you admire the most?

DD: Eric Clapton, John Mayall's Bluesbreakers... Eric was really my first

guitar hero, and reading interviews with Eric Clapton made me aware of all of the black American blues artists like B.B. King and Freddy King. It's funny, because I think a lot of white American guitarists got hip to the blues through these British guys.

VG: B.B. King addressed that in his interview with this magazine; he observed that the British players "re-imported" the blues.

DD: Absolutely; those of us growing up in white neighborhoods and households weren't exposed to any blues or R & B music unless we found a particular station on the radio.

VG: When did you begin to concentrate on playing blues guitar?

DD: After I graduated from high school, I moved to the San Francisco area. Since my folks were involved in

the Hollywood scene, I kind of wanted my own identity; I was trying to find myself as a person and a player. San Francisco had a big allure at the time as having a really creative music scene; there was a lot going on. But I did go to college up there and worked, and I bought myself an electric guitar; there was a blues scene going on up there that was pretty exciting to me. There was Mike Bloomfield and Nick Gravenites in the Electric Flag, Charlie Musselwhite.

VG: Here's the first, um, "gender-specific" question: Why the blues, when there are other musical genres that seem to have been more female-oriented in terms of performers?

DD: When I was really getting into wanting to play electric lead guitar, there really weren't any girl groups; there was nothing around as far as women playing. I could have picked anything; this was way before the Go-Gos. The only women I knew about in music were Bonnie Raitt, who was playing the kind of music I *loved,* and the two girls in Heart, the Wilson sisters. I'd played an acoustic guitar in high school, but the more I got into electric, the more I began to love blues, because it's such emotional music that can be conveyed on an electric guitar so well.

VG: What about your guitars, from your earliest acoustic on?

DD: My first guitar was a *horrible* Japanese in-

TOP: *Photo by Pat Johnson Studios*

LEFT: *Photo by Cari Pike*

strument; my dad said that if I practiced for a year with that thing and showed them I was really serious, he'd get me a real guitar, and he kept his word; a year later I got a 1964 Martin 00-18, and I still have it.

I bought my first electric from a guy I was dating; it was a l964 Gibson ES-330. It was tobacco sunburst and had black pickups. My amp was a blackface Bassman; it got a *great* tone. The 330 has a very different "personality" from something like a 335. I practiced as much as I could, trying to learn anything from anybody. Once I started getting more into the band scene, I started running into feedback problems a little bit, so I told myself I needed to get a solidbody guitar. I sold the 330 and got a really cheesy Music Man guitar; I had no idea about the vintage value of the 330 and I don't think a lot of people knew back then how valuable certain guitars would become.

I would go to a blues club north of San Francisco and check out a lot of the players touring the West Coast back then; Albert Collins, Buddy Guy and Junior Wells, Koko Taylor, Etta James, Gatemouth Brown, plus the white cats like Bloomfield and Butterfield. All of the guitar players I heard live back then were heroes. I went through "phases" where I was trying to learn all of a certain player's licks; B.B. King, Albert King, then Stevie Ray Vaughan and the Texas thing. There are so many great players down there; I love Anson Funderburgh and Jimmie Vaughan. I also had a heavy Magic Sam phase. When you really get into somebody's playing, you may have a new hero, but when you shift to somebody else, all of the previous influences *remain* heroes.

VG: Ultimately you settled on a Fender Stratocaster as your main guitar. Were there any guitars between the Music Man and a Strat?

DD: I realized I wasn't getting a great tone from the Music Man, so my next guitar was a 1973 Fender Telecaster; I still have it. It's got a maple neck and light creme finish. It's got a good neck with plenty of meat on the back of it. I played it for quite a few years, and then something happened; I sort of got "Strat-mania". (chuckles) The different sounds you could get with a Strat really started appealing to me, and a lot of my favorite players were playing one at that time, so I felt like I had to have

(Both photos) Debbie performing with the legendary Albert Collins. Photos by Mike Cruz.

one. The first one I got, which I also still have, was a 1972 hardtail. I played that one for quite a while, including when I was playing in a band with John Mayall's wife. Then I got invited to play with Albert Collins, and during my tenure with Albert I was approached by Fender, and I signed on with their Artist Relations program; Mark Wittenberg was very supportive and helped me out a lot.

VG: Obviously, I need to inquire about how your association with Collins came about.

DD: Well, in working with Maggie Mayall and the Cadillacs, I became involved with John Mayall's guitar player, Coco Montoya. Coco had played drums for Albert Collins in the Seventies, so I met Albert through Coco. Coco and I were doing some little bar gigs between the Mayall tours, and Albert heard me; he was knocked out by what I was doing. We became friends; he'd invite us up to his house for barbecue with his wife. He invited me to sit with the Icebreakers several times, which was really a thrill for me; he'd been one of my early, early inspirations. He got to a point where he was making some changes in his band, and I got a call asking if I wanted to go on the road. I said: "Oh, *yeah.*" (laughs)

When Fender approached me while I was with Albert, I got another Strat; this one was from their Custom Shop. They made the neck identical to the neck on my hardtail; I wanted to have two guitars set up the same in case I broke a string. It has a "Mercedes Blue" custom color and a mother-of-toilet-seat pickguard. Other than that, it's kind of like a '62 reissue as far as its hardware and the way it's set up.

VG: Are those two Strats your main studio guitars as well as your main touring guitars?

DD: During that whole time, I always had wanted a *vintage* Strat as well, and I had two friends, one in Los Angeles and one in San Francisco, that had each gotten into the business. Chris Cobb at Real Guitars is a great guitar player and a really good friend; he knew what I *couldn't* afford, so he called

me when he found a great 1965 Strat that wasn't completely stock; the tuning heads and one of the pickups had been changed. That's my main axe now; I take it and the Custom Shop Strat on the road. I leave the hardtail at home; it *is* heavier, and playing night after night means I'd rather be wearing a lighter guitar. That's my '65 on the cover of *Loose Tonight*; that's the only guitar I used on it.

But I recently got a hold of a vintage Gibson guitar that I've been messing with lately; it's a 1960 Les Paul Special. It's got two P-90s in it, one of which is a replacement. The two pickups have different outputs, so when you put it "in the middle" it has an out-of-phase sound. It almost sounds like an old thin-bodied hollow guitar; really cool.

VG: What kind of amplifier are you currently using?

DD: I use a 1967 blackface Super Reverb; I also have a new Super that Fender makes. Sometimes I run both of them together, but usually I use them separately.

VG: Did you depart the Icebreakers due to getting your own record deal?

DD: No, it was just getting to be that time where I wanted to try and do my own thing full-time. Between tours with Albert I'd still been trying to work with my own band; I didn't have a record deal when I left, but I knew I *wouldn't get* a record deal if I didn't make a full commitment, and Albert was very encouraging to me about my decision.

We stayed in touch; there were times when my band would open for his. In June of the year he died, we did a festival in Santa Cruz; I was one of the earlier acts and he was the headliner, and I got up and sat in with him. I was very concerned about him that day; I felt like something was wrong; he didn't look or seem right. Nobody agreed with me; they were saying he was fine, but I was thinking "I don't think so"; I'd traveled with him for three years. Then in August he collapsed in Switzerland, and that's when they discovered he was ill; he died in November.

VG: Comments about your nominations for W.C. Handy Blues Awards? Another periodical observed that your category was somewhat "sparse".

DD: I've been nominated three times for Contemporary Female Blues Artist. It's kind of wide-ranging if performers like Marcia Ball, Koko Taylor, and Etta James are nominated for the same award as me; it's an honor to be nominated with those great blueswomen, but sometimes I feel like there should be more categories.

VG: Has your vocal style been compared to any other blues interpreters by acquaintances or other publications?

DD: I don't think so; everybody hears something different.

VG: Stereotypically, the blues seems to be somewhat chauvinist at times; if someone heard a female singing the blues they might expect to hear something along the lines of "that man done me wrong". It seems like the first two tracks on *Loose Tonight*, "I Don't Want No Man" and "Wrong Man For Me", are somewhat "assertive," for lack of a better term.

DD: Well, I was hoping to take that stance on this record. For one thing, I was trying to sort of "turn the tables", doing a female version of what guys do in the blues, but it's part tongue-in-cheek, too; I had a lot of fun with it. But I didn't want it to be too "victim-oriented," and I think anybody can sometimes think "that man done me wrong" or "that woman done me wrong", because it's *so*

true when it happens. (chuckles) Anybody can get their heart broken; anybody can sing about it.

VG: Another track on the new album is called "A Mother's Blues," but you don't have any children yourself, do you?

DD: No I don't; it was written from an "observation" standpoint. The crux of it is about women who have been real involved in careers, and have made the decision to give that up for motherhood. How it's difficult once you've been out in the world and have gotten your personal identity from your job, and suddenly you're staying at home with your baby, and you're not seeing that many people. The song is about the difficulty and the incredible reward of the experience of motherhood.

VG: Overall, are you pleased with *Loose Tonight*?

DD: Yeah, I was real happy with the way it turned out. I went into this record trying to concentrate on writing, and I ended up writing seven tunes; I was real pleased with that because I'm not the world's most prolific writer; I've worked real hard on my playing so writing has sort of lagged behind in a way because I'm on the road so much.

I was also pleased with my co-producer, Billy Rush; he's a great guy and we worked really well together. He's very creative and very sensitive to the whole production process. The players and the guest artists on it were great, too.

VG: We've been talking about how your career began in California, but a while back you relocated to the Northeast.

DD: Well, it was pretty hard to tour from California; the blues scene was not really happening as far as clubs; there were a lot more bands than there were clubs. When I got the record deal with Blind Pig, the idea was to play a lot of dates in support of the record. If you take a map of the United States and draw a line down the middle then look to the left, there's a lot of wide open spaces! (laughs) It's really not cost-effective when you're touring; you're driving *so far* for each gig. But look at the Eastern part of this country; it's dotted with towns. I moved here to have a touring base, where it would be easier to make a living. Plus, my record company told me that their biggest sales are on the Eastern seaboard. My management is also on the East Coast, and it's a little closer to Europe, which is another market I've been playing.

VG: It sounds like you're staying busy.

DD: Yeah; at some point I'm going to try to slow it down and prepare to do another record. I've been in a "touring whirlwind"; I'm starting to get some ideas that are coming together about what I'd like to do.

I just hope to continue to become a better player; that's the personal goal, and of course the other goal is to advance my career and make more money (chuckles); you always try to do that!

Debbie Davies may be a musician in a genre that's primarily noted for its male performers (to say nothing of the gender ratio concerning electric guitar players), but so what? If any purveyor of blues music can write and perform with the meaningfulness and confidence that Ms. Davies proffers, he/she is doing it right.

Davies later toured Europe (including parts of the former Soviet bloc) and began work on her third Blind Pig album.

Spencer Davis
Gimme Some Guitar

The circumstances and location from which the *Vintage Guitar* interview with Spencer Davis was recorded were quite possibly the most unique in this publication's history.

Our conversation with the veteran British guitarist/singer/producer/A&R executive was done via long distance telephone from *VG*'s Southern Regional Office to California. Mr. Davis set call forwarding to his cellular phone (hmm.... interesting... and expensive, too!) and when *VG* called, he was stationed near his beloved Morris-Cooper automobile at Universal Studios, having been asked to loan the British-made vehicle to the studio for a video project. There were several other classic English vehicles there, including a Morris Traveler, a Ford Cortina, a Ford Consort, and other collectibles. Davis opined the vehicles were being used for something important, videowise. And some weeks later he called *VG* to aver his suspicions had been confirmed: the vehicles had been rounded up for a video for the new Beatles song "Free As A Bird." (Cool!)

Anyway, Spencer Davis has worn many hats in his musical career, and shows no signs of slowing down, even after decades of hard work. As guitarist for the Spencer Davis Group, he was in the middle of the British music scene in its glory days

of the 1960s. His primeval, distorted guitar can be heard on hits such as "Keep On Running" and "Somebody Help Me," and the now-standards "Gimme Some Lovin'" and "I'm A Man." The vocalist for the first edition of the Spencer Davis Group was the redoubtable Stevie Winwood, who wasn't old enough to have a driver's license when the band first formed.

At times during our conversation, Davis was actually talking while driving his Morris-Cooper, but he handled both chores with ease, detailing his experiences and the guitars he used (the Morris-Cooper is a right-hand-drive car, by the way).

VG: I have a policy of asking all veteran British interviewees about skiffle and/or Radio Luxembourg.

SD: (chuckles) Well then, you already know the answer! What really got me started, though, was my late Uncle Herman, who would bring his mandolin over to the house when I was about four or five years old. He played songs like "With Someone Like You," and I remember watching and listening. A friend of mine had a guitar that I liked when I was about 11, but that was a bit early; most people started playing when they were 13 or 14. I told my parents I wanted one, but they got me an accordion. I learned some Christmas carols on it, and went out door-to-door. In Britain you do that the week before Christmas; it's like trick-or-treating in America, but the people give you money,

RIGHT: *The original Spencer Davis Group participated in the 1965 movie* Go Go Mania. *(Left to right) Stevie Winwood, Spencer Davis, Muff Winwood, Peter York. Note that Davis and Stevie Winwood are playing Harmony guitars.*

so that was the beginning of making music for a living.

VG: When did you finally get a guitar?

SD: When I was 16. I went up to London and bought a *horrendous* cheap guitar for five pounds. It had a butterfly transfer on it. I was into skiffle and blues, so to me it was wonderful. Later I got a Hofner guitar and mounted a pickup on it. By the time I was 18 or 19, I was really into Leadbelly, so I got an old Stella. The first electric guitar I bought was a Harmony Stratotone. I still have it.

VG: How did the original Spencer Davis Group form?

SD: I was into Big Bill Broozy, Muddy Waters and Lightnin' Hopkins, as well as Leadbelly. I used to go around with a guitar and a harmonica around my neck before I'd even heard of Bob Dylan; I got that from Woody Guthrie. Sonny Terry and Brownie McGee were also my heroes.

I didn't get the Stratotone until the Spencer

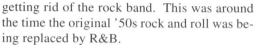
BLUES RE-UNION
CROMWELL MANAGEMENT
THE COACH HOUSE, 9A THE BROADWAY
ST. IVES, HUNTINGDON, CAMBS. PE17 4BX
Tel: (0480) 65695

Davis R.B.Q., for "Rhythm & Blues Quartet," was formed. I was in university in Birmingham, in the Midlands, and I used to sit in with the Excelsior Jazz Band, which played New Orleans traditional jazz. I'd sing gospel songs like "Just A Closer Walk With Thee" and "Precious Lord."

In the interval, the stand-up bass player and I would do Leadbelly songs like "How Long Blues"; Willie Dixon tunes as well. Around

the end of '62, I went into a club called the Golden Eagle, on Hill Street in Birmingham; there was a rock and roll band onstage called the Renegades. I volunteered to go on during the interval and do some blues tunes, and one of the songs I did was "I Got my Mojo Workin'," which at the time was like the national anthem of the R&B movement in Britain (chuckles). It worked. The crowd went nuts, and the promoter wanted me to come back the next Monday night, because he was getting rid of the rock band. This was around the time the original '50s rock and roll was being replaced by R&B.

VG: Did you use your Stella?

SD: By then I had a Zemaitis, a custom-built guitar. I now have two of Tony's guitars.

When I got the gig full-time, I needed to find a band to help me out, and I found a combo called the Muff Woody Jazz Band, in another club. Muff Winwood was playing guitar, and his younger brother Steve was playing piano. Steve sang like Ray Charles and played like Oscar Peterson. It was exactly what I needed for the Golden Eagle. I asked Steve to join, but I wasn't particularly interested in bringing Muff along. But Steve didn't have a driver's license, and Muff offered to switch over to bass, so I recruited both of them. Their band was more into swing and even some be-bop type of material, so there were some unusual roots for our combo.

Another guy I'd played with from time to time in the university jazz band was a drummer named Peter York. I got him to play with us, and we would practice at Steve's house, learning Jimmy Reed and Chuck Berry songs. We were more into R&B instead of pop music, as were the Animals in Newcastle and the Rolling Stones in London. It was like that for us in Birmingham. The Spencer Davis Group was never compared with a band like Gerry & the Pacemakers, for example.

VG: If I remember correctly, "Keep On Running" and "Somebody Help Me" were hits in

An aspiring player checks out one of Spencer Davis' 12-string guitars in the mid-1960s. That's the "Mark I" version of the Spencer Davis Group checking out her chops.

England *before* "Gimme Some Lovin'," but those two songs charted in the U.S. *after* "Gimme Some Lovin'" was a hit.

SD: That's correct. "Keep On Running" was our first number one in the U.K. and the rest of Europe. In America, it was released on Atco, and when it came out it was played on black stations; Steve sounded so much like Ray Charles. Probably 70 percent of the material we did was "ethnic," inspired by everyone from Big Bill Broonzy to Jimmy Reed.

Steve and I wrote "Gimme Some Lovin'," and we wrote "I'm A Man" with the late Jimmy Miller. We'd been on Island Records, which eventually ended up being sold to Polygram, and I couldn't think of a better place to be. Those earlier songs are *still* being used in movie soundtracks and other projects. A new movie starring Richard Dreyfuss has "Keep On Running" in it.

VG: Once the band had some big hits, did you step up from your Stratotone?

SD: Yes, I did. I bought a Stratocaster; Steve got a beautiful pair of Strats. Mine was stolen at the Rose Bowl in Pasadena. I started collecting guitars. I bought a late '50s sunburst Les Paul from Tony Hicks of the Hollies, around 1965 or '66. I paid £250 for it, and we all know what those are worth today! (chuckles) It was a beautiful guitar; very heavy. I had to sell it when times got a bit tough due to some management problems. Today that guitar would be in the $30,000 range. I used that Les Paul when we did the soundtrack to *Here We Go 'Round The Mulberry Bush.*

VG: The band is shown in the book on Burns guitars as being an endorser of their amplifiers.

SD: We got two guitar amps – one for me and one for Steve. I thought they had a great sound. Real different. They were covered in black vinyl, and the grill was silver, in a material that was almost like a Cinemascope screen.

VG: There were other Spencer Davis Group albums after the Winwoods left; I recall one named *With A New Face On.*

SD: I've always referred to the original band as the Spencer Davis Group Mark I. There were 42 titles done with the Winwood, Winwood, York and Davis lineup. The next version, the Spencer Davis Group Mark II, had Phil Sawyer and Eddie Harding in it. Pete York stayed with me.

Pete and Eddie left for a while in the late '60s, and I had Dee Murray and Nigel Olsson in the band before they went on to join Elton John. Then there was Alun Davies, who played guitar with me and was replaced by Peter Jamison, who was famous for bottleneck slide. I've had some great musicians with me over the years.

In 1970, I moved from England to the United States. I did an album with Peter [Jamison]. There was one song I recorded that featured Barney Kessel as a guest. It was an instrumental called "Balkan Blues," an inspiration I got when I was doing a gig in Hungary with the Mark II version of the Spencer Davis Group.

There was a 5-piece Spencer Davis Group at one time. I worked with Peter York, Eddie Harding, and Ray Fennig, who was a fabulous guitar player out of a Dutch band; he was an English guy but he was living in Holland, and Charlie McCracken, who was with the late Rory Gallagher.

VG: You eventually got into producing as well.

SD: While Steve was still in the band, we toured with the Rolling Stones, and I got into producing a band called the Habits, which was a project of Bill Wyman's.

But in '75, I made a big move. For a brief time, I got out of playing completely. I went into translating, using the language degree I'd gotten at university, to support my wife and three kids. Soon afterward I went to Island Records, and helped out in Artist Development and A&R. I did that from '75 to '79. I was involved with Bob Marley, Robert Palmer, Eddie & the Hot Rods, and Steve Winwood with his solo act.

VG: Did you ever see the picture in an old issue of *Creem* that showed you and a couple of the Hot Rods? You were looking at your watch, and the caption read something like: "Spencer Davis gives two members of Eddie & the Hot Rods exactly five minutes to hang out in L.A."

SD: (laughs) No, I didn't. I wish a had a copy of that! *Creem* was an *incredible* rock and roll magazine.

VG: What did you do following your association with Island?

SD: I did independent production work with

a guy named Paul Corder, among other things. I did some recording for Janus Records, then I moved to Pacific Video, which was a video post-production unit. I saw the boom of music videos on the horizon. I brought in Rod Stewart and did a big Linda Ronstadt project. I'd already produced videos earlier for the Spencer Davis Group – one song called "Time Cellar" was sort of a fantasy piece along the lines of the Beatles' "I Am the Walrus." The B-side was a song I wrote with Eddie Harding called "Don't Want You No More," which the Allman Brothers recorded. I got to know Duane and Gregg. Their new guitar player, Warren Haynes, is wonderful; I'd like to meet him some day. He's a great slide player.

Then I co-founded a record company called Allegiance Records. John Stewart was on that label. We bought Takoma Records while I was there.

And every year since '84 I've gone to Europe, as regular as clockwork twice each year, to tour with Peter York.

VG: What about the formation of the Classic Rock All-Stars?

SD: I toured some in the mid-'80s with the "American" Spencer Davis Group, and toured with Peter York and a left-handed bass player named Colin Hodgkinson. Then I did a live-in-the-studio album with my California band. The next year, for the European tour, Peter, Colin and I added Brian Auger and called it Blues Re-Union.

I worked with a band called the Franklin Brothers; I still work with them sometimes. About 3½ years ago, I found Mike Pinera and Jerry Corbetta working with Peter Rivera; Mickey Dolenz had guested with them as well. I worked with them, and we got a live album out of it. The producer, Kevin Beamish, was quick and wonderful; he was brilliant. When I'm in a band I step away from the production part.

I was hoping they would do some new material. We went all over the country and all over the world; Japan, Australia, Europe. But it got to be so much like a 'repeat performance' I had to make a move, and I was offered a deal by CMC International in North Carolina. I'm also working on a project called Desert Rock Television, from Sho-Pro, Inc., based out of Dallas. I'm the host of a show

called "Desert Rock"; we've shot two pilots.

VG: The most recent performance photos of you have you playing a Squier Stratocaster.

SD: I bought that in Germany in '83. It's a JV series; one of the better ones that was assembled in Japan from American parts. One day I took it to the Fender factory and they almost cried when they saw how good it was! I've already been offered $1,000 for it; I won't part with it. The other day I got another JV with a rosewood board and Lace Sensor pickups. I've got a "real" 1959 Strat that I bought from Norm's Rare Guitars. I've also got a National steel, a Guild 12-string that I also got from Norm's, a Yamaha that I got 25 years ago for £25, a Hofner that I got in a pawn shop, a '52 reissue Telecaster, reissue Stratocasters... I'm still building a collection.

VG: Had you ever been to a vintage guitar show prior to attending the one in Santa Monica in the summer of '95?

SD: No. I was blown away! I was disappointed that I couldn't stay longer, but I was on my way to Europe. My son was also thrilled; he's a guitar player as well.

VG: You've stayed busy over the years; I can't imagine that someone like you would consider retirement if and when you felt like slowing down.

SD: Not unless somebody nails me to a wall! (laughs) Music's given me a hell of a lot, so I'm trying to give as much back as I can. I'm on the go all the time.

Pete York and I have a joke about how "Keep On Running" was our first number one hit, and how we did the Keep On Running Tour in '84, and in '96 we're probably going to do the Keep On Walking Tour! Someday we'll do the Keep On Standing Tour, and eventually we'll have to do the Keep On Lying Down Tour! (laughs)

Spencer Davis may not be in the pantheon of guitar gods, but he's participated in more facets of the music business than most players, and his exuberance and eloquence made conversing with him an enjoyable experience. Since our conversation, Davis has informed *VG* that Island Records is planning to issue a double-CD boxed set of Spencer Davis Group material, including rare outtakes and BBC live recordings, so there is another facet of Davis' efforts that should merit checking out.

The Seymour Duncan Factory

The Sound of California...heard around the world

Recently *Vintage Guitar* magazine had the opportunity to visit the factory where dozens of unique-sounding pickups are designed and manufactured under the expert eye of one of *VG's* own writers, Mr. Seymour Duncan. Located on the California coast in Santa Barbara, the Seymour Duncan facility has a reputation for producing high-quality pickups for guitars, basses and many other instruments as well. Our guide was Mr. Duncan; Seymour can be seen at many guitar and music events, including vintage guitar shows.

Our conversation began in Seymour's office, which is casually furnished with music memorabilia featuring Seymour's collection of over 3,000 guitar records that ranges from dozens of Ventures albums to Gabor Szabo records to a rare copy of the James Burton solo album. "I'll buy just about any album that's got a guitar on the cover," chuckled Seymour. "I've had some of them since I was twelve."

From among the memorabilia, Seymour pulled old photos of himself posing with the likes of Leo Fender, James Burton, Ricky Nelson, Jimi Hendrix, Jeff Beck, etc. "I was a young player in England," he told us, "and I always tried to hang out with other guitarists and guitar people. This is how I got to know Roger Mayer, who was Jimi Hendrix' guitar tech, and Richard Cole, who was a guitar tech for the Yardbirds. I finally met Jeff, and really loved how he played that old Esquire; I was fascinated by the sounds he got out of that single pickup, and that's why I play an Esquire today." Seymour now owns Jeff's well-worn '54 Esquire — it was a gift in appreciation for the "Tele Gib" that Seymour made Jeff (first heard on the *Blow by Blow* album). The Yardbird Esquire can be seen on the *Vintage Guitar* magazine cover for March, 1993.

As we walked through the factory, Seymour explained the building was new and they had moved to the facility in October 1993. He told us that the old facility proved, "too spread out,

Seymour W. Duncan

and this building features our manufacturing facilities on one floor and the business part on the other." He noted that the new facility is about 20,000 square feet in size.

After watching some of the design team working with their computers, we stopped at a small room where prototypes of new models are kept—under lock and key! Most of the prototypes we saw were new "Antiquity" series pickups. (More about those later...)

The Seymour Duncan Corporation has been in business since 1977, growing from a garage downtown to its new facility with 60 employees and company reps around the world. (Seymour's been winding since 1966). The main production area has as many as eight people winding pickups at any one time. "Employees are cross-trained to do more than one job," said Seymour, "so they can fill in at another station and guarantee quality control every step of the way." All pickups are hand-built and hand-assembled. There are nearly 200 different models available, including pickups for acoustic guitars. The company also builds acoustic amps and active circuits for certain instruments. One of the folks we met was long-time employee and engineer Kevin Beller, who designed the company's active pickups and acoustic amplification systems. Seymour has designed many of the company's most popular pickups, including the "'59 Humbucker" and the "JB Model" (originally custom-made for Jeff Beck).

Around the production areas, boards containing working samples of pickups are found, but employees know their craft so well that they rarely refer to them. Throughout the facility, you can find high tech side-by-side with old-fashioned and natural ingredients; we were shown a solution made from paraffin and bee's wax they use in potting pickups.

As we made our way around, we asked Seymour about the most unusual custom pickup job he's done. It was for *Star Trek: The Motion Picture*. "They used an instrument called the 'Cosmic Beam.' It was about fifteen feet long and made of steel I-beams with ten strings. It was played with an aluminum bar and put out these weird harmonic tones that they used for sound effects."

In another room just off the main production floor we saw another example of a Seymour Duncan product being installed into an unusual instrument. The Custom Shop's Brian Birmingham was busy putting an accelerometer/sensor with an active pre-amp in a Lyon & Healy renaissance harp. The harp was a 100-year-old replica of a 16th century instrument, according to artist Lisa Franco, who was watching Brian's efforts.

As mentioned, the business offices of the Seymour Duncan enterprise are on the second floor, which is actually a mezzanine overlooking the main production floor. Company records, promotional material, etc. are organized in an efficient manner, yet for all of the company's high tech organization, some things are *extremely* casual in this writer's opinion: All one meeting area has for seating are a half-dozen purple bean bags arranged in a circle! (A "formal" meeting room with a large conference table is also on the premises, however...)

The latest "buzz" from the Seymour Duncan facility — as many *VG* readers already know — involves the new "Antiquity" series pickups, which were introduced at January 1994 NAMM Show. These startlingly accurate reproductions of classic pickups are handmade by Seymour and longtime employee Maricela Juarez. Each individual pickup has its own "characteristics," just as the originals did. Seymour told us that "the same manufacturing techniques that were used when the originals were made are used in making the Antiquity series," and it really shows. The last step is to "age" each pickup about 40 years. Then every Antiquity pickup, autographed and numbered, is slipped into its own drawstring pouch and tucked inside a box sporting the classy Antiquity logo. "It's really like a sub-company," said Seymour, "and we've been just swamped with orders." Right now about twenty Antiquity models are available.

Before leaving, we watched Seymour do some pickup winding on his machine A guitar fan might wonder how many of the great songs heard over the years have sounded a little better due to the efforts of this musician/craftsman known the world over. Seymour Duncan's love affair with guitars and their electronics has come a long way since he worked on pickups for Hendrix, Page, Clapton, Beck, etc. at the Fender Soundhouse in London. His dependable and innovative products are now known and respected around the world, but the company shows no sign of resting on its reputation. The reception received by the new Antiquity series is proof that even "pre-aged" reissue pickups by this company are viable. It will be interesting to monitor the future innovations from the Seymour Duncan organization.

"Antiquity" pickups spend some time outside following processing.

Elliot Easton

Lefty Goes to the Left Coast

The affable countenance of former Cars guitarist Elliot Easton has been seen many times at guitar shows; his predilection for fine fretted instruments has a "southpaw perspective," since he's a left-handed player.

And the viewpoint of a left-handed player was just one of the facets *VG* pursued in a recent interview with the knowledgeable and eloquent guitarist. Easton has moved around a bit during his career; he's originally from Massapequa, Long Island, New York, which is also the home of Brian Setzer ("another member of the guitar-playing brethren," observed Easton. "Must be something in the water — Jerry Seinfeld's from there, too."). Some time ago, Easton moved to the Los Angeles area, but before *VG* got into a historical interrogation with Easton our first inquiry concerned a recent event, which was Easton's first effort at being a father:

VG: First and foremost, how's parenthood?

EE: It's such a cool thing I can't put it into words; we've got a little girl named Sydney. It's a fulfilling, joyous thing for us. She's got me wrapped around her little finger! (laughs) I'm glad I waited this long, because I don't think it would have been fair to have a kid while I was touring constantly when I was with the Cars. It was like I'd be real busy for a year and then not much would go on for a year; the cycles would continue. Now I'm at a better pace in my life where I can appreciate being a parent.

VG: A lot of people know about the Cars coming out of Boston, but how many members were from there?

EE: Only one. Boston had a lot of colleges with a lot of kids from all over, and there was a great atmosphere. The Cars *were* a Boston group, I guess, and Aerosmith was a Boston group, too, but I think Steve [Tyler] is from someplace like

Yonkers. Peter Wolf of J. Geils is from the Bronx; that's another example.

I moved to Boston in '72 to go to the Berklee School of Music. Most of the bands working on the South shore of Long Island were cover bands doing Top 40, whereas Boston embraced bands playing original music, and you could eke out a modest living, which seemed pretty incredible in those days.

VG: What about your "pre-Cars" bands and instruments?

EE: Well, I started out with a Mickey Mouse when I was three, then I got a Roy Rogers; I went from plastic to wood at age five. Little League and a few other things intervened for a few years, and just prior to the British Invasion I got "re-interested." At that time, to my utter disgust, my parents got me a nylon-string classical guitar. There's nothing wrong with a gut-string guitar; I use one in the studio all the time, but back then I wanted something like a Mosrite, or at least a Fender Mustang.

For my thirteenth birthday, which was my Bar Mitzvah, I got a Japanese electric of the St. George/ Kingston variety; it was the kind of electric guitar you'd see in a department store, not a music store. It had *huge* chrome pickguards, three pickups and a black-to-red sunburst. I played that until I was about sixteen; around then I was into Dylan, Delta Blues and fingerpicking, so I wanted a good flattop. I had a job, and for the first time in my life, I ordered a left-handed guitar. It was a Favilla; he was friends with D'Angelico; he was another Italian immigrant who built mandolins and beautiful

TOP: Easton cops an attitude backstage at the "Fridays" television show, 1984. Photo by Joel Bernstein.

RIGHT: *A 1986* Musician *magazine party included noted players like John McCurry (to the left of Easton), Les Paul (center) and Al DiMeola (to the right of Mr. Paul). Photo by Larry Busacca.*

guitars. Those guys seem to have a gift for it. I got their cheap, all-mahogany acoustic, but that's all I could afford. Yet it opened a door for me; it was my first good left-handed guitar, and I still have it.

I was going home after school each day and comping licks from records. At a certain time in my life, virtually all of my heroes were Tele players; even Bloomfield played one at one time. There was Jesse Ed Davis, Robbie Robertson, Roy Buchanan, Clarence White, James Burton. I decided I had to have one; I washed dishes at a restaurant to be able to get the money, and I ordered a left-handed blond Tele from a classic New York music store in Freeport called Gracin's Music; your New York readers will probably remember it. I was so in love with guitars by then I'd take a bus to Gracin's just to hang out; I'd sweep his floor or just stay out of the way, just so I could be around guitars. You can't imagine how many times I called them, wanting to know if my guitar had come in! (laughs) I must have driven them crazy, but they were always so nice to me.

VG: Did you know from the Mickey Mouse guitar on that you were a left-handed player?

EE: Yeah; we have photos of me when I was three holding that guitar left-handed.

VG: Do you do everything left-handed? I know some folks, for example, who write left-handed, but they play golf right-handed.

EE: No, I'm a "hard-line lefty." I can't tell you about all the places my left hand has been. (laughs)

VG: On your earlier guitars, did you just reverse the nut and strings?

EE: I didn't even do that; I was on a path to being the next Albert King or Otis Rush, or so I thought. I just figured out the chords upside down, but then it reached a point where I felt like it was holding me back. I wanted the same advantage as a right-handed person, so I started turning the strings around, and then I actually started getting lefty instruments.

VG: Once you started reversing the strings, how long did it take you to "adapt," for lack of a better term?

EE: Probably a few weeks; at that point all I knew were a few barre chords. I was turning the strings around by the time I was thirteen or fourteen.

VG: What about the bands you played in before you went to Berklee?

EE: My first band was probably like a lot of people; a couple of guitar players through one little Fender Vibrolux amp, playing on the patio for our friends. The repertoire could have been anything from "Pipeline" to "Kicks" by Paul Revere & the

Raiders. I had a band in high school that actually did pretty well locally; it was called Washboard Slim. It was sort of a San Francisco, acid-rock vibe; people would probably surprised to know that I was a real Dead freak in that time period; I loved Moby Grape as well.

Washboard Slim was runner-up in a county-wide "Battle of the Bands" in '71, and the prize was a five hundred dollar gift certificate from Sam Ash, so each band member had a hundred dollars to spend. I was thinking about Mike Bloomfield and Frank Zappa a lot, and I decided I wanted a Goldtop; At that time, those guitars had the small humbuckers. So I sold my Tele for a hundred and fifty, my mom gave me fifty bucks, and the hundred dollar credit meant I walked out of Sam Ash with a brand new, left-handed Les Paul Deluxe Goldtop for $297. Those were the days!

VG: What made you head to Berklee?

EE: I knew that I wanted to be a professional musician; as much as the education part was a desire to be out on my own. I really enjoyed my experience at Berklee.

VG: The next obvious question is how the Cars formed.

EE: (Laughs) That's a bit of a convoluted story! I was rooming with a friend who answered an ad in *The Boston Phoenix* for a sound man, and he invited me to come along with him and see this band called Richard & the Rabbits; it included Ocasek, Orr, and Hawkes. I really liked them, and I recognized that there was some great writing going on. Later, that band broke up, and Ric and Ben started playing as a semi-acoustic duo; they did some of Ric's songs and some covers, at a place called the Idler in Harvard Square. My roommate was also involved with them; after he had the sound mixed right, he'd run onstage and play congas. I started coming to their gigs just to listen, then later I started bringing my guitar down, after I'd jammed with them at Ben's house. At that time I was playing a '72 Strat that I'd bought new from Manny's; it had a natural finish and a "bullet" and three-bolt neck.

VG: What do you think of the bullet truss rod/

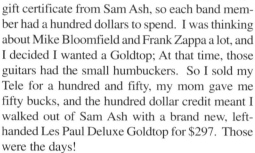

The Cars in 1984: Ben Orr, Greg Hawkes, David Robinson (front), Ric Ocasek, and Elliot Easton. Photo: George Holz.

three-bolt neck configuration on Fender instruments?

EE: I think they got it worked out better at G & L than Fender did. The idea of a tilt-adjustable, bolt-on neck is good, because you don't have to do any shimming, but on the Fenders the neck didn't seem to be very secure. I didn't have any problems with mine, but I would rather have had an earlier version of a Strat, but I couldn't afford the three hundred bucks a '64 Strat would have cost back then. (laughs) I can remember back at Gracin's when new Strats were two and a quarter, and Teles were one sixty; one seventy five.

I had that Goldtop from Sam Ash when I graduated from high school and when I went to Berklee. I traded it for a 335, and somehow I scraped the money together for a Tele. The 335, Tele and a Twin amp were my gear, and my apartment got ripped off; all of those pieces were stolen. I went back down to New York, and the best I could come up with was that Strat, which I was using with Ocasek and Orr.

That expanded into a band called Cap'n Swing, but it wasn't a swing band; I think the name came from some kind of Beat literature that Ric read. That band was kind of like "Velvet Underground Meets Steely Dan"[with] Ric's songs, which are quirky and tend to explore the dark side a bit, but the band wasn't a precise pop band like the Cars were; it was more of a jamming band. We'd take off on musical "excursions," and it got to the point where we were able to do a showcase at Max's Kansas City in New York, which would have been around '76. We played for a lot of big-name rock management companies like Aucoin and Leiber & Krebs. They all said we were good, but there were

too many "diverse images" in the group; one guy looked like he should be in the Grateful Dead, another like he should be in the Velvet Underground; they said: "We just don't get it." In hindsight, I guess we took it in a positive way, as constructive criticism. We eliminated some of the members of the band who we felt would be resistant to adapting and changing; Greg Hawkes was brought back in. In the interim, Greg had played sax with Martin Mull & His Fabulous Furniture. He also played sax on the early Cars records.

VG: Right or wrong, the Cars will probably be forever stereotyped as a so-called "New Wave" band. Did the term even exist when you finally gelled, personnel-wise?

EE: I don't believe it did. When we formed the band, it was right at the beginning of the Punk thing, but personally, I took music too seriously and was into it too deeply to want to be a three-chord basher. I'd already been learning pedal steel licks on my Tele. I think "New Wave" was probably some journalist's tag as a reaction to Punk. Any band that came out around '77 or '78 got called a New Wave band. We never tried to be some skinny-tie, Knack-type of group; we were weirder than that. (chuckles) We never sat down and had a discussion about being tagged as a New Wave band; it was probably a joke to us.

VG: The Cars did a "Midnight Special" show with no dialogue; the graphics had something like "Tonight, the Cars present the future of music," and there were some, uh, "unique" acts like Iggy Pop and Lene Lovich. Why did you opt for such a concept?

EE: Because we refused to do things like cut to a commercial going (Easton does an credible wolf-like howl) "AHH—OOOOOO!" with Wolfman Jack. We said that if we were going to host the show, we weren't going on with that putz; we weren't willing to make that kind of show-biz concession. That kind of hoopla was anathema to us. It was an unusual move, and I think it was well

TOP (both pages): *Easton rocks out onstage during the 1982* Shake It Up World Tour *with a Les Paul and an early '70s Gibson ES-355 (Mono w/ Varitone!) that was not completed by Gibson until 1981. Elliot describes this guitar as "the best ES series instrument I've ever owned."*

received. It was where someone was trying to do something a little different. I still have a video of it; it was great fun.

VG: Do you have a favorite Cars album and song?

EE: Probably the first album, *because* it was the first. My other favorite record in terms of craft would be *Heartbeat City*; those are the two best records we made. As for songs, I tend to think more about favorite guitar solos; I'm real proud of the work I did in the Cars. I like *all* of our songs, but my favorite *solos* are on songs like "Best Friend's Girl," "Touch and Go," "Tonight She Comes," "Shake It Up," "Since You're Gone"...lots of them.

VG: And since the Cars were mainstays of MTV, do you have a favorite video?

EE: Probably "You Might Think," because it was a real breakthrough for us, and it won "Video of the Year" the first year MTV had their awards; I've got my little spaceman on my bookshelf.

VG: The band played at Live Aid. Comments and observations?

EE: That was really exciting; it was one of those days that you'll never forget. I saw the Zeppelin reunion from the wings; all sorts of bands all day. Other than our part of the show, I hung out on the bleachers on the side of the stage all day; it was amazing. Backstage was like a trailer camp.

VG: You played a red Telecaster at that event.

EE: It was Fiesta Red; that guitar's also in the video for a song called "Magic." John Page is my oldest friend in the guitar industry; he's been building guitars for me since around '79. I was one of the first guys to play the Lead I and Lead II for Fender. Since I was a lefty and sort of a guitar connoisseur, I was asking them to build me instruments that they wouldn't normally be making; in essence I was treating them like a Custom Shop before they *had* a Custom Shop. When the '52 Telecaster reissue first came out, John got me the Fiesta Red lefty with a single-layer white pickguard.

I still have that guitar, but now it has a lime-green metalflake paint job with pinstriping and a Jazzmaster rhythm pickup. Some people will put a humbucker there, but putting a Jazzmaster pickup there helps the instrument retain its "Fenderness," and it sounds *outstanding;* it gets a bigger rhythm sound.

VG: I can recall how the Cars used aesthetically interesting guitars in concert, in videos, and on album covers. The *Panorama* cover is a handy example, as is the video for "Drive," but I forgot what you were holding in that scene where the band was supposed to be wax figures.

EE: That's a Guild Duane Eddy DE-500; the only lefty ever built. In the early Eighties Guild started building them again, using hardware from the old days; they made it for me then.

VG: Tone-wise, a lot of your guitar work on Cars songs has a bright and "up-front" sound. A lot of guitar players would probably think you used a small amp in the studio. Did you have a particular favorite studio setup?

EE: No, I used whatever would produce the sound I would be hearing in my head for a particular guitar part, and it could have been *anything*, and to be honest, I used 4 X 12s more than small amps. "Shake It Up" had a Deluxe Reverb; I think I used a V-4 for "My Best Friend's Girl."

VG: What about "Good Times Roll"?

EE: Well, for the whole first album, a friend got us a deal on some Ampeg amps; a VT-22, VT-44, and a V-4, and I think we had a Marshall half-stack and a Twin. My arsenal consisted of a Les Paul Standard and a Telecaster, a Morley echo pedal and an early Roland chorus ensemble.

VG: The reason I asked about "Good Times

BOTTOM (both pages): *Whole Lotta Lefties: Elliot Easton in his back yard in Weston, Massachusetts, 1981 (no wisecracks about "Easton from Weston," please). Photo: Jonathan Postal.*

Roll" is that it's an example of a song that sounded a lot "heavier" in concert on the *Live in Houston* video. Why wasn't the Houston show released as a live album?

EE: The band could rock a lot more live than it did sometimes on record; we sounded more "guitar-heavy" live. It never even came up about releasing the Houston show as an album; it was never even discussed, and it wasn't the first time the band had done a remote recording. We had done a couple of King Bisquit shows and some other live broadcasts, but we never talked about releasing a live album.

VG: When the Cars broke up, it was reported that the reason was dissatisfaction within the band about the way the *Door to Door* album turned out. Comment?

EE: That was only one facet of things; it was a lot more complicated. To say that the band broke up over the way that album turned out would be a huge over-simplification.

VG: I've seen solo albums from members of the Cars, some of which were out before the band officially broke up. What about you?

EE: I did one around '85, before the band split; it was called *Change No Change*, and it was on Elektra Records. Rhino is seriously considering releasing it on CD. I co-wrote the songs with Jules Shear; he's been a fine songwriter for other artists, as well. We'd written this huge batch of songs, just as friends, and they weren't necessarily designed for *me* to sing, but I was in a position where I could do a record, so I did. It did okay; there was a single called "Wearin' Down Like A Wheel," and the video got medium rotation on MTV. I put together a band and toured, but Jules didn't go out with me.

VG: I saw your name associated with an album called *The Guitars That Conquered the World*.

EE: That was something *Guitar World* magazine put together. It had one track each by twelve or thirteen guitar players. I contributed an acoustic guitar piece; a Bert Jansch kind of thing. It was in kind of an English folk style. I figured some of the others would take their track and blow their brains out, playing all their hot licks. No pun intended, but I thought I'd take a left turn and contribute an acoustic piece. Dickie Betts and Warren Haynes had a nice track on that album.

VG: What prompted your move to the Los Angeles area?

EE: Nothing really earth-shaking —

VG: (interrupting) Now *that's* a bad pun!

EE: (laughs) Aw, man... my wife and I just felt like a change. I had an experience putting an act together and getting it signed to Atlantic. I went through the whole process of making an album with Roy Thomas Baker producing. I had Stan Lynch on drums, Benmont Tench on keyboards; it was kind of a duo album with me and a singer named Danny Malone. We were called Band of Angels. We even had the artwork done, then Atlantic decided they weren't going to release it. It was supposed to have come out at the same time as a Mick Jagger solo record.

That represented a couple of years of writing, shopping for a deal, etc., and to have it not come out really kind of put me off, and I felt like I didn't want to start all over again from New York. I just didn't have the desire, so Los Angeles seemed like the right move. And it *was*. Los Angeles has always been sort of a spiritual home to me,

since I was a huge fan of the pop culture of Southern California when I was growing up. Everything from Ed "Big Daddy" Roth to surf music to cool cars. I loved all of that stuff, and I still do. Some of those things have come to fruition; I've had the pleasure of working with Brian Wilson. There's not a lot of that around today, but there are a lot of people who were directly involved with it that I've gotten to know; the stories are great.

VG: Are you saying that area still has an "ambience"?

EE: It does, and you can *create* that ambience. If you're driving down the P.C.H. and you put on a great instrumental record, how different is it? Just cruisin'!

VG: If I remember correctly, you once told me that one of the first things you did when you got to L.A. was a Sam Kinison tribute.

EE: Someone asked me to come down to a jam; it was just another opportunity for me to meet some of the local players. That's what I did when I first got to L.A. My long-time friend Alan Kaufman – who was the roommate back in Boston that took me to see Richard & the Rabbits and works with celebrity jams at a club – and I formed an eight-piece band with a horn section and a Hammond organ. I was playing a Tele, and we were doing everything from Stax/Volt and Barkays stuff to Grant Green, Blue Note boogaloo to "Goldfinger." Toward the end I got a lefty bajo sexto from Fender and ran it through a Vibro-King. We were called the Tiki Gods.

VG: We're at the age where as far as we're concerned, Sean Connery will always be James Bond.

EE: Absolutely. I think a lot of that has to do with the fact that those movies were made while Ian Fleming was alive; he was involved with the casting.

The Tiki Gods went on until a few months ago, when I got too busy. But the list of people I got to play with was incredible: Herbie Hancock, Billy Preston, Jeff "Skunk" Baxter, Robby Krieger, Smokey Robinson, Tom Arnold, Gary Busey.

VG: In one of the last "preliminary" conversations we had, you noted that you were playing with Creedence. Details?

EE: It's the original rhythm section, Stu Cook and Doug Clifford, a fine singer named John Tristao, Steve Gunner on keyboards and other instruments, and me. It's called Creedence Clearwater Revisited. We've played a few gigs in Vegas and Reno, and a festival in Idaho. We met Col. Tom Parker in Vegas.

I've also been producing and doing some session work. My producing partner is Gordon Fordyce; he's British and he apprenticed under Roy Thomas Baker. Once Gordon and Roy and some other friends took me to Liverpool while we were recording *Heartbeat City*. We visited places like Penny Lane and Strawberry Fields, and there was a Beatles convention going on at the Adelphi Hotel; I met Gerry Marsden. I had the time of my life, and that's how I got to be pals with Gordon. He's a crack engineer and a good hands-on guy with computers and technology, and I'm more of a musical guy. I'll be working with the guitar player or drummer, getting into a groove, helping them come up with hooks. So Gordon and I are a very complimentary team.

VG: Let's talk about your guitar collection. Quantity, rarest piece, favorite piece?

EE: My collection is like an amoeba; it's constantly changing shape. These days I've got about 50 or 60 instruments. I can name two that are both "rare" and "favorite"; it's a toss-up because they're both incredibly rare and wonderful guitars. I have a 1950 left-handed 000-28L that's in museum-quality condition; it doesn't even have a pick mark on it. I've also got a '58 Tele that's my ideal Tele: light blond, single layer white pickguard. It's in almost the same condition as the Martin. I love those kind of Teles even more than the butterscotch, black-pickguard ones. Both of those guitars have incredible tone, as well.

To open up the "circle" a little more, I have a '64 or '65 Strat that's in mint condition. It's a better player than the Burgundy Mist one I sold a few years ago. The Burgundy Mist one was *too* new. The frets were still scratchy on it! John Peden photographed it; it was a "centerfold." It even came with a white Tolex case that "creaked" when you opened it.

I have a really cool '61 Gibson first-issue Barney Kessel with PAFs. It's the Custom, with a spruce top, bow-tie inlays, and a brown case with pink lining. It's got a wide, flat neck; it sounds like "a jazz guitar meets a Les Paul." It's a fine instrument; some people think those are ugly but I think they're beautiful. That Kessel is *quite* elegant.

VG: In the *Vintage Guitars in America, Vol. 2* video, you were opining that it's difficult to find left-handed vintage pieces.

EE: Well, there's certainly a fraction of what there is in "righty." I can't imagine what it must be like to live in a world where you can walk into any music store and pull most anything off the wall and try it (chuckles). When I walk into a music store, there's usually nothing there for me to play. Here's all these cool, sexy guitars, and for me, they're all backwards.

VG: I can't say that I've ever noticed any left-handed instruments from the old Chicago-area budget manufacturers like Harmony, Kay and Valco.

EE: As a matter of fact, I was just talking with Scott Jennings from Route 66. He just came back from the Arlington show, and he found two lefty Harmony Rockets. I've also seen a lefty Stratotone. There are these little "pockets" of funny things that you see in lefties. One of those companies you mentioned must have done a run of lefty electric mandolins because I've seen a few of them.

VG: But when you were growing up, did you ever see something like a left-handed Silvertone/Danelectro with the amp in the case?

EE: No, I've never seen a lefty Danelectro of any type.

VG: At one time, you had a Kramer signature model guitar.

EE: That was something that I designed with Tom Anderson, who's a fine builder. The guy who was running Kramer at the time, Dennis Berardi, loved to hang around rock bands; I don't know any other way to put it. He was a nice guy, and he offered me the opportunity to design my own signature instrument. I took it as a challenge to come up with something for Kramer that had more of a traditional vibe. At the time, they didn't offer a guitar that *didn't* have a Floyd Rose. So I designed a guitar with a Tele-style bridge. It was available in two models: The Tele bridge and Seymour Duncan Quarter-Pounder system with a five-way switch for a lot of sounds, or with a humbucking-single-single pickup setup with a Floyd Rose. I thought such a guitar might have some appeal to country players and roots rockers who might go for the Tele configuration.

Looks-wise, I was inspired at the time by that orange Jackson guitar Jeff Beck was playing around the time of his *Flash* album. I wanted something that looked "like it could have existed, but didn't." The pickguard on the Kramer is an example; Fender could have done that with their Tele, but didn't.

Mick Jagger played one of the Tom Anderson-built prototypes in the "Mixed Emotions" video. Tom built fabulous guitars, and I can't honestly say that the production guitars had the "magic" of the Anderson-built ones. That's not to put Kramer down, but you're talking about two completely different setups; one is an artist in a small shop, building one guitar at a time, the other is a huge factory, which by its very definition has to turn out a lot of instruments. In effect, Fender has gotten around the same potential problem by offering the Custom Shop; they don't ask you to expect the same thing out of a Mexican-built Strat as one that Jay Black builds for you (chuckles).

VG: Haven't you been a Gibson clinician at times?

EE: I have, and I still do those occasionally. I usually take a Les Paul with me. Right now, Gibson is building me a red Epi Sheraton – an American-made lefty.

VG: In your search for vintage lefty instruments, have you ever encountered a counterfeit?

EE: No, the only time something's ever smelled rotten is when I'll go into a store and the guy says he's got a guitar that I used to own and he wants me to sign it. But when I look at the guitar, it's something I've never had. That seems to happen because there aren't too many left-handed collectors, but fortunately it's a rare occurrence.

VG: Are there any instruments you're still seeking?

EE: Yeah. May I use this interview as a forum to list three instruments?

VG: Absolutely.

EE: The first guitar is one that everybody's going to laugh about, because nobody wants them anyway: I'd love to have a Sixties Fender acoustic flat-top, like a Kingman or Malibu or Villager 12-string. One of those that were designed by Roger Rossmeisl. Some lefties were built; there was a Malibu in your magazine that I missed getting by a day. I've been looking for one of those forever.

I'm also looking for a clean ES-330, and an SG Standard from around '64, like what's seen in the "Rain" and "Paperback Writer" videos, with a long Vibrola tailpiece. Of course I'd always like to have things like Brazilian D-28s. I've got a '61 now.

VG: It sounds like you've got plenty to keep you busy these days, family-wise *and* business-wise.

EE: Here's hopin'! There's a Cars anthology on Rhino that's just been released, but now that we've got a baby, I've got to bring home the bacon.

VG: Uh, with all due respect to your heritage, "bringing home the bacon" is a bit of a contradiction.

EE: Well, maybe I should say we're Reformed...(laughs).

In spite of being more or less limited in his access to classic guitars, Elliot Easton's enthusiasm and eloquence concerning such a subject is an inspiration to other guitar lovers, left-handed *or* right-handed. We'd briefly conversed with Easton at numerous guitar shows, but once we were able to coordinate an interview, the wait was worth it.

Duane Eddy
Of DeArmonds and Details

The temptation to get the word "twang" into the title of this interview is obvious, but that term has been applied to Duane Eddy's guitar style so often that its use here might seem hackneyed to veteran guitar music fans.

Yet that particular low-end guitar string tone is Eddy's signature sound, and his 1993 box set release on Rhino Records is called *Twang Thang*. Consisting of forty tunes on two Compact Discs (a total of eight bonus tunes are on the CDs compared to the cassette anthology), *Twang Thang* is a definitive history of one of rock music's first guitar heroes. Its fifty-two page booklet contains an informative narrative written by Dan Forte (a.k.a. Teisco Del Rey, a previous *Vintage Guitar* interviewee); Forte was also responsible for the compilation of the anthology.

Utilizing the anthology's booklet as a prime source, *Vintage Guitar's* conversation with Duane Eddy took an approach of asking for details concerning guitars, tones, and history, but our first inquiry was about *Twang Thang* itself:

VG: "Last things first," for lack of a better phrase. Are you satisfied with the way the *Twang Thang* anthology turned out?

DE: I'm *exceptionally* happy with it; I got to remaster forty tracks with Denny Purcell of Georgetown Mastering. Dan Forte, who wrote the liner notes, called me up one day and told me that the anthology was in the works; he wanted to give me his thinking on how it might be done. I made a couple of suggestions, including how much I'd love to re-master those songs and get them right for a change. It seems like nobody ever does that; I've heard some packages that still have pops and crackles where the songs were taken directly off a record. So Dan called Rhino; they were happy about the idea, and Denny and I

did the re-mix *analog* first, and then *digital,* so it sounds like it used to sound, even if it's played on the new state-of-the-art digital equipment. It's got all of the original warmth and strength, but at the same time it's compatible with the new audiophile equipment.

VG: Dan Forte's liner notes in the booklet are pretty thorough.

DE: He's an old friend; we've known each other since the mid-Seventies. He came down here and stayed with us for a few days; he went through all the old photos that my wife pulled out, and in the evenings we sat around and talked; he based most of his liner notes on those conversations.

I'm real happy with the reviews the anthology got around the country; some publications were calling it the best sound they'd ever heard on a re-issue package. [See Jim Hilmar's review of *Twang Thang* in the October, 1993 issue of *Vintage Guitar.*]

VG: I'm going to take the "details" questions pretty much on a chronological basis whenever possible. Do you remember the brand of the lap steel you got for your ninth birthday?

DE: It was an Electromuse; my aunt bought it and sent it to me; I don't know whether she got it from a store or a catalog. I used an E6 tuning for Hawaiian stuff and an A tuning for country.

VG: Did you ever think you'd want to be a steel guitar player instead of a Spanish guitar

TOP: *Modern Motoring - Duane Eddy with a New Gibson Custom Shop Corvette; the idea for this guitar came about in his home. Photo by Miki Slingsby, London, England.*

RIGHT: *Duane is playing his famous Gretsch and using a Howard amplifier, late 1958 or early 1959. Photo appears in booklet accompanying the CD* Twang Thang *and is courtesy the Duane Eddy Collection.*

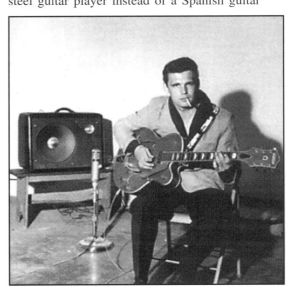

player?

DE: No; I'd played around on an old Dobro at one time, and that's why my aunt bought me that lap steel. My parents liked Hawaiian guitar and wanted me to take lessons, but I wanted to play what I called "guitar," meaning Spanish-type. I argued with my folks about it, and I ended up not getting any lessons on any instrument! (chuckles)

VG: When your family moved to Arizona when you were thirteen, there weren't stations like WCKY, WWVA and WSM to listen to anymore. What did you listen to once you were relocated to the Southwest, and what influenced your playing?

DE: I heard Mexican radio stations for the first time and loved the music, but country music was the biggest influence, and I listened to the country stations constantly. I used to come home from school, turn on the radio, pick up my guitar and play along with the records I liked.

VG: The move put you between Nashville and the West Coast, but closer to the latter, which had the Western Swing sound during those times; Hank Thompson, Spade Cooley, etc. Did that influence you?

DE: I started working in clubs when I was fifteen; by the time I was seventeen or eighteen I was a full-time musician, playing for dances and on local T.V. and radio shows. We always had drums in our band, which I suspect was a nod to the Western folks instead of Nashville. We did do Hank Thompson and Bob Wills tunes; there had to be drums for dancing. We were also doing rockabilly, though we didn't know at the time that's what it was called. (chuckles) Since we did have a drummer we weren't as "authentic" as a Nashville group with no drums, but we did all of the Top Ten country songs when we played, which were all out of Nashville, and we still played them with drums.

I talked with Glen Campbell years later, and at the same time we were doing that kind of music for Western dance clubs in the Phoenix area, he was do-

ing the same thing for the same kind of clubs in the Albequerque area.

VG: Was your Les Paul Goldtop your first electric instrument?

DE: Yes; I bought it at an appliance store. They had about four or five instruments hanging in there; I wanted an electric guitar and it was

the only electric they had, so I bought it. I didn't really know much about guitars then. My first amp was made by a local guy that the appliance store told me about; he had chicken wire across the front of the cabinet to protect the speaker. (chuckles)

VG: In addition to your other talents, you've had an essay of yours published, and that was one of the Forewords for Jay Scott's Gretsch book. In it you discussed when you traded in your Les Paul for your Gretsch 6120. One veteran guitar dealer told me that Gretsch guitars tended to have a wide variance in the feel of their necks since they were hand-made, and you wrote about the 6120's neck in that Foreword.

DE: I'm convinced I got lucky with the 6120's neck; the music store also had a White Falcon I tried the same day I bought the 6120, and the White Falcon's neck felt like a baseball bat! You could play it, but it wasn't "user friendly."

VG: When you traded in your Les Paul, did you note any difference between the P-90 pickups on the Les Paul and the DeArmonds on the 6120?

DE: Well, at the time it was simply a trade for a new guitar; I liked the way the neck felt on the 6120 plus the fact that it had a vibrato bar. I suppose I noticed a difference between the sound of the two guitars, although the amp I had wasn't that wonderful. (chuckles)

VG: You also noted some modifications that you had done to a Magnatone amp in that Foreword. Why did you have those things done to it?

DE: I got the Magnatone around the same time I got the 6120, and a guy named Dick Wilson, who was a great jazz player, and a guy named Buddy Wheeler, who was a steel player in town, hopped my amp up to a hundred watts. They also put a fifteen-inch JBL speaker in it plus a tweeter, and they recovered it in black

TOP: *The cover of Eddy's great 40 song anthology.*

LEFT: *Duane posing with the Electromuse lap steel that he received for his 9th birthday, 1947. Photo appears in booklet accompanying the CD Twang Thang and is courtesy the Duane Eddy Collection.*

Naugahyde with white grille cloth, so it looked really sharp. Since Buddy was a steel player, he was looking for a clear, clean sound, so that's why a tweeter was put in it. In those days we thought it also made a Spanish electric guitar sound glassy and warm. Buddy ended up playing electric bass on "Rebel Rouser" and most of the hits I cut in Phoenix, using an amp as powerful as mine with *two* fifteen-inch bass range JBLs and a tweeter, which was the "click" sound you hear on those records. Those amps looked a bit like some of the early Standel amplifiers, only a lot more luxurious. I don't know if Buddy and Dick had seen a Standel at that time or not. I know I didn't see one until a couple of years later.

VG: Is that the amp shown on Page 25 of the anthology booklet? The grille cloth has been removed.

DE: That's a Howard amplifier. Buddy and Dick got tired of modifying amplifiers, so they designed their own circuitry and power pack, and hooked up with a guy named Tom McCormick, who manufactured their design under the Howard brand name. Two pages over, on Page 27, there's a picture of the modified Magnatone; I'm running one of my Dano six-string basses through it.

VG: The "outboard" DeArmond tremelo unit you used seems like a fairly unheralded gizmo; John Fogerty mentioned it in a 1985 *Guitar Player* interview.

DE: It was definitely part of our sound back then. I've still got one, but I don't know if it works or not. I had another one, but a while back Ry Cooder and I plugged it in, and it went up in smoke! (laughs)

VG: The use of the empty water tank in the studio as another important facet of your sound was noted in the anthology notes, but what kind of reverb units did you use in concert back then?

DE: If I remember correctly, both the Magnatone as well as the Howard amplifiers I used back then had echo chambers built into them, but I never did use the units built into amplifiers for recording; I used studio effects. In those days the spring echoes built into amplifiers didn't work well for recording.

VG: While the Guild Duane Eddy Signature Model electric guitar is seen on the cover of *Twang Thang*, the only time it's seen inside the booklet is in a couple of early Sixties RCA publicity photos.

DE: And you'll notice that the Gretsch is on the back cover and is seen many more times in the booklet! (laughs)

VG: What can you tell us about the Guild endorsement guitar? Did you have any input into the design?

DE: Yeah, somewhat, but they screwed it up right at the beginning and reversed the location of the master volume knob and the pickup switch. I wanted the pickup switch on the upper part and the master volume on the lower cutaway, just like my Gretsch, so the publicity photos on the cover of the anthology show the guitar set up the wrong way. I sent it back to factory and made 'em change it.

I kept the design of that guitar pretty much like the Gretsch; it had DeArmond pickups but I had wanted it to be a deeper guitar than it turned out to be; the company fudged on that part of my design. Other than that, there were some cosmetic things, such as the original gold and black color scheme. That was supposed to be the only color combination at the time, but they took it upon themselves to decide to make the model in other colors as well. The deal I made with them was that the one like I played would sell for around seven hundred dollars, and they were to build a cheaper version that still had a Bigsby vibrato for around four hundred dollars, for kids that were learning to play. They fudged on that too; the four hundred dollar guitar ended up with a plain tailpiece for the most part; although I did see a few with a Bigsby on them.

VG: At the same time your Guild signature guitar was released, the company also marketed a George Barnes model. I've read that you played with the likes of Barney Kessel and Howard Roberts, but did you ever play with George Barnes?

DE: No, I never had the honor of even meeting him. The owner of Guild, Al Dronge, was cool, and *very* interested in producing a Duane Eddy Signature model guitar. On the other hand, his son Mark had a very snobbish attitude towards Rock & Roll. He told me at the time that he was much more interested in making guitars for the New York jazz players such as George Barnes and Tal Farlow.

VG: Regarding your use of Danelectro baritone guitars/six-string basses back in the late Fifties, what do you think of the resurgence of interest recently in that type of instrument?

DE: I think it's great; I love the sound of them. Danelectros were probably the funkiest-sounding ones due to those lipstick tube pickups. There's a guy here in the Nashville area, Jerry Jones, who's building Danelectro reissues; I haven't played one yet but they look like they're great guitars. George Harrison has a Fender Bass VI which I played; it has a much more mellow sound than the Dano.

VG: In addition to all of the other notable guitarists cited in the anthology booklet, who else have you played with that you think should be noted?

DE: Larry Carlton, Robben Ford, Albert Lee and I all did concerts together. I've done studio work with Steve Cropper, John Fogerty, and others.

VG: Do you collect?

DE: Not really, but I've kept every one of my own guitars throughout the years, with the exception of the Les Paul I traded in on my 6120. I had two Martins that were in a California store needing some work, but the store burned down, so I lost those; that was several years ago. The only new instrument I have is a fine solidbody Valley Arts guitar that was the last instrument Mike McGuire made before he left the company. I think Valley Arts is about the top of the line in solidbody guitars these days.

VG: It's been a few years since you wrote the aforementioned Foreword for Jay Scott's book. Any comments about the products the new Gretsch organization has introduced since then?

DE: They had an acoustic White Falcon at the recent Nashville NAMM show; it looked very nice, as did another red-colored acoustic at their space. But I didn't get to spend a lot of time at the NAMM show, so I'm going to take a run down to Savannah sometime in the near future to try out some of their new guitars.

VG: When and why did you move to the Nashville area?

DE: About nine years ago; we were living in Lake Tahoe,

and decided to move here because everybody had started calling me a recluse for living up there. (laughs) Nobody could find me, and I was tired of being retired. I got to looking at my phone book and realized that I knew a lot more people down in this area than I did in Lake Tahoe or anywhere else. Things started to happen right after we got settled in here; I did a recording with the Art of Noise.

VG: And that still would probably strike many popular music fans as one of the most unusual collaborations of all time.

DE: (chuckles) I know; they were pretty avant-garde; in fact, there was a pun going around about me saying: "Avant-garde the faintest idea of what they're doing"! (laughs) But it worked out really great; there was a live concert recorded in Newcastle, England that was shown on a national television show called "The Tube." They really know what they're doing; Anne Dudley is a skilled and educated musician; she arranges for the London Philharmonic and does a lot of session work. She wrote the music for *The Crying Game* and several other movies. J.J. Jeczalik has produced groups like the Pet Shop Boys; he's very clever with his computers and Fairlights. They had gotten some movement on the dance charts, but their record company felt that needed to "hook them up" with another name to get some attention. My friend, Eddy Pumer, who was there at a meeting happened to mention that he'd spoken to me the previous day, and Derek Green, the head of China Records, jumped up and said: *"That's it!"* The Art of Noise liked the idea, and when I heard what they did I thought it was far out and different, but I thought such a joint venture would work well. It was a remarkable experience.

VG: Any comment about the resurgence of interest these days in guitar instrumental music, even though such music might appeal more to players rather than to Top 40 listeners?

DE: I certainly haven't heard any Top 40 instrumental guitar hits lately, but I think it's the cleverest thing in the world when players can pick up an instrument that has basically the same six strings and neck length, and can get so many different kinds of music and sound, and express so many different feelings with it. It's truly amazing. Each person can get his own sound with his personal touch and technique. It makes for fascinating listening; you can go from guitar player to guitar player and still say "Look at what he's doing."

One thing I've noticed about some of the players in the Nashville area since I've moved here is that some of the stars are not only great singers and songwriters, they're phenomenal players as well. Guys like Vince Gill, Steve Wariner, Ricky Skaggs; it seems like they can do it all. Get them with someone like Albert Lee and they'll blaze you right off the planet! (chuckles)

VG: What's kept you busy recently?

DE: I've been real busy this year; I played on a track with Carl Perkins and the Mavericks. Carl's not working too much these days but he's feeling great. He rests up between gigs so he can give it his all when he does perform; he's an inspiring person. The track we did was "Matchbox"; it's as good as I've ever heard him sing it. The Mavericks were great to work with! The track is on the album *Red Hot + Country*, and we're doing a T.V. special as well; it was filmed live at the Ryman Auditorium in Nashville.

I also recorded a track with Foreigner; Mick Jones had been kind enough to induct me into the Rock & Roll Hall of Fame in January of last year. Rod Stewart, the Grateful Dead and the Animals were among the other inductees. John Fogerty was going to induct me, but the earthquake happened two days before the event and did a lot of damage, so he and Rod Stewart stayed home with their families; it was a pretty traumatic experience for them.

Mick Jones did a fine job with my induction; it was a hell of a nice evening. I sat with Eric Clapton, Jeff Beck and Mick; over at the next table were Dion and Chuck Berry, so I had old friends and new friends there. Later Mick came down here and we recorded a track named "Until the End of Time", which was released in January of *this* year. They're totally professional and extremely talented. Mick and Lou Gramm are fantastic men to work with.

We're in the working stages of preparing to do a T.V. special, doing my old hits with some guests. Carl Perkins, Chuck Berry, the Everly Brothers, and Roy Orbison all had somewhat similar projects. It'll be probably be sort of a "rockumentary" and we'll also do a live show. Hopefully it'll turn out to be an interesting event.

VG: James Burton told me that the jam that he and Bruce Springsteen got into at the end of "Pretty Woman" on the Roy Orbison Cocoanut Grove concert was unintentional; Orbison had forgotten to end the song like T-Bone Burnett had told him to.

DE: Well, I don't blame Roy for forgetting, since he was standing there looking at all those famous people; that could make you a little nervous! (chuckles) Knowing James, though, that jam session is an excellent example of how he can jump right on something and make it work. I wouldn't have known about that song's ending being improvised if you hadn't told me.

So last year was pretty exciting; another plus is that I've had songs in three hit movies during the past few months. First, "Rebel Rouser" was in the movie *Forrest Gump* and also on the soundtrack album that went to Number Two and is *still* in the Top Fifty! Then three of my tracks were used in *Natural Born Killers*; "Rebel Rouser", "Shazam", and "The Trembler." I also had a track in the movie *Milk Money*.

Two commercials used the Art of Noise/Duane Eddy version of "Peter Gunn" this past year; Bud Lite and Mercedes.

So it's been good, and it promises to get even better as 1995 wears on. At the moment I am talking to a label about doing a new album, and there's also a CD-ROM project in the wind. Hopefully all of these things will work out, and I'll be very busy in the forseeable future.

If any guitar player that's noted for a certain "tone" can maintain the respect of fans and other players for as long as Duane Eddy has, the term "legend" doesn't seem inappropriate. Eddy's playing and distinctive sound is (as of this writing) once again on the charts for the umpteenth time in many decades, and another group of listeners is being made aware of the Twang King, who shows no sign whatsoever of abdicating.

Mark Farner

God, Guitars, and Grand Funk

One of the most successful power trios in the annals of rock music (and probably one of the *loudest* bands of all time, regardless of the number of members) was Michigan's Grand Funk Railroad. Roaring into prominence with a "breakthrough" performance at a 1969 Atlanta pop festival, the threesome's flat-out, no-holds-barred music was a staple of Seventies FM radio, and their concerts enthralled millions of fans worldwide. The trio's albums were released on a steady basis and were incredibly successful; millions of Grand Funk albums were sold around the globe.

Guitarist Mark Farner is still rocking these days, albeit in a different musical genre and for a different goal. Farner and his band Common Ground are recording and performing in the burgeoning Contemporary Christian musical phenomenon (his logo includes the phrase "Rock and Roll since '64 — Rocking now Forever more"). The affable and eloquent guitarist recently talked at length about his decades of experience and the guitars he played. His usual stage outfit during his Grand Funk days was comprised of pants and no shirt (the lack of which was somewhat offset by Farner's waist-length hair). Accordingly, our initial question was inspired by the fact that the guitarist appeared to be in better shape back then than the vast majority of Seventies rock stars:

VG: The bio I skimmed said that you took up guitar due to a football injury. A lot of males our age who *weren't* jocks probably picked up musical instruments as a way of meeting girls; if you hadn't been injured, do you think you would have stayed a jock and not ever played guitar?

TOP: *Mark Farner with his current performance guitar, a Peavey Impact 2.*

RIGHT: *Get Down! Mark Farner during the glory days of Grand Funk with his Messenger guitar. Its holes have been taped up to prevent feedback.*

MF: Well, I really loved the excitement of hearing my name called out over the loudspeaker at games; "That was number 66, Farner, on the tackle." I was defensive linebacker over center, and our team was undefeated. We kicked butts and took names, but we were all a bunch of misfits. (chuckles) A lot of us smoked cigarettes and got some older guys to buy beer for us, but as a team we hung together. Hearing the crowd roar whenever I made a tackle and hearing my name over the P.A. really thrilled me, and of course, it's a similar situation whenever you're playing a concert and you finish a song.

VG: Are you saying the "adulation," for lack of a better term, was as inspiring when you played concerts as when you played football games?

MF: Absolutely, *particularly* the *first time* it happened in each circumstance; that's something you never forget. In both situations, I said to myself: "This is what I want to do!" (chuckles) I was fifteen when I started playing guitar, and Grand Funk's first album came out when I was twenty; those five years went by *fast*.

I've learned how to play to an audience; how to get the most participation and the most communication between an audience and an artist. On the earliest Grand Funk albums, I was doing about ninety-nine percent of the writing; I think those songs were saying what people wanted said about things like politicians and the Vietnam War. We sold millions of albums without having a Top Forty hit. Up until *We're An American Band* we

were pretty much a "people's band."

VG: What about your first guitars, "pre-Grand Funk"?

MF: The very first one was a Harmony that we got from Fingerhut. It had a single pickup, and I played it up until I got a Messenger.

VG: Those are fairly rare instruments. How'd you settle on something as unusual as that guitar?

MF: A promoter in Michigan was also the Messenger representative; he gave me one to check out. It had a fuzztone built into it; when it was working right it made you sound just like Jimi Hendrix. I said: "I gotta have this!" (chuckles)

VG: Were you using that guitar during your stint with Terry Knight & the Pack? Were they sort of a circuit band?

MF: I was using the Messenger by then. Back then there were venues where kids from about fourteen to twenty years old would go to dance; we played a lot of those places in Michigan and towns like Dayton, Ohio. Bob Seger was on the circuit; the Amboy Dukes with Ted Nugent, the MC5, the Rationals, SRC, the Stooges....

VG: Those are mostly Detroit bands; in his *VG* interview Ted Nugent cited those bands as part of the "Detroit sound." Do you think Terry Knight & the Pack were part of that sound?

MF: We were on the same circuit but we didn't sound like anybody else. One of the last things we ever played just before Grand Funk got going was as the Fabulous Pack, minus Terry Knight, down in Ann Arbor where a lot of those bands had played.

VG: Did Grand Funk form under the "guidance" of Terry Knight, for lack of a better term? He produced your first albums.

MF: He was the "idea man." The reason we split from him when we were in the Pack was

we all decided he couldn't sing; there were some business disagreements as well. But Terry's gift was that he was creative; he had the gift of gab and could really hype something. He was "a con man in a businesslike way." (laughs) He was definitely a great promoter; I believe that if it hadn't been for Terry's promotion and ideas, Grand Funk wouldn't have been nearly as successful.

VG: Mel Schacher's bass tone had a distorted sound, à la Felix Pappalardi of Mountain. Was that part of Grand Funk's signature sound?

MF: Absolutely; it was balls-to-the-wall bass guitar. We used West amplifiers, which were Michigan-made and were all-tube. He'd run everything up to "10" on his Fillmore model; I used that model as well. He had a P-Bass that he'd also put a humbucker in; the sound he got using the humbucker with the regular P-Bass pickup was unique.

VG: On a lot of songs your guitar seemed to have a slightly distorted sound, but during the same tune an even more distorted sound would kick in. Maybe a definitive example would be the live version of "Paranoid."

MF: That was the Messenger; I'd reach back about three inches from where my right hand would be resting and flip a toggle switch, and the guitar would be in "Overdrive."

The neck on that guitar was symmetrical all the way up; it didn't get fat up at the top. You could play the same way all the way up the neck and you never ran into any wood until you ran out of frets, so you never got into any trouble by having to conform your hand to fit where the neck met the body. Plus, once that neck got inside the axe, it was an A-440 tuning fork. I don't know what that did for it; it was part of the hype, man! (laughs)

VG: Most readers will probably remember that Grand Funk's "breakthrough" performance was at a 1969 Atlanta pop festival, and I know the band made a triumphant return the next year, but some of my acquaintances think that the first live album was recorded at that second Atlanta festival.

MF: It was actually recorded all over the country; we took the best cuts from the best nights.

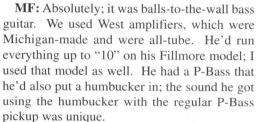

TOP: *Farner in the mid-Seventies with a Veleno.*

LEFT: *Farner and his custom-made Gibson L-5S.*

VG: Back then you were cranking out albums on a fairly frequent basis.

MF: In our first three years, we put out two albums a year plus a "greatest hits" album. When we weren't in the studio, we were on the road. I think the longest it took us to do an album was two weeks, and the shortest time was five days. I think *E Pluribus Funk* was the shortest one; it came together quickly.

VG: The band went on to use other producers after parting ways with Knight; some of the others were notable musicians themselves.

MF: Todd Rundgren was the first on *We're An American Band*; Jimmy Ienner produced us as well. He did "Bad Time," and I got an award from BMI because that song was the most-played BMI song in 1975. It wasn't a Number One tune; I think it got as high as Number Ten.

Frank Zappa worked with us on *Good Singin', Good Playin'*. He came to Michigan to see if he could work in our studio; we'd originally built it as a rehearsal facility, but with the intention of doing rehearsals *and recording* there in the future. Before he got there, we were thinking: "This guy's a musical genius, but he's so off-the-wall he's gotta be on drugs" (chuckles), but he was as straight as he could be. The only thing he was "on" was *coffee;* he had a portable thermos to keep his supply hot, and when it got half-empty he'd send the engineer out to brew him some more. He was *never* without a coffee cup in his hands; he was a real "bean fiend"! (laughs)

VG: When and why was Craig Frost brought in as a fourth member to play keyboards?

MF: In 1972; it was against my wishes. I wanted to keep the band as a three-piece, but when we split with Terry Knight the other two guys wanted to do something that sounded different. I felt like we didn't need to change anything since we were so successful, but I was outvoted; the band was a democracy.

VG: I saw the band on "In Concert" around the time of the *Phoenix* album; Freddy King was the opening act, and you were promoting an anti-drug house.

MF: That was Phoenix House. The concert was done at Madison Square Garden. We also did things like help promote blood drives for the Red Cross.

VG: After Grand Funk split, you did a couple of solo albums. How did those differ from Grand Funk's efforts?

MF: Well, musically, Don Brewer wasn't there kicking the beat off with those drums; I don't believe the energy created by Mel Schacher, Don Brewer and me could have ever been duplicated by any other three people in the world. The first solo album had a keyboard player on it; it was produced by Dick Wagner, who played with Lou Reed and Alice Cooper. He also wrote a big hit for Air Supply. The second album was mostly three piece; Andy Newmark played drums. He'd played with Sly & the Family Stone and John Lennon and worked out great on that second album.

VG: Then there was the Grand Funk reunion in the early Eighties, minus Mel Schacher. My perception was that it didn't last too long.

MF: Schacher told us that he didn't want to fly. The same guy who played bass on my solo albums, Dennis Belinger, played with Don and me. We were on the Full Moon label, which was a subsidiary of Warner Brothers; it was Irving Azhoff's label, but after he signed us he left Warner Brothers, leaving us and a couple of other bands with nobody to "carry the ball"; there was nobody "in our corner."

VG: You had a born-again experience in 1983 and are now actively involved in playing Christian rock. How many albums have you done since your personal experience happened?

MF: Three; *Just Another Injustice*, *Wake Up*, and *Some Kind of Wonderful*, all on Frontline.

VG: Any comment about some artists who are famous within the Contemporary Christian music phenomenon yet are relatively unknown to "secular" audiences? I'm thinking about groups like Geoff Moore & the Distance and D.C. Talk.

MF: I know Geoff Moore and Mike from D.C.

TOP: *Farner onstage in the mid-Seventies with a Veleno.*

Talk; they're good guys. In this industry, there are "Christians that just happen to be musicians" and there are also "musicians that just happen to be Christians"; it just comes off that way.

I look at music as a *tool* in my hands; it's not a *gift,* because the Bible has all gifts listed. If people tell me I'm a gifted musician, I say: "You'd better read your Bible." (chuckles) I believe I'm supposed to prosper my Savior; He wants an increase in the investment that He's made in me. I see it as an opportunity to reach somebody that's hurting; to say some things that will provoke somebody to think. A lot of people are so locked into the values of *this* world they haven't thought about the next one.

I just think that a lot of Christian acts have geared themselves to *entertain* a Christian audience, which is fine; it's valid and necessary, and it works. On the other hand, I look at what I do as music to entertain Christians, but also to be used as a tool. Hopefully, it'll help me store up a little bit of treasure in Heaven, so I won't feel so bad when I go Home, and I'll be able to "collect" on it!

VG: The flip side of talking about artists that have always been pigeonholed in the Contemporary Christian genre is to cite artists like you that were successful in secular music, had a born-again experience, and are now active in CCM. I recall seeing Maria Muldar in a magazine, and Dion's been in that mode for decades.

MF: Somebody you'd probably remember is Domingo Samudio, a.k.a. Sam the Sham. That guy's in Memphis, Tennessee, on the streets with a little trailer that he sets up. He's told me not to ever go back, because the world's got a trap set for us. He helps gets street people that need help to a house that's there; he's helped everybody from winos to prostitutes. He's really got a heart for people, and he's in the *trenches* out there.

VG: Is your band still called the Godrockers?

MF: No; the band had that name for a while, but *everybody* who rocks for God or believes in this music is a Godrocker, so we now call ourselves Mark Farner & Common Ground.

VG: And you *do* still play selected Grand Funk songs in concert, right?

MF: "Are You Ready," "Footstompin' Music," "Rock & Roll Soul," "Hooked On Love," "Mean Mistreater," "Some Kind of Wonderful," "Locomotion," "I'm Your Captain," "Heartbreaker," "Aimless Lady" ...plenty of 'em!

VG: The story I read about you in a CCM magazine said that you recognize Vietnam vets whenever you do a concert.

MF: That's an ongoing thing with me; we've done some benefit concerts for Vietnam veterans associations around the country. The song "I'm Your Captain" meant so much to those boys; it was a song that I had prayed for back before I was serving the Lord; I guess I would pray every night just for the "fire insurance"! (laughs) I got up one night and wrote the words, then got up the next morning, grabbed my old American George Washburn out of the corner of the kitchen, and started strumming. It came together that fast. That Washburn was my "baby."

VG: We've already discussed the Messenger guitar you used during your earlier years with Grand Funk; let me give you some names and brands of other instruments I saw you playing, and you can comment on each; when you played them, what albums or tours you used them on, etc. First, Micro-Frets.

MF: I picked one up, and was intrigued by its tunable nut; the way that G string part looked. Usually if you were playing with a slinky set of strings and did an open E chord, that G string would go sharp, but you could adjust that nut so the guitar would play in tune on a E chord and the rest of the way up the neck, and I loved that idea. I played two of 'em, a red one and a blond one. I went from the Messenger to a Micro-Frets; they had a unique sound.

VG: Gibson L-5S solidbody.

MF: Gibson custom-made that for me; the wood that they picked to use was fifty-five years old, so the wood was already "vintage" when the guitar was made. (chuckles) I still have that one and I still use it in the studio.

VG: Veleno.

MF: I had three of those, including the very first "Traveler" model. I worked with John on what I wanted to get; the chrome one I had was neck-heavy, but I *loved* the way they sounded; they would sustain *forever.*

The reason I got the Traveler was I needed a smaller-scale guitar that I could take on airplanes. I would get ideas for songs on airplanes, and using headphones through a small instrument meant that I could work out the ideas right when I came up with them. I'd run the headphones through a tiny practice amp someone had built for me; it didn't have effects or even a volume control; you'd use the controls on your axe. I liked the "V" in the headstock, and John promised to put me a V on it someplace; it ended up

Farner onstage in the mid-Seventies with a Micro-Frets guitar.

on the body. The Traveler was tuned in G; it was a *screaming* little guitar. You had to watch your bends on it because it was such a short scale instrument that you could bend past your note real easily; same for doing a vibrato on it. I heard that he made several more of those after he made the one for me.

VG: Peavey.

MF: The first one I had was a custom-made Mystic; it had racing stripes on it. I've been endorsing that brand since 1981. I've also played other models, including the one I use now, an Impact. It has sort of a Strat body plus a phenolic fretboard, which I *love;* you can't wear that sucker out, and it also makes for a real unique sound. I had an Impact I which is now my spare; I locked down the vibrato on it because I'm famous for breaking strings (chuckles). The gauges I use run .048, .038, .028, .018, .015, and .010. So I got an Impact 2, which has a bridge that can be fine-tuned, and I like that because you can hold a chord on the guitar, reach down and "tweak" it out when you're performing. It's my favorite guitar; it came out of the box ready to go, practically playing itself! (laughs) It was set up perfectly; when I checked the intonation, it was calibrated precisely for my gauge of strings.

VG: Have I left out anything?

MF: I have a "bullet" Strat that was electronically customized for me in 1976. Our staff engineer Jim Fackert did the work on the axe after I questioned him about "activating" its stock pickups. It's one of the best sounding Strats in the universe, and it's fed its power on the signal cable from the guitar to the preamp. The DC current doesn't interfere with the signal when they cross paths in the cable. My biggest gripe with this axe is that the neck takes a flop at the most inconvenient times.

VG: Do you have a collection?

MF: I did at one time; I also used to collect guns. I had over three hundred long guns, pistols and revolvers. But you need to take care of those things, and these days I've pretty much gotten rid of the guitars that I don't use. One nice old guitar I had was a three-pickup white Gibson SG that I got from Stevie Marriot of Humble Pie. I cut *E Pluribus Funk* with that guitar.

This ad for one of Farner's solo albums features his "Bullet" Strat.

VG: Do you still have the old Washburn you used to write "I'm Your Captain"?

MF: No, that was stolen; there's a certain airline I need to thank for what happened ....I *do* still have an old three-pickup Supro Val-Trol; it's absolutely pristine. I got it with the original case and all of the original literature. However, I got rid of all of my guns except my "shooters," and with the exception of the Supro and a couple of others, the only guitars I've kept are my "players."

VG: Future plans?

MF: I'm gonna keep rockin'. We're finishing up a recording studio in my house; it's both digital and analog, so I can write and record there.

I believe that prayers being taken out of schools in 1963 was the beginning of the downfall of our nation; Thomas Jefferson said that the Constitution was written solely for the governing of a moral and religious people, and was inadequate for any other type of people. And man, I don't believe we've got too many moral and religious politicians these days; they don't know what it is to be a working man; they ain't never had a blister on their hands. I've got to stand up for what made us great to begin with; if I can just provoke people to think, I'll be doing good.

It's obvious that Mark Farner is committed to his calling by sharing his beliefs through his music, and while his conversational abilities also aver his spiritual quest, he comes across as self-assured and confident, and without finger-pointing or proselytizing. For all of his mega-success in the past, one gets the feeling that Mark Farner is certain that his best days are still ahead, so it shouldn't be surprising that this interview's sub-title is "prioritized."

The concert photographs appearing with this interview are reproductions from Mark Farner's personal scrapbook.

Shortly after this interview was conducted, Mark Farner called Vintage Guitar's *Southern Regional Office to advise us that he'd signed on for the 1995 edition of Ringo Starr's All-Starr Band. Among the other veteran musicians committed to this project are John Entwistle, Felix Cavaliere, and Randy Bachman; a two-part interview with Bachman appeared in VG's January and February 1992 issues. In the summer of 1996, the original three-man line-up of Grand Funk Railroad toured; it was the first time Mel Schacher had been on the road on a major tour in twenty years.*

Billy F Gibbons
From Willy G. To Willie G.

It's been a long time comin'. ZZ TOP's Billy F Gibbons is, of course, considered one of the finest contemporary guitarists in the world, and most guitar lovers are also aware of his stature as one of the preeminent guitar collectors on the planet.

Mr. G., standing at the crossroads of the vintage guitar phenomenon for quite some time, is a stalwart supporter of *Vintage Guitar*. This interview culminates a work of magnitude recorded during the ZZ TOP World Tour supporting their most recent release, *ANTENNA*, for BMG. This writer conferenced at long length with Reverend Gibbons, and the interview is accurately recorded in three segments, which will be spread over the next three issues ...a logical engagement, considering the range of information and inquiries prepared for the guitarist! The conversations comprise the most in-depth interview to appear in *VG* to date (the aim of this reporter's design). This first part of our interview with the affable and eccentric Texas guitarist delves into the earliest of origins of his legendary Lone Star trio, "THAT LIL' OL' BAND FROM TEXAS":

VG: Billy, what initially inspired your attraction to the guitar?

BFG: ELVIS, ELVIS, ELVIS, ELVIS, ELVIS! Elvis Presley and a string of Blues players longer than a Mississippi freight train ....and, of course, a host of broadcasts on radio delivering those great sounds. And ...lo and behold ...a fine guitarra del electro with that obscene control marked "Loud"!

(grins)

VG: From my sources, it's suspected you come from a family of entertainers.

BFG: Yes, quite a long line of entertainers. An English dad and my mom being Southern handed me a great heritage, DNA-deep. It be in the genes.

VG: So, we may assume you were pursuing guitar stuff right away?

BFG: Yes, I'm fortunate to have that Texas upbringing; a fine, funky point of embarkation, for sure. And early on, there were regular round trips to Hollywood, too, that got me deep off in it. I remember, along with little sister Pam, being let loose on the set design lots, sound track trucks, wardrobe lot, the scoring room ...you name it! So, yes, I got the start up on it really early.

VG: Your interest in "rock" obviously paralleled an interest in "blues" music. Did "rock" appear first, with an awareness of the "blues roots" a bit later?

BFG: Well, blues and rock were yet to be defined. A lot came from Memphis' Sun Studios ...definitely a combo of blues and "hillbilly hot rod" stuff everywhere. When Elvis skyrocketed, he really took the spotlight and ultimately picked up on a big batch of blues from Chess, RPM, Modern, Ace from Mississippi; all of it highlighting the regional thing. All this stuff was being felt from radio, night spots, record shops, and certainly the street. One favorite story flourishes along the lines of "Yeah, I was told not to listen to that kind of music..." (grins) We found those mystery radio stations late at night when we could get away with it. All of that music was inspirational, and at the time there wasn't much attention given to "naming" it. It was a nat'chul thang.

VG: What was the first instrument that came your way?

BFG: Man, I spent about a year hinting hard 'bout a set of drums and electric guitars. Everyone can relate to that. And,

TOP AND RIGHT:
Photo by James Bland

come Christmas Day, a sunburst Melody Maker with a single cutaway showed up backside the tree in a "fake gator skin" cardboard case. Next to it lay a Champ amp sayin' "plug it in," and I about fell out. Jimmy Reed, Ray Charles, here we come!

VG: We're definitely talking pro-style beginning?

BFG: Yeah, tough stuff, American-style that's well "in that groove." So, by Christmas afternoon, the Jimmy Reed I-and-IV change was down! And then, Eddie Taylor's "Easyman V" topped it completely. ZZ TOP is still into the "I-IV-V," *hypnotize!*

VG: How about your playing experiences, "pre-Moving Sidewalks"?

BFG: The first pro "gig" lineup was known as The Saints. The front line guitar work came from David Crosswell and Phillip Taft. They were influential, showing me how to get past the first couple of frets on guitar. We seldom passed the seventh fret, but playin' that "low-down" sound, we didn't want to! (laughs) Holding rhythm section was Mr. Steve "Tamale" Mickley, who specialized in Professor Longhair/Caribbean beats. That Texas-Louisiana exotic thing. Still on line. Most cool. In fact, I'm still on 24-hour call to hit it and git it with those guys, just for playin' loud and blue, and shuckin' tamales, too.

VG: Speaking of hot fare, tell us about the inside cover of *Tres Hombres.*

BFG: That layout's the product of a fine Houston establishment, Leo's Mexican Restaurant. Started by Señor Leo Reynosa, one time a rider with Pancho Villa and *totally* into Tex-Mex and blues. Leo's is a great stop on the hot sauce trail.

VG: Back to The Saints line-up; didn't mean to get sidetracked.

BFG: Well, there were four members and an "open spot" for whoever would show up. We played Jimmy Reed-style with the tone knob down toward the darker side 'til somebody sat in with a proper Precision or whatever. Big Mike Frazier eased on the scene with a longneck '57 Fender, and the sound got really "tuff." We played jobs that sometimes got a bit wild; the predictable "raid and riot." Many a night spent scrambling over fences, guitar in one hand and amp in the other, walking and hitch-hiking home, landing a few laughs ....and gettin' paid in green, to boot!

TOP AND RIGHT:
Photo by James Bland

Then The Saints developed a big, big revue, Billy G. and the Ten Blue Flames. Kelly Key Parker and Bobby "Blue" Braden on the stand with us ....just jelly, jelly, jelly. Real tight stuff. Keep in mind, my partners, Dusty and Frank, were starting their careers in Dallas with many of the same influences. They started the Warlocks up in Dallas and then became the American Blues with another great Texas blues man, Rocky Hill. And down in Houston, we evolved into the Moving Sidewalks. Then, some fine changes started breaking musically, worldwide.

VG: The Moving Sidewalks actually did some records, and now there's some advertisements for Sidewalks recordings on CD.

BFG: There's a French and an Italian reissue. Sounds just as it was laid down, too.

VG: The story's been told before about how the band appeared with Hendrix, and he made some favorable comments about your playing. Details?

BFG: Yeah, that was a great time. There's the new book, an unauthorized biography of ZZ TOP, by our original lighting director, Dave Blayney. Most interesting history; there's a few of the secret stories ...no long shoes to walk in ...just a lot of good trash and treasure, and a favorite picture of the Sidewalks and Jimi.

The Moving Sidewalks were included along with the Soft Machine in the Hendrix tour package. There was lots of hard work, luck, and lots of great energy. We worked on and off with the

Experience for months. The proper tour was booked a year out; we'd go out for three weeks and then get a week off.

VG: Back during those times there were some Texas-based bands that got a large amount of national exposure. In particular, I'm thinking about The Sir Douglas Quintet and the 13th Floor Elevators.

BFG: Sir Doug hit the Top Ten with "She's About A Mover," "I'm A Tracker" and "Mendocino." The Elevators, chief exponents of psychedelia, had an unbounded vision, so to speak. They hit with "You're Gonna Miss Me" and broke right out. The Texas record label, International Artists, had an interesting line-up: The Elevators, Endil St. Cloud and the Rain, and one of our particular favorites, the Red Krayola. They not only put out music that made you feel good, they used a lot of "escalated imagery" that made you *think* good. The great thing about this Texas lineage is that it still followed a "gunslingin' thing" ....six shooter/six string; same thing. The musicianship and camaraderie from then is still solid.

VG: Sir Doug Sahm is still active with the Texas Tornadoes, isn't he?

BFG: Yeah, they're tearing it up everyway, everywhere. They're playing in London tonight with the exposition that's been going over gang busters called "The American South." Junior Brown and his "git-steel" is rockin' it and so is Tish Hinojosa's outfit.

VG: So how did ZZ TOP get together?

BFG: The Moving Sidewalks and the American Blues were on the circuit with the Chessmen, featuring Jimmie Vaughan, Doyle Bramhall, Billy Etheridge and Tommy Carter. Then came the original ZZ TOP line-up; it was superb. Dan "The Man" Merrill Mitchell on drums and Lanier Greg on Hammond B-3 and bass pedals. It was a "trio del maximo," fo' sho'. All of us happened to be playing in the same place at the same time. The introduction with Frank and Dusty was luck, fortune and voodoo.

VG: So technically, you're the "lead-man" member in ZZ TOP?

BFG: Yeah, it's a cool arrangement. The original line-up is on the first ZZ TOP single called "Salt Lick" on the Scat label. Then, Vaughan recommended another guitarist from the Chessmen, Billy Etheridge, to take the bass guitar slot with us. The early incarnations of ZZ TOP continued to spin ...I think it changed about every Sunday morning! (laughs) We were visited by Cadillac Johnson, and then the trip was complete when Frank and Dusty arrived from North Texas.

VG: Where did the name come from?

BFG: Aw, it's a fraternal secret. Last night we were filmed in performance for the flick with Pauly Shore. Somewhere during the show, a hat flew through the air and landed stage center; not just any hat, but one carefully decked with the Zig Zag Man, and Top rollin' papers. Perhaps someone's inspiration from our name? Ain't shedding no secrets ...then again, that's steps ahead of the "how and why" ...(laughs)

VG: With attention to your "working" instruments, is the main one for you still the infamous Sunburst, "Pearly Gates"?

BFG: Yes, "Pearly" is the cornerstone of tone; the main line to this interest in instruments. There's another great Texan I hang with, Reid Farrell, who became known as Red Pharaoh playing guitar with Archie Bell and the Drells of "Do The Tighten Up" fame. He rang me up after finding a guitar with "big fat pickups." (laughs) During the Moving Sidewalks days, I switched to a Fender Stratocaster. Then, Reid told me: "I think I've found something for you; a guitar with the

TOP AND LEFT:
Photos by James Bland

same pickups as Clapton's." Pharaoh gave me a '58 Flying V; the first real Gibson humbucking slammer. It's pictured on the cover of ZZ TOP's *FANDANGO*. It has the sound.

Time was well spent experimenting with Telecasters and Esquires. Always will be. Then, I was turned on to "Pearly Gates," following up on one of those stories about a Les Paul ...forgotten in a farmhouse, off up in the attic. For sure, Sunbursts were a mystery, but the guitar had those "big fat pickups." So, the deal was struck, and "Have mercy...!"

VG: I asked if "Pearly Gates" is one of your main guitars. Is it also a *favorite* guitar?

BFG: Lord have mercy, most certainly. And, in addition to Fifties and Sixties vintage guitars, there's a lot of choice stuff available right off the shelf now, equally radical like "Pearly Gates."

VG: As far as stage instruments go, you and Dusty use many custom instruments; everything from Explorer-things to "giant crazy cowboy" styles with the Mississippi River running throughout the fretboard design.

BFG: Yeah. As these "irreplaceable and embraceable" instruments came into vogue, we began creating unusual Sixes and Fours, with a wildly diverse manufacturing support from some real heavy-hitters: Peavey, Fender, Gibson, Bolin, Dean, Hamer, PRS, Parker, Fernandes, National ...Lord have mercy, you name it, there's some fine ones. We still have the customized Texas-shaped Gibson, *Guitar World's* Texas issue centerfold. Bo Diddley may let us put fur on that one, too!

The *ANTENNA* Tour's got some monster axes workin'. The Fender Custom Esquires and Fender Basses, and Gibson's "workover jobs," a pair of rare '61 SG-LPs, and EB-3s; twin matched pairs. We're workin' some real "off the wall" playing technique with 'em. Exaggerated tunings and weird string alloys; gotta stand up to them Mexican pesos, don'cha know! (NOTE: Rev. Gibbons' performance pick is indeed a peso that has been "modified" to a traditional, plectrum-like shape). The rest of the array is straight ahead. Simple ...powerful.

VG: Is there a certain track or recording that you think put the band into modern prominence?

TOP AND RIGHT:
Photos by James Bland

BFG: Yeah, "LaGrange," the first "Top Ten." The artist and poet, Waltaire Baldwin, a long-standing associate from Memphis, persuaded a promoter, Steadman Matthews, to include ZZ TOP on a blues program billing. Waltaire showcased our first record for Steadman. That show became our first appearance outside Texas, and was our first opportunity to get to know all of the great blues artists in Memphis. When we arrived there, we were hustled up at showtime, onto the main stage. The performance seemed to please all of them Memphis blues players. "Mint Man" Robert Johnson, the "modern" Robert Johnson, that is, introduced us to the hot players around town, and their acceptance was roofline! It represented the point where we felt like gold. Then the hit record came right after. Terry Manning's master-mind, from down over at Ardent.

VG: Is this the same Robert Johnson that has the very nice 'Burst collection?

BFG: Yeah, sho' nuff. He's still got the most unreal stuff. He's "Mint Man," fo' sho'.

And now, this point is where all of this Texas/Memphis/Mississippi stuff gets *way* interesting, possibly the first opportunity to illuminate an aspect of what founded the vintage guitar "industry." There is Mike Ladd of Memphis; he is the originator of Mike Ladd's Guitar City, a specialty guitar and amplifier dealership and custom shop. At one time, the front door looked right into Elvis' front yard at Graceland. Of course, it's now the Elvis Mall. When Mike decided to go into busi-

ness, he said: "Since I'm doin' this guitar thing, I'm gonna do it right. I'm gonna check in with Elvis mornin', noon and night." In addition to a roomful of vintage gear, he kept two Harley Davidsons parked out back. The "badass" one belonged to Elvis. Without warning, Elvis would slip out at night and come in to talk guitar and glide. Then, of course, he would get to snarlin' (Gibbons does an Elvis voice): "Hey, 'Guitar-man' ...it's a quarter-to-two. Let's roll." That was the start of it. At Ladd's.

VG: Do you consider the band's activities to have "mutated" through more than one "phase"? For example, it's known you all went into seclusion and took an extended time off, following the *TEJAS* Tour.

BFG: Yeah, a three year seclusion. 'Til then, we toured incessantly for seven years, straight ahead. We took time to chill and enjoy; we emerged with the new material delivered to Warner Brothers in California ...*DEGUELLO*.

VG: You also emerged with an aesthetic look that is still part of ZZ TOP: Top hats, cheap sunglasses, and beards that look like they were inspired by the Smith Brothers.

BFG: (Laughs) Heh, heh, heh ...I do believe we've heard that before!

VG: The band "steadfastly" selects certain associations carefully, right? We've seen the periodic magazine covers with ZZ TOP and car parts, lap steels, fine art, gorgeous women, big fast Fords, Ferraris, and jewelry.

BFG: Yes, unique special moments. A kind of tradition now, doing the odd and unusual, which is another detail of ZZ TOP. It's to the point where "odd" and "ZZ TOP-like" meet and mean the same thing.

We *did* make the Gibson catalog that had their artists like Muddy, Wes, Les, B.B., Keith and Allman ...all the way back to Charlie Christian.

There's a new movement of guitar makers creating world class product. The outfits of Dave Wintz and Bart Wittrock, Jake Stack, Bolin, and "Strong." Workin' the upscale and experimental stuff comin' out of back rooms. New leaders in the spotlight. There's super support systems for electric guitarists — like Soldano, Groove, Mesa, Marshall, Kendrick, Cesar Diaz, Stackhouse, Angela, City, Mojo, Orange, C & R, GHS, Nady, Digitech, Zoom, Real Tube, Statesboro, Classic, Big "R," Roland and Future Funk.

VG: To highlight ZZ TOP's current World Tour; I know that you've discussed recording specifically, and in my opinion, *ANTENNA* is yet another full-out "tone fest" like all of the ZZ TOP recordings.

BFG: Yes, indeed! It's simply "tech" with tubes. BMG Records (USA and International) supports us "Doin' the Do"! For the *ANTENNA* record, we gained entry to the "house instrument" stash for some groove gear, and started grindin'. Beard played every drum by every drum maker known, like Twenties to the Sixties. Dusty was playing a nameless amplifier and a "full Martian" bass guitar. I lucked out with Steve Cropper's Esquire and a thrashed Fender Dual Professional amp seen in the Rod and Hank's store in Memphis. It's the amp up from the river bottom. It started this real trip about the V-front Dual Pro and Esquire connection. Tweed, "tens," and twang ...too chromin' cool, mane.

VG: Is this interest in '40s and '50s Fender Dual Pros a new facet of your interest in collecting vintage guitars and amps?

BFG: Yes, the V-front freak-out fanned from the *ANTENNA* sessions. The amp I'm talkin' about is that mangy Mississippi one. The tone spilling out of that amp was disgusting, but nice and predictable. So, a search for another real good model began.

Anything untouchable/unavailable/unfathom-

TOP: *THE ODDS HAVE IT! According to Rev. Gibbons, this recent publicity photo was processed backwards; i.e., that ain't a left-handed Fifties Telecaster he's holding! Photo by James Bland*

LEFT: *Photo by James Bland*

Photo by James Bland

able is the passion of the pursuit! (Laughs) And now, seeing the return of quality items for the future, applies to guitars, amps, and, FX, as far as I'm concerned.

Dudes like Kendrick's Weber and Cesar Diaz are tube and circuit experts. Among other things, they're wailin' on our Dual Pros now. A thorough and extensive "bench-test" is what they doin'. They're also into building some terrific amps of their own. Lord 'a' mercy! Getting solder points, proper tubes and wirelines correct, fully dressed and "dragstrip ready"! (Grins) And to really throw 'nitro', dig this ...Guitar Oasis in Huntington Beach loaded a '50-'51, 2 X 10, Fender 'Super' V-front cab with a Bluesbreakers Brain from a '66! This Kendrick is dubbed, the "Do Awl"; Cesar's wicked wonder's called "The Diaz ZZ Top 30"; and, Guitar Oasis sent their ZZ Special under the name Dual Blues Professional Breaker. It's really crazed. T-Bone Walker meets MC 900 Ft. Jesus.

VG: And when and how did you start collecting guitars?

BFG: The fierce technique of Clapton, Peter Green and Mick Taylor from the "Bluesbreakers" recordings started it off. The suggestive clue appeared in the photo of Clapton playing a 'Burst through a 2 X 12 combo. The assumption being his wonderfully wretched sound emanated from the combination of "big fat pickups" and that alien Marshall amp setup. That assumption, of course, set the stage for playing on the Flying V, which led to the quest for the 'Burst. When we got word about an certain available Sunburst, we followed up, which led to the acquisition of the guitar pictured on the cover of *ZZ TOP's FIRST ALBUM*. The guitar that we know and love as "Pearly Gates." (Grins) That marked the date of the first ZZ TOP recording.

VG: When did you decide collecting the hardcore stuff was for you?

BFG: Well, after scoring "Pearly Gates" we wanted more. It took us into the deepest, darkest sections of pawn shops, thrift shops and second-hand stores. For a while, I latched on everything with two humbucking pickups on it feeling the sound like "Pearly." Of course, that was the first experience discovering those things called "old git-tarzz" offer incredible varieties of tones. Even

now, I'm among the many guitar players constantly humored that supposedly identical instruments can sound rad different.

VG: Is it fair to say that you've always had a preference for dual humbucker guitars?

BFG: I prefer the way the bridge-position reacts. I seldom venture into "Dual Pickup Land," because the bridge pickup effect is where the thrill is at. Most instruments are outfitted with humbucking pickups in pairs; I just never bothered to leave the "back bridge" position.

VG: George Gruhn related a story during his seminar at a guitar show of you playing your '50s Gibson Explorer in concert. When you came backstage, somebody asked if it was a Hamer or an Ibanez! Comment?

BFG: Yes, George's profound recall is reassuring. That's a fact. That put me on notice to distinguish vintage sounds and aesthetics different from newer instruments suddenly being made. It was the spooky era when the primary American guitar makers were ensconced in a "tumultuous turmoil." A "second wave" of guitar manufacturers realized that there was an increasing interest in vintage instruments, and *YO!* Look out. From 'no Explorers' to 'Floors of Explorers'.

VG: I usually ask in interviews if vintage instruments are used in the studio and in concert. I know that's the case for you. Are you using any "new" instruments in the studio?

BFG: Yes indeed. As noted earlier, the *AN-TENNA* sessions began with Cropper's '56 Fender — I don't know which was put to the test more, player or instrument! (Laughs) Before the sessions were over, the fine folks at Fender presented the band with a selection of "ZZ TOP Specials" that are new interpretations of an Esquire design and a slightly deviant Bass design: Small headstocks, early-style necks and plain slab bodies. We're using those instruments constantly. They're inlaid with some choice silver and pearl and creme binding under black lacquer, MetalTech Twist-o-Grip knobs and Seymour's stacked humbuckers, which have the "Pearly Gates" winding. We're also into the power versions of those pickups with Fender and EMG as well. There are loads of variables! Signal readers, power meters and "mean mistreaters." The real test is sussing out 'what's what'. We like whippin' "MIDI into MUDDY."

VG: Speaking of Seymour, when I toured his factory a while back, he showed me the pickup that you gave him years ago that he keeps submerged in what looks like a Mason jar full of red water. Water's so rusty I thought I was looking at a jar of salsa. He pulled it out and put it on a meter and it's still got output.

BFG: It's got the Seymour hot sauce sound, too! (Laughs) I've heard that every once in a while that pickup gets extricated from "the depths below" just to prove it works. An obvious good choice for surf work.

VG: You're considered to be one of the major collectors in the world of Rock. Comment?

BFG: I like all the madness, the maniacs and mystics that gain enjoyment from loads of instruments or simply one special, favorite. For instance, Bonnie Raitt probably has her favorite instrument or so, but she can stone cold walk up to a "sit-in" and get right down to tearin' it up. Peter Buck, R.E.M.'s guitarist, same thing. Buck can color the sound to fit the band and complement Stipe's singing, and it's all by hand. Same ax. Same with Al Jourgenson from Ministry and his lineup of "REV-CO" guys, or, say, the "B-SURF" bunch. A real signature sound from old Mosrites and Strats. The tunings are not of this earth, but the guitars are a universe. Whatever works whenever it does is all you need (laughs).

I will mention that each instrument gets a kind and dignified treatment and they get the predictable thrashin', too! Ain't none bein' overlooked. (Grins)

VG: You mentioned "tried and true" instruments in your collection a second ago, but don't you also have some oddball pieces, — specifically some Russian-made guitars?

BFG: Yeah, before the Wall was dismantled, some arrangements were made to barter for some instruments from behind the "bricks." A curiosity stimulated by an article that had appeared in a quarterly publication from the Smithsonian about electric guitars from the Soviet Union and East Germany. Warner Brothers' European Division even made it possible to actually speak with some players who were becoming popular due to their Western music stylings. They told me if you "turn it up to 10" ...Whoa, dude! Instant inspection from the authorities (laughs)!

The details of the exchange were burdensome and bizarre; the deal was a trade of "equal value" goods ...but ...the stuff had to appear trashed and banged-up to enter Soviet territory. Anything ...guitar, amp or FX ...that we sent in had to "hyper-chill". My contact inside the country had some very specific requests on his "shopping list." A hand written footnote at the bottom said: "Billy, please make sure that you have a friend who's handy with a hammer; these exchange items must look well-beaten!" So, I had Dusty use the instruments prior to the exchange. 'Nuff said!

VG: Movin' on ...I'd like to ask about your ownership of a '50s Gibson 'Moderne' thing! Is that photo of this instrument with that weird shape and the other instruments with you in your convertible for real?

BFG: Yeah, the 'Sailfish' looking thing ...Let me put it to you this way: No one that I know has come up with a Gibson Moderne from the '50s. There is an instrument that has the Gibson Marque that is probably from the '58 "trade show" display that produced the short run of original Korina Flying Vs and Explorers. Probably, more than those two designs were actually created. So far, just a few patent references show the Moderne in a blueprint stage, or the prototype stage. I've been invited by the experts for speculation on the peculiar-but-fine-playing instrument's origin. It looks gross, but there's no question of its cool tone and feel. I'm hooked on the Moderne. No doubt about it.

VG: My perception is that recently you're increasingly interested in amplifiers. The Dual Pro collection, for example, is obvious.

BFG: Just the loud ones. Gunfire and shiftin' sands. Light 'em up. Amps are like guitars, and, in fact, each one does have its own personality, most appreciable with vintage amplifiers, late '40s - early '50s with glowin' coke bottles. The old Dual Pro fixation/fascination has an interesting bit of background. My pal, Pete Anderson, sent word over to the house with invitation to stop in at the Capitol Tower near Hollywood and Vine for a Dwight Yoakam session in Studio A. So, I came 'round, makin' my way down Sunset with the "must do" stop-ins at Guitar Center, Jimmy's Rare Guitars, Albert at Guitars-R-Us, Johnny Guitar, Valdez and Amp Crazy. All them joints.

Arrived at the studio to hear Pete soloin' with Dwight and the boys, flat out sizzlin' with the 'Two-Ten Esquire' "thing." He's been solid on that set-up forever, and knows how to use it. Sounds killer. Anderson's work with Bruce Zinky over at the new Fender Custom shop in Scottsdale has resulted in the Dual Professional reissue. Quite a hot rod. Goes right alongside Bruce's invention, the new Tone Master. It's a great pairing when you get great guitars and great classic amps together. Check out the James Harman hard-harpin' "Masco" set. Way rare. These Mosvalve rigs are big and fat, too. Stuffed in a small package for carry out. The giant sound.

And for guitars, a recent rendezvous 'sez' it all. I checked out Portland, Oregon at a place called Guitar Crazy, and Bob, Doug and Richard wanted to know if there was anything I was especially looking for. I slipped in a request for the Alamo Fiesta, made in San Antonio, with little likelihood of any being about the Pacific Northwest. Then they asked if I wanted a single or dual pickup model. They had both (laughs)! One more shining example of how deep the awareness of fine instruments is. For instance, Dave's, in La Crosse, stayed open one night 'til we tried out the entire barrel from the back room. Vintage deals deluxe.

VG: Are there any instruments that you passed by that now capture your interest?

BFG: Well, who wouldn't want the Billy Strange "theme song guitar" from the James Bond soundtracks! Anything in Angela's or Briggs' showroom.

There was one guitar seen at one of Charley Wirz's guitar shows — the 1990 Dallas show, which is now under the capable direction of Mark Pollock. Near the closing of the first day's session, I saw a gent walking at a brisk pace with a Goldtop that had creme-colored P-90s, a Tune-o-matic and stop tailpiece. Visually, it was the most right on instrument I'd ever laid eyes on! It descended beneath "visual art" and "fashion." (Laughs) The owner was relishing the compliments put on possessing such an innocuous piece of wood and metal. Rightly so, Amigo!

Later, I bumped into the same guy and the same guitar. I took the guitar, he took the dough ...and you know how the story go. I took that mess straight into the studio and ignited one of the blues tracks

Photo by James Bland

on *ANTENNA* entitled "Girl in a T-shirt." *KILLER!*

VG: (Interviewer scat-sings a portion of the introduction to "T-Shirt"...)

BFG: (Laughs) That's it! That guitar looked terrible/wonderful/worse and it sounds terrible/wonderful/wicked! '56 cracked-top...

VG: Do you have the plans putting your collections in a book?

BFG: You know, it'd be all right to offer a presentation of the stranger items, and I suppose some individuals might say ain't no time better than the present, to do it. Hopefully, we can get a little more specific about that in the future. I fully support anything concerning the "vin-tique mystique."

VG: Are there any other collections and/or collectors you admire?

BFG: 'Sho' nuff. Certainly Brock's cool. And you gotta have Gil ...where the cool man thrives. Jesse Jay Adams at Roadhouse, Texas, has *the* Mary Kaye '57. Quick exchanges I've had with Beck, Clapton and Richards always seem to bring about discussions of the six-string and let me tell you, them dudes don't hesitate pulling out any guitar to fill the bill for the sounds they're seeking. They don't mess around. Neither does Alenov. Gimme Jimmy Brown and we'll go to town.

VG: I've seen photos of Clapton playing his '50s Explorer in concert, and it's got a slightly different body style. It appears to have been contoured or rounded on the upper bout of the body.

BFG: Yeah. I know the instrument well. It was acquired through Willie Spears from Texas. It's the record cover guitar of Don Nix, who saw the guitar make it to Eric's possession. I think it was another case of "Here, take this; I'll go get that," same as El-Raunch-o-Rama Goldtop used on "Girl in a T-shirt." I think Nix landed an equally unusual instrument as a result of that transaction with Clapton. The photos of Eric playing that guitar look like he's having a fine time. Killer!

VG: I've had a few opportunities to play the '50s Explorers for extended periods of time and I've noticed the neck on the mahogany Explorer reissue is quite different. How do the original 1950's Explorers compare?

BFG: Well, every Explorer and Flying V I've had an opportunity to play required a lumberjack grip. (Laughs) Those guitars have railer-high frets on a neck a bit wider than the '60s production necks; the contour is pure "telephone pole." The "retro-repros" are fine guitars and they have a feel similar to an original.

VG: Do you have a crewman or a guitar tech that knows vintage instruments?

BFG: Now, everybody knows. (Laughs) During the rigors of the road, we're sometimes asked to do a TV/Club/Radio impromptu appearance. If that opens up, it offers opportunity to check out a few shops. One could hire a "legion of lookers," but in the final analysis, trust your own judgment. I guess I'd rather examine or play a guitar or amp personally.

VG: Would you want to guess where your collecting thing might detour?

BFG: Well, I'll take a point that offers: "Wait a minute!" Just about the time you think you've seen it all, there's the unexpected funk pack ....As evidenced by Gruhn's presentation of the Slingerland Electric Spanish guitar featured at the Houston show. It's a Spanish, slab body, fully electric instrument and is in the catalog from 1938! Now, that's fine. And, just about the time you think you've heard it all, out of the blue comes somethin' new like Long John Hunter, playin' his blues with a Borderland twist ....His records prove there's more than a groove. Always somethin' gonna make you move!

VG: One of Gruhn's recent finds is the 1957 prototype Flying V priced around $150,000.

BFG: Yeah! Righteous. And somebody will no doubt have the distinction of enjoying the ownership of that rarity real quick. Some smart buyer's gonna know the asking price is quite in line with the unusual value. Savant? I always think wherever there's a question about anything, consult a pro. And you can always just grab the guitar, plug it in, and turn it up to '10'.

VG: I heard the news ZZ TOP's haberdashery, Nudie's Rodeo Tailors, over in Hollywood, is in transition... Porter Waggoner, lookout!

BFG: Well, the good news is Nudie's successor and visionary, Manuel Cuevas, is operating in Nashville, so the tradition is ongoing and continues doin' it best. Nudie was our first tailor and our "sharpdressed" man with a plan. And, 'Manuels' laid the rhinestones and stylin' stitches on us desert dudes 'way back'. Miles-o'-style, à la Nudie, à la Turk. Ah yeah, Manuel!

VG: I understand that you were awarded the patent for design on the warped "Generator" guitars series. Would you fill in some details?

BFG: Those designs, commissioned for construction and later a brief production run, were sought after by a group of backers. Great guitars. Visual mutants... put together well and play loud! They're an 'aesthetically correct and ergonomically incorrect' design (laughs). An awkward-but-lovely effect, fortunately! That's the interesting period of design, just prior to ZZ TOP's videos, around '82-'83.

VG: The band is associated with numerous charities. The most famous, of course, is the Delta Blues Museums' Muddywood celebration.

BFG: It's fate that the opportunity for an association with the Delta Blues Museum showed up. It did and the Blues Museum forum is now generously offering education, scholarship and college fund support throughout the Delta region. It supports bands, it supports a learning experience.

VG: Generally speaking, do musicians pay attention to the art maintained in the "blues"?

BFG: Yes. Fortunately, the release of the Robert Johnson boxed set as well as the Delta Blues Museum's working, living representation are great additions. Up until then, there may have been confusion about 'what is what'. But tangibly, the music is about and there are workin' members of the 'original cast' to thank for this stuff. There's opportunity to "feel the feel" and figure it all out, and that means one's interpretations can be true to the attitude, and ultimately, the spirit of them blues.

VG: What are the details of the association with the Delta Blues Museum and ZZ TOP's donation of the "Muddywood" guitar?

BFG: Yeah, ZZ TOP's foray into the deep end of the Delta that led to the Delta Blues Museum party, news coverage over the world, the Hard Rock Cafe's "Muddywood World Tour," and the Clarksdale Bar-b-que, is well documented.

We arrived the day Jim O'Neal, the founding editor of *Living Blues Magazine*, was meeting the Museum Director, Sid Graves and driving to Stovall's for possible preservation and restoration on Morganfield's cabin. They were interested for the area had recently been shaken by high winds, which lifted the roof! So, we accepted an invitation to come out. Hi-way 49, so fine.

Fortunately, clearing had been done so they could conduct a proper inspection, and it was decided the structure could remain. The roof timbers lay piled up, waiting to be taken away, and a Muddy-wood piece was offered up as a memento. On the return way to Memphis, thought was, it'd be real nice to pay back a piece of the blues and make a guitar from the Muddy Waters' house. Rick Rayburn of Pyramid Guitars in Memphis completed the construction and assisted with the presentation of ZZ TOP's gift to the museum; it's a centerpiece.

VG: There's two Muddywood creations, yes?

BFG: Correct; and, a lot of cussing while makin' sawdust and strafin' steel (laughs)! The Blues Museum original and the experimental one. Didn't expect what lay ahead... nails, knotholes and a lot of broken blades!

VG: A lot of players really admire that guitar. Any chance for a production run?

BFG: It's in the works. Coming soon are the production and special edition "Muddywood" blues guitars, constructed at Peavey down in Mississippi. Each instrument will have something from the Morganfield place at Stovall, and detailed exactly like the Delta

Blues Museum's "Muddywood" guitar. The Peavey edition aims to be a functional, playable, 'Down in the Delta' instrument for a living, working concept relating to that thing called the blues.

VG: Wonderful! How 'bout a comment on ZZ TOP as a hard working show business giant.

BFG: What really counts is the music, and we love it. There was a time when a musician was expected to arrive for the gig, plug in, then play. A lot has progressed. Entertainment presentation with full-blown, full-attention comprehension. The L'IL OLE BAND FROM TEXAS is right on into it. There's also that cinematic side. Film and video came up with an escalation of live presentation productions. Really powerful. ZZ TOP began doing some things and then... Lookout!... the advent of videos, MTV, and 'music uplinks', really took hold.

VG: Regarding ZZ TOP and the advent of MTV and music videos. Your band has some of the most easily recognized images associated with the music video phenomenon; there's your famous Fords, Harleys, and the gnarly Cadzzilla, furry Explorers, the drop-dead bevy of blondes, the aforementioned Smith Brothers Cough Drop boxtop beards, cheap sunglasses... (I see the band's wearing Ray Bans!... Caballeros, no doubt). My perception is that the band shifted into high gear and released the mega-million selling *ELIMINATOR,* at exactly the time MTV was really catching on. Is there a possibility that "visuals," from films and 'vids', can be as influential as the music?

BFG: It's an invitation to get real, real, seriously good as a player. You've identified videos as a special "extension" for musicians. The range of presentation gets 'wide'. You're hearing music, you're seeing visuals, all with interpretation by directors, musicians and artists.

ZZ TOP, first recognized as a musical aggregation, expanded on in front of the camera. We've met some fine musicians that improved their playing after working on camera. After hittin' on the video scene, they picked up on technical jammin' and slammin' the chops! That's uplifting — an added benefit of film making and recording.

VG: There is some "live" material from *Fandango* on one side captured in New Orleans. Comment? More to come?

BFG: There is live material from Europe and Australia. There are recordings from several tours... *ELIMINATOR, AFTERBURNER* and *RECYCLER*. The Dallas Deep Ellum live material does exist for mastering. This tour is recording tracks every night, as well. If ZZ TOP prepares a release of a "live" recording, a simultaneous offering on video and audio might be cool. Portable video players, portable CD players and "back pocket" tape decks make multi-format releases a necessity! (Laughs) Grab what'cha got; run what'cha brung.

VG: Speaking of live performance, the band played "The Tonight Show" with Johnny Carson hosting. During the performance, the camera cut to a shot of Johnny Carson and Doc Severinson, both wearing beards. Carson wore sunglasses, too! It looked like a fun moment.

BFG: (Laughs) Man, that was truly fine. When the monitors caught sight of them, it tore the place down. It was the best.

VG: *THE ZZ TOP SIX PACK,* released as a set, brought your analog recordings into a true digital domain. Yes?

BFG: Correct. It completed a CD offering of the entire ZZ TOP catalog. Coming next is the blues compilation from Warner Bros. entitled *ONE FOOT IN THE BLUES*. A handpicked package from *ZZ TOP'S FIRST ALBUM* all the way through the bad boy blues tracks from *ANTENNA*. Dripping, just drippping!

VG: Yes, some great sounds in the ZZ bag. By the way, are there any details about the other instruments and effects y'all use?

BFG: Oh, yeah. Blowin' harp, mostly usin' Lee Oskar's, and Hohner's amped through a taxicab-dispatcher's mic... make it real dark... totally dark. Diaz is making a stompbox tremolo called the Diaz' Texas Tremodillo. Real authentic sound. Just bring it on... we'll trash it. Boogie's got a pretty crunch pedal with that "lots-o-watts" sound. Ummm... Marshall Supa-Fuzz, the Real Tube pedal.

VG: You've discussed Memphis with B.B. King in an interview for *Guitar Player* Magazine. I'd guess at least part of the answer would be the same reasons that made you want to play the guitar, the blues and Elvis.

BFG: And you'd be right. The Baldwin-Matthews Blues Night Show led us to discover Memphis' many great musicians and guitar fanatics during that first trip. It set the stage for diggin' Memphis. It's like the comment by Ry Cooder 'bout how you get the "musicness" of Memphis when you arrive. It just keeps bringing us back.

VG: We've come to know you by many names... "Hollywood Willy," "G-man," and, one of our faves, "The Right Rev. Gibbons." Are they surrounded by a secret?

BFG: Well, they've accumulated over time. I consider them gifts from sincere, true friends.

VG: I'm hearing a lot of ZZ TOP songs being played by talk show radio and even TV hosts. Comment?

BFG: Hmm.. mm.. m.. well, just so they play it loud! (Laughs)

VG: Speaking of your film careers, what was it like working the *Back to the Future* project?

BFG: Well, a most interesting outing, to say the least! As is came down, Steven Spielberg sent director Bob Zemeckis to secure the writing of the "Theme song" and soundtrack work with ZZ as the way to go on it. And, as it were... a quick trip up around the set in Sonora, California came up for the Band to check up the "feel" and thrash on a tune. So, here we are... on the set, inside a western town out in the middle of the northern California Badlands, taking a stroll on location, leaning on a corral post, lookin' things over. Middle of the day, blaringly hot, during the cast-call for lunch "break." Next thing, we're hustled into a wardrobing car, outfitted in turn of the century cowpoke threads. And, there was much "to-do" about looking "period" and what, and fuss over appearing much like a scruffy musician of the time. Later, the big discovery was, as we're hangin' 'round... the director, Bob "Z-Man," and the "A.D.," Bob Gayle, spotted us, out in the pony arena... middle of the scenic. "Bob Z" says, "Uh... er.. who'er those guys... ...to which Bob Gayle responded... "Bob,... that's ZZ TOP... the guys hired on to score your 'opener'...!" "Oh... yeah! Those 'beards'... uh... they'll be just fine... save a bit on costuming... Uh... get 'em in the picture." So, roundabout, we became his 'town band'! Brilliant! Steve and Bob Zemeckis, are the coolest! As was the stars in the project. Great film. Loads of fun, that!

VG: Any extra remarks from your perspective?

BFG: I'll say it here: anyone who wants to learn about the wild world of vintage instruments needs to read *Vintage Guitar*. You might learn something new... you'll always learn "something vintage"! (Grins)

VG: We'll take that with compliments.

BFG: Absolutely!

It's obvious from conversing with Rev. Gibbons that he is an active, aggressive advocate of alliteration when he does interviews. He's got a monster guitar collection. He's also a prodigious purveyor of prestidigitation (he demonstrated several card tricks backstage following a concert). That he is a gifted and dedicated musician goes without saying; his eloquence during our conversation simply reinforced the image.

(For coordination assistance in this interview with Billy F Gibbons, *Vintage Guitar* thanks: BMG, the fine folks at Peavey Electronics, Ford Heavy Trucks, Fender Guitars and Amps, Gold Star Sound Services, Gibson Guitars, Billy F Gibbons Production 1, Inc., Federal Express, Kinko's, MTV, American Motion Picture Archives,... "and all the fine folks who support us doin' what we love... spankin' the plank, and playing them blues".)

For information on the Delta Blues Museum, contact: The Delta Blues Museum, 114 Delta Avenue, Clarksdale, MS 38614. Telephone: (601) 627-7341.

The ZZ Top Fan Club can be reached by contacting: ZZTIFCI, P. O. Box 19744, Houston, TX 77024, Telephone (713) 461-9851.

The quest for fine equipment can lead to the most extraordinary people and places. It is a pleasure to thank the following associates and friends for their assistance in obtaining many of the pieces mentioned in this article:

• Rod and Hank's Vintage Guitar, Memphis, TN
• GuitarsWest, San Marcos, CA
• Scott Liebow, Guitar Center Hollywood, Hollywood, CA
• Brent Magnano, Guitar Oasis, Huntington Beach, CA
• Cesar Diaz, Diaz Amplifiers, East Stroudsburg, PA
• Mark Pollack, Greater Southwest Guitar Show, Dallas, TX

• Andy Marshall, THD Electronics, Seattle, WA
• Gerald Weber, Kendrick Amplifiers, Pfluglerville, TX
• Steve Brown, One World Music, Austin, TX
• Karry East, East Coast Guitars, Christiansburg, VA
• Buzzy Levine, Lark Street Music, Albany, NY
• William Busalacci, Seattle, WA
• Chuck Seward, Mosier, OR
• **SPECIAL THANKS TO BILL LLOYD, HOUSTON, TX**

— Billy F Gibbons

David Alan Grier

"Men on Guitars"

Most *Vintage Guitar* readers can probably ascertain what the formal guidelines for potential interviewees might be. In fact, *VG*'s policy is so liberal, it's almost a matter of what *doesn't* qualify a person as an interview subject instead of what *does*! One generalization that is applicable to potential interviewees is that if the person only plays an Ibanez guitar with a Floyd Rose whammy bar, he/she probably doesn't fit *VG*'s format.

But what about someone who has been successful in another facet of entertainment besides music? Actor/comedian David Alan Grier is probably best known for his efforts on Fox TV's "In Living Color," but he's been seen in movies and on stage as well. He also does stand-up comedy, but he has maintained a love of guitars and music since his childhood days in Detroit. At a recent Pomona guitar show (Grier's attended more than one), the versatile and affable entertainer's exuberance for old guitars was evident during a short conversation with *VG*:

VG: I assume acting is what brought you to California.

DAG: Right; I moved to New York in 1981 and stayed there about seven years, but when I was in college I used to come to New York on weekends. The first time I came to New York was 1976, and I was hanging around 48th Street, and you could still see D'Angelicos in the windows for anywhere from $1800 to $3000.

VG: Did it seem like an outrageous price back then?

DAG: Sure; I would ask "Who's this guy D'Angelico," but look what's happened to the prices since then! I was in *Dreamgirls* in 1986, and I saw a blond Switchmaster with PAFs in excellent condition on 48th St., and the dealer wanted $1700 for it. It was such a weird looking guitar I thought I'd never play it, so I didn't buy it; I recently bought one just like it and paid a *lot* more than $1700. The one I got probably isn't as clean as the one I saw on 48th St. It's amazing what prices have done over the last several years.

VG: What stimulated your interest in guitars?

DAG: I'm not a very good player, but I've been a *lover* of guitars ever since I was a little kid. When I was around twelve years old I starting

sending off for Fender catalogs, and I played in garage bands. Now that I've gotten a bit more financially able to cultivate a collection. It's almost like guitars are my "toys" (chuckles).

As a kid and even now, Jimi Hendrix was really the guy who got me excited. Before he came along, the electric guitar sounded one way, and after him, it sounded different. No one ever made it sound the way he made it sound; he was a milestone. It took me a long time to appreciate Eric Clapton; I thought he was overrated, but he seems to have aged well and I admire his playing immensely now.

I still listen to new players, and many of them are exciting. There's a guy named Jeff Linsky from the Bay Area who plays the requinta, which is a South American instrument that sort of like a classical guitar except it's three-quarter size. I mostly listen to jazz and blues: I don't like "metal." My taste has changed; these days I listen to a wide variety of players; everybody from Carlos Barbosa Lima to Joe Pass to Danny Gatton.

VG: What about portrayals of guitar players in your acting career?

DAG: The closest I ever came was an audition in New York; a guy had written a script about the life of Robert Johnson, who in terms of blues guitarists is the ultimate. I have the "complete recordings" CD collection of his stuff; his slide is so delicate and so sweet, it sounds like two guitars on some songs he recorded by himself in a hotel room in 1936. I was excited that I got to audition for the part, because Johnson is a brilliant American artist that I think everyone should know about.

VG: Then there's the comedy character on "In Living Color."

DAG: That's Calhoun Tubbs, but his whole thing is he's a bad player; he was inspired by some players I remember from Detroit like One String

David Alan Grier. Photo by Willie G. Moseley

It's obvious that Mr. Grier has a penchant for natural-finished instruments! On the floor is a 1970 Gibson ES-150DN, and standing behind it ar (Left to right) a 1960 Gibson ES-5 Switchmaster, a 1966 Gibson L-5 CESN, a 1966 Gibson super 400 CESN, and a new resonator guitar.

Sam; of course, Sam told everyone he knew Robert Johnson; "He taught me this chord!", Sam would say (laughs). Yeah, right.

When I was doing a movie up in Toronto, there was a flyer up for a performance by an old black blues player; my wife and I went to see him in some coffeehouse full of college kids sitting at his knees, and he had to be the worst player and singer I've ever heard in my life (laughs), and yet everybody in the audience thought he was the legitimate article. That experience influenced the creation of the Calhoun Tubbs character as well.

VG: What kinds of instruments did you play in the Calhoun Tubbs skits?

DAG: We used to rent them; I used to play a non-cutaway sunburst L-5 from Norm's Rare Guitars. A couple of times I played something like a Paramount, and I thought the cheaper, the better, because if they were old and dried-out, they had a great sound. But I could never riff on the show, because that wasn't part of the character. Then when I went into guitar stores and picked up an instrument, it surprised some people to find out I really can play.

On the show, I usually played in an Open D tuning with a bottleneck; at least I knew what I was doing, even if I couldn't riff.

VG: My perception from preliminary conversations with you is that you like archtop guitars. Tell me about you collection.

DAG: I've got about twenty-five instruments; mostly archtops, including a 1966 Super 400 CESN, a 1977 Super 400 CN, a 1969 L-5 CESN, the Switchmaster I mentioned earlier. It's hard to find good archtops anymore because the market is very small. I was on tour last year doing standup, and would call a lot of shops, but no one seemed to have any.

VG: At a show here a year ago, you were eyeballing a *new* Super 400 at one exhibitor's booth.

DAG: Yeah; at that time, Gibson had just announced their Historic Collection. I was thinking about buying a new one just because the old ones are so hard to find and so expensive.

VG: Why archtop, "jazz-type" guitars?

DAG: I guess everybody has a favorite type of instrument; I know guys who are into Les Pauls and Strats. Plugging an archtop in and getting that warm sound out of one just thrills me, so that's the "niche" I'm pursuing.

VG: What's the best deal you think you've ever gotten?

DAG: I've got a Rickenbacker 360-F that I got on 48th St. for $500. It looked like a weird guitar, so that's what brought me into the store, but it had a warm, funky sound. Usually they were Fireglo or blond, but this one was factory black. When I moved out here, the same models were hanging in music stores for $2000! Now, I buy guitars that I love: I wouldn't mind having a D'Angelico, even though I didn't always appreciate them .

VG: Are you buying any new archtops from lesser-known makers?

DAG: I got a guitar from Mark Lacey: he makes incredible stuff. I also recently ordered a Heritage "Super Golden Eagle Custom," I think it's called. It's an 18-inch guitar that was around $3200. I think Heritage guitars are very underrated. The builders had been with Gibson for *years and years*, and the craftsmanship and sound of their instruments is beautiful. At $3200, I thought my guitar was a steal. Maybe in the years to come, people will come to appreciate them.

VG: What sort of projects do you have lined up in the future? Are any of those projects musical?

DAG: Well, I think it's obvious that even though I wanted to be a singer and songwriter when I came to New York, acting is what is going to pay the bills. I'm in a new movie with Daman Wayans called *Blankman*, and I'm about to start on another comedy called *In the Army*.

VG: You've done a military role before, but it was in a drama called *A Soldier's Story*.

DAG: One thing I liked about that movie was how well it adapted from the stage play. Another reason I liked it was that it was a drama, about all I've done for the last four years is comedy, so I'd like to think it's time to get some drama back into the mix.

Even though like I said earlier, the market is small on archtops, I'll still keep looking around for those, too. The love of guitars is something I don't think many people ever outgrow.

David Alan Grier's enthusiasm and eloquence concerning guitars is refreshing. He hasn't made his mark in the entertainment world as a musician, singer or songwriter, but his appreciation of fine fretted instruments is an admirable facet of his show business career.

George Gruhn
Half A Decade Later

The July and August 1990 issues of *Vintage Guitar* featured a two-part profile of Nashville vintage guitar dealer George Gruhn; his pronouncements on the then-current state of the vintage instrument business comprised the entire first half of his profile (the second half dealt with the history of Gruhn's guitar business).

It goes without saying that a lot of changes have occurred with the vintage guitar business since Gruhn sat down for a chat with *VG* at a 1990 Atlanta guitar show. This time, we opted for an interview instead of a profile, yet the 1990 Gruhn profile was the foundation on which this "update conversation" was based. As might be expected by long-time old guitar aficionados, George Gruhn's comments were straight-forward, potentially controversial, and important:

VG: Let me start by getting your comments about two quotations of yours that opened your 1990 profile, and how such observations could be updated five years later. First, "At the rate things are going, five years from now there will be virtually no vintage instruments left here."

GG: It is my opinion that the market today is very different from five years ago. During the period 1985 through the first quarter of 1993 prices were escalating very rapidly. Many items went up 50 percent per year and some as much as 100 percent. This was a period in which the Baby Boomers who had dropped out of the market from 1975 through the early 1980s were re-entering. They were more affluent than ever before and were pursuing their hobbies with a vengeance. As a result prices escalated rapidly. Prices started to level off during the first quarter of 1993. Since that time prices have remained relatively stable. Some items have appreciated but certainly not at the previous rate and many items such as D'Angelico and Stromberg and other fine archtop acoustic guitars have not appreciably changed in value since the end of 1992.

The overseas economy in both Europe and Japan has been relatively poor; although the dollar has gone down significantly with respect to the Japanese yen and European currencies in the last few years the pace of foreign buying of high value collectibles has slowed drastically. Foreign buyers continue to buy utility grade instruments pri-

marily in the $2,500-and-under price bracket, but their purchases of expensive pieces are a small fraction of what they once were. In the case of the Japanese market, the CITES Treaty has created a further impediment to shipping instruments to customers there, because the vast majority of collectible instruments made prior to 1970 contain Brazilian rosewood. The Japanese government has used the CITES Treaty as a non-tariff trade barrier and has demanded import licenses above and beyond any required by the treaty. These licenses are extremely difficult for Japanese citizens to obtain and have obstructed trade.

When my original comment was made five years ago it certainly did appear that at the rate things were going supplies here would be drastically diminished. What happened, however, is that within 2$^{1}/_{2}$ years of the time my statement was made, conditions changed and the outflow slowed down because the foreign buyers were pulling back on expensive purchases. In addition, several major collectors have greatly slowed their purchasing. One major Japanese collection has been returned to the United States for exhibit here.

The fact remains that vintage instruments of quality are more expensive and more difficult to obtain today than they were five years ago, but the supply has by no means totally dried up. Fine 1950s electric guitars and pre-World War II acoustic instruments are indeed more difficult to get today than five years ago, however, the market has broadened such that many dealers today are specializing in used late 1960s and 1970s instruments rather than the ones which I would have regarded five years ago as being truly collectible.

VG: "Is the market going up, up, up, with no end in sight? No; some people are going to get their fingers burned and it won't break my heart to see that happen."

GG: To some extent I just answered that. It is clear that the market today is very different from five years ago. We are seeing a great proliferation in the number of dealers both large and

George Gruhn

TOP: *Gruhn Guitar's Second floor showroom, which features high-end collectibles.*

RIGHT: *George's personal 1924 Gibson K-5 Mandocello (in back) and 1928 Gibson L-5.*

small advertising in publications such as *Vintage Guitar* magazine; we also are seeing a fiercely competitive market in which it is not possible for all of these individuals and businesses to thrive. It is my opinion that many individuals and dealers are asking highly speculative prices, and frequently enough are making very speculative purchases which have the potential to backfire. In my own business I try to be more conservative and to purchase items which I think have solid market value. It is my opinion that if a dealer prices an item too high, not only does it not sell, but ultimately it creates ill will.

VG: What has happened to the market since the summer of 1990 regarding demand for specific brands and models?

GG: Some of this we have already discussed. In general, most of the items in demand in 1990 would still be very strongly in demand today. I have seen a weakening of demand for archtop acoustic guitars in the past two years. In 1990 Les Pauls appeared more popular than Stratocasters with many players, whereas today both are popular, but Stratocasters and Fender guitars in general have a very dominant position in the electric guitar marketplace. It has been my experience in observing the market for over thirty years that Gibson and Fender tend to leap-frog in popularity in four or five year cycles. In general, the acoustic market remains strong, and overall those items which were of value in 1990 are still valuable today. If any particular models have really crept up in the past five years I would say that in Fender guitars, Jazzmasters, Jaguars, and Mustangs have been the big growth area. While these instruments are not, in my opinion, on par with the classic old Telecasters, Stratocasters, Precision Basses, or Jazz Basses, they appeal to the new wave players and the grunge rockers.

VG: What has happened to the market regarding *price*? Do you think people are still hung up on that one five-letter word?

GG: I think that it is an unfortunate fact of life that the majority of people who wheel and deal guitars and even many who claim to be collectors are more concerned with price than with quality, artistry, history, or any other factors. This is, in my opinion, no worse a problem today than it would have been five years ago, but the situation is still similar. Needless to say, there are indeed individuals who are sincerely interested in instruments without focusing solely on price. I think that it is critically important that there be end consumers, and instruments must not be regarded solely as "hot potatoes" to be kept only for a short period and then quickly dumped. Ultimately, for this market to have any long term stability there must be customers who enjoy and appreciate the instruments for their own merits, regardless of monetary value. These pieces after all were designed as musical instruments and were intended to be functional tools.

VG: What about the changes in foreign markets? Foreign buyers are still an integral part of your business, aren't they?

GG: The foreign market continues to be very important, however we are by no means dependent upon it, and we find that to a greater extent today than five years ago, the finest quality instruments are being sold in the USA rather than strictly to foreign buyers. While export continues to be important, the total percentage of my business volume done as export is somewhat less now than five years ago.

VG: Another phenomenon that has occurred in the last half-decade has been the advent of guitar auctions. Some of them, in my opinion, had seemed to be a bit dubious. Comment importance of auctions? Some items, such as the circa 1949 Fender Broadcaster prototype, didn't sell.

GG: It is my opinion that auctions have not been nearly as significant in the guitar market as they have been in the violin market. There is little doubt that a significant portion of the violin market today is devoted to auctions. In the case of the guitar market, various auction houses such as Sothebys, Christie's, Skinner, and Guernsey's have heavily solicited consignments and have stated that they would get record prices for consignors. The basic premise appeared to be that the auction houses would attract a new clientele with a high degree of sophistication and a great deal of money. In effect, the auction houses stated that they would be able to reach out beyond the standard guitar-buying clientele and bring in a new and better quality clientele. It has been my observation that they have failed to come through on this promise. The buyers of violins have shown little interest in guitars, and the auction house clientele for jewelry, fine art, coins, stamps, and other collectibles has not rushed in to spend money on guitars, banjos, or mandolins. If anything, prices have been a bit over my normal wholesale but less than my retail. Effectively, instruments have sold at auction for a price equivalent to that which I would normally net a consignor here. This means that, in effect, the consignor is getting less money than if they consigned to a dealer such as me. The auction house typically gets 10 percent commission from the buyer and 10 percent commission from the seller, therefore they are getting a 20 percent commission. If they sell an item for the same price I would have netted the consignor, the consignor is actually getting 20 percent less than if he had sold it through a dealer such as me.

It has also been brought to my attention that in some cases when an item did not sell at auction, consignors have been charged for storage and insurance. While many auctioneers put considerable effort into pre-auction publicity, it should be borne in mind that the item is actually on the block for a minute or less. It is only logical that a skilled dealer given a few months to sell an item should do better than an auctioneer given a minute or less. One should also keep in mind that even though the item may be on the auction block for less than a minute, the auction house requires the consignor to leave it with them several months in advance so they may photograph it, catalog it, and promote the auction. The instrument is tied up for quite awhile, whereas if it is consigned with a dealer it can be listed for sale immediately.

While auctioneers have not been particularly successful with selling vintage guitars, they have done extremely well in the memorabilia market. It would appear that Rock 'n Roll memorabilia attracts quite a different clientele from the typical vintage guitar buyers. Memorabilia buyers are not particularly interested in quality of musical instruments as much as association with a star. They are equally happy to buy clothing, photos, signed albums or posters, or other artifacts as well as musical instruments.

VG: The increasing interest in vintage guitars has meant more guitar shows, and in 1990 you had opined that there were already too many. One point that might need to be made is that some of the more unusual or rare items might show up at smaller shows. How many shows do you and your associates now attend?

GG: Certainly the number of guitar shows has greatly proliferated in the last five years. Now there's at least one per week and some weekends there are as many as three at the same time in different areas of the country. It is impossible for any one person or business to cover all of them. It has been my experience that it is increasingly difficult to find truly fine vintage collectibles at many of the shows. At some of the better shows I used to be able to purchase fifty or more instruments in a weekend. Now it is a struggle to pick up twenty, and the quality of the pieces is on average down. The shows remain a good place to pick up utility used instruments but are not near as good as they used to be for picking up the finest unmodified vintage originals. In spite of any reservations I may have about shows, we do continue to attend at least a dozen of them per year. It is my expectation that as time goes on there will be a weeding out of shows and promoters. The strongest will survive along with some who simply have low overhead and can make it in a leaner environment.

VG: Is "star power" still a factor in the vintage market? How important is it; how important should it be?

GG: Today just as five years ago and for that matter just as ten, fifteen, or twenty years ago, the market is influenced by who plays what on stage. Manufacturers of new instruments have always been aware that endorsements are important. Gibson had Nick Lucas as an endorser in the 1920s and Bacon & Day had stars such as the cowboy artist Montana as an endorser equally early. During the 1950s Bill Monroe was a powerful force in revitalizing interest in vintage mandolins, and Earl Scruggs and Don Reno greatly influenced the banjo market. This trend continued on up through the folk boom and into the Rock 'n Roll era and is certainly alive and well today. Whether it's good, bad, or indifferent, it is a fact of life that the market is influenced by performers use of instruments on stage.

In the vintage market another powerful influence is the effect that a few collectors with large amounts of money can have if they choose to specialize in particular models or makers. The price of D'Angelico and Stromberg guitars, as well as some of the Gibson archtop models such as Super 400s, was powerfully influenced by a few avid collectors who spent large amounts of money building their collections. When some of these people slowed down on their purchasing a couple of years ago prices on these instruments stabilized. Three or four years ago numerous people were saying that archtop acoustic guitars were the "new adult toys," whereas today the market for them is slower than three years ago. Certain rare models can constitute such a small market that a single purchaser can vastly influence that marketplace. In a sense, a collector can be a star in this marketplace and have every bit as much influence as a performer.

VG: There are more *dealers* in the business these days. What's your perspective on that, as a *veteran* dealer? You've been in the biz a quarter-century...

GG: While I have been in the marketplace for over thirty

years as a collector and have had a shop since January, 1970, I frequently feel that seniority does not necessarily equal security. In business, unlike in politics or frequently in the academic world, seniority does not necessarily guarantee success. If a newcomer has skill, understands financing and the products, and has good sales skills he can rapidly establish himself in the marketplace. In our free enterprise system this is as it should be. I have no complaint against dealers who operate a legitimate business. I am concerned that numerous small time wheeler-dealers are entering the business without providing good customer service or operating according to what I would consider to be normal business practices. In my case I have a shop with thirty employees. We pay withholding taxes, corporate taxes, sales taxes, workman's compensation, and we provide employee benefits such as paid vacations, and health insurance. We conform to federal labor law on such matters such as overtime pay. I resent having to compete with dealers who operate in a strictly cash-and-carry manner, providing no receipts, no guarantees, collect no sales tax, pay their employees in cash with no benefits, no overtime, and no income tax, and simply do not conform to legitimate legal business practices. It is my opinion that if people are going to advertise a service in a na-

TOP: *Gruhn Guitars' main showroom.*

RIGHT: *Gruhn Guitars' current Location 400 Broadway, Nashville, Tennesee.*

tionwide publication and do hundreds of thousands in business a year that they should conform to normal business ethics and the law.

I find that numerous individuals use blue books and frequently my own price list as a guide in pricing their merchandise. In many instances they are not providing the same service that my shop does. When we sell an instrument it is set up in playing condition and is to the best of our ability restored to proper structural and cosmetic condition. I find that numerous individuals are offering instruments with no guarantee of full authenticity and frequently in need of considerable work for prices equivalent to what we charge for fully restored properly set up examples.

I accept that in an open market, competition is a fact of life and is in reality healthy. No marketplace can thrive without competition. As the marketplace has become more sophisticated numerous reputable dealers have emerged on the scene. The buyer has many options. It is wise to check the reputation of those with whom you choose to deal.

VG: Tell us about your move down the street to 400 Broadway. Results?

GG: Two years ago we moved from 410 Broadway to 400 Broadway. The old building consisted of three floors and was very long and narrow. The lot was only 20 feet wide and 129 feet deep. Our showroom in that shop had narrow dimensions of about 17 feet by 45 feet. The rest of the building was devoted to offices, storage, repair, and other backup facilities. The new building has four floors with 12,000 square feet

of space, has much higher ceilings, and is fully renovated and up to codes. It is much more comfortable. It permits us to exhibit much more merchandise in a more attractive environment. We have more and better of everything. In addition, we have our own parking lot in the rear providing free customer parking. In a downtown setting this is an important feature. The new building has permitted significant growth. Since we purchased the building there has been considerable change in the neighborhood immediately surrounding us. The Ryman Auditorium which formerly housed the Opry has received an eight million dollar renovation. It is located only about 150 feet from our back door. The new Bell South Tower is less than a block away. It was an 100 million dollar project. A new 120 million dollar Arena is being erected one block from us. The Wildhorse Saloon and the Hard Rock Cafe went in two blocks from us. A new Planet Hollywood is moving in directly across the street. Numerous other changes are taking place. Hundreds of millions of dollars of development is occurring in a two block radius around us, and much of this started within a few months after we purchased the new building. Our timing could not have been better.

VG: You'd noted in an article you wrote in another publication that you had resumed collecting instruments. Comments and details?

GG: I have recently started collecting again. From 1963 through 1976 I amassed a large collection consisting of pre-World War II pearl trimmed Martins as well as some fine banjos and mandolins. In 1976 I sold most of the collection and purchased a building and a house. In the past couple of years I have resumed collecting and have concentrated primarily on banjos which I personally enjoy playing and Loar signed and dated mandolin family instruments. My goal in collecting has not been simply amassing an expensive collection but has rather been directed toward acquiring instruments which I personally enjoy. In addition to vintage guitars, banjos, and mandolins, I have also retained the hand-made prototypes of models that I designed for Guild and some instruments I have designed since that time. While I am confident that my collection is a good investment, the primary motivation has been for personal enjoyment.

VG: What about some of the specific acquisitions your store has made over the last years? How'd those come about?

GG: We are constantly buying guitars. I try to acquire at least fifteen instruments per day. Obviously, some have greater value and greater historical significance than others but all help add to the bottom line. Some of the most significant pieces I have uncovered recently, in my opinion, would be the 1957 Prototype Gibson Flying V, Ray Whitley's small "party guitar," Grady Martin's double neck Bigsby guitar, a Prototype Gibson Super Jumbo Flattop labelled L-5 Special, an original hand-made Orville Gibson guitar, a Bacon & Day Ne Plus Ultra #9 tenor banjo, as well as a number of very fine D'Angelico, Stromberg, and Loar-signed Gibson instruments. Since we handle several thousand instruments a year it is difficult to come up with a list of only five or six that are truly the "notable ones." After so many years of total immersion in this marketplace I have established excellent contacts. We are offered a large number of fine instruments, and we always strive to acquire the best offerings.

VG: You've released three books in the first half of the Nineties. Are you satisfied with the way they turned out and the market's reception? What other writing projects do you have in the works?

GG: I have been well pleased with the public reaction to the three books I co-authored with Walter Carter, *Gruhn's Guide to Vintage Guitars*, *Acoustic Guitars and Other Fretted Instruments: A Photographic History*, and *Electric Guitars and Basses: A Photographic History*, from Miller-Freeman Publishing.

I will have other works coming out in the future. We are planning at some point to do an update and revision on the *Gruhn's Guide to Vintage Guitars*, as well as a compilation of some of my previous magazine writing, and another photo book. These projects will take time, and I do not have any release dates at this time. In addition to book projects, of course, I do numerous magazine articles and the monthly question and answer column for *Vintage Guitar* magazine.

VG: One of your ads listed the "segments" of the market: Professional musicians, weekend players, collectors, if I remember correctly. Have the percentages of each segment changed in your business over the last five years? What about the observation that "the only difference in men and boys is the price of their toys"?

GG: The market has always been in a constant state of transition. During the early to mid 1970s professional rock and pop musicians accounted for a very high percentage of our market, whereas today they are a rather minor component. Collectors remain of considerable importance in purchasing the upper level pieces, but by far the greatest percentage of our business is done with amateur players who want good quality instruments which are fun to play. Foreign buyers continue to be important to us, but as I have previously stated the greatest percentage of instruments we export are what I would classify as used rather than true vintage collectibles.

Regarding the quote "The only difference in men and boys is the price of their toys," how applicable is that statement to the vintage guitar market? While this is a statement I have heard numerous times it is not one attributed to me. I personally do not think that price alone determines merit of an instrument. I enjoy dealing with people who have a sincere love of the instrument and are concerned with workmanship, artistry, sound, playability, and historical significance rather than price alone. Needless to say, it is true that some of the finest pieces are priced out of reach of many consumers. We are still happy to provide information and talk to people who are not wealthy. We should also recognize that young players should be encouraged and given information so that as they become more sophisticated and wealthier over the years they will retain an interest in our products.

VG: You were recently on the cover of *MMR* magazine (*Music Merchandise Review,* a music retailer trade publication). Comments regarding the profile of your company that appeared in it?

GG: I was very pleased with the *MMR* interview. I felt that it was one of the best profiles done on me and my company which has ever appeared in print. *MMR* is widely distributed to music stores but is not sold on the newsstand and therefore is not seen by the general public or most musicians. I would have liked to see this piece get wider coverage, but I thought *MMR* did an excellent job. Since the interview was accompanied by a cover photo and was distributed at the summer NAMM (National Association of Music Merchants) show it received as good coverage as could have been provided by any music trade magazine.

VG: Would you support a standardization of what constitutes instrument condition ratings; "MINT," "NEAR MINT," "EXCELLENT," ETC.? How would such be accomplished?

GG: While I think it would be desirable to have standardized descriptions of condition, the simple fact is I don't expect it to happen. In my own business at this shop we try to be as consistent as possible in providing descriptions of condition. In order to do this one must not only judge the cosmetics but also the structural condition of an instrument as well as its degree of originality. This takes experience and skill. Even if uniform industry-wide standards could be established, the fact is not all dealers have either the knowledge or the integrity to apply them.

VG: Along the lines of the previous question, at one point there was an organization being formed called the Association of Vintage Instrument Dealers (AVID), but you later advised that it didn't get off the launching pad, or words to that effect. Why didn't such an organization succeed? Is there a need and/or place for such an organization? Why or why not?

GG: AVID simply never got off the ground. It was originally proposed to help with the difficulties encountered as a result of the CITES Treaty. If anything, what we found is that many dealers and traders simply don't trust each other or communicate with each other well enough to form the basis for an industry-wide organization. In order for there to be an association of dealers, the dealers must wish to associate with and cooperate with each other. With the exception of problems encountered as a result of the CITES Treaty there have been few industry wide issues that would form the basis for cooperation. While some of the larger dealers have shops that operate according to standard business procedure, many independent wheeler-dealers are counterculture renegades who would fight any attempt at organization.

VG: What do you think is the greatest challenge that will be facing the market in the coming five years?

GG: Historically, it has been the Baby Boomers who have supported the vintage guitar market. It was Baby Boomers who were at the forefront of the acoustic "folk boom" from 1959 through 1963 as well as the Beatles and Rolling Stones type rock boom of 1964 through 1970 and the folk rock scene of 1970 through 1975. From 1976 through the early 1980s many of the Baby Boomers dropped out of the market. The typical guitar buyer was male and, after they reached an age bracket in their mid-20s the typical player acquired an expensive wife, children, house, car, and upward mobility in his job. When he came home at night he was tired. If he opened up a guitar case and played it, it made noise which woke up the children, which frequently upset the wife, who made him put the guitar back in the case. For the previous two hundred years fretted instrument sales had been primarily to young players and a smaller secondary market of retirees. Starting in the mid-1980s an entirely new demographic trend took place. For the first time in human history people sixty-five years and over outnumbered teenagers, and the middle-aged Baby Boomers outnumbered everyone else combined. The Baby Boomers have leisure time and money and started to pursue their hobbies more vigorously than ever before. It was Baby Boomers re-entering the market who played a large role in driving the vintage market from 1985 through the present time. The Generation X buyers showed relatively little interest in vintage collectibles from 1976 through 1984 and seemed not to acquire much interest in these products after the Baby Boomers re-entered the market. It has been my experience that the younger buyers are very much interested in music and are quite willing to spend money on good utility grade instruments to play, but they have not been willing to pay premium prices for vintage collectibles. It was the re-entry of the Baby Boomers into the market during the mid-1980s and onward that caused the rapid appreciation of vintage instrument prices.

At this point in history it would appear that virtually all the Baby Boomers who are going to re-enter the market have already done so. The oldest of the Boomers are now approaching fifty years of age. For the vintage market to prosper in the future, interest in these products must jump from one generation to the next. It is the Baby Boomer's children, more than the Boomers themselves, who will determine the marketability and value for fine vintage instruments twenty years from now.

For any market to be healthy there must be a steady infusion of new buyers. It is not sufficient to simply preach to the already converted. When the Boomers re-entered the market they were eager to acquire instruments. It is much easier to sell someone guitars when they have one or two or even five or six instruments and are looking to complete their collection than it is after they already have twenty-five or more and are relatively satiated. Unlike a bottle of fine wine or gourmet food which once used is consumed, a musical instrument can last hundreds of years with proper care.

There is a great wealth of information available today in the form of books, magazines, recordings, etc. It is critical that those of the Baby Boom generation who are avid collectors and dealers reach out to the younger generation to perpetuate interest in the market. In the coming decade the torch must pass from the Baby Boomers to the next generation if the market is to remain healthy.

VG: Wanna do this again five years from now, in the year 2000?

GG: I'm sure five years from now there will be plenty to talk about. If anything is constant it is change. I have no doubt that the future will hold surprises.

Warren Haynes
OF Mules and Macon–Based Boogie

Slide-meister Warren Haynes has been a busy player during the Nineties. Not only does he command the other guitar slot opposite Dickey Betts in the Allman Brothers Band (his musical association with Betts precedes his joining the veteran Southern rock band), he released a solo album in 1993, and he and Allman Brothers bassist Allen Woody have formed an offshoot trio with drummer Matt Abts called Gov't Mule.

Relaxing in his hotel suite prior to an Allman Brothers concert, the affable guitarist reviewed all of his musical efforts and the guitars he used (and uses) in an easygoing and cordial conversation with *VG*.

VG: Are you originally from the South? What about your earliest bands and guitars?

WH: I'm originally from Asheville, North Carolina. I started out at about age eight, wanting to be a singer; I listened to a lot of Motown and Memphis soul. I guess the "transitional" performers for me were B.B. King and Ray Charles, because they were singers *and* they played instruments; B.B. had his voice *and* his guitar. I played in local and regional bands.

My first guitar and amp were a Norma set, from a Lowe's hardware store; less than a hundred bucks for both of 'em (chuckles). After that I got a Lyle SG copy, then a SG Jr., and after that a three-pickup SG Custom which was walnut with gold hardware. I think it was made around '69 or '70, and I believe they're kind of rare. I broke the neck on mine and had it fixed, and it wasn't the same afterwards, but I still wish I had it. Woody recently got one just like it, and I'm trying to talk him out of it!

Then, I got a late Sixties Gibson ES-150; the thick, double-cutaway model with the master volume control. And at that point I thought I'd really accomplished something, since I still had an SG; I actually owned *two* guitars.

VG: Didn't you have feedback problems with the ES-150?

WH: Yeah, but I had a guy put some 1/8-inch plywood that was painted black into the f-holes; it still looks like regular f-holes. I still have that guitar.

VG: Did you have a proverbial "big break"?

WH: When I was twenty, David Allan Coe asked me to join his band; I wasn't thinking I'd fit into a country band, but he told me he wanted a blues/rock player to round things out. I played with him for about three years.

VG: Were you playing slide by then? Had slide players been your guitar heroes?

WH: I started playing slide early on, but I didn't play it much with Coe because he had a pedal steel player. My early heroes had been Clapton, Hendrix, Duane and Dickey, Billy Gibbons; I listened to *everybody,* and read a lot of guitar magazines. Because of interviews with players like Clapton and Duane, I became aware of the "original" players like Albert King and Freddy King.

VG: What about tunings, then *and* now? Any particular setup?

WH: Ninety-five percent of the time I'm in Standard tuning, and that's how it's been, when we play live *or* for recording. Occasionally I'll drop either E string down to D. I've played in Open G and Open E, but when I've done that I've found that my "vocabulary" was limited.

I've never had a specific setup; I just keep my action a little high.

VG: There *is* a Coricidin bottle shown with the collage of backstage passes, picks, etc. on each *An Evening with the Allman Brothers Band* inside cover.

WH: (chuckles) That's mine. I had a few that used to be Duane's, and I got some reissues as well. One of the ones that had belonged to Duane was stolen and returned to me; the guy thought he was just getting one of my slides, but when he found out it had been Duane's he felt so bad he gave it back.

VG: So how did the affiliation with the Allmans transpire?

WH: After I played with Coe, I moved to Nashville; at the time I thought I wanted to be a studio musician, and I did that for a few years but I got more work as a background vocalist; I think my guitar sound was too "aggressive" for

Warren Haynes, onstage with the Allman Brothers Band. Photo: Jack Pearson.

Nashville back then. I finally decided I'd rather be in a band where I was the singer or *one* of the singers; I didn't want to be a "hired gun." Around '86 or early '87 I was about to sign as a solo artist, but I got a call from Dickey. We'd met when I was with Coe, and Dickey was about to record his first solo album in nine years; his bass player had kept telling him about me. So I put off my record to do *Pattern Disruptive*. Matt Abts, who's in Gov't Mule, was the drummer.

I played in the Dickey Betts Bands for about two and a half years, and when that started winding down, Dickey called me about the Allman Brothers Band getting back together. It's strange; the whole time we were in the Dickey Betts Band there wasn't any talk of the Allman Brothers being put together again. But it was a smooth transition; Dickey and I had built up a great guitar rapport in the years we'd played together in his band.

VG: *Seven Turns* was generally hailed as the best thing the Allmans had done in years, and the follow-up, *Shades of Two Worlds*, sounded like the Allmans of old as well, in my opinion. Were there supposed to be any specific differences in those two albums?

WH: *Seven Turns* was probably more of a "song" album; *Shades* was more improvisational. We felt like we had grown, so we stretched out. "Kind of Bird," for example, was a tribute to Miles Davis and Charlie Parker. Dickey and I spent two weeks writing that song, and whenever we'd take a break we'd listen to Charlie Parker records.

TOP: *GOV'T MULE – Warren Haynes, Matt Abts, and Allen Woody. Photo: Danny Clinch.*

RIGHT: *Warren's 1993 solo effort, Tales of Ordinary Madness*

VG: Interesting marketing concept concerning the live albums; they were sub-titled *First Set* and *Second Set*, and there was a studio album, *Where It All Begins*, between them.

WH: Well, the original intent was to release a double CD, but the feedback we got was that the economy might not support it. Then we thought about releasing two live albums back-to-back, but we'd been writing a lot of new songs, so we decided to do *Where It All Begins, then* the second set live album.

VG: Some of the songs from that studio album showed up on the *Second Set* live album; songs like "Soulshine," "Sailin' 'Cross the Devil's Sea" and the title track; they seemed to translate well in performance.

WH: Dickey wrote "Back Where It All Begins," but it was my idea to solo in different keys. Mine's in E; Dickey's is in A. We did the same thing on "Nobody Knows" earlier; Gregg's solo is in F, mine's in A, and Dickey's is in D.

VG: I *do* need to inquire about any comparisons listeners and longtime fans made between you and Duane Allman, and if some fans considered such a "proximity" to Duane Allman's playing to be "heresy," for lack of a better term, although in my opinion you've got your own niche, sound-wise.

WH: Well, maybe for the first year some people might have said things like "Wow, this guy sounds like Duane," but I think it's evolved beyond that. If you listen to us play for two and a half hours and still walk away thinking "Duane," you haven't paid attention. There's all kinds of guitarists to be influenced by, but there's only a *handful* of *slide* players, and of course Duane's at the very top of the list. But over the years I've also listened to Lowell George, Muddy Waters, Elmore James, and Ry Cooder. David Lindley's been a melodic influence, and one of the more recent slide players I like is Sonny Landreth, who used to be with John Hiatt; he now has his own band.

VG: This may take a while, but I need to inquire about some of the brands of instruments you cited in the liner notes on recent albums. First, Gibson.

WH: That's where I started! I have two '59

Les Paul Custom Shop reissues; one made in '89 and one that's about a year and a half old; the newer one has the original-style neck joint, which helps its resonance. I've got Seymour Duncan "Pearly Gates" pickups in one reissue and Gibson "Classic '57" pickups in the other.

VG: Paul Reed Smith.

WH: I started playing those when I was in Dickey's band; Paul's a true craftsman. I've got four of them, but recently I've been concentrating more on playing my Les Pauls. I *would* like to have a McCarty model P.R.S. like Dickey's got; I like the 22-fret neck on it instead of a 24-fret, and I think the stop tailpiece also helps it sound better.

VG: Acoustic brands like Alvarez, Takamine, and Washburn.

WH: An Alvarez is what I played on "Dolphineus" on the *Gov't Mule* album. That's a Takamine on "Midnight Blues" and "In Memory of Elizabeth Reed" on the live albums, and on the *Live at Great Woods* video. I've got a couple of Washburn Cherokee models; they've started manufacturing in the U.S. again and their stuff is really nice.

VG: Lesser-known guitar brands like Chandler and Fodera.

WH: Paul Chandler made me a cool, Tele-type guitar; he makes great stuff. Vinnie's building me a guitar that looks like an oversized, hollow Tele with a resonator in it. I haven't gotten it yet, so maybe thanking him was a bit premature (chuckles).

VG: How many vintage or collectible instruments do you have?

WH: Not a lot. Gibson-wise, I've got a cherry '61 Dot Neck, a '62 SG with nothing original left on it except the wood (chuckles), and a Les Paul Artisan with the fancy fretboard inlay; that's the heaviest Les Paul I've ever played. I still have my ES-150, and I've got a P.R.S. that was custom-built for Dickey; I also have one of the four P.R.S. Artist prototypes. Fender's Custom Shop built me a Strat that's half-American Standard, half-Eric Clapton.

VG: One of the photos in the *Second Set* album showed you playing an old Fifties National Reso-Phonic; the solidbody with a resonator in it.

WH: I love that old guitar; I've actually recorded with it. I've also got a new National steel-bodied guitar, and some new acoustics.

VG: You finally came out with a solo album in 1993; some of it sounds a bit different from your work with the Allman Brothers. "Fire in the Kitchen" ain't a Southern boogie, for example.

WH: I'd written some of the songs before I joined the Dickey Betts Band, but about half of the tunes on it were new. In general, I was going for an alternative sound, but there *are* some songs on it that could be done by the Allman Brothers or maybe on one of Gregg's solo albums; if I write a song and think it would be a good song for the Allman Brothers, I'll present it to the band for their consideration.

There are some things on that album I might have changed, but for the most part I'm happy with it. It was done more like a studio album, whereas songs that get recorded by the Allman Brothers or Gov't Mule get "road-tested" before they're recorded. *Where It All Begins* and *Gov't Mule* were both cut live in the studio, and I didn't use headphones when we recorded them. I like recording that way.

VG: The *Gov't Mule* album sounds like a no-frills, "loud, heavy blues album" by a power trio. What inspired you to do an album like that?

WH: Seeing younger bands like Blues Traveler, Widespread Panic, Phish, and the Dave Matthews Band, and the way younger listeners would respond to their jams. But what *influences* Gov't Mule were bands like Cream, early ZZ TOP and Hendrix; trios as well as bands like Free and Led Zeppelin, which were trios with a lead singer. The main impetus, though, is the chemistry between Matt and Woody as a rhythm section. Some listeners who like the "country" side of the Allman Brothers — songs like

"Ramblin' Man" — might not get it, though.

VG: Comments on some of the cover tunes on the *Gov't Mule* album?

WH: I've always been a big Son House fan, and wanted to get one of his songs on an album. One night onstage somebody must've had some kind of equipment problem; maybe I broke a string; at any rate I started singing "Grinnin' In Your Face" acapella, and Woody and Matt liked it so much they wanted it on the album.

I like the message of "Mother Earth"; I'm familiar with Memphis Slim's version more than any other, and nowadays it's more timely than ever. I was intrigued by the piano part on Memphis Slim's version, so we put that part on the bass and played it at half the speed of the piano. I think that adds to the urgency of it. Some journalists try to incorporate an environmental message into it, but the world's gotten so crazy anyway.

A friend of mine named Don Butler hangs out with us whenever we're on the West Coast, and he was on the bus with us once while we were going from L.A. to San Diego. We'd forgotten to bring along some CDs to listen to, and he had a cassette of songs by Free with him. We heard "Mr. Big" and thought it was a cool song; this was right around the time we were talking about forming Gov't Mule, and we did "Mr. Big" the first time we played.

VG: There've been some "doubled-up" gigs where Gov't Mule has opened for the Allmans, right?

WH: Ten shows. Gov't Mule has done about a hundred shows total, and we'll be going out after the Allman Brothers tour winds down. We're opening for Blues Traveler on New Year's Eve; John Popper played harmonica on "Mule" on our album, and I played slide on a song called "Mountain Wins Again" on their latest album.

VG: Are there any instruments you're still seeking?

WH: I wouldn't mind having an old Firebird and maybe an old 'Burst, but the prices on 'Bursts have just about gone through the roof. I still collect old Gibson amps; I've got a '58 Vanguard, a '61 Vanguard, and a Fifties Skylark amp with a six-inch Jensen in it that I used a lot on *Seven Turns*. I know everybody's always interested in old tweed Fenders, but some of the old Gibsons, especially the little ones, can sound really nice.

VG: Sounds like you'll be busy at least through the end of the year.

WH: Beyond that! The next Gov't Mule album should be out around September so we've got to get to work on that, and there's another Allman Brothers record in the works, and *that* one may be out even earlier.

It might appear that Warren Haynes is burning the candle at both ends, around the middle, and in between, but he's having a great time doing it. His confidence and dedication is obvious in his guitar playing and song writing abilities, and it's evident in his conversational abilities as well.

Warren Haynes and Allen Woody ultimately left the Allman Brothers Band to concentrate exclusively on Gov't Mule.

The Allmans' 1994 release, Where It All Begins.

Steve Howe
"Fill in the Blanks"

In our preliminary discussion with respected British guitarist Steve Howe prior to going "on the record," the interviewer noted that the main focus of the questions he'd prepared were oriented at accomplishing the, ...um, "concept" that's the subtitle of this article, because guitar lovers and music fans around the globe are probably familiar with the musical stylings of the man whose amazing guitar technique made such memorable recordings with bands such as Yes and Asia.

So in an interview somewhat along the lines of previous *Vintage Guitar* conversations with guitarists like B.B. King and Duane Eddy, we asked Steve Howe for information concerning his instruments and recordings that would be of the most interest to guitar lovers, which might not have been detailed earlier by the erudite and gifted Howe. When *VG* spoke with Howe, he was in the middle of a recording project utilizing guitars from the Scott Chinery Collection; the CD was slated for release in conjunction with the collection's photo book. It was after midnight when our cassette recorder started work, and Howe was still in the studio (he'd already been there for over 12 hours).

The available information concerning Howe's music and instruments includes the excellent photography book showcasing his amazing guitar collection; the photos were taken by Miki Slingsby, who also photographed Duane Eddy for a *Vintage Guitar* cover (an article showcasing Mr. Eddy's historical instruments appears in the current issue of *VG Classics*; those guitars were also photographed by Mr. Slingsby). Our initial inquiry to Steve Howe concerned a comment he'd once made about modification of vintage guitars:

VG: You stated in the past that you didn't have a problem modifying older instruments if it helped their sound. Do you still stand by that viewpoint? I'm asking this because of your current effort with the Chinery guitars.

SH: Well, I can give you a classic example that happened about a half hour ago. I was playing a 1934 Martin OM-45; it's one of my favorite guitars from Scott's collection. It's in original condition, but the tuning pegs slip. That's where I'm coming from; if a great vintage guitar is meant to be played and something about it doesn't work, it could be frustrating. New machine heads would be vital to some guitars; after 40 or 50 years, some parts wear out.

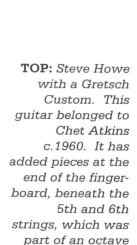

I liken it to having an old car; would you want to drive one for years without changing the tires or the oil? I went a bit far with my Broadcaster; it's my most modified collectible guitar, but it still works for me. And I've learned things; I don't claim that everything I've done is right, and some guitars in my collection had already been modified when I got them. Practically all of the guitars in my collection have had their tuning pegs replaced; the replacements are *much* better than the "three-on-one" heads.

VG: How much of your "pre-Yes" material is available on Compact Disc?

SH: There's a really good CD that I put out in England last year called *Moth Balls*; it's available from a distributor called Feedback. There are 25 tracks from the '60s on it, and a large amount has never been released until now. I was very happy with the consistency of these tracks; it's a lot of fun. There are tracks from Bodast, Tomorrow, The In Crowd, and even the Syndicats; all seven tracks I recorded with them had never been available be-

TOP: *Steve Howe with a Gretsch Custom. This guitar belonged to Chet Atkins c.1960. It has added pieces at the end of the fingerboard, beneath the 5th and 6th strings, which was part of an octave divider effect.*

LEFT: *Steve and Martin working out the leads.*

fore. There are also two solo tracks that had never been released; I'd forgotten that I'd recorded one of the solo tracks called "You Never Can Stay In One Place;" I thought I remembered everything I'd ever recorded (laughs)!

VG: Is it fair to say that the most complex recording you've ever done would have been *Tales from Topographic Oceans* with Yes?

SH: Yeah, *within Yes.* I'm one of the few lucky people who has the 28-minute version of Side One, which was never released. Back then you had to think of a record in terms of about 20 minutes per side. It was a very good project, and was a bit like what I'm doing now and like I've done all the way through my career; I've looked into my collection and played lutes, Danelectros, Spanish guitars, Les Pauls, 175s, L-5s.

Topographic was a big deal, and I just played Side One live on stage recently with Yes; it's a nice piece to play. In a way, we were getting complex with "Close to the Edge" and "Awaken" as well, and I think one track that "sums it up" for me is "To Be Over," from *Relayer*. Not only does it have some writing that I did that I'm fond of, Jon also wrote *around* it and wrote *for* it. The complexity and arrangement is such that it's multi-layered; bells, guitars, drummers. To me, that's a classic track that doesn't get mentioned often. It doesn't have the wonderful Rick Wakeman on it, but it certainly has a group that was tight.

VG: What's the story on your recent performance with Yes? That's the first I've heard about it.

SH: We did three shows in early March in San Luis Obispo, California; we recorded them and also did two studio tracks which total 30 minutes. There should be a double CD with live material and the new studio tracks out this summer; it's called *The Keys to Ascension.*

VG: Who's in the band?

SH: Jon Anderson, Chris Squire, Rick Wakeman, Alan White, and myself.

VG: Speaking of live performances, I'm aware that the "Asia in Asia" MTV concert was

released on video, but why wasn't it released as an album?

SH: That's a good question; I think it *will* be released sometime soon. Sometimes there was a very "dull" approach to managing groups in the '70s and '80s; it was kind of mundane. We did albums, we did tours; we were creating "bits of history" at times but nobody really thought of exposing such things through all of the formats that were available.

Another example is an album of mine due out soon on Caroline; it's called *Homebrew*, and is a collection of my own studio tapes. There are five or six songs from the Anderson, Bruford, Wakeman, Howe period that should be quite surprising to listeners, and other tracks. I wanted to put this out to show how I write songs; "this is what I do at home." It starts outs with six instrumentals that feature a lot of guitars; there are times when I'll be playing two electric guitars in a duet, for example.

VG: Your previous solo albums were released in '75, '79, '91 and '93. What were the similarities and differences in them, and was there one where you were more satisfied with the results?

SH: Well, there was also the 1994 album, *Not Necessarily Acoustic*, which was a live album from my first solo tour of America. To be honest, I like all of the music I've recorded to different degrees, but the one that I still like a lot is *Turbulence*, because it was something that I "detailed;" I recorded the album then went back and "touched it up" by adding a bit here and there,

TOP: *Steve in the studio lounge with a 40's Selmer Jazz Model.*

RIGHT: *Steve with a D'Aquisto Teardrop.*

and I did the same thing when I mixed it. It's satisfying when you do things right; there have been some albums that I've done with bands like Asia and GTR that weren't mixed in my style.

I'd waited a long time to do an album like *Beginnings*, and I kind of went mad and did a "variety" album (chuckles). *The Steve Howe Album* was a little more streamlined but still had the same breadth, and that's why I enjoy *Turbulence*; it's much more focused and is mainly about one style of music. *The Grand Scheme of Things*, the '93 release, was a big project that didn't get much exposure, but I think the instrumental work on it is enjoyable; it was kind of a synopsis of my work up to then. It had a lot of influences, and inspired me to release different kinds of albums after that.

There was the live solo tour album, and I did an album with Paul Sutin called *Voyages* on CNC Records; it features a lot of Danelectros and a Steinberger 12-string. It's a bit more "New Age-y" and melodic.

VG: New Age-wise, you were also on a benefit album called *Polar Shift*.

SH: Paul Sutin was on that track, as well. I've also been working with Annie Haslam; she used to sing with Renaissance. We did a jazz gig in New York called *Lilies in the Field*; it was a benefit album to raise money for the children in Bosnia.

VG: Some years ago I interviewed Jeff Berlin, who was the bass player for an Anderson, Wakeman, Bruford & Howe broadcast concert; he said he was called in because Tony Levin couldn't do the performance. Berlin said he had to learn the material very quickly; what's your perspective on that episode?

SH: Tony was the perfect bass player for us at that time, but he got a mild case of hepatitis. We didn't know who to call; we may have even talked about calling Chris Squire, but that didn't happen. I like Jeff, but in a way he didn't have enough time to settle in and make as much of a contribution as he was capable of doing. He did a fine job and got all of his parts right.

VG: Have you ever done any instructional videos?

SH: I did one that I don't care for too much, called "The Turbulent Plan;" I think it's a bit "flaky" (chuckles). Some parts of it are fun, though, and I still do guitar clinics. I enjoy doing those, but sometimes I think I'm going to talk for a short time, then I go on for *ages*; it's almost like someone is tempted to drag me off! I like being able to prepare thoughts on a certain angle of guitar playing, and being able to share those thoughts. Since I'm self-taught, I can't really talk about learning how to *play* the guitar.

VG: Any comment about how the 4-disc *Yesyears* anthology turned out?

SH: Well, I think there were some mistakes made on it; I really pushed for the complete version of "America," with the introduction and the guitar solo, but the version that was on the anthology was the one that had been released as a single to try to get some airplay.

One thing that I *was* happy about was the inclusion of "Montreaux's Theme;" it's the only existing copy of a very intricate piece of music that we wrote. I enjoyed that kind of playing; I think I played a Stratocaster on that piece. I didn't play a Stratocaster much with Yes; I recall using one on "Parallels."

VG: Your book also noted your use of a Strat on the *Drama* album.

SH: That's right; I view the *Drama* album as having been made by a special and unique band, almost like a "supergroup Yes," since the Buggles were in with us. Having Geoff and Trevor was like injecting Yes with liquid mercury!

VG: There was also a *Yesyears* video.

SH: (chuckles) I could talk a lot more about the CD anthology. I think there's a lot of "chat" on the video that is unnecessary. I don't think musicians look that good when they're talking about themselves, particularly on television. Radio's not a bad medium for talking, but sometimes even that gets overdone. What a musician *plays* is important.

VG: How did the project with the Chinery guitars evolve?

SH: I met Scott through some friends in New York; we did some guitar business, and then he asked about playing his collection on an album. I though it was a lovely idea, but I told him I had a bit of a problem with the repertoire. I don't play tunes by other people all that much, but I know a few songs. So after some exchange of ideas, it was decided that I'd produce the album and make some appearances on it, and I approached Martin Taylor about being on the album as well; I'd produced his 1992 album *Artistry*. He's an exceptional jazz guitarist, and it's a good team. We've gotten seventeen tracks done as of today. We do some duets, and there are a couple of tracks where I'm on my own, but the bulk of it features Martin. This is a showcase for Martin, and for Scott's guitars as well.

The record is almost wrapped up, but we haven't recorded the track with the "blue guitars" that Scott commissioned; we'll do that when all of those guitars are ready.

VG: Any plans to tour with Taylor to promote the album?

SH: This has been fun; it could be interesting to see what develops. Obviously, Martin and I don't need the Scott Chinery Collection to play duets, but this collection has presented an opportunity for us to play together, and there are some amazing instruments that we've been able to use. The Chinery collection is quite astounding; it's quite broad, and we had a lot of guitars to choose from when we recorded.

VG: As for any other possibilities in the future, what about plans for Yes? The news that you recorded in San Luis Obispo was a complete surprise to me, and it will probably surprise a lot of our readership as well.

SH: I think we'll record again, although when and where and who will be involved isn't settled. There were some rumors that Rick wouldn't be able to go any further, but I think he was quite excited about doing the shows and the recording, so maybe there's a future in it for everybody who was together in early March.

Steve Howe's recording projects are as eclectic as his playing style, and he's passionately dedicated to doing his professional best with whatever instrument he's playing in whatever genre, yet Howe's playing simply can't be pigeonholed. That's always been the case for the veteran guitarist, and considering his future prospects and projects, the breadth of Steve Howe's stringed instrument abilities will also mean that it's highly unlikely his playing will *ever* be pigeonholed. And thank goodness for that.

Tom Johnston
Doobie Redux

It had been a busy year for Doobie Brothers guitarist Tom Johnston when *Vintage Guitar* chatted with the veteran player while the band was taking a break from touring; 1995 promised to stay hectic for the legendary rockers, as an overseas tour was in the offing shortly after the short hiatus. From his home in Northern California, Johnston discussed his years of experience with the Doobies as well as his departure in the late Seventies for a solo career that yielded a hit single. The guitarist opted to participate in a reunited Doobie Brothers band in the mid-Eighties, and it's been a steady ride since then:

VG: What were your musical influences when you were growing up?

TJ: I grew up in central California, in the agricultural belt between Fresno and Bakersfield. My influences were all R & B; mostly blues. The earliest stuff I listened to that I liked were songs by Little Richard, Bo Diddley, Jimmy Reed, and Freddy King; later on I got into James Brown, which wasn't a guitar influence, but it was great R & B.

VG: During your youth, wasn't the Bakersfield area noted for singers and players like Buck Owens and Merle Haggard? Mosrite guitars would have been made in that area around that time.

TJ: Yeah, it was "Nashville West." Mosrite was considered the big surf guitar when I was in high school, but the first guitar I had was a broken archtop Harmony that I bought from a friend for twelve bucks. I never did fix it; it played fine but it had a crack in the top. From that I went to a Kay single-pickup electric and some funky little amp. That was followed by a Kent with two pickups, after which I got a 335 and a Bandmaster amp, so I was finally playing some decent stuff. That would have been in 1964; I was just playing in high school bands. We played a lot of pop stuff, and if I had anything to say about the song list, as much R & B

Freeze Frame: Tom Johnston performs with the Doobie Brothers on "The Tonight Show" in July of 1995.

as possible. I was in one band that played half Beatles, half James Brown. Later on, I ended up in a Mexican wedding band, and a soul band that only played in black bars in Tulare.

VG: The liner notes on one of the Doobie Brothers CDs noted a band you were in called Pud.

TJ: That was in 1969, when I moved to San Jose to go to San Jose State. We had a horn section; we were kind of rock and soul and wrote all of our own stuff. It was sort of along the lines of something like the Sons of Champlin. We even had chick singers, and that ended up getting pared down to a hard rock trio. I played in several bands at one time back then, and eventually John Hartman, Dave Shogren, Pat Simmons and I formed what became the Doobie Brothers.

VG: One of the things I'd heard about the earliest days of the band was that you honed your chops in biker bars.

TJ: Well, we played bars and bikers showed up; there was one bar in particular; the Chateau Liberte up in the Santa Cruz Mountains. We *did* go to one Hell's Angel's convention, but we didn't actually play because another band was so high they wouldn't quit; they were *wired.* (laughs)

VG: The first album's lineup had the foursome you just mentioned, and the song "Nobody" got a bit of airplay. There was "loping" or "chugging" guitar style on that song that ended up as a "signature" on many Doobie Brothers songs; tunes like "Listen to the Music" and "Long Train Running."

TJ: That was basically my rhythm playing, which comes from the R & B background, but by then I was playing a lot of acoustic guitar and doing a lot of writing on acoustic. I'd also played solo acoustic guitar in clubs; Pat was also "acoustically-oriented" when we ran into him, but he wasn't too much into the rhythm thing; he was into finger-picking. Both of us "transferred" our playing styles to electric as well.

VG: What kind of acoustic guitar were you playing then?

TJ: I had a Gibson J-50 that I dearly loved; it got ripped off in 1974.

VG: What about your equipment setup when the Doobies got going?

TJ: I still had the Bandmaster, and was playing an SG by then. I'd started with an SG Special and I moved up to an SG Standard later. I loved their long necks and tone, but one problem was that you couldn't push on the body; they acted like they had a whang bar even if they *didn't* have one! (laughs) But they were fun to play and they weren't very expensive. Later, I switched to Ampeg amps and I also got a Goldtop Les Paul.

VG: The Doobies were a guitar-oriented band, then *The Captain and Me* had some Arp synthesizer on some of the tracks.

TJ: That was on maybe three songs; I ended up playing it myself. It was pretty much the producer's idea.

VG: I don't think I've asked an interviewee this before, but based on some concert footage and photos I saw back then, it looked like the band members would sweat a awful lot. Were there ever any physical problems like heat exhaustion onstage?

TJ: There were some times when you'd just about pass out onstage, and that still goes on. (chuckles) If you're playing in the South and the temperature is about ninety degrees and the humidity's around a hundred percent, the stage lights can add another ten or fifteen degrees. Back in those days, playing in clubs could be pretty hot as well. There've been gigs where I think I've lost about eight pounds.

VG: Back then the band appeared on shows like "In Concert" and "Don Kirshner's Rock Concert"; why wasn't any live material released from the days of your first tenure with the Doobies?

TJ: I don't have any idea. We did a couple of "Midnight Special" shows too; Burt Sugarman's show.

VG: When you quit the band in the mid-Seventies, is it fair to say that Jeff Baxter took your place?

TJ: That wasn't the case at all; he'd come on board in 1974, and had gone on the road with us

some in 1973. He'd actually played on some of our songs as far back as *The Captain and Me*.

VG: If I remember correctly, the press cited your departure from the band as being for "health reasons."

TJ: More like "health and sanity." (laughs) I'd been on the road for six years; I was "toast." I just needed to get away from it for a while; I got into lifting weights and I *put on* some weight; played baseball and football. Then in 1979 I did my first solo album, and I did another one in late 1980.

VG: The first one had the improbable title of *Everything You've Heard is True.* How was that title supposed to be, uh, "interpreted"?

TJ: "Musically or other ways." (laughs)

VG: When that album came out, the Doobies were more into a "blued-eyed soul" facet, in my opinion, thanks to the presence of Michael McDonald. Did you set out to make your album to sound more like the Doobies used to sound?

TJ: Well, it probably did sound that way, but I just did what I always did, plus a couple of things I'd always wanted to do, like "Show Me" by Joe Tex, and I used the Memphis Horns quite a bit, but the rhythm style that we discussed earlier was obviously still there. The Doobies had used the Memphis Horns on two albums, and they'd toured with us, too.

VG: Your first solo album came out during the halcyon days of Disco, and the hit, "Savannah Nights," *does* have a dance beat.

TJ: Well, it didn't originally; I got nicked on that when I wasn't looking. That's not the original drum beat I was looking for at all, but that's the way Teddy [Templeman, the producer] decided it ought to sound. I remember coming into the studio one day and saying: "What the hell is that kick

Album photography from the Doobie's The Captain and Me, *released in the early 1970s.*

drum doing in there?" I think they were looking to get a song on the charts as a result of what was going on in the music world those days, but that was the only song on the album that had that kind of rhythm. Basically, there wasn't anything added but the kick drum, and that's what Disco was all about anyway.

VG: I thought "Show Me" might have charted if it had been released as a single; it was a great cover.

TJ: I was real pleased with it too; the Memphis Horns are on it, and Billy Payne from Little Feat played some great piano on it. There are a lot of all-stars on that album, including Jim Keltner and Bob Glaub.

VG: What about the second album?

TJ: It was called *Still Feels Good*, and I might as well have not made it because it sure as hell didn't get any airplay. I'm always shocked if a fan brings a copy for me to autograph, because not many people have that album.

VG: What kind of equipment were you using by then?

TJ: I was playing a Firebird that I got from Johnny Winter and using Music Man amps. That guitar was stolen as well.

VG: You appeared on the live album that was the supposedly the "farewell" venture for the Doobie Brothers in 1982.

TJ: I was invited over; I played on three songs and sang on two of them. They were serious about packing it in.

VG: When and why did the first reunion event take place?

TJ: In 1987 we got together to do a Vietnam veterans benefit. Keith Knudsen was the one that organized it, and we had almost everybody who'd ever played in the band up on the stage at one time. Four guitarists, four drummers, two keyboard players, bass and percussion. Two more benefit gigs followed that one, then we did ten more gigs to pay for all of it. After that, we did a concert in Russia that was a Bill Graham project.

As for recording, the *Cycles* album in 1989 was a reunion of the "early" band; then we did another album in 1991 called *Brotherhood*.

VG: At one point you also did a benefit for the family of Bobby LaKind, the percussionist who had inoperable cancer.

TJ: Bobby was on the *Cycles* album, but wasn't with us after the first leg of the first tour to support that album. After we found out he was sick, we did some concerts, and he played them; he hung in there. That was kind of like the 1987 Vietnam veterans benefit; *everybody* who'd been in the band showed up to play. Bobby died on Christmas Eve of 1992.

VG: Once things got going again in 1989, was the band trying to get the same "feeling" as the Seventies albums had?

TJ: The reunion of the "early" band was Teddy Templeman's idea, but he didn't end up producing *Cycles* after all. We used three different producers on *Cycles* including Rodney Mills, who produced all of *Brotherhood*. I think "The Doctor" sounds like "China Grove" in reverse. (laughs)

VG: By the time *Cycles* came out, music videos were a factor in the business. My perception was that "The Doctor" and "Need A Little Taste of Love" were both performance videos; one studio, one concert. "The Doctor" showed you apparently ad-libbing to the camera, as well as John Hartman chasing the "track camera."

TJ: "Need A Little Taste of Love" was done at that resort where Stevie Ray Vaughan did his last show. There were cameras flying all over the stage where we did "The Doctor"; they were filming from at least four different angles. Chasing the track camera was just an example of John being John... (chuckles)

VG: You were seen playing Paul Reed Smith guitars by then.

TJ: That's about all I play now. I started using them around late 1985 or early 1986. I went on a USO tour around the time I bought my first one; I took it and an Explorer along. The more I played the P.R.S., the more I liked it, so I got another one that I liked even better; I still have that one and I now have a total of six.

VG: How did *Brotherhood* differ from *Cycles*?

TJ: A *lot*! (laughs) We were trying to go in another direction; we wanted to get away from the "standard Doobie sound". I wrote a song with Jerry Williams called "Excited"; I was real happy with that, and I liked a couple of songs I wrote for that album as well. I'd been inspired by Eric Clapton's *Journeyman* album; I'm an *avid* Eric Clapton fan, and Jerry had written five of the songs on that album, including "Pretending" and "Alibis."

VG: One reader wanted me to inquire about some European dance re-mixes of some older Doobies material like "Listen to the Music" and "Long Train Running." I'm not familiar with them.

TJ: (chuckles) Unfortunately, I've heard them. I'm not real thrilled at all with what I heard. I may make royalties off of such, but I don't like the idea. All it is is Disco; they've used the original lead vocals, background vocals, and conga drums, which they've bumped *way* up in the mix; I'd forgotten they were even on the track. They've added things like a new bass; the drums are the worst-sounding things I've ever heard in my entire life.

VG: You're about to embark on a tour with Foreigner to Europe.

TJ: This should be interesting; we're playing a lot of places that we haven't played before, like Copenhagen and Glasgow. Another difference is we'll be doing it by bus instead of airplane.

VG: Do you collect guitars?

TJ: I used to have tons of them, but I got rid of most of them; they were just sitting around, so I figured I didn't need them if I wasn't playing them. They were taking up too much room in my studio here in my house. I've still got my Les Paul, a 1956 Strat, and a hand-built Strat-type guitar with EMG pickups that a friend of mine who used to be one of our roadies made; he's a hell of a guitar tech. I got another Firebird to replace the one that was stolen, and I've still got a 335, a Telecaster, a Dobro, three Martins. I've even gotten rid of some Paul Reed Smiths I had; I suppose if someone wants to decorate their house with guitars, that's fine, but that's not my thing.

VG: Future plans besides the European tour?

TJ: We're going to be recording at European concerts, then we're going to Australia. Warner is putting out a boxed set as well; the live stuff is being recorded to be used on it. There may be some unique things like acoustic versions of some songs. We'll be recording when we get back, so it looks like we'll be busy for most of the year.

Tom Johnston's distinctive singing and guitar playing have been important facets of Doobie Brothers songs for many years, and he looks to future projects with eager anticipation. He's got a commendable work ethic for a famous musician, and his ongoing career just keeps "chugging along"....just like his playing style.

Mick Jones
"Concert for the Kinfolks"

Veteran guitarist Mick Jones' most successful band is back in action with its original singer. The multiple-platinum band Foreigner is out on the road with vocalist Lou Gramm back on board; Gramm had departed the band to pursue a solo career, and Foreigner had actually recorded one album, *Unusual Heat*, with another singer. However, Jones and Gramm worked out their differences in 1992, and when we interviewed Jones the band was in the middle of an extended tour.

Our interview situation with Jones was a bit different from others. The circumstances involved sort of a "family affair" for the guitarist, not just because his brother Kevin is the tour manager, but also because their mother's cousin resides in the town in which we caught the band's performance. We had a backstage pass for the show, but the Jones brothers had some relatives to visit with before our interview could be recorded. Kevin Jones and this writer decided that the best opportunity would be back at the hotel, so Mick Jones was the first performer that this reporter interviewed *right after* a performance. Nursing a Bud and munching on a submarine sandwich, the guitarist reminisced about his decades in the music business, and what it's like to be back out on the road with the original lead singer back in the band:

VG: How did relatives of yours end up here?

MJ: My mother's best friend was her cousin; we used to call her "Auntie Joyce," and she's now known as "Mama Joy" here. She married an American and came over here after the War. She's lived in California and other places; turned out they settled here. She and my mother still write and talk with each other quite often; they're still quite close. When we knew we were going to play here I knew we'd need to see her; they roped off a special section at the venue tonight for my relatives.

VG: I'll go ahead and ask you about Radio Luxembourg; I usually ask every veteran British player about the music they heard when they were coming of age, and they all cite that station.

MJ: Same for me. Chuck Berry, Gene Vincent & the Blue Caps, Buddy Holly.

VG: What about your earliest experiences in British bands? Any British players that influenced you?

MJ: My "mentor" was a guy named Colin Green; he played with Georgie Fame and the Blue Flames. He was a couple of years ahead of me in school; we lived in Portsmouth, south of London. When I was about fourteen, he would take me up to London on Saturdays where they would get tours going; I'd see Gene Vincent and Eddie Cochran getting on their busses. I decided that was what I wanted to do for my life's work (chuckles).

My first band was called Hogsnort Rupert; I was playing with them by the time I was sixteen. We played American blues, R & B, soul music. Then I joined Nero & the Gladiators, which was an instrumental band, but we were doing a different thing compared to the Shadows. We'd do pop versions of classical music; things like "Hall of the Mountain King" by Grieg and "Entry of the Gladiators."

VG: That sounds like an early version of a band like the Vanilla Fudge.

MJ: It was! After I joined them, they eventually became a soul band and dropped the instrumentals. One reason for the change was because I couldn't play all that fancy ****. (laughs)

VG: What about your progression of instruments back then?

MJ: My first instrument was a Hofner Senator, which was a semi-acoustic. Then I had a Burns two-pickup solidbody; I've forgotten what the model was but it was a cherry red color.

Then one day I walked into a store on Shaftsbury Avenue in London; that's where all the music stores were. Jimmy Page and Jeff Beck were in there and they'd just gotten their Danelectro double-octave guitars from the States. But I spotted an SG/Les Paul, and I got my father to sign for it on credit. I used that guitar for the next four or five years.

It's also the guitar that I dropped onstage when

Mick Jones. Photo courtesy of Atlantic Records.

I was opening for the Beatles (laughs)! I was in a band that was backing a French singer named Sylvie Vartan at a Paris performance; she later married Johnny Halliday and I played behind him as well at one time.

VG: Wasn't he like "the French Elvis"?

MJ: He still is (chuckles)! His fiftieth birthday was this year, and they had a *huge* celebration in Paris.

Now, when I was backing Sylvie Vartan as an opening act for the Beatles, on the second night the curtain came down between us and the Beatles and caught the headstock of my SG; it dragged it to the floor. John Lennon came up to me and inquired if I was English; he invited me to "have a drink with the lads after the show." I was seventeen then and of course totally in awe of the Beatles; I mean, who *wasn't* back then? This was right before they came to America; they took me under their wing, and I literally lived *A Hard Day's Night* for several weeks (chuckles). We still keep in touch; I played on a couple of songs on George's *Dark Horse* album.

VG: What about recording? When did that start?

MJ: I formed a band with Gary Wright called Wonderwheel after the original version of Spooky Tooth split; we did some of his solo stuff. Then Chris Blackwell at Island Records suggested that Spooky Tooth re-form; by that time Luther Grosvenor had taken the stage name "Ariel Bender" and was playing guitar for Mott the Hoople. I was Spooky Tooth's lead guitarist on three albums, *The Mirror*, *The Witness* and *You Broke My Heart So I Busted Your Jaw*. After that I did an album with the Leslie West Band; that lasted about nine months to a year, and I was so frustrated about how things went with that, I was thinking about getting out of music altogether. Than I started to write songs.

VG: Is it fair to say that up to that point you'd been pretty much of a sideman?

MJ: Not exactly; in many of my situations I had to take a back seat, so to speak, but I'd been the "musical director" and "arranger" for such

bands. It had been quite a rollercoaster experience, but I was trying to learn my craft.

VG: For all of your experience and frustration, Foreigner's first album must have seemed to make it all worthwhile, since it established the band as a major act immediately.

MJ: The album was produced by Gary Lyons and John Sinclair with Ian McDonald and me; Ian had played with King Crimson and he played guitar and sax with us. He and I had done a lot of mixing, and late one night I sat down and listened to the final version of the first album before it was released. I thought it was the best thing I'd ever done in my life, and I felt so high just listening to it. Whatever had happened to the first album sales-wise, I was completely satisfied with how it sounded. I'd never done anything up to that point that made me feel like I'd achieved something, but this album gave me a great feeling. I suppose the record-buying public agreed, considering the sales of it.

VG: Around that time, there was a television special hosted by Edwin Newman called "Land of Hype and Glory." I heard Foreigner was originally supposed to be a band cited in that documentary, but the producers opted for KISS instead.

MJ: I wasn't disappointed by that situation at all. You know, the way I felt the band should be "presented" caused some problems, including some problems between Lou and me. I always thought the band shouldn't push any personalities; we never thrust ourselves forward as a "visual" or controversial band. So for that attitude we eventually became known as a "faceless" band.

VG: I was discussing "arena rock" bands with Gary Richrath, the former guitarist for R.E.O. Speedwagon. We agreed that "arena rock" wasn't always a complimentary term, and he opined that the "Big Four" of the genre were R.E.O., Styx, Journey and Foreigner. He said that there were other terms some critics used about such bands and that maybe "faceless" was one of the other descriptive terms. Comment?

MJ: I think it needs to be noted that I was from the "English school" when it comes to the use of the word "faceless," the way Pink Floyd was a "faceless" band, for example. The American use of the term seemed to mean "bland," so I resented that term a little bit if it was used in the American context. My idea was to keep us private, and to let the music do the talking. Looking back, I can see we've matured and I'm proud of what we've done, just as I'm sure someone like Dave Gilmour is proud of what he's done.

VG: What was the largest gig Foreigner ever did?

MJ: California Jam 2, which was pretty soon after we broke. We did songs like "Cold as Ice" and a primitive version of "Hot Blooded"; the studio version hadn't been recorded yet.

VG: As far as large events go, it seems like I read you were rebuffed by Bill Graham about playing at Live Aid, but you did do the first Farm Aid concert.

MJ: We weren't "rebuffed," we weren't asked. I got a bit put out about it, but it seems like there's always a trendy little group of elitists who always want to do all of these wonderful things for humanity. Your Stings, your Peter Gabriels... it seemed like at Live Aid anybody who was a "hustler" could get on the bill, but we weren't hustlers.

VG: I think your band did a real classy thing by shuttling a choir onstage during "I Want To Know What Love Is." Was that a regular feature on that tour?

MJ: Yeah; we didn't know what to expect at Farm Aid, but it was great. We'd played a show in Kansas City the night before, flown in at 3 A.M., then we had to go to Nebraska to do a show that night. We were wondering about Farm Aid being more country or folk music-oriented, but the place went bananas; we had a tremendous time.

VG: A few years ago, you had a solo album out, and I saw two videos of songs from that album. The one of "Just Wanna Hold" appeared to be sort of an "all star" effort.

MJ: Billy Joel and Christie Brinkley were on it; I'd produced Billy's *Storm Front* album. Sean Lennon and Ian Hunter were on there as well.

VG: In that video you were playing a Les Paul Jr., and I saw a Gibson endorsement poster of you with the same model. What appealed to you

about the Junior?

MJ: It had a raw, basic, funky sound. Over the years, however, I've really only used about three guitars; in Spooky Tooth I played a Gibson Stereo that had originally belonged to Big Jim Sullivan. I bought it in 1969 and used it until about 1974; it was stolen in Buffalo, New York. I've got a three-pickup Les Paul; I took the middle pickup out of it. It has a *great* neck on it. There's also a custom-made two-pickup SG that I had made for me last year.

VG: I read that Lou Gramm and you had been talking to each other, and apparently things are going well once again.

MJ: Right; this tour is running like clockwork, and we'll be recording again soon as well.

VG: Not to sound like a cliché, but are you saying "It's good to be back"?

MJ: Well, you were at the concert tonight. What do *you* think? (smiles)

Indeed, perhaps the most memorable image of the aforementioned Foreigner concert was that of dozens of outstretched hands pointing in the direction of the stage as a beaming Mick Jones flung guitar picks in their direction when the concert was over. He looked like he was having the time of his life. For all of his experience, Mick Jones is still committed to making music to the best of his ability, and he wouldn't have things any other way. He's developed his "craft" to a successful and enviable level, and he anticipates further success in the future.

John Kay
The Steppenwolf Story

John Kay with his Rickenbacker 381JK Limited Edition.

...and that of the Sparrow as well. Veteran rocker John Kay has been active in the rock music scene for decades, and Sparrow was a pre-Steppenwolf Canadian group that achieved a modest amount of success; members of Sparrow formed the "core" of Steppenwolf, which exploded onto the late Sixties music scene with the now-"anthem status" hit, "Born to be Wild." The band experienced mega-success, and as is usually the case, experienced personnel changes as well, until calling it quits after numerous gold and platinum albums.

Ultimately Kay ended up back recording and touring with a band known as "John Kay & Steppenwolf;" the reasons for the slight name difference were detailed during our interview. John Kay now resides in the Nashville area, a great distance from where he was born; as we settled into our interview, *VG* began by inquiring about Kay's heritage, which we had forgotten was non-Canadian:

VG: You're originally from Canada, aren't you?

JK: Actually, I was born in Prussia, which up until World War II was the eastern part of Germany. The Russians were coming in, so my mother and I fled; I was just a baby at the time. We ended up stranded in East Germany for several years, then in 1949 we escaped to West Germany, where we stayed until I was about fourteen. In 1958 we moved to Toronto, Canada, where I spent my high school years, and then in 1963 we came to Buffalo, New York. I stayed there about a year and met some great musicians; I was just starting to get serious about playing music then. I ended up going to Los Angeles and other places around '64 and '65,

and in 1965 I went back to Toronto for what was supposed to be a visit, but I ended up playing in coffeehouses and ultimately joined Sparrow before the year was out. So I've been around (chuckles)!

VG: As "transient" as you were, what kind of music do you recall hearing?

JK: With my European upbringing, there was a German folk music background; stuff that was passed on from generation to generation in schools and within families. Around 1956, I stumbled across rock and roll due to the Armed Forces Radio Network; I heard Little Richard on the radio around the time rock and roll motion pictures began to be shown in Germany. *Don't Knock the Rock* for example; Little Richard was in that picture. During the last two years I was in Germany, I became a collector of singles; albums were out of the question due to my modest finances! I listened to Radio Luxembourg as well, although I had to do it somewhat surreptitiously late at night, under my bed covers with an earphone (chuckles).

It was quite different once I got to Canada. I listened to not only Canadian stations but Buffalo stations as well; there were rock stations in both Canada and Buffalo, but I'd also listen to Buffalo stations that played R&B, black gospel, country and western. All of those styles had something to offer, and the first year I was in Toronto I didn't know many people my age, so I immersed myself in listening to the incredible variety of music on the radio; I'd never heard anything like it. I soaked it up like a sponge. Around that time I got my first guitar, which was an acoustic Kay. A new friend in school gave me a Hank Williams songbook, which had chord diagrams. That was the next step; learning to play chords so you could sing along with what you were strumming.

VG: What about your first electric instrument?

JK: I got an inexpensive Harmony around 1961, along with a Harmony amp that had one twelve-inch Jensen speaker. The guitar was black with two pickups and a sort of pearlescent pickguard; it had one of those somewhat "ungainly" shapes, but it wasn't ugly enough to be one of those "hip" models that we now admire like some Supros and Silvertones. It wasn't horrible, but it wasn't distinguished in any way, shape or form. I did the best I could with it; I didn't know much about string action. Lonnie Mack had "Memphis" out back then, so I'd see how much of it I could accomplish on the Harmony.

As it turned out, when I came to Buffalo I completely abandoned electric instruments; I sold what I had and got my first *decent* guitar, a Gibson J-45. Before that, I'd played in a trio where all of us ran through an Ampeg amp that I'd gotten to replace the Harmony amp. I bought the J-45 when I came to Buffalo because I got interested in the folk music phenomenon; Peter, Paul and Mary, the Kingston Trio. I checked out a lot of albums from the public library; I learned about Appalachian dulcimer music, bluegrass, etc., but what really made me sit up and take notice was listening to old Delta blues recordings. I even heard some early recordings by McKinley Morganfield; he was recorded by John Lomax; it was a "field recording." From there I got into Robert Johnson, Son House, Bukka White, Leadbelly, Mississippi John Hurt, Sleepy John Estes; the list is almost endless.

VG: Was McKinley Morganfield the name on the label, or was it Muddy Waters?

JK: McKinley Morganfield; it was a Library of Congress recording of "I Can't Be Satisfied" and one or two others. Later, when I started to listen to Chicago blues by artists like Little Walter, Howlin' Wolf, and Sonny Boy Williamson, I realized that Muddy Waters and McKinley Morganfield were the same man. Yet at the same time I was listening to music by artists like Richard and Mimi Farina, Tom Paxton, and Len Chandler; folkies. So I kind of had a "dual education."

VG: Was it the folk movement that took you to L.A.?

JK: Well, a friend of mine from Toronto picked me up in Buffalo; we went across the country in his Triumph TR-3. We went to places like Santa Monica and Hermosa Beach and listened to some of the West Coast surf bands. It wasn't quite what I was into, but it was interesting. We were out there for several weeks, and when we got back I came to the quick conclusion that what Buffalo had to offer musically paled in comparison to what I'd just seen; while on that vacation I'd heard an incredible variety of music. Since I'd graduated from high school, I informed my parents that I wanted to move to the West Coast. They informed me that in my absence, they'd had a chat and had decided for their own reasons that they wanted to move to that area as well, so we all migrated out there together. We settled in Santa Monica in the late summer of 1964.

I tried to get my bearings soon after we arrived; I started scanning the local newspaper, looking for ads for folk clubs and coffeehouses. I began hanging out at clubs like the New Balladeer and the Troubadour; people that were around back then included David Crosby, Jim McGuinn, Tim Hardin, and Taj Mahal. I began playing such places myself, and later I hit the road and more or less worked my way across the country back to the East Coast; all I had was my J-45. I stopped back in Buffalo for a while; it hadn't changed much. Then I went up to Toronto; I got a gig in a small coffeehouse there and met a singer named Johnny Seay, who got me into the folk club scene in New York for a while. Seay played the Bitter End, and I got to see Woody Allen doing some stand-up comedy there, working on some of his material. It was an exciting time, but I eventually got my gig back at the Toronto coffeehouse. While at a party upstairs at that club, I met the keyboard player for a Canadian rock group called the Sparrow. He told me he liked the way I played harmonica, and invited me

Steppenwolf poses for a Rickenbacker publicity photo in the late Sixties.

The current line-up of John Kay & Steppenwolf is (left to right): Michael Wilk, Rocket Richotte, John Kay and Ron Hurst.

to sit in with them.

VG: Sparrow didn't get a record deal until you joined; I thought you were a founder.

JK: No; they'd been around for a while. I jammed with them on some blues tunes, and soon afterwards the keyboard player left; they replaced him with Goldy McJohn and added me as well. Goldy, as you probably already know, made the transition to Steppenwolf.

VG: He also had a big Afro for a white guy.

JK: (laughs) It was out to his shoulders! I put a DeArmond pickup in my J-45 when I joined Sparrow.

VG: Seems like I saw a photo of you playing that instrument with Sparrow at some debutante ball; the photo was in some publication like *Life*, *Look*, or maybe the *Saturday Evening Post*.

JK: We'd been to New York before to record some demos, and we eventually played there often; we played places like the Barge out on Long Island, where the Rascals had supposedly been discovered, and Arthur, which was Sybil Burton's jet-set discotheque. The debutante ball was for the Woods family's daughter; I don't think they were even from New York, but it was a big coming out party for her. The Peter Duchin Orchestra was there for the "society music"; we showed up in Mod outfits with our Fender Bassman amps.

I have to admit, though, that the younger contingent was a lot more hip to what we were doing, their income bracket and monkey suits not withstanding (chuckles). They not only knew about the Rolling Stones covers we were doing, they knew about players like Paul

Butterfield; I was pleasantly surprised. All we did were two twenty-minute sets, and we not only had a good time, we were compensated quite well (chuckles)!

VG: Did you play the J-45 throughout your venture with Sparrow?

JK: Well, I convinced the band that the West Coast was where things were happening, so we migrated out to there and checked into the Tropicana Hotel on Santa Monica Boulevard in L.A., like most out-of-town bands did back then. Another band called the Poor had also just come in from Colorado; most of them eventually went on to play in Rick Nelson's Stone Canyon Band except for Randy Meisner, who ended up as the bass player for the Eagles.

The J-45 was stolen from a club soon after we arrived in L.A. We were signed to Columbia, so with the CBS connection we were able to get some Fender equipment. I got a Telecaster, which was so nondescript-looking that I stripped off the finish to the bare wood and stained the instrument a walnut color; I had to hock it after Sparrow broke up, which was before Steppenwolf formed.

VG: Did Sparrow break up while in L.A.?

JK: We'd moved up to the San Francisco area and had rented a house in Mill Valley. We got into the Frisco music scene, playing places like the Avalon, the Fillmore and the Matrix. Steve Miller sat in with us a lot; he had a great band and he was a terrific harmonica player. Sparrow broke up in the Spring of 1967; Steppenwolf didn't form until late summer. There was a three or four month period between bands, but a lot of people think Sparrow simply "evolved" into Steppenwolf, which wasn't the case. Dennis Edmonton, the lead guitar player, got a solo songwriting/recording deal and changed his professional name to Mars Bonfire. Nick St. Nicholas, who had been the bass player, started playing with a local band called Time. That left Goldy, drummer Jerry Edmonton, who was Dennis's brother, and me; we sort of went our separate ways but kept in touch.

VG: How did the formation of Steppenwolf occur?

JK: I'd gotten married; we were living in a small apartment over a two-car garage in Hollywood. A neighbor of ours was Gabriel Mekler, a producer for ABC/Dunhill Records; his wife was also Canadian, but he was born in Israel. We got to talking, and he asked me to play him some of Sparrow's material. He thought it was interesting stuff, and asked if I was still in touch with the other guys. I got hooked up again with Jerry and Goldy; we got two local guys to complete the band, Rushton Moreve on bass and Michael Monarch on guitar. Michael was only seventeen; he'd sat in with the Sparrow some. We did some demos and Gabriel convinced ABC/Dunhill to sign us.

Things were still snug in the money department; my Telecaster and my Showman amp were still in hock. My wife had taken a job as a cocktail waitress, then she got pregnant with our daughter. ABC/Dunhill loaned us some equipment that they'd purchased for another band. There were Jordan amplifiers, a Fender Esquire which Mike got, and some other stuff. I got Mike's "Mos-Vox," which was a Mosrite body with a Vox neck; it was, shall we say, "unique" (chuckles). But I was from the "acoustic school"; it worked for me when I put heavy-gauge strings on it; I still use heavy-gauge strings.

The first album was recorded in four days on an eight-track machine for a cost of $9,000. We cut seven tracks the first day, four tracks the second day, I did eleven vocals the third day, and we mixed all eleven songs the fourth day. Everything was recorded "live" with the exception of some vocals. We got by with minimal equipment; Goldy's organ was a Lowery that was cranked to distortion. He made it sound like a Hammond with that percussive style of his; he and Jon Lord from Deep Purple were probably the two most percussive keyboard players around back then.

VG: "Born to Be Wild" and "Hey Jude" were *the* songs heard on Top 40 radio during the Summer of 1968.

JK: In fact, "Hey Jude" kept us out of the Number One spot; it was Number One and "Born to Be Wild" was Number Two for weeks. When "Magic Carpet Ride" came out, it zipped up the charts a lot faster since it was following behind "Born to Be Wild," which was our ground-breaking hit. "Magic Carpet Ride" also topped out at Number Two; I think the Number One song was one of the Supremes' biggest-ever hits. In the final tally, "Magic Carpet Ride" outsold "Born to Be Wild" by about 300,000 units.

VG: I've always suspected that the *Early Steppenwolf* live album was technically the Sparrow.

JK: It was; by the time *Early Steppenwolf* was released, Nick St. Nicholas was Steppenwolf's bass player, so four-fifths of Sparrow were now in Steppenwolf; the only one not around was Dennis Edmonton, alias Mars Bonfire, who had written "Born to Be Wild"; he also played rhythm guitar on "Magic Carpet Ride." You couldn't get much closer than that.

The record company had contractual rights for two albums a year from us. By the third album things were getting "spotty"; some of the tunes on *At Your Birthday Party* are still among my all-time favorites, while others were without question filler material. That album had a short-lived "up and down" time span on the charts. The company was wanting another album out soon, and the fellow who had been the manager of the Martix in San Francisco approached ABC and told them he'd recorded the Sparrow every night we'd played there without telling us; he had two mikes hidden in the ceiling. We listened to the tapes and didn't like them, but the

company decided to issue a "collector's item" album to help out for a while before we came out with another new album. We didn't have any control over it.

VG: "Born to Be Wild" has been covered by many other name bands, including the Blue Oyster Cult and Slade. Have you ever heard any covers of Steppenwolf material that you thought were commendable?

JK: I liked Humble Pie's version of "Desperation"; there's also an interesting version of "Magic Carpet Ride" that was recorded by Billy Paul, the singer who did "Me and Mrs. Jones"—

VG (interrupting): You gotta be kidding.

JK: (chuckles) Nope. There's also another recent cover of "Magic Carpet Ride" on the *Coneheads* soundtrack that was recorded by Slash from Guns & Roses.

VG: When did the band officially split?

JK: After an album called *For Ladies Only*.

VG: That was the album that had the phallus-shaped automobile on the inside cover.

JK: Ah, yes; the infamous "Richard-mobile" (laughs). That photo was taken in front of Graumann's Chinese Theatre on Hollywood Boulevard during a Sunday matinee. When people exited, some laughed, but some were taken aback. The L.A.P.D. descended on the vehicle like a plague of locusts, trying to bust the driver for some infraction, but he had everything in order, even back-up lights. One policeman was really hassling the driver; the driver told the policeman: "If you think this is interesting, you ought to see the garage I park it in!" (laughs)

Shortly after that, everyone in the band pretty much realized that we were drained of inspiration and creativity, so we went our separate ways. I did a couple of solo albums, but after about a year and a half, we did a Steppenwolf tour of Europe with the John Kay Band as the opening act so I could promote my solo career. That tour led to the reuniting of Steppenwolf in the mid-Seventies; we did three albums.

After that we went our separate ways again; I spent a lot of time with my family, because my daughter was at an age where I wanted to be around; plus I wanted to get my batteries recharged. We traveled a lot in our RV, and flew to Hawaii several times. In 1978, after writing some new tunes, I recorded a solo album in Muscle Shoals called *All in Good Time*.

VG: We haven't discussed the instruments you used throughout your Steppenwolf days.

JK: Well, I got the Telecaster out of hock (chuckles)! I used it a good bit, then our management worked out a sponsorship deal with F.C. Hall of Rickenbacker. I used several of their instruments, and we also used those unusual Transonic amplifiers; I think Led Zeppelin and us were the only ones to use those through Rickenbacker's sponsorship. We were sponsored by Sunn amps at one time as well.

I had a few Dan Armstrong clear-bodied guitars; I used those for things like slide on "Magic Carpet Ride"; I played in standard tuning, but when I play blues with a slide, I prefer open tuning. I have a 1938 Dobro *metal-body* guitar at home that I really enjoy playing; it's a rare instrument because most of the Dobros back then had wood bodies. Only about eighty of those were made.

VG: Do you collect?

JK: Not really, but I do have a few old instruments. I have a fairly old L-5, a 1942 D-28, and others. I like those guitars, and I *use* them; I'm not one to buy guitars and put them away. I'd like to get some National guitars, a tri-cone and the other style. I just read Bob Brozman's book on Nationals; it's really well done.

VG: Are there any guitars you've gotten recently that you like?

JK: About a year and a half ago I got an all-black Gibson J-200, which is probably the only guitar I've ever bought because I wanted to have one; I remember seeing Elvis playing one in *Loving You*. It's a Bozeman-made guitar with a piezo pickup built into the bridge.

VG: Your current performing outfit is called "John Kay & Steppenwolf"; is that due to some kind of legal hassle about the Steppenwolf name?

JK: That came about in 1980, because when I was doing my solo thing in the late Seventies, we got wind that there were a couple of bogus Steppenwolf bands out there. I went out with that new name to stop what I considered to be the systematic destruction of the band's name and reputation, but a lot of damage had been done. We hit the road like a young band, criss-crossing the U.S. and Canada several times for four and a half years; we also went to Europe a couple of times. We painstakingly built our reputation back up, starting with what were "toilets" and working our way up to concert venues.

One of the things I've stressed from the get-go is that we're not a nostalgia band; we've recorded some albums and are ongoing. We're not just playing our old hits. At this point in my life I'm not interested in continuing to play only what I've already done. I'm still writing songs and I'm looking forward to recording again as well.

VG: A while back in *Bass Player* magazine, a letter from a reader complained that the current band doesn't have a bass player; apparently the bass parts are sequenced. Comment?

JK: Since 1985, the bass chores have been handled exclusively by our keyboardist, Michael Wilk. He plays keyboard bass live on some songs; the bass part is a completely separate set up with its own amplification. There are some songs where the bass part is sequenced, because Michael's playing full-bore on a Hammond B-3 or he's playing alternative parts.

We have a variety of bass samples available to us; Fender and Rickenbacker, among others, depending on what the song calls for. The point is, Michael himself has created those bass lines; I can understand why bass players might have a problem with that, but it's not a new phenomenon. Everybody is already aware that the Doors had a keyboard bass, and Jimmy Smith played the bass pedals on his organ. The decision to go that route in '85 was an economic one as much as any other reason. I don't buy into the "techno-phobia" or "organic" school of thought that thinks things shouldn't change. Granted, there are some people who go to the other extreme, trying to create music with nothing but machines, eliminating human beings; I don't buy into that line of thinking either. I think of the new technology as another tool for musicians.

VG: As far as traditional-style guitars being created with some

modern innovations in their construction, your signature Rickenbacker might be an example to cite. How did that come about?

JK: John Hall contacted me in the late Eighties; we'd known each other for years. He told me about Roger McGuinn's limited edition twelve-string, and would I be interested in discussing a similar project? Out of all the guitars I'd ever played, the Rickenbacker 381 was probably the most unique, because of its style as well as its sound. I also liked the fact that Rickenbackers were American-made and hand-made as well. John told me that their Research and Development was right up there with every other manufacturer's, so we started planning on a guitar with an unusually broad range of tonal choices.

The 381JK had two humbucking pickups with a four position switch to give choices between single coil and humbucking sounds, active and passive choices, and a phase switch. The one that I got has a built-in Nady wireless system, but that isn't a standard feature.

I think it's important to point out that Rickenbacker and I worked on this instrument piece by piece; another thing we collaborated on was the color. I told them I needed a high-contrast instrument so I could see what I was doing onstage; I'm legally blind and have been since birth. The 381JK was black with a silver pickguard and chrome hardware; it also had special inlaid fret markers. And *I play this guitar onstage every night;* it doesn't sit in a glass case in my house.

VG: Why did you move to the Nashville area?

JK: After twenty-two years in the Los Angeles area, a lot of changes had taken place, and not all of them were to my liking. I'd reached a point where I wanted to deal more with music instead of the business of music. Around here people still make a lot of great music for the pure enjoyment of it. I live out in the country; there's no hot air or B.S. like one encounters all too often in the L.A. music scene.

VG: Any other recording coming up? Other future plans?

JK: We'll be mixing our first live album in twenty years soon; there's a 24-track studio across the lake from where we live. The tracks were recorded over the last two years. We still have a hardcore base of fans, and we have a small but very efficient organization, including the road crew and musicians.

I've been very lucky in a lot of ways; these days I think it's fair to say that I'm comfortable but not complacent. I'm still married to the same woman after twenty-seven years, and our daughter has grown up; in many ways she turned out better than we might have hoped, so we must have done *something* right as parents (chuckles). I'm able to continue writing and playing while being able to *enjoy* what I'm doing; I think a lot of people might not realize how important the "enjoyment" aspect is to a musician. I've been very fortunate.

John Kay knows what it's like to have been up and down in the music business. These days, he is going at his own pace and on his own terms, which many musicians aren't able to do. While he still may be in a "journeyman" status with his current musical venture, if such a situation suits him fine (even as he aspires to larger accomplishments), he's got it better than a lot of players.

Mike Keneally
On Beyond Zappa

The cover of Mike Keneally's latest album, *Boil That Dust Speck*, is chock full of symbolic imagery that's primarily people-oriented. A pair of scissors is prominent, and the working title of the album was *Snip*, for more than one reason: Keneally's father and Frank Zappa (for whom Mike was the lead guitarist on the avant-garde icon's final tour) both died while the album was being recorded; on a more positive note, Keneally's daughter Jesse was born during the recording of *Boil That Dust Speck*. Accordingly, the scissors not only represent the severing of "generational apron strings," but the cutting of an umbilical cord as well (Jesse's sonogram is also found inside the album).

Mike Keneally was born on Long Island, but his family moved to San Diego when he was eight; he describes himself as "virtually a Californian." He states that his "pre-Zappa" playing experience was "as obscure as obscure can be. I was playing in Top-40 clubs; occasionally I got to play original material in showcase clubs, but it was a time when there wasn't any kind of a scene surrounding 'original rock' in San Diego. So I was either playing original music that nobody ever heard, or Huey Lewis tunes in cover bars," he laughs.

The direct step from that environment to Frank Zappa's band was as improbable as some of the music that Zappa and Keneally made. "I called his office and asked for a job," Keneally relates. "It was a case of the most fortuitous timing imaginable. Frank had toured in '84 and lost money, and said he'd never do it again. Then I heard in '87 that he was getting a band together. My reaction was that I'd get to see him play again, but then I decided that if I was ever going to realize my dream, I had to take a big step then. I told his office that I played guitar, sang and played keyboards, and was familiar with everything Frank had ever done. What I *didn't* know, and didn't find out until quite some time later, was that he'd had a guitarist/vocalist in the band who'd disappeared that week, as well as a keyboard player who'd been asked to leave. So there was some 'guiding force' at work there.

"Frank evidently got the message; he called back two days later, telling me to get to his place and prove I was familiar with his material. My brother drove me up while I sat in the back seat of the car and practiced all the way from San Diego to L.A.," said the affable guitarist.

Keneally had first heard Zappa's material around 1970 or '71, when he was nine years old. The first album he heard was the Mothers of Invention's *Freak Out!*, which was the incongruous band's first release, but it was several years old when it caught Keneally's attention. "It was new to *me*," he says. " 'Help I'm A Rock' was the first song I heard. I was a strange kid anyway, and it seemed to fit in so well with my lifestyle. The next album I heard was *We're Only In It For The Money*; I had no idea you could do that kind of music on record. From that point on, I was hooked for life."

Other guitar proteges during Zappa's career included Adrian Belew and Steve Vai. "I don't get compared too much to Adrian except maybe in terms of songwriting; Adrian and I share a deep love of the Beatles, and that really shows more in his songwriting than it does in mine. But Steve and I both grew up loving Zappa, so naturally that influence shows up in our playing. I'd have to say that Frank was far and away the largest influence on my soloing and improvising."

The guitars utilized by Mike during his tenure with Zappa actually belonged to the late composer/musician/artist; the main two guitars were a Fender Tele and Strat that had been modified with parametric EQ devices. "I was a babe in the woods regarding tone," says

Mike Keneally.
Photo by Victor Molina

Keneally, "and I had to learn; in fact, you never stop learning." Keneally's current setup includes a Clapton Strat as a primary guitar, run through a Rivera 100 Duo-Twelve and a Fender Blues Deluxe; "It's not a stereo signal," he states.

Other Keneally guitars include a Heartfield Talon, a Fender Reissue '53 Telecaster, a Hamer Duo-Tone, and a Fender Custom Shop guitar made by Mike Stevens.

Keneally still has access to the aforementioned Zappa-owned Fender guitars anytime, because among his post-Zappa projects has been an association with Ahmet and Dweezil Zappa in a band called Z. He's also recorded with Screamin' Jay Hawkins and Marc Bonilla, among others; his own band for solo projects goes by the name of Beer For Dolphins.

In a review of *Boil That Dust Speck*, *Bass Player*'s Jim Roberts says that Mike Keneally "gets my vote as Frank's heir apparent." Keneally expressed disbelief about the comparison: "I'm flattered; having worked with Frank and having been familiar with his music for twenty-four years, I know that *there is no heir apparent;* there will never be another Frank. I think in my own way, I'm paying tribute to

Frank by trying to be as creative and interesting as possible when I do my own music. I'm tremendously honored by a compliment like that."

Among Mike Keneally's *non-playing* ventures is writing a column for *Guitar Player*. Keneally has plenty of projects in the future to keep him busy, and if such activity is as unique as what's heard on *Boil That Dust Speck*, it should make the days ahead quite interesting for the guitarist. The eclectic mix of music on this album ranges from goofy fun to serious, competent chops; one of the thirty (!) tracks is all of eight seconds long. One listen is all is takes to make it obvious why the Zappa comparisons are valid.

But ultimately, *Boil That Dust Speck* might best be described as a high-tech audio equivalent of an old-fashioned county fair spookhouse ride; i.e., "Strap yourself in and hang on, 'cause ya don't know what's comin' up around the next corner."

Yet for some strange reason, you find yourself wanting to ride it again.

Keneally parted ways with the Zappa family/ organization in the Spring of 1996.

TOP LEFT: *Mike Keneally.*

TOP RIGHT: *Mike Keneally (center) onstage with Frank Zappa (left foreground) in the late Eighties. Photo courtesy of Society Pages.*

Anthony Kenney
Full Circle with a Fender Bass

Technically, bassist Anthony Kenney is a new member of the Kentucky Headhunters, but his playing experience with Greg Martin, Richard Young and Fred Young (the remaining 'Heads following the departure of the Phelps brothers in mid-1992) goes back for decades, since Kenney was a member of Itchy Brother, the combo that beget the Kentucky Headhunters. Not surprisingly, he's kinfolks as well; the Young brothers are his first cousins.

Prior to a recent concert, Anthony Kenney relaxed in the motel room he was sharing with Greg Martin (who was interviewed by *Vintage Guitar* in 1992), and detailed what it's been like to come full circle with a band that he began in before he was a teenager:

VG: Were there any relatives of yours from the previous generation that inspired you and your cousins to play?

AK: My dad was a local rockabilly-type performer at a "jamboree"-type place up the road in Cave City, Kentucky; he'd take me up there when I was three or four, and I'd beat on this upright bass that was there. I guess that old "doghouse" bass inspired me; my dad also showed me some chords on a guitar. I'd show those chords to Richard, and then Richard took some formal lessons from a local guy, so we decided we'd save money if he'd show me what he'd learned (chuckles).

VG: What about instruments back then?

AK: The first guitar I remember was an old blond acoustic Silvertone with f-holes that my father owned. My own first electric was a Silvertone electric that my father bought me when I was about

five; even at that age I went straight to an electric; I didn't get an acoustic first.

VG: So when was your first public performance?

AK: When I was about eight or nine; Richard, Fred and I played a Fall festival for a grade school. I think Fred had a fourteen-dollar set of drums, Richard had something like a Univox copy of a

Gibson 355, and I had a Teisco with four strings on it. I think we played "(I'm Not Your) Stepping Stone" by the Monkees and maybe "Louie Louie."

Eventually I graduated to a Gibson EB-0; this would have been around '69 or '70; I was using a Vox transistorized amp with one eighteen inch speaker and a G-note tuner built into it.

VG: Was the band called Itchy Brother by then?

AK: No, it was called Truce. Around the time I got the EB-0, Greg started coming into the picture; he'd always gone to school with Richard and Fred. Greg had moved to Louisville, so he'd bring down cool albums like ones by the Cream; we were a little behind the times in our area (chuckles). Greg was playing that Gretsch Silver Jet of his back then.

We recorded a 45 at a small two-track studio, and put it out on our own "King Fargo" label. We had to come up with a name, and one of Fred's favorite cartoon characters had always been Itchy Brother from the "King Leonardo Show," so we used that name for the band. We had the minimum of copies of the single pressed, which was probably five hundred, and we sold maybe ten copies (laughs). We'd throw copies of the single from the stage when we did gigs at shopping centers.

Greg's move to Louisville finally meant we had to get another guitar player. During that time I sold the EB-0 and bought a two-pickup Epiphone bass that looked sort of like a P-Bass; it had two pickups and a bolt-on neck. I used a Sound City hundred watt head and something like a six-ten cabinet for

Top: Itchy Brother waxes unserious in 1983 - Anthony Kenney, Greg Martin, Fred Young, & Richard Young (left to right) This photo was taken for a reunion show.

Left: Current publicity photo for the Kentucky Headhunters. Pictured from left to right, Fred, Mark, Greg, Richard and Anthony.

the latter days of disco, it was impossible to get a deal.

There were times when Greg would move back to Louisville, and I'd have to take over the guitar player position; we'd bring in a bass player. I'd use Strats and Les Pauls; we did that several times. We had a good demo tape that Thoroughbred made, but nothing ever happened, so we all sort of went home and did our own thing. But that tape was partly the reason that Richard, Fred and I got signed as staff writers for Acuff-Rose Publishing in Nashville. We met a guy named Mark Orr, who's now the Headhunters' singer. We got him to sing on those Thoroughbred songs; we got him to come to our old practice house, and man, he could *wail*! He was as excited as we were; he thought he'd finally found a band that was headed in the same direction he was. We did more showcases, but nothing ever happened again, so Thoroughbred disbanded, but we kept in touch with Mark.

VG: Had you or the Young brothers moved to Nashville by then?

AK: No; we just did our writing there in Kentucky and drove down to Nashville whenever we needed to; Mark and I ended up in a regional band called Daddy-O; Kevin Woods, who wheels and deals in guitars, was the other guitar player besides me.

Around this time, Greg and Richard called me about getting Itchy Brother back together, but I'd just gotten married and had a pretty secure "day job" at the time, managing a hardware and lumber store. I'd didn't want to go out on the road for weeks at a time, so I passed. Greg had been playing with Ronnie McDowell, so I told him I thought Doug Phelps, who was Ronnie's bass player, would work out real good for them, which he did. So the Headhunters started out as a four-piece, but Doug eventually brought his brother Ricky to a practice session to jam, and he ended up being the singer.

VG: It wasn't until around then that the radio show got going, right?

AK: Yeah, and I was the producer/engineer for it; I could handle it since it was one night a month. I was still working at the hardware store and playing in Daddy-O, but based on how well the radio

an amp.

Eventually, Greg came back into the scene; I was maybe twelve or thirteen by then. Greg was the only one old enough to drive, so we started playing places a bit further out like Louisville. We bought an old van to haul our gear, and started playing sort of a club circuit.

VG: All of you were underage.

AK: We never did have any problems with the club owners; we always had an adult go with us. Some of our parents would go; they were real supportive. Itchy Brother disbanded several times over the years; the main reason being members having to get jobs, but Fred and I were still in school, so we couldn't go out and do a week-long gig at a club.

At one point, Mitchell Fox from Swan Song Records came to Louisville to hear us at a club called the Sound Stage. He got real interested and took tapes of us back to England for Peter Grant to hear, but John Bonham died around then, which put things in turmoil for that company. We were sort of disillusioned, and went our separate ways for a while. About a year and a half later we got back together, but we called ourselves Thoroughbred; we were looking for a name with a Kentucky image. Mitchell was involved then too; he brought us to New York to do some showcases, but since this was still during

TOP: *Itchy Brothers in 1977 - Greg Martin, Anthony Kenney, Richard Young and Fred Young.*

RIGHT: *This cover for an Itchy Brother 45 rpm record dates from 1973, Anthony Kenney is sitting in front; behind him are Richard Young, Fred Young, and Greg Martin.*

show had gone over, Ricky called me one night and offered me an opportunity to be the band's producer/sound man. But I still didn't want to get involved with something like that, which would foul up the other things I had going on.

The Headhunters got signed to Mercury, so Greg had to leave Ronnie McDowell, and I told Greg that I'd be interested in taking his place in Ronnie's band, because that *would* be something that was "musically secure," so to speak. So I auditioned for Ronnie's band and got the gig; I was his guitar player for three years.

VG: What sort of instruments did you play in McDowell's band?

AK: I used a late Sixties Strat, and then I got some reissues to take on the road because I didn't want to take my old guitars out. There were some occasions where I'd use a '66 Telecaster, too. It was the kind of gig where you'd travel as light as possible (chuckles). I used a Mesa-Boogie amp for a while, and I also used one of the reissue Bassmans that Fender had started making; I never did like the channel-switching idea on amps. I've always felt like if you want it your guitar "clean" you turn it down; if you want it "dirty" you crank it up.

VG: Have you always used tube amps, regardless of whether you were playing guitar or bass?

AK: The only time I didn't was when I used an Acoustic 370 bass head for a while during the Thoroughbred days. It was four hundred watts; the speaker cabinet had four fifteens in it; two front-loaded and two folded-horn types. Other than the Vox I had way back, that's the only transistor amp I've used.

VG: How did the Headhunters gig come about?

AK: Someone told me the Phelps were going to leave; I watched something like a press announcement on a Nashville show; maybe it was "Crook & Chase." I called Fred up to ask what was going on, and Fred told me to get ready, because Richard, Greg and he wanted me to come play bass for the Headhunters.

VG: And I'm sure it wasn't too difficult to get used to bass once again, considering the other musicians in the band.

AK: And it made me realize that it would be hard for me to pick up a bass guitar and perform with someone other than Fred Young playing drums. We think so much alike, doing "kicks" and things. We'd played with each other since we were three.

VG: So if you were to get a call from someone saying something like "Aaron Tippin needs a bass player for his road band," you'd decline?

AK: Absolutely. (pauses) Now, if the Rolling Stones called... (laughs). I found out while playing "country bass" in other gigs before I joined the Headhunters that it sort of stifled my writing a bit; I could be a lot more expressive when I was playing guitar.

I'll have to say, though, that my favorite bass players are ones that are simple, in-the-pocket players like Bill Wyman, and Joey Spampinato from NRBQ.

VG: What adjustments did you have to make getting back into bass playing?

AK: Interestingly, I use a pick with a bass live, but recording *Rave On* and the Johnny Johnson album, I found that using my fingers got a little bit warmer sound and cut down a bit on noise. But as hard as this band goes at it live, I have to use a pick, and our sound man knows what to expect.

VG: What about instruments?

AK: When the Headhunters called me, all I had was a Yamaha in my home studio. I had some Strats that I'd used with Ronnie, and I took a blue sparkle one to Jimmy Brown at Guitar Emporium in Louisville, and we worked out a trade for a white '57 reissue P-Bass with a gold anodized pickguard. It played good; it had a maple neck, and I prefer rosewood necks, but it was all he had at the time. For amplification, I ended up getting two Ampeg SVT-2 rack-mounted tube heads, and Ampeg cabinets.

I told Ronnie about what was going on; he'd been really good to me and I wanted to help him find someone to replace me so the transition would be as smooth as possible. It turned out that Kevin Woods took my place with Ronnie, and he's still with him.

VG: I've seen you playing a sunburst P-Bass as well.

AK: Richard set me up with Mark Wittenberg of Fender, and Mark sent me a sunburst '62 reissue P-Bass. It's my favorite bass of all time, and I've got a black one as a spare. It's not "broken in" like the sunburst one is. To be honest, that sunburst '62 reissue is probably the best P-Bass I've ever played, and that includes the old vintage P-Basses I've tried. Fender's been real good to me; they're putting out some fine reissues. I've also got one of their new SRV Strats.

VG: Have you ever owned any collectible instruments?

AK: At one point I had a Hofner violin-shaped bass like Paul McCartney has, and a '66 Strat, and a P-Bass. They were in my home studio of my new house when a main plumbing shut-off valve blew out while we were off doing a VH-1 special. It destroyed all of them; I had insurance but those instruments were irreplaceable. Since then I've been a little leery about collecting. If I was playing *guitar* instead of *bass*, I might want more instruments. I wouldn't mind having one of those Danelectro reproductions that Jerry Jones makes, though; and that's because of Joey Spampinato; he uses flat-wounds, and he gets one of my favorite tones. Every member of the Headhunters is a *huge* NRBQ fan. I've tried some Danelectro shorthorns from Guitar Emporium, but I haven't the right one yet, which is why I might want to think about a Jerry Jones.

VG: What's up next?

AK: We've got a "greatest hits" album due out next, and we've recorded a couple of cover songs that may end up on it. We're thinking that it's time for a live album too. We're still writing new stuff, but it's been hard to write since this season's been really busy for us; we recently did twenty-three gigs in Canada, for example. The last Canadian performance was near Seattle, and the next gig was in Orlando four days later; that's how long it took us to get there (laughs)! And it ended up getting rained out!

We'll be going back into the studio, so there's that to look forward to as well. We'll be staying busy; we've already got gigs lined up in '95.

Anthony Kenney is a veteran guitarist and bassist who's in a current situation that probably suits him just fine. It's all the more of an enjoyable gig since he's playing with the kinfolks with whom he grew up, and his eloquence in recounting the development of the Itchy Brother/Kentucky Headhunters aggregation was straightforward and expressive, just like his bass playing.

B.B. King
...and the "B.B." stands for "Birthday Boy"

Riley B. King was born on a cotton plantation in Indianola, Mississippi on September 16, 1925. Following a childhood spent in poverty, he made his way to Memphis in 1946, where he forged a career in the music business, under the stage name of B.B. King (the "B.B." stands for "Blues Boy"), and he's been playing, touring, and recording almost non-stop ever since; he'll be seventy years old this year.

But most *Vintage Guitar* readers are probably already aware that the King of the Blues was playing, touring and recording before the vast majority of them were even born. They're also probably already aware of Mr. King's pronouncements on the blues (who can have 'em, who can play 'em, etc.).

Accordingly, when *Vintage Guitar* was able to arrange an interview with B.B. King prior to a recent concert (he still performs about 250 times a year!), our approach was to inquire about facets of Mr. King's fabled career that would be of the most interest to guitar players, since *VG* is a "specialty" periodical.

We were escorted into a small, private dressing area following a press conference; a relaxed and eloquent Mr. King patiently answered our questions in a courteous and efficient manner. Some of his responses were somewhat surprising:

VG: The story of your dash back into a burning nightclub in Twist, Arkansas to rescue your guitar is well known to most of your fans, but do you remember the make and model of that guitar?

BBK: I remember the make but not the model; it was a little black Gibson guitar. You can see it in some old pictures that we've had made up; my name was put on it with a paint brush. It was an acoustic, believe it or not, with a DeArmond pickup on it to make it into an electric.

VG: Let me ask about some of the other instruments that I've seen you playing in some older photographs. There's that famous picture of you performing onstage in shorts; you're playing a big three-pickup Gibson ES-5.

BBK: (laughs) That picture still haunts me! One of the reasons I liked that one was because my idol T-Bone Walker had one; he was so *flashy* with his. I liked it, but it just never seemed to "fit" me right. It was big; I had one that I gave to my father, and when he died I got it back. I still play it sometimes. When the guitar that became the "Lucille" model came out, that was the one for me; that did it.

VG: Do you remember which pickups you used the most on the ES-5?

BBK: No; I don't know much about the electronic parts of a guitar. If something went wrong with my guitar tomorrow, and I couldn't find anybody to fix it, I'd be in big trouble! I like guitars where the neck feels right in my hands; that's what's important to me. Since '49 I've played all kind of guitars, Epiphone, Fender, you name it.

VG: There's another historical photo of you playing a single-pickup Fender Esquire.

BBK: That was one of the first ones that came out.

VG: When the Gibson came out with their thinline semi-hollow series, which model did you start out with?

BBK: The 335; it was like somebody knew what kind of guitar I'd been wanting. The 355 "Lucille,"

with no f-holes, is what I play now.

VG: Do you use the Vari-Tone on it all that much?

BBK: I never use it at all. I think of this guitar as sort of a big brother to the Les Paul; to me, the Les Paul guitar is one of the best guitars that's ever been built, and the neck of the 355 is similar to the neck of the Les Paul. I like the larger, "butt" part of the 355 body, because it fits under my arm real well (pats right side of rib cage).

VG: Did you make your first recording in l949?

BBK: It was the latter part of '48; I made my first record for Bullet. The first four sides were "Take A Swing With Me," "Miss Martha King," "How Do You Feel When Your Baby Packs Up To Go," and "I Got The Blues."

VG: What about the amplifiers you've used over the years? That photo of you in shorts with the ES-5 showed you playing through a Fender tweed amplifier.

BBK: Yes; the old Fender amplifiers were the best that were ever made, in my opinion. They had a good sound and they were durable; guys would throw them in the truck and they'd hold up. They had tubes, and they'd get real hot, but they just had a *sound* that is hard to put into words. The Fender Twin was great, but I have an old Lab Series amp that isn't being made anymore. I fell in love with it, because its sound is right between the old Fender amps that we used to have and the Fender Twin. It's what I'm using tonight.

VG: You mentioned T-Bone Walker being an idol of yours; he was from Texas instead of Mississippi, and he played unique chords and did arrangements, instead of "three-chord-and-three-string" blues songs.

BBK: Well, he was just *one* of my idols. Lonnie Johnson was another; so was Django Rheinhardt; so was Charlie Christian. I also liked Chet Atkins; there was Blind Lemon Jefferson out of Texas.

VG: Some people differentiate between what they call "Texas blues" and "Delta blues."

BBK: (chuckles) Well, I don't agree with that; I think it's the *person*. There's a lot of us from Mississippi, and we all don't play alike. John Lee Hooker and I don't play alike; Muddy Waters and I didn't play alike. I knew about Robert Johnson, but I wasn't crazy about Robert Johnson like a lot of people are; I knew he was great, but my "Johnson" was *Lonnie;* he's the one I was crazy about.

I've always been wanting to play better; I was crazy about a guy named Johnny Moore, who had a group called the Three Blazers, which included Charles Brown. Johnny Moore was the brother of Oscar Moore, who was the guitar player for the Nat Cole Trio.

VG: Oscar Moore was usually seen playing a big Gibson L-5, I think.

BBK: And Johnny Moore had one just like it! He taught his brother how to play.

There are many other guitar players I could talk about that never made a name for themselves, and I listened to a lot of them as well.

VG: How did you get yourself into other performance venues other than what was known as the "chitlin circuit"?

BBK: I augmented my group; we started to be like a Big Band, kind of like Count Basie. I was still able to play places where we'd played before, but we got into some new places. For example, there was a club in Chicago called Mr. Kelly's; they'd never had blues in there; it was always jazzed-up. When I augmented my group, they brought me in. That was the first time that club went from strictly Jazz to a different sound. Elvis came on the scene around '54, and after that the British bands "re-imported the blues," as I call it. Then I started playing places like the Fillmores.

VG: Back then, you made a comment that Peter Green was a player who could make you "sweat," so that's at least one white British player who was playing what you considered to be "authentic" blues.

BBK: The thing is, I didn't think about what color he was, and I don't think about such now. So when I said that, I didn't mean he should be thought of as a white player, but just as, excuse the word, a *damn good player.* He could really get me excited. He was a great player and a good friend. He hasn't been playing any lately; I saw him about two or three years ago, and he was working as something like a pallbearer in a graveyard.

VG: How many albums have you recorded?

BBK: Seventy-four.

VG: A lot of guitar players are partial to live albums, and at your press conference earlier this evening, you alluded to the possibility of another one coming up. I'd like to ask about a couple of them; for example, your bio refers to the *Live at the Apollo* album as a "Big Band" album.

BBK: Yes; that was done with an eighteen-piece all-star orchestra; every guy on that stage was a star in his own right.

VG: The guitar tone on the San Quentin live album seems to have a bit more of an "edge" to it. Any reason why?

BBK: (chuckles) No; it was just the way I was feeling, the type of amp I had, and the facilities. Like I said earlier, the technical stuff is something I don't think about; it's just whatever's sounding good to me *now* (laughs).

But there *are* a couple of sounds on albums that I made that stand out in my mind. I don't really talk about it, but when I did "The Thrill Is Gone," I thought I had a good sound. When I did another tune called "Blues At Midnight," the sound of that amp was exactly like I like. There's been another song or two, but other than that it's just a case of me feeling good and the amp sounding good. Those songs just stand out to me as having a sound I wish I could get more often.

VG: You were interviewed by Billy Gibbons for *Guitar Player* magazine, and when I interviewed him for this publication, he cited Ry Cooder's observations about the "musicness" of Memphis. Comment?

BBK: When I first got to Memphis in '46, I heard sounds that I thought were heavenly; sounds I'd never heard before. The musicians weren't putting on; they were just playing casually, like they were playing cards, and it sounded better than anything I'd ever heard. From time to time, you can *still* hear that. There are a lot of musicians that are in Memphis that have that sound that you wish you could have every day, but they don't want to travel; they just hang around Memphis.

VG: You've participated in some notable charity events, such as Live Aid and the first Farm Aid. There were a lot of different types of acts, but I thought "How Blue Can You Get'"'s line about "I gave you seven children and now you wanna give 'em back" was *still* the showstopper that it always seems to be.

BBK: (laughs) It *is* one of my favorites. A lot of people don't know that tune was written by a famous music critic, Leonard Feather, for Louis Jordan, who used to do funny things like that. But I heard it and liked it so well I decided I'd record it; I think many of the best recordings that I've done through the years have been tunes that were written *by* somebody else, *for* somebody else, and I happened to hear it, but it seemed like the songwriter was asking me: "B., is this the way you want it?" (chuckles)

VG: Another musician I once interviewed offered the opinion that "the blues always seems to come around and shake things up a bit whenever it's needed." (Mr. King laughs) It *does* seems like the interest in blues music has been somewhat "cyclical," for lack of a better term.

BBK: I don't quite agree with all of his comment, but part of it I *do* agree with; it *does* seem to shake up things from time to time. I think what happened is there have been times like when the British bands came over in the early Sixties, and they made the U.S. as a whole aware of blues, when the blues had been there *all the time.*

VG: I've interviewed American players who acknowledged that the British bands made them aware of the blues; one of them told me that he was made aware of the original blues musicians, right here in his own back yard, so to speak.

BBK: Right; that's exactly what we're talking about. So when a lot of them stopped playing it, then a lot of Americans thought that the blues had gone away, but the rest of us that had been here all along were still playing it, and we never stopped. Sometimes they use the word "resurgence" when they talk about the blues, and I have a bit of a problem with that, because today the blues is more popular than it's ever been since I've been trying to play it. And a lot of it has to do with the young people who are playing it and supporting it.

VG: You're coming up on your Seventieth birthday; you're not ever going to retire, are you?

BBK: I don't see any reason to, as long as people still want to hear me. What else would I do? I was a disc jockey once; that's the only other job I'd like. I was born on a plantation; worked on a plantation. It was hard work, but it prepared me for what I do today, and I don't regret any of it.

There are so many young players that are great; they'll keep the interest in the blues going. Stevie Ray Vaughan was one of the best blues players *ever.* Then there's another young man named Robert Cray, and a young man out of Canada named Jeff Healy. (appreciative whistle) He's *mean!* These players are superstars with the youth; in my case, I'm not a superstar, I'm just a guy that's been out there for a long time; I've been doing this for forty-five years, so I might as well keep on.

VG: With all due respect, I think most blues lovers would debate you concerning your statement that you're not a superstar.

BBK: Well, thank you (smiles).

Following our interview, B.B. King and his band put on a show that ran almost twice its scheduled length. Mr. King plans on staying active; his future plans include not only the aforementioned live album, but a CD-ROM as well, and a possible autobiography. He's a busy man, but is that any surprise? That he is able to look back at decades of accomplishments yet still look ahead to future projects is admirable, particularly since many blues lovers consider B.B. King to be the pre-eminent purveyor of the musical genre that he himself loves so much.

Vintage Guitar would like to thank Mr. Sherman Darby and New Era Promotions for their courtesy and help in arranging the interview with B.B. King.

King was one of the Kennedy Center Honors inductees in 1995. He also toured constantly, taking out his Blues Music Festival in 1995, 1996 and 1997. He was seen on several TV shows, and did some funny commercials for companies such as Wendy's, and for products like M & M candy.

Kostas

The Songwriter As Eclectic Collector

It may seem like a bit of a paradox that a single-monikered songwriter of Greek extraction has written best-selling hits for some of the biggest names in Country music, but that's exactly the case for Montana-based Kostas (who frequents California and Nashville as well). His 1994 album, the cryptically-titled *X S in Moderation*, includes liner notes from Dwight Yoakam, Patty Loveless (who also appears on the album), and Marty Stuart (whose extended narrative details the growth of Kostas's guitar collection, among other things).

Other songs written by Kostas have been hits for Travis Tritt, Holly Dunn, and McBride & the Ride, and many other artists. Kostas was named 1990 NSAI Songwriter of the Year, and has received other honors and awards as well. Not bad for someone who was raised in a small town in Montana.

Kostas' Montana childhood was the prime reason he got into Country music; "Country music was about all anybody listened to back then," he says. "As a kid, I'd sell papers and shine shoes, then sneak into bars and sing 'On the Wings of a Dove'. I wasn't writing back then, but I was learning about music."

These days, Kostas spends his summers in Montana, just outside of Bozeman, site of the Gibson acoustic guitar factory. While that may sound like a convenience to a serious guitar lover like Kostas, he noted: "I was there before they were" with a laugh. "All of my friends that used to be musicians are working at the Gibson plant."

While Kostas' songwriting abilities have enabled him to build a large collection, he says "I've always had a passion for guitars, mandolins, and banjos, plus other instruments. I like the older ones; they don't have to be 'precious'; they just have to have been played by someone and enjoyed. If someone wants to discard something like that, it's got a new home if I find it."

Kostas collects both acoustic and electric instruments; at a California guitar show (the first he'd attended) he purchased a circa-1916 Gibson harp guitar and a Rickenbacker double-neck steel guitar.

The interest in classic American fretted instruments parallels Kostas' feelings about the music such instruments played. "I think American music from this century has influenced the world in many ways," he opined, noting that "American instruments are the best. Whenever I find something that's old and unusual, I'll usually pick it up." Accordingly, his extensive collection includes practically-extinct instruments such as old tiples and plectrum guitars. He *does* wheel-and-deal in an effort to improve his collection, but admits with a chuckle: "I've bought more than I've sold."

The number of instruments in the songwriter's collection is now considerably more than the highest figure cited in Marty Stuart's linear notes, but Kostas says: "I don't sit around counting them." The assortment includes a Martin guitar made in 1860, and a Civil War "squeezebox" that he describes as "unbelievable; it's mother-of-pearl and brass inlaid; just beautiful." When queried as to the favorite instrument in his collection, (the ol' "if you-were-stranded-on-a-desert-island-and-could-only-have-one-instrument" scenario), Kostas responded: "It would have to be something that I could play *and sing* with," ultimately deciding on his 1941 Gibson SJ-200; "It sounds and plays good"; he noted.

As eclectic as Kostas' collection is, he's still seeking other unusual instruments. "I *love* the old National cast-aluminum lap steels; they've got kind of a 'art nouveau' look to them."

X S in Moderation (produced by Val Garay and Kostas) is an excellent sampler of Kostas songwriting abilities, but it's also a fine album from a musical viewpoint. It's chock full of

Kostas with his favorite guitar, a 1941 Gibson SJ-200.

think he/she is hearing a vocalist possessed by the ghost of Roy Orbison.

Kostas plans to keep writing and performing; when asked about branching out into other genres besides Country, he stated that while he's not known in the Pop or Rock fields at the present time, word is getting around about his tunes. "I don't really write Country; the songs may end up *being* Country once they're written, but I'm as capable of writing in other 'directions' as well," he said confidently. "It's all music to me."

The affable songwriter/collector may not fit many persons' image of a stereotypical "human Nashville hit machine," but Kostas' guitar collection isn't very stereotypical either. He anticipates further success in his songwriting and recording career, and his passion for his craft, like his passion for American instruments, is one of Kostas' biggest assets.

fiddles and steel guitars, but it's Kostas' plaintive singing that gets the point of each song across. On ballads like "If You Think" and "That's What I'm Gonna Do," a listener might

Kostas with one of his finds at the guitar show in Pomona, California

Robby Krieger

Different Doors, Different Directions

The mysterious, sitar-like intro to "The End." The lyrical guitar solo in the extended version of "Light My Fire." The howling slide tone (replete with a tremelo) that shrieks out from a live cover of "Who Do You Love."

As most readers probably already know, guitarist Robby Krieger is responsible for those licks and many others on classic songs by the legendary L.A. quartet the Doors; other members included Ray Manzarek on keyboards, John Densmore on drums, and the late Jim Morrison on vocals. Krieger also wrote or co-wrote a large number of the band's tunes as well. He was born and raised in Los Angeles.

Since that band's demise in the early Seventies, Krieger has ventured through other musical "doors" in an effort to apply his guitar playing and songwriting to different genres. In fact, his playing experience prior to his association with the Doors wasn't what most folks might think, but when Krieger called at the appointed time for his interview, naturally our first inquiry was Doors-related:

VG: Over three years ago in this magazine, I noted a Doors concert video in a column. The video was from a '60s television show; I think it was Ed Sullivan's show. The song was "Touch Me," and there was a string section plus a solitary sax player who did the solo at the end of that tune. It appeared that you had a hell of a black eye

whenever the camera showed you playing. What's the story on the shiner?

RK: I get asked about that a lot, and the TV show was the Smothers Brothers show, not the Ed Sullivan show. Jim and I had a fight, and I wouldn't let the makeup people put anything on it. I figured that if I left it alone, twenty years later somebody might ask me about it, and that's definitely how it's turned out (chuckles).

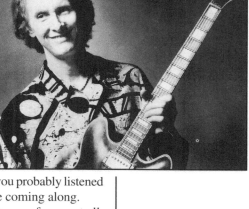

VG: It would be logical to assume that since you're originally from L.A., you probably listened to surf music when you were coming along.

RK: That really wasn't the case for me at all, although I was aware of that kind of music. What really made me want to play guitar was hearing flamenco music. I listened to players like Sabicas, Carlos Montoya, Serrano. My father happened to go to Spain on a business trip, and he bought me a hand-made Ramirez flamenco guitar; I still have it. He paid two hundred dollars for it; it's probably worth about five thousand now.

After that I got into jazz guitarists; Kenny Burrell, Joe Pass, and Herb Ellis, for example. Years later, after the Doors had split, I really got into high quality guitars, and I got instruments like a Super 400, a Johnny Smith, and a Barney Kessel with the double cutaways, long scale and "bow tie" inlays.

As far as playing guitar in a rock band, the guy who inspired me to play that type of music was Chuck Berry. He was on the bill of a rock concert I went to at the Santa Monica Civic Center, and when I saw him play I told myself that I'd better try out that kind of music. I really didn't play in too many bands before the Doors got going.

VG: Just about everything that is a part of the Doors' history has been documented in books, movies, whatever; I think it would make sense to concentrate on other aspects of your career, but is there any "anecdote" about the Doors that you can tell that some readers might not have heard

TOP: Robby Krieger with his favorite guitar, an early Sixties Gibson ES-355 (mono). Photo by Heather Harris.

LEFT: Morrison and Krieger onstage during the glory days of the Doors. Photo courtesy Elektra.

before?

RK: I think it's just about all been said; I can't think of any "rare story."

VG: Why did the band opt not to have a bass player?

RK: When we played live it sounded better with Ray playing keyboard bass rather than having a bass guitarist. We *did* use bass players in the studio; Larry Knechtel, who was known around the L.A. studio scene as a keyboard player, actually played bass on some of our songs, as did some other session players. In fact, I played a rented Fender P-Bass on some songs.

VG: Back then you were seen playing an SG.

RK: I did the first couple of albums with a cheaper SG that had single-coil pickups; after that I stepped up to an SG Standard that had humbuckers. I played slide on a Les Paul; you can hear that guitar on live cuts like "Who Do You Love" and "Little Red Rooster;" John Sebastian sat in with us on the latter song.

VG: If I remember correctly, the band attempted two albums as a trio after Morrison died, and the last one had some kind of "moving picture gimmick," for lack of a better term.

RK: We did *Other Voices* then *Full Circle*, which had a zoetrope that you'd put on your turntable; the figure would go through a full life cycle from birth to death. After that we officially broke up, but we did get back together in the late '70s to record the music for *An American Prayer*, which was Jim reciting some of his poetry.

VG: What was your first musical project after the Doors' demise?

RK: John and I had a band called the Butts Band that did two albums; it was a unique outfit because we were one of the first U.S. bands to do reggae, which was really happening in Jamaica. We recorded in Kingston, and stayed in Chris Blackwell's house.

VG: You've released solo albums since then, right?

RK: Pretty much. I did *Robby Krieger and Friends* with a bunch of L.A. studio musicians in 1977; it was a fusion-type album. It was right around then that I started getting into good guitars, as I mentioned ear-

lier, and I got two great semi-solid Gibsons; a rare ES-355 that's a mono guitar; it's not stereo and there's no Varitone. I think it's a '63 or '64 model. I also got a blond 1959 ES-335 "dot neck."

VG: Is that the instrument that's pictured on the cover of your *Versions* album from the early '80s? That album seemed to be perhaps ahead of its time, since it was all rock instrumentals and it came out several years before the I.R.S. "No Speak" idea.

RK: That's my 335, and that was sort of the intent of *Versions*; to do rock songs as instrumentals, with a little bit of fusion in there. That was a fun album!

VG: Sometime in the early '80s I saw a documentary on the Doors, and you were commenting that you were working on a dance instrumental album. Which album did that turn out to be?

RK: That never really happened; I *did* put out a single called "Nasty Kinky," which was my tribute to Nastassia Kinski (laughs). But I gave up on the "dance" concept; it seemed to be too hard to incorporate the guitar into those types of beats and still come up with something that was melodic-sounding.

In the mid-'80s I put out an instrumental album called just *Robby Krieger*, and it was kind of unique. It was recorded direct to a two-track in the Variety Arts Theatre; we did it when the place was empty, and the hall had terrific ambience so it was sort of like a direct-to-disc, "live-in-the-studio" album, but in this case a empty theatre was the location. That album was a jazz/fusion type.

VG: Around that time the first *Guitarspeak* album came along. What instruments did you use on "Strut-A-Various?" For what my opinion's worth, that was one of the best cuts on the album.

RK: I played my 355, but some time ago I'd gotten a '61 Strat, which I used for rhythm, and that's still the way I record today. Other people

have told me they liked "Strut-A-Various," and I think one of the reasons it might be notable is because I actually went to the trouble of spending some money; hiring a horn section, doing a real "studio trip." Some of the other guys probably just did something in their home studios. I also did an instrumental album in the No Speak series called *No Habla*.

VG: You also went on the "Night of the Guitar" tour. Comments?

RK: That was an interesting idea. Each guy did two or three songs; everybody used the same back-up band. I played "Love Me Two Times" and "Strut-A-Various," but without the horns; it still sounded okay. We'd all jam together on songs like "All Along the Watchtower" and "Rocky Mountain Way." There was a total of about thirty gigs on the European continent and England. We were supposed to have done the same thing in the U.S. but it never did come off.

VG: What were you doing when the '90s came around?

RK: I played with Eric Burdon's band for a couple of years; we did mostly his songs plus a couple of Doors tunes, and some blues as well. We did a lot of touring; it was billed as "Eric Burdon with Special Guest Robby Krieger."

VG: What was the extent of your involvement with the Doors movie?

RK: I was a music technical advisor; I just hung around and made a nuisance of myself (chuckles), telling them: "This is wrong, this is wrong, this is wrong." I *did* do some of the music; what they mostly used were outtakes of the old stuff, with Val Kilmer actually singing over the old music. I played all of the "incidental" guitar music that you hear in the movie.

VG: Were you satisfied with the way the movie turned out?

RK: I thought it turned out like it should have; a lot of people like to put that movie down, but it seems to still be popular whenever it plays on TV. In a lot of respects it wasn't an accurate portrayal, but considering that it was a Hollywood movie, it was probably as accurate as Hollywood could make it (chuckles).

VG: What about your latest musical effort?

RK: I've got a trio called the Robby Krieger Organization; it's a trio with me on guitar, Skip Van Winkl on organ and pedal bass, and Dale Alexander on drums.

VG: The lack of a bass player is obviously going to lead to comparisons to the Doors by some listeners.

RK: I wasn't going for that when I set it up; we do a number of Doors songs, but other things we do go off on a completely different tangent. We do a lot of fusion and some straight-ahead blues as well.

VG: There's another guitar player named Krieger that I've read about; I saw your son Waylon's picture in *Fender Frontline*.

RK: I tried to get him interested in playing when he was a kid, but he didn't get into it until some of his friends started getting into music about the time he was fifteen, which was pretty much the same age I got into the guitar. He and Berry Oakley, Jr., who's my godson, played in my band for a year and a half; they now have their own band called Bloodlines. I knew Berry Sr. and all of the other Allman Brothers, they all went fishing with me on my boat a couple of times. Berry Jr. is really into his father's history; he has some of the old basses his dad owned.

We did some Allman Brothers tunes in my show when Berry Jr. was with us.

Waylon primarily plays rhythm guitar with Bloodlines; Smokin' Joe Bonamasa plays lead. Waylon started out years ago on one of my Les Pauls, then he went to a Strat.

VG: The Doors were inducted into the Rock and Roll Hall of Fame in 1993. What was the ceremony like?

RK: It was a lot of fun; it was the first time in about five years that the Doors had played together, and Eddie Vedder from Pearl Jam sang.

VG: His picture was on the cover of *Time* magazine a while back; he was cited as being at the forefront of the current musical movement. What was it like having a younger-generation vocalist?

RK: It was cool; I was flattered that he wanted to do it. He does borrow a lot from Morrison, and he was really into the jam. He picked my brain for three or four hours in my hotel room about not only the history of the Doors, but the whole rock and roll trip and what to expect. He's a very serious person; he's a lot like Jim in some ways. Another great thing about the ceremony was getting to see Cream perform.

VG: What about collecting instruments?

RK: I have about fourteen instruments, but I don't consider myself a collector; I don't like to keep guitars around if I'm not playing them. I don't have any of the old SGs I used to play; they all got stolen at one time or another; I really didn't consider them to be "historically important" back then; I figured if you lose a guitar you get another one (chuckles). It wasn't until I got my 355 that I realized the importance of having a favorite guitar. You'll see various SGs at some Hard Rock Cafes around the country that are supposed to have been my guitars, but they're not.

In addition to the 355 and the 335, I've got two Les Pauls and various SGs, among other guitars. I had an old ES-345 that had been custom-ordered with an L-5 neck but it was sold. One of the SGs is a one-of-a-kind with a graphite neck that Gibson made for me. It was supposed to have been my "signature guitar" but Gibson ended up deciding not to make it. I think they said it would be too expensive, but I think it's a great guitar; I really like the way it feels.

VG: Future plans?

RK: I'd like to get more into soundtracks; I did the score for a documentary about Harley-Davidson called *The American Motorcycle*, and it's coming out as a soundtrack album soon on Cabin Fever records.

The band is going to tour in Europe, and after that we'll be touring the U.S. We've got a live album in the works; it'll be out internationally before it's released in the States. So there's several things to look forward to.

While the songs listed at the outset of this interview are probably indelibly etched on the minds of most Classic Rock fans, Robby Krieger's more recent efforts merit listening as well. His playing is as expressive as ever, and Krieger looks forward to continued success with not only his own musical projects, but those of his son as well.

Bruce Kulick

No Kiss-Off

This is one of those "deadline dilemma" articles. Just a few days before this issue of VG was to go to press, media reports said guitarist Bruce Kulick and drummer Eric Singer had left Kiss, and a phone call to ESP's Matt Masciandaro confirmed such. Because Kulick's interview was recorded prior to his departure, it was decided to run the interview as it was recorded. At the very least, the opportunity for an update from Kulick is now in the offing.

The bottom line is that Kulick had been in the lead guitarist slot with Kiss longer than anyone else when our conversation was recorded at a large guitar show. Since he usually brandished modern-looking guitars onstage (with one notable exception), it might come as a surprise to some readers to discover that Kulick is a vintage guitar enthusiast and collector. His pride in his accomplishments after years of hard work was evident when we began our on-the-record-chat:

VG: I've asked other New York players about what kind of influences came from being brought up in such a large, diverse metropolis.

BK: I was born in Brooklyn; moved to Queens when I was 10. There's no doubt the Beatles were the first big thing that got my attention. But my older brother, Bob, loved music, and thanks to him, I heard about the Yardbirds with Jeff Beck and Jimmy Page. He used to take me to a lot of concerts; I saw one show, for example, where the Young Rascals headlined, and the opening acts were Cream and the Who. I was about 13 or 14.

I heard a lot of stuff I wouldn't have heard if it hadn't been for my brother. Originally, we were listening to folk music, then the Beatles, then all of a sud-

LEFT: *1984 - Bruce Kulick (center) onstage during his first tour with Kiss. At left is Gene "Ol' Titan Tongue" Simmons; Paul Stanley's on the right.*

den he was hip to every British band in existence, and hanging out in the Village all the time! He's got some great stories; he told me about a lefty black guitar player who'd play with his teeth; that was Jimmy James and the Blue Flames, of course. I learned how to play "Hey Joe" from my brother, who'd heard Hendrix playing it in the clubs. I was exposed to a lot of stuff, and about the only American guitarist that made an impact on me was Leslie West. I thought Mountain was great, but they were some guys from New York "doing Cream" ...and doing it very well, but I also had the Vagrants' singles.

So I began frequenting the Fillmore; I'd listen to anybody from Miles Davis to the Allman Brothers to Humble Pie with Peter Frampton. I was there on New Year's Eve when Jimi Hendrix recorded *Band of Gypsies*.

The British Invasion really affected me; I didn't have any real affection for the Beach Boys or other American stuff. I loved Clapton in Cream, and Jack Bruce, too. In fact, my first good instrument was an EB-3; my brother was playing guitar so I figured I'd play bass.

VG: Was that EB-3 your first instrument?

BK: No, the first guitar I picked up was the hand-me-down, nylon string acoustic that a lot of players wish they still had, for sentimental reasons. I wore holes in it playing the two chords to the Dave Clark Five's "Glad All Over" (laughs). I played a bit in high school; I borrowed my brother's Epiphone Riviera. The

cover band I was in did dances, and we even did the Circle Line, which was a boat that would cruise around Manhattan. By then I had the EB-3, and I got a Plush amp, which was tuck-and-roll like a Kustom, but Kustoms were more expensive. I think playing bass strengthened my guitar playing, and I felt like I got better than the lead guitar player. To this day, I still play bass on occasion, even on a Kiss track, sometimes.

VG: What was your first electric guitar?

BK: A '65 SG Special. It meant a lot to me, and I used to polish it every night. I modified the bridge and tailpiece, but as I got into collecting guitars sometime later, I bought a completely original one and left it alone. The first real "pro" gigs I did were backing up disco artists like George McRae and Andrea True. I was the "rock guitar player in a disco dance band."

VG: The disco connection is going to surprise some readers.

BK: I know, but you have to remember that Top 40 in the mid-'70s was disco, and I wanted to work. I'd heard Beck's *Blow By Blow* with all of those creative chords, and as it turned out, the band would have to play for a half hour before George McRae would come onstage, so we did Beck covers.

Did I want to be in those bands? No, but it was *experience*. I did it to learn how to "land on your feet" in almost any situation. With McRae, I played in a giant, sold-out stadium, and I also did a concert with an orchestra, which was exciting. I didn't enjoy the Andrea True gig; we played nice places where she'd had big hits, but we also played Air Force bases. At times it was like Spinal Tap (laughs)!

After I got through with those gigs, I knew I needed to get a Strat, so I bought a stripped '63 model for $400. I also got a Les Paul Pro around that time, and a B.C. Rich. Then my brother and I both went out with Meat Loaf on the *Bat Out of Hell* tour, which was great.

VG: Your brother is enough of a "player's player" to where I've seen him in some endorsement ads.

BK: He's been in Washburn ads and others. Ironically, he auditioned for Kiss the same day Ace did, and they ended up going with Ace, but Bob kept in touch with the band, which kind of opened the door for me later. I'd gotten to know Paul through Bob. Bob was in a band called Balance, which had a hit called "Breaking Away," and his last band was called Murderer's Row; I wrote a song for them. He's currently producing some bands in L.A., so he's

still pushing forward.

By the time I got into Meat Loaf's band, I knew what to expect, and this tour was the real thing. He'd had a huge radio hit, and we were selling out arenas around the world. It was a year long, and we'd had enough by the time it was over, but it was a professional effort.

My next band was called Blackjack, which had Michael Bolton in it, but he was called Michael Bolotin back then. We were like Bad Company; we got a big record deal on Polydor, and our lawyer handled Led Zeppelin and Bad Company for Swan Song in America. Tom Dowd produced our first album, but I was really intimidated; that was one area where I *wasn't* experienced. Being in the studio, doing my music for a famous producer wasn't a fun time, and Michael didn't enjoy it either, but we did the best we could. We did another record with Eddie Offord, from Yes, producing; he was another hero of mine, but it also wasn't what I expected. I was kind of dejected after that, so I joined the Good Rats.

VG: The Rats had a "core" or "cult" following for some time, didn't they?

BK: Yeah, it was a regional thing, and the clubs were changing around then. I did one gig where the Rats were second-billed to Ozzy when Randy Rhoads was still alive, and Motorhead opened the gig. Let me tell you, Lemmy didn't like that too much (laughs)! By then, I was playing a Les Paul Custom and a B.C. Rich Eagle Supreme; I had a good sound. I was with the Rats from '80 to '82.

VG: Had you already started collecting by then?

BK: Not a lot, but I'd already started holding on to a couple of things. I had let some other guitars go in the past. Once I got into Kiss, I was a lot smarter about getting collectible guitars.

By the early '80s, Michael had changed his last name to Bolton, and he got a gig to open for Bob Seger on a big concert tour, so I went with him, and I played on his record. I used the same rig I had with the Rats, but a lot of it

Kulick meets the namesake of several of his Gibson guitars.

Kulick works out with his Les Paul Custom.

got stolen in Manhattan. Around then I also recorded with Billy Squier, and he wanted me to tour with him, but I said no. His next record really hit big, so I might have regretted my decision, but I guess it meant I'd end up being available for Kiss.

VG: And obviously we'd want to know how that transpired.

BK: I got a call from Paul in late '84, asking me to fill in for their guitar player, Mark St. John, who was sick. They realized they had the right guy, after they'd had some changes in their lead guitarist and drummer slots.

By '79 or '80, Kiss was not Kiss anymore; they just didn't get along, and that's why they did the solo albums. And that was good for them, but when they tried to put things back together, things were very difficult. So Peter Criss left, then Ace. Eric Carr, God bless him, was on drums by then, and they finally went with Vinnie Vincent, because he was writing some decent songs with them. So he got involved with *Creatures of the Night*, but there's a lot of different players "ghosting" on that album, just like my brother ghosted on *Alive II*. He played on some of the studio tracks.

They took off the makeup and did *Lick It Up*, and Vinnie left; I don't want to get into the reasons. Then I think they wanted to find somebody who was really fast and extreme, and Mark was on a list of names that Grover Jackson gave them. I have a lot of respect for Mark's playing, but he was like Alan Holdsworth, which didn't make a lot of sense to me as far as Kiss went. You wonder how it might have turned out if he'd stayed healthy. Because of his illness, I played on a track on *Animalize*, and then Paul told me, "Don't cut your hair" (chuckles).

Three months later, they asked me to go on the road with them to Europe. We started on September 30, 1984, in Brighton, and I was really excited; that was where all of those years of performing in stadiums or for small audiences that didn't give a **** paid off. But it still didn't mean that I knew how to *perform* with Kiss immediately, but within a week I was comfortable being onstage with the guys.

VG: The first indication I saw that there had been another change in the lead guitarist slot was the *Animalize* concert video, which I saw on MTV.

BK: We recorded that in December of '84, after the European tour. As for guitars, I had nothing at that point. I had kind of a Strat with a Floyd, and I might have still had a Les Paul, but I really didn't have much gear then. Paul told me to go over to Manny's and pick out whatever I liked. I got a gold Charvel with an angled headstock, another Charvel, and a B.C. Rich, so those were my guitars for the road. Unfortunately, most of the guitars I had then were stolen from our warehouse a couple of years later, and that's when I really started collecting guitars to use in the studio, but not to take on the road. It was around that time that time that ESP started getting into some "Charvel-ish" or... I hate to use the word, "heavy metal" guitars. The quality was great, and I knew Richie Fliegler, who was working there at the time, so that's when I hooked up with ESP.

VG: Albums and tours you've done with Kiss?

BK: *Animalize, Asylum, Crazy Nights, Hot in the Shade*, and *Revenge*. All of those albums had tours, and there was a record called *Smashes, Thrashes and Hits*, which was a greatest hits album with two new tracks. The tribute album doesn't count, even though we backed up Garth Brooks on it; Garth's a great guy. *Alive III* was from the *Revenge* tour. Then there was the convention tour, which relates to the new *MTV Unplugged* album.

VG: On a video of a live version of "I Love It Loud," it looked like most of your guitars were of the "Super-Strat" configuration, but I thought I saw what looked like a Les Paul Jr. as well.

BK: That's right. Through the mid-'80s I used an ESP Horizon with a stop bridge if I needed a guitar without a Floyd Rose. It worked, it behaved, and it was perfect for live work. I broke a collar bone in '89, and heavy guitars had always bugged the hell out of me anyway, so I went on a quest for light guitars. In '89 and '90, I bought a Custom Shop Explorer that was made from Korina, but it wasn't loud enough to use live. I bought a Moderne when they were cheap; 600 bucks. During the most recent tour I got a '57 Les Paul Custom reissue from the Custom Shop; it's a perfect weight for me, and it sounds great.

But the other "find" was at Guitar R' Us in Hollywood; it was a beat to **** Les Paul Jr. that had a neck which had obviously been broken in three places, but it had been repaired pretty well. It had the wrong kind of bridge, and had already been routed for a humbucker, *which I would never do.* The pickup was a Patent Number, the pickguard wasn't original, and it already had Schallers on it. Albert had it on consignment, and he told me to take it home and try it. That guitar ended up as one of the main guitars on the *Revenge* tour, and I've done some other recording with it since then.

VG: What about other guitars you've collected?

BK: I've got to mention Ed Seelig at Silver Strings Music; I've done a lot of guitar business with him over the years. Around '90, I asked him to find me a utility Les Paul Special, and he found a gorgeous '58 one that was *mint.* I paid market value for it then, but I don't play it. One time when I got it out I put a tiny scratch on it, and nearly had a heart attack. That's why something like that Junior is perfect for the road.

Ed also got me a clean '60 ES-355; I used it on "Domino" and the new studio record, but you'll never see it onstage. I also found and bought a clean, *stock* Les Paul Jr. while we were on the road; it must have belonged to some church guy because it had .012s on it!

Then I started re-living my teenage years by getting into SGs (chuckles). I got a gorgeous '64 SG Jr., and a '65 SG Standard because of Harrison. It had a reset neck; I try to stay away from such things like that but the front of the instrument was beautiful, and it had a combination of chrome and nickel parts. I finally found a '65 Special that was like the one I had when I was a kid; it had a stop bridge on it.

One Les Paul I need to tell you about is a "Frankenstein"; it's a converted '53 my brother got back in the early '70s. Someone had put some PAFs on it, and the guitar also had a ****ty sunburst refin. I finally found the right nickel parts to go on it, and I got Gibson to refinish it for me; it's gorgeous. This thing has even been on *Alive II*, when my brother used it. It's the most "important" guitar I own.

I also bought a Korina Heritage V that showed up on a "Monday Night Football" promo a couple of years ago. Most of the tour guitars I take out are some great ESPs and a couple of Gibsons.

VG: Tell me about the 1995 "convention" tour.

BK: We'd finished touring South America, Japan and Australia; those were regular concert dates. It was Gene's idea to come with something that meant we could spend some time with the fans. We didn't want to do a full concert in a hotel, so we decided to play unplugged; we kind of said: "Let's show 'em we can do it." I'd used a Chet Atkins acoustic solidbody on "Forever," so that's what I took, along with a Marshall Acoustic Artist amp and a SansAmp. We had about 12 songs prepared, and we took requests. There was an Eric Singer drum clinic, I did a guitar clinic, and we signed autographs and answered questions.

VG: The attendance was limited to specific numbers, and there were some questions about the admission fee.

BK: In some towns, we could have easily pulled a couple of thousand fans into a hotel ballroom, and there was no way that could have been handled. We had 1,300 people at the Chicago event, and it was scary. I had mixed feelings about [charging] $100 per ticket, but I know the fans got their money's worth. It was a 6-hour event; we performed for two hours, and it was an intimate setting. The ticket price was an issue in the band, but we didn't want just anyone; for that kind of money we got the real diehards (laughs)! It was hard work for us, but it was a lot of fun and very rewarding for us *and* the fans. I think we proved that the '90s Kiss could really play, and could play songs from any era.

The convention tour was very successful, and I know of some other bands that are interested in doing the same thing. They've contacted Gene and said "How the hell did you do this?"

VG: That tour begat the *MTV Unplugged* album. Did your equipment setup differ from the tour setup?

BK: When MTV came to hear us, they were impressed, but they wanted us to do it *really* unplugged, so I went through "guitar hell" over the Chet Atkins acoustic; it *was* a solidbody instrument and they didn't want me to use it. I was asking myself how I'd bend strings, play lead, tune down a half step, and manipulate an unwound G string on a typical Martin, a typical Takamine, or a typical whatever. I tried a lot of brands, but I couldn't keep them in tune and I didn't feel comfortable playing leads on them. I wound up using an Ovation, which wasn't my favorite-sounding guitar, but it was the most "friendly" for what I was doing. It didn't feed back, and I could rip all of the leads without it going out of tune. The neck was almost like a Charvel; the fretboard was a big piece of rosewood with big frets and fast action. The Ovation I used was great. I used a different SansAmp for the MTV concert as well; the one I used on the convention had some distortion capability, and MTV wouldn't have gone for that, either (laughs)! SansAmp is a great company.

The *MTV Unplugged* album is more extended than what was seen on the MTV special. It's an hour of music; 15 songs. There were some songs that we were kind of fooling around with that weren't included; for example, we did a country version of "God of Thunder" (chuckles). The band worked really hard while performing, then Ace and Peter came out and did "2000 Man" and "Beth," then all six of us did "Nothin' to Lose" and "Rock and Roll All Night." I'm really proud of it. There's also a long-form video of it that will be available.

VG: Do you collect amps as well?

BK: I've got a lot of little "tweed guys" (chuckles). I had a great birthday last year; Gene bought me a reissue Rickenbacker 12-string, and Paul got me a gorgeous '54 tweed Deluxe. I also have a lot of old stomp boxes; I love those things.

VG: Any guitars that you're still seeking?

BK: I've got a soft heart for Epiphone Casinos, but they're way overpriced. I like Rivieras as well, but they're hard to find. I just like a nice, clean, round neck.

VG: Do you think the necks on Epiphones are different from those on Gibsons made during the same time, like an ES-330?

Bruce Kulick with the protoype of his ESP signature model.

BK: No, I've played some clean 330s, but I can't believe the sounds the Beatles got out of their Epiphones; twangy, weird stuff! But if I saw a clean 330 at the right price I'd get it; I'd want one with a stop tailpiece.

VG: Tell me about your new ESP signature model.

BK: I'd been an ESP endorser for some time, and when I finally started designing my own signature model, it took about a year to get it done. I grew up with an SG Special, so we knew that would be a part of its look, and I always loved B.C. Rich guitars; I always thought some of their late-'70s and early-'80s models were underrated. Matt Maciandaro, with ESP, is a terrific guy; he and I started looking at SGs and B.C. Riches in order to utilize all of the features I liked. The first prototype was a neck-through with great access, and two humbuckers. We've been working on a bolt-on model; I wanted something that would be less money, but that's going to be tricky. They should be in stores before the end of the year.

VG: Why double parallelogram markers?

BK: I always thought they looked sexy on 345s. But this guitar is "between a powerful SG and a powerful B.C. Rich," so I'm happy. After all the years of buying, selling, and collecting, I'd better love something that I helped design!

VG: So your current activities seem like a bit of a paradox; you're introducing a loud solidbody electric guitar, while the band is releasing an acoustic album.

BK: But I still see that as a one-off for the band, even though it was "groundbreaking" for a lot of our fans, and we've got a new studio album coming out; I used my signature prototype on it. This band is constantly evolving. Some people only know of the band from the days when they wore makeup, or as a heavy metal band. But Kiss had a hit with a song called "Beth," they had a disco hit, they had heavy metal hits, they had a hit in the '90s with "Forever." We can't be pinned down; we can't be "pidgeonholed." No way.

As Kulick himself noted, guitar lovers shouldn't expect to see his collectible instruments onstage at a Kiss concert. But his respect for classic guitars and his use of them in the studio is a surprising and admirable facet of his career. Stay tuned for further information.

The October 1996 issue of Vintage Guitar *featured the preceding interview with veteran guitarist Bruce Kulick, the lead guitarist for Kiss when our conversation was recorded. Just prior to press time, Kulick left that platinum-selling band, and* VG *opted to run his interview as it was recorded. The introduction to the interview noted Kulick's recent career move, and stated that the opportunity for an update from Kulick was in the offing.*

And such was the case when Bruce Kulick called Vintage Guitar*'s Southern Regional Office soon after his interview was published. In a brief and cordial conversation, he filled us in on the details of his departure from Kiss, and his future plans:*

VG: Well, we had time to change the text to note your departure from Kiss, but we didn't have time to change the artwork, since it was the color centerspread. The interview's subtitle was "No Kiss-off." Ironic, ain't it?

BK: (laughs) Yeah, but I thought it turned out really great, and I've gotten some comments from other people who enjoyed it. The point is, I really was proud of what I'd accomplished in that band, and I still am.

VG: Since we last talked, I've seen an old video of Meat Loaf's "Paradise By The Dashboard Light." Is that you playing the Strat or the Les Paul?

BK: Neither my brother or I are in that video, even though we were on the *Bat Out of Hell* tour for a year. Bob and I were in the studio with another singer, but his career didn't go anywhere. They got two guys that sort of looked like us; people *do* think it's Bob and me.

VG: You noted in your interview that you saw the *MTV Unplugged* album as being "pretty much a one-off for the band." Is that what the reunion/ "makeup" tour was supposed to have been, as well?

BK: It was originally presented to me as "we're just going to do this for a year." I wasn't happy about it, but I was getting paid. But the next thing I knew, the "makeup" tour was being touted like it was the second coming of the Messiah. It *is* kind of cool as a nostalgia trip, but they're not doing any new music. They're only doing material up to 1980;

what about the other 16 years that the band sold gold and platinum records?

The success of the concert ticket sales put me more in a position of thinking that the band would want to stay in its makeup for awhile, and I started to ask: "What about *my* career?" We'd done a brand new album with 12 songs, and I co-wrote nine of them, which was the most co-writing I'd ever done for a Kiss album. I sang a song called "I Walk Alone," which, come to think of it, was probably a prophetic title (chuckles)! I thought that album really helped in an attempt to bond with Kiss fans. Some fans have gotten bootleg copies of the album, and I've heard that "I Walk Alone" is one of their favorite tracks.

I wasn't planning on staying inactive during that year, but then I was told that the new album was going to stay shelved indefinitely; no release date.

VG: Was that the proverbial "last straw?"

BK: Once I saw that the focus of the record company was on the "makeup" phase when they released yet another live album, I figured a new album from the "makeup" version of the band would be an obvious followup when they got through touring. If it did happen, it wouldn't do anything for me. I couldn't have gone from more of a "high" about the new record to more of a "low," considering what's happened, in terms of my commitment to the band. It was a very awkward position to be in. I need to create music; I can't sit around. Without any guarantee of knowing when the "makeup reunion" would run its course, I figured it was time to move on.

VG: Did you discuss the situation with Eric Singer (Kiss drummer who departed same time as Kulick)? Was it a mutual decision?

BK: I can't say which one of us was more frustrated. We decided to put out one press release at the same time, because things weren't working for either of us. He's an extremely talented drummer, which I think is very evident on the *Unplugged* album.

Actually, the whole band discussed the future; it wasn't like Eric and I were plotting behind anyone's back. We all got together and talked about things; I didn't get any guarantees, so it was time to look at other options.

VG: And I understand you *haven't* stayed inactive; you told me when we did the first interview that you were going to Europe to do some clinics.

BK: Actually, I've been there twice. The first time, I did 21 clinics in five countries. It was really exciting to play for the fans; I don't think Kiss has played in Europe often enough.

When I got back, I got hooked up with a singer named Lenita Erickson, whose album was produced by Curt Cuomo, who's a good friend of mine that co-wrote some songs with Paul Stanley and me. Lenita was going to Europe to do some promotional concerts, and she needed an acoustic guitarist to accompany her. I'd seen her in Curt's studio; she's quite talented, and sings kind of like a female Rod Stewart. To me, it's real heartland music; it's not trendy or "alternative." We did 10 shows in Europe, and it was a challenge, because it related to the *Unplugged* experience. It was great fun, and once plans are set for her here in America, I'm definitely going to be involved.

VG: Other future plans?

BK: I've got a manager named Larry Mazer, who worked with Kiss and Cinderella; we're real hungry to do something. I'm doing some writing, and have got the "nucleus" of a band together, but it's too soon to say who. I want to get a record out that's comprised of some great melodic rock, and the band that records it will be able to kick some serious musical butt.

And by the time this interview comes out, Eric Singer and I will have done some clinics in Australia. When we were there a couple of years ago, we sold out some huge arenas and did multiple-night gigs, and we don't have to go down there in makeup for the fans to support us. Eric and I will do our individual clinics, and will do some jamming together.

I've produced other artists this year, and I've got a website; the address is http://www.nextlevel.com/brucekulick. We got over 20,000 hits on it in the first two weeks. So I haven't been on vacation this year, and I'm willing to have a lot of pressure on me, because that's when I'm at my best; I'd go crazy if I was hanging around the house. I'll be sure to let you and your readers know what's going on.

Greg Lake

"Welcome Back, My Friends"

Bassist/vocalist Greg Lake was in an ebullient mood when he called *Vintage Guitar* to talk about the newest offering from the redoubtable English progressive trio Emerson, Lake & Palmer. The band regrouped in the early Nineties for a studio album (*Black Moon*) and a world tour; a live album recorded at the Royal Albert Hall in London during that tour is a tour-de-force performance that was the band's most recent release. However, Lake was upbeat about a new retrospective multiple-CD effort called *Return of the Manticore*, which includes remastered ELP tunes plus new material consisting of some unique cover songs as well as a heretofore never-before-recorded *studio* version of "Pictures at an Exhibition."

The release of *Return of the Manticore* was pending when *VG* talked with Greg Lake, and the details of the effort were noted in our conversation. Before present and future projects were discussed, however, we asked him to harken back to his English childhood in an attempt to let us know how his interest in playing and singing unique music came about:

VG: What part of England are you from?

GL: Originally I was from a seaside town called Dorset. Several other players come from there; people such as Bob Fripp and Andy Summers. In the summer there was always work for musicians since it was a tourist area.

VG: Considering the genre of bands in which you've played, most people would assume that you've had some kind of classical music training.

GL: Not really; Bobby Fripp and I were childhood friends, and we both took guitar lessons from a man named Don Strike. He was actually a banjo player, and consequently Bobby and I both picked up a sort of cross-picking technique.

When I listened to music back then, I'd end up with a bit of classical music in with everything else. That's still the case today; I enjoy classical music, but I haven't had any formal music training on "symphonic"-type instruments.

VG: As far as *pop music* memories go, I need to make a token inquiry about Radio Luxembourg.

GL: That was the *only* place where one could hear contemporary American rock music; it was the "source" of knowing what was going on. I could reel off names of early influences; Roy Orbison, Chuck Berry, Elvis, Little Richard. Those performers kind of shaped one's image of what rock music was and should be. As for guitar players, Hank Marvin inspired me when I was very young, as I'm sure he inspired many English kids (chuckles), and later I became aware of players in my own era such as Hendrix and Jeff Beck.

VG: What kind of songs did you and Fripp learn from your teacher?

GL: (chuckles) Everything from "Red Sails in the Sunset" to violin exercises by Paganini; it was a weird concoction of music. You were supposed to read the music, but I tended to play by ear. Anytime the teacher saw me wandering away from the score he'd placed in front of me, he'd hit my fingers with a ruler, *WHAP!* He was a bit of a disciplinarian (laughs). Ultimately my style developed by playing by ear, because all live performance for a rock band is based on that. In the case of playing something like "Pictures at an Exhibition," *you've got to remember what goes where.* I've sort of developed a technique of remembering things in what I'd call "blocks."

VG: What about the brands and models of guitars you used back then?

GL: I was "into" Fenders very quickly; before that I went through some silly stuff like a Futurama and a Hofner President.

VG: What about "pre-King Crimson" bands?

GL: Just what I'd call childhood bands; a group of kids get together for two or three months, then somebody leaves; innocent fun.

VG: The English equivalent of "garage

bands"?

GL: Yeah, but in my case they were more like "bedroom bands" or "kitchen bands," because those were the places we practiced (laughs)!

VG: When did you begin concentrating on bass?

GL: Bob called me up; he'd been in a band called Giles, Giles and Fripp; they'd done an album called *Cheerful Insanity* for Decca Records. The album was "commercially ridiculous," and Decca told Bob that unless they came up with something that had at least a vague correlation to what was going on in the real world, Decca would drop the band. Decca suggested that the band get a decent singer, so Bob asked me to sing, but he also said: "The only thing is, we don't need two guitar players, so would you mind playing bass?" I agreed; they had a record deal and I told myself that it couldn't be too difficult, since a bass had four strings instead of six. Twenty-eight years later I'm still playing the bloody thing (laughs)! But I'd never played bass before I joined Bob's group, which became known as King Crimson.

VG: So it's logical to assume that your guitar playing most likely influenced your bass playing style.

GL: And the choice of bass as well; the first one I had was a Fender Jazz. It had a slim neck; more like a guitar than other models I tried. I also went for wire-wound strings; I couldn't stand the tape-wound types. I played bass from a "guitar perspective," I suppose; I was doing things like playing chords, which was wrong, but it worked. I played with a pick for the most part as well.

VG: King Crimson probably had a number of terms that listeners might have used to describe the band; terms like "art rock" or "progressive rock." Are there any adjectives you might use to describe the version of that band with which you were associated?

GL: Well, it was a very unique band with unusual people in it, and I think one term that might have applied could be "anarchistic"; if something made sense, then we wouldn't play it (chuckles). It was a struggle to find something that really didn't work, then finding a way to make it work.

Let me give you an example: In live performance, there'd be one song where there was no key, no time signature; it would be counted in and you'd simply start playing. Then it would be a question of which musical "thread" prevailed; then you'd either subscribe to what

someone else was doing or someone else would subscribe to what you were doing. On occasion, some amazing things developed, and that really is the wonderful aspect of free music; it has a spirit of its own. If players can *listen* to other players instead of simply *playing,* the music can be taken to places that no individual player could probably reach.

VG: After the first two albums with King Crimson, there was the first incarnation of Emerson, Lake & Palmer, which lasted about a decade. What about the instruments you played with that band?

GL: Let me point out that I didn't play bass on *In the Wake of Poseidon*; I just sang. I was still playing a Fender Jazz when ELP formed; it was dependable. One knew where one stood with a Fender. In the mid-Seventies I used a Gibson Ripper; it was a well-proportioned instrument that had some tone switching capabilities that made it interesting, but I didn't play it too long; I came back to a Jazz.

VG: You also played a Zemaitis acoustic guitar around then.

GL: I spent a while with Zemaitis guitars; acoustics *and* electrics. They were very nice, decoratively-speaking, but when it comes to acoustics, it seems like I've always gone back to Gibson guitars, just as I did with a Jazz bass. In the same way that it seems Fender has got electric six-strings "covered," Gibsons have got acoustics covered; they're dependable and they sound wonderful.

The electric guitar heard on the "Welcome Back My Friends" part of "Karn Evil 9" was also a Zemaitis instrument. He made a series of electrics back then; such guitars had a Les Paul shape and a highly-engraved metal front, which was either aluminum or titanium, and two

"Baby, It's Cold Outside": Lake mugs while filming a video for "Fanfare for the Common Man"; he's holding his custom-made Alembic eight-string bass.

humbucking pickups. Ronnie Wood was in the Faces then; he had one just like mine.

VG: How many people have told you that the live *Pictures at an Exhibition* album made them aware of classical music, or at the very least, aware of Mussorgsky and other Russian composers?

GL: Well, we know that the sales of the symphonic version of *Pictures at an Exhibition* doubled during the prime of our version. I think our album drew listeners' attention to the fact that the piece had a wonderful melody. It seemed to let people know that even if one was a teenager, one could still have an appreciation for classical music. It appealed to young people without sounding stuffy or pretentious.

VG: One of the last albums from the original incarnation of ELP was another live one called *In Concert*, and it opens with "Peter Gunn." The bass on that cut has a remarkable tone.

GL: That was probably an Alembic eight-string bass; I had three Alembics at one point, two four-strings and an eight-string. They were custom-made; Alembic was really the first company to use beautiful woods. They worked with me closely; the instruments were wonderfully precise; the active circuitry was another high-quality feature. Those were beautiful and high-quality instruments!

VG: During the decade that the first version of ELP was together, do you recall your largest, best and worst gigs?

GL: The largest was probably the California Jam, which had hundreds of thousands of people. That was the performance where the "flying piano" made its appearance.

It's difficult to cite a "best" gig, although I've been asked that a lot of times. ELP had a remarkable run of success back then; places like Madison Square Garden, the Isle of Wight, California Jam, and the Olympic Stadium in Montreal were all fantastic, but I really couldn't pick one concert, because some of the smaller events we would play in places like the Midwest were great as well.

We always tried to stage the performance where the visuals would add to the drama of the music. Our production was never gratuitous, and I think we were one of the first bands to take out what is now considered to be a "standard" rock and roll production.

The worst gig *is* easy to cite, however (laughs). We were scheduled to do a show in a stadium in Italy, and the promoter told us not to bring our own staging and lights, because they'd supply them. We agreed, but when we got to the stadium at about one in the afternoon on the day of the concert, there was no stage, no lights and no promoter. We sent the road crew to look in every restaurant in the town; they found the promoter and brought him back to the stadium. His face registered shock and horror when they brought him through the tunnel; he'd gotten the dates mixed up.

He got a building company to erect a scaffolding-type stage. There wasn't time to do anything about lights, so we had to play using the football lights.

VG: You would have had every right to cancel the performance, in my opinion.

GL: Well, we didn't want to disappoint the 40,000 fans who were coming. We went ahead and did the show, and one of the features toward the end was always Carl's drum solo. Keith and I would go offstage and wait on our cue to come back out. So I'm standing in the wings, watching Carl play, and Francesco, the promoter, comes up to me and puts his arm

TOP: *Greg Lake onstage in the early Seventies with his engraved Zemaitis electric guitar.*

RIGHT: *Emerson, Lake & Palmer. Photo courtesy Victory.*

around me; I told him: "Don't touch me!"

"No, no," he said, "You'll forgive me when you see the surprise I've got for you at the end of the show!" I'm asking myself what it could be; dancing girls? So Carl finishes his solo and we go back out and resume playing.

All of a sudden, this huge skyrocket comes roaring right between my legs and right out into the front of the audience! I'm not talking about some firecracker you'd get from a news agent; this was a *mortar!* Then the entire stage explodes with fireworks. What the promoter had done was erect a fireworks display during the concert, without telling us, on a wood scaffold behind the scaffold stage they'd built earlier in the day. But when he set it off, it fell over, so the whole display blew across the stage and out into the audience! I felt like I was in combat; Catherine Wheels were spewing out of the drum kit (laughs)! It's funny now, but at the time it was incredibly frightening. Remarkably, no one was injured.

VG: You put out a solo album around 1980, if I remember correctly. How did it differ from your previous efforts in a band format?

GL: It was kind of like being the "son of a rich and famous father." Coming out of a band like ELP, I was in some ways musically disoriented; I felt like I had something to live up to in some ways. I think I was probing new directions for my music in a simple way. I did things like a country song, and I got into stuff that was virtually heavy metal; I began working with Gary Moore, who is a *fantastic* player. It was pretty much of an "experimental" album, and I went back to playing guitar on it; I was using a Fender Stratocaster. (NOTE: Lake actually put out two solo albums in the Eighties)

VG: In 1983 you had a very brief association with Asia. Was it just for that MTV "Asia in Asia" broadcast from the Budokan in Tokyo?

GL: That was all there was to it. They had had a falling out with Johnny Wetton, who's a very good singer and player in his own right; oddly enough, he comes from the same part of the world as Bobby, Andy and I. He also had the King Crimson experience; Johnny and I have been close friends for many, many years.

Carl Palmer called me up and said: "Could you do me a favor?" I thought he wanted to borrow a guitar or something (laughs)! He told me about the MTV broadcast from Tokyo with the whole thing set up and booked, and could I do it, since they'd fallen out with Johnny. At first I didn't want to, since Johnny is a friend of mine, but I called him up and he told me to do it. I did the show, and we discussed the possibility of making an album, but they wanted to go in a "pop" direction, which I couldn't do; it never went any further than that.

VG: You played a Steinberger on that broadcast.

GL: I liked the Steinberger because it was different; it was modern and accurate. The only problem was its balance; there was nothing to stabilize the right arm. I didn't stay with it.

VG: The next time you were heard from, it was another ELP variant, only this time it was Emerson, Lake and *Powell;* Cozy Powell had been a drummer for the Jeff Beck Group and had a hit single in the early Seventies called "Dance with the Devil."

The token re-worked classical piece was "Mars, the Bringer of War" from a suite called "The Planets" by Holst. In my opinion, ELP has shown a penchant for playing classical pieces with a lot of "Ooomph" to them, for lack of a better term. Russian works, for example, and "Mars, the Bringer of War" is like an inexorable march. Did *any* incarnation of ELP ever consider doing some "lighter" classical works along the lines of "Water Music" for example?

GL: Few classical pieces translate well on rock instruments in a three-piece band. I think how a piece sounds *rhythmically and melodically* are the two issues. "Pictures at an Exhibition" fits into the category of a symphonic piece that can be played by three people; it's got a very definitive melody. Other classical pieces we've recorded are of the same type.

VG: "Louder" classical works aside, has ELP made an effort to record classical works that were "concepts" such as "Pictures at an Exhibition," or parts of concepts such as "Mars, the Bringer of War," which was a movement from "The Planets," because such music might appeal more easily to rock fans?

GL: (chuckles) We don't go actively looking for classical things to do; we don't try to put a token classical piece on each ELP album. But if you were to come into one of our rehearsals, many times you'll hear Keith playing something from the classics to warm up or for his own amusement. Sometimes we'll join in, and we'll discover something that "clicks," so we'll use it. "Fanfare for the Common Man" was something that happened like that.

VG: And I believe I read that Copland got to hear it before he died.

GL: Yes he did; I think what he liked about it was that it was presented in a way that he never envisioned, and I think the free form stuff at the end amused him; he probably never expected someone to express his composition like that! I played the Alembic eight-string bass we discussed earlier on "Fanfare."

VG: On the "Touch and Go" video you were playing a white Spector NS-2.

GL: Those were nice instruments but I didn't play them too long.

VG: The next time I saw Keith Emerson, he had re-united with Carl Palmer in a band called the 3, but you weren't around; there was another bass player. It had to seem a bit like musical chairs, but ultimately the original ELP line-up got going again.

GL: (chuckles) It *was* like musical chairs. I don't know much about that other band that Keith and Carl had; I never heard the album and I never saw the band perform.

A friend of ours named Phil Carson, who was the head of Atlantic Records in Europe, came to us a couple of years ago and proposed that we do a film score, which we'd never done—

VG: (interrupting) And that's a bit of a surprise; I'd have thought that ELP would have been involved with making music for films at some point during its history as a band.

GL: True, but that never happened. We decided to give Phil's idea a go, but after we'd been in the rehearsal room for four or five weeks, what we'd written was the substance of an *album* instead of a soundtrack. When Phil heard it, he said we should put out an album, which we did; the idea of a film score got shelved. That led to a tour, of course, and it's gone on from there.

VG: When I first heard about ELP reuniting and the new *Black Moon* album, I saw a performance clip-type video on ABC's "In Concert"; the band was doing "Fanfare for the Common Man," and you were playing what appeared to be an orange Fender P-Bass.

GL: (chuckles) Actually, that was a borrowed instrument. All of my equipment was being shipped over from England, and somebody borrowed, or maybe rented, that Precision. It was quite a nice bass.

VG: I'll resist the temptation to refer to Prokofiev's "Romeo and Juliet" as the token classical piece that appears on *Black Moon*.

GL: (laughs) Thank you! It did work out quite well, I think.

VG: What about the tour results after *Black Moon* was released?

GL: Understand that the original lineup of ELP hadn't been out in ten years, and we had no idea what the reception would be. What we decided to do was concentrate on somewhat smaller venues, like theatres; we didn't go for stadiums; we were conservative. The tour was quite successful since we approached it in that manner; the concert market has been quite unpredictable, and at a time when tours were being pulled off the road, we were adding dates. We ended up adding a second leg, and played 140 cities total. I'd rather play to a full theatre than to a half-empty arena, and I think that playing arenas is contigent on having current album success. We made the right decision.

VG: And now comes *Return of the Manticore*. How does it differ from the other ELP anthologies I've seen?

GL: It's a unique retrospective of the band. There are some previously unheard recordings and some new recordings as well. I've always wanted to do a studio version of "Pictures," and we recorded that in Dolby Surround-Sound; "Pictures at an Exhibition" is an ideal piece of music for that kind of technology.

We also recorded one track each from bands we were in prior to ELP. We did "Hang On To A Dream" from the Nice, which Keith was in, "Fire," from Carl's association with The Crazy World of Arthur Brown, and there was an abbreviated version of "21st Century Schizoid Man" for me. Those were fun to do, and there's lot of other great stuff on there as well.

VG: What instruments are you playing these days?

GL: I've been through a lot of brands, most of which have been very good guitars and basses. Currently I play Tune basses from Japan; they're beautiful basses. The woods are fabulous, the electronics are fabulous. They've really come up with a unique instrument; it has an unusual shape but it conforms to what is needed in a bass guitar; the balance, tone and stability are there. It's hard to come up with something new, but Tune has done it.

VG: Do you collect instruments?

GL: I try not to, but I'm forever seeking out high quality *new* instruments, and I still have some of my older instruments. Recently I bought a small Collings guitar; the craftsmanship on it is exquisite.

VG: Are you planning on touring to support *Return of the Manticore*?

GL: Well, yes and no. We're going to be doing a quick world tour not to do concerts, but to do playbacks of "Pictures" in SurroundSound; the Dolby people are involved with this project; we'll do interviews as well.

We're currently working on a new album which is due to be released in the late Spring of 1994; after that there's another world tour.

VG: I've got to ask if you've got another classical piece on the upcoming album.

GL: We've got a lot of things that we're experimenting with, but I wouldn't want to predict how the album will turn out. I do, however, think that it will be an unusual record for ELP. We're looking forward to 1994; it should be quite exciting.

The live ELP album recorded at the Royal Albert Hall during the *Black Moon* tour is indicative of how potent ELP's sound still is. Songs such as "Knife Edge," "Lucky Man" and excerpts from *Tarkus* are as strong as ever, and newer material such as "Paper Blood" stands on its own. For all their years of experience, Emerson, Lake and Palmer is still a talented and innovative trio, and Greg Lake's bass playing and singing still ranks among the world's best. That he can also give an eloquent interview is a bonus!

ELP's next studio album was titled In the Hot Seat. *The studio version of "Pictures at an Exhibition" appeared on the CD version of that album as well.*

Howard Leese

The Heart of the Matter (Concerning Guitars)

This writer's reaction upon receiving the package of photographs from Howard Leese of Heart (to accompany the guitarist's interview) was to invoke the two-word expression of nonplus made famous by Charlie Brown in the "Peanuts" comic strip: "GOOD GRIEF!"

Leese does indeed have a commendable collection of classic instruments; so much so, he advised *Vintage Guitar,* that Japanese publications have made regular pilgrimages to his house to photograph some of his guitars. He has been the guitarist and keyboard player for Heart for over two decades ("I was the last original member to join"), and has accumulated an enviable assortment of equipment.

Heart is currently on hiatus (for reasons detailed in our discussion), but before we delved into the details about Howard Leese's collection, *VG* asked about his history with the platinum-selling band that came to national prominence in the mid-'70s with hits like "Magic Man" and "Crazy on You."

VG: Are you originally from the Pacific Northwest? Is that where you were living when you joined Heart?

HL: No, I was born in Hollywood, California; I grew up in L.A. I moved up to Vancouver, Canada around 1970, after I got out of college. My long-time partner Mike Flicker, who was a drummer, went too. We were a production team, and we got an opportunity to go up there and work in a studio. We started our own label, Mushroom Records, and Heart was one of the bands we signed.

VG: What got you started wanting to play music?

HL: Well, I was with my mom one time at a friend of hers; I was nine. They had a piano in their living room, and I sat down and began plinking around on it, and before I knew it, I'd picked out the Davey Crockett theme, and my mom's friend showed me a couple of chords and scales, and I could play them right back to her. So I took a couple of years of piano, but I got bored with that around the time the big guitar boom started.

VG: Tell me about your earliest guitars.

HL: I've been playing professionally since I was 11. I moved away from home when I was 17; I've been supporting myself by playing guitar ever since then; never had a real job (laughs). My first guitar was a St. George with a matching amp. My first *good* guitar was a 1966 Gibson 335 in cherry. I talked my folks into getting it for me; at the time my band got a chance to play at the Teen Fair in L.A., which was a "big" gig, and I couldn't do it with the cheesy little guitar I had. We got the 335 at Ace Music in Santa Monica; I still have it.

Another guitar I got was a Telecaster from Mars Bonfire, who wrote "Born to Be Wild" for Steppenwolf *on that guitar*; he was the drummer's brother, and was in the band when they were called Sparrow. Then I went to a pawn shop in L.A. and got a ragged old 4X10 Bassman. That was the rig I used non-stop for some time, including the first Heart recordings; songs like "Magic Man," "Crazy on You" and "Barracuda"; total investment three hundred dollars.

I got to sit in with Steppenwolf when I was about 17; it was a big thrill to be able to play "Born to be Wild" with that band, using the guitar on which it was written.

VG: It's interesting that old 4 X 10

TOP: *Leese shows off his own hand-made H.M.L. guitar, ser. #001. All photos courtesy of Howard Leese.*

LEFT: *A mid-'80s publicity photo of Heart (left to right): Nancy Wilson, Mark Andes, Ann Wilson, Howard Leese, Denny Carmassi.*

Bassmans have become quite desirable in the vintage amp market.

HL: I know; what's so funny is that at the time it was just a cheap, affordable amp. I wanted something that would "break up" with distortion a little bit. I paid a hundred and sixty bucks for it; it was ragged when I got it and it's worse now, because it's been around the world a bunch of times, but I still have it, it still works, I still use it in the studio, and it still sounds great.

VG: Details about your Canadian recording and production venture?

HL: Mike was a drummer and I played everything else. We'd play the tracks for singers; we were making singles for Canada and were doing pretty good. Heart's *Dreamboat Annie* album was the ninth record we released.

VG: Had you joined the band by then?

HL: No, during the recording of the album I was a "hired hand," but when it was finished they asked me to join. At first I said no, because they were playing six nights a week, five sets a night in clubs, and I was doing two or three sessions a week. A few weeks later when the record started getting on the radio, it looked like they might go somewhere, so I eventually joined.

VG: Roger Fisher was the other guitarist back then; how did you two cooperate regarding guitar parts in songs?

HL: The solo on "Crazy on You" is a duet; both of us together. We actually recorded that together *live*. It's mostly me on the single of "Magic Man"; on the long version there are breaks that have both of us. Back then we split solos pretty evenly. I did a little more on the records; he did a little more live, because I had to play keyboards too.

VG: I recall a controversy about the marketing of *Dreamboat Annie*; an ad hyped something about "the Wilson sisters' first time," which had a bit of a sexual innuendo feel to it.

HL: I vaguely remember that. The cover of *Dreamboat Annie* is the girls'

faces and bare shoulders. It's tame by today's standards. If you look at the outline of their heads, it makes a heart shape, and that got totally overlooked. I think one of the guys at the record label came up with the "first time" idea because it was our first album, but there *is* a double entendre to it. That was back in the days where we were working so much that at times we didn't even know how well we were doing or what was going on; we'd be in Europe and would hear about what was going on back in the States. Things were happening fast, and by the time we found out about some of the business parts, it was too late to do anything about them, but I don't think Ann and Nancy were too happy about that.

In fact, at that time, two women in a rock band was a novelty anyway, and some people didn't take us all that seriously until they heard the music, because back then, girls were pretty much tambourine-playing back-up singers. A couple of good bands like Big Brother and the Airplane had female singers, but that was about it.

VG: There was another controversy about the *Magazine* album when it was released.

HL: That was a big legal mess, but the story is pretty simple. After *Dreamboat Annie* was a big hit, we began recording the second album. We recorded four basic tracks but didn't finish them; we went back out on tour. We were in Europe when our accountant contacted us. Even though we owned the label, we now had other people running it for us, and when we did some checking up, we found we were really getting screwed. So we signed with CBS and began recording *Little Queen*. In the meantime, the old label took those four incomplete studio tracks and four live songs from a club date recorded a long time ago, slapped it together and put it out behind our backs. We thought it wasn't fair to our fans; they deserved a

TOP: *"Tip of the Iceberg" - Howard Leese with just a few of his classic guitars.*

RIGHT: *Leese with Heart stage rigs.*

fully-recorded record, so we sued to stop the distribution. That was the first album to actually be recalled; we didn't want people to think that it was our sophomore effort.

We finished *Little Queen*, and after a year or two of legal wrangling, we made a settlement, got the tapes back, and finished the four songs as best we could, and put *Magazine* out again. The original versions of that album are collectors items of sorts.

VG: So that would have been you on piano on the live version of "I've Got the Music in Me," which was a fine cover tune, in my opinion.

HL: Yeah; I played the guitar solo on "Mother Earth Blues." That song was recorded by the band Mother Earth back in the '70s; Mike Bloomfield did the solo on it. I couldn't get enough of "Down So Low" back then.

I got to see Tracy Nelson onstage at the Newport Pop Festival in '69; she was jamming with Eric Burdon and Jimi Hendrix. She's an incredible singer, and "Mother Earth Blues" is our tribute to her.

VG: The band went through some personnel changes, and you settled into the lead guitarist slot by yourself.

HL: When Roger was in the band, he and I would play electric and Nancy would concentrate on acoustic stuff, but when Roger left, Nancy started playing more *electric* rhythm guitar. She still plays electric but she's back into acoustic a lot now.

VG: Did you add a keyboard player for tours?

HL: No, I'd play guitar and keyboard at the same time. I'd hit a big power chord with my left hand and get it to sustain, and my right hand was free to play keyboards. Or sometimes some songs would have a piano intro, but when the rest of the band came in I'd switch to guitar.

VG: A while back *Vintage Guitar* published an interview with Mark Andes, who played bass with Heart for about ten years. Any comments?

HL: "Mark, I miss ya!" (chuckles) He's a great guy; when Mark and Denny Carmassi joined, I was able to pick them both. The girls asked me to fix the band; it was "broken." I think the band we put together was a fine unit; we worked really hard and did well for years.

Denny Carmassi is in Whitesnake now. He did the *Coverdale-Page* record, and when they split up he went with Coverdale.

VG: He did the studio work for Ted Nugent's new album as well, but he didn't go out on tour with Nugent's band.

HL: We go way back with Ted; I've known him forever. He's real dedicated and works really hard.

VG: What about the evolution

of your instruments through Heart, after the "Born to Be Wild" Tele and the 4 X 10 Bassman?

HL: Well, I bought myself a nice old 'Burst as soon as I could afford one. I got a '60 model from Larry Briggs in Tulsa, in 1980. I paid $4,800 for mine, and what the prices have done since then is pretty scary! Now, they're like $48,000, but there's nothing like them, so I guess it's whatever the market will bear. If you're really serious about getting that tone, there's only one way to do it.

I use that 'Burst a lot in the studio; I use a '58 V for the rhythm tracks because it's got a nicer power chord tone. I use a Strat now and then for the clean stuff, but when we're making an album we'll bring fifty, sixty, seventy guitars to the studio because they all sound different. If you have lots of guitars and lots of amps, the combinations are endless. It's important to be able to come up with a lot of different sounds; some of the songs have as many as seven guitar parts. I don't use racks of outboard equipment or effects; my rig is really straightforward.

VG: Was the largest performance you did at California Jam 2?

HL: Cal Jam 2; biggest paid gig ever! They had to bring us in via helicopter. The attendance count stopped at about 350,000 people. It was so big you couldn't see the end of the audience from the stage. They had a P.A. system every quarter-mile, and they were time-delayed so there wouldn't any echo problems. Every band in the world was there; Nugent, Aerosmith, Journey,

TOP: Leese with early handmade PRS guitars.

BOTTOM: (left to right) 1967 ES-345; rare Pelham Blue finish. 1960 Special and Junior. 1957 Les Paul Standard - Refinished Burgundy Metallic in 1967. Late 1960 Les Paul Standard w/no fade on its top.

Foreigner. It was a fantastic day.

Ted had to fly in from Africa, where he was hunting, and the government of the country where he was on safari *collapsed,* and he had to run for the border (laughs)! They had to smuggle him out, and he had to fly for about 25 hours. He landed at Ontario about 10 minutes before he was supposed to go on; his band did the soundcheck without him. No one had heard from him, but he showed up in a helicopter and went right onstage.

VG: Any particular best or worst gigs can that you can recall?

HL: I love playing live, so *most* of the gigs have been "best" gigs. The worst gig was probably one in Kyoto, Japan. It started raining really hard; about six inches in 20 minutes, and the stage collapsed while we were playing. A lighting truss fell down and hit the drummer on the head. There have been some other crazy ones where people have jumped onstage. We've done so many shows that probably anything that *can* happen *has* happened. I've ripped my pants; I've tripped over a monitor and landed on my face (chuckles).

VG: Are there any Heart albums that are your personal favorites?

HL: I like the *Brigade* record, because it was produced by Richie Zito, who's a guitar player; he played with Elton John for a couple of years. He had lot of simpatico for me, so there's a solo on every song on that record. Guitar-wise, that's my favorite.

The Road Home, which we have out now, is an acoustic live show that we did in Seattle with some members of the Seattle Symphony, and that album was produced by John Paul Jones from Zeppelin. It was a lot of fun; it was all "pure."

No pickups; everything's miked. There's a video of it as well, which has been on the Disney Channel and VH-l. We're really proud of it.

VG: You've done some endorsements in the past; Carvin, for example.

HL: They built me a beautiful 12/6 double-neck that I still use. It's got quilted maple, and it "out-Rickenbackers" a Rickenbacker in the studio; it has a real "shiny" or "chimey" sound.

I've also endorsed Paul Reed Smith; I have the first two maple-top PRSs. Carlos Santana, Al DiMeola and I were the first three people to get those hand-made Paul Reed Smith guitars. That was my main guitar for years; that first Golden Eagle is on a lot of our records. The new Santana models are like those early hand-made ones Paul made before he opened the factory. They're as thick as a Les Paul and they have a slightly different shape. One of the two I have was made from a three-hundred-year old dresser; it has a little plug in it where the drawer pull went! I bought it after the guy in Maryland he made it for turned it down, and I liked it so well I got him to make me a single-pickup, single-knob version. After he finished it, he got me to loan it to Carlos while Carlos' guitars were being made; Carlos recorded *Zebop* with it.

I got that second guitar back from Carlos, but recently the two guitars Paul made for him back then were stolen. So I loaned Carlos "Number Two" again, while they made him some more guitars. Now, the factory's making a Santana signature model. Carlos has actually played that single-pickup maple-top of mine more than I have.

VG: How many instruments do you have? Any other "rarities"?

HL: I've got about a hundred and fifty instruments. I've got a Rickenbacker "light show" gui-

tar, and a single-cutaway jazz-type Rickenbacker that is one of three that were made in a blond finish; most were Fireglo.

I've got a lot of Les Pauls; a '58, the '60 we discussed, a '57 that was refinished Burgundy Metallic in '67, others. I have three Firebird VIIs; a white one, a black one, and a sunburst one that's perfect; it's *new*. I also have a Cardinal Red Firebird V, a '58 330 that's mint, and a Pelham Blue 345 that's the only one I've ever seen.

As for Fenders, I've got a Broadcaster, a '61 Mary Kay, two Fifties Strats in Candy Apple Red, and a Rosewood Tele, and others.

VG: What about basses?

HL: I have one of the early hand-made Paul Reed Smith basses, a '56 Precision, a '68 Paisley Telecaster bass and a matching Telecaster.

VG: Do you have a favorite piece, from a recording/performing perspective versus a collectible perspective? Can one differentiate between such?

HL: I don't think so; I think each guitar has its own personality, but some may have more value as a collector's piece, like that "light show" guitar. It's not much of a guitar to *play*. Another example might be the Vox organ guitar I have; it must weigh thirty five pounds! It wouldn't get played much, but it's kind of neat.

I'd have to say that my PRS "Number One" maple-top is my all-time favorite guitar. I've used it the most; made the most hit records with it, and I've had it since it was new.

VG: I know such guitars like the early hand-made PRSs were custom-made instruments, and I want to ask about other custom-made instruments, I toured the Gibson Custom Shop in late 1990, and they had a red prototype of a guitar made for Nancy Wilson; its profile looked like a

LEFT TO RIGHT:
Telecaster - this guitar and amp was Leese's original "rig" for years. The Tele was formerly owned by Mars Bonfire. 1956 and 1957 Strats in Candy Apple Red. 1960 Custom Telecaster and Custom Esquire. Rickenbacker "light show" guitar.

female torso. Other than the Carvin, have you had any major manufacturers that have made custom instruments for you recently?

HL: I've had some guitars made for me at Custom Shops here and there, but they're not necessarily original styles. The one for Nancy was a prototype of a guitar she designed, but it didn't go into production. The one they delivered to her was black, and as far as I knew it was the only one. Maybe that's an example of Gibson making prototypes in pairs; you never know.

Fender's made a couple of metalflake instruments during the last couple of years; a Tele and a pair of left-handed purple metalflake Strats; I just think they look cool upside-down.

But I've also started making guitars myself. I made a couple by myself, and now I'm working with a great luthier here in Seattle named Jack Pimentel. I came up with a design that looks like a cross between a Les Paul, a mandolin and a violin. The body has a Les Paul shape but it has five chambers under the top; it has a F-5 style headstock, and I use fantasic maple that I got from the Amish people. I use coca bolo for the fingerboards. I've only made a handful of them; I play the first one onstage now. It's got a PAF in it. I don't think I'll market them but I'll make some for people I know who can do the instruments justice.

VG: Do you prefer single-pickup guitars for recording and performing?

HL: Well, when I'm playing heavy rock with Heart I generally use just the bridge pickup, and I like for a guitar to be as simple and as light as possible.

VG: Sounds like the pickup philosophy of one Billy F Gibbons.

HL: "Never use more than one pickup and more than four chords." Words to live by (laughs)! If you don't need it, you don't need it.

VG: Is Heart going to do an acoustic tour to support *The Road Home*?

HL: We filmed the show in Seattle, and it's like the film is doing the tour for us. The band is in hiatus right now because Nancy's taking a year off to start a family. In the meantime, Ann and I have put together a kind of rock and rhythm & blues revue; it's a ten-piece band with horns; We'll be playing odd shows just to stay sharp. I think we'll begin work on another Heart studio album when Nancy's ready to start working again.

VG: You do attend guitar shows, don't you?

HL: Yeah; I've been to some here and I went to Dallas for the first time in '95. There were people there that I'd heard about for years, but had never met. But when you talk with such dealers and players, it's like you've known each other for years, because you've got so much in common. I love that.

And it goes without saying that Howard Leese loves guitars as well. His collection is quite enviable, but he uses his guitars as well; he doesn't just "hoard" them (RE: Rick Nielsen's *VG* interview in early 1992). That's the mark of a true professional who deserves what he's acquired.

Vintage Guitar would like to thank Bruce Hastell for his help in securing our interview with Howard Leese.

TOP: *Leese on stage.*

BOTTOM: *(Left to right) Two 1961 Les Paul Standards. 1958 ES-330TDN and 1960 Epiphone Sheraton (one of three). 1960 Gibson Les Paul Standard (A.K.A. "The Grail", says Leese).*

Lemmy
Icon with an Iron Fist

"Be sure your Last Will and Testament is order," said Malc (who is this writer's musical and philosophical peer), upon hearing that an interview with Motorhead's bass player/vocalist was in the offing.

Lemmy Kilmister has been described as "an old man in a young man's game," "the godfather of Metal," and "the Clint Eastwood of head-banging heroes" in various periodicals, and the veteran Rickenbacker basher is taking such terms literally, as the World's Most Brutal Heavy Metal Band is approaching its twentieth anniversary with a vengeance. Motorhead has been forging a new album on an almost yearly basis since the early Nineties, when their career got back on track after numerous legal hassles.

When *Vintage Guitar* talked with Lemmy (who prefers to go by his given name), a recent earthquake in California had rattled his apartment; "Some things fell off the walls, but it didn't do any structural damage," he advised. A 1991 concert video called "Motorhead Live: Everything Louder Than Everything Else" also contains some interview footage with band members; some of the comments from that video served as a foundation for certain questions in our own interview, an example of which was the first inquiry:

VG: How did you know Hitler was a vegetarian and didn't smoke or drink?

L: I collect German and Nazi stuff; I've been collecting flags, daggers, swords and medals for about four years. It's an interesting field.

VG: What about your instruments and playing experiences "pre-Hawkwind"?

L: I'm from North Wales; that's on your left (chuckles). The first guitar I had was a Hofner Club 50, then an EKO, which had four pickups and ten buttons; only four of 'em worked (laughs)! Then I got a single-cutaway Harmony Meteor; that was a good guitar. I traded it for a Gibson 330; I was playing rhythm guitar in those days. I was playing mostly blues; "Smokestack Lightning," "Good Morning Little Schoolgirl," Yardbirds and R & B-type stuff. I traded the 330 for a maple neck Telecaster.

VG: One of the other band members makes a comment on the '91 concert video about your

bass playing; he says (interviewer attempts a British accent):"'E don't play bass, 'e plays rhythm guitar." How did your bass playing style develop?

L: Phil Taylor said that. I was used to playing chords; I've got a very good sense of timing. When I went over to bass guitar, I didn't play "strict bass;" I played a lot of open strings to fill in, a lot of chords. I do a lot of things that you shouldn't do, which is great fun.

VG: Did you have to audition for Hawkwind?

L: I was still auditioning when I was fired, actually; they never told me I was in the band, and I played with Hawkwind for four and a half years (laughs)! I was on everything from *In Search of Space* through *Warrior on the Edge of Time*.

VG: You've stated that if one listened to Hawkwind, there was a three-piece rock band inside, and that when you were coming along, you wanted to be the MC5. Why did that band appeal to you?

L: They were "actual;" they did two and a half good albums. They were raw, exciting, nasty. They were like a punk band years before punk came along.

VG: And it's been over twenty-five years since *Kick Out the Jams* was recorded.

L: Is that right? I wish you hadn't told me that (laughs)!

VG: Yep; November of '68 if I remember correctly. It's finally out on Compact Disc.

L: It still holds up, as does *Back in the U.S.A.*, but I wouldn't think *Kick Out the Jams* would be as good on CD.

VG: By the time you were playing in Hawkwind, you were sporting a Rickenbacker bass. Have you always played that brand, and why did you choose it?

Tools Of The Trade: The Lemmeister with a rack o' Rickenbackers. Photo courtesy of Rickenbacker International Corporation.

The World's Most Brutal Heavy Metal Band (left to right): Phil Campbell, Lemmy, Wurzel, Mikkey Dee.

L: The first bass I had was a Hopf, a German brand. Del from Hawkwind got it for me at an auction, and I still owe him for it (laughs)! Then I got a Rick; they're very good instruments for a guitar player-turned-bass player. They've got very fast and skinny necks, which I like. Also, they've got a weird shape; I buy guitars as much for the look of 'em as for the playing. You can always switch pickups.

VG: What kind of strings have you used over the years?

L: Rotosound up until about three or four years ago; then we switched to Dean Markley.

VG: There have been tales about neck tension problems on older Ricks due to certain types of strings. Have you had such problems?

L: No; I've had my number one bass since 1979; I've had my *old* number one bass since 1971.

VG: What about the "Born to Lose/Out to Lunch" bass?

L: That Rick is the "mystery bass." It's got a maple neck, and I've never seen another one. I got it for eighty five pounds in 1978 or '79. Somebody had made it into a fretless bass by ripping all of the frets off the neck (chuckles). It also had about ten holes in the headstock where a lot of machine heads had been. It has the "Rick-O-Sound" double input, so it's definitely a Rickenbacker; I think it must have been a prototype or a special order instrument.

VG: Seems like I recall hearing that Motorhead was the official band of the Hell's Angels motorcycle outfit at one time.

L: They used to come to a lot of our gigs, and I used to share a house with two of 'em. We were the "unofficial" band, I guess.

VG: Most people probably think that Motorhead's original lineup was "Fast Eddie" Clarke on guitar, Phil Taylor on drums, and you, but wasn't Larry Wallis the first guitar player? Was this before he played in Pink Fairies?

L: Actually, the original lineup was Larry Wallis, me, and Lucas Fox on drums. Larry was in Pink Fairies *before and after;* in fact, he was even playing with *both* bands for about three weeks.

VG: Of the albums you recorded with Clarke and Taylor, which ones are your favorites?

L: Probably *Ace of Spades* and *No Sleep 'Til Hammersmith.* A music media person in England was kind enough to say that *Hammersmith* would be the "yardstick" by which live albums would be measured in the Eighties and Nineties; it was recorded in 1981.

VG: There are two other older Motorhead albums about which I need to to inquire; one was a cut-out I found called *Beer Drinkers* which had an instrumental called "Instro" and the Z.Z. Top title cut on it. With all due respect, I didn't think it was so hot.

L: Those were outtakes from the first album; the record company released 'em later.

VG: What about the live *What's Words Worth* album? I've seen it with three different covers, one of which shows a four-man band, but it was recorded when the band consisted of Clarke, Taylor and you.

L: It's getting re-released all the time. It was a gig we did for the Wordsworth Museum in England; it was a benefit, and we even played under a pseudonym, "Iron Fist and the Hordes from Hell."

VG: After Clarke left, you had former Thin Lizzy guitarist, Brian Robertson, in the band for all of one album, and after that Wurzel and Phil Campbell came onboard. Seems like I read you couldn't decide between the two players so you went with both of them.

L: And that was on the day Phil Taylor left for the first time (chuckles). Campbell and Wurzel have been with me five years longer than Eddie Clarke was.

VG: The band did a tenth anniversary gig in the mid-Eighties, and according to your onstage comments, everyone who'd played in Motorhead showed up except for Larry Wallis.

L: He should have. Phil Lynott was there as well; that was the last gig he ever played.

VG: Why was Bill Laswell chosen to produce *Orgasmatron?* He was known for dance/pop and avant-garde jazz stuff.

L: I'd never heard of him, but the management said he was good. He worked out all right;

it's an excellent mix, and he recorded everything very well.

VG: At one point, apparently due to more legal entanglements, two live albums got released back-to-back in the late Eighties.

L: There was *No Sleep At All*, which was supposed to be released, and *The Birthday Party*, which was the tenth anniversary gig that was recorded *before No Sleep At All.* We held up *Birthday Party* for months but we couldn't stop it.

VG: You were an interviewee in a documentary called *The Decline of Western Civilization*, and one Motorhead song, "Cradle to the Grave," appears on the soundtrack.

L: That was the B-side of a single; it was a good song but it never ended up on one of our own albums.

VG: That doesn't sound like a Rickenbacker bass on "Cradle to the Grave." Have you ever used any other brands to any extent?

L: That was a Rickenbacker on that song. With Hawkwind, I used a Thunderbird now and again; I've still got a Thunderbird but I don't use it. I ought to sell it; it needs to be working.

VG: What can you tell me about the Lemmy Limited Edition that Rickenbacker is going to make?

L: I haven't seen it yet; what I've asked them to do includes some hand carving on the top, and it's supposed to have Bartolini pickups.

VG: Refresh my memory about why you set your microphone in a high position, pointing downwards.

L: It helps me breathe better ...also, I don't have to look at the audience (laughs)!

VG: For the all the delays you might have had in the past, it seems the band has been making up for lost time, since *1916, March or Die,* and *Bastards* have all been released about a year apart.

L: We always put out an album a year, except when we were in legal problems. If you remember, bands used to put out an album a year all the time. I don't know why it takes people three years to do an album; if a band can't put out an album a year, then they ain't workin'.

VG: When it comes to songwriting, why is so much of your stuff oriented towards warfare?

L: I was born the last year of the war, in '45, and I guess my generation was closer to it. I think the trappings and the romance of war are fascinating. The best **** always comes out of wars; I mean, we probably wouldn't yet have the jet plane yet if it hadn't been for the Second World War. Great innovations happen during war; heroic deeds are done; people wave white handkerchiefs on the station platform while the train pulls out. It's all great stuff; it's very intense.

Sometimes when I hold some of these daggers I own, it almost seems like they're vibrating, because they've done something; been somewhere. War is the ultimate combination of emotions together: Hate, fear, love and death, all at the same time. It's an amazing experience. We haven't had a war since the Second World War, but we probably will, 'cause we can't stop ****in' with each other.

VG: An interviewer on the '91 concert video asked about your outlook for the future, and you said things like "We're all gonna go down in a soup made of ourselves" and "The human race is stupid." That tour and interview took place during the Gulf War.

L: And I stand by that. Every generation thinks it won't get killed.

VG: A song on *Bastards*, called "Don't Let Daddy Kiss Me," is what I'd call morbid-but-sincere. Why did you opt to write a song about incest?

L: Because I felt very strongly about the subject. Why would people want to molest their own children? What made me write the song was seeing a twenty-three year old girl on TV who'd been married a year; she said she'd been assaulted every night since she was five until the night before she got married. I mean, what the **** is *that*?

You might like the song better if someone else did it besides us, because we're associated with a certain thing that's expected by our listeners.

VG: But you've got to admit that given Motorhead's reputation, it's difficult to imagine the band trying to become "socially relevant," for lack of a better term.

L: Well, I've always been writing anti-heroin songs; "Dead Men Tell No Tales," "Dancing on Your Grave" and so forth.

VG: What about "White Line Fever"?

L. "White Line Fever" is about speed, actually (chuckles).

VG: The band has gotten into using acoustic guitars and recording ballads; that's a bit of switch.

L. I don't see why we shouldn't; every time the Beatles came out with a new album it was like they were a different band. I like doing power ballads; they've got a "heavy" middle part.

VG: It'll soon be the twentieth anniversary of Motorhead. I was telling a friend of mine that this interview was upcoming, and his response was: "Lemmy *is* Motorhead, period." Comment?

L: I may be the band's main voice, but it's not like that within the band. We fight like cats and dogs sometimes, but we try to keep it a democracy ...or maybe it's what might be called a "benevolent dictatorship!" (laughs)

Readers may have noticed that most of Lemmy's responses were similar to the lyrics of songs he's written: short, straightforward and to the point with no frills. Somehow, we anticipated such an attitude, and it made our conversation with the "grizzled veteran" (another phrase from a Motorhead concert review in another periodical) all the more interesting. Motorhead's latest bio describes Lemmy as the band's "frontman/founder/lyricist/icon," and in the opinion of many people, that ain't no hype.

Motorhead pared itself down to a trio format following VG*'s interview with Lemmy (Wurzel's outta there), and subsequent album releases included* Sacrifice *and* Overnight Sensation.

Michael Lutz

Bass Beyond Brownsville

The interviewer took a bit of a risk, declining a steak dinner with Ted Nugent in order to converse with musician/producer Michael Lutz (we were on a bit of a tight schedule for family reasons). While Mr. Lutz is currently ensconced as Nugent's bass player and producer of the *Spirit of the Wild* album, his history as a player in the public eye dates back to the days when he was a member of another Michigan-based kick-ass rock and roll band, Brownsville Station.

Lutz still lives in Michigan, and is an avid guitar enthusiast. We sat down backstage prior to a concert featuring Nugent's band and Bad Company; Lutz noted that he had run track in high school, and still runs; "I've run in a few marathons, and qualified for Boston once," he noted. That gave *VG* the opportunity to refer to another Michigan-based interviewee:

TOP: *Lutz cops a stereotypical (for the times) rock star image and attitude in this mid-Seventies photo. Photo courtesy of Michael Lutz.*

RIGHT: *Spirit of the Wild participants: Michael Lutz, Ted Nugent, Derek St. Holmes, and Denny Carmassi. Photo courtesy of Michael Lutz.*

VG: Mark Farner noted in his interview with this publication that he was a jock who took up guitar because he got hurt playing football. Was there any "jock-musician" transition for you as well?

ML: No, I got into track and cross-country because I was good at it, and I'd been involved with music since the fourth grade; I picked up the clarinet and sax. I've had some formal music training, but I try not to let it get in my way (laughs).

VG: What about the transition to rock and roll?

ML: One of my idols was Rick Nelson, for two reasons: I wanted to be able to sing like him, and I wanted to be able to play guitar like James Burton; he totally blew me away. There were so many guitar players that I liked, but only

a few had their own unique sounds; guys like Burton, Scotty Moore, Duane Eddy. Those Telecaster sounds that James Burton got on early Rick Nelson records still hold up today; people are still striving to get those kinds of sounds.

VG: Did those guitarists and recordings inspire you as a fan, or did they make you want to play guitar?

ML: Well, I was into music in general, and when I decided to teach myself to play guitar and keyboards, it wasn't like I dropped the other instruments, but eventually I *did*, because there wasn't enough time; the more I got into the rock and roll end of things, the less time there was to concentrate on other instruments.

Once I got into the "band/guitar" thing, what intrigued me about the Beatles was the *sound* of their guitars; it was one of the first times I'd heard a Gretsch guitar sound like that. When you listen to "She Loves You" or the opening to "I Want to Hold Your Hand," that's a *real* distinctive guitar sound.

VG: Were your first bands "garage bands," for lack of a better term?

ML: Sure; I played in a band in high school called the Talismen; we played a lot of high school functions, and we ended up putting out a couple of 45s on Hideout Records, which was Punch Andrews and Bob Seger; Glenn Frey was around back then, too.

VG: What about instruments?

ML: Well, I still have the very first electric guitar I ever bought, a Gibson ES-125TDC; what a great guitar! I don't have the first amp I bought, which was a Bandmaster. I like hollow-bodies; Scotty Moore played one, which wasn't the same model or thickness as the 125, but I was always intrigued by his sound, and I liked the idea that I could practice on it without having to plug it in. Later on I got a Fender Jazzmaster. When the Talismen broke up, I was in and out of a couple of different projects, then I decided to form Brownsville. That's too long of a story to get into (chuckles), but the original Brownsville drummer and I had been in a trio; I had switched over to playing bass by then. I was playing Hagstrom basses, a four-string and an eight-string. I still have the eight-string. We lined up Cub Koda on guitar, and Tony Driggins from Jackson on bass; I went back to playing guitar.

VG: Is it fair to say that Brownsville Station was a "Detroit sound circuit band" like the MC5, the Rationals, SRC, etc.?

ML: Sure; that's how we broke out. Our first album came out on one of Punch's labels, Paladium, which was sold to Warner Brothers. Detroit was a "hotbed" back then, and we were into big-time theatrics, climbing on P.A. cabi-

nets, hooking twenty-five cords together... that was before wireless days (chuckles)!

VG: When you said "theatrical" I thought you meant something more along the lines of Alice Cooper, because Brownsville *did* tour with the Cooper band around the time of the *Love It To Death* album.

ML: That album came out almost a year before "Smokin' [in the Boy's Room]"; we were booked out of the same agency.

VG: Around the time the band broke nationally, it had been pared down to a trio.

ML: By the time we recorded the *Yeah!* album, which had "Smokin' in the Boys' Room," Tony had left the band. Instead of trying to find another bass player, I just switched over to playing bass, which I'd done before, and most people don't know that I'd done a lot of the studio work already on bass for Brownsville.

VG: The next album, *School Punks*, had some songs that got some airplay as well.

ML: "Leader of the Gang," "Kings of the Party..." we'd actually gotten a hit from *Yeah! before* "Smokin' "; it was an old Jimmy Cliff tune called "Let Your Yeah Be Yeah."

VG: Right or wrong, is Brownsville Station perceived by most folks as having been a One-

LEFT: *Mid-Seventies Brownsville Station fanzine.*

BOTTOM: *Analog Jungle: Michael Lutz in his home turf, Tazmania Studios. His instruments are (Left to Right) a '62 P-Bass reissue, a custom-made stage bass, a '68 Gibson EB-2, a late Sixties Hagstrom 8-string, a '65 Gibson ES-125 (his first guitar), an '85 Paul Reed Smith (the 49th one made, according to Lutz), a '65 Gretsch Tennessean, a '59 Les Paul (formerly owned by Mike Bloomfield), a Conklin fretless, a '67 Gibson ES-330, and a '64 Gibson Thunderbird. Lutz is holding his Rickenbacker "light show" guitar. Photo: Bob Alford*

TOP: *1995 -
Michael Lutz
onstage w/Ted
Nugent in support
of the* Spirit of the
Wild *album.
Photos courtesy of
Michael Lutz.*

Hit-Wonder due to "Smokin' In The Boys' Room"?

ML: Of course; to this day it's still one of the all-time best-selling rock and roll singles ever.

VG: Of course, the royalties from Motley Crue's cover don't hurt.

ML: Nope, not at all (chuckles).

VG: Did it surprise you that they recorded a version of that song?

ML: Not really; I knew that someone somewhere was going to do it; a single like that will be re-done every ten or twelve years.

VG: What type of bass or basses did you play in Brownsville?

ML: Initially, I was playing a Hayman bass; it was distributed by Dallas Arbiter. The pickup had a *huge* magnet; it sounded great and was louder than ****. I was playing it through Sunn rigs.

And here's a story for you: We were doing a show at the L.A. Coliseum, and I was trying out some new front-loaded eighteen cabinets. The Hayman had an incredible amount of gain; the magnet was about three by five! In the middle of the third song, the crowd went *bananas,* and I thought we were going over great. But one of the cones in those front-loaded eighteens had caught fire, and when I turned around, my whole rig was in flames (laughs)! The audience thought it was part of the show; "what a concept."

Studio-wise I was using Haymans and a couple of old P-Basses; I still had my eight-string Hagstrom, and it ended up getting used on a couple of things early on that never made it onto a record. I've always had one or two

Thunderbird IIs hanging around as well. They've always been the "reverse," style; that's the only way to go. It's a sweet instrument, but I can't even reach the last tuning peg (chuckles). I have one that is totally pristine; the headstock's never been broken. Those are tough to find. Its finish has been taken off; that's the way I bought it and I'm sure that helped its sound; it *snarls.* It sounds a lot different from other old Thunderbirds, and I don't use it in concert; I can't find a newer Thunderbird that sounds like this old one, for that matter.

VG: When did Brownsville split?

ML: Our last album was in 1979 for Epic; we broke up in early '81.

VG: What did you do before you began your association with Nugent?

ML: I took it easy for a year; I wasn't really sure if I wanted to jump right back into the music business. I did a few projects; did a lot of writing. One day Ted called me about playing bass on a song he'd written called "Fred Bear," and he discovered that I was into the recording/production aspect, and that started our affiliation. That would have been in late '88. Production-wise, I've had a hand in everything we've done since "Fred Bear." It went one step further when we decided to do the *Spirit of the Wild* album; we designed and built our own studio.

VG: During sound check, you were playing what appeared to be an Ibanez bass.

ML: That's an Ibanez neck, but the basses are custom-made. I designed them; the wood comes from a friend who collects wood out in California; it's alder. They were put together by my tech in Ann Arbor, Tom Pellarito. I have two of those that are exactly alike. They have Bartonlini active pickups; a P-Bass type in the neck position and a Thunderbird type in the bridge position. There's a blending pot, and a tone pot that just rolls off high-end, as opposed to the standard rolling-on-and-off of high-end and rolling-on-and-off of low end. The other feature that I love is the wireless transmitter, which is built into the body of the bass.

Other than that, I use a '62 reissue P-Bass that I use on "Stranglehold" and a '77 maple-neck P-Bass as a backup.

VG: You *do* have some collectible guitars and basses, don't you?

ML: It's more than a collection; I play a lot of guitar in a lot of the projects that I'm involved in when I'm producing. I've got a Rickenbacker "light show" guitar; I had a light show bass that was stolen. I've got a '64 Tennessean, and a '59 cherry sunburst Les Paul that used to belong to Mike Bloomfield. In the mid-Seventies I had the pleasure of visiting the Fender factory, and at the time they were thinking about making an all-maple solidbody Telecaster; they had about fifty or sixty blanks sitting around but they never got into it. They gave me a blank, and I made a guitar out of it. It's a *beast;* the heaviest guitar in the world! It's got a 1962 rosewood Strat neck on it, a Schaller bridge and tailpiece, an old, original DiMarzio PAF in the neck position and a DiMarzio Super II in the bridge position; it's a *kahuna!*

Bass-wise, I've got the Thunderbird II, and an original single-pickup Ibanez copy of a Thunderbird which is a really nice bass; its made out of great wood. There's the Hagstrom eight-string, and a nice Hamer Impact bass that's a mahogany neck-through; it records really well.

I don't stash guitars and basses away. Everything I've got, I use.

VG: Tell me about Tazmania Studios.

ML: When we decided that I would produce the record, we had some time, and I know Ted's aversion to hanging out in big cities, and I'm the same; I get claustrophobic after two or three days in a big city. We'd already done some things for his bowhunting venture; "Sunrize" was done on a half-inch machine in my living room.

The studio we built is forty-eight track, analog. [I] don't believe in digital. I don't think they've got digital down right, and there's an ineffable quality to analog. Digital is unforgiving; it's like a FAX. Why would you want to have a copy of something when you can have the real thing? They haven't gotten the technology to the point where digital can understand all of the intrinsic qualities of an analog sound. I could show you in the studio where, let's say, the reverb is trailing off on a vocal, and digital can't decide what's going on, because digital is just "on" and "off."

VG: The analog advocacy of yours will probably surprise a lot of folks, considering how modern recording is probably more digital-oriented.

ML: All they have to do is listen to the record and hear how honest and punchy it is, because it's analog. Obviously, to end up on CD, the mixes have to be dumped to a digital domain, but up to that point, it was all done analog, including the mix-down.

I also believe in using a lot of vintage gear; old tube compressors, etc. And I think the only pedal we used on tunes that made it onto the record was an old Roland CE-3 chorus pedal that we used to get stereo out of two 5150 heads.

Dave Gilbert asked me in an interview for *Guitar World* how we got all of these varied guitar sounds; what did I tweak in, EQ-wise, and I told him I don't believe in it; I'm looking for *authenticity* in sound. When you hear different guitar sounds on the record, *it's because it's different guitars.* I don't sit there trying to artificially create something with EQ. I'm a believer in doing a judicious job of miking, and then if you want to change sounds, change guitars. We had all of these old Les Pauls, Gretsches, Byrdlands, and some Paul Reed Smiths at our beck and call, and we used them. We take the essence of what the old guitars and amps are, and leave the sound up to them.

VG: Future plans?

ML: After this tour, Ted is thinking about doing an album that's tentatively titled *Earth Tones* which will have a lot of hunt music. I've also been getting calls from several bands about doing some producing. I should have plenty to keep me busy in the future.

The so-called One-Hit-Wonder designation of Brownsville Station aside, Michael Lutz's ruminations about instruments and recording techniques are noteworthy, and he's got the right attitude for a veteran rocker, so he should indeed have plenty to keep him busy; he deserves it.

SIDEBAR: When Ted Nugent returned from dinner at a local steakhouse, he made it obvious that it had been an enjoyable experience; Da Nuge sauntered back into the dressing room at the venue and announced (while patting his stomach): "Now *that* was dead meat done right!"

HARVEY MANDEL

The Chicago-California-Florida Triangle

Veteran Chicago guitarist Harvey Mandel is still alive and well. Having first come to prominence in the late Sixties with his critically-acclaimed solo albums, Mandel ultimately wound up in Canned Heat, and later with British blues godfather John Mayall. He's been active all along, but has kept a relatively low profile. Much of his time has been spent in Florida, but when *Vintage Guitar* interviewed Mandel, he was living in the Bay Area of California; he'd lived in California previously, and had relocated there to nuture his playing career, which appears to be the upswing:

VG: Is it fair to say that you were a contemporary of Mike Bloomfield's when you were growing up and beginning to play in the Chicago area?

HM: I think so; he and I used to get into black clubs on the West Side to play the blues, and I think we were the first white kids to do that. One of my first gigs was at a club called Twist City, and that's where I met Buddy Guy; I must have jammed with him a million times. It was the kind of club that used to change headliners every week, so I met and played with almost every famous blues performer that was alive back then.

VG: What made you want to play guitar?

HM: Actually, I was a late starter; I began playing when I was sixteen going on seventeen. A friend of mine was playing rhythm guitar and I was playing bongos, of all things (chuckles), in a little folk music duo. I used to hang around his house, and one day he showed me how to play a chord on it. I guess I just got "hypnotized" by a guitar's sound, so I got my first one soon after that; it was a Harmony. I got my first electric guitar at Sears; I also got one of those amplifiers of theirs with two twelve-inch speakers.

VG: Describe your "progression" to better-grade guitars.

HM: My next one was a nice Guild that was similar to a 335 or 345. Then I eventually got an actual Gibson; I played 335s, 345s, and 355s for years. I used Strats on occasion as well; in fact, I played one of those at Woodstock with Canned Heat. (NOTE: Mandel can be seen on a video called *Woodstock: The Lost Performances* playing a black Fender Stratocaster. On the same tune, a revved-up version of "Goin' Up The Country", bassist Larry Taylor is bouncing around onstage with a sunburst Fender bass, and the now-deceased Al Wilson is playing a worn Fifties Les Paul).

VG: What about your earliest recording and playing experiences?

HM: The first album I played on was with Charlie Musselwhite's South Side Sound System. A couple of years later it started becoming a hit in the San Francisco area, so we got a gig at the Fillmore out there. The bill had Cream as the headliner, then the Electric Flag; Mike Bloomfield was playing with them at the time. Then us, which was billed "Charlie Musselwhite's South Side Sound System Featuring Harvey Mandel".

VG: So the first time you played the Fillmore, both Clapton and Bloomfield played on the same bill?

HM: Yeah, it was real cool; it was being promoted as a super guitar show, and Clapton was like the king of the hill at that time. I remember when I got there, all I had was this tiny Fender amp that I'd been playing in clubs back in Chicago, and there was Clapton's wall of Marshalls. (chuckles) He knew who I was, and he let me use a half-stack for the gig.

After that I moved to California; I began working on some solo projects. I also played with the Barry Goldberg Reunion a bit, then I got into Canned Heat in the late Sixties.

VG: Excuse my naivete, but I don't know what "Cristo Redentor" means. (NOTE: *Cristo Redentor* is the title of Mandel's first solo album).

HM: I think it means "Christ the Redeemer"; it's the title of a jazz tune written by Donald Byrd.

VG: The cover of *Cristo Redentor* showed you playing a thinline electric.

HM: That was a Gibson ES-355; by then I had four Gibsons. I believe *Cristo Redentor* is still available on CD.

VG: There was an album back then called *Two Jews' Blues*; the artists were noted on the cover as "Barry Goldberg And....", if I remember correctly.

Were you the "other one" besides Goldberg?

HM: No, that was Mike Bloomfield; I don't think his name could appear on the album because of contractual reasons. I played with Goldberg for a short time after that; it was mainly a recording effort. I only played a few gigs with him before I joined Canned Heat, which I did just before Woodstock; in fact, Woodstock was my second gig with them.

VG: An obvious question would be why you'd opt to join a band, replacing someone, when you were in the midst of a solo career; you had already recorded and released solo material.

HM: They were really at a "peak" back then; when the opportunity came, I figured it would be nice to travel with a group that was known world-wide. I hadn't traveled much in any of my previous efforts. I replaced Henry Vestine.

VG: This publication has already gotten Leslie West's perspective on Woodstock; what about yours?

HM: It was pretty wild; just getting there was an experience! I remember flying into some little airport in New York and being picked up by a helicopter not long before we were due to perform. The copter literally took us to the stage area. Not long after that we got up and played, which of course was like being on an acid trip without taking acid! (laughs) There was every conceivable kind of person there, from your basic "San Francisco hippie" to straight-looking people; a real "collage" of humanity. I don't think any of us realized the significance of the event at the time; it was bigger than anyone ever dreamed it would be. Some folks might have thought there'd be other Woodstocks, but nothing ever came close to it as a cultural event, in my opinion.

VG: How long did you stay with Canned Heat back then?

HM: About a year; I joined them again for about a year in the mid-Seventies, then about three years ago I joined them again for about a year and a half. I'm not "officially" with them anymore, but on occasion I'll do certain tours with them if it works into my schedule. I just went on a European tour with them a while back.

VG: There was also your association with John Mayall back around the same time as your first stint with Canned Heat.

HM: I went straight into Mayall's band from Canned Heat; Larry Taylor, Canned Heat's bass player, went along too. I did two albums with Mayall back then, *USA/Union* and *Back to the Roots*.

Working with Mayall was a great experience. It was another "traveling band"; we toured Europe and Japan back then. I stayed with him about a year, then in the late Seventies I joined up again for about a year.

VG: What else have you been involved with over the years?

HM: I recorded on the *Black and Blue* album with the Stones; not long after that I moved back to Chicago but I didn't get to get into recording any solo stuff for a long time. So I pretty much worked around Chicago and did pretty good due to my past reputation.

Then for family reasons I moved to Florida for a number of years. Living in Florida was like being in another country. (chuckles)

VG: How so?

HM: It seemed to be "musically cut off" from the rest of the country; what was going on in places like Chicago, New York or San Francisco didn't seem to affect Florida; it was like nothing existed except what was down there. They had their own club scene, for example; only a couple of clubs would bring in out-of-

town blues acts. I worked continuously when I was down there, but it was like nobody anywhere else in the country knew I was alive.

Then I got hooked up with Dave Gross, who became my manager; he heard me in a club one night and was familiar with my past stuff. He got me several gigs in the San Francisco area; those went over real well, so I eventually moved back to this area. Around the time my solo career got going again thanks to those San Francisco jobs, I joined up with Canned Heat again for one of those tours I was talking about earlier. So things started coming back around in more than one area of my music.

VG: One of the most recent recordings I've heard by you was an instrumental called "Snakebite" on the *Guitarspeak II* album.

HM: While I was in Florida, I really got into experimenting with MIDI, and I'd recorded an entire album of MIDI stuff. When I.R.S. got in touch about the *Guitarspeak* album, those songs were the most recent ones I had, so I sent them some tapes, and "Snakebite" was the one they picked. I never did release the MIDI stuff as an album; I did those recordings using MIDI primarily as a writing venture, with the intention of going into a studio and recording those songs again with live musicians.

VG: What kinds of guitars have you been using recently?

HM: I used Chandlers for a while; I had an endorsement deal with them. A while back, though, I switched back to Fenders. I have two guitars from the Fender Custom Shop that are my main guitars, a Danny Gatton Telecaster, and a Stratocaster, which is my main, "all-around" guitar. I'm also considering an endorsement deal with Gibson.

VG: Do you collect?

HM: Not really; I've got about five instruments that I'm going to keep permanently. Of course, if I still had all of the ones I've been through, I could open my own store! (chuckles)

VG: What about upcoming recordings and other future plans?

HM: I've got a new blues album coming out soon with nine songs on it; it's basically done except for a couple of possible re-mixes. Eight of the songs are vocal, and there's one instrumental. I'm thinking about calling the album *Twist City* after that club I mentioned earlier.

I've been playing pretty much in the San Francisco area; the furthest we've been so far has been Hawaii and Alaska, but when this new record comes out I hope to go out on more of a world-wide basis. I'd like to think that my playing has progressed *light years* beyond what I did over twenty years ago; I was young back then, so hopefully I've matured as well. I think if people liked my solo stuff back then, they'll like this new record.

Harvey Mandel has played with some of the greatest names in the business, and has the experience that most guitar players can only dream of attaining. He looks forward to a resurgence in his career with an admirable attitude for a veteran guitarist.

Mandel's new album was indeed titled Twist City; *he also recorded a direct to hard drive album (using retro miking techniques) called* Snakes & Stripes, *and a reissue two-CD set of his earlier instrumental efforts was also released; its title was* The Mercury Years.

Joey Molland
Golden Apple Days

Fans of the legendary pop/rock band Badfinger readily recall the English quartet was one of the most successful acts on the Apple Records ros-

ter, which was owned by the Beatles. After years of litigation, albums from that company and label are finally turning up on compact disc. One *new* anthology, *The Best of Badfinger*, contains 21 tracks from the four albums Badfinger recorded for Apple (*Magic Christian Music, No Dice, Straight Up*, and *Ass*).

Badfinger guitarist Joey Molland is still active; he's writing and recording on a regular basis. He's also got an enviable collection of classic guitars, and in a recent conversation with *Vintage Guitar*, he discussed his band's history and his instruments. Like the quartet that owned the record label for which his band recorded, Molland hails from Liverpool:

VG: What was it like growing up in the middle of what was dubbed the "Mersey sound?"

JM: It was exciting; I was 15 or 16 years old when the Beatles started to hit. I'd also been listening to Elvis and Chuck Berry. The first guitar I had was one my brother, Chris, made; he'd also had a Höfner Committee. The first good guitar I got was a cherry red Gibson ES-345. I had a Selmer amp with preset tone pushbuttons on the top, and I also used a Vox AC-30. Radio Luxembourg was what all of the musicians listened to in England and in Europe, because they played R & B records; it was a *big* influence.

VG: What about your "pre-Badfinger" bands?

JM: I played in a band called the Masterminds; we did a record for Andrew Loog Oldham, the Rolling Stones' manager. It was on Immediate; it was a Bob

TOP: *Molland on stage with a '59 Les Paul Standard.*

RIGHT: *Joey Molland's current arsenal includes a 1961 335, a '55 Goldtop, a '61 Special, '66 Flying V, a '61 Custom, a '61 Standard, two '64 Firebirds and a '92 Classic, plus old HiWatt and JCM-800 amps.*

Dylan song called "She Belongs to Me." Immediate has just put it back out on a singles collection CD. We did a Rolling Stones TV show back then; it was live and really scary (chuckles)!

The Masterminds broke up after a couple of years, and I got a job backing up a group called the Merseybeats, which became the Merseys when their singers formed another group after the Merseybeats broke up. Then, I joined a group called Gary Walker and the Rain, which was an offshoot of the Walker Brothers. We made a whole album, and that was one of my best experiences up to that point, writing and playing guitar.

VG: Were you still using the 345?

JM: No, it was stolen a few months after I got it. My brother, Chris, got me an SG Special, and I played it for a long time. Eventually, the keyboard player for Wayne Fontana & the Mindbenders sold me a tobacco sunburst Les Paul Standard. I used that all through the time with Gary Walker, up to about '67 or '68. The band broke up and we were all broke, so I traded the Les Paul Standard for one of those SG/Les Pauls and another AC-30. That's what I had when I joined Badfinger in '69.

VG: Was the band still called the Iveys when you joined?

JM: It was really right in the "transition period;" they were looking for a new name, and they'd already signed with Apple. I think the name came from Neil Aspinall, who was the Di-

rector of Apple Records at the time; he'd been one of the Beatles' roadies. He's still with Apple Records.

VG: Who was the first Beatle you met?

JM: That would have been George. A couple of months after "Come and Get It" hit, we went into Apple, and George was coming down the stairs. He congratulated us, and said "Well, you know that from now on, you'll have to play that song every day for the rest of your lives!" (laughs).

VG: My perception was that the band was slagged a good bit in the British press as copying the Beatles, but Badfinger was more accepted in the United States. Comment?

JM: First of all, when we played to a lot of college audiences in America, there would be all sorts of music in our shows, and I think the American audiences were more open to that kind of a band. We did acoustic songs, songs with a piano, or outright rockers. We found that in England, we were expected to play straight ahead pop music like "Come and Get It." England was *very* possessive of the Beatles, and anybody who came anywhere near them was looked on as "infringing." They were comparing us to the Beatles some in the press, and that may have led to sort of a "backlash." We never did achieve the popularity in England that we had in America.

VG: Then let me really go out on a tangent and ask if you heard a band in the late '70s called Klaatu.

JM: Like everybody else, I thought it was the Beatles. Their songwriting really did sound like Beatles songs at times.

VG: What about working with some of the Beatles on solo projects?

JM: Tommy [Evans] and I played acoustic guitars on "Yellow Sky" and "Don't Want to be a Soldier" for John's *Imagine* album. I used a D-35; Tommy had a real nice D-41. We also played acoustic guitar on George's *All Things Must Pass* album.

VG: Once Badfinger broke out, what other guitars did you acquire and use?

JM: When we came to tour in America, I'd get the Yellow Pages out of the phone books wherever we were staying, and go down the pawn shops and music stores. I was picking up Les Paul TV models in beautiful condition with brown cases for three hundred bucks. In 1973, I had five '50s model Les Pauls; you could go into some shops and see five or six great old Gibsons hanging on the wall. You don't see that now, unless you go into some big store like Gruhn's.

I've had a lot of classic guitars, and I still have some good ones. Back in those times everything I bought was used; I never bought a new guitar. By the late '60s, everybody was starting to get hip to the old '50s Les Pauls. The Bluesbreakers' record with Eric Clapton had that Les Paul stuck "up front" in the mix, and we'd seen people like Beck playing them, as well. Townshend was playing Rickenbackers, and George was playing Rickenbackers and Gretsches.

VG: There's some slide guitar on songs like "No Matter What" and "Suitcase." Was that you or Pete Ham?

JM: I played slide on "No Matter What," using a Gibson lap steel. It had a hell of a pickup on it; it had normal tuning except for the E string

TOP: *Playing a white '61 Special.*

MIDDLE: *The original Badfinger (clockwise from top center) Tom Evans, Mike Gibbins, Pete Ham, Joey Molland. Evans and Ham are now deceased. All photos courtesy of Joey Molland and Crosstown Management.*

LEFT: *Badfinger hangs out with George and Patti Harrison (that's Joey Molland second from left).*

tuned down to D. Pete played slide on "Suitcase."

VG: Are there any memorable concert performances you want to note?

JM: The Carnegie Hall show was a favorite, because it's such a historical place. The O'Keefe Center show in Toronto was a great one, as well. We played at a club in New York called Ungano's, around '71, and Harrison came to the gig. He sat down in front with an open briefcase that had a cassette recorder and a couple of mics in it. That was something; a Beatle recording one of your shows!

VG: How did your involvement with the Bangla Desh benefit come about?

JM: After we finished playing the acoustic guitars for *All Things Must Pass*, we came to America and did a tour, then we went back to England to start making a new record. George was producing us, and about halfway through the recording, the Bangla Desh tragedy happened; millions of people dead. Ravi Shankar asked George if there was something he could do to help, and George got into it *immediately*. He apologized for leaving us in the middle of a recording, and Todd Rundgren finished the production; he was a good friend of George and an excellent musician. George had produced some songs like "Day After Day" and "Suitcase;" Todd did the final mixes on them.

George began organizing the Bangla Desh concert, and he called everybody that had played on his records to help out, and of course, everyone said yes. The band got bigger, and we rehearsed for a week. At the dress rehearsal on Saturday, Dylan showed up! He got onstage with Leon Russell, George, and Ringo while everyone else was taking a break, and they must have played for about an hour; it was like a private Bob Dylan concert!

VG: Badfinger didn't appear as a separate act, right? Wasn't it just a big "super-band?" Did any Badfinger songs get played?

JM: No, it was all just one big effort, but it's kind of funny because at the time, we were the only performers that had a hit record on the charts. I think some people might have expected us to do "Baby Blue."

There was a documentary film that is finally coming out on video; there's supposed to be some added footage, and it's been digitized; "cleaned up."

VG: Are there any post-Apple Badfinger albums that you want to note?

JM: I think both of the albums we did for Warner stand up well today; *Wish You Were Here* has a more "gutsy"/"ballsy" sound. Then we did an album called *Airwaves* that got some good reviews, but it was a bit disappointing when it wasn't more successful. We *did* get a couple of Top 50 hits out of it, but they didn't chart as high as the earlier hits.

VG: What about the live Badfinger album? Isn't that a fairly recent release?

JM: I got that out a few years ago; the original shows were recorded in Cleveland in 1974. I had the 16-track masters, and we were seeing a lot of Badfinger bootleg concert albums in the '80s; there wasn't any "regular" Badfinger live product available. Mark Healey and I spent about 225 hours working on that album.

The original concert was recorded 16-track, with open mics; there weren't things like noise gates in those days. We dumped it over to 24-track, and cleaned up the tracks by *manually gating* them; we switched the tracks on and off ourselves. Peter had played an old Strat that night that was buzzing and farting, and his vocal mic was open, so every time he moved away from the mic, a lot of other noise would be heard. We took a long time working on it, and Ryko agreed to release it. We didn't think it would sell that well, but it did. It was simply a reaction to all of the bootlegs that had been around.

VG: And there was never a "Badfinger's greatest hits" anthology, until 1995.

JM: There was a lawsuit involving Apple and EMI that went on for eleven years, and all of the Apple artists product was taken off the market. Once it was settled, Apple began gearing up for reissues. They actually sent us a new record contract and upped our royalties; it was a major boost, and they've been doing a good job ever since. Yet, there isn't a Mike Gibbins song on *The Best of Badfinger*, and it might have been an unintentional mistake to leave some of his songs off, but I think it turned out good.

VG: What instruments do you use when you perform these days?

JM: I'm using a couple of reissue Standards; one is a Custom Shop with a flame top. I actually implanted some Patent-Applied-Fors in it, so it's more or less a 1960 Standard. I've got a refurbished '63 Firebird V; the finish got beat to hell, so now it's a beautiful Candy Apple Red color.

VG: What about guitars that you use in the studio, and don't take on tour?

JM: I've got an SG/Les Paul, a '61 Special, a couple of Harmony Stratotones, others.

VG: Didn't I hear that you played a benefit in Miami awhile back?

JM: That was a big biker rally for Toys for Tots; there were maybe 50,000 guys there! Thousands of Harleys parked in a field; unbelievable! I played with Mike Pinera, Bobby Kimball from Toto, and Nick St. Nicholas from Steppenwolf.

VG: What about other tour plans?

JM: I don't know what Mike wants to do about touring, but I've been on the road for the last five or six years playing, trying to keep it going. He and I did some shows together in Florida a while back; it was a lot of fun.

Kenny Loggins is putting together a new label; they're interested in doing a Badfinger/Joey Molland record, so I've been in the studio recording some new songs. My wife and I are setting up something to go on the Internet.

I've been a musician all my life, and as I get a little older I get more happy about the fact that I've been able to maintain that vocation. I don't have any intention of slowing down at all.

Joey Molland has the kind of dedication many veteran rockers would do well to emulate. He's played on some classic hits, and has some classic guitars, plus he's staying busy. That's an admirable mix, as is the effort heard on Badfinger's live album, and the same goes for the assortment of songs on *The Best of Badfinger*.

Vintage Guitar would like to thank Bruce Hastell for his help in securing our interview with Joey Molland.

Ronnie Montrose
Motor Scooters and Rifle Guitars

Veteran guitarist Ronnie Montrose is still rocking and still recording. The renowned player's fret efforts first came to public attention with Van Morrison over two decades ago, and his further ventures are probably known to (and have probably been heard by) many *Vintage Guitar* readers.

Recently *VG* had the opportunity of talking with Montrose; we conversed about his history and his ongoing musical efforts; he advised that he was born in San Francisco but spent most of his earlier years in Denver; he returned to the Bay Area around the beginning of the Seventies:

VG: Had the San Francisco "acid rock" phenomenon influenced you enough to make you want to move to that area?

RM: I moved back right around the end of that time; that type of music never did really appeal to me all that much, but I knew there were a lot of musicians in the area. I picked up the guitar when I was seventeen; I'd only been playing a couple of years when I moved out here. I wasn't really playing professionally; I was looking for people to jam with and thought it might lead to something.

VG: Once you started playing, who were your influences?

RM: Just about everybody I'd listened to when I was a kid. Elvis, the Beatles, the Stones, Chet Atkins, Johnny Smith, even Hank Williams. I was basically working out chords when I started, as opposed to trying to be a blues player with a vibrato style. I fell in love with the guitar the first time I picked it up and hit my first 'E' chord.

VG: Did you say to yourself: "This is what I want to do for a living"?

RM: Absolutely not. I didn't consider that being a full-time player might happen until I got an offer to play with Van Morrison in the early Seventies, although I think my first "big gig" was with Edgar Winter.

VG: What about your instruments, "pre-Edgar Winter"?

RM: My first guitar was a Gibson Melody Maker that I got at a pawn shop for sixty dollars; I was really brazen, and I put a set of humbuckers on it. Then I got a Goldtop Les Paul Deluxe around the time they began introducing them; I put full-size humbuckers in it as well. Later I had it refinished in a dark sunburst like an old Gibson L-4;

I'm still very partial to that look. I have an old "Banner series" Gibson SJ in a dark sunburst that's my favorite guitar.

VG: How did the gig with Van Morrison come about?

RM: I was doing carpentry work to make money; I'd do work for Bill Graham and his partner, David Rubinson. It was a trade-off; they'd let my band rehearse in their office space at night.

One day David asked if I'd like to play with Van Morrison; I thought he meant that my band would *open* for Morrison's band (chuckles)! I went to the audition determined to get the gig, and I got it. I owe a lot to David; he also got me my first recording session. I was with Van a little less than a year. After that I toured with Boz Scaggs right after his *Boz Scaggs and Band* album came out. We did some recording in Muscle Shoals, and in Kansas we opened a show for Edgar Winter. That's how the gig with Edgar came about.

VG: An obvious question would be why Winter wanted to shift gears from an R & B-type band with horns to a small rock combo.

RM: He just wanted to try a rock style, and they were looking for a young rock player, so I passed that audition as well (chuckles).

VG: If I remember correctly, the original lineup was you, Winter, Dan Hartman on bass, and Chuck Ruff on drums.

RM: Not quite; in the original lineup Dan and I both played guitar, and Randy Hobbs, who'd been in the McCoys and Johnny Winter And, played bass. One night in Texas, Randy had a seizure an hour before we were supposed to go onstage. Dan filled in on bass, and it worked. Randy wasn't in good health at the time, so we decided to stay a four-piece. (NOTE: Both Hartman and Hobbs died in 1994.)

VG: I recall seeing the band on the old "In Concert" series, and there was a song where you and Hartman switched instruments in the middle of a song; I think it was called "Let's Get It On."

RM: That *was* the song; you've got a good

memory! I'd go play bass while Hartman would play with his teeth; that kind of schtick (laughs). But there's a sad story about that part of the performance. We were playing in Dudley, Massachusetts one night; I was using a '58 Les Paul Sunburst that I'd gotten from J. Geils. When the time to "switch" came, I put it on a stand like I'd always do; I went over and played bass while Dan played a white Strat. When I came back over to get my Les Paul, it was gone; there was just a strap there. That was in the days of no security, and I never did get that guitar back.

VG: So you were into vintage, great-sounding guitars by that time.

RM: Yeah, I'd gotten into them around '73 or '74; I'd seen Eric Clapton, Jeff Beck and Duane Allman all playing Sunbursts. I could never afford them for the longest time, and I finally bought one once I was a full-time musician. I remember calling my wife from New York, telling her that I couldn't believe I was getting paid to play music (laughs)! That was when I first started playing for Edgar. Another rare instrument I had was a transitional reverse Firebird with a straight headstock; I was so upset that the Les Paul had been stolen that the next night onstage at Philadelphia I trashed the Firebird; it was a "youthful fit of anger," I guess.

VG: Once you could afford good guitars, used *or* vintage, did you have a preference for Gibsons?

RM: I sure did. I had two or three Les Paul Juniors, a Les Paul TV Special, and three Sunbursts. Robert Johnson of Memphis got me my '58 Flying V.

VG: You only played on the Edgar Winter Group's first album. I need to inquire about your departure.

RM: Well, it was one of those things where there wasn't enough room for everybody's "growing pains." I was thinking that it was still sort of a "sideman" gig; between Edgar and Dan, there was a lot of writing power in the band. I put out the word that I was going to do something different,

and I got a lot of phone calls, including one from Sammy Hagar. I was on vacation from the Edgar Winter Group for about three or four months; I rehearsed with Sammy, Denny Carmassi, and Bill Church, and committed to doing the Montrose band with them, but I went back and did six or seven more gigs with Edgar.

VG: Before I forget about it, I want to inquire about a particular sound on the first Montrose-album. I've seen Hagar doing the "Bad Motor Scooter" intro in concert on a lap steel. Is that how you did it on the first album?

RM: Well, one thing you ought to know is that the song almost didn't make it onto the album (chuckles)! We thought it was a "loser" track; just a little ditty that Sammy had written, but it was missing something. Then one day I was sitting with my red, double-cutaway Les Paul Junior, and a Electro-Harmonix Big Muff fuzztone, and the one amp I wish I'd never got rid of, a three-ten tweed Fender Bandmaster. I'd gotten it for ninety dollars, and when I bought it, it was covered with woodtone contact adhesive paper! The contact paper peeled right off; it didn't leave any residue and the tweed looked brand new. I used that amp so much I blew it up several times before I finally got rid of it.

I tuned the Junior down to Open D, and started dinking around with a slide; I was probably doing Johnny Winter riffs. I happened to hit something that sounded like a motorcycle, and everyone yelled "STOP!" all at the same time (laughs). We all knew where that riff belonged, so we changed reels and did it as the intro to "Bad Motor Scooter."

VG: How many albums did the original Montrose band do?

RM: There was never the same "cast of characters" on more than one album. Bill Church was replaced by Sammy's friend Alan Fitzgerald on the second album; Alan played keyboards as well as bass. We did a European tour, and Sammy and I had a real falling out; it was somewhat like what happened while I was in Edgar Winter; band members tend to get growing pains. There have been a total of five albums by Montrose; all lineups.

TOP: *CIRCA 1980 - Ronnie Montrose with a 1958 Les Paul Standard. He purchased it in 1977, and retired it after seven years.*

RIGHT: *Cover art from the "Music from Here" album.*

VG: Did you hear about any feminist protests concerning the cover of *Jump On It*?

RM: Sure did (chuckles). We had hired Hipgnosis, who'd done album covers for bands like Led Zeppelin and U.F.O.; great stuff. We gave them the title of the album, and when they sent it back the album was ready to be released, and we opted to go with it, even though we knew it might be controversial. I had one call from some feminist group. David Rubinson had a comment; he said they'd done a good job airbrushing my ****s off of the cover (laughs).

VG: *Open Fire* was released around 1979, and it might have considered to be ahead of its time, since it was an all-instrumental album; I'm thinking about how instrumental albums have gotten more popular since then.

RM: Well, it wasn't ahead of *Blow by Blow*. I was at a point in my career where I wanted to make that kind of album; I've always followed my muse. It seemed natural to do an instrumental album like that at that time. I may not be on the tip of everyone's tongue as their favorite guitar player, but I get a lot of letters from other players telling me that they respect what I do, so that helps sustain me. I *did* get a strange mix of comments when *Open Fire* was released. Some people said they couldn't stand it and that I was going to lose all my fans, and others told me that I'd finally grown up and started playing decent music (chuckles).

VG: You were also on the first *Guitarspeak* album.

RM: One of the best-kept secrets of the Eighties is that I did three albums on Enigma; I got a good response to the guitar work on *The Speed of Sound*. Edgar Winter played sax on the *Territory* album.

VG: You've chosen some unique songs to cover, including "Town Without Pity" and "Telstar."

RM: Such songs simply have a melody that I like. I was actually working on a song in 6/8 time like "Town Without Pity," and we opted to record the "original," because it has a great melody and structure. Edgar helped to arrange it and did a great job.

VG: How do you feel about collecting guitars?

RM: After that '58 Les Paul got stolen, I got real uptight about taking valuable instruments on the road. I'm known as a player, not a collector, and I look at instruments from the viewpoint that they should be played; I don't look at them from a "commodity" viewpoint. Now, if someone wants to collect instruments and keep them like they're works of art or maybe Americana items, I respect that, but there's a difference between such a collection and buying and selling guitars as commodities. I've been through a lot of guitars; these days I've only got about a half dozen instruments, the oldest of which is my Gibson SJ. I've kind of spoiled myself as far as getting into vintage pieces goes, because some years ago Grover Jackson made a Strat neck for Warren DeMartini that was too wide, so he sent it up to me. It was beautiful and it was $1^7/8$ inches at the nut, which is *very* wide, but that's what I like; with my reach I do a lot of thumbing and "wrapping around" on the neck. I have three custom-made Fender-style guitars; a Tele-style, a Strat-style, and an Esquire-style that has a B-Bender. Almost every pickup in every guitar is made by Seymour Duncan .

I also have a guitar that I designed with Steve Klein that we call the M.K. Steve then modified that design, and it became the Klein electric. I use "parts guitars," but a lot of fine builders and technicians like Glenn Quan, Mike Gardner, and Chris Hutchins have been involved in making them. That way I get what I want. I still appreciate vintage instruments, but right now it seems like most of them aren't comfortable for me.

VG: What's the story on the rifle guitar?

RM: That was made by a builder named Gordon Branch. I met him about ten years and discovered he not only built guitars, he was also a gunsmith. I'd always wanted a guitar that looked like a rifle, and some had been marketed but they weren't very good. The one Gordon made is more for concerts, of course; at one point it had a working laser inside the scope, and Steve Klein recently put a Steinberger vibrato on it.

VG: Even though you don't collect anymore, what do you think of what prices have done, especially on some of the models you used to own?

RM: I've taken guitars apart all the way down to the last screw, and I know many of them are now considered works of art, but as a player, when I go to guitar shows and see people bringing guitars in and thinking of them in terms of nothing but dollar signs, it's somewhat depressing. There isn't really any single person that's responsible for the prices being driven up, it's the fantasy of certain people who have to have a certain instrument or instruments.

VG: To wind things up, what's the story behind you falling off of a stage with your '58 V?

RM: We were opening for Journey in front of 50,000 people; this was in the early Eighties. I jumped over the monitors and headed towards the front of the stage, but I fell through a piece of shabby plywood. All I remember is that my instinct of reflex was to lift the guitar over my head; it was a thirty-foot drop. I caught my leg on some other plywood and scraped my back. I was dangling there and nobody in the audience knew I'd missed a beat; they thought it was part of the act. I had to go to a doctor for a couple of weeks because I tore a muscle in my leg, but I saved that V (chuckles)!

VG: Future plans?

RM: I had an album released in the Spring called *Music from Here*; it was done a bit differently from some of the other instrumental albums, because the songs are mostly straight jams. We did a lot of writing in the studio and I *did* do some overdubs, but it was very loose and a lot of fun. We usually tour around the Bay Area to support my newest releases, but this year we've been touring all over the country.

I've also been doing design and consulting work with Big Industries on an amp they've built. It runs on a nine-volt battery and it looks like a work of art. It weighs about ten pounds and has a six-inch speaker. It sounds really great and it's *loud*. It's called the Ronnie Montrose Signature model. So I'm keeping busy and still having a good time.

Ronnie Montrose is indeed respected by many guitarists for his past efforts, and his ongoing efforts are respectable as well. He has a commendable attitude concerning music and guitars, and such straightforwardness is also respectable.

For information about Music from Here, *contact: Fearless Urge, P.O. Box 2595, Petaluma, CA 94953-2595.*

Ted Nugent

Mo' Motor City Madness

Hiatus! Hiatus!" exclaimed Damn Yankees drummer Michael Cartellone. He was explaining the current status of the supergroup to us

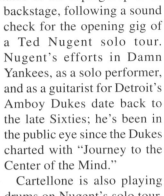

backstage, following a sound check for the opening gig of a Ted Nugent solo tour. Nugent's efforts in Damn Yankees, as a solo performer, and as a guitarist for Detroit's Amboy Dukes date back to the late Sixties; he's been in the public eye since the Dukes charted with "Journey to the Center of the Mind."

Cartellone is also playing drums on Nugent's solo tour, and the bass player for this tour is Michael Lutz, whose name may be familiar to some readers as a founder of Brownsville Station (Lutz's sense of humor was evident, as we wise-cracked about his royalties from Motley Crue's cover of "Smokin' in the Boy's Room").

The aforementioned sound check featured roaring versions of many Nugent classics, including "Snakeskin Cowboys," "Free for All," and "Cat Scratch Fever." Nugent is an avid outdoorsman; the "gimme" cap he was wearing sported the logo for his Ted Nugent World Bowhunters organization, which publishes a full-color bi-monthly magazine for a membership base of approximately 20,000. The guitarist/entrepreneur's reputation as a "beast of bludgeon" is well-known in the music business, and such notoriety is also applicable to his conversational abilities (which we expected). Nugent's pronouncements were, uh, "straightforward," to say the least.

TOP (both pages): *Photos by Scott Leibow, all photos courtesy of Ted Nugent.*

VG: If Damn Yankees is in hiatus, what are its members doing?

TN: Tommy and Jack are working on a duo album right now, and my solo album will be out this Winter. I'll probably tour and do my radio show through '95, and at some point in late '95 or early '96 the Damn Yankees will probably do it all over again. We don't feel like we've even warmed up yet.

VG: Are you originally from Detroit?

TN: I *am* Detroit; they named the city after me, as in "Motor City Madman." I've lived in Michigan all my life.

VG: Who were some of your earliest influences?

TN: The answer to that is "yes" (chuckles). Everything from short skirts to train wrecks to every guitar that would twang in between. From Duane Eddy and the Ventures and Dick Dale & the Del-Tones to all of Motown. Seeing the Beatles on *Ed Sullivan* was a big turning point, but before that, seeing Elvis on TV staggered me. He made an impact on everybody!

VG: In my opinion, there *was* sort of a "Detroit sound" for rock bands in the late Sixties; bands like the MC5, the Stooges, SRC, the Rationals, the Amboy Dukes.

TN: Absolutely. There was a real "competition" factor among Detroit bands; it was a "race" and led to a very aggressive sound; everybody was really into live club bands. The competition between individual musicians and all of the bands was unprecedented and was very

volatile. A lot of people mistakenly equated the intensity of Detroit rock and roll with the "industrial" element of Michigan, but that wasn't the case. The energy inspired everybody to just cut loose, and that's still the case. I'm sorry to have to tell you this, Willie, but *you haven't witnessed rock and roll until you've been to one of my shows in Detroit.*

VG: Around the time of the Detroit rock and roll sound, Savoy Brown noted the Detroit audiences in liner notes and some onstage commentary on the *A Step Further* album, so there's corroboration from a British source.

TN: They were probably referring to the Grande Ballroom; we played there a lot in the old days too. I don't think there's a place in Detroit that has electricity that hasn't had to deal with me at one time or another.

VG: During your Amboy Dukes days, you were noted for your "howling" guitar tone. What motivated you to acquire that signature sound, and how did you get it?

TN: What motivated me was a desire to play on the edge of volume and the edge of tone, to where it can get out of your hands. I also attribute it to the use of a Gibson Byrdland; I'm the only guy on the planet who can grab a Byrdland and do what I do with it.

VG: There were some other players who had an "oozing" signature tone back then as well; Randy California, for example.

TN: Randy was good; another good example was Randy Bachman on "American Woman" (Nugent scat-sings the signature lick from the song). I don't know how he got that sound, but it was great.

VG: What about amplifiers back then?

TN: I used Fenders, but right now I'm using

Peavey 5150s, and I'm not only duplicating the sound I got back then, I'm increasing the depth of it. But I've used Marshalls and Fenders, and I still do on occasion.

VG: On the instrumental "Scottish Tea," was the guitar supposed to represent bagpipes?

TN: Well, I don't know about that, but that's a great song, and it's a fine example of how that bass pickup on a Byrdland has a rich, open, round, and unique tone. You can hear the "hollow" sound; you can hear the spruce. A spruce-top Byrdland sounds quite different from a maple-top Byrdland; I have eleven Byrdlands, and all of them have spruce tops.

VG: One thing I've wondered about is the introduction on the live *Survival of the Fittest* album; after the M.C. or whoever says "Hello" to the audience, somebody responds by yelling "**** you," I think.

TN: (chuckles) That was actually somebody in the band, not the audience, but I can't remember who it was.

VG: By then the band's moniker was "Ted Nugent and the Amboy Dukes."

TN: Did you notice that? I thought that was kinda cute. I put my heart and soul into anything I do, so that's one reason the name change came about; if you **** up, I'll mow you down.

VG: The cover of that live album showed you with a bow and quiver.

TN: I've been into bowhunting since I was born; I've been playing the guitar and shooting a bow since I could walk.

VG: Why wasn't "Journey to the Center of the Mind" on the live album?

TN: We were just trying new things; I *did* play some of the licks from "Journey" at the beginning of the first song. We sometimes play that song even today, but I've always liked to be adventurous. We were fooling around with it during the sound check earlier.

VG: I also heard "Shapes of Things," which was a bit of a surprise.

TN: That came from a jam session while we were rehearsing for the tour. It sounded good, so we put it on the set list.

VG: There were some "guitar wars" staged

LEFT: Family Man: the entire Nugent clan participates in the patriarch's various entrepreneurial adventures. Even Rocco (on Dad's shoulders) has been seen modeling Ted Nugent World Bowhunters merchandise!

between you and other players at one point; I think it was before your solo career.

TN: Wayne Kramer from the MC5 was one, and also Mike Pinera from the Blues Image. To be honest, it was an idea of a booking agent named Dave Leone; he figured it was a way to get people more interested in bands like the Amboy Dukes and the Blues Image. It was promoted like a boxing match, but it was basically a jam session.

VG: How many albums have you put out in all phases of your career? Any favorites?

TN: Twenty-five if you include the two Damn Yankees albums. I'd say my favorite would be either the first solo album or *Cat Scratch Fever*. The tones are rich on them; the production was respected. I think I've written better songs, though; I think "Little Miss Dangerous" may be my best composition ever, but the production on it didn't capture what I call the "fibre" of the instruments. I've never been a nut for detail; I'm more into the groove of a song rather than the sound, and maybe sometimes that's been a mistake. That's why this next album is *so* important.

VG: Weren't you a fairly early endorser of Paul Reed Smith guitars?

TN: Paul came around to see me in 1973 or so; he was just a snotty-nosed kid and he said that he made guitars and offered to make me one. I said "Sure." I still have that instrument; it's one of his earliest guitars, so I bet it'd be worth some money these days. When I first got it back then I could tell he was an artist; I could tell he had a feel for utilitarian instruments for musicians, and I was impressed. I've monitored his progress, and I'd be very comfortable in saying that he makes the finest instrument on the planet. I've got about a dozen PRSs, and I used them exclusively for about the last ten years. Some of 'em are painted with zebra striping. I didn't really use any of my Byrdlands during that time; I must have been out of my ****in' mind.

Even Paul told me just last week: "Ted, I'm very proud you play my guitars, but if you don't pick up that Byrdland, I'm gonna kill ya. I miss the Byrdland." So I'm meeting with Paul soon, and we're going to create a Ted Nugent/PRS "Birdman"; that's the tentative name. It's going to have an arched spruce top and my type of neck; Paul is the *master* of necks, as far as I'm concerned.

VG: What instruments are you taking on this tour?

TN: PRSs and Byrdlands; four of each; Michael uses mostly Thunderbirds. We're tuned down to E-flat; that's the first time in my life I've tried it that way.

VG: What about collecting instruments?

TN: I've got an old Strat, two Les Pauls; a '57 and a '58. A couple of old Fender basses, and a Fender six-string bass. I've never been much of a collector, but if I still had all of the guitars I've ever owned, I could sell them and build a new home (chuckles)! Michael has one of those Rickenbacker "light show" instruments, by the way. I've got probably about thirty instruments total.

I'm still looking for old Byrdlands, and I'd like another six-string Fender bass; one with four switches on it. It has what I call a "granite meets glass and chrome" sound; I recorded an instrumental called "Sunrize" with the Bass VI I already have.

VG: Didn't you also record an instrumental for your daughter Sasha at one time?

TN: I sure did; she's on this tour, helping with backstage management.

VG: You alluded to your upcoming album a bit earlier. Why is it so important?

TN: For one thing, it just *reeks* of wood. Michael and I co-produced it; we built our own studio called Tazmania Studios, and we really *captured* the sound. If you like "Cat Scratch Fever," "Stranglehold," or "Great White Buffalo," you're gonna have to own *two* copies of this next album, which is called *Spirit of the Wild*. I can't believe I ever put that Byrdland down; Mike inspired me to pick it back up. There are some PRS guitars on the new album, but it's what I'd call "90% Byrdland."

VG: Back around 1970, when *Creem* magazine was still newsprint with a tabloid format, you were already espousing a "drugs suck" attitude.

TN: Absolutely; all my life I've been *militantly* against abuses of my senses. I know the issue you're talking about; I was on the front in a fishnet outfit.

I consider my senses to be gifts from God, and I would never give the Lord the finger by poisoning my senses. I'm fortunate to have them as well as my motor drive; being a hunter from early on taught me that you have to have reverence for life forms, and it has to start with your own. I've never touched a drug in my life.

To witness the vulgar tragedy of trendy, transparent drug infestation by what I call the "pierced-nipple brigade" in this industry has made me do sort of a combination of laughing and puking. I think that anybody that poisons their system with drugs, alcohol or tobacco is a lesser human being, and I'll spit on their graves.

VG: I take it, then, that you ain't too broken up about Kurt Cobain's demise.

TN: I have no patience for maggots like that. I consider him to be a perfect example of a bad human being; he's what wrong with our species. He had the *nerve* to make a list of complaints and then poison himself with heroin? **** him. I wouldn't even waste my spittle on his grave.

VG: We've just about covered everything, including your future plans. Anything else we need to know about?

TN: I'm working with Gibson on plans to replicate some of my Byrdlands. We went by the factory during this tour and they're going to blueprint some. One of the ones they'll be making for me will be in a cherry-stain finish, which will be a first for a Byrdland, as far as I know.

VG: Is the term "conservative rock and roller" an oxymo-ron? The only examples I can think of are you and the late Lee "Backbeat" Atwater.

TN: Well, I don't really have an answer for you, but I do know of some people in this business who are responsible musicians; my own band for starters. Some others seem to have their act together fairly well, even if they had to learn the hard way. Eddie Van Halen, who's a virtuoso, and the guys in Aerosmith, for example. The guys in Z.Z. Top seem to be pretty much family-oriented. Sammy Hagar has a work ethic that the rest of the world could learn from.

It seems to me that if MTV and other liberal pieces of **** wanted to get the facts representing the real hard-working, hard-playing people in this business, they only need to go to one place, and that's to Ted ****in' Nugent, because I have maintained my focus, my identity, and my integrity as I've done the breast stroke up the white, frothy rapids of indecency in this industry. And I've made it, not by myself, but with others like Michael Lutz and the guys in Damn Yankees, who have also maintained their focus, identity, and integrity.

VG: One last inquiry: You're the official musician of the Excellence in Broadcasting Network. Does Rush Limbaugh, as he claims, play "the best bumper music in talk radio"?

TN: No, I do. I mentioned my own radio show earlier. It's national, and Rush was a guest on it. I only went to 39 markets; this Winter I'll be on *hundreds*.

I'm 45 years old, and I haven't even gotten started yet. This new album that will be out later this year proves it.

Suffice to say, a conversation with da Nuge-meister is quite an experience, but like all too few persons in the public eye, Nugent has facts to back up his pronouncements, no matter how blunt some of his statements are. He's definitely one of a kind, and not just because he plays loud rock and roll on a Gibson Byrdland.

Persons interested in Nugent's bowhunting organization should contact:
Ted Nugent World Bowhunters
4133 W. Michigan Ave.
Jackson, MI 49202
ph. (517) 750-9060

Vintage Guitar *would like to thank Jeff "Arafat" Carlisi for his help in arranging the interview with Ted Nugent.*

HARTLEY PEAVEY
The Sound of the South

The sub-title of this interview could just as easily be something along the lines of "The Mississippi Maverick," but that would put such a sub-title too close to the sub-title of a dealer profile that appeared in an early 1993 issue of *Vintage Guitar* (Fly-By-Nite Music's profile was sub-titled "The Missouri Maverick"). At any rate, most readers are probably already familiar with Hartley Peavey and the myriad of musical products that are manufactured in Peavey's sprawling complex in Meridian, Mississippi.

Since many guitar dealers and enthusiasts tend to use the quarter-century mark as a loose definition of differentiating between instruments that are "vintage" vs. simply "used," some of Peavey's earlier amplifiers are just now entering the "vintage" category; he started his company in 1965. When we visited Hartley Peavey in Mississippi's "Queen City," we began our interview by discussing the history of this modern American success story in the musical instrument and sound reinforcement business:

VG: Here's your opportunity right at the outset to comment about the two-part article on Peavey instruments that appeared in *Vintage Guitar*.

HP: I thought the article did a good job discussing the instruments, but I sort of found myself wishing that it had discussed the company's contribution to guitar manufacturing. We were the first company in the world to adopt modern construction techniques for guitars; that was what made the T-60 and the T-40 bass unique.

VG: Well, that's why I'm here; perhaps the factory tour today will enlighten our readers. You've got to admit that many people wouldn't have thought that a manufacturing company from the Deep South could have accomplished what your company has accomplished.

HP: When I first started out, everybody said: "That Peavey kid down in Mississippi's crazy"; that I couldn't make a go of making musical products where I was located. But what about the locations

of where most kinds of American *music* evolved? You can draw a square that's about two hundred and fifty miles long on each side, where the "bottom" borders the Gulf of Mexico, the "west side" is just on the other side of the Mississippi River, the "north side" is the northern border of Tennessee, and the "east side" goes down from the eastern border of Tennessee. Inside you've got Louisiana, Mississippi, Tennessee, Alabama, and maybe a bit of Missouri.

Think of the musical styles that came from that area: Jazz from New Orleans, Country and Gospel from Nashville, Delta blues, and "blends" of all those types of music. And where is Meridian in that "square"? Dead center. We're in the middle of the heartland of American music.

VG: What about your own musical experiences before you settled in to manufacturing instead of playing?

HP: My father played saxophone in a Swing band; they toured all over the Southeast, playing places like Coral Gables, Florida. When he got off the road he worked at J. J. Newberry's, which at the time was what was known as a "five-and-ten-cent store." Then he opened a music store in 1938 here in Meridian with fifty dollars and a second-hand piano.

I came along in 1941, and my father was too old to be drafted during World War Two, so he tried to

TOP: *Check out the name tag - everyone in the Peavey organization is on a first-name basis, including the founder. This photo is circa the early Eighties.*

RIGHT: *Melia and Hartley Peavey today.*

make a go of the retail music business, even though you couldn't buy instruments during the War. He'd go out into the countryside and buy old player pianos and refurbish them. So I was literally raised in the music business.

The interesting thing about having been born in 1941 is that my teenage years happened to coincide with the birth of what we now know as rock and roll. My father wanted me to play in the school band; he promised to buy me a car, which was also important to a teenager (chuckles)! I started out on clarinet, which a lot of sax players do. I didn't like it; I thought it was a sissy instrument, and it seemed like I was always biting holes in the reeds. Ultimately I played trumpet in the marching band, but I still hated it; I didn't want to march at football games or dress up in a monkey suit with a tassle on my head (laughs); but I was working for that car!

My grand-dad died when I was in the seventh grade, and I sort of inherited his hand tools; I was pretty handy and used to build things like model airplanes and science projects; I'd win some science fairs not because I was smart, but because my projects looked really good.

VG: So how did your involvement with playing guitar come about?

HP: My father's store was also a Magnavox dealer; I got to work on a lot of hi-fis, converting them to stereo in the late Fifties. We used to get records in the store; I remember I got goose bumps the first time I heard Ray Charles' "What'd I Say." I did some D.J. work as a teenager as well, and one of the stations where I worked switched to a Country format two or three weeks after I went to work there. I was all ready to quit, but then I realized

they were getting all kinds of records into the station, and they were literally throwing away all of these great rock and blues records. Greed got the better of me; I was like the old Allstate logo with the hands (laughs)! I'd walk home every day with a ton of great records; classic labels like Blue Note and Excello.

In 1958, I went down to Laurel, Mississippi to a Bo Diddley concert, and that just blew me away. Bo had an amplifier about the size of this desk, and a Les Paul-type instrument covered in rabbit fur! He had just come out with the album with that rocket-shaped guitar of his on the cover. I went home and pestered my father to give me a guitar, but he said I had to learn to play before he'd give me one; he also said that guitar players didn't pay their bills (chuckles). He finally gave me a Suzuki classical; it was the first Japanese guitar I'd ever seen, and I didn't know you weren't supposed to put steel strings on it, which of course I proceeded to do; of course the bridge came right off (laughs)! So that was my introduction to the wonderful world of guitars.

VG: What about your first electric instrument?

HP: I was a horse trader; I went through several, but I remember that the first *decent* electric guitar I had was a mahogany Les Paul Special. I liked the way Gibsons sounded, but I didn't like the way they looked; I thought Fenders were cool so I carved out a place in the back of the Les Paul and painted it white with Krylon spray paint. I ended up giving it to a friend of mine named George Cummings, who ended up playing lead guitar for Dr. Hook and the Medicine Show. George was down here visiting me a few weeks ago, and he told me he still has that guitar.

VG: I assume you played gigs like fraternity parties with "show bands."

HP: Yeah, but I was never very good. I built an amp from a Mullard schematic that had four twelves and a couple of horns; it also had an RIAA E.Q. curve in it that was a piece of crap. A friend said he'd give me some lessons if I'd build him an amp, so I did. As it turned out, I ended up building gear for almost every band I played with, then I'd go to practice one day and they'd have some new guitar player who could blow me away, so I'd be out. The first time, I said something to myself like;"That's life"; the second it happened I said something like:

TOP: *Hartley poses in the early Eighties with one of his original-style instruments, the Mystic.*

LEFT: *A younger Hartley Peavey at his craft.*

"Boy, this is a string of bad luck!" But the fourth or fifth time it happened I said: "You know, I think these people are trying to tell me something!" (laughs).

VG: According to literature I've read about your company and personal history, you started your amplifier building company right out of college.

HP: Right; I stopped playing in bands when I was a Junior, and I took a personal "inventory," trying to decide what I wanted to do with the rest of my life. I decided that I was good at building things, and I loved music. Leo Fender was my idol; I had all of his catalogs. I could tell you all of the dimensions, weight and tube compliments of his amps; I could even draw the schematics for most of them. I'd actually gone to a local vocational school starting in the summer after I finished the sixth grade, taking electrical courses, and by the time I graduated from high school I could run a lathe and a milling machine; I could work sheet metal and fix a radio or a television. All of that, combined with my experiences in my dad's music store, gave me a well-rounded approach to my efforts.

VG: Other than your location, which we've alluded to earlier, how did you try to be "different" when you first began making amps in the mid-Sixties?

HP: I'd played in bands for about eight years before I quit, and all that time, almost every musician I talked to told me the following statement or some version of it: "I wish that somebody would make good gear at fair and reasonable prices." I've always used that as a cornerstone of my company's philosophy.

VG: Obviously you've gotten a lot of folks who took you up on that philosophy.

HP: Yeah, but I still get somebody every once in a while who'll say something like: "No offense, Peavey, but I tried one of your amps back in 1967 and to tell you the truth, I wasn't impressed."

My usual response is to ask if such a person's guitar playing has improved since then, and the reply is something like: "Of course I've gotten better!"

To which my next response is: "So have I."

VG: You began making solid state amps before tube amps.

HP: Yes; keep in mind that in 1965 solid state was still new to everybody, and many of the other amplifier companies tried on more than one occasion to manufacture and market solid state amps with disastrous results back then. Mine were pretty damn good for those times. I set up shop over the music store, which by then had been sold by my father, and I made one amp at a time. I began selling "direct from the manufacturer," such as it was (chuckles); I'd take my amps to regional dealers in towns like Tuscaloosa and Montgomery. Mississippi Music, who bought my father's store, was also one of my first dealers.

VG: A lot of the stories about your company's history have already been documented in various publications, including the issue of your company periodical, *Monitor*, that was published for your company's 25th Anniversary celebration. Is there any anecdote that some people might not have heard that you can tell us?

HP: I think the story of how I got my first salesman is kind of funny. Around 1966 or 1967, the manager of the music store below my shop called me one day and asked me to come down; there was a salesman down there claiming he had the best-sounding amp in

the world. The salesman said it would blow any other amp away; that it was better than Fender, better than Vox, better than anything. The music store didn't have a guitar player on the premises, so they called me to come down and try it out.

I walked downstairs, and there sat this tuck-and-roll pleated Kustom monster on casters with two Altec speakers in it. The salesman was bragging about it, and told me to turn it on. When I hit the switch, the amp went **"KA-POOK! Sssssssss";** it was noisy as hell and it had no definition. The salesman wanted to know my honest opinion, and I told him I didn't think it sounded worth a ****. The salesman got agitated, obviously (chuckles), and when I told him I had an amp that sold for less than half of what the Kustom would retail for, he dared me to bring it out; he said something like: "Roll it on out here, sport."

I brought down a 65-watt solid state amp with four ten-inch Utah speakers in it; I couldn't afford Altecs. I turned it on and blew his ass out of the room (laughs). I mean, the blood drained from his face! He didn't say a word; he just packed his bag and rolled his Kustom out the door. I went back upstairs feeling sorry for the salesman and a bit embarrassed, but he made me do it.

A few minutes later, the salesman's brother, who was traveling with the Kustom salesman, came up to my shop. The Kustom salesman's name was Bob Belfield, and his brother Don was also a traveling salesman, but didn't have a line at the time. Don was also in the store when my amp blew away the Kustom, and he came scurrying up to my shop, begging me to let him sell my amplifiers. I didn't know how desperate he was (chuckles), and he didn't know how desperate I was, because I didn't have any money. But he took my amp on the road, which left me more time to build amps, so it worked out well for both of us.

VG: And things have just gotten bigger since then. What about your current facilities, and the evolution to your current size?

HP: In 1968 I borrowed $17,500 and built my first plant; a few years later I bought an old corrugated cardboard factory as we got bigger. Then in 1973 I built the first part of the big yellow building that now comprises our largest facility; we've kept adding on to it over the years. We now have twenty-one separate facilities with a total square footage of 1.2 to 1.3 million. All of our factories are here in Meridian with the exception of a speaker plant in Foley, Alabama and a factory/warehouse in Corby, England, which is about ninety miles northeast of London. The British plant makes microphones, speaker enclosures, and some electronics, and they do the distribution for the European continent.

VG: Forrest White told me that he admires your success; he called you "the modern Leo Fender." He also said he introduced you to Mr. Fender at a NAMM show.

HP: That's a true story; I decided when I was a young pup that I wanted my company to be like the old pre-CBS Fender company, and I've tried to maintain that attitude as we've gotten bigger. Of course, our sales have far surpassed what the Fender company did, but to be fair they weren't making things like signal processors and synthesizers (chuckles)! Yet I've got to think that had the old Fender company not sold out to CBS they would have eventually gotten into manufacturing such products.

I finally met Mr. Fender in the Eighties; by then we were already making guitars. He gave me some advice about how to maintain control of my company from the viewpoint of "one old man," to use his words. It was the only time I've ever gotten goose bumps talking to someone; that's never happened before or since. I mean, what do you say to a living legend?

VG: Your company has a myriad of endorsers; apparently you are quite active in soliciting famous names. Who were your first endorsers, and what was one of the most interesting endorsements you got?

HP: The Nitty Gritty Dirt Band was the first "big name" act I got to endorse my amps. Back then we had them play a concert here, and Steve Martin was their warm-up act; he was just becoming known nationally back then. He was a banjo player; John McEuen taught him.

One of the most unique endorsements was a recent one, where Eddie Van Halen collaborated with us on the "5150" amplifier. You see, Eddie wanted a rugged, powerful and dependable amp, but he wanted the speakers in it to sound "broken in," for lack of a better term. I compare it to buying shoes; a pair of shoes will feel different after they've been worn for a while, but how do you get a set of speakers to sound like that right out of the carton?

We did a whole new special Sheffield speaker for Eddie, and that did the trick, combined with our "Resonance and Presence Control" circuit inside the amplifier; it helps a player adjust the sound of the speakers. Van Halen was delighted with the way it turned out.

VG: Considering the title of this magazine, none of your guitars are old enough to merit "vintage status" yet, but you know how most of the desirable vintage pieces are U.S.-made, and your company is still domestic. Comment?

HP: Most of the "vintage companies" aren't with us anymore. With the exception of Rickenbacker, domestic companies have either sold their names to other companies that don't give a damn about guitar-making, and/or they've gone running off overseas using cheaper labor. How they can put a classic American guitar maker's name on such instruments seems almost unethical to me. It's almost like some guy on the street trying to sell you a so-called Rolex watch for twenty dollars. Yeah, it may have the Rolex name on it, and it may look like a Rolex, and it may keep time, but in your mind, is it really a Rolex?

I have an enormous amount of respect for the Hall family and the way they've run Rickenbacker. They've kept the faith with their customers, and they've never stooped to what some of the other guitar companies have done.

VG: Let me put myself on the hot seat here a minute. I've opined in writing that the T-60 could have been to the Eighties what the Danelectro-made Silvertone "amp-in-the-case" guitars were to the Sixties; "everybody's first electric guitar." Is that a fair statement?

HP: Not really; I think you were probably thinking about price versus the way they were made. Nat Daniels wanted to make something as cheap as he could, so he used poplar and Masonite. My guitars were lower-priced than my competitors, and I'd be happy to compare the quality of my instruments to theirs. In fact, the price and manufacturing of electric guitars in the mid-to-late Seventies were what inspired me to go into the guitar-making business.

I know a lot of luthiers won't like to hear this, but I'll debate till I'm blue in the face that bodies and necks can be made better using computer technology, which does a better job in turning out consis-

tent products.

VG: Was there any other product that inspired you to apply its manufacturing techniques to guitars?

HP: I like tinkering with firearms, and some of the tolerances used in making guns fascinated me. I did a little research and found out that things like rifle stocks are made with a machine called a copy lathe; gun manufacturers put a two-by-four on such a machine and carve out a rifle stock. It works in sort of a panographic way, and the finished piece of wood is several thousandths of an inch from the size of the final product; all they do is a bit of final sanding.

Nobody had ever tried to build guitars the same way. I went to Germany and bought a Geiger copy lathe; we set it up to do four necks at a time. It had a rotating cutter, and a sander built into it as well.

VG: Your "pre-installed" truss rod, for lack of a better term, was another innovation.

HP: We realized that a lot of people were installing truss rods after the neck was carved; after the fact. A truss rod is literally a bent piece of steel, and it pre-tensions the neck. If you install a truss rod after a neck is carved, you get an artificial force that is added. We carve the neck with the truss rod in it, so that means when we carve the surface of the neck, it's already pre-tensioned. Nobody had ever built a neck that way before; at least if they had, I didn't know it.

VG: Any other machines and/or innovations you use?

HP: We bought a numerical control profiler, which differs from a router. A router goes forward and backwards, and right and left; what we call an "X" and "Y" axis in manufacturing. Our profiler also goes on a "Z" axis, which means that you can carve the top of a guitar body at the same time it's being cut out. One operator can make three hundred solid guitar bodies a day.

VG: Are you saying that you proved people who said "you can't make guitars using computers" wrong?

HP: We were really talking about different things. They were talking about making *guitars* with computers, and I was talking about making *guitar parts* with computers. You have to differentiate, and sometimes that difference has gotten overlooked.

And what is it that transforms a pile of guitar parts into a guitar? A pair of human hands. I believe that human hands should be used for what they do best: assembling and setting up, and not correcting slop, which as far as I'm concerned is what a lot of hand-built pieces have to have done to them. I know a lot of your readers won't like to hear that, but I'm fully prepared to sit down and show anyone which can make a more precise instrument time after time: man or machine.

VG: I'm sure that's not the first time you've said something that might be interpreted by some folks as controversial. Another controversial item was the "Why?" ad some years ago.

HP: (chuckles) My philosophy has always been to build the best products I could; they just happened to be priced less, because I cannot let my company charge more than a fair price for our products. That ad you're referring to pointed out such differences in our T-60 and two instruments by my friendly competitors; our T-60 included a molded case, and we were the first company to manufacture blow-molded guitar cases as well.

VG: Not to harken back to the Danelectro comparison again, but is the perception that Peavey guitars are more budget-oriented valid?

HP: Absolutely not. We build durable, quality equipment at a fair price for working musicians. Of course, every once in a while someone will still tell me something like: "You know, Peavey, you build great stuff," then they'll add: "For the money." Well, bull****. We build good stuff and it holds up. It represents *value*.

You see, consumers can tend to be somewhat fickle, and sometimes it seems like musicians can lead the pack. I've brought out products for working musicians just like Leo Fender did; when he introduced his Broadcaster it sold for what, about $165? It was a no-frills "breadboard" instrument that probably looked cheap to people used to big archtop electrics with binding. It's interesting that the year Mr. Fender sold his company to CBS, 1965, was also the year I went into business; sometimes I think that maybe that's the year Mr. Fender "put his torch down," and I picked it up.

So it really bothers me when someone says my guitars are "cheap." The T-60 makes a Broadcaster look crude and cheap, so whenever someone starts comparing our earlier instruments to Danelectros, I feel like I've been kicked in the butt.

VG: A lot of people consider your earlier Classic tweed amplifiers to be "up-and-coming collectibles," for lack of a better term. Are there any fretted instruments that you've built that may become collectible, in your opinion?

HP: When we first started out making guitars, we built a few small instruments that were in a T-60 configuration; they were almost like 6-string mandolins. We opted not to pursue building them because it cost about as much to build one of those as it did to build a regular-size guitar, and the perception of the public was that such instruments were novelty items. Maybe those might become interesting, considering how few of them were made; they're out there in the market. Speaking of Classic model amps, we're building them again with even better circuitry, albeit in an old tweed-looking case. This new circuitry produces a modern, contemporary sound, as well as the sweet, vintage sounds produced by those amplifiers of "yore."

VG: One publication noted that your company has done some progressive things for your employees, like initiating a literacy program.

HP: I want you to notice in the factories that everyone's name tag has their first name on them; everyone's on a first-name basis. There are no "Misters" at Peavey, and I've taken that attitude since I first started the company.

Of course, when I first got going I had hair down to my shoulders, and in those days in a small Southern town everybody thought you were a hippie if you looked like that (chuckles)! But hippies didn't work, and I worked my butt off. I hired people regardless of how long their hair was, what color their skin was, or whether they were male or female. I told anybody that went to work for me that we all had a job to do, and whoever did an outstanding job had a future with this company in a position of responsibility if he or she wanted it. We take care of our people; that's the way it started out, and that's the way it is now.

VG: Are there still times when you're still considered to be an "upstart"?

HP: You'd better believe it. My response to that kind of attitude is to state that I've been in this business for over twenty-eight years.

I invite anybody who thinks this company is still a "fledgling" or "upstart" corporation to look around the musical instrument manufacturing business and tell me which companies have the same owners they did almost three decades ago and are still going strong. I can't think of anybody except Rickenbacker, Jim Marshall, and Zildjian. How many others are in that situation? We're one of the few companies that have actually *increased* the state of the art. We're pioneers in computer-integrated manufacturing; the product is actually built inside a computer before it's physically built. We have over a hundred engineers, and we go around the country for IBM, helping them give seminars.

VG: You've got a relatively new type of guitar for your company that's been on the market for a while, the "Ecoustic" electric/acoustic. Have you ever had any inclination to build and market arch-top guitars or "thinline" electrics like the Gibson ES-335?

HP: No, because my perception is that those types of products sit in dealers' stores too long. As I said earlier, we build equipment for working musicians, and the vast majority of working musicians prefer solidbody instruments.

VG: Are there any other products you may consider getting into down the road?

HP: Well, we've been quite satisfied with how our keyboards have done, and we got into making synthesizers and pianos after we began making guitars. You see, I'm never satisfied. We're continually developing new products in our computers; we're forever making prototypes of instruments. We've come a long way, but "the fat lady hasn't sung yet" (laughs)! The one slogan that will always keep me looking forward is: "If it makes sound, it's fair game."

Before we departed Hartley Peavey's office, he showed us two guitars that were perhaps the antithesis of each other; neither was a Peavey-made instrument. He proudly displayed his recently-acquired Heritage arch-top electric with his name on the truss rod cover, and then showed us a cheaply-made flat-top tenor guitar; inside the soundhole was a black label with the familiar Peavey "lightning bolt" logo, along with the words "Hecho En Venezuela." It was an obvious counterfeit; Peavey doesn't even know who made it.

Hartley Peavey can take a certain amount of pride in the counterfeit Peavey flat-top as well. Anytime a guitar manufacturer has become established enough in the market that someone opts to make phony instruments bearing the company's name, it's a back-handed compliment of sorts. Such "respect" for a company may be somewhat off-the-wall (not to mention illegal), but the *legitimate* respect for Peavey products and the company's success in marketing durable, well-made American instruments and sound reinforcement products show no sign of stagnating.

In the mid-Nineties, Peavey opened another guitar factory in Leakesville, Mississippi. The company also began importing Scandinavian-made acoustic instruments, then finally opted to import electric guitars from the Far East; such instruments were known as their "International" series. Peavey landed the guitar endorsement of Eddie Van Halen as well. The newly-designed guitar was called the "Wolfgang" in honor of Van Halen's son.

Joe Dan Petty
"Techin' it Twice"

It's been "full circle more than once" for bassist/"guitar tech" Joe Dan Petty, of Macon, Georgia. "Guitar tech" is in quotes because during his first stint as a member of the road crew for the Allman Brothers Band (he's on the back cover of the *Fillmore East* album), his job description was the less-refined "roadie."

But, contrary to popular belief, Petty was a bassist *before* and *between* his associations with the standard bearers of Southern Rock. In a recent telephone dialogue, Petty discussed his years of playing and road work in a cordial conversation with *Vintage Guitar*.

Joe Dan Petty is originally from Bradenton, Florida, where he played in a self-described "kid band."

"We played high school proms and skating rinks," he said. One of his peers in those days was Dickey Betts, and Petty advised that Betts' father played fiddle at barn dances attended by Petty's mother.

"The first real professional band I played in was called the Jokers," says Petty, "which wasn't the same Jokers that Dickey played in when he was in Indiana; he formed this band after he moved to Florida. I could only play marginally when I started hanging out with Dickey, but he taught me a lot."

Another "pre-Allmans" venture for Petty was called the Thunderbeats, which included lead guitarist Larry Rhinehart, who went on to subsequent fame with bands such as Iron Butterfly. Later, Petty and the Thunderbeats' other guitarist, Mac Doss, went to the Jacksonville area, recruited a drummer, and began playing nightclubs, using the same moniker. Another Jacksonville musical aggregation for Petty was known as the Gold Rush, a blues-based combo.

Yet another Jacksonville-area band of Petty's was playing regularly at a St. Augustine club when the venue shut down for two weeks for remodeling. "The Brothers came through town during that time," Petty relates, "and asked me if I wanted to go to Miami with them; they were doing some recording. I went along and never went back to my band."

Petty's earlier basses included his first instrument, a '50s Gibson EB-1.

"You could mount a stand on the bottom of the body and play it like an upright, and it was a dream to play, but I didn't like its sound. It was too 'muddy,' and I never could get it to sound like I wanted. I bought a Jazz Bass, but the neck on it was so screwed up that it wouldn't play in tune. There was a hot bass player around Jacksonville, named Chuck Parrish, who I really admired; he played a Precision, and I *loved* the tone of that instrument. The guitar player in his band sold me a Precision, but the pickup didn't work, so we installed one of the pickups from my Jazz, and it sounded great!"

The switch from a short-scale EB-1 to a full-scale P–bass initially proved daunting.

"I'd take it to a club date, and could only play it one or two songs before it was *killing* me," he said. "The neck was longer and wider, and it took awhile to get used to it, but once I got to where I could play it all night, I retired the Gibson."

Eventually, Joe Dan got another Precision, which he kept until it was stolen while he was playing in Grinderswitch (more about that band later). That particular P-Bass was a totally stock model in a sunburst finish.

As for his "roadie" days with the Allman Brothers Band, the erstwhile bassist averred that he was at some of that band's earliest rehearsals in Jacksonville, and he recalled the Second Coming, a band in which Dickey Betts and Berry Oakley played just prior to the formation of the Allmans. Petty noted that in those days, the term "tech" didn't exist.

"When I started, people who worked on the crew were called 'roadies,' but just prior to that, 'roadie' was what a band's *road manager* was called. That was when bands didn't have people handling their equipment. As 'equipment managers' we ended up being called 'roadies.' I think the term went through some changes.

"When I went back to work for the Brothers in '89, I was called a 'guitar tech,'" he said with a chuckle. "I haven't been a 'roadie' in quite some time."

Joe Dan Petty's original assignment within the original Allman Brothers Band was to set up Butch Trucks' drums, but he noted that among the roadies, "everybody did a lot of everything. "The 'amp line' roadie was Kim

Payne, Red Dog set up Jaimoe's drums, and Mike Callahan did sound, but we all helped each other out. The band took care of their own instruments. If they wanted something, like the pickups changed out, they didn't hand the instrument to us, but in some cases we'd help if something needed to be modified.

"Berry Oakley was really into his rig," Petty continued. "And he was always modifying things, trying to get a better sound. He had some older, vintage basses that he didn't mess with, but when he'd been in the Second Coming he'd had a blond Guild hollowbody bass with a big black pickup, and he had somebody put that Guild pickup onto a fairly new Jazz Bass he owned. That bass is still around; his son has it and still plays it." [Ed. Note: Berry Oakley, Jr. is the bassist for a band of second-generation musicians called Bloodlines.]

Duane Allman and Dickey Betts, Petty noted, pretty much stuck with Les Pauls.

"Duane had a Goldtop he traded for a Sunburst," he said. "But he liked the pickups in the Goldtop better, so he and Kim Payne switched the pickups in a motel room in Daytona. Dickey was playing an SG, then he got a Les Paul in Detroit, but he never did warm to it, and got another Les Paul. Dickey gave Duane his SG, and Duane set it up for slide."

Petty also offered his input on the "Big House" in Macon, noting that both Gregg and Duane lived there "at times. Mike Callahan and I lived there off and on, and Kim Payne lived there most of the time," he said. The permanent residents were Berry Oakley, his wife and his sister, according to Petty, and the house wasn't the proverbial "crash pad."

"Sometimes, somebody might end up sleeping on a sofa," he said. "But there weren't a lot of mattresses all over the floor."

The largest performance for the Allmans was at the Watkins Glen pop festival, and Joe Dan Petty was there. "I thought it was pretty well organized," he said. "You have to remember that it was really only one day of performances, but we'd arrived a couple of days before. There were over 700,000 people there, and I think about 90 percent paid admission; usually such big concerts ended up becoming free festivals. It was amazing to stand onstage and look out at the audience.

"After about the first 10,000 people, the rest looked like wallpaper," he chuckled. "I know they had at least two delay towers, and they may have had more than that. The day of the concert, the only way for us to get there was by helicopter."

The circumstances that led to Joe Dan Petty's departure as an Allman Brothers Band road crew member germinated while the band was taking some time off.

"I was hanging around Macon, and I thought I might like to get a band together," he said. The combo that became known

as Grinderswitch ended up recording some demos, and ultimately Capricorn Records offered them a record deal. Petty had some decision making to do, and when he told the band he wanted to try his luck at being a player once again, they patted him on the back and wished him the best.

"The last show I did as an Allman Brothers roadie was on a New Year's Eve at the Cow Palace in San Francisco," he said. "When the Brothers went back out on the road the next March, Grinderswitch went out as their opening act."

Petty notes that Grinderswitch still did its share of stereotypical "Southern boogie" material, but the band was, in his opinion, a bit more country-oriented in its overall sound and songwriting. Some of Grinderswitch's albums have been re-released on compact disc, including a live-in-the-studio FM simulcast performance.

After Grinderswitch played itself out in the early '80s, Joe Dan formed a group called the Lifters, which he says did a lot of covers and played at a lot of what he termed "corporate" events.

It was quite lucrative, he noted, but in the late '80s, he got a call from Dickey Betts.

"I'd told Dickey years ago that if they ever got back together, I wouldn't mind going back out with them. He remembered that, and called me when the Brothers were going out to support the *Dreams* boxed set Polydor was releasing," he said.

"That's all they were going to do. At that time, Dickey had a record contract, and so did Gregg, but the Allman Brothers Band didn't. Things went so well, they decided to keep the band going on again. I left a couple of times to finish up some commitments I had with the Lifters, but I'm back with the band permanently. And like I said earlier, these days I'm known as a 'guitar tech'."

Petty's main duties these days involve the guitars of Dickey Betts and Gregg Allman. He averred that Betts was still using his '57 Goldtop, which went by the name of "Goldie," at the inception of the band's reunion, but that instrument has since been retired. Betts favored Paul Reed Smith instruments for awhile, but he is now playing a Gibson ES-335. Gregg Allman's instruments are primarily acoustic, such as the Gibson J-200 he plays on "Midnight Rider," and Petty stated that Allman "also has some Taylors and Washburns he likes."

So Joe Dan Petty is back on the road with the preeminent purveyors of the Southern sound. His decades of experience, both onstage as a performer and backstage as a road crew member, have served him well, and he's probably had more unique experiences than most people can imagine. And it sounds like he's still enjoying the ride, especially the current incarnation of the Allman Brothers Band, which is putting out some incredibly potent music in concert.

Mike Pinera
Images of Iron, Etc.

Veteran guitarist Mike Pinera has come a long way since he first entered the popular music arena with the Blues Image. The Florida-based band charted (as most readers probably already know) with the smash single "Ride Captain Ride," but Pinera was also a guitarist for Iron Butterfly and other bands.

His current musical venture is somewhat unique as well, and *Vintage Guitar* recently chatted at length with Pinera about his past, present, and future:

VG: What about your musical history, "pre-Blues Image"?

MP: When I was eleven, my folks got me an electric guitar with the amp built into the case from Sears. I'd sit and listen to the radio; I'd copy stuff I heard. Then a few months later, it got to the point where I wanted to play in a band; I grabbed Mel Bay's chord book and got into that. I think my playing ended up being fifty percent by ear and fifty percent by theory.

The first band I played in was called the Impalas; we were all really into playing and worked really hard. There was a place in the Tampa area called the Clearwater Auditorium; all of the major artists from that era would play there, and part of the package deal was that the promoter would supply the band; we would back up singers like Gene Pitney, Fabian, and Bobby Vinton. Not only did we back up pop idols, we played behind R & B singers like Ben E. King and Jerry Butler. Meeting stars like those inspired us to want to push harder. I started writing original material, and we got to be the most popular band in the Tampa area.

A promoter wanted us to move to Miami, since a lot of people from New York vacationed down there, and it might offer an opportunity for us to get a break that might develop nationally. By then we'd changed our name to the Blues Image, and we'd also gone on the road with some other bands. We'd even gone as far as Reno on some gig that didn't work out; I was in junior high at the time! We stuck it out for a month and played some, but we ended up taking a train back home and moving to Miami.

VG: Hopefully that went over better than the Reno venture did.

MP: We became really hot in Miami; one reason was our bass player, who was from Wales. He brought us records like the Bluesbreakers album with Eric Clapton, plus rough cuts of Hendrix. We listened closely; it sounded a lot like what I was playing because I'd learned a lot of tricks from black guitarists like Bobby Bland's guitar player. He'd told me to do things like turn my Fender amp up to "10" to get a great tone (chuckles).

VG: What kind of guitar were you using by then?

MP: I'd jumped right from the Sears guitar to a Gibson ES-335; I had actually made money as a player, so my parents realized I needed a better instrument. I think it cost three hundred and nineteen dollars, and I can still smell that cherry finish when I opened the case for the first time! I was listening to players like Travis Womack and Lonnie Mack, and I was experimenting with feedback and blues licks that I heard by players like Little Johnny Taylor and B.B. King. I ended up getting an ES-345 with a Varitone as well.

We ended up at a large club in Miami called the World; we were opening for bands like the Vanilla Fudge and the Rascals. We did that for about a year, then a promoter came up to us and told us we were so popular that we should open our own place, and he'd help us. We leased a vacant bowling alley in north Miami Beach, took out all the lanes and set up a stage; it would accommodate about fifteen hundred people.

The club was called the Image, and we were the house band, of course; we opened for everyone from the Cream to the Grateful Dead to the Yardbirds. We were in awe of these guys, and we got to jam with most of them. The very first national act we had was the Mothers of Invention.

VG: Were there any players who were younger than you showing up as "spectators,"

Mike Pinera sports an Aria thinline in this earlier publicity photo.

The Classic Rock All Stars: Mike Pinera, Jerry Corbetta, Spencer Davis, and Peter Rivera.

for lack of a better term, that ended up becoming noted guitarists?

MP: Gregg and Duane Allman would come to hear us. We had two drum kits going; we'd gotten that inspiration from James Brown and thought that was the biggest sound we'd ever heard for rhythm, but we used it on blues shuffles like "Parchman Farm"; it sounded *huge.* Once we were doing a Spencer Davis B-side called "Don't Want You No More" when the Allmans were there, and they asked us what the song was when we took a break; most Allman Brothers Band fans are aware of what that band ended up doing with that song (chuckles).

After we ended up moving to L.A., we ended up with a club situation just like what we'd had in Miami; the club was called the Experience. One night the jam session included Jimi Hendrix on guitar, Eric Burdon and Jim Morrison on vocals, Keith Moon on drums, and Noel Redding on bass, plus the Blues Image.

VG: The Blues Image was ultimately signed to Atco, right?

MP: Right; we'd moved to L.A. because a lot of people told us we could make it, but once we got out here we had trouble getting signed, as I'm sure was and still is the case for a lot of bands. We recorded a demo and took it around to all sorts of management companies. We were at Eric Burdon's company, where the manager turned us down, but Burdon had been in the next room and happened to hear the demo, so he got his manager to help us out; this was before that jam at the Experience. About all that manager did was get us a gig at the Whiskey A Go Go, but while we were there, Lee Dorman, the bass player for Iron Butterfly, heard us, and he got us signed with their management company. Iron Butterfly had just been awarded the first platinum record in history for *In-A-Gadda-Da-Vida,* and we ended up opening for them.

To show you how much pull Iron Butterfly had back then, they got Ahmet Ertegun and Jerry Wexler from Atlantic/Atco to come out to our house in the Valley to hear us play some songs; it was really a thrill watching those limousines pull up to our garage. A week after they heard us, the management company said Atco wanted to sign us.

VG: Describe your recording experiences once you were signed to a major label.

MP: The first album was a critical success but didn't sell; it was a progressive blues record that had weird time signatures and Latin-Afro rhythms against blues patterns. It might have been considered "too jazzy," since we were doing things in 7/4 time, for example, but to this day, a lot of *musicians* who've heard our stuff tell me it's their favorite album of that time.

By the time it was time to do the second album, we realized that we needed a commercial hit single; being a good band like the Dead or the Cream wasn't enough. Another problem was when we got off the road from opening for the Butterfly, we were supposed to go right into the studio because Atco wanted our next record in sixty days. All of a sudden we were in the studio with no material, whereas the material for the first album had been "fine-tuned" over a period of two years before it was recorded. Since I was the main songwriter, I wasn't used to writing under that kind of pressure.

We'd jam in the studio, but it didn't feel right. I'd go home and write at night, and little by little the second Blues Image album started to take shape, but it didn't have the soul or the warmth of the first album. Yet the songs were a little more commercial. The band started to experience a lot of disharmony; the business was definitely taking its toll on us.

VG: But that second album yielded "Ride Captain Ride," which put the Blues Image into the "One-Hit-Wonder" hall of fame.

MP: (chuckles) Talk about pressure! The producer who was working with us was also producing Three Dog Night, who were having hit after hit. He told us we still needed a hit single; even though we had one day left in the studio before Atco wanted us back out on the road, the producer threatened to give that last day to Three Dog Night if we couldn't come up with anything. So in a matter of ten minutes, Skip, the keyboard player, and I whipped up "Ride Captain Ride"; we recorded it that day. There was a third Blues Image album, but I wasn't on it; I left right after the second album sessions to join Iron Butterfly.

VG: Didn't another player named Rhino join around then?

MP: Rhino came into Iron Butterfly at the same time I did; he was also from Florida and had played with Gregg Allman; the "southern rock" school. Our styles complemented each other really well because he was really "fluid" and played a lot of slide, whereas my style was very choppy and staccato. The first album I did with Butterfly was their fifth one, *Metamorphosis*. There's a picture of me on the inside cover; I'm playing a Dobro that Jimi Hendrix gave me.

Things ended up with the Butterfly a lot like they did in the Blues Image; all work and no play. One day Doug Ingle, the keyboard player, walked in and announced he'd had enough. The band decided to "take a break" rather than "break up" so Doug could chill out and so our contract could expire; there was about a year and a half left. One thing that kept me busy around that time was discovering and co-producing Black Oak Arkansas. Lee Dorman and I worked with them on guitar arrangements, among other things, when we produced their first album.

VG: The one with "Lord Have Mercy On My Soul" prefaced by that monologue about the Halls of Common?

MP: That's the one; it ended up going gold. It was on Atco as well.

VG: How did you manage to mike Jim Dandy Mangrum's washboard?

MP: (laughs) I'm glad you remember that! We actually did have to try out several types of microphones before we found one that worked well on getting the right sound out of that washboard.

After the Butterfly broke up, I got a call from Mitch Mitchell, who'd been Hendrix's drummer, asking me to join a band he was forming called Ramatam; the other guitar player was a girl named April Lawton; she was really good. But the problem with that effort was that it really wasn't a band; it was more like a "project." Ramatam did a second album but I'd already left.

Right around then, I got a call from Tim Bogert and Carmine Appice to join Cactus, but that happened right as Jeff Beck called them; they'd just cut *'Ot & Sweaty* when I was invited to join them, but before I got there, they'd been called the same week by Jeff to form Beck, Bogert & Appice. Carmine told me to stay with Cactus's keyboard player Duane Hitchings, and Peter French, the singer, and we had permission to call it The New Cactus Band. We did an album called *Son of Cactus* but Pete French wasn't on it; I brought in a drummer I knew and Duane bought in a bass player he knew. We toured with the Amboy Dukes; Ted Nugent and I got into some great jam sessions; some of those were promoted as "guitar wars."

VG: Weren't you also in a band called Thee Image?

MP: We'd let the bass player go from the New Cactus band; Duane was playing keyboard bass, and the drummer and I made us a power trio. We felt that the Cactus name was holding us down; Cactus had originally been known as an underground boogie band, and we wanted to get onto the Top 40 charts. We started talking with Emerson, Lake & Palmer's management, and they agreed with us that a name change would be in our best interest, so the trio changed its name to Thee Image and put out two albums on ELP's Manticore label; we did a lot of

touring with them as well. But we didn't have any hit material; we were told we were too "progressive." After that I went solo.

VG: Still with the 335 and 345?

MP: Yep; I had some studio guitars like a Stratocaster and a Roland synth guitar. When I played with Alice Cooper in the Eighties, I started using Aria instruments.

I did a solo album for Capricorn, then another one for Spector Records; no relation to Phil Spector (chuckles)! In the middle of recording the second album I got a call from Duane Hitchings, who was then forming a new band for Alice Cooper; this was in 1979 and Alice remembered jamming with me at the Experience club back in Hollywood.

I played with Alice from '79 to '82 and was on two albums, *Zipper Catches Flesh* and *Special Forces*; I also went on a couple of world tours while in that band. At the time, Alice was listening to a lot of punk rock, and didn't want to do anything "commercial," so those albums kind of got shelved and didn't get promoted too much.

After Alice, I tried another solo thing but it didn't work out; at the same time I was starting to learn as much as I could about music videos; it was like I was locking myself in editing labs for months at a time (chuckles). It was during the mid-Eighties that I decided to get totally clean and sober, and I've been that way for six years now.

VG: A lot of musicians seem like they've had to go through that experience; fortunately most of the ones that I've interviewed have had an "upbeat" attitude about learning from their past.

MP: Same for me; you can take what you've been through and hopefully let others know about the down side of such experiences. Just last night, for example, I did a benefit concert at a rehab center on the corner of Hollywood and Vine; it's one of the only nonprofit places in California. A kid came up to me and told he'd just checked in there, and that the reason he did was when I played there a few weeks before, I had given his girlfriend my autograph; he figured that if Mike Pinera could get clean and sober, he'd give it a try. The longer I stayed clean, the more I got into doing benefits and speaking to kids at schools; the fact that I've come from such a wild background helps my message to be more valid than if I was a straight drug counselor.

Around 1988, I started doing some classic rock reunion package tours. They were a lot of fun; there were performers along like Mitch Ryder, Badfinger, the Surfaris, even people as diverse as Mickey Dolenz and Tiny Tim! That went on for several summers; we'd do state fairs and such. It felt good to me to be a solo performer with a backup band, and I noticed how the classic rock style was making a comeback and a lot of kids were rediscovering it; kids who were fourteen years old were asking me about my experiences jamming with Jimi Hendrix!

In 1991 it occurred to me that we were taking about twenty-five people on the road, packed into two Greyhound busses, to get about ninety minutes worth of Top Ten hits, and I realized that no one had ever put together a "classic rock supergroup" of several individuals that had a lot of hits between them.

I called Spencer Davis, Jerry Corbetta from Sugarloaf, and Pete Rivera, who was the drummer and lead singer for Rare Earth. That was the hardest part; finding a drummer who was also a lead vocalist for hit songs. We got a sideman on bass, and we called it the Classic Rock All-Stars.

VG: What's been the reaction?

MP: We started out with the summer fairs again, but it's caught on so strongly we're booked solid for months. We just got through with a seventeen-date run; we'll take a short time off and then go back out for another couple of weeks. So people can come hear two hours of Top Ten hits from several bands, played by *one* band made up of former members of the original bands.

VG: Any recording plans?

MP: Already done it! We just cut a live album; it's the best of what you hear at one of our shows. We're going to do something a bit brash regarding marketing it; we knew that we were not going to be signed by a major label; major labels aren't interested in "rock and roll vets" who are over forty years old (chuckles). So I convinced our management that the way to market this album would be on television, using an "800" number. We got signed up for some air time on late night television with a big firm.

VG: You ain't talking about a half-hour infomercial, are you?

MP: (laughs) No, no; just a one-minute spot!

VG: What instruments are you using with the All-Stars?

MP: My old 335 was broken several times and the airlines lost it more than once, so I couldn't stand worrying about it anymore. I got a Yamaha SA-2100, which is a replica of the 335, that I take on the road with me; I also take a Stratocaster. As far as what I'm doing now, I'm on the road 99 percent of the time and in the studio one percent, so I try to carry durable, road-worthy guitars; not instruments that are so delicate or valuable that you have to be almost *too* careful with them.

VG: Do you anticipate the All-Stars keeping on with this concept until it's either no longer commercially viable and/or no longer fun?

MP: Absolutely; we've worked ourselves up into a circuit to where a lot of the fair promoters and casino booking people are already booking us well into 1995, so we're at the point to where we can do this for years to come.

We *have* been working on original material; we all still write.

If and when we do some contemporary recording, we might want to consider a name change for the band, but I was wondering how we could put out something new without confusing or alienating the fan base that we have now. One solution might be to drop "Classic Rock All-Stars" for new material but maintain the *initials;* "C.R.A."

Regardless of what happens concerning the name, the chemistry and friendships within this band mean it'll keep going for a long time. We can rely on each other; we can trust each other. We're treating this like a business, and it's paying off.

Another facet is that all of the years I was educating myself about video production may pay off as well; I've been taking a broadcast-quality camera on the road. We still do shows where there are other bands on the same bill; for example, we just did a gig in Cancun, Mexico with Blood, Sweat & Tears, Kansas, and R.E.O. Speedwagon, among others, and I filmed the whole thing. I edited it down to a program that might be called "Classic Rock in Cancun."

VG: Are you going to market videotapes of it via an "800" number, too?

MP: I'd like to specialize in compilation albums and videos, to be marketed through T.V. There are a lot of friends of mine who have been out there since the Sixties, like me, and they're still writing original material and still playing great stuff, but the record companies aren't interested because they're "yesterday's news." I think it opens up a whole niche that's never been explored; it's an opportunity for veteran performers who are still active and for fans as well. I'm really excited about the future possibilities of this! And I'm just as excited about being in the Classic Rock All-Stars; it's the best musical opportunity I've had in years.

If every veteran rocker had his priorities as organized as Mike Pinera does, it would make for a potent musical entity in the worldwide entertainment market. His innovative concepts in music as well as marketing the sounds of classic bands is respectable, and it should be interesting to follow the progress of Mike Pinera's band and his business ventures.

Obviously, the interview with Mike Pinera was recorded before the one with Spencer Davis...

Mick Ralphs
Still Keepin' Bad Company

When rock music fans look back at what might be considered the "tone age" of British guitar players, usually the names that will be cited include the likes of Eric Clapton, Peter Green, Jimmy Page, Jeff Beck, etc. (NOTE: The writer acknowledges that the name of such an era is also found in the title of a fine instrumental album by Jay Lacy, but the album's title, *Back to the Tone Age*, refers to the fact that all of the tunes on it are played on vintage guitars.)

And if such a "concept" is extended into the mid-Seventies, other names that might pop up would include Andy Powell and Ted Turner of Wishbone Ash, or maybe Rory Gallagher (actually, Gallagher is Irish, but a minor technicality such as that shouldn't be applicable in this scenario).

But what about Mick Ralphs?

Ralphs' ferocious lead guitar was a staple of the first six Mott the Hoople albums, after which he went on to platinum status with Bad Company (the original incarnation included former members of the Free and King Crimson). After that band parted company (pun intended), Ralphs was involved in other projects before Bad Company cranked up again in the mid-Eighties. *Vintage Guitar* recently conversed with the veteran player prior to a concert; Bad Company was opening for Lynyrd Skynyrd. Our interview took place in the hotel bar, and as perhaps a sign of more responsible behavior on the other side of forty, Ralphs had coffee and the interviewer had a club soda with a squeeze of lime:

VG: I'll put myself on the "hot seat" at the outset: I'd written in 1990 that I was had yet to see *Brain Capers* on Compact Disc, and that to me, it was the definitive early Seventies British hard rock album. I found a copy about eight months ago; it's the only copy I've ever seen, and hearing it again in this new format simply reinforces my opinion that you and Ian Hunter have never sounded better.

MR: (chuckles) Then I suppose you're already aware that I only stayed around for two albums after that, neither of which were produced by Guy Stevens. We had a really wild

sound when Stevens produced us, and things certainly sounded different on *All the Young Dudes* and *Mott*. Guy Stevens had produced our first four albums.

VG: What part of England are you from?

MR: Herefordshire, which is a county in the Midlands; I was raised in a farming community. There weren't many big cities around; the closest was Birmingham, about 50 miles away.

VG: Here's a token inquiry about whether or not you used to listen to Radio Luxembourg.

MR: Absolutely; that was the only station you could hear decent music on. It was basically like a pirate station broadcasting offshore, but Luxembourg was actually a small country on the European continent. They played the American charts, which you'd never hear on the BBC. In those days, you couldn't buy American records or American guitars in England. I'll never forget the first time I saw Hank Marvin playing a Fender Strat; I had his picture on my wall, and a guitar like that was every schoolboy's dream. Cliff Richard had bought that guitar for him on a visit to the States.

VG: Why weren't American instruments for sale at that time?

MR: Some trade regulations that were later resolved in around '62 or '63. I used to send away for music distributors' catalogs, and all they offered were European brands like Hofner, Framus, Eko and Davoli, all of which were quite dreadful. Then around 1962, a company called Selmer began introducing Fender and Gibson instruments in their catalog. Up until then we'd had to put up with guitars that were awful; I remember my first guitar had action like this (holds thumb and forefinger approximately 1 1/2 inches apart); it was a cheese slicer (laughs)!

VG: What brand and model was it?

MR: It was an Italian guitar called a Rosetti "Lucky Seven"; it was appropriately named

Mick Ralphs

TOP: *The original lineup of Bad Company (left to right): Boz Burrell, Paul Rodgers, Mick Ralphs and Simon Kirke*

since you were lucky to get any music out of it (chuckles)! But it *looked* good; a spinster auntie of mine bought it for me.

VG: How old were you when you first began playing?

MR: I didn't really start until I was around eighteen. I liked music but didn't consider becoming a player until I heard *one song* that *really* motivated me, "Green Onions" by Booker T. & the MGs. Up until that point the music I'd grown up with was basically done by a singer with a band backing him up, like Cliff Richard and the Shadows. But when I heard Steve Cropper on "Green Onions," I said to myself: "Now *that's* different!" Until that time, a lot of the popular music was a bit too "syrupy" for me to get interested in being a player. Cropper's guitar on "Green Onions" had a "style and attitude" that got me into examining blues and R & B recordings quite quickly, and the first good guitar I got was a Telecaster.

VG: What about "pre-Mott" bands and instruments?

MR: I played in a local band for a long time; members would come and go, as is usually the case. I used the Telecaster and a Vox AC-30 amp, set up on a chair. The band went through several different names, and we toured Germany a bit. With the exception of Ian Hunter, it was the band that became Mott the Hoople.

VG: So how did the addition of Hunter come about?

MR: We were doing club dates and trying to get our foot in the door in the business, but up in Herefordshire there weren't any FAX machines (chuckles)! I was the one who had to go down to London with demo tapes; those were some discouraging times but I didn't give up.

I happened to know Dave Mason and Jim Capaldi, who were in Traffic at the time; they were originally from Worchester, a town near where I was from, and we'd known each other from "local band" days. They helped me out with Island Records; we were eventually signed to that label.

We were assigned to be produced by Guy Stevens, who was a brilliant man; he's now deceased. He told us he wanted the band, but not the singer. So we advertised for a singer; Stevens had a vision of us being like a "Bob Dylan *Blonde on Blonde* period" electric band, and he wanted a singer to go with that idea. Ian Hunter looked the part, and he'd written some good songs as well.

VG: Once you were signed, what sort of guitar do you end up playing?

MR: By then I'd progressed to an SG/Les Paul, then a Goldtop Les Paul. I tried to make guitars last as long as possible; even then I could never afford more than one.

VG: Back to my earlier opinion about you never having sounded better than on *Brain Capers*; what was the setup you were using?

MR: That was a Les Paul Jr. through a Sunn amp; I was inspired get into Juniors when I saw a player your magazine has recently talked to, Leslie West (points to copy of November 1993 *Vintage Guitar* brought by interviewer). We came to the U.S. in 1970 and toured with Traffic and Mountain; I saw and heard what Leslie was doing and said: "That's it" as far as tone went; he was getting that sound out of a slab of wood with one pickup and two knobs. I bought one at a pawn shop in New Orleans for seventy-five bucks. In fact, there's a photo of us in concert on the inside cover of *Wildlife*, the third album, and I'm playing that Junior. There's a live version of "Keep A-Knockin'" on that record, and I played the Junior on it. I don't have that Junior anymore, but I've had several since; they were great.

VG: I've seen pictures of (bassist) Overend Watts and Hunter playing custom-made instruments.

MR: Overend used Thunderbirds a lot, then he got into having basses made; he had one made called the "Swallow" which was shaped like a bird. It was unwieldly, but he had the idea back then of having the tuning pegs on the body. The neck was so long he couldn't reach the pegs, so he had them build it that way, "pre-Steinberger." The strings were anchored on the headstock; the tuning pegs were on the body.

Ian's "H"-shaped guitar was a horrible instrument; it was really more for "effect."

VG: You did some lead vocals on occasion, didn't you?

MR: Yeah; I did a lot of writing for the band with Ian, but he did most of the singing. I sang songs like "Thunderbuck Ram" and "Darkness Darkness" in that high-pitched, weedy voice of mine (chuckles).

VG: It seems a paradox that *All the Young Dudes* was much more successful than *Brain Capers*. Not to flog a dead horse, but in the aforementioned commentary I called the Bowie-produced album an "insipid, sissy-sounding melange."

MR: Well, it was. You see, up until that point the band was a commercial disaster. We were on the verge of packing it up, then David Bowie sent me a letter with a tape with two songs on it, "Suffragette City" and "All the Young Dudes." He wrote that if we were going to break up, could we record these songs before we did, and he'd produce them if we wanted. I still have the letter and the demo tape.

We did *All the Young Dudes* and let David produce it because we were looking for some kind of commercial success to keep the band going. It worked, but the band changed. It wasn't a radical, full-tilt thing anymore; instead we got "stylized" and Ian started to try writing hit singles. He'd ask me to write a guitar hook, which I was happy to do, but I was losing interest quickly; I wanted to get back into something a bit more "raw."

VG: Did you go straight into the Bad Company venture after you departed Mott the Hoople?

MR: I'd already been working with Paul (Rodgers); I'd been writing songs all along that didn't fit into what Mott was turning into, and I couldn't sing that great. Paul had a band called Peace after he left the Free; they were an opening band on one of Mott's tours. I played him the demos of songs like "Ready For Love," "Can't Get Enough," and "Movin' On." We started working on them; he could sing those songs much better than I could. Simon (Kirke) showed up one day at Paul's house while we were working on songs, and Paul finally stated that we needed to form a band. We auditioned several bass players, and ended up with Boz Burrell, who'd been in King Crimson. His style was quite innovative; he played a fretless Ampeg with

a scroll headstock like the bass player in The Band had.

VG: You had more commercial success with Bad Company than Mott ever had, yet you were playing the "raw" songs you wanted to do.

MR: Yeah; it was perfect. We came out with the first album in '74, and did six studio albums; the last one came out in 1980.

VG: I'd have expected a live album during the duration, or at least one after the band split.

MR: We should have done one. We recorded every gig on cassette; I've got hundreds of tapes in boxes with labels that say things like "El Paso 1975," but we never tried to do a major effort to record and re-mix. The next album for the current band is a live album, however. But with the original band, we had a lot to do in a short amount of time; it was always like "Album, tour, album, tour, album, tour."

VG: Why did the original Bad Company split?

MR: I think Paul wanted time off; I think he got tired of the pressure. Since the first album had done so well, we felt we always had to try and make the next one even better. The touring was pretty relentless as well. At the time, we figured he'd want to come back in about a year; we never officially disbanded.

So in the early Eighties I did a solo album, and I produced a band that Simon was in for a while. Paul did a solo album as well. None of those projects really did anything. I think it's obvious in this business that a band is bigger than any of the solo projects its members might do. I never wanted to do a solo album, but I had all these songs I'd written that I needed to record.

VG: Next time I heard you, and *saw* you as well, was on the *About Face* David Gilmour concert video.

VG: Two of the players in David's touring band were also in my band; Mickey Feat on bass and Chris Slade on drums. Chris is in AC/DC now, and he also played in the Firm with Paul and Jimmy Page. In fact, the other guitar player in the current version of Bad Company, Bucket, was also in my band, but back then nothing was happening, as I just noted. Dave told me: "Listen, you're wasting your time doing this; save yourself a lot of money and come on the road with me, and I'll take your bass player and your drummer as well." It was really great working with Dave, after the responsibility of having my own band and having to be the leader; it was fine with me to work for someone else.

VG: So you didn't mind being, for all intents and purposes, the rhythm guitarist in a band?

MR: Not at all; I've always been a sort of rhythm-oriented player anyway. I learned to play rhythm guitar before I learned to play lead, and I do a lot of lead work off of chords. I think Dave's style and mine worked well on that tour; he wanted a player with a sort of "chunky" rhythm style so he could play lead over it. He *did* give me one lead solo each night, however, and I "made a meal" of it (chuckles).

VG: The version of "Comfortably Numb" at the end of that video is probably my favorite version of that song; Nick Mason sat in on drums.

MR: It *was* good, and I think that tour made Dave realize that more people knew Pink Floyd than knew David Gilmour; when we were in Europe the posters had "David Gilmour from Pink Floyd" on them. So he decided to record again but to make it a Pink Floyd gig; he got Nick and Rick Wright back in, and he also told *me* that I ought to be doing a Bad Company gig; he thought that was what I did best. So I got involved with this reincarnation around 1985, after the Gilmour tour.

VG: How did that come about?

MR: Phil Carson from Atlantic Records told Simon and I that we ought to get a band together along the lines of Bad Company. We auditioned several singers and bass players; we had actually recorded the first album, *Fame and Fortune*, and the band still didn't have a name, and we were still *not* planning on calling it Bad Company. However, when we came to America to mix the album, the managers and the record executives told us that if we called the band Bad Company we'd have a "head start."

I objected, since only Simon and I were in the group. Boz was "drafted" back in to give the name some credence, but he only lasted about six months; he hated it. He now plays stand-up bass in a jazz band; that's always been a dream of his.

I think that perhaps tacking the Bad Company name onto that first album after it had been recorded may have been a mistake. Once we got ready to record the second album, we got more focused towards the old Bad Company sound, and it's worked out great since then. Brian Howe has always been our singer in this reincarnation, and he's done a tremendous job.

VG: Isn't it about time for another album?

MR: We're just about to release a live album called *What You Hear Is What You Get*; as I said earlier, the original version of Bad Company never released any live material.

VG: Same album title as an Ike and Tina Turner live album.

MR: Is it? Oh, ****; I didn't know that (laughs)!

VG: Plans after the live album?

MR: You know, 1994 will make 20 years since the band first formed; there's all kinds of things we could do. Maybe come out with a boxed set or some unreleased material; there's *loads* of stuff that the original band did that never came out. It would be nice to get together with Paul and do some shows next year; we'll probably look into doing something to mark the occasion.

VG: You do collect, don't you?

MR: Yes; right now I've got about thirty instruments. My favorite "Gibson year" is 1959; I find guitars from that year are the best for me, *regardless of the model*. I have a ES-335 blond dot-neck that's in mint condition, a Les Paul Standard sunburst that's the nicest of several that I've had over the years,

a double-cut TV Junior, and some Epiphones from that year as well; they have the small "New York"-type pickups but they were made by Gibson. I really like those types of Epiphones; if you know anybody who's got a '59 Epiphone, put them in touch with me; they're great guitars (chuckles)! I've got a '64 Gibson Country & Western acoustic, plus some others. Certain guitars in my collection I'd never sell but others come and go, as I'm sure it is with many collectors.

VG: Do you take any of those 1959 Gibsons on the road?

MR: No, I usually take out six instruments: Three reissues of the '59 Les Paul Standard; they're Custom Shop models and are *very* close to the real thing. Tom Murphy at Gibson is a great guy to work with. I also have two Esquires that I use for slide; one is an original 1957 model and the other is a reissue. I *do* take one of my '59 Epiphones along; I used to use it for slide but haven't done so for a while, so it's in the case at this point.

VG: You're still having a good time doing this, aren't you?

MR: Absolutely; I think this version of the band just keeps getting stronger, and there's finally a live album. We're still enjoying the ride!

About three weeks after our conversation with Mick Ralphs, we were able to listen to the brand new live album from Bad Company; in addition to the personnel mentioned by Ralphs in the interview, veteran British bassist Rick Wills is also a member of the live ensemble. A line at the top of the CD booklet's back cover states: "THIS ALBUM IS A TRUE LIVE RECORDING." It shows.

Mick Ralphs appreciates old guitars, and he appreciates the opportunity he's had as a musician. He's got a good perspective on his past, present, *and* future, and the 20th anniversary of Bad Company should be eagerly anticipated by the band's fans, just as the event is eagerly anticipated by Mick Ralphs. Stay tuned.

Vintage Guitar would like to thank Jeff "Arafat" Carlisi and Gary Gilmore for their help in setting up the interview with Mick Ralphs.

Bad Company underwent further personnel changes (see interview with Rick Wills). An interview with Dave "Bucket" Colwell is "in the can" as of this writing; when Colwell was interviewed, the band was in Nashville, recording an album that featured a power ballad version of Vince Gill's "I Still Believe in You." Gill and Allison Kraus put in guest appearances on a version of "Oh Atlanta."

Jimmy Rip
"Retro" Ain't the Word For It

Los Angeles-based guitarist Jimmy Rip's new album *Way Past Blue* has the distinction of being one of the initial three releases on the House of Blues label, and when one discovers how the album was recorded, and why it was recorded that way, it makes for very intriguing listening.

Rip is originally from New York City, having migrated to the Left Coast around the advent of the '90s. While growing up in Fun City, his older brother, who also played guitar, took him to concerts by famous blues musicians.

"New York has never been a great blues town," observed Rip. "I don't think there's more than two or three places to play, but my brother had real good taste in music, and he used to drag me around to shows featuring players like John Lee Hooker and Paul Butterfield. Back then, a lot of artists used to play New York, even though there wasn't much to the local blues scene."

The guitarist began doing studio work when he was 17, and recorded and toured with quite a few New York acts. "I guess my name is probably on the back of sixty or seventy albums," Rip opined. He still has his first guitar, a Zimgar. "I inherited it; it went from my father to my older brother to me," he says. "I pull it out now, and am kind of amazed at what sold for twenty-nine dollars then. It looks kind of like an early '60s Byrdland; thin body, single round cutaway, beautiful sunburst, herringbone binding. It had a DeArmond pickup stuck on it."

Since the Zimgar, the guitarist has been through over 200 other guitars, and he still owns (and uses) some great ones.

One of Rip's most distinctive assignments was as guitarist on more than one Mick Jagger solo album, and as musical director for one of his tours. "I met him when we were doing a Bette Midler video," recalled Rip. "The director cast me as a guy who looked like a guitar player; I was playing behind Bette, who was doing a cover version of 'Beast of Burden.' Later I added some guitar parts to one of his albums, and when he was planning a tour of Japan, Australia, and Indonesia, he asked me help him put a band together.

"The bass player was Doug Wimbish, and the lead guitar player was a guy no one had ever heard of named Joe Satriani. I think that's the best I've ever heard him play guitar."

Rip didn't mind being the rhythm guitarist, because "three-fourths of the show was Rolling Stones songs, and I wanted to do the Keith parts!"

At times, *Way Past Blue* may sound somewhat "Rolling Stones-ish" or "Jagger-esque" (for example, "State of Mind" might recall "You Got to Move"), but Rip noted that while he was of course inspired by the Stones, he was also inspired by the original bluesmen who inspired the Stones themselves; an example cited by Rip was Fred McDowell.

Mick Jagger *does* guest on *Way Past Blue*, playing harmonica on "Mojo" (more about that tune later) and singing backing vocals on "Insanity Please."

Jimmy Rip's prime guitar (for studio work *and* live performance) is a stock 1956 Stratocaster. He also owns a blond '61 Strat, and both instruments have "C"-size necks.

"I've got big hands," he said. "And if I could find a 'D', I'd buy it." Many interesting guitars appear on *Way Past Blue*. For example, the electric slide guitar heard on "It's Goin' Round" is a National Silvo from the late '30s; "Cold Comfort" features a '58 P-Bass.

One guitar that appears in the album booklet is an old Telecaster decorated with dice decals and the name "Lucky," and Rip is soliciting more information about its previous owner(s):

"It's a '53 Tele that's all straight, except the Bakelite guard is gone; at one point, the guitar was painted a Kelly Green color. I got this guitar through Lloyd Chiate at Voltage; I've bought around a hubdred guitars from him over the years. Apparently, it was owned by a country player named Lucky Miller; I heard that he got it new when he was a kid and had done all of those cosmetic modifications to it; it looks like a kid would have done things like that. I've heard that he's deceased, but he used to be a noted Nashville/Grand Ole Opry kind of player. Some people have said they remember hearing about him, but it's minimal information. I'd *love* to have a picture of him playing it."

To say that the recording quality of *Way Past Blue*

Photo by Melissa Behr.

TOP: *Jimmy Rip with Don Henley at the 1996 VH1 Honors. Jimmy performed with Don on his recent Greatest Hits album.*

RIGHT: *Jimmy with Mick Jagger at the House of Blues Music Company launch party.*

is "primitive," "retro," or "authentic" is an understatement, and that's exactly how Jimmy Rip intended it to sound. A noticeable example is the vocals; sometimes there's outright distortion in the singing. "It was completely intentional," says Rip. "I like distorted vocals; the sound of a singer overpowering a microphone is exciting, and it was inherent in the equipment being used." While an expensive Neuman microphone was used, taped next to it was an old '50s Shure "green bullet."

"My harmonica player gave it to me," noted Rip. "He got it from an old L.A. Transit bus. The green bullet was plugged into an old Champ amp, which was miked in another room, so I had one clean mike and one distorted one. We put them on two separate tracks, and mixed one louder than the other, depending on the song."

The mixing board used on the album was from the old Record Plant mobile truck. It's an historical piece of recording equipment; many live albums were done on the Record Plant's mobile unit. "That truck went all over the country," observed Rip.

Rip's main amplifier on *Way Past Blue* was a 1958 Fender Deluxe; the rhythm guitarist and harmonica player also used '58 Deluxes. Live, Rip counts on a '58 tweed Twin.

Another unique item is the bass used by Denny Croy, Rip's bass player. "Interesting instrument," said Rip. "I guess it's from the Mosrite-period of Dobro. It looks like a regular upright, but the body's about 1/3 as thick. It has a really cool pickup system; there's nothing showing on the instrument, except for a couple of dials. I heard they made about a dozen of them around '68 and '69, which is the Mosrite period. I also use a 12-string resonator guitar that was made around the same time; it's heard on 'State of Mind'."

Perhaps the most eclectic track on *Way Past Blue* is "Mojo." An initial listening seems to indicate that it's a remake of "I've Got My Mojo Workin'" done in a minor key, accompanied by a American Indian/Native American beat. But there's more to it than that.

"There's an interesting story about how that whole track came about," said Rip. "My girlfriend had a documentary about Marie Laveau, who was the recognized queen of the voodoo cult from New Orleans. In this documentary, an actual voodoo ceremony was shown, and the beat was fascinating; I recorded it from the documentary and brought the tape to the studio one night. I handed out per-

cussion instruments to all of the guys in the band, and for six minutes we just let the tape roll while we laid that beat down. I didn't know at the time that it was going to be 'Mojo.' I knew no one could ever do 'I've Got My Mojo Workin' as well as Muddy, and I had also been inspired by Lightnin' Hopkins' 'Mojo Hand.'

"When you get into the *lyrics* of 'I've Got My Mojo Workin', it's a *very* dark and mysterious song; it's about voodoo and putting a spell on your woman. I thought: 'Why not do it in the spirit of the lyrics?' I added a few new lyrics; even though most versions of it are uptempo, it's a mysterious and evil song." Rip's interpretation does indeed aver that the tune has a "darker side."

Jimmy Rip still has quite a few classic guitars, and there's one that he's still seeking.

"I'm looking for an ES-330 with a big 'baseball bat' neck, which I guess would mean it would be a late '58 or '59. I want the 2-pickup model; I have a single-pickup one that I used for rhythm on 'Walk'. I'm not much of a Les Paul man, but I do have a '57 Goldtop that I used for Average White Band-type rhythm on songs like 'Layin' in the Cut'. Somebody modified it in the '70s; it's got a PAF in the bridge and a Firebird pickup in the neck position. That's one of the coolest combinations I've ever come across. Sometimes PAFs in a neck position can get too fat, too dark, too tubby. The Firebird pickup sounds great there."

Rip plans on touring to support *Way Past Blue*. "I gotta get out there about 390 days a year," he said with a laugh. "There's also another Mick solo record down the line sometime; hopefully it'll sound as great as *Wandering Spirit*."

Rip played 90% of the guitar on that album.

The use of older recording equipment, older guitars, older amplifiers, and older recording techniques adds to the "authenticity" of *Way Past Blue*, and Jimmy Rip wouldn't have it any other way. Ultimately, this "retro" recording comes off as a unique tribute to the legendary blues masters of bygone days, and serious blues fans should be impressed by Rip's sincere effort.

Lee Ritenour
"...Rit on the Right"

The subtitle of this interview also notes the channel in which the interviewee's guitar is heard on the *Larry & Lee* album; what's more, Ritenour was interviewed first (two days before our conversation with Larry Carlton took place).

The subject matter for both interviews was quite similar, because both guitarists have forged similar paths as preeminent session players in the kaleidoscopic Los Angeles studio scene, followed by respected solo careers and other musical ventures.

Now in his early forties, Lee Ritenour has been active for decades, and our initial inquiry concerned his beginnings; he was born and raised in the L.A. area:

VG: My perception is that you started playing guitar at a very young age.

LR: I think it goes back to when I was putting nails on the ends of broomstick handles and stretching rubber bands across them when I was about four or five (chuckles). When I was around seven I got my first guitar; it was a folk guitar that was nothing special. I started playing folk music by groups like the Kingston Trio, and when I got serious about playing, my parents were very encouraging and supportive. They found the best teachers, and by the time I was twelve I wanted to make it my life.

VG: What was your first electric guitar?

LR: A Sears & Roebuck; the kind that the amplifier built into the case. I wish I still had it. My first jazz guitar was a blond Belwin that was used; my dad bought it in a music store when I was about eleven or twelve. By the time I was thirteen, I'd gotten two guitars that I still have; one was a solidbody Ampeg by Burns of London. It had a five-way switch on it with one sound that was called "Wild Dog." It didn't turn out to be much of a guitar that would last over time, but it got me through my teen years.

But the other one was and is a "main" guitar, a 1950 L-5 that I bought from a Las Vegas musician. It had a Johnny Smith pickup on it; it was about fifteen years old when I got it. It's been on all of my records; the new

Fourplay album, the album I did with Larry Carlton, and it's all over albums like *Wes Bound* and *Stolen Moments*.

VG: So is it fair to say that by then you were already going in a jazz direction? Why did you go that way instead of towards rock and roll?

LR: Well, I really had a "split personality" during that time. When I picked up that L-5, I wanted to play and sound like Howard Roberts, Joe Pass, and *especially* Wes Montgomery; Kenny Burrell and Jim Hall, too. At the same time, when I would pick up the solidbody guitar, I was being influenced by the rock and roll of those days, especially the British Invasion, which included Clapton, Beck, and Peter Green.

And growing up in L.A. in the late Sixties meant checking out the Hollywood scene; I would go to concerts by Canned Heat and I'd see the Byrds hanging out at the local music store called Wallick's Music City.

I was a young teenager, and these guys were in their twenties, and I'd hear one good player after another. That had an influence on me as well, but not as great as jazz did, because jazz was more sophisticated, and my head was already into listening to jazz radio more than pop radio. I love *the sound* and *the power* of the rock & roll guitar, but I love *the sophistication* of the jazz guitar. Early in my career I started combining the two elements, which was around the beginning of the fusion movement. When people like Larry Coryell and John McLaughlin came along, they were *very* influential.

VG: By the time your first album came out, hadn't you settled into using a Gibson 335?

LR: Yes; in my late teens I acquired my first 335, then I got a red 335 that I've played throughout my career; it's a dot-neck. I think it's a 1960 model; I can't see the serial number on the label because the f-holes have been

The 1981 album Rit featured "Is It You," a Pop chart hit for Lee Ritenour

stuffed with foam. I play it and the L-5 more than any other guitars, even today.

VG: Didn't your association with Dave Grusin start fairly early in your career?

LR: I met Dave when I was twenty; he was already very influential as a composer, arranger, and keyboardist in the Los Angeles scene. He played on my first album, *First Course*, and he and his partner, Larry Rosen, co-produced my third album. Larry was an engineer, and he and Dave later formed Grusin-Rosen Productions; the three letters became GRP, which is the record label a lot of contemporary jazz artists recorded for; I'm still on the GRP label.

VG: How old were you when you did your first session?

LR: I did a bunch of demos, but the first "big one" was when I was in a band that was being produced by John Phillips of the Mamas and the Papas; we recorded at his home studio in Bel-Air. I was about fifteen; some of the tracks were used by the Mamas and the Papas, but I don't think they ever got released; I remember being disappointed that I couldn't go get the record. Nevertheless, those tunes had real session musicians on it, and I was so young. By the time I was twenty I started to play on some Sergio Mendes records, and things started to branch out very quickly; by the time I was twenty-one or twenty-two I was doing a lot of session work.

VG: When *First Course* was recorded, was there any "feel" you were going for?

LR: Well, I was very nervous about doing the first album, as any artist is; I was especially nervous because I felt like I was coming into my own as the number one session guitarist in Los Angeles; the previous number one guitarist had been Larry Carlton. But those years, '76, '77 and '78, were *prime* years for me as a studio musician, and I was doing as many as fifteen sessions a week. So when I did the first album, I really wasn't prepared as an "artist"; I was still thinking as a "studio musician," and I was very worried about hav-

ing my own identity on the guitar, because up until that time my job as a studio musician had been to be a "chameleon."

VG: Doing what people told you to do?

LR: Either that, or bringing what I wanted to a record that would compliment their record; playing a Clapton-type style or a Chet Atkins style or jazz or classical.

At the same time, I was playing in two jazz clubs called Dante's and the Baked Potato; Dave Grusin, Harvey Mason and Ernie Watts were playing in that band. Later Patrice Rushen, another great keyboardist, played in it. We were forging a sound that would become popular, but it wasn't until several years later that I felt more comfortable with who I was stylistically. Yet when you go back to *First Course*, the Lee Ritenour style is there.

VG: The opening cut on the second album, *Captain Fingers*, is the title track, and it has an almost "progressive rock/Yes-type" sound; very aggressive and complex.

LR: It's very fusion-oriented; I wrote that tune after I had the title, whereas most other tunes get written, *then* you come up with a title. It was a nickname that the cartage guys came up with when they had to carry around this big case that had fifteen guitars in it. I wrote "Captain Fingers" because I wanted to come up with a "pyrotechnic" tune (chuckles). I remember taking some heat on the first album that it was too "soft" and lightweight. So I made sure I got more aggressive on the second album, but it was also part of the times. The Mahavishnu Orchestra was out there; Al DiMeola had come out with his first album around the same time I did; Larry Coryell had turned to more of a distorted, fusion sound. The sound of the guitar was "rock," but what we were playing was "jazz," so in essence it was called "fusion" at the time.

I was very proud of the album; I felt like it put me into the "artist mode." After that album came out, the production company I was with went out of business, so I became a "free agent" and signed with Elektra Records, where I remained for seven years. *The Captain's Journey* was the first for Elektra; that was in 1978, and was really when I decided to "turn off the faucet" on studio work and concentrate on being an artist.

VG: Some of your albums may have been considered "concept" albums. *Festival* was a Brazilian music-influenced album, for example.

LR: Throughout my career, Brazilian music has played a strong motif. The first album I did with a Brazilian flavor was one called *Rio* in 1979. That was my first acoustic album, and it's stood the test of time. Almost ten years later I revisited that area on *Festival*, and I worked with some Brazilian artists on that album; a very famous singer/songwriter named Caetano Veloso, and Joao Bosco, a talented acoustic guitar player. They're very big stars in Brazil. The Brazilian culture has become a major part of my life; I married a Brazilian citizen. Musically, I'll probably revisit that territory again.

VG: Obviously, *Wes Bound* is a tribute album, and one would assume that you just used the L-5 on it.

LR: Almost exclusively, except for one song.

VG: Didn't you have a single that made it onto the pop charts once?

LR: Yeah; I did an album called *Rit*; it was the first time I crossed over and did a vocal tune with a singer named Eric Tagg from Texas. The song that Eric, Bill Champlain and I wrote called "Is It You" became a Top Fifteen single and I think it was a number one R & B single. That was a big album for me, and it was interesting because at the time, the only other person who had used vocals to cross over from contemporary jazz was Grover Washington, who did it with Bill Withers. Of course, [George] Benson had done it in '76, but he was singing and playing, whereas Grover and I were using other singers, and this was in 1980 for me; Grover had done it in '79. It was an unusual turn of events.

VG: So technically, I guess you qualify as a One-Hit-Wonder.

LR: (laughs) Right, although I think the next year a tune from the *Rit II* album called "Cross My Heart" was on the pop charts but didn't get very high. The *Fourplay* material has been on the pop and R & B charts quite a bit, but that happened years later.

VG: When did you go from Elektra to GRP Records?

LR: In 1985; Dave Grusin and I did our first and only collaboration album called *Harlequin*. It was also a Brazilian-oriented affair; we worked with another singer/songwriter from Brazil named Ivan Linns.

VG: There was also the *GRP Live* album with you, Grusin, and Diane Schuur, among others. You played a version of "Dolphin Dreams" from the *Captain Fingers* album; you used a guitar synthesizer.

LR: That was a Synthaxe. There was a live video done as well; it was recently on something like the Discovery Channel. It was recorded at the Record Plant in Los Angeles.

VG: My perception is that you were an early user and/or proponent of guitar synthesizers; you were holding one on the cover of the *Earth Run* album.

LR: That was a Synthaxe as well; *Earth Run* was the first time I'd really used it extensively on an album. I go all the way back to the 360 Systems in 1976 or '77; you can see one on the back of the *Captain Fingers* album. I've had a sampling of all of them; I've had quite a few Rolands, the Yamaha GR-10, the Synthaxe. I currently use the Gibson MIDI-Max, which is also not being manufactured anymore, but as far as I know it's still the best of the analog versions. I also have the current Roland model, the GR-1, in my rack.

Unfortunately, the guitar synthesizer business kind of fell apart, except for Roland; people couldn't afford to keep it going and do the research that was needed. It definitely turned out to be a more complex situation that anyone imagined.

VG: Some people might opine that the technology got outmoded fairly quickly, as is often the case in electronics.

LR: There was the tracking problem, and all of the particulars of a guitar that didn't translate very well to MIDI. I use my guitar synthesizer almost exclusively in programming my computer. I *do* record with it, especially for background material. I don't use it live very often anymore, but it *is* an integral part of my computer system, which is fairly complex.

VG: Are you doing any session work at all anymore?

LR: I'm pretty much doing my solo career; once in a while I'll do a guest spot on somebody's record, or if Dave Grusin has a movie that needs something special I'll do that for him. But my own career takes up more than enough time (chuckles).

VG: A lot of people aren't aware that you were on Pink Floyd's *The Wall* album.

LR: I don't remember the names of specific tunes; there were some background singers and maybe a keyboardist and myself, but none of us got credit, which is kind of unusual. A lot of people *do* ask me about that album, because it's listed in my credits. I definitely spent some nice time working with David Gilmour and those guys, overdubbing various acoustic parts and an occasional electric part. It was like working with Steely Dan; the pieces are so intricately woven together, it's a "mosaic" of many parts. Pink Floyd, like Steely Dan, would concentrate on one little rhythm guitar part that was eight bars long for two days; they would agonize over every inch of it, which is fine. I appreciated that way of thinking, but for the most part I'd rather do that on my own record than somebody else's.

VG: One of your other ventures is the Fourplay band; when did it get going? [Note: the other members of Fourplay are keyboardist Bob James, bassist Nathan East, and drummer Harvey Mason.]

LR: I believe our first album was released in '91; our third album was just released. We're about to go out on tour to support it.

VG: What about the album project with Larry Carlton? How did that come about?

LR: We knew each other for many years, and we grew up near each other in the South Bay of Los Angeles, but we never got a chance to work with each other because our careers were so similar. We were two lead guitar players; calling two lead guitar players to a session would be like having two baseball pitchers on the same mound! We both had solo careers, and if there was any "competitiveness" it was from not working with each other.

But our friends were always asking us when we were going to record together; once we ended up on GRP it became a reality, and we finally did the album last year and toured quite a bit this year.

VG: You each produced the songs that you wrote.

LR: Pretty much, but we were very involved in each other's tunes, because they were mostly cut live with the band, so we were constantly making suggestions to each other, but our rule of thumb was whoever's composition we were working on had the final word and production control.

VG: It certainly doesn't sound like a "showdown" or "show-off" album.

LR: It didn't turn out to be a "showdown" because Larry and I don't think about music that way. Those kind of albums bore us when we listen to two guitar players rattling off a million notes; we're much more musical than that. Most of the time in the studio it was "You take the first section and I'll take the second..." "No, *you* take the first, and *I'll* take the second..." We were being overly polite, to the point where the band would say *"Somebody* play the melody!" (laughs).

VG: There *are* some harmony guitar parts on the album; did both of you work those out within the individual compositions?

LR: Yeah; Larry wanted to have a chance to write for what he calls a "mini-guitar orchestra." Here was an opportunity for him to write some harmonies and take advantage of those once we went on the road. So his tunes like "Closed Door Jam," "Lots About Nothin'" and "Up and Adam" have a lot of that; my tune "L.A. Underground" has a lot of unison playing. We were both constantly thinking about the orchestra-tion of the guitars.

VG: Your current guitar arsenal is listed on the CD cover of *Larry & Lee*; do you have any others in your collection?

LR: Well, I have an old Strat that didn't appear on the album; I don't play it too often these days. I don't know what year it is, but I do know that the serial number on it is 0335 (laughs). That's not the reason I bought it, but when I was trying it out, I flipped it over and saw the serial number, so I figured that helped me decide to buy it.

VG: Your son's name is Wes; it's obvious where the name came from, and he's shown with you on the album cover. Do you think he'll grow up to be a guitar player?

LR: Only if he wants to be. I can certainly help him in that area, and it's for sure that music's in his blood; he's already dancing and strumming on guitars.

The musical symbiosis of Lee Ritenour and Larry Carlton is not only evident on their collaboration album, but in their attitudes and conversational abilities as well (a definitive example being Ritenour corroborating Carlton's "guitar orchestra" statement *before* Carlton was interviewed). The solo careers of Ritenour and Carlton are laudable, but the fact that two titanic guitar talents can create an album as listenable as *Larry & Lee* is icing on the cake as a tribute to their professionalism... but it probably wouldn't be out of line to opine that the album was an enjoyable and fun experience for Messrs. Ritenour and Carlton as well.

Neal Schon
The Journey Continues...

...and it just might include a revitalized band that goes by the name of Journey. Neal Schon, as most readers probably know, is noted for being that platinum-selling band's lead guitarist, and many music fans are also familiar with his other ventures such as a brief stint in Santana, and in more than one (so-called) "post-Journey" aggregation.

When *Vintage Guitar* conversed with the Bay Area guitarist, he was upbeat about an altogether different musical effort of his, a solo instrumental album called *Beyond the Thunder* (Higher Octave Music). He chatted amicably about his past, present and future:

VG: Are you originally from the Bay Area?

NS: I'm an Air Force brat; I was born in Oklahoma City. We also lived on the East Coast, and we moved out here to the West Coast when I was about eight or nine. Years later, I moved up to Marin County to live with Gregg Rolie.

VG: You got an early start with famous players; weren't you a teenager when you joined Santana?

NS: I was fifteen; I'd been playing around San Francisco for about a year before that. I played with B.B. King, Elvin Bishop; there were some jam sessions at Mike Bloomfield's old club. I was a hotshot kid that other players would try to "out-gun."

VG: What about your earliest guitars; "pre-Santana," for lack of a better term?

NS: My first was a Kay acoustic from some store like a K-Mart; it was one of those awful ones that gave you calluses real fast (laughs)! The first electric I had was a Japanese model; I can't recall the brand name. It was a semi-acoustic and was a little bit better than the Kay. The first decent instrument I got was a used 335 that my dad helped me buy. I was about twelve when I got it; I really liked the way it felt and sounded.

VG: Your bio noted that you were listening to bands like Cream and Hendrix; that was probably true for a lot of aspiring guitarists back then.

NS: I listened to a lot of the music that was coming out of England in the late Sixties; it was blues-rooted but more electric, and there was a lot of improvising going on. I've been a fan of improvisation ever since I began playing, and I've been getting back to that more than ever. I got into a "song mode" as Journey went along; it was what I call a "structured confinement," but lately I've been getting into other ventures where I get to improvise more.

VG: Back when you were jamming with famous guitarists at such an early age, is that how you honed your chops, or did you have bands as well?

NS: I've always had bands from the beginning; there was a kid's garage band, and I joined an instrumental band in the Bay Area that went by the name of Anthrax. After that I joined a band called Old Davis; we did R & B tunes, and I played electric blues over the top of it. That was actually a really good band, and it helped me meet other musicians.

We were playing down in the Peninsula at a club called the Poppycock, and the bass player, Bob Woodridge, was friends with Gregg Rolie and Michael Shrieve from the Santana band, he'd invited them to check us out. They must have liked what they heard, because they stuck around, and we ended up jamming all night, after everybody had left.

VG: Of the famous names you jammed with, Gabor Szabo was a bit different from the likes of B.B. King, Albert King, and Buddy Guy.

NS: He was a Gypsy jazz player; right now I'm working on a record with a band called Abraxas, which is almost everyone from the original Santana band except Carlos, and there's a song on there I dedicated to Gabor called "Cafe Szabo." He improvised completely, every night he played. I was interested in *any* player who could improvise; who could get completely lost and then make sense of it.

VG: When did you officially join Santana?

NS: The night after I played with Derek and

the Dominoes at the Berkley Community Theater, and Eric asked me to join that band. The Santana guys found out about it, and asked me to join them right after that so I wouldn't join Eric's band. I was really excited about playing with Eric, because he'd taught me so much through his records about improvising. I'd spent *hours* listening to the live record in *Wheels of Fire*, learning how he'd twist rhythms and play cross-rhythms over the top of the drums; it completely opened my mind up to the possibilities of improvisational guitar-playing.

I first played on Santana's third album, after *Abraxas;* the Tower of Power horns were on there. I also played on *Caravanserai*, and the last project I did with Carlos was the live album with Buddy Miles recorded in Hawaii at the Crater Festival.

VG: What kind of instruments were you playing during your tenure with Santana?

NS: I was playing a reissue Goldtop Les Paul; I still have it. It had creme-colored pickups; I've stuck humbuckers in it since I bought it. I also had a Fender Strat when I was in Santana.

VG: You and Rolie departed Santana around the same time; had you already decided to form what would become Journey?

NS: No, I actually got involved with several other things. I was playing with Larry Graham and Greg Errico, the original rhythm section for Sly & the Family Stone, in a power trio that was really hip; I wished we'd continued doing it, but Larry felt like he wanted to do something than was more "normal R & B." Larry also had that baritone voice; up until then I'd never heard of a power trio with a baritone lead vocalist, but it sounded great. It's funny, because this was before Mother's Finest had come along, and what we were doing sounded quite a bit like them. Cream influences, Hendrix influences, and funk influences, and I was still doing a lot of impro-

vising.

But Larry wanted to do what was more straight-ahead R & B, so he formed Graham Central Station; I played in that band for about three months, but I felt like the reins were a little too tight, and I wasn't getting to improvise that much. When I *did* get to take a solo I got chopped off after about four bars, which I wasn't used to; so I quit. The guy who started off as my guitar tech had become my manager, and he started to put a band together with me. He brought in Prairie Prince, the drummer from the Tubes, Ross Vallory on bass, and George Tickner on rhythm guitar, who had written some interesting songs. Soon afterwards, Gregg Rolie was added, and we began playing around a *lot*. I think our first gig was at the Crater Festival in Hawaii, where that live album with Carlos and Buddy had been done earlier; they used to have those festivals every year.

VG: The music on the first Journey album had some extended pieces on it that indicated an improvisation-oriented guitarist like you would have felt right at home.

NS: That's the way it started out. Aynsley Dunbar had become the drummer; we'd grab a song, figure out a good solo section, and then Aynsley and I would go to town on it.

VG: How many albums did Journey do in that configuration and that "mode," for lack of a better term?

NS: The first al-

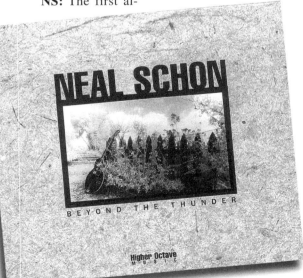

bum, *Look Into The Future*, and *Next*. After that Steve Perry was brought in as lead vocalist. We did *Infinity, Evolution*, and *Captured*, which was a double-live record. Shortly after that Gregg wanted to leave; he felt like he needed to start a family;

TOP: *Photo by Karen Miller*

RIGHT: Beyond the Thunder, *Neal Schon's new release.*

he was tired of being on the road. At that time the Babys had been opening for Journey, and I'd gotten to know Jonathan Cain, and I asked him to join us.

We did *Escape, New Frontiers*, and the last one was *Raised On Radio*.

VG: During your tenure with Journey, you were involved with more than one off-shoot project. One of them was a collaboration with Jan Hammer; there was even a video for a song called "Lies."

NS: That actually did really well at the time. It was when MTV had just started, the video went to Number One on MTV and the song went to Number One on A.O.R. radio. I did two records with Jan Hammer; I sang and there was also a lot of instrumental stuff.

VG: You participated in some kind of "guitar greats" concert with the likes of David Gilmour, Link Wray, Steve Cropper and Brian Setzer; the concert was shown on MTV.

NS: That was a one-off; Jonathan and I had written a couple of songs to play at that show. We didn't have a band; we had everything in the computer; it was just the two of us playing. And half of the computer went down right before we played, so half of the parts weren't there (chuckles)!

VG: You appeared to be playing something like a Schecter Tele-style guitar.

NS: I think it was a Charvel Tele. I used mostly Les Pauls and Strats in Journey, then I came out with my own brand of guitars, and I used those, but I've gotten back to the Strats and the Pauls again.

VG: What about the band called Bad English? There was a Babys connection there as well.

NS: I had done a solo album called *Late Night*, and I got a call from Jonathan, who said he was putting a band together with John Waite, and did I want to come check it out? I brought along a drummer, and we all made a go of it.

VG: Had Journey split by the time Bad English formed?

NS: We've never split; we stopped playing together and stopped making records but there was never anything official about the band breaking up. It's been a long hiatus, but we're getting ready to start it up again.

VG: The last videos I saw of Journey showed you, Cain, Perry, and what appeared to be a "substitute" bass player, Randy Jackson, as well as a "sub" drummer.

NS: At that point the band was really in sort of a state of "winding down"; the last record we made wasn't the easiest one that we'd ever done. The whole band wasn't getting along; Steve was producing and he felt that things would sound better with a different rhythm section.

VG: I'm not familiar with another venture of yours called Hardline.

NS: That was a little project that I produced; my wife's brothers were two guys that were in Hardline. Actually, at that time she wasn't my wife; I'd met them through her. I thought they'd done some interesting work as far as songwriting; I wasn't doing anything at the time so I started working with them, and I ended up *writing* songs for them, and I ended up playing a lot of guitar on their demos. They ended up getting a record deal

and I produced the record. I went out on tour with them and killed my ears (laughs); they're a *very* loud band. We opened for Van Halen in Detroit, but we needed to play more bigger places; their music was more "concert-style"; it was not meant for little clubs, but those were most of the places they played and it was rough on my ears. I've already been through that, and right now I'm interested in keeping the amount of hearing I have left intact!

VG: Other than the late Roy Buchanan, you're probably the only famous modern guitarist who's had a bona fide *brand name* electric guitar line that had your moniker. What were you trying to accomplish with the design of Schon guitars?

NS: I was trying to come up with something that could get several different tones. It actually sounded more like an SG instead of a Les Paul, but you could get "Stratty" tones out of it as well. I think it ended up with its own, distinctive sound.

To try and come up with something that looks different and sounds decent is really very difficult; I was happy with the original design, as far the sound, the look, and the way it played. In the initial stages I had a good thing going; when we did the first NAMM show in Chicago with the line, I sold a half-million dollars worth of guitars. As it turned out, the builder couldn't come up with the guitars, so store owners got pissed off at *me*, since it was my company. That was a lesson; it was a long, drawn-out battle; I was in litigation for four years, trying to recover some of the money I'd lost.

VG: Any idea how many Schon guitars were made?

NS: I really have no idea; I sold more in Europe than in the States towards the end, right before I stopped building them.

I've seen a lot of players using Schon guitars; the instruments have a certain "thing" about them that some players like. I used a Schon exclusively on the Bad English record, and those are all my brand on my *Late Night* solo record.

VG: How and why did your recent instrumental project *Beyond the Thunder* evolve?

NS: To tell you the truth, I didn't expect to do something this different. I started out doing what I usually like to do; a lot of wailing and a lot of improvising; it was much more of a high-energy fusion record. I shopped it but I wasn't getting any bites; companies felt like the market had been completely flooded on the "heavier" instrumental stuff, but they *did* like the melodic, "jazzier/bluesier" material that I had. So I decided to go in that direction; I already knew I could do the other stuff, and at that point in my career I didn't feel like I had to prove that I could do every lick I ever knew on every record. It was a good learning lesson to concentrate on what I was going to do; keeping it consistent from beginning to end. I think this record had a great flow.

VG: You're on the same label with *Beyond the Thunder* as Craig Chaquico, whose *Acoustic Highway* and *Acoustic Planet* albums were quite successful on New Age charts. Any connection with him concerning your signing with Higher Octave?

NS: I've known Craig for years. I think that since they had a lot of success with Craig's albums, that meant they more interested in hearing what I could do in this genre than other companies were, and I had gotten more interested in Higher Octave than any other company.

VG: For what my opinion's worth, *Beyond the Thunder* isn't quite as New Age-ish as some other instrumental guitar albums; there's some uptempo music on it as well. But as we speak, isn't your album doing well on the N.A.C./New Adult Contemporary charts?

NS: It's been moving up consistently. It's in a completely different market than what I've been used to for the rest of my career, so it's new and strange to me; it's been very interesting. I'm glad I did this record; almost everyone who listens to it really likes it, because it wasn't what they expected. Everybody knows I can do the wah-wah thing and the shredding, but I felt like nobody knew I could play tastefully, too. There's a couple of solos on the record that cut loose; I've still got to let people know I can do that, but I didn't feel the need to have it *all over* the record. But the next record I do is going to be a bit more "out there."

VG: "Out there" meaning what?

NS: I want it to be a bit spacier, futuristic... but you never know what you're going to get when you say "out there" (laughs)!

VG: The songs on *Beyond the Thunder* sound like they'd fit onto more than one chart.

NS: That's what I was going for. Not just N.A.C., but I wanted to cross over to regular Adult Contemporary, and some urban stations as well, and that happened recently in New York City. "Cool Breeze" went Number One on some major urban jazz stations; it's got a funk bass line and a kind of Wes Montgomery thing over the top, along with some "rolling blues" stuff that I like to play.

VG: What about the guitars that you used on that album?

NS: I used Tom Anderson Strats, a '65 Fender Strat, and one of those weird-looking Roland 707s; it's a synth guitar but I used just the guitar part on several tracks; it sounds wonderful. It's got a warm sound, and it's great for the "clean" stuff and the rolling, bluesy parts of some songs. Each note is really even up and down the neck; it records wonderfully. I also used some Yamaha acoustic guitars.

VG: There are some unique instruments shown in the cover photography; a big black Gibson archtop electric, for example.

NS: I use that a lot at home when I'm writing. I tried it on a couple of tracks but didn't end up using it; I'm probably going to get into using it more. I've got that guitar rigged up with a synth pickup, by the way. A couple of my Andersons also have synth pickups built into them, and some of my acoustic have synth pickups too.

VG: There's also a very old Gibson acoustic with a scrolled body shown on the cover of *Beyond the Thunder*.

NS: That's part of my collection. It sounds wonderful, but it's very hard to play; the neck is huge and you run out of frets (chuckles)! It's in mint condition; I'll probably never sell it. I believe it's a 1913 model.

VG: Any tour plans to support *Beyond the Thunder*?

NS: I'm going to go out, but I want to get another record under my belt; one like I was talking about earlier. I want it to be a bit more uptempo, so when I *do* go out and play I'll have some stuff that I can improvise on.

VG: I heard that you *have* been touring with Abraxas.

NS: Yeah; I just finished a tour with them, and we're currently in the studio finishing a record.

VG: How and why did Abraxas form?

NS: It was just for fun; I was finishing up *Beyond the Thunder*, and Michael Carabello and Chepito Areas came in to put some percussion on a couple of tunes. We started playing, and I went "Wow"; it brought me right back to my roots. It was a good feeling; it was very musical, and when you play with percussion, the labels get taken right off. It's no longer "rock & roll" or "pop music," it's almost like "world music." I went right up to Gregg Rolie's house and said: "Listen to what I just did with these guys. We should call everybody up, get together and write some songs real fast, and see what we come up with, just for the hell of it." We did that, and wrote some real interesting stuff. There's a market out there for the type of music we've recorded. Abraxas is everybody who was in the original Santana band except Carlos and Dave Brown; Alphonso Johnson is playing bass in Abraxas.

We don't have a record deal yet, and we're even talking about putting the album out ourselves. Between that and the possibility of getting Journey going again as well as the solo albums, I've got plenty to keep me busy!

Absolutely. Neal Schon has already played in famous bands and with other famous guitarists for so long, he would have an enviable career to look back on if he chose to hang up his guitar. But somehow Schon's enthusiasm for his future projects indicates that such an option isn't under consideration in any way, shape or form.

Journey's "reunion" album, Trial by Fire, *was a mega-hit, and Schon subsequently released a two-CD follow-up instrumental album on Higher Octave titled* Electric World. *An album by Abraxas was also released.*

Leland Sklar

"I Can't Even Make A Chord On a Guitar"

The interviewer's attempt at humor upon being introduced to Leland Sklar was somewhat lame: "Yeah, Leland, I know who you are; you used to sing with the Oak Ridge Boys." Whereupon Sklar noted that he'd not only recorded with the Oak Ridge Boys, he'd actually posed with the vocal group in lieu of William Lee Golden (the singer to whom Sklar bears a passing resemblance due to his long hair and beard) for a gag publicity photo.

So it shouldn't come as any revelation that the veteran bass player has recorded with dozens of the biggest names in the music business; he's still one of the top session players on the West Coast, and he travels to Nashville and other locations on a regular basis. Most music fans have probably noted Sklar's visage onstage with the likes of James Taylor, Jackson Browne, and Phil Collins, but that's only the tip of the proverbial iceberg in his career (about the only revelation that should come as a surprise to most readers would be his comment that's the subtitle of this article). The erudite and eloquent bassist recently sat down with *VG* for an enlightening look at his efforts and instruments; Leland Sklar was born in Milwaukee, but his family moved to the Los Angeles area when he was a small child:

VG: One would assume that growing up in the Los Angeles area meant there were plenty of guitar-playing or bass-playing influences available.

LS: Actually, my first musical influence was Liberace. I studied piano from the time I was five until I was fourteen; I used to watch Liberace's television show. I was really quite successful as a child pianist; I won the Hollywood Bowl Association award for the most outstanding young pianist in L.A.; I did a lot of recitals.

But when I went into junior high, there were fifty other piano players ahead of me, but they had no bass players, and I was asked if I would like to play string bass. I said "Sure"; they brought one out, and I looked at it and said "You've got to be joking" (laughs). But I had a wonderful teacher named Ted Lynn; all of my earliest lessons were with him, and he re-

ally inspired me. And I fell in love with the "psychology" of the bass more than the piano, so I eventually weaned the piano out of my life in order to concentrate on bass.

VG: The "psychology of the bass" as what?

LS: I like the responsibility that comes with it; holding the fundamentals together instead of being the front guy. That *definitely* became apparent when I started playing rock & roll.

VG: How did that transition come about?

LS: I credit that to the Beatles. Up until that point I'd pretty much been playing in jazz quartets and trios; I was never a fan of people like Elvis. I

didn't *dislike* that kind of music, but I wasn't a snob about playing classical and jazz, which was where my focus was. I'd played a bit of surf music, but the Beatles really turned me around; I still look at McCartney as one of the greatest electric bass players ever, from a melodic structure standpoint.

VG: What about your first electric bass?

LS: It was a St. George with a Melody amplifier; I fell in love with it. I miss playing upright bass at this point in my life, from a bowing standpoint, but I know too many great upright players out there, and it's not like riding a bicycle; you don't just "hop right back on it." I've still got a couple of basses at home that are pretty funky; I sold my best bass years ago to a friend, and I regret it to this day; it was a mid-1800s Czechoslovakian model and it was beautiful, but from that point on, I just focused on electric.

VG: What sort of instruments did you get after the St. George?

LS: I was so inspired by McCartney that I wanted a Hofner but couldn't afford one, so I got an Eko violin-shaped bass that was fun. After that, I found a '62 Fender Jazz bass for sale,

Barefoot Servants: Ray Brinker - Drums, Ben Schultz - Guitar, Jon Butcher - Vocals, Guitar, Leland Sklar - Bass. Photo: Marty Temme

and bought it for ninety bucks. That's been my instrument of choice ever since, and I still have it; I carved it up, in a fit of stupidity back in 1966 (chuckles). It's got peace signs on it, and I used to have a picture of Zappa decoupaged on the back because I was into the Mothers. An instrument based on a '62 Jazz bass is what I use now.

VG: Was there any problem adjusting to the Jazz's 34" scale as opposed to the Eko's 30" scale?

LS: None whatsoever. I never even give a thought to scale length; I don't even know how many frets are on a bass. It doesn't matter to me; I'll play whatever I'm handed, from a Jerry Jones to a Thunderbird.

VG: So you don't fit the stereotype of a lot of electric bass players who are/were converted guitar players.

LS: I can't even make a chord on a guitar. I'm *strictly* a bass player.

VG: How did your electric bass playing develop?

LS: I used to sit at home and play all of my albums at 45 r.p.m. instead of 33, Working on my chops. I listened to the Righteous Brothers, and I loved all of the bands out of San Francisco. Then I'd slow the records back down to 33, and I had all of this "space" to deal with. I *loved* Tim Bogert's playing on the first Vanilla Fudge album, and I loved the playing of Bob Mosley from Moby Grape, Jack Bruce... there's an amazing family of bass players out there in so many different styles that excite me; players from McCartney to Victor Wooten.

VG: Any particular memorable "firsts"?

LS: I remember my first session; I'd played around doing gigs with Chicago George Smith and Albert Collins; there were times when I was in eight or ten bands at one time! But my first recording gig was for a Brian Hyland session that Del Shannon produced; that was around the time I started with James Taylor.

And I have to give credit there; playing with James Taylor was really what brought me to

any prominence. When I started working with him, our careers sort of took off at the same time, and to me, James is still the most gifted singer/songwriter that I've ever worked with.

VG: Is it fair to say that the same thing happened for Danny Kortchmar?

LS: And Russ Kunkel, and Craig Doerge; the whole group. We actually formed a group called the Section, which came about from being on the road with James; we did three albums. What we did seemed to surprise everybody, because having been with James, it was probably expected that we would be an Eagles-type group, but we brought in a sort of pop/fusion, which may have been a little ahead of its time. That material is still selling, though; particularly in Japan. They keep calling us; wanting us to come back and do some more work over there. I don't think we ever will, but you never know.

VG: One of the cover photos on Jackson Browne's *Running On Empty* showed you playing an exquisite, apparently-hand-crafted double-neck bass.

LS: It had a regular neck and a piccolo neck; it was built by Steve Helgeson up in Arcada. His company was called Moonstone. The body was burl bird's-eye maple that was carved to look like an eagle in flight; the main neck was ebony with mother-of-pearl inlay, and the piccolo neck was rosewood with abalone inlay. He carved two eagle heads out of burl walnut with Mexican fire opal eyes that fit over the headstocks. It was the most beautiful bass I've ever seen, but it was not a great player. As of now, it's hanging above the entrance to the Boston Hard Rock Cafe. I still own it, but it's on loan to them; they have it well-displayed as you walk in the door.

VG: What were your primary instruments during your "Taylor and Browne years," studio *and* concert performance?

LS: For years now, my main instrument has been a bass with a '62 Precision neck that we cut down to the shape of a '62 Jazz neck; the body is an early Charvel alder P-Bass style. The pickups are very early EMG P-Bass models that we placed where Jazz pickups would normally go. It's got a Badass bridge, and like all of my basses, mandolin fret wire, which is the smallest fret wire you can get. I love it and swear by it; it's almost like having a fretless, but the accuracy's still there; it's fabulous. That bass also has a D-tuner on it. I'd say that probably 90% of what I've done over the last twenty years has been on that bass.

VG: How did the Phil Collins gig come about?

LS: Phil and I had met when we both played on a Lee Ritenour track; Phil knew my history from James and Jackson, and I knew about him because of Genesis and Brand X. We hit it off, and he originally called me in 1980, but I couldn't work with him because James was working at the time. Then he called again in '84, and I did *No Jacket Required* and the tour.

VG: A concert video from that tour was released; why wasn't a live album forthcoming as well?

LS: I have no idea, because we *did* record one; it was just never released.

VG: There's a song on that video that I'd never heard before which was a unique effort; it's called "Hand in Hand," and it has an almost "African" feel to it.

LS: I don't know if that's on one of Phil's albums. We opened each concert with that song; Chester Thompson would play some kind of kalimba-marimba instrument.

VG: That's not the opening song on the concert video, however.

LS: It seems like some things always get taken out of context and moved around, and it pisses me off when that happens, because when you're doing live shows, you're creating a certain momentum. Another example of that is when we did a James Taylor show in Boston for PBS. When we finally showed the edited version, it had been rearranged to fit their programming.

VG: Another facet of the Collins concert video was your use of a Steinberger bass.

LS: I ended up using it for "shock value." The Steinberger I have is serial number One. I had two prototypes before that; I was trying to help Ned with the development of it. So there's an intrinsic, collector's aspect to it, but for the most part, I'm still a wood instrument player.

VG: Some years ago, Jeff Berlin opined that Steinbergers were probably very accurate, but in a studio environment they were too "brittle"-sounding.

LS: They're almost clavinet-like. One thing that's great about them is if you tune them up, you can do a whole tour and never have to re-tune. They're really quite amazing for their properties; it's not my instrument of choice, but when it's the right instrument for a certain track, it's great.

VG: For all of your projects with Taylor, Browne and Collins, you've always been doing all sorts of studio work as well. I need to ask about several facets of your session work; first, what do you think might have been your favorite session?

LS: One of my favorite sessions was Billy Cobham's first album, *Spectrum*; I think it's still a milestone album in the progressive fusion area. We did the whole album in two days; those are almost all first takes on it. Tommy Bolin was the guitar player on it, and I still consider Tommy to have been one of the greatest guitar players who's ever lived, and I miss him dearly.

VG: Worst or hardest session?

LS: That's an area that is a bit funny, because there can be hard sessions for *different reasons*. Sometimes they're *emotionally* hard; sometimes they're *musically* hard. I just finished

doing the soundtrack for the new *Highlander* movie; J. Peter Robinson, who used to be the keyboard player with Phil, did the music for it. It was difficult, because Peter wrote parts for it on synthesizer, quantized it, then bumped it up to speed. We had to do it note-for-note, and it took *forever* to suss it out.

VG: He plays the artsy director in the "Billy Don't Lose My Number" video; you're in it as well. There's that sequence where Collins and Robinson are trading off names of Westerns and actors; a lot of people didn't know who the last person cited is; Collins and Robinson say his name simultaneously.

LS: (laughs) That was Mal Craggs; he was our road manager. He's in the video as well; in the *Road Warrior* sequence, he's driving the truck, playing the Mel Gibson part. It was "inside" stuff (chuckles).

VG: What about sessions where people might not have expected Leland Sklar to appear?

LS: I did an album with Ted Knight from "The Mary Tyler Moore Show," called *Hi, Guys*. I'm getting ready to start an album with Andy Griffith; I just finished doing some work in Nashville with Mark Collie and Lorrie Morgan; I've worked with Reba as well. I do a lot of work there. I used to do all kinds of cartoon shows; "Ghostbusters", "Groovy Ghoulies," "The Archies," all of the Filmation stuff.

I'm a real worker, so I'll take anything that comes along. Basically, whatever calls come in, I'll go do it, and I'm always surprised and pleased when it ends up being something a little left of center.

VG: My perception is that your association with the Barefoot Servants was more of a "group" thing rather than as a back-up and/or session player.

LS: Exactly; I wasn't hired as a sideman, I came on as a member. The producer sent me some tracks while I was in San Francisco, doing an album with Linda Ronstadt. He wanted to know if I'd be interested in doing the record. As soon as I heard two notes, I called him back and told him to count me in, and it was one of those things that progressed. Ben (Schultz) is a wonderful musician and writer, and I've been a fan of Jon (Butcher) for years. I was committed only to doing the record, but I told them: "If you guys would like to take this on the road, I've love to do it, instead of you having to hire somebody else."

We had some disappointments last year, but I'm not completely discouraged by it; we did tour for three months with the Southern Spirit tour. The band is great; it's the kind of music I'd listen to myself. I've always been a ZZ TOP fan and a fan of blues/boogie bands. I'll listen to either that or Aaron Copland and Gershwin; not a lot in between.

VG: Does your collection consist primarily of utility instruments or collectibles?

LS: I have a lot of instruments; a few are collectible; most are ones that people have sent me to try out. I end up giving a lot of that stuff to children who want to learn to play. I have a '62 Jazz bass which I bought from George Gruhn a number of years ago that's almost mint; it still had the cover plates and the original LaBella strings. It's got spring-loaded mutes; everything's intact.

I've also got a January of '62 Precision that has a fingerboard that looks like teak. It was in mint condition; I couldn't figure out what that fingerboard was, so I called the Fender archives. They looked up the serial number and said it was an experimental bass. I found an old Kay acoustic bass from the Fifties at a flea market, but I've never been a big collector.

Basically, I have four basses that cover about 99% of what I do. There's the "hybrid" we discussed earlier, a John Carruthers five-string, a Yamaha TRB-5 five-string fretless, and an old BX-1 that I made into a piccolo bass. I have a Washburn AB-45 acoustic bass, which is a beautiful instrument that I used a lot with Lyle Lovett.

So I try to have enough instruments to cover what's required, but I'm also a firm believer in what my role is when I show up. I don't like playing six-string, and I don't like playing five-string unless I absolutely have to.

VG: So is the controversy about keyboard bass and/or MIDI, which has been going on for some time, a sore subject?

LS: No, not at all. Life's too short to worry about whether synth players are going to take bass players' jobs, or whether bass players are going to be MIDI, so they can blow synth guys away. To me, as long as you diversify, there's enough stuff out there to do. I've covered myself; for the past fifteen years I've been going to Nashville on a regular basis. I'm always looking for touring projects to do; I work here in L.A. regularly, and when I'm not busy I work on cars and my house (chuckles)! I still see guys panicking about synthesizers, but I think synthesizers have settled into their own space, and these days you see folks pulling out B-3 organs and Wurlitzer or Fender/Rhodes pianos; they're tired of listening to the "generic synth sound"; they'd rather have the "personality" of the real thing.

VG: So for all your years of playing, has the experience given you what might be termed "callouses" when it comes to discussing where the music business has been as well as where it's headed?

LS: I've got leather skin (laughs)!

Well-stated, as is Leland Sklar's bass playing. He's every bit as eloquent in his ruminations about sessions and touring as he is when he's *playing* in such sessions or tours. Either way, Sklar's statements are important as well as enjoyable.

Bob Spickard
Two More Sides of the Chantays

Bob Spickard has been involved in playing music ever since the "glory days" of surf music. He does, however, have a "day job" (more about that later), and his children are also involved in music as well (more about that later, too):

VG: As was the case when I interviewed another veteran surf music guitarist, I don't think we need to re-hash the history of surf music due to Robert Dalley's book being available; however, is there any comment you have about the history of the Chantays as presented in *Surfin' Guitars?*

BS: It's pretty accurate, although there were a couple of things that I believe he took out of context. It's my understanding that Bob now has a publisher, and he's going to come out with a revised and updated version of that book, and that it's going to be hardbound. I talked with him in June of 1993; I gave him some updated information on our efforts. Bob lives in Utah, but he came out here for a "Surf Battle" concert at the Huntingdon Beach High School football stadium. Performers included Jan and Dean, Dick Dale and the Del-Tones, the Tornadoes, the Kingsmen, and us. We also did a performance down at Jack Murphy Stadium in San Diego for a Padres game with Jan and Dean and Dick Dale; both of those were fun.

VG: What first inspired you to play guitar?

BS: Well, my father played guitar; when I was about three years old my mother gave my father a Martin D-18. So there was always a guitar around the house, and my dad showed me my first basic guitar chords. But I think I was more inspired to get serious about playing after I heard a local band called the Rhythm Rockers, which as you probably know had Brian's brother Steve playing sax. They were playing at local teen dances and looked like they were having a good time plus making some money! (chuckles)

As for *players,* the Rhythm Rockers played some Freddie King songs that I really liked, so I started listening to things like "Heads Up", "Sen-sa-shun" and "Hideaway." From there I went on to listening closely to Johnny & the Hurricanes, Duane Eddy, and the Ventures, naturally; I think I bought every record the Ventures ever put out! So I had a local band that inspired me to become a player, but there were several nationally-known players that I think

influenced my playing.

VG: What about your first electric guitar?

BS: It was a single-pickup Barth that I got for my fifteenth birthday, and I still have it. My dad and I went to a music store in Costa Mesa, and the Barth felt nice, sounded nice, and was within our budget; I think we got the guitar and a Barth amp for $125. My dad always said it was the best $125 he'd ever spent (laughs)! Originally it was a blond color; Brian refinished it for me in the mid-Eighties. In fact, it sat in pieces for a long time before I put it back together after Brian painted it red. I never really thought about it being a collectible guitar, even though Barths are kind of rare, but I kept it because it's the guitar that I used to write and perform the original version of "Pipeline."

VG: Did the Chantays form with the idea of becoming a surf band?

BS: Not necessarily; we just got together to play music, and the surf music fad happened to coincide with the time when we were forming a band.

VG: The photo of the Chantays in Tom Wheeler's *American Guitars* shows you and Carman holding Stratocasters with dark pickguards; the book states that such guitars were unusual for the time.

BS: Those were tortoise-shell pickguards. Shell pickguards were part of the Custom Color program at the time, but sunburst Stratocasters came with white pickguards. I honestly don't remember whether or not the retailer got them from the factory like that or the shell pickguards were installed by the dealer; those guitars were custom-ordered from a music store in Santa Ana. Brian already had one on order, and I came up with the money to get one too, but I didn't tell Brian I'd ordered one. Both of the instruments were ready at the same time from the store. That would have been in 1962.

VG: Do you still have that guitar?

BS: No, but I have another '62 Strat that I got in 1967; a while back Steve Soest found an original tortoise-shell pickguard and put it on the guitar. It's the guitar I almost always use these days.

VG: I was listening to a double-album length Chantays CD the other day, and there are several

Publicity photo from later 1964, Top to Bottom: Brian Carman, Steve Khan, Rob Marshall, Warren Waters, Bob Spickard. By this time, Khan had replaced Bob Welch as the Chantay's drummer.

cover songs on it. When the Chantays performed live, what percentage of tunes were original versus covers?

BS: I'd say about fifty-fifty. We wrote a lot of other instrumentals that didn't end up on albums. That CD is the first two albums; there was a third album that was released in Japan.

VG: One of the cover tunes on that double-length CD was "Three Coins in a Fountain"; the song included an organ dominating the melody and there was a weird "dripping" sound heard.

BS: At the time, Steve Khan was playing with us, and that was our "tribute" to his dad, Sammy Cahn. I showed Steve some of his first guitar chords and turned him on to Wes Montgomery; he's a great fusion player in New York now. He played in one band called Eyewitness, and has put out several solo albums, as well as doing studio work for a multitude of artists such as Billy Joel, Steely Dan, etc.

The "dripping" sound was a studio effect that ended up making the song sound hokey; I thought it sounded like roller-skating music (laughs)! All too often back then we didn't have much say-so whenever we recorded, and that song is an example of something not turning out like we wanted.

VG: Do you recall your best and worst gigs?

BS: (chuckles) That's a tough one, because I can't really think of an outstanding example of either a best or a worst performance. Almost all of the gigs were and still are good; I have a good time whenever we play. I talked in Dalley's book about those performances in Japan when "Pipeline" was just about the number one song in the country; those would of course have to be considered as memorable. One performance was in front of 24,000 people. The only time I recall a bad experience was when we were playing in Washington state, and we were late due to a driving rainstorm. We had to unload in the rain and set up; we had to play while we were soaking wet.

VG: What about your "day job" these days?

BS: I own a company that manufactures, distributes and sells high-pressure cleaning equipment; steam cleaners, pumps, car wash equipment, and related industrial equipment. Here in California there's a large demand for mobile detailers; that's a portion of our market.

To be honest, I wish we could play more these days; we all seem to have done pretty well in our respective "day jobs," and I'd rather be playing guitar than peddling industrial equipment (chuckles). Three of the original members are currently involved with the band, and sometimes a fourth one gets to play with us. I enjoy the camaraderie and I enjoy playing for people.

VG: Do you rehearse all that much?

BS: Sometimes we'll decide what we're going to play five minutes before we go onstage (laughs)! We've all been together so long, about thirty two years, that it doesn't take long for us to figure out songs.

VG: There seems to have been a resurgence in instrumental guitar music that came along in the late Eighties, and surf music was instrumental guitar music about a quarter-century earlier—

BS: (interrupting): You mean like Joe Satriani? *Surfing with theAlien*? (laughs)

VG: Not hardly; I was thinking more along the lines of the I.R.S. *Guitarspeak* series, but some modern instrumental surf music has been heard as well. Any current bands or players that you've heard who might be noteworthy?

BS: There's a band I've heard called the Insect Surfers who are a modern surf band, but they're pretty good; they have what I'd call a "genuine sound." I really liked their CD when I heard it.

VG: Dick Dale and the late Stevie Ray Vaughan covered "Pipeline" for the *Back to the Beach* movie. Comment?

BS: I'm glad it got nominated for a Grammy; it was good to hear it in a different venue. It came out sounding different from the way I thought it would, but I wasn't disappointed. I didn't really hear it enough to critique it; I'm an avid Stevie Ray Vaughan fan, and I don't think it sounded anything like him; Stevie usually sounded more funky. But it was an interesting match-up.

VG: Do you collect instruments?

BS: I've acquired a few over the years. I've got a '62 ES-335 with a stud tailpiece, a 1919 Washburn acoustic, and I have that 1946 D-18 of my father's. I also have another Martin guitar, a '72 D-35, and an old Fender Shenandoah 12-string, plus a Tele. Then there's the Barth, as well as that '62 Strat that I use in concert. I've had some others but sold them; one was a beautiful ES-175 jazz guitar. Overall I think I've got a good, basic assortment of guitars.

There's one unique thing about my Strat that I think is interesting; the neck plate was signed by Leo Fender with an engraving tool. Brian and a former Fender employee named Babe Simoni got him to etch his name on there; Mr. Fender said that he thought it was the first time he'd ever done that.

VG: You advised me in our preliminary conversation that you're a grandfather; are any of your children involved in music?

BS: All of them play; my son is more involved with film, but he recently did a commercial for a new band called the Stone Temple Pilots. Their album recently went platinum, and he's hoping to do something along the lines of a video with them. He won a Gold Award at the Houston International Film Festival last year for a documentary he did. He's also an excellent keyboard player; he's put soundtracks onto some of his own video projects.

My older daughter plays guitar and drums, and my other daughter is an excellent bass player, piano player and singer; she does a lot of weddings.

VG: What about *your* future musical plans?

BS: Well, we've been doing so many concerts recently that we've just about decided it's time to go back into the studio and do some modern recordings. Obviously, an updated version of "Pipeline" is one tune we'd do, but updated versions of other older songs would be pretty high on the priority list as well. It's gotten to the point where we all may have a bit more time to devote to the music business, which as I said earlier I wouldn't mind doing (laughs)! We've had such a good response to the concerts we've done that it's obvious to me that there's a definite market for the sound and the product!

Yet another veteran of a specific genre of music, Bob Spickard is still enjoying his guitar playing, even though it's not his "day job." However, if one asked him if he'd prefer being a full-time musician, it's easy to surmise what his response would be!

The Chantays released a modern album in 1996 called Waiting for the Tide.

Chris Squire
Backstage Bassics

"I m sorry; you don't fit the profile of the magazine."

That remark by this writer drew nonplussed looks from Tony Kaye and Alan White, keyboard player and drummer, respectively, for the legendary British progressive rock band Yes; the reporter had flashed a then-current issue of *Vintage Guitar* at the two musicians, evoking a chuckle from both of them when they saw the guitar on the cover.

Obviously, we were seeking a member or members of the Yes that *did* fit the format of *VG*; and after encountering White and Kaye in a hotel lobby during the band's 1994 *Talk* tour, we arranged to meet bassist Chris Squire backstage at the venue. Prior to settling into Squire's dressing room for the interview, we happened to run into Kaye again. Tony Kaye was Yes' original keyboard player, and had formed a group known as Badger following his departure from Yes in the early Seventies. Badger's first album was a live effort that featured Kaye's extensive use of a now-antiquated keyboard device known as a Mellotron, and we remarked that in perusing the stage setup for that evening's concert, we didn't see any Mellotrons. Kaye responded with a laugh that at one point, he had actually programmed a Mellotron sample into one of his MIDI keyboards (talk about time warp technology!).

Chris Squire has been described by one of this writer's former bandmates as "a giant; literally and figuratively" among bass guitarists. Witnessing the ensuing concert averred that a full-scale bass does indeed resemble a standard-size guitar in the hands of Squire, but he's also considered a legend in terms of his innovative style and tone (utilizing a Rickenbacker bass for most of his career). Yes has been a viable musical entity for over a quarter-century, and Chris Squire is the only individual who's been on all of the band's albums. The band has enough legendary status to have merited a multiple CD/cassette boxed set (*Yesyears*), and a portion of Squire's early musical ventures are discussed in the *Yesyears* booklet; we began by asking for details:

VG: What was your earliest instrument?

CS: Well, if you go back to the very beginning, my first bass was an Italian-made instrument called a Futurama. I started playing bass pretty much from the start; the only band I was in before the Yes was a band called the Syn, and when it formed, the friend of mine who had played classical guitar for a long time and was going to be the band's guitar player told me: "Well, you're tall and you've got big hands; you should play bass" (chuckles).

VG: Are you satisfied with the way the *Yesyears* boxed set turned out?

CS: Yeah, we were consulted on it; a guy at Atlantic Records asked for our input and if we had any obscure tapes. I'm satisfied with the music that ended up in the set. There was another sort of anthology that I compiled in the early Eighties called *Classic Yes*; it was smaller, but it had some live tracks that hadn't been released until then.

VG: One of the band's first important concerts was opening at Cream's "farewell concert."

CS: It was an exciting time for us; we were just getting recognized around town. It was a great opportunity.

VG: Some of the earliest Yes recordings were cover tunes, and the *Yesyears* booklet mentioned influence from the Vanilla Fudge. Comment? Any favorite covers that the Yes did?

CS: We used to listen to the Vanilla Fudge a good bit in those days, when they had those big hits like "You Keep Me Hangin' On"; I've met Tim Bogert. I enjoyed playing the Beatles' "Every Little Thing," which was on our first album, and "Something's Coming" from *West Side Story*. In fact, we used to do other songs in concert at places like the Marquee; songs like "Eleanor Rigby," but we never got around to recording them. I think those old covers songs

Chris Squire with his Rickenbacker Limited Edition, Model 4001 CS.

still hold up.

VG: There was a time before the Yes got going that you did about a year of "woodshedding." Is that when you developed what is considered to be "the Chris Squire sound," using a Rickenbacker bass and a pick?

CS: I think so; I was about nineteen or twenty; trying to decide what I was going to do. I think I had the third Rickenbacker bass that was imported into England. I was working as a shop assistant in a music store that sold violins and stuff like that, but there was a "rock" music store down the street that belonged to the same owners, and that's where I got the Rickenbacker. I think the guy from the Kinks had one and John Entwhistle had one, then I got mine.

VG: Your only solo album, *Fish Out of Water*, is finally available on CD, isn't it?

CS: I know it's out on a Japanese Compact Disc; I think it's out here in the States now as well. The Japanese disc has a really good sound. It's now twenty years old, and I think it holds up as well. I'm thinking of doing another one, since it's been so long since I did *Fish Out of Water*.

VG: You've never really done that many solo or side projects.

CS: The year before last, I did a solo tour; a total of seven performances. One show was in Phoenix and the rest were at clubs in southern California. You'll see a guy onstage tonight named Billy Sherwood; he's like the sixth member of the Yes when we tour; he plays acoustic guitar and other instruments and sings backup. He and I have known each other for several years and have done some writing, so a couple of years ago I told him we should go on the road with the material. Alan White came along to play drums, and Steve Porcaro went out with us as well. We did completely new material that no one had ever heard before; it was billed as "The Chris Squire Experiment," for good reason (laughs)!

VG: A few years ago, you played on a benefit re-make of "Smoke On The Water."

CS: That was for the Armenian earthquake disaster; I went to London to do it. I don't really know how well it sold.

VG: Over the quarter-century that Yes has been in existence, is there any least favorite Yes song you can cite, perhaps due to its complexity?

CS: I can't say that there's a "least favorite," but "Topgraphic Oceans" was more than a little tricky (chuckles)! It's probably the most complex thing we've ever done.

VG: On the flip side, any favorite or perhaps "definitive" Yes song, in your opinion?

CS: Well, maybe "Heart of the Sunrise." We're still playing it; you'll hear it tonight. Of course, many people consider "Roundabout" to be the definitive Yes song, and on the new album we have some really good stuff that might eventually become what some people would call definitive Yes songs; they have the potential to be such.

VG: I've always wanted to know about the so-called "XYZ Band;" there were a lot of rumors going around at one time about a short-lived collaboration with Jimmy Page, and the name of the band supposedly had a particular meaning attributed to the letters.

CS: That was after John Bonham had just died, and Page was a bit low, obviously. It was 1980, and was after the *Drama* album and tour for the Yes, when Trevor Horn had been in the band. We decided to take a sabbatical and cool off for a while. Jimmy had moved close to me, and invited me to do some jamming with him. Alan and I actually put down four tracks with Jimmy; songs that I wrote, and I did the singing as well. They've never been heard, but we've still got the tapes, and Jimmy probably still has the masters in his studio. The name of the band was to stand for "Ex-Yes/Zeppelin."

VG: About the *Union* album that came out; cynics would have noted that such a lineup probably wouldn't have lasted, since it was an attempt to combine eight people from two bands.

CS: Well, I think it's important to note that on the album there was no point where the eight of us were playing together on any one song. It was really like Jon was going back and forth between the Anderson, Wakeman, Bruford & Howe band and us like a loose cannon (chuckles).

VG: Let's shift gears and talk about instruments for a while. One of our previous interviewees was Rickenbacker's John Hall; he and I discussed some stereotypical things that some musicians might think about Rickenbacker basses, including the use of roundwound strings straining the old truss rod system as well as fret wear. Hall's response included citing your use of Rotosounds on your Rickenbacker; he stated that the truss rod system was refined to accommodate any kind of string, and that Rotosounds, which are almost pure iron, would wear out any type of fret wire faster than nickel strings. Hall said Rickenbacker uses some of the hardest fret wire in the industry. Comment?

CS: (chuckles) Strangely enough, my instrument always held up okay, but originally I think John Hall hated me because of that. I went to the factory one day, and he showed me a bunch of 4001s that had been sent back because the frets were worn down; he said: "This is your fault" (laughs). But John ultimately marketed a limited edition based on my bass.

VG: Details?

CS: It's unusual that they would want to make a guitar like that. Originally, I went through a period where I was putting "flower power" stickers on my instrument, then I stripped those off and put silver-colored stuff all over it. I stripped that off as well, and ultimately a Chinese guitar repair guy put a solid creme-colored finish on it. That's the color it's been since then, and when Rickenbacker copied my bass, they used that creme color; they've never had a stock finish like that. The limited edition also has vermilion "wings" on the headstock.

The limited edition is great, but unfortunately what they can't copy is the "crappiness" of the old electronics inside my original, which gives it its own sound. Of course, it wouldn't be fair if they tried to "age" the electronics in the limited edition.

VG: I was perusing the stage setup, and noted all of the basses lined up over on Stage Left. Let me give the names of some of them, and you can comment accordingly. First, there's the unusual green Mouridian bass that was seen in the "Owner of a Lonely Heart" video.

CS: Jim Mouridian is out of Boston; he's a bass player himself, and fancied himself a guitar builder. That's an original design that I did with him. He went into business for awhile, then I think he decided he didn't want to have to contend with a factory, employees, and taxes (chuckles). I think he built around a hundred instruments. A band called Extreme used Mouridians as well. I've had that bass for over ten years now; I've really gotten to like it and I use it on three songs on the current tour.

VG: Tobias. You were holding one in a recent Ampeg endorsement ad.

CS: The four-string in that ad, which I use on a couple of songs in concert, is my version of a "four-string five-string bass" that Mike made me (chuckles). It's strung B-E-A-D; has extra-wide frets on it as well. I also have a regular five-string red Tobias on tour; they're well-made instruments.

VG: Ranney.

CS: That's an eight-string bass by a guy in Chicago; he also made me a twelve-string guitar. They're fantastic instruments, and I think that's all he's ever made.

VG: One bass I *didn't* see was an Electra Outlaw MPC you were seen playing some time ago.

CS: That was an experiment; apparently for the company as well as me, I suppose. It had a flap in the back where you could drop in all sorts of modules; flanger, octave, etc. I think the company decided that it was going to be too expensive for the market, since it was an imported model.

VG: You were playing a Kramer/Ferrington acoustic bass in the "Love Will Find A Way" video.

CS: I still have that, and I also have an old Ernie Ball Earthwood bass in my house back in England.

VG: Do you collect?

CS: Yeah, I've got about forty or fifty instruments, including some nice ones like a blue Gibson Thunderbird. I used to have one of the old Gibson violin-shaped-basses; I have other old collectible basses as well.

VG: Haven't you done an instructional video?

CS: I did one for Star Licks; I wasn't that pleased with it. It seems like I've always felt that if people came to see a show they could copy what they see there; it's difficult for me to sit down and say "This is how I do this" (chuckles).

VG: For what my opinion's worth, the *Talk* album is easier for longtime Yes fans to get into right at the outset than some other albums.

CS: We're quite pleased with the results and the reception to it. After this tour I think I'll really work towards a new solo album; since as I said earlier *Fish Out of Water* is twenty years old, it's about time for another one (chuckles)!

VG: One last observation: Big difference between the Roger Dean cover art of most Yes albums and Peter Max's cover art for *Talk*.

CS: Another example where it was time for a change (laughs)!

The subsequent Yes concert proved why the band is still a viable musical force after a quarter-century and it proved why Chris Squire is indeed a "giant" (musical connotation only) among bass players; such would be the case even if Squire was of diminutive physical stature.

The Yes went through more personnel changes, and it should be obvious that the interview with Steve Howe was recorded after the one with Chris Squire.

Frankie Sullivan

Second Survivor

...not that there's anything secondary or subordinate about this Chicago-born guitarist's stature in the platinum-selling rock band that bears the moniker in this interview's subtitle, but Mr. Frankie Sullivan is, as long-time *Vintage Guitar* readers have probably already surmised, the second member of Survivor with whom we've conversed. The band's keyboardist/guitarist, Jim Peterik (who's also a veteran of the Ides of March), was interviewed by *VG* in 1992.

Fact is, Peterik seems to concentrate more on keyboards these days (at least one Survivor album's credits cite him as keyboard player only), which means the lead guitar duties are almost exclusively the domain of Frankie Sullivan.

Like Peterik, Sullivan still resides in the Chicago area, and he has a lot of great-sounding classic guitars. In a recent conversation with *VG*, Frankie noted how his interest in fretted instruments began, and how his philosophy concerning collecting may differ from other players/collectors:

VG: What motivated you to take up guitar?

FS: Three of my four sisters are older than me, and when the Beatles were happening, they were *bonkers* about that band. I remember asking myself why they were acting *so weird* when the Beatles played the Ed Sullivan show (chuckles). I thought the Beatles had cool-looking hair, and I was seduced by that whole episode. I'd like to think that I started developing an ear for music by listening to my sisters' Beatles records.

Then I got into the Rolling Stones; I remember telling my friends in the neighborhood that the Beatles were okay, but the Stones were

cooler. The whole Keith Richards vibe; the way he wrote songs, the alternate tuning; it was more rootsy and bluesy.

Then Cream came out, and it was all over as soon as I heard four bars of "I Feel Free." I heard them and other players like Zappa, Hendrix and the Nazz on the radio, and was amazed at all of the sounds a guitar could make. I asked my mom and dad for a guitar, and I got a Hagstrom guitar and a Silvertone amp with an eight-inch speaker for Christmas when I was 14. I spent a lot of time concentrating on listening to guitar players who were into that deep, rootsy kind of vibe, and of course that led to discovering blues players like B.B. King, who'd influenced the likes of Eric Clapton. And there were a lot of "great unknown" blues guitarists who played in the Chicago area. So while I appreciated what a guitar could do, I began to try and teach myself what *I* could do with one.

VG: What about guitars that came along after the Hagstrom?

FS: My sister was dating a guy who was in a band called the Renegades; he's now my brother-in-law. The Renegades were a local band that was pretty well known, and at the time he had a '61 Dakota Red Stratocaster, which he still has. It's been refinished; I don't know why we let that happen (chuckles). He let me use it back then; he left it at our house and I played it every chance I got; I *worshipped* that guitar! At the time, most of the guys were playing Gibsons, but I noticed Jimi Hendrix playing Fenders. We both know he played Flying Vs and SGs, but his main axe was a Stratocaster, so I figured he knew something important about that model!

VG: Were there any other Chicago-area players or bands, besides the blues guitarists, that influenced you back then?

FS: There was a band called Bangor Flying Circus that was like an "underground" group; their lead guitarist used SGs and Marshalls, and I really liked his sound. When they did "Born Under a Bad Sign" they sounded just like Cream. He "did Clapton" real well.

VG: Tell me about your professional playing experiences, "pre-Survivor."

FS: By the time I was 16, I was playing in an

eleven-piece horn band; we did a *lot* of Tower of Power stuff. We were the house band at a club, and I had to go in and out through the back door because I was a minor. The only other thing I'd done prior to that horn band was a garage band.

Then I joined a band, called Mariah, during my senior year in high school. The band got signed to United Artists, and we recorded a couple of albums. So by the time I was 17, I was making a record. The first album didn't sell well, but that wasn't the point; I was in a studio, doing something I'd dreamed of doing for years. I was kind of in awe of the tape machines and the producer, but I have some really good memories of my first recording experiences.

We played around a lot; we went to California for six months and played a *bunch* of club gigs. When we got back to Chicago, there was one night when we were playing at a club downtown, and Jim Peterik's band, not the Ides, was playing downstairs. He came upstairs and watched one of our sets, and he and I started keeping in touch, and in the late '70s we started Survivor.

VG: Peterik and I discussed Survivor being designated an "arena rock" band in the "history of rock;" did the media cite the band as such?

FS: I don't know that a band goes for a particular sound; I think that when a group of players gets together, who they are and who their influences are determines what kind of sound they have. David, the lead singer, was the last addition to Survivor, and maybe that had something to do with our being known as an "arena rock" band.

And I remember the term "faceless rock" as well; we had a Number One record and I did an interview with *Rolling Stone*. When the issue came out, the damn headline said "Faceless Rock Lives" (chuckles). I can laugh about it now, but I remember thinking something like "what the hell is *that*?" when it came out. I took that stuff with a *major* grain of salt; if you choose to be in the entertainment business, you have to understand and realize that you've got to take some lumps sometimes.

VG: Were you the lead guitarist for the band from its inception?

FS: When we did the first record, Rob Nevison produced it; he was and still is a brilliant producer. He did records for UFO, the Babys, and Bad Company, so he knew what it was like to work with guitars! When we were in the studio, Rob started designating more of the guitar playing to me. Jim played some guitar, but he started playing more keyboards as time went on. I guess it was sort of an evolution of the band's sound.

VG: Was there any live material recorded with the idea of turning it into an album?

FS: Not an album, but there *is* a video that was recorded live in Japan in '85. We did the "King Bisquit" show, too.

VG: The band went on hiatus for awhile, and re-grouped in the early '90s.

FS: We hadn't worked together for three years, then our label wanted to put out a greatest hits album. We wrote a couple of new songs that were a little more rootsy, and we recorded them in a couple of days; it was effortless. Then we decided to do some dates, and we went to Europe, which is a good market for Survivor; it always has been. It's gone on from there.

VG: Before and after the hiatus, what kind of instruments did you use in the studio and on tour?

FS: From '84 on, I would take my sunburst Dot, a '59 Les Paul, a '58 Strat, and a '59 Telecaster on the road, because I loved the way they sounded. Then on one of the tours, one of the P.A. columns fell over before we went onstage, and missed my guitar rack by about three inches! My guitar tech, who has found almost all of my vintage instruments, ran into the dressing room; he was as white as a ghost. He told me everything was almost ruined, and the next week he found me some reissues; stuff that was semi-expensive.

So now I use my vintage stuff primarily in the studio. In addition to the '58 Strat I used to take on the road, I have a '58 non-trem that I love. My '59 Telecaster is the type where the strings don't go through the body. I love those '58 and '59 Fender necks; when they got rid of those V-necks, the next ones were real nice and flat. I had a 1960 Les Paul in tobacco sunburst that was stolen; it was a beautiful. I also had a very early Charvel that was stolen; I think it was made when Grover was still working in his garage. I had a '70s Explorer that was stolen as well.

Around '89 or '90, I met Tom Anderson, and he started making some guitars for me. I still take my '59 Telecaster and at least one old Strat out on the road, though.

VG: How many instruments do you have?

FS: My collection changes from time to time, but I have a "core" of guitars I call "The Dirty Dozen"; 12 pieces that are really "blue chip." I go for *quality,* not *quantity.* I have a '52 SJ-200 that's unbelievable; a rare '55 blond J-185, a '56 all-gold Les Paul with a Tune-O-Matic; those are getting hard to find. I also have a couple of 'Bursts, some Stratocasters, and a couple of nice new guitars from the Fender Custom Shop.

So I'm pretty happy with what I've got. I'm not a "maniac" collector (laughs), but I just got a nice addition recently. It's an early '63 ES-335 with block inlays; I'd been looking for one of those for some time.

VG: Why one with block inlays?

FS: Well, for one thing, they're going up in price, and there aren't that many of them. I was talking to George Gruhn the other day, and he said he just doesn't get them. I looked around for a few months; I wanted an early '63 in red, which is more collectible. The one I bought is really clean, and has one PAF and one Patent Number. As far as I'm concerned, the early Patent Number pickups are the same as PAFs.

I look at guitars in kind of a "black or white" way: you can buy six $1,000 guitars, or a blue chip $6,000 guitar that is really a fine piece. I'm real picky about the stuff I buy; I'll ask questions like "have the pickups ever been out of the guitar" or even "have the pickup *covers* been taken off of the guitar?" There are ways you can tell; you can turn the pickups over to see if the solder's been broken and re-soldered. I actually get that picky.

VG: Have you ever been to guitar shows like the one in Chicago each Spring?

FS: Yeah, but I've got a bit of a problem with the guitar market these days. It's dried up considerably, and I'm one of those people who's particular about what he buys. It's become extremely difficult to find instruments that aren't refinished or repaired, and I'm not interested in those kinds of old guitars. To each his own, though. It seems like the pieces I'm interested in have become unbelievably expensive, too.

But if I get a vibe about wanting a certain piece, like that 335, I'll find one and pay a lot for it if it's exactly what I want. I honestly think those early block-inlay 335s will become as collectible as the dot-necks; maybe more.

And another thing I look for in a blue chip piece is that it had better play great. Once I bought a 1960 Les Paul that was dead mint, but I learned something: if it had been sitting around that long and no one had ever played it, it might not be a good player. A guitar may look good and may be worth a fortune, but what if it doesn't play good?

VG: You also know some other previous *Vintage Guitar* interviewees besides Jim Peterik; folks like Jeff Carlisi, Dave Amato, and Howard Leese.

FS: Jeff's a great guy and a great guitar player. Jim, Jeff and I have written songs together; a while back we were all over at the studio, and Jeff was playing some *great* licks on a late '60s Tele Thinline we had there.

Jim and I have been in the studio a lot lately, and Dave's in California doing the same thing right now, so he's been kind enough to check out a guitar or two that I've heard about; he's someone I can trust.

I met Howard through Denny Carmassi, and Ron Nevison produced Heart as well. I got to play on one of their records; it was a real treat.

VG: Do your future plans include another record?

FS: Yeah, and we're going to play some dates this summer; that's being firmed up as we speak. Jim and I are really concentrating; other than the greatest hits album, we haven't had a record out since '89, and that's long enough!

VG: Peterik made a comment in his interview about how no band ever breaks up for good anymore.

FS: People may get to the point where they tire of each other and they go their separate ways, then they realize that not only is the grass not greener, it ain't even there (laughs)! A band is a great outlet, not only for creativity, but it's like being a member of a winning baseball team or football team: When the chemistry's there and you're working hard, there's nothing in the world like it.

Frankie Sullivan's love of his career and his guitars is evident. To some guitar lovers, his approach to collecting might seem a bit different, but it should be considered a laudable perspective by anyone with an interest in classic fretted instruments.

Martin Taylor
All that Jazz from the British Isles

Scottish jazz guitarist Martin Taylor is a well-respected player in his own right; so much so that he's collaborated with the likes of Stephane Grappelli, Chet Atkins, and David Grisman, as well as Steve Howe in the Scott Chinery Collection recording project. His perspective differs from a stereotypical guitarist from the British Isles, as does his playing.

In a recent conversation with *Vintage Guitar*, Taylor detailed his love of jazz and the reasons he chose to play it. The interviewer had noted that Taylor was from Scotland, and opted to base his first inquiry on that country, only to be set straight by Taylor at the outset:

VG: Did growing up in Scotland mean that your musical inspirations would have been different from someone growing up in England or Ireland?

MT: Well, actually I grew up in a small town about 30 miles out of London, but I've lived a greater part of my life in Scotland. My mother is English, and comes from a musical family; her grandfather was a violinist and her uncle a professional cellist. My father's family was also musical; they were traveling folk from Ireland and Scotland, and like all the nomadic people of Europe, had a very strong musical tradition. My paternal grandmother and great-grandmother were very good singers, and my father, Buck Taylor, was quite a well-known jazz bass player in Britain.

I was brought up listening to jazz, primarily the Gypsy guitarist Django Reinhardt, and also American jazz musicians like Art Tatum, Louis Armstrong, Fats Waller and Ben Webster. So I

was obviously greatly influenced by the music my parents listened to, rather than the surroundings that I grew up in. The music of my childhood and youth was the Rolling Stones, the Beatles, and Jimi Hendrix; I enjoyed that music also, and had the great privilege of seeing Hendrix play in London when I was about 13. But the music that really moved me, and that had a musical language that I understood best, was jazz.

VG: What about your earliest instruments and experiences?

MT: My father gave me a ukulele when I was about three or four, and he showed me a few chords. He also played guitar, and I would strum away on his brand new 1959 Hofner President. My family was quite poor, but my dad wanted to encourage me to play, so he bought me a Russian classical guitar from a friend at a fairground. It was practically impossible to play; terrible action, but I fell in love with it and played it until my fingers started to bleed. If there was anything that should have put me off from playing, it was that awful guitar, but I loved playing from that moment on.

A few years later I got a German guitar called a Framus, then when I started to do gigs at around 12, I bought myself a Guild Starfire. I was playing in my dad's band by that time, at weddings and village dances; music for dancing. It was a great experience and I look back at those days with a great deal of fondness.

By the time I was 15, I had decided that I wanted to pursue a career in music, and at that time it was possible to leave school at 15, so I took up an offer to go on the road with a band playing around England during the summer. Then, in the winter, we took up residency on the Q.E. 2, and sailed to New York. I'd always dreamed of going to America, and it was a very exciting time sailing into New York at sunrise; I had never seen anything like it. One of the

TOP: *Photo Courtesy of Linn Records.*

LEFT: *Martin Taylor & Steve Howe, Martin relaxing with Steve's legendary '64 Gibson ES-175D.*

first things I did was to head down to 48th Street and buy a guitar. I bought a 1964 Gibson ES-175, the same year model as Steve's [Howe], although it wasn't as good as Steve's. His guitar is *amazing*.

I played on the cruise ships out of New York for a couple of years; we played a lot of jazz in the group, and on one jazz cruise I got to play with the Count Basie Orchestra. I got to hear a lot of great jazz musicians at places like the Village Vanguard, and in my mind there was no question that I should play anything but jazz.

VG: Once there was "no question" that you'd be a jazz player, what other instruments did you acquire?

MT: After the ES-175, I bought a 1971 Gibson Johnny Smith, which I used for a long time, until British guitarist Ike Isaacs gave me a 1964 W.G. Barker for my 21st birthday. I used the Barker for many years; all of the tours and recordings I made with Stephane Grappelli were on the Barker.

VG: Earliest recordings?

MT: My first album, *Taylor Made*, was recorded in London in 1978 for Wave Records. In 1981, I recorded *Skyeboat* for Concord Records out in San Francisco, and I did many records with Grappelli on various labels. I played on several of Stephane's collaborations with Yehudi Menuhin, and Stephane and I made a duo album in the early '80s for EMI, called *We've Got The World On A String*.

I also recorded several albums in the early '80s with clarinetist Buddy de Franco, and I had some success in the U.S. with an album called *Sarabanda*, which had John Patitucci on bass, Paulinho da Costa on percussion, and was produced by David Hungate, from Toto. I didn't really enjoy recording in those early days; it's only in recent years that I have felt at ease in the studio. I like recording now, and am reasonably happy with my newer recordings.

VG: How and why did you first come to the U.S. to record and further your career here?

MT: My first trip to the States was in 1972, but I didn't spend much time; it wasn't until 1979 when I made my first tour with Stephane Grappelli that I got to stay here for an extended visit. I did about 11 or 12 tours with Stephane, I played a couple on my own, and I also came over on three occasions to play duos with the late Emily Remler. She and I played well together; I loved her playing and it was a great tragedy that her life was cut short.

It was very important for me to come to the U.S.; it's the home of jazz and blues, and most of the musicians that have inspired me over the years were American. My career back home began to take off in the late '80s, so my trips to the States became fewer. I was doing a lot of solo concert tours around Europe, the Far East and Australia, so all my time and energy was taken up with that. At home I play theatres; in concert settings it's to quite large audiences, so it has been very important for me to pursue that area of my career, as I was getting a larger following and selling a lot of albums in the U.K. Recording *Tone Poems II* with David Grisman and collaborating with Steve on the Scott Chinery project has really whetted my appetite to play in the States again; I plan to make regular visits again.

VG: You've also been associated with Chet Atkins; I saw you on a Nashville Network program with Mr. Atkins and Vince Gill, among others.

MT: I was playing at a guitar festival in Israel a few years ago, and met Marcel Dadi,

TOP: *Martin with a '50s Gretsch White Penguin.*

RIGHT: *With a Larson Bros. "Big Boy."*

the French guitarist. He invited me to play at the Chet Atkins Appreciation Society's guitar festival at Issoudun, in France. I met a lot of great guitarists at Issoudun; Thom Bresch, Brad Jones, and the president of the Society in the U.S., Mark Pritcher, who invited me over to the Nashville Convention. I had already met Chet many years before in the States, and in fact we recorded a track together at Chet's studio in 1987; the tune was "Here, There and Everywhere." I put it on my latest solo album, *Portraits*, along with two new duets that Chet and I recorded last year in Nashville.

I've been a Chet fan since I was a kid; it's funny, because on that TV show, Chet and I were both interviewed, and there was one moment where I suddenly felt overwhelmed by being on TV with the great man himself. I've seen a video of it since, and you can't see it but for a moment; I just couldn't believe I was on American TV with Chet. He's such a hero of mine!

VG: On that show you were playing a large, blond archtop. What was the make and model?

MT: The guitar I used was the prototype of a guitar I designed, along with Martyn Booth, for Yamaha. It's called the AEX1500; in the U.K. it's known as the Yamaha Martin Taylor. It's now available in the States and I am very proud of it; it came out well.

I've been a Yamaha endorsee for six or seven years. I have two AEX1500 production mod-

els; one blond, one sunburst. I also have two prototypes, the blond one you saw on TV and a black model. I have another Yamaha archtop guitar called an AES1200, an APX10 steel-string flat-top, a nylon string APX10, and an APX8C, which I use with my band, Spirit of Django. Yamaha has been very good to me!

VG: What other guitars are in your current "arsenal"?

MT: Besides my Yamahas, I still have my father's 1959 Hofner President; although I don't play it, I could never part with it. I have the 1964 W.G. Barker from my Stephane Grappelli days, a Benedetto Cremona Bob made for me in 1988, and my newest addition to the "family" is a 1929 Martin 000-45, which Scott Chinery gifted to me from the Chinery Collection; a very generous gift, which I treasure.

My Gibson 175, the Johnny Smith, and a couple of other guitars were all sold at different moments of poverty! I regret parting with them, but I had a family to feed at the time. I was given a Selmer Maccaferri "D-hole" guitar once at a Stephane Grappelli concert; the owner told me he liked my playing so much he wanted me to have it. I played it for several years, then when I met up with its owner again I talked him into taking up the guitar again and gave it back to him.

I find it difficult to think of guitars in monetary terms; I could sell a couple of my guitars and buy myself another house or another Mercedes, I guess, but money can't replace the pleasure I get from these instruments.

VG: Which instruments do you take on the road?

MT: I only travel with my Yamahas. If something happened to my Barker I wouldn't be able to replace it. The Yamahas are practical; they're easy to play and they sound consistently good no matter where I'm playing. I know that sounds like an ad, but it's true; that's why I play them.

VG: How did the *Tone Poems II* collaboration with Grisman transpire?

MT: David Grisman and I first met in 1979 in California; Stephane had told me about David. Stephane just loved David's playing,

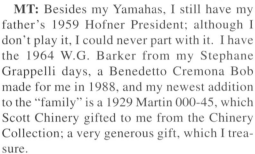

and a Grisman gig was always the highlight of a U.S. tour for us. David and I became friends and always kept in touch; I played on some of his albums like *Dawg Jazz/Dawg Grass* and *Acoustic Christmas*.

David heard my solo album *Artistry*, which Steve produced, and wanted me to make a solo album for his Acoustic Disc label, but I was signed with Linn Records and I have a good relationship with them, so I didn't want to rock the boat. I suggested that I record an archtop version of *Tone Poems I*; since it was to be so different from my recordings for Linn, they agreed to release me to make it.

When we talked about material, it was very easy to come up with the tunes, particularly for guitars and mandolins from the '20s, '30s, and '40s, as that was the Golden Age for American songwriting. I like to play a lot of that older material, which is probably why David thought it a good idea that I record the archtops. I loved *Tone Poems I*; I'm a big fan of Tony Rice.

VG: How far back does your acquaintance with Steve Howe go, and how did the Chinery Collection effort come about?

MT: Steve and I first met around 1988, in London. Yamaha invited us both to look at a prototype MIDI guitar they were developing, because we had both had experience using guitar synths, and they wanted our opinion. Steve came along to a gig I was playing that night, and we just became friends and kept in touch in the same way that my friendship with "Dawg" developed over the years, through a mutual obsession with music. When Linn Records asked me to make a solo album, which ended up being titled *Artistry,* I asked Steve to produce it.

I was doing a lot of solo concerts at that time, and Steve was very interested in my thoughts and experiences on solo playing, as he was contemplating going out on the road solo himself. We exchanged a lot of ideas; I'm proud that I managed to convince Steve to "take the plunge," and he now does a lot of solo gigs.

Last year Steve introduced me to Scott Chinery. Scott had already approached Steve about recording the Chinery Collection, and apparently Steve suggested that I was the man for the job. I flew up from Nashville to meet Scott and Steve in New Jersey to discuss the recording project. Scott's collection is *staggering!* When I walked into the guitar room, I couldn't speak for about 30 minutes! I've never seen anything like it. D'Angelicos, D'Aquistos, Gibsons, Martins, Benedettos, you name it; the finest guitars in the world. Scott got me to play the D'Angelico Teardrop, and then, from what I remember, asked me about recording the guitars. I must admit I was in a bit of a daze being surrounded by those guitars!

VG: Howe said, in his interview, that he wanted you in on this project because you were more into "standards," whereas Howe has his "own" repertoire. Comment?

MT: I guess that's correct, in that I come from a jazz tradition which draws from the standard repertoire, so I am very much at home in that environment. But as it turned out, I wrote a few tunes for the project, and Steve and I wrote a couple of tunes together. Steve even got me to play a tune where I showcased all of my country licks...all three of them! He really stretched me out on that one!

I've written a fair amount of music for TV over the past few years, and I enjoy being given a brief to write to. In this case, the "brief" was the guitar collection, writing music that suits each instrument. I found that to be interesting and challenging.

VG: How did the Chinery recording differ from *Tone Poems II*?

MT: With *Tone Poems II*, David and I decided that the "thread" linking the guitars together should be a piece of music written around the time that the instruments were made and were popular. The aim of the Chinery project was to play music that we felt was *appropriate to each instrument,* not necessarily because an instrument might be connected to a particular time period.

Tone Poems II was more jazz-oriented, I guess, although there are a lot of jazz tracks on the Chinery project. They are quite different recordings. On *Tone Poems II* I played a total of 23 guitars, and on the Chinery recordings, a total of 67 instruments, including baby guitars, mandolins, banjos, basses, pedal steel, etc. My favorite guitar on *Tone Poems II* was the Gibson Lloyd Loar, and on the Chinery project, a 1931 D'Angelico, a D'Angelico Excel, and the Martin 000-45.

VG: As we're doing this interview, the recording utilizing the "blue guitars" Chinery commissioned is still pending; what song or songs will you be doing?

MT: We're still having thoughts about that. We need to find a way of recording the guitars so that they are all heard equally at their best; I have some ideas, and so do Steve and Scott.

VG: Future plans?

MT: I've just returned from Paris, where I was recording a new album with my band, Spirit of Django; the album will be called *The Gypsy*. Stephane Grappelli plays on three tracks, and we recreated the Hot Club of France version of "Undecided" from 1934; it was fun playing Django's solo.

I'm still playing a lot of solo concerts and my last solo album for Linn Records is selling well. I'll be recording the Chinery "blue guitars" soon, and a U.S. tour with David Grisman is scheduled for November of this year. I'll also be making my annual trip to Chet's convention in Nashville in July.

Next year, Linn will be releasing a compilation CD to mark my 25th year as a professional musician, and I'm searching my attic for any of my old recordings to go on the CD.

In general, life is treating me well; I am *very* lucky to be involved with such great musicians as Steve, David, and Chet, and as I approach my 40th birthday, I feel as if my life has only just begun.

It's always gratifying when someone as eloquent on the fretboard as Martin Taylor is also eloquent when he/she does an interview. Taylor's reputation is international, and his effort on the Chinery Collection guitars will simply add to his stature around the globe as a gifted guitarist.

Robin Trower

More Than Twice Removed From Yesterday

Longtime rock guitar lovers are probably aware the title of Robin Trower's first solo album (released in 1973) is included in this interview's title. Trower had previously been the guitarist for Procol Harum of "A Whiter Shade of Pale" fame (although he didn't play on the song), and some of his collaborations over the years have included the likes of Jack Bruce and Bryan Ferry, but Robin Trower's solo albums and comparisons to Jimi Hendrix have been at the core of his respected efforts, for decades .

While recording his latest album (which contains a couple of surprises), Robin Trower took a break to converse with *Vintage Guitar* in a relaxed and eloquent conversation via trans-Atlantic telephone. The affable guitarist was born in south London, but his family moved to Canada when he was two, and from there they moved to New Zealand, then back to England, settling in Essex, where Trower still resides.

VG: I always ask every British interviewee about Radio Luxembourg and/or skiffle.

RT: Well, Radio Luxembourg was where you could hear most of the American music; all of the rock and roll stuff, because the BBC was pretty "square" (laughs). So Radio Luxembourg was the happening thing, but you couldn't always get a good signal. It was part of my

"education." I never really liked skiffle; I was a rock and roll fan from the start.

VG: Tell me about your earliest guitars.

RT: The first guitar I got was a cello-shaped Rosetti; I got it at Christmas when I was 14. I got a pickup put on it and bought a homemade amplifier. The next guitar I got was a solidbody Rosetti which had a couple of pickups, then I got a German-made Strat copy that had three pickups and a toggle switch for each pickup. It was still an inexpensive guitar; this was around 1958, and it wasn't until quite sometime after that when I saw a real Fender in this country.

VG: What guitar did you consider to be your first "professional quality" instrument?

RT: A Gretsch Chet Atkins solidbody. Then I got the first Country Gentleman that came into the country, and after that I went on to an old two-pickup Les Paul with humbuckers, and a SG/Les Paul, then a sunburst Les Paul with white pickup surrounds. I started playing Strats when I was in Procol Harum.

VG: The liner notes to a British CD anthology of yours state that prior to Procol Harum, you were playing in an R & B combo called the Paramounts. I've talked with other British players who talked about having played in "soul bands" during those times; were there differences between mid-'60s British R & B bands and soul bands?

RT: The Paramounts were more blues-based. We used to do a lot of Chuck Berry, James Brown, Bobby Bland, a bit of Ray Charles.

All photos courtesy of Derek Sutton.

There were soul bands at the same time we were doing R & B, but I think the soul bands were doing more pop; they had horns and were doing Sam & Dave-type stuff.

VG: Didn't you join Procol Harum when the band first formed?

RT: They had already released "A Whiter Shade of Pale," but they hadn't really formed a band when they recorded that song. When it became a hit, they decided they needed to make an album, so they sought out other musicians. I did five albums with them.

VG: Is it fair to say that Procol Harum was more of an "art rock" band that was quite different from your experiences *before* Procol Harum, as well as your solo career *afterwards*?

RT: Definitely; they were more "European."

VG: And is it fair to say that back then, Procol Harum wasn't a guitar-oriented band?

RT: Yeah; their sound had more to do with the fact that they had a piano and an organ. They definitely had a keyboard sound; I was just there for a bit of embellishment (laughs).

VG: But there were some songs, like "Juicy John Pink," on *A Salty Dog,* that had some notable guitar licks. That particular one started off with nothing but your guitar and Gary Brooker's vocals. Do you remember your instrument setup on that song?

RT: I think that was the first song I wrote with Procol Harum. At the time I was playing a blond Les Paul with two P-90 pickups through a small Gibson amp.

VG: Is the fact that Procol Harum was a keyboard-oriented band the reason you departed?

RT: The truth of the matter is that I'd started to write more songs than I could play in that band. It could've worked if they'd done one or two guitar-oriented songs on each album, but I was very prolific around that time, and I needed an outlet, so I decided to go out on my own.

VG: Were you already into your Hendrix influence by then?

RT: After Hendrix died, Keith Reid, Procol Harum's lyricist, thought that he and I should do a tribute track, so I studied the first three albums. We wrote "Song for a Dreamer," which is on *Broken Barricades*, the last album I did

with Procol Harum. We did one concert with Hendrix, two weeks before he died.

VG: You've heard the Hendrix comparisons from the outset of your solo career, but I thought James Dewar had a much more soulful voice than Hendrix did, so that was a difference, in my opinion.

RT: I wasn't trying to imitate Hendrix; I was trying to create the music I wanted to make. I was into singers probably more than I was into instrumentalists. It was a combination of the songs I was writing, with Hendrix influences on guitar, but the vocals were more influenced by Donnie Hathaway, Marvin Gaye and Otis Redding.

VG: Personally, I never did care much for what I heard of Hendrix's work following *Electric Ladyland*. When your first albums came out, I found myself saying something along the lines of "that's where I wish Hendrix had gone, musically."

RT: I appreciate that. The first three albums of his are "the ones;" after that, I think there was definitely a decline.

VG: Around 1975, *Guitar Player* put out a Jimi Hendrix special edition, and one of the comments from a noted player quoted in that issue referred to you as Hendrix's "spiritual double."

RT: Robert Fripp, from King Crimson, gave me that issue, but I don't remember that comment. You have to feel complimented if you're compared to somebody who was that brilliant, but I've always said that if it hadn't been for

RIGHT: *20th Century Blues participants Livingstone Brown, Robin Trower, Mayuyu.*

players like Hendrix, Albert King, B.B. King, Bo Diddley, and Chuck Berry, I wouldn't "exist" as a musician. That's what influences are all about.

VG: What did you think of Frank Marino?

RT: I never really heard a lot of his material, but I did a couple of shows with him in the '70s. When he was playing Hendrix songs, you couldn't tell the difference. It was amazingly close; a lot closer than I ever got (chuckles)! He didn't try to duck the comparisons, and he was great at it.

VG: What was your setup in the early days of your solo career?

RT: On *Twice Removed From Yesterday* I was using Marshall 8 X 10s, but I was blowing them up too much (laughs). So I'd switched to 4 X 12s by the time we got to *Bridge of Sighs*. I had a booster/overdrive unit custom-made for me, a wah-wah, and a Uni-Vibe, and just Strats for guitars.

VG: Has there ever been any time during your solo career where you've made a serious attempt to utilize another type of guitar, other than a Strat?

RT: Not really. I bought another SG/Les Paul, but I never really used it. At one time I had a great collection of vintage Strats, but they were all stolen; about 18 of them. So I decided to play brand new guitars after that, and Fender's been really great to me. They've built some great instruments for me.

VG: You and Marino also participated in the IRS *Guitarspeak* project.

RT: Miles Copeland asked me to do an instrumental, and when I handed it in, he didn't like it too much, but he put it on the album anyway (chuckles).

VG: Then there was the Procol Harum reunion album, *The Prodigal Stranger*. Why did you opt not to tour with them?

RT: By that time, I was co-producing an album with Bryan Ferry, and I was committed to that project. I went out on the second leg of Bryan's world tour, which took us to Scandinavia, Holland, Britain, Singapore, Australia, Japan, Florida, Argentina, and Brazil. I was a sideman; it was fun.

VG: The bassist on your most recent album, *20th Century Blues*, is Livingstone Brown, who was on IRS *Guitarspeak* projects as well. Is that how you hooked up with him?

RT: Right; I did a "Night of the Guitar" tour, and Livvy and Mayuyu were the bassist and drummer, and I decided to use them on my next album. Livvy took the vocals, we "toured" the material and "broke it in," then went into the studio and laid it down in just a few days. It was more or less recorded live in the studio. It was a three-piece idea again, like the early days, but the material was coming from a different place. I think it's a bit less rock and roll, and a bit more R & B.

VG: Brown's vocals are somewhat "raspy"-sounding, and some of the material reminds me of tunes like ZZ Top's "Fool For Your Stockings."

RT: Well, I think it's in the same "ballpark." They're a very blues-influenced rock and roll band. I'm a *big* Billy Gibbons fan.

VG: You've played Squier Strats, as well.

RT: Yeah, when I couldn't get decent American-made ones. At one point the American Strats were not made well at all, and it wasn't until the company was bought back by the work force that they started to make decent guitars again.

VG: What's keeping you busy these days?

RT: At the moment I'm working on a blues record; I think it's my first "real blues" album. I'm using new Fender tube amplifiers, and a beautiful Strat the Custom Shop built for me. It's pretty much stock, but it has a flatter neck, jumbo frets, and locking tuners. I've been using some Fulltone devices; a Deja-Vibe and his new overdrive unit. They've got a beautiful sound.

VG: A lot of manufacturers are attempting to get back to "retro" sounds these days; tube amps and reissue devices like you just cited are examples.

RT: Well, those were the times when we were hearing the best tones; the best music; the best sounds from electric guitar. I still listen to players like Cliff Gallup with Gene Vincent; he used to get some *incredible* sounds, and from what I could tell, it was just a Strat through an old Fender amp. I'm really into the sound I've been getting out of these new Fender amps.

VG: Other details on your upcoming album?

RT: I'm going to come over to the States and try out a couple of Hammond organ players for some songs on the album, and I want to mix in America, as well. This will be the first album where I've done the vocals, and I'm using the original drummer from my solo career, Reg Isidore. Paul Page, the co-producer, is playing bass.

VG: You hit the half-century mark a while back, but my perception is that you haven't slowed down a bit.

RT: I think I'm working harder now than I ever did; I'm doing more things, what with producing Bryan and being on the road with him, and doing my own thing. I'm really excited about this new blues album; I've been promising myself for about 20 years that one day I'd have a go at this, and it's been enjoyable.

Up until now, Robin Trower's "musical eloquence" has been heard via his guitar playing; i.e. "he's done his talking through his Strat," for lack of a better phrase. That he's now assuming vocal responsibilities as well as recording what he terms a "real blues" album is indicative of his forward-looking vision, especially when you consider how long he's been a respected player.

Rick Vito

Veteran

Guitarist Rick Vito is more of a veteran than some music fans may realize. While perhaps best known for his efforts in a recent incarnation

of Fleetwood Mac, he's had decades of experience, and is still active following his departure from "the Mighty Mac."

Recently *Vintage Guitar* had an opportunity to talk with Vito; the soft-spoken yet enthusiastic player was quite eloquent about his guitar-playing history since the Sixties; Vito began by advising that he is originally from Philadelphia:

VG: Were you involved in the Gamble & Huff, "T.S.O.P." phenomenon?

RV: No, I'd already moved to California by then; I came out here in 1971.

VG: What about your earliest musical and guitar-playing memories?

RV: Christmas morning; my parents gave me a Stella acoustic. My first love was Stella, along with fifty million other guys (laughs). I was really into the Ricky Nelson show, with James Burton; I've been able to play with James on several occasions. "American Bandstand" was in Philadelphia, and I knew people who knew people who went on the show (laughs). My father was in the nightclub business so it seemed like I was close to show business before I ever

TOP: *1980 - Rick Vito onstage with Bonnie Raitt.*

RIGHT: *Rick, Albert Collins and Juke Logan*

got into it.

My mother played the Hawaiian lap steel, so I was always plunking on it. I think, though, that Elvis is probably the one who made a lot of the "masses" want to play guitar. Even though his guitar was a prop, he made people associate the guitar with performing rock and roll.

VG: What was your first *electric* guitar?

RV: It was a Gibson ES-125; it had one pickup near the neck, a big fat body, and no cutaway. I ran it through a little wood-colored Alamo amp with a ten-inch speaker; I wish I still had it; back then it used to do those annoying things called "overdrive" and "feedback" (chuckles). I wish I'd known how to control it back then.

VG: First performing experiences?

RV: My first onstage experience was with a doo-wop group; I was the lone guitar player for five guys with slick hair, Cuban heels, and leather jackets; they were doing a Frankie Lymon-type thing. I was playing that ES-125, and it was a magical experience, as I would think any musician's first time performing in front of people would be.

I joined a band when I was sixteen; we played clubs around the Philadelphia area doing cover material. We did a lot of Rolling Stones songs; I just read the latest interview with Keith Richards; I think it's true that the Rolling Stones were probably more responsible for making American kids take a closer look at the blues, which is right here in our own back yard. It was easier for "middle class ears" to listen to the Rolling Stones first and then get indoctrinated to the real thing.

VG: What instrument did you play with that "club band"?

RV: I was taking lessons from a guy named Kirk Hamilton, who was a big Telecaster fan; he played one and convinced me that a Tele was *the* instrument of choice. I sold the Gibson and went down to a pawn shop on South Street in Philadelphia; they had about six old Teles on the wall, ranging in price from $100 to about $160. I played all of them and bought a '61 model with a creme finish and a huge slab board; it played great and sounded great, and I ended up using it for a number of years.

VG: I mentioned the Gamble & Huff scene at the outset; did you ever think you might have missed an opportunity by moving to the Left Coast?

RV: Not really, because by the time I was in college I was pretty much of a blues purist; I played in a band called The Wright Brothers Blues Band, and we did songs by B.B. King, Freddie King, and Jimmy Reed. Around that time we got to see the "original" Fleetwood Mac with Peter Green, and he *really* motivated me; he was doing faithful interpretations of the genre, but with his own style. Even the songs he wrote were faithful to the blues. He had that tremendous-sounding Les Paul, and while he had his own style, the style was nevertheless respectful of the roots; respectful of players like B.B. King and Otis Rush.

VG: There's a song on the old *Fleetwood Mac in Chicago* album called "Homework"; if someone had never heard Peter Green's playing, that song would probably be the one I'd play for such a person. Green's solo on that song makes the hair on the back of my neck stand up.

RV: That's a perfect example; I liked that song so much I recorded it myself.

VG: You played with several "name" bands over the years, didn't you?

RV: When I first moved to L.A. I got hooked up with Delaney & Bonnie and Friends, who were still together at the time; Eric Clapton had done a tour with them, and Delaney produced Eric's first solo album. I really liked their style, which was sort of R & B and blues-based, with a bit of gospel as well. So that was the first tour I ever did with major artists.

That spun off into a gig with Bobby Whitlock, who had also been in Derek & the Dominoes. In 1975 I joined John Mayall and did four albums with him, *New Year, New Band, New Company*, *Notice to Appear*, which was produced by Allan Toussaint, *Banquet of Blues*, and *No More Interviews*. At the time, John wasn't exactly in

the "apex" of his career (laughs).

VG: Another recent *Vintage Guitar* interviewee, Harvey Mandel, had also played with Mayall during that decade.

RV: I knew who Harvey was; he'd been in John's band before I came along back then. He was the first guy I ever saw who did fingerboard tapping, *way* before Eddie Van Halen popularized that idea.

After that I did an album on CBS with Roger McGuinn in a group called Thunderbird; that year I also met Bonnie Raitt and substituted for her guitar player on one of her tours.

I've done a lot of session work over the years as well; I've recorded with folks like Roy Orbison, Leon Russell, Rita Coolidge, Dolly Parton, even David Soul; I played on his Number One single "Don't Give Up On Us." That was my first and only Number One (laughs)!

I got going with Bonnie Raitt again, and I played with her for two years, in '80 and '81. That led to a gig with Jackson Browne; I was on an album called *Lawyers In Love* with him. Following that I was with Bob Seger. I did about four albums with Seger; "Like A Rock" is now a Chevy truck commercial (chuckles)! I had played slide on that song. After I toured extensively with Bob I met up with Fleetwood Mac.

VG: Which, right or wrong, is probably the musical entity with which you're most often associated, but it seemed like it was for a relatively brief time.

RV: I think it's important to stress that they were the first *band* I ever joined; all of those other gigs were as a sideman. The general public knows more about me because of the four years I spent in Fleetwood Mac than anything I'd done previously.

VG: How did that association come about?

1975 - Vito (third from left) during a stint with John Mayall.

1989 publicity photo of Fleetwood Mac - Left to Right - Stevie Nicks, Mick Fleetwood, Rick Vito, Christine McVie, John McVie and Billy Burnette

RV: I'd done a session for Billy Burnette once, and Mick [Fleetwood] was the drummer; it was basically a demo session. We hit it off, and a couple of years later, Lindsey [Buckingham] left. About a week before that happened, Billy and Mick came into a club in Sherman Oaks where I was playing; they sat in and once again it was fun for all of us. Mick called me up soon after that and said Lindsey had left, and that Billy was going to join but he didn't play lead guitar. Mick said: "I know you like the Peter Green stuff, so do you want to learn some songs and come down and play with us?" I said sure, so I learned about a dozen songs, went down and played with them, and it was a great time for everybody. We all got along well from the first day, and they already had a tour booked. But as I said earlier, I joined as a full-fledged member, not as a sideman for that tour. I was to be included in the recording, songwriting, merchandising, the whole shot.

VG: Soon after the new lineup was introduced, I saw a performance clip on TV, and you were playing a bizarre-looking orange and black electric guitar onstage that had a body that looked sort of like a solidbody that had been "divided" down its center line, and the halves were offset.

RV: That was from the *Tango in the Night* concert tour video. It's coral, black and creme-colored; I was trying to get a really Art Deco look. I've got a patent on its style and also on another I had built. Both guitars were made by Toru Nittono of the L.A. Guitar Works in Reseda. I've always played old guitars, but I also always wanted to have something that was *noticeably and specifically mine.* Toru's an excellent craftsman; he built those for me after I got off the Seger tour, and he did a finer job than I would've ever hoped for.

VG: On the *Behind the Mask* album, Burnette's roots are showing somewhat; "When the Sun Goes Down" has a definite rockabilly feel.

RV: I was practicing at home, and came up with a line about "when the sun goes down and the moon shines bright"; I thought that would be something Billy would be interested in co-writing, so I let him join in. That song was one of the first we "pitched," and everyone in the band wanted to do it; it's a fun tune.

VG: You mentioned playing slide a while back; do you use any certain tuning?

RV: Actually, I've used several over the years. I like A, E or D, and I still like to play slide in standard tuning, *particularly* in a song that's in a minor key; that opens up a lot of possibilities and a player can really get innovative.

VG: Was the Art Deco guitar your main concert guitar with Fleetwood Mac? What other guitars did you use on tour and in the studio?

RV: The "Streamliner," which is the name I gave the Art Deco guitar, was my main performance instrument. I'm a big fan of Les Paul TV Juniors for slide; I've used those for a long time. I also have a guitar that I got from Norm Harris when he was marketing his own brand some years ago; it's gotten to be more of a Frankenstein over time (chuckles). It's basically a Tele-style with two humbuckers and a Strat pickup in the middle; it's a real versatile guitar that I used on tour. I use a 1959 Gibson J-45 as my main acoustic. I also have some vintage guitars that I use more for recording; I don't take those on the road.

VG: Examples?

RV: I've got a late Fifties sunburst Les Paul, a Broadcaster, a '54 Stratocaster, and some others. They are, of course, unbelievably unique-sounding guitars. There's an old National Style O resonator guitar that I own that's on the cover of *Behind the Mask*: I use that in the studio a lot as well. In fact, it's heard on that album in what I'd call "subtle" ways; we also used a Coral Electric Sitar on one cut, but I don't own that instrument.

VG: I've got to inquire about your departure from the band.

RV: Well, let's just say that there wasn't a great deal of communication at the end of my stay, so it's something that I don't have a completely clear picture about. I put out a solo album called *King of Hearts*, and it might have caused some bad feelings. It left me feeling very disappointed with the original members as people. Stevie Nicks had done a duet with me on my album called "Desiree"; it got a bit of movement, which was gratifying. She's got a good heart.

VG: What's kept you busy since you left Fleetwood Mac?

RV: I was trying to promote that solo album; it's basically all self-penned songs, and I produced or co-produced all the tracks. In this economy, it seems that the record companies are promoting proven acts that have a large following. I understand that, but it makes it hard for new groups and new ideas to get heard.

I'm still playing around the L.A. area; I have a band called Rick Vito & His Mondo Rhythm Kings. Right now it's a three-piece group; basically what I'm doing is what we talked about earlier. It's blues-rooted music that takes a step or two towards rock and roll. I'm producing a record of a blues artist named Son Richards that I'm very excited about.

VG: What brought you to the guitar show in Pomona in February of 1993?

RV: I'd never been to a guitar show before. I've almost always been a vintage guitar lover and collector, although I did get away from the market for a while. When I renewed my interest, I realized I had for all intents and purposes been away for a *long, long* time, considering what the prices had done (chuckles)!

You see, a while back I considered myself to be in a select group of people who were "in the know" about old guitars. In fact, I wrote an article on rare guitars that focused on Norm Harris which was published in *Guitar Player* in 1975. I think it was one of the first articles they ever ran on vintage instruments. Now, it seems like there's all sorts of people from all over who want classic instruments.

VG: What about the Dallas show the next month?

RV: Norm's partner Danny invited me to go; I knew Mark Pollock and the Dallas folks made arrangements for me to play with James Burton and Seymour Duncan, among others. I knew Seymour when he was back in Wildwood, New Jersey; he was taking guitars apart then. He gave me proof sheets of photos of the Rolling Stones he'd taken, and I still have them.

VG: You were playing a turquoise-colored guitar onstage at that jam session, but you were jumping around so much I couldn't tell what it was.

RV: (chuckles) "Ants in my pants and I gots ta dance." I found a totally trashed Junior that I tried to salvage; Jackson Browne gave me a pickup for it and Seymour gave me another. Toru did another great job on it.

VG: Louise Burton, James' wife, had some kind words about your playing; she said you had a very melodic style.

RV: Bless her heart. That's a wonderful compliment, especially coming from her. I got a lot of education from listening to her husband's solo album; I picked up a lot of stuff about slide dobro.

VG: What lies ahead?

RV: I'm looking to make another record; I've got a few deals in the works. As far as guitars go, I've got some nice ones but I wouldn't mind having a Custom Color maple neck Strat. But you know something? I don't think I could look for something to buy at guitar shows; I'd rather find pieces in pawn shops or in some home where a guy has owned a guitar twenty five years and is now wanting to sell it; there's a sort of "spiritual" quality to an instrument like that.

I found a guitar in Cincinatti in 1990 that had belonged to a bluesman since 1960. I had to do a lot of restoration to it, and I played it for the first time a few weeks ago. The bluesman has since died, and it's like that man's spirit was in that guitar. That may sound corny to some people, but I really feel that way.

Hopefully I'll be able to get things organized well enough to where I can eventually move to the country. I'd like for my kids to be able to ride horses somewhere other than Griffith Park.

VG: But some years ago an MTV veejay made a comment that "every band in the world comes from L.A.," although he had a saracastic tone.

RV: Well, every band in the world comes *to* L.A., to try and make it. How many of them actually succeed is a completely different matter, in my view (chuckles).

Rick Vito has the perspective of an educated journeyman guitarist. He's played with the best, and is still seeking to hone his craft at every opportunity, utilizing his custom-made and vintage guitars. He knows his trade well, and he knows how to have an eloquent conversation about guitars as well.

Steve Wariner

Hoosier Hotshot

Students of American popular music history might already be aware that a novelty act from the Forties was indeed known as the Hoosier Hot Shots; in fact, Cincinnati jazz guitarist Cal Collins noted that combo in his own *Vintage Guitar* interview (June 1993).

But the phrase is certainly applicable to Steve Wariner, since he hails from Indiana and is one of the current Nashville area guitarists who, according to Duane Eddy in *his VG* interview (June 1995) "can do it all" (more about the Eddy opinion later).

Wariner's accomplishments (so far) as a singer/guitarist/songwriter/producer include twelve Number One singles and twenty-eight Top Ten singles, eight BMI songwriting awards, a Grammy, and a Country Music Association (CMA) award. That he also has a guitar collection that numbers around seventy instruments (as well as a signature model guitar by Takamine) is also a plus, considering the format of *Vintage Guitar*. The lightning-fast picker utilized a lot of his instruments on his most recent recording, an instrumental album called *No More Mr. Nice Guy*. Among the other guitarists that appeared on this new effort (released March 12, 1996) were Chet Atkins, Larry Carlton, Vince Gill, Richie Sambora, Lee Roy Parnell, Leo Kottke, and other notable musicians. Steve Wariner's exuberance about this new and different project was obvious when we recently conversed:

VG: Your reputation precedes you a bit, since several other interviewees have mentioned you, and I'd like to get your side of the anecdotes or comments they made about you. First, Richard Young of the Kentucky Headhunters told me about a trade he made for one of your Telecasters; he managed to find you an 1800s Martin acoustic.

All photos courtesy of Steve Wariner and Arista.

SW: That's true; my brother Terry played with me on the road for years, and he lives close to the Headhunters. He was sort of the "middleman" in that trade. Terry and I have always traded guitars back and forth; he's a Fender guy all the way and has a lot of nice old Strats. He's got a '59 that I'd *kill* for (chuckles); in fact, I used it on a couple of tracks on the new album. So Terry did the leg work on the swap. The Martin has one of those "casket" cases; it was made in 1870 to 1890 era; that's as close as we can get to dating it. It's a neat little parlor guitar; it's not fancy, but it's a cool instrument.

VG: Duane Eddy discussed his move to the Nashville area in his interview with this publication, and noted that "some of the stars are not only great singers and songwriters, they're phenomenal players as well. Guys like Vince Gill, Steve Wariner, Ricky Skaggs; it seems like they can do it all."

SW: That blows me away; I didn't read that or hear about it. I'm really flattered by that remark; I grew up sitting by the stereo, playing along with Duane Eddy records like a lot of other players. I love those old Gretsches he played.

VG: And finally, Larry Carlton noted your vocals on the re-recorded theme for "Who's the Boss," as well as his participation on your new solo album. How did the TV theme singing effort transpire?

SW: At one time I was recording for MCA, and Larry was on their "Master Series" label. I think Tony Brown, who was heading up A & R as well as producing me, threw my name in the hat when Larry made it known he wanted to re-do the song. At this point Larry and I hadn't met, but I'd always been a super fan of his playing. When I was on tour in California, he and I hooked up in the studio. The TV people liked the version we did and used it; ever since then Larry and I have been good friends. In fact, the song on the new album that Larry played on is called "The Theme"; it also sounds sort of like a show theme.

VG: Was your "youthful musical career" in Indiana oriented more towards Country or Rock? What about instruments?

SW: I was fortunate, because when I was a kid my dad had a band that played on weekends, and they practiced at our house. I started playing when I was about nine or ten, and the first instrument I ever touched was a four-string Danelectro bass; it was a late-Fifties single-cutaway that was copper colored. If I can ever find one of those, I'll buy it for sentimental reasons.

But I realized that I was just playing single notes on a bass, and there were six strings as well as chords on a guitar (chuckles)! My dad played all kinds of music, but he loved guitar players. He had records by Chet Atkins, Duane Eddy, Merle Travis, and even Jerry Byrd. He played a lot of Country, but he was really into Bob Wills and other types of music. He wasn't too much into rock and roll, but it was just beginning to happen.

Then around 1961 he bought a brand new Fender Jazzmaster at Arthur's Music in Indianapolis; my dad got a good deal because someone had thrown a brick through the front window where the guitar was on display and nicked it. I still have that guitar, of course; it's the one that my brothers and I learned how to play on. I played with my dad for a long time, and I usu-

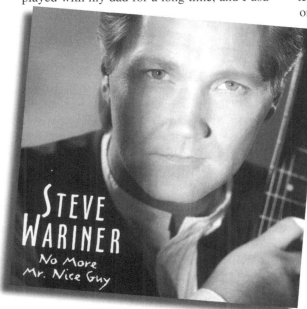

ally played guitar, but sometimes I played other instruments like drums; I played drums in my brother's rock and roll band when I got a little older. Once I got into high school I started playing some clubs in Indianapolis, and that's how I started meeting people from Nashville.

VG: How did you end up getting permanently hooked up with your Music City connections?

SW: One of the clubs in Indianapolis was called the Nashville Country Club; they'd bring in a big name Nashville act every couple of months, and that's where I met Dottie West. I

was playing guitar, but her band was looking for a bass player, and they offered me the job. I also played bass for Bob Luman's band, and I also played bass for Chet [Atkins]. I was playing a '61 or '62 Fender Jazz Bass that's Olympic White; my uncle Jimmy bought it new along with a matching Fender Jaguar and a Showman amp. He gave me the bass when I was in my early teens; I still have it, and I still use it. I play bass on a lot of Chet's records; I played on four songs on the *Neck and Neck* album he did with Mark Knopfler. I always use that bass for session work, unless I need a five-string. I've got a Peavey five-string bass, and I also have a '59 Precision that I've recorded with on occasion.

VG: How did your association with Atkins come about?

SW: I met Chet when I was touring with Dottie. A lot of RCA artists went to Europe on a tour; Bobby Bare and Jim Ed Brown, and Chet was on part of the tour. That's when we first met, and of course I was in awe of him, but he was really nice to me. Later, we met again when I was playing on a Bob Luman album. Paul Yandell, who's Chet's sideman and a fabulous fingerpicker, was also on the session, and he heard some of the songs I'd written and asked me to get him a tape of them so he could take them to Chet. To make a long story short, we met several times, and one time he asked me to come down to a session at the old RCA studio. I walked in, and the only other players there were Chet and Jerry Reed. Chet asked Jerry to give me a guitar so I could sing something, and I'll never forget what Jerry said when I got through; he looked at Chet and said: "Chet, sign this boy up; what do you want, *blood*?" (laughs). So that's how I got signed to my first contract.

VG: There's an anthology of some of your

TOP: *Steve Wariner and Chet Atkins.*

LEFT: *Steve Wariner's latest Arista release.*

earlier solo material that shows you with a red Peavey T-60 on the cover.

SW: I had a great association with Peavey, and I still do. I used that T-60 when I first started doing my own dates; they also made me a black, one-of-a-kind guitar later, and I used Peavey Special 130 amplifiers for a long time. I'm a big Hartley Peavey fan; he's a classic American success story. His company has been great to me over the years.

VG: What was your most successful album, and your favorite album?

SW: The most commercially successful was *I Am Ready*, and I don't know what my favorite one is. I never listen to my stuff once it's out; the only one we ever play around the house is my Christmas album.

VG: How do you feel about music videos as a facet of Country music?

SW: Well, from a business point of view, they can be a wonderful tool to introduce a new artist to the marketplace. Other than that, I'm not sure. When videos first began to be made, Conway Twitty said that a song ought to be left to the imagination of the person that hears it; that a video shouldn't "fill in the blanks," and in a lot of ways I agree with him.

I've never really talked about this, but I think the "visual" part of Country music has gotten to be predominant because of videos. In other words, when acts are being considered by record labels, the company people want to know what he/she looks like; does he/she need to lose weight; that kind of stuff is more important than the music. I don't think that's necessarily the right way to consider a performer.

VG: One video that looked like it was a lot of fun for you was the New Nashville Cats' "Restless," which also featured Vince Gill, Ricky Skaggs, and Mark O'Connor.

SW: Mark and I are old friends; I've known him since he was about fourteen. A lot of people don't know he's also a great guitar player as well as a great fiddle player. He called me about the New Nashville Cats project he was getting together; he asked me to write some songs for it, and he kept one I wrote called "Now It Belongs To You," about a fiddle that's passed down from father to son. He also got me involved with an old Carl Perkins song called "Restless," and I went to the studio not knowing who the other musicians would be. You can tell that we were just jamming and having fun, but it won a Grammy and a CMA award.

VG: The video for "Crash Course in the Blues" showed you playing what looked like a red Stratocaster with some custom fretboard inlay.

SW: That's a Joe Glaser guitar with a B-bender in it. He also made me a Tele-type with an extra pickup and a B-bender; I've played that guitar more than any other for the last several years. He made the Strat copy for me a long time ago; the inlay was done by an artist named Diane Patrick. It's really ornate and I don't play it very much.

VG: Any recent custom-made guitars you've acquired?

SW: Fender made me a brand new Telecaster with a B-bender and three Texas Special pickups, so I can get some Strat-type tones. The body is little thinner than a regular Telecaster, and it has a "V" neck.

VG: It appears that red is your favorite guitar color.

SW: Well, this new Fender's a deep blue; I decided to do something a little different... but I haven't decided on whether to keep it that color (chuckles). I also just got a couple of those Relic Fenders; they're unbelievable. My '52 Nocaster Relic is incredible.

VG: For what my opinion's worth, I think your vocals sound a lot like Dave Loggins at times. Haven't you recorded some of his material?

SW: I did a song of his called "Married to a Memory" on *Drive*, which was the last album before the instrumental one. What a great song... and I wish I knew how many times I've sung "Please Come to Boston" (chuckles)!

VG: The video for the title track from *Drive* has a lot of vintage stock car racing footage in it. Did your upbringing near the Indianapolis 500 as well as NASCAR racing being another Southern tradition have anything to do with that video concept?

SW: Actually, I did two versions of it. I was asked to do that video by MBNA Bank. It wasn't a commercial; it was more like something to be used for their promotional purposes. They're heavily involved with NASCAR, and having been raised in Indiana not too far from the track, I could identify with their concept. The other version was what became the video that was seen on CMT.

VG: One fairly recent collaboration in which you participated was the Chet Atkins "Read My Licks" TV Special. What was that like?

SW: That was about a year and a half ago. It was fabulous; I've known Eric Johnson for a while, but I'd never met Earl Klugh until then; I'd always been a big fan of his. He's a gentleman. I wish they'd aired the entire concert, because some of the stuff that got edited out was tremendous. It could easily have been shown as an hour-and-a-half show.

VG: Of all of the people I've interviewed, I don't think I've ever met anyone who's "into" his music as much as Eric Johnson is.

SW: He really is an artist; he's very technical, but he plays with a lot of passion. He was supposed to play on the instrumental album, but he was sick when I recorded it.

VG: How did the *No More Mr. Nice Guy* instrumental project develop?

SW: I'd been wanting to do this for years, but the Mark O'Connor project really inspired me and brought this idea even more "up front." I went to Tim DuBois, who's the head of my record label, about three years ago, and told him I wanted to do a guitar album. Tim's a great musician and a great friend, and he thought it was a great idea. I did a little bit of work on it, but then Tim called me in for a meeting and convinced me to put it on the "back burner" for a while.

Two or three years went by, and *Drive* had just about run its course, and I felt like the timing was right. I did the tracking at a big studio, and the rest was done here at my home studio. Arista was very supportive; Tim had no idea that all of those players would end up on the album. They all came here to record at my home studio, except for Richie Sambora and Larry Carlton.

Richie was in Singapore on tour with Bon Jovi, and Larry was still in California. I sent them tapes, and they did their parts on ADAT and sent them back to me.

VG: Most listeners would probably opine that the most "unique" song would probably be "Next March," and in some respects that's not surprising, since it features Bela Fleck.

SW: I love the Flecktones and Victor Wooten. I thought it would be neat to have a funk kind of piece with Bela playing five-string banjo it, instead of some traditional bluegrass song; that would have been too predictable.

VG: The title track is a duet with you and Vince Gill, and has the same kind of rapid, country-shuffle beat that "Crash Course in the Blues" has.

SW: It's kind of a "train beat" thing; we wanted to open up with something that "burns." Vince is a great player; he was playing his old '52 Telecaster, and I played my Glaser Tele with the B-bender in it; I knew I wanted to play some bender licks on that song.

VG: Aren't you a Takamine endorser?

SW: I have my own model; they're doing a new run on them that will be out in April.

VG: Let's talk about your collection; favorite and rarest pieces, etc.

SW: I've added a few pieces recently, so I think I've got over seventy instruments. My favorite guitar is my dad's old Jazzmaster, for sentimental reasons. I've got a White Falcon that Chet gave me several years ago; it's an early Sixties model, and he signed it for me. I have the #1 serial number guitar in my Takamine series. That old Jazz bass is pretty special, too; it's been all over the world a lot of times.

VG: I'm sure you use a combination of your custom-made guitars and vintage guitars when you're in the studio.

SW: Right; another favorite of mine is a '62 Strat that I use almost anytime there's a call for a Strat sound. And I've got a rehearsal to do today for a special called "Legends of Country Music"; they asked me to do a segment that's a tribute to Chet, so I'm going to drag out one of my old Gretsches.

And that was another fun part of doing the instrumental album; I got to pull out guitars I hadn't touched for a long time. I dragged out some of my old Strats, and I used a 335 on "Next March"; it seems like I never play a 335, so that's what made this album a lot of fun. I used a lot of different guitars to get the right sounds I was looking for.

VG: Any plans to tour to support *No More Mr. Nice Guy*?

SW: We're talking about it, but I don't know how extensive it will be. I'm going to be doing my "regular" touring, but we've been discussing some instrumental performances in small, 3,000 seat theatres with Chet, Leo Kottke, and me; Larry Carlton may participate as well. One of the venues where we'll be is the Ryman Auditorium here in Nashville.

VG: As far as your love of guitars goes, any final anecdote we ought to hear?

SW: One of the biggest thrills I ever had was going to lunch with Leo Fender. We were playing in Santa Ana, and my brother Terry and I were put in touch with G & L by the owner of the club where we were playing; Dale Hyatt was along as well. Unfortunately Mr. Fender really couldn't speak because of his Parkinson's Disease; this was a few months before he died. Of course, I had about six million questions I would have liked to ask him, but couldn't, but it was still a lot of fun. When I told him about my old Jazz bass, his eyes lit up. It was an experience I'll never forget.

Normally, this writer knows to leave the album reviews to John Heidt, but hopefully Mr. Heidt will understand if an opinion is rendered herein that *No More Mr. Nice Guy* is a tour-de-force guitar performance from Mr. Wariner and friends. The production and picking that are heard on that album do indeed add leverage to Duane Eddy's opinion that Steve Wariner is one player who, as Eddy said, "can do it all."

LESLIE WEST
Mountain Man

"I've only really played in three bands; the Vagrants, Mountain, and West, Bruce & Laing," says Leslie West. Yet all three of those combos achieved a considerable amount of prominence, and West's legendary, passionate guitar playing was an integral part of such bands.

Leslie West is still performing and recording; we talked with him when he'd returned from a performance in Florida. He resides in a small community north of New York City, where he was born and raised, and his hometown upbringing was the starting point for our conversation:

VG: As a native New Yorker, you must have had all kinds of sounds you heard that probably influenced your playing and the first bands you played in.

LW: The main players I used to listen to were Albert King, Eric Clapton, and Keith Richards. The Vagrants were the first band I ever played in, and we were trying to sound like British bands; groups that were getting all the attention. It was more like national and international bands that influenced us, as opposed to New York bands.

I think it's fair to say that the kind of sound we were trying to get was whatever you could get by plugging three instruments into one amplifier (chuckles)!

VG: What about your first instruments?

LW: The first guitar I had was a '58 Stratocaster. It was an old, beat-up guitar, and when my brother and I were going to get in with this group that ended up becoming the Vagrants, I wanted to have a new instrument, so I traded that beat-up Strat for a shiny new Kay.

VG: The Vagrants had more of a regional reputation, but you did play both Fillmores, didn't you? I saw the band's name on an old psychedelic poster.

LW: We played the Fillmore West and the Winterland, but we never played the Fillmore East; it was called the Village Theatre at the time. I think the other bands that played with us when our name was on that poster were the Who and the Nice.

VG: Any other instruments that you used with the Vagrants?

LW: It was pretty much the Kay, but I also played a Hagstrom, and I had a Teisco 12-string that looked really strange.

VG: In a recent interview with the magazine, Tim Bogert stated that the Vanilla Fudge formed with the idea of being an R & B band, but two bands that played the Hamptons a lot, the Young Rascals and the Vagrants, inspired them to get more "refined." Comment?

LW: Maybe they noticed us because we were wild and reckless; we took chances musically because nobody was good enough on their own instruments to know any better (chuckles). My brother Larry was the bass player for the Vagrants; he has as good of a vibrato on the bass as I do on the guitar.

VG: In the late Sixties, some rock magazine opined that Canned Heat would fill the "gap" left by Cream disbanding. Most guitar fans would probably consider Mountain to have been the ultimate "pretender to the throne," for lack of a better term.

LW: (chuckles) Their producer was our bass player, so we had to expect such comparisons. I'd rather be compared to Cream than Three Dog Night or the Buckinghams! In their time frame, Cream was the biggest band in the world. (Note: The producer/bass player was the late Felix Pappalardi).

VG: Wasn't one of your first performances at Woodstock?

LW: Yeah, that was Mountain's third show. We were on right after Canned Heat; we were the first band to go on when they turned the lights on. Halfway through our set the lights really began to take effect. Jimi Hendrix's agent was our agent, and they got us a really good spot on the show on Saturday night.

VG: How organized were things backstage?

LW: Well, it was about as organized as you

could expect (chuckles). I remember Janis Joplin walking around with a gorgeous female friend; I think everybody there wanted to be with that girl. There had been some food Saturday afternoon but it was all gone by the time we were around. I remember our manager brought us some chicken; we had our own helicopter so he made a food flight. We were starving.

VG: You were known then for playing Les Paul Jrs., but you were seen playing other models as well. What about your Flying V?

LW: I bought the first and second guitars of the reissue series. I gave one to Felix and I kept one.

VG: Didn't I read that you removed the bass pickup on your V and used the cavity as an ashtray? Most collectors would cringe if they heard about something like that being done.

LW: Well, that's what I *said* I'd done to it; I put a Junior pickup in it. I've got some strong feelings about collecting guitars: If you're going to collect something for *value*, diamonds are worth a lot more and they're a lot smaller. I think guitars should be *played;* locking them in a display case is a crime.

I also can't stand seeing some player who might collect guitars, and when he plays in concert he's got thirty guitars on stage with him. Seems he's changing guitars every song! With all of the distortion devices and effects that are out there today, you can't tell me you can tell the difference between guitar changes.

It's not right to make some kid in the audience drool by showing off all your guitars; that kid probably makes $1.90 an hour and knows there's no way he'll ever be able to afford a guitar like any of those. I don't mind a guy getting on stage and making two or three changes; maybe a Les Paul to a Strat to an acoustic. But *every song?* It's like players bring their entire net worth on stage.

VG: Didn't you use an Ampeg/Dan Armstrong plexiglas guitar for slide?

LW: Yeah; Felix got the prototype of the bass guitar from Danny Armstrong; Danny used to be signed to Felix's production company. I used the plexiglas guitar on songs like "Crossroader."

VG: Felix was noted primarily for playing a violin-shaped EB-1; was it also one of those reissues that came out in the late Sixties?

LW: Actually, he started out with one of the old original ones with the banjo tuners and a large brown pickup. We rented it from a musical instrument company to use during the sessions for my first album; I ended saying to Felix: "Look, tell them the instrument was stolen, pay for it, and keep it" (chuckles). I knew he'd never find another one like it; I have that bass now. He bought a couple of those reissues later on.

VG: Many fans would probably opine that live performance was one of Mountain's strong points, and the band did put out a disproportionate amount of live material. A while back I bought a cassette of the double length live album *Twin Peaks,* and the song "Nantucket Sleighride" fades out on Side One then back in on Side Two. How long was that particular cut?

LW: About a week and a half (laughs)! That album was recorded at the Budokan in Japan; you can hear Felix speaking in Japanese on it. It's available on compact disc, and "Nantucket Sleighride" is one continuous song; it's not cut in half.

VG: I saw some concert footage of you in some obscure movie on the USA cable network late one night a while back; I think it was called something like *The Day The Music Died,* and the basic plot from what I could tell was about some activists taking over some concert or pop festival that apparently wasn't well organized anyway. What other movies have you been in?

LW: I'm not familiar with the movie you're talking about. I was in *The Money Pit* with Shelley Long and Tom Hanks; I played a transvestite musician; that was a off-shoot group I was in called the Cheap Girls.

VG: Another opinion that long-time fans would probably have would be that West, Bruce & Laing wasn't all that different from Mountain. Did you expect your next musical venture to be so similar to the previous one?

LW: Yeah, because Felix didn't want to go on the road anymore, and Corky and I wanted to keep on going. The obvious choice was Jack Bruce.

VG: Is the white finish on the Les Paul Jr. on the cover of West, Bruce & Laing's first album an original finish?

LW: No, somebody gave me that guitar; they got it for me down on 48th Street. It was a factory refinish job, though.

VG: Didn't you audition for Lynyrd Skynyrd at one time?

LW: I never did audition; Ronnie Van Zandt asked me to join the group but their manager thought my ego was going to be a problem. That plane crash happened about two weeks after things fell through about my joining, so ultimately I was glad I didn't join.

VG: Are there any other bands of note you've played with where your work might not have been publicized?

LW: I played on "Won't Get Fooled Again" and "Behind Blues Eyes" on the *Who's Next* album. The Who came to New York to record and didn't want to do any overdubs. They were recording at the Record Plant, and their producer Kit Lambert called me up. I said "You've got to be kidding; this is fantastic!" So I did the sessions, but when they got back to England, I think Glyn Johns was the one who re-recorded those songs to get my part out; he thought my lead playing didn't belong on an album with Pete Townshend, but Pete had wanted me to do it! In fact, at those sessions I gave Pete a Les Paul Jr. and a Fender Tweed Champ amp. I still have the original version of those songs on tape.

They wanted an organ player as well for those sessions, so I told them that Felix played organ a little. Turned out Kit Lambert thought I was talking about Felix Cavaliere from the Rascals (laughs)!

Another thing I did a while back was to arrange and record "Wild Thing" for Sam Kenison.

VG: Oh, no — (laughter).

LW: I saw Sam play guitar on "Saturday Night Live" one night when he hosted, and he and I hung out at a NAMM show. One of the big events was a Kramer party; Van Halen, Bon

Jovi, Sambora and others were on stage, so I made sure Sam got to play. He called me up after that and wanted me to help him get a band together, so when he did an encore at places like the Universal Amphitheatre in L.A., instead of telling more jokes he'd play music. I got him to do "Wild Thing," then on his next album he did "Mississippi Queen"; he re-wrote the words and I played guitar and bass on that song.

VG: You and Laing did a tribute album following Pappalardi's death, didn't you?

LW: No, it wasn't a tribute; we dedicated the album to him. I don't really believe in "tribute" concepts in recording.

VG: More recent projects include ones with I.R.S. and Passport. You appeared to be playing a Steinberger M-style guitar as well as some Strat clone.

LW: I used Kramers some, but it's pretty much been Steinberger exclusively for about the last six years. The liners notes for the *Theme* album were done by Howard Stern; he's a great, great friend.

VG: What about current projects?

LW: I just finished doing Billy Joel's album. I think it's due out in late summer; it's called *River of Dreams*. I played on four songs; to me those songs are reminiscent of *Fresh Cream* or *Disraeli Gears*.

VG: Joel's going for a sound that "hard"?

LW: Yeah; we've been friends for decades. He used to be in a band called the Hassles that used to open for the Vagrants.

I recently had a live album released on Shrapnel, plus a studio blues album that's also now out. My current band still plays, and Corky and I have been working on a Mountain boxed set that hopefully will be out sometime this year. He and I still go out occasionally as Mountain as well, so I'm staying very busy.

VG: To sum up, I've heard some guitar fans talk about certain players whose tone and style are instantly recognizable; they can "say it with three notes." Persons I've heard cited include Steve Cropper and David Gilmour. What if someone wanted to put you on such a list?

LW: Well, I only play with two fingers, so maybe that has something to do with my tone and style.

Let me give a story about "tone and style": A long time ago, I went to a club in the Village called the Cafe Au Go Go when I was first starting out. In fact, it was the week I first saw the Cream at the Village Theatre we were talking about. There was a jam session at the Cafe Au Go Go; Elvin Bishop was there, Bloomfield, Clapton, Hendrix and B.B. King too. Hendrix plugged into his pedals and played everything he knew around a twelve-bar progression; everybody got up and played *every lick they ever knew* in about thirty seconds. Then came B.B. King's turn, and of course he wasn't a "speed demon" but he had a certain style. He hit *one note,* got it to feedback and sustain, and held that one note throughout the entire progression.

The place went absolutely crazy! Now, if that's not "saying it," I don't know what is!

Leslie West is a true veteran who's still got a lot to offer; his two newest albums and his recent recording projects are proof positive he intends to stay active of the guitar scene. Overall, he's got quite an enviable resume for a player who traded a '58 Strat for a Kay...

Kris Wiley

Regarding the "Blues Guitar Gender Gap"

When Kevin Seal was introduced as a new MTV veejay some years back, a viewer might have gotten the impression that lurking behind Seal's "average guy" facade was an on-the-edge mind of an axe murderer. Something about his countenance was, for lack of a better term, "subliminally creepy," and MTV seemed to hype such a perception when promo clips about his new job showed him cackling maniacally while cranking up a chain saw.

But Seal turned out to be a sardonic wiseguy whose observations were usually on the money whenever he offered an opinion about the popular music business, and the one quote of his that I thought was the most succinct and erudite was his smart-*** sneer about how "every band in the world comes from L.A."

I even broached that remark to one *VG* interviewee who was thinking about relocating from Los Angeles to the country; he said: "I'd like for my kids to be able to ride horses somewhere other than Griffith Park." When I reminded him of Seal's comment, the interviewee said: "Well, every band in the world comes *to* L.A., to try and make it. How many of them actually succeed is a completely different matter, in my view."

Well put, and for the balance of this essay, the term "make it" will appear in quote marks, not because I'm being sarcastic about the phrase, but because "make it" may mean many things to many people in the music business, and the amount of success (financial and otherwise) a band or individual thinks is necessary to "make it" is probably as varied as those bands and performers that are indeed trying to "make it."

Vintage Guitar does have some specific guidelines concerning whether or not a person might fit the magazine's format as an interviewee or profile subject, and sometimes those guidelines do get stretched a bit, but it's gratifying that nowadays many public relations and management firms are contacting *VG* about artists; not long ago, it was the other way around.

But what if an unsigned artist is trying to "make it" in the Los Angeles music scene, and she's in a definite minority within the musical genre in which she's firmly ensconced? Kris Wiley didn't have a long way to go to get to the L.A. music scene (she hails from Redondo Beach), but as a female blues guitarist, she's definitely a rare breed, if one opts to pay attention to gender in the blues genre.

The first I heard about Ms. Wiley was when a videographer, who's also a guitar buff, sent me an unsolicited videotape of her performance at B.B. King's club in L.A., where she's appeared on a regular basis for over a year. The enclosed note said that while Wiley was unsigned, everyone who'd heard her felt like she was "going to make it."

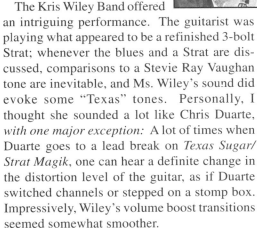

The Kris Wiley Band offered an intriguing performance. The guitarist was playing what appeared to be a refinished 3-bolt Strat; whenever the blues and a Strat are discussed, comparisons to a Stevie Ray Vaughan tone are inevitable, and Ms. Wiley's sound did evoke some "Texas" tones. Personally, I thought she sounded a lot like Chris Duarte, *with one major exception:* A lot of times when Duarte goes to a lead break on *Texas Sugar/ Strat Magik*, one can hear a definite change in the distortion level of the guitar, as if Duarte switched channels or stepped on a stomp box. Impressively, Wiley's volume boost transitions seemed somewhat smoother.

Another interesting aspect was that for the balance of her performance, Ms. Wiley's eyes were closed. She seemed to be concentrating intently on evoking the most appropriate and meaningful music from her guitar; I didn't get the feeling the "playing blind" imagery was put-on, nor did it seem like she was trying to act aloof from the audience. It just seemed to be her style, period. The other members of the band were quite competent, and the audience at B.B. King's was enthusiastic.

Ultimately, I was able to converse with Ms. Wiley to suss out the details about her equip-

Kris Wiley

ment and her music. Her main performance guitar is a '72 Strat that has indeed been refinished; her main amplifier, for the last four years, has been a '64 blackface Fender Super Reverb that she got from Coco Montoya, and she also uses a Dunlop wah pedal plus a Tube Screamer onstage. She is a Seymour Duncan endorsee, utilizing "beefed up" Antiquity pickups.

As was the case when I interviewed Debbie Davies (January, 1996), I did ask a couple of "gender specific" questions when Kris Wiley and I talked; she stated there were only a few female guitarists in the L.A. blues scene, and that some of the other "girls" (her term, not mine) were oriented towards a more traditional, "T-Bone Walker-type" guitar style, whereas Ms. Wiley feels more influenced by players such as Stevie Ray Vaughan and Jimi Hendrix. "Maybe I'm a bit wilder," she said with a laugh.

Wiley's aggregation has played quite a bit in California, and as I write this, she's supposed to be performing at B.B. King's club in Memphis and other possible locations in the South later this year.

I've written previously about acknowledging the debt owed by many rock guitarists to legendary blues players, and of course, one can't acknowledge such legends without noting (at least mentally) that the progenitors were black. I still feel like music should count for what it's saying, not because of the color of a musician's skin (regardless of the genre, for that matter, but blues music is an obvious focal point of such examination, which could lead some folks into a collective guilt mode).

But sometimes I still stumble and say something I might later regret (although to what extent I feel guilty about such a foible is another matter). A definitive personal example for me was found in the interview with B.B. King: I mentioned that some time ago, Mr. King had stated that Peter Green could make him "sweat," and I observed: "So that's at least one white British player who was playing what you considered to be 'authentic' blues."

Mr. King didn't miss a beat. "The thing is," he said, "I didn't think about what color he was, and I don't think about such now. So when I said that, I didn't mean he should be thought of as a white player, but just as, excuse the word, a *damn good player*."

Lesson learned, from a teacher who's pre-eminent in his field.

And why shouldn't the same line of thinking apply to female players? The videotape of Kris Wiley's performance cranks off with an instrumental song that's chock fulla wah-wah, and in a curious experiment, I dubbed the audio to cassette. Cueing up the introductory tune, I played it for several fellow guitar lovers, asking them: "Tell me what you think of this player" (note the non-gender-specific terminology). All of the listeners were male, which shouldn't be surprising, so any comments were male-oriented ("That guy sounds pretty good," "He sounds like _____," etc.), and I guess such comments shouldn't be all that surprising.

The note from the videographer contained a comment attributed to another L.A.-area musician who plays in a "second generation" combo. According to the videographer, the musician saw Kris Wiley in concert and opined, "She plays just like a dude!"

I asked Ms. Wiley about that remark, and she said: "I think it's great, because it breaks down the gender walls."

It remains to be seen whether or not guitarist Kris Wiley is going to "make it," but her playing and singing can stand on their own merits, and not just because she happens to be a female musician in a genre that happens to be almost exclusively male. I, for one, plan to monitor her progress.

So I'm telling you that you shouldn't check out Kris Wiley because she's a woman. You should check her out because she is, excuse the word, a *damn good player*.

(A tip of the hat to Mr. King for the plagiarism...)

Rick Wills
Bassically Bad

Okay, so the sub-title is a bit corny and plagiarizes somewhat from the sub-title of a previous interview in *Vintage Guitar* with Chris Squire ("Backstage Bassics," December 1994 issue).

But even though Rick Wills and Chris Squire are veteran bassists from England, that's about all of the common ground they share. Whereas Squire has spent the last quarter-century with the Yes, Rick Wills has been with several notable bands, as well as some combos (Cochise, Parrish & Gurvitz) that achieved a nominal amount of success in his native country if not world-wide. Squire favors Rickenbacker basses and a pick; Wills uses P-Basses and his fingers, and thinks of himself as an "in-the-pocket" player.

And the aforementioned notable bands to which Wills has belonged have been quite successful around the globe. We discussed them in chronological order with Wills prior to a concert during a tour by a revitalized Bad Company in support of its new album, *Company of Strangers*. We'd interviewed lead guitarist Mick Ralphs about a year and a half earlier (June 1994 issue); since that time Bad Company had released its first live album and had changed lead singers. Rick Wills was in an upbeat mood about the Bad Company's new effort with a new lead vocalist:

VG: What part of England are you from?
RW: My hometown is Cambridge. I spent a

lot of time in the States when I was in Foreigner; I lived about nine and a half years up in Westchester County just above New York City. When things quieted down with touring with Foreigner, I got to the point that I felt like there's really nothing like your own home; England had that "pull" on me. I wanted my kids to do *some* of their growing up in England, because they'd been in the States since they were babies, and for all intents and purposes they were American; they spoke with an American accent!

So we went back; I still live in Cambridge but I must admit the winters do get me down; I've been thinking about buying a place in Florida (chuckles). Musically, Cambridge is probably best known for being where Pink Floyd started. Syd Barrett, Dave Gilmour and I grew up with each other; we used to hang out at the same stores together. We were in competing bands, then Dave and I got to play together in Jokers Wild. The opportunity to get out of Cambridge came for Dave long before it did for me; he was a good singer and good player. He went off with Alexis Korner for about a year and a half before he got the call from Pink Floyd to take Syd's place.

VG: I have a policy of asking every British interviewee about Radio Luxembourg.

RW: I was a classic case, with the radio under the pillow, listening to the Top Twenty countdown at ten o'clock; hearing the music drift in and out on those medium-wave airbands. But it was magic; no one else was playing that kind of music.

VG: What about your first instruments?

RW: Well, I was originally a rhythm guitar player; my first instruments weren't too special! My acoustic guitar was a 666 model; it didn't really have a brand name. From there I went to a Futurama, which was my first electric. It was advertised in the Selmer catalog, and was a "poor man's Fender," because Fend-

TOP: *Photo by Aubrey Powell.*

RIGHT: *Bad Company - Rick Wills' current venture with, from left, Dave Colwell, Wills, Simon Kirke, Mick Ralphs, and Robert Hart.*

TOP LFFT: *Rick with a Rick - Onstage with Cochise, ca. 1970. That's B.J. Cole on steel guitar behind Wills.*

TOP RIGHT: *From a Small Faces tour book: Rick with the Gretsch bass he played with that group.*

LEFT: *Publicity photo for Foreigner's Head Games album (Wills' first effort with the band). From left, Ian McDonald, Wills, Dennis Elliot, Mick Jones, Al Greenwood, and Lou Gramm.*

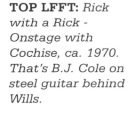

ers were kind of new and expensive in those days. I think Cliff Richard brought the first one in to give to Hank Marvin of the Shadows. Bruce Welch, the Shadows' rhythm guitarist, still has that very one; it now has a lovely see-through cream-type finish; the neck has got a lot of bird's-eye maple; all the fittings have been goldplated. I've got a picture of me playing it; I did an album with Bruce.

VG: I've heard the Shadows referred to as "the English Ventures" by more than one music fan.

RW: They *were*, but they were different. They were one of the most precise, accurate bands I've ever heard, and they still are. They had *two* careers, one as Cliff's backing band and they'd also tour themselves, because they had so many instrumental hits, the first one being "Apache." Like a lot of players, I was crazy about the Shadows.

VG: Earliest bands?

RW: Just local bands in Cambridge; the first one was called the Sundowners. All I wanted to do was play; school went out the window (chuckles). I finally got my own Strat and my own AC-30, then trends changed; rhythm guitarists became unfashionable in bands. Three-piece bands became the thing when Hendrix came along.

I quickly realized that I wasn't the greatest guitarist in the world; I could play rhythm but I could never really come to grips with playing lead. I always liked the sound and the look of a bass; it was a cool looking instrument. So I went up to London and traded my Strat in on a Precision Bass, and never looked back. That would have been around '66 or '67. I played bass in one band for a while, then Dave and I did Jokers Wild.

VG: Did Jokers Wild ever do any recording?

RW: Yeah; we did some stuff in France, but it never got released. It was demo-type material. When Dave left to join the Pink Floyd, I went back to Cambridge and played with a band called the Soul Committee for a while, then I met up with Tim Renwick and Jerry Shirley, and we got a band up called Little Women... strange name for a bunch of guys (laughs). I loved the way those guys played; they were doing Doors songs and were into Hendrix, whereas I had been doing soul and dance things. Jerry ended up in Humble Pie, and Tim's a fantastic session player who was in Sutherland Brothers & Quiver, and he's been on the recent Pink Floyd tours. Right now he's working with Mike and the Mechanics.

I played with those guys for about eighteen months to two years, and when Jerry left to form Humble Pie, that's when I first met Pete Frampton and Steve Marriot. I played with different bands in and around Cambridge, and then when Pete left Humble Pie he asked me if I'd like to make a band up with him, and we formed what was called Frampton's Camel around '71. The first song we ever wrote was "Do You Feel Like We Do."

We came over to the States and started touring and touring and touring (chuckles); that's all we ever did. That went on until about '74 or '75; I was burned out from all the touring, and while I thought Pete was a tremendous guitar

player, I had some difficulty with some of his lyrics. He overheard me saying what I thought of his lyrics, and that was the end of our relationship for a while (laughs)! After that I played with Nicky Hopkins a bit.

VG: Hopkins is now deceased.

RW: Yes he is; it was very sad to hear. He was a very lovely person and a great piano player; all of that music he did with the Stones was great.

I did that for a while, then I spent a little time with Roxy Music.

VG: Were you back in Cambridge when the offer to join that band came about?

RW: No, I was in London; the Roxy Music gig came out of the blue. A friend of my wife worked in the office of Roxy Music's management. We happened to see her at a Paul McCartney and Wings concert at Hammersmith-Odeon, and she told us that Roxy Music was currently auditioning bass players. That was the last band in the world I thought I'd ever be in (chuckles)! All of the top session guys like Phil Chen were ahead of me and I figured there was no way I'd get the job, because those guys were *killer*. But they chose me; the drummer, Paul Thompson, said: "That's the guy."

VG: Obviously, that was a different musical direction for you; more of an art-rock style.

RW: Yeah; they had a "look." They were a glam-rock band, with the makeup and the clothes, and that never appealed to me. But having said that, I think it was fun to have played with them; they were very nice people and their music was interesting and different. Once I got into playing it, I found there was more to it than I'd imagined. After two tours of America and one European tour, Bryan [Ferry] pretty much called a halt to Roxy Music.

VG: Around the late Seventies you did what was for all intents and purposes a Jokers Wild reunion with David Gilmour and Willie Wilson on Gilmour's solo album.

RW: That was just a one-off; Willie had also been in Sutherland Brothers & Quiver, too. We'd always talked about doing a reunion like that, but we didn't look at it as being a career move; we just wanted to enjoy making the album. There was no question that Dave was going to leave the Floyd to do this, but we did some videos.

VG: There was even some advertising here in the U.S. along the lines of the "Is-it-real-or-is-it-Memorex" audio cassette campaign; I saw some magazine ads that said something like "Is it David Gilmour or is it Pink Floyd."

RW: I wasn't aware of it; I think it was probably done over here to call attention to the fact that "David Gilmour" on its own probably didn't ring too many bells unless you put "the Pink Floyd" with it.

The album was something that Dave had time to do, and that we all wanted to do. To be perfectly honest, we didn't take it that seriously, but we had a lot of fun doing it, and it turned out pretty good.

VG: Isn't that the way some projects ought to be handled sometimes?

RW: Absolutely; I think there are some nice songs on there. Dave and I have always been very close friends; I was his best man.

VG: What was your next "permanent" band project?

RW: I got home from touring with Roxy Music and was just hanging around, then I got a call from Steve Marriot at four in the morning; he said: "Me and Ronnie

TOP: Rick Wills (upper left) with the Soul Committee, ca. 1969: The saxophone player next to him is Dick Parry, who played the sax solo on the original version of Pink Floyd's hit "Money." Parry also toured with the Pink Floyd during 1994.

RIGHT: Roxy Music 1976-1977 with Andy Mackay, Bryan Ferry, Eddie Jobson, Wills, Phil Manzanera, and Paul Thompson.

[Lane] have just had a falling out; would you fancy playin' bass with the Small Faces?" I couldn't believe that call; I *loved* the Small Faces!

VG: I've always thought that the earliest Small Faces songs were tremendous pop tunes that hold up to this day. "I Feel Much Better," "Itchykoo Park."

RW: "Tin Soldier," "Lazy Sunday" ...they were all great. The songs that Steve wrote with Ronnie were killer. Steve wanted me to come to the studio *right then* at four in the morning! I *did* go down there the next day, and I was pretty nervous, but they were quite nice.

One thing I did do differently in Small Faces was to put down my Fender bass for a while because of the size difference in the band; I was taller than the other guys, so to kind of "counter-balance" that look I got an old Gretsch bass that had a big soapbar-type pickup and a great, warm sound. We did a couple of albums for Atlantic. Steve's not with us any longer, either, which is very sad. He was a tremendous talent. I feel very honored to have been associated with those guys.

After the Small Faces kind of fizzled out, I was wondering what I was going to do next. I opted to go to New York and stay with Jerry Shirley, who was living there at the time, to see if anything was happening there; I was also trying to get some royalty money that I was due because Peter Frampton's live album had been a huge success; "Doobie Wah" and "Do You Feel Like We Do" were on it.

I've been very lucky at times, because the first week I was in New York I got a check for $35,000 as a partial payment for the songwriting. I'd never had that kind of money in my life; *and* I spoke with Mick Jones in Foreigner; they'd decided to change bass players and were holding auditions that week. I knew Mick from Paris way back in '67, when I was there with Dave Gilmour; he was backing singers like Johnny Halliday and Sylvie Vartain.

I was the first bass player to audition, and Foreigner's drummer, Dennis Elliott, said: "He's the bass player." But they *did* need to audition the others who'd signed up, so it took about three weeks before I knew I had the job.

VG: Why do you think some bands have settled on you as a bass player so quickly?

RW: I honestly don't know; I guess it's the way I play. I use my fingers; I used a pick early in my career but I always thought you got the nicest sound by using your fingers. I've always tried for a "feel"; I've always been more of a "feel" player than a technician. I've never been one to whiz all over the fretboard, trying to prove I could play faster and better than anybody else. I like to be in the pocket, sitting back and grooving with the drummer.

VG: The association with Foreigner went on for quite some time.

RW: Thirteen years. Joining Foreigner was a complete change; instead of traveling in busses, they had their own airplane. It was first-class, royal treatment everywhere. I'd never played sold-out shows in front of that many people; it was incredible. But it was a good experience, and I was ready for

it. It didn't freak me out, and it didn't make me change.

VG: Were you still relying primarily on P-Basses?

RW: Right; I've always had basic, sunburst P-Basses over the years. I've used a Jazz Bass on occasion, and I had that Gretsch with Small Faces, but I've always gone back to P-Basses, because they're "straight-forward." The one I'm using now is actually a Squire bass that Mick Ralphs found for me in London. It's Candy Apple Red, and was custom-made for a guy in the shop where Mick found it. It's been modified; it's got a Jazz pickup as well, and three controls; two volume and one tone. It's got a nice sound, and it's a bit lighter than a regular P-Bass.

VG: For all of the success Foreigner had, my perception that things sort of "fizzled out" with that band as well.

RW: It started with sort of "ego" problems between Mick and Lou; it was a sad and confusing thing to watch. Lou wanted to do his solo thing, and Mick was distraught when Lou left; Lou's voice had been one of the band's strong points, and he was Mick's writing partner as well. We got Johnny Edwards, a wonderful singer, as a replacement, and did an album called *Unusual Heat*. No offense to anybody, but it really wasn't a true Foreigner album. We did our best, though. Dennis's heart wasn't really in it anymore, and after we did a tour, he left.

Then it was *my* turn to be distraught, because he was such a great drummer; very accurate and precise; a wonderful musician. We did a bit more with a session drummer, but it just wasn't the same.

I'd been threatening Mick [Ralphs] and Simon [Kirke] for many years about wanting to play in Bad Company; I've known those guys from *way* back, from their Mott the Hoople and Free days. I'd always loved Bad Company's music; it's so infectious. They didn't want to mess up anything with Foreigner, but they told me if I was sure this was the right time, they were about to go on tour in support of *Here Comes Trouble*.

VG: So you left Foreigner to go *directly* to Bad Company; there wasn't any period of inactivity like there had been for you in the past when you were between bands? And Foreigner went into "hiatus"?

RW: Right; Mick and Lou eventually met in Los Angeles and worked out their differences; they decided to build a new band around them. I haven't seen them in a long time, but we're doing a show together soon. It ought to be fun to get together.

The decision to go to Bad Company wasn't easy for me, however. But the timing seemed to be right, and it's worked out great for all concerned. Simon and I hit it off like that (snaps fingers); he's the most laid-back drummer ever; he *never* rushes any tempos and has a lovely way of holding back. It's a pleasure to play with him.

VG: In addition to the Squire P-Bass, what else are you using on this tour?

RW: I've got an old Telecaster bass; the square-bodied one with the big white scratchplate, and a '57 reissue P-Bass; I used that all of the time I was in Foreigner. I've got a five-string Music Man that I used on the tour when we made the live album, but I've gone back to using just a four-string bass. I used Ampeg SVT amps for many years, and for this tour I changed over to Marshall; they've brought out a fantastic new bass amp series, and I've got a sponsorship deal with them.

VG: Do you collect?

RW: I did for a time when I was in Foreigner; I bought some instruments from Pete Alenov up in Minneapolis/St. Paul. A black Les Paul, a nice old Custom Tele. I had an old black '63 Everlys acoustic which I sold to a friend of mine in Florida a couple of years ago. Recently I bought a J-160E, one of the acoustics like the Beatles used; I've always wanted one of those. They're not the best-sounding acoustic in the world, compared to a J-45 or a Country & Western, but it's immaculate.

VG: Since you joined Bad Company, the band has gone through the same experience as Foreigner concerning a change in lead vocalists.

RW: I knew Robert Hart from the auditions to replace Lou in Foreigner; he very nearly got that job but Johnny Edwards had a higher range. Robert's full of enthusiasm, and is a *great* singer; he isn't road-weary... he's also ten years younger than me (laughs)!

VG: I'd imagine you use a minimal number of basses in the studio as well.

RW: Just what I mentioned earlier. Our music is so basic that when you get into a groove, there's really not a lot that you should be messing with.

VG: This tour is in support of the first album you've done with Hart as the lead singer.

RW: We're *very* happy with it; we went back to the old way of recording. It sounds very much like the first Bad Company album; that was the sound we went for and the vibe we wanted. We just found out that the first single, "Down and Dirty," is the Number One most-added song on A.O.R. radio in America, so it's a fantastic start. And the reviews have been great as well; they're saying things like "Isn't it great that a band can get itself together and go back to where it belongs!"

We went about recording with the drums in a nice, loud room for the ambience; the bass in a booth; the guitar amps tucked away in different places. We recorded live with very little overdubs; just solos.

We're happy that things have been going so well; each show on this tour has been better than the previous one. Everybody in the band is committed, and there's been a lot of strong songwriting as well. I think that by getting back to a classic Bad Company sound, we'll be going on for some time. We're all quite excited about it.

Rick Wills' current musical venture seems to be in the groove, which is exactly how the veteran bass player would prefer his career to be, just like his playing. Wills's confident-yet-excited-and-upbeat demeanor when giving an interview is also a reflection of his playing style, and *Company of Strangers* heralds a "new-yet-retro" (i.e., very listenable) phase for Bad Company.

Vintage Guitar would like to thank Sid Pryce for his help in coordinating the interview with Rick Wills.

David Wintz

Reversal of Fortune

...not that there was anything wrong with the business fortunes of the President of Robin Guitars & Basses to start with. Instead, the subtitle of this interview is a "double pun" concerning two facts: (1) Robin brand instruments were originally made overseas and are now completely handmade in Houston, Texas, and, (2) Robin instruments were the first to have an entire line with "reverse-style" headstocks; the earliest Robins had a slightly down-sized, "Explorer"-type headstock, and the whole lineup maintained an upside-down look until recent times.

Conversing with the contemporary guitar builder in his Houston office was an enlightening experience. Wintz was born and raised in Houston; there *was*, as most readers might suspect, a connection with the local musical instrument retailer known as Rockin' Robin (details later), but we began by asking Wintz about times prior to the Rockin' Robin connection:

VG: What about your guitar experiences *prior* to the Rockin' Robin days?

DW: I started playing guitar when I was thirteen; it was strictly a British Invasion thing. It wasn't long after seeing the Beatles play on "Ed Sullivan" that I got hooked on wanting to play the guitar. My first guitar was a used pre-CBS Mustang, which was actually a loaner from a music store until my shiny *new* red Mustang came in. I even remember at the time that the new one was "funky," in the negative sense, compared to the pre-CBS one; I didn't like the CBS one nearly as well. The fingerboard looked dried out, and it wasn't nearly as comfortable. As a kid, I was thinking that a new guitar should have been better than a used one, and looking back, I remembered such things about good features of vintage instruments when I began designing my own brand.

TOP: *This early Nineties photo of David Wintz also appeared in the revised version of Tom Wheeler's* American Guitars; *he's holding an early Robin RV-2 made around 1982 (left) and the company's innovative Machete model.*

LEFT: *Eric Johnson onstage with a Robin RV-2. Photo taken circa 1982.*

I traded the CBS Mustang in on an Epiphone Casino; the Beatles influenced that choice as well (chuckles)! In the late Sixties I got out of playing for a few years. Then around 1970 a friend of mine took me to Specialty Guitar Shop here in Houston; they had a lot of old stuff and it really zapped me; from that moment on I was a "guitar hound," going into pawn shops on a regular basis. I bought things like a mid-Sixties orange Gretsch 6120 with painted-on f-holes, and a mid-Sixties Epiphone Sheraton.

VG: What about your playing experiences?

DW: Around the time I went into Specialty, I was just starting to play again, so the interests paralleled each other. I haven't worked at any job since then that didn't have to do with guitars. I played in a local band; it was all original music that was basic rock and roll, then we got into art rock, Yes-type stuff. We didn't play a lot, but it was a good experience. Then in the summer of 1972 Bart Wittrock and I started up Rockin' Robin.

VG: Where did the store name come from?

DW: The song; "tweet-tweet" (chuckles). It fit the image of what we were trying to accomplish. Bart and I hit it off from the very start, and worked together for years; we moved to about five different locations as the business grew.

VG: The next obvious inquiry is about the advent of the Robin brand.

DW: We were at a NAMM show in Chicago; Tokai was exhibiting there. They were exhibiting some funky-looking new models, but we'd

seen their cool replicas of old Strats, and we asked why they didn't have any there. They escorted us into a small room in their exhibit, which was chock full of replica guitars like that "Love Rock" Les Paul style they made, plus Strat copies. The bottom line is that we ended up buying everything they had there; about twenty guitars. Once we sold those, we opted to get Tokai to manufacture some of our own designs, which included a smaller, reverse-Explorer type headstock. We went through hundreds of names, and settled on "Robin," which wasn't the same as "Rockin' Robin," but it was similar. We didn't want to use either of our last names, and my middle name is Gibson, so that got ruled out as well (laughs)! The name Robin can apply to a man or a woman; it's a folk hero's name; it couldn't be misspelled or mispronounced.

This was still kind of a part-time thing; there was no long-term plan and we weren't a couple of luthiers.

VG: The photo of you in the updated version of *American Guitars* shows you with the first Robin guitar; in addition to the reverse Explorer headstock, it appears to have a bound, Strat-shaped body.

DW: Exactly; that's an '82 guitar. Due to copyrights, we couldn't do a traditional-looking Strat copy. We were definitely the first to have a reverse headstock on a bolt-on neck; Firebirds were sort of reversed but had banjo-type tuners. There wasn't any "deep" marketing concept behind the reverse headstock; we just thought it looked cool. We couldn't tell that there was any audible difference; it was strictly visual. I know some companies since then have said that a longer string length on the bass side gives a different sound, but our headstock was marketed for its aesthetics.

The two things that *are* true about a reverse headstock is that it goes "against the grain" of what players had been conditioned to seeing, which is exactly what we were trying to accomplish, but a reverse headstock on a guitar is also easier to tune; a player's arm doesn't have to twist like it does on a conventional headstock.

VG: I've got to play devil's advocate at this point and note that an issue of your company's newsletter that I perused announced that you were switching to a conventional-style headstock. Comment?

DW: We're not trying to tell people that "this is the way it ought to be;" marketing research indicated that conventional headstocks would probably get a better overall reception by the public.

VG: What about the switch from a foreign manufacturer to domestic production?

DW: We used Tokai for a while, then we got some stuff from them that didn't meet our quality standards. I went over to Japan; I'd just started the Allparts company, and went over there looking for parts as well. I ended up turning down an entire shipment of guitars that was ready to be shipped to us. Later I switched to ESP, and other companies as well. I still had one foot in the Rockin' Robin retail part; we were using the back part of the store to set up the imported guitars.

Around 1987, the dollar took a nose-dive against the Japanese yen. Prices got so high I figured it was either time to get out or go on and start a factory, and I was a glutton for punishment (laughs). I'd made guitars before, but not on a *production* scale. Once that decision was made, there were a couple of years of transition; the guitar facility moved to a separate location from the store, of course. So it was "Bye-bye, guitar shop; hello, production!" Bart and I have remained on great terms; we're best friends.

VG: Did you start out making the same styles you'd been importing?

DW: Yes, we made neck-through-the-body archtops; we'd been making a similar guitar in Japan called the Medley Custom, so we called the domestic one the Medley Custom TX, for "Texas." That's an expensive type of instrument to start out with; we made a few of those then decided to go with bolt-on, which is okay for the hard rock look; the Medley was oriented towards that market.

VG: Is this facility your first location?

DW: No, we've only been here since the first

of '94. The first location was sort of built up as we went along; one thing on top of another, but when we moved out here we laid it out like we wanted from the beginning; it's a "user friendly" shop and we're really happy here.

VG: Let me ask you about some particular Robin styles; you can let us know whether they are/were domestic or imported, and comment about each. First, the Artisan; it looked like a bound SG.

DW: That was an imported model; there were only about a hundred and fifty of them made. People who own them are *nuts* about their Artisans; I still get calls about them. Michael Stevens, a Texas luthier who was with Fender's Custom Shop at one time, actually made the prototype.

VG: Is the Medley your longest-running style?

DW: No, the Ranger is; we started those *really* early; around 1983. The Ranger has proven real successful over the years; we've introduced a baritone version of it. With its pickup configuration, a Ranger is an extremely versatile instrument.

VG: Are the Medley and the Ranger your most popular models?

DW: Well, the Avalon is coming on big time; we're back ordered several months on it. It's something a bit different for us; it has a 24³/₄ inch scale, and a single-cutaway carved top on a body that's wider and thinner than a Les Paul. The series is set-neck. The Custom Classic and Custom have mahogany bodies and mahogany necks; and the Deluxe and Flattop have a swamp ash body with a mahogany neck. We're the first to offer that kind of wood combination; obviously the Flattop doesn't have a carved top (chuckles).

VG: The Wedge was a bit unusual-looking.

DW: Imported, discontinued, radical. Obviously, it was oriented towards the "glam metal" bands, but it was actually quite comfortable.

VG: There was a model that I only saw in a bass; it was called the Freedom. It had a great-feeling neck on it, in my opinion.

DW: That wasn't domestic, either. It was only available in a bass; it was supposed to be a cross between a Music Man and a Tele bass. It had two Double Jazz-type pickups, and they were active; it was so powerful you could plug a set of headphones right into the instrument; you didn't even need a preamp! The first Freedoms had real wide necks, then they went to more of a Jazz shape; you probably played one of the latter types. It might not have sold well because of distribution; I think it still has potential and we might try it again, but we're definitely more of a "guitar company" than a "bass company."

VG: The Machete is an original, domestic style that seems to have done pretty well for you.

DW: Absolutely. I saw a guitar that another company was making; it looked nothing like the Machete, but it inspired me at the right time to come up with a new shape. I went home and came up with the Machete in about thirty minutes. The view from the rear end of it is unique; it has three "stairstep" drops of a quarter-inch each, and that look is fully patented. Something like a Firebird has one drop of maybe a sixteenth of an inch, but the Machete really has a great aesthetic. It comes in set-neck and bolt-on versions. The "four and two V" headstock is from a guitar I made for myself in 1974.

VG: Back to the Avalon for a minute, since it's your most recent model. Details?

DW: Some of the other details you need to know is that it has a straight pull on the strings to the tuners, and single Kluson-type machine heads. The headstock has a fourteen degree pitch and a sort of a "deco" bevel on the back of it. The nut is like a Martin nut in that it sits on the headstock instead of the fingerboard; it's a little harder to do it that way, but we pay attention to details.

VG: The Octave Guitar isn't in your current catalog.

DW: No, but we still make them as custom orders; in fact, we're working on one today out in the shop that I'll show you. It's a cool instrument for studio doubling and "chicken pickin'," but it's a specialty item, like a twelve-string guitar.

VG: You had to have been pumped up when an MTV Mardi Gras special some years ago showed Stevie Ray Vaughan and Jimmie Vaughan playing "Pipeline" on a double-neck Robin that had a regular neck and an Octave Guitar neck.

DW: You bet! There were only about twenty-five or thirty of those doubles made; that sequence is well-known by a lot of people.

VG: What about the dolphin inlays I've seen on some instruments?

DW: Originally, those appeared on Medleys, but I don't remember if they were designed specifically for Medleys or not. It's an option for Medleys and Avalons; it's standard on an Avalon Custom Classic, which is top-of-the-line. A guy cuts the dolphin inlays for us locally; they're very exquisite and very detailed.

VG: What about endorsers?

DW: We're getting back into that; sometimes we're so busy that endorsement activity has to go on the back burner, so to speak. Recently the guitarist for White Zombie has been using a Machete; that's a big plus.

VG: Your video discussed custom orders. Comment?

DW: That's not a large portion of our business, but I think any guitar builder has to consider that part of the business. Many players are willing to pay a premium to get exactly what they want, and while custom orders take *as long or longer* than the time frame promised, the owner is so delighted with the instrument he's a "convert" (chuckles).

VG: This may sound like "the reverse of the original reverse situation," but what about the export of your U.S.-made instruments?

DW: They go primarily to Europe and Asia. The Europeans buy a lot of Medleys; recently Rangers have begun selling well in France. The markets overseas depend a lot on the value of the dollar, of course, so prices can still fluctuate; some things don't change.

VG: Recent projects and future plans?

DW: We wanted to come out with a classic-looking 24³/₄ scale instrument, and the reception to the Avalon has been gratifying. I may look at something like the Artisan again as a next guitar style, but right now we've got some great-looking instruments that are extremely high quality. We've just begun distributing Rio Grande pickups; those are selling well, too. I'm proud of what we've accomplished, but we're not resting on our laurels at all.

Robin evolved into Alamo Music Products, which also began making a second brand of guitars called Metropolitan, which have a cool "retro-vibe."

Allen Woody

Of Short-Scale Basses and Long, Long Songs

Like his bandmate, Warren Haynes, bassist Allen Woody is burning the proverbial candle at both ends, around the middle, and in between; he pulls "double duty" in the same two bands that Haynes does (The Allman Brothers Band and Gov't Mule). Accordingly, it took some time for *VG* to catch up with Woody, but the wait was worth it.

Allen Woody is a long-time guitar lover, and his collection currently numbers around 300 instruments. Details concerning his collection and his playing experiences (as well as his tenure as an employee of a certain Nashville vintage guitar store) were part of an extended telephone conversation while Woody was taking a few weeks off between practice sessions and performances. He was born in Music City ("Same hospital that Duane and Gregg were born in," he noted), and such a beginning prompted the obvious first inquiry:

VG: How did growing up in Nashville affect your interest in playing music?

AW: When I was a kid, Ernest Tubb lived down the street from my mom and dad; I used to watch him on TV. He had great players, and I think it's fair to say I loved what might be called "Old Country." I really liked Buck Owens and the whole Bakersfield thing; Don Rich and sparkle Teles.

There was a player in Nashville named Jimmy Colvard who played with a band called Barefoot Jerry; he also played the lead on Dave Dudley's "Six Days on the Road." He was a *monster* guitar player; unfortunately he went the same route as Danny Gatton; he ended his life about 10 years ago. Barefoot Jerry was a country band that really *rocked*. They had Russ Hicks on pedal steel; Wayne Moss thumbpicking a Jazzmaster. For a while, the term "country rock" meant the Eagles, but these guys were the real thing.

So I liked traditional or "real" country music; Hank Williams Sr. was the real thing; so was Pasty Cline. Guys like Harold Bradley doing the Danelectro 6-string bass tic-tac thing; I found out later that those guys would take a doghouse bass and play the bass track, then double it with the 6-string tic-tac to get those sounds.

So it was a pretty natural progression to go from "real" country music to rock and roll, and it's ironic that my dad was the one who turned me on to blues players like Muddy Waters. He'd been a truck driver, and would listen to WLAC in Nashville when he traveled; it was one of the last clear-channel blues stations, and it could be heard all over the United States. Billy Gibbons has cited that station.

And back then Johnny Cash was doing a TV show from the Ryman Auditorium, and he was featuring rock acts on some of his shows. My mother took me to see Derek & the Dominoes on the Johnny Cash show when I was 14; I was in Gruhn Guitars the same day and Clapton was in there buying a Strat. What was so cool was that after they taped the show, Derek & the Dominoes played for two hours for the kids that came to the show. I still have a cassette tape of that performance.

VG: Earliest instruments?

AW: My first electric guitar was a Kingston, which I wish I still had because it was a Hound Dog Taylor kind of instrument. I had a matching bass that was a Tuxedo brand name. When I was in the ninth or tenth grade, I went into Madison Music in Nashville, and they had a late '60s Hofner bass. Raised logo on the headstock, pickup rings that resembled Gibson pickup rings; not quite a "Beatle Bass," but real close. I traded in both of my Japanese instruments and gave them $100 for it, and I still own it. That was the first *good* bass I got.

As for my first *good electric guitar*; I was studying music in Nashville at Blair Academy, and my grandfather picked me up from school one day and took me to a Boy's Club, of all places. Vox had given them 100 guitars; "Bulldog" and teardrop-shaped models. They were all sunburst except for one red teardrop and one white teardrop. I wanted the white one because of Brian Jones, of course, but the red one and the white one were factory seconds; the rest of the guitars were marked seconds but there was nothing wrong with them. Vox was going out of business so that's why they were all marked like that. I sat there for two hours and tried out *all 98* of the sunburst guitars (chuckles) and picked out the one I liked; my grandfather paid $60

Allen Woody with a '60s Epi Rivoli short-scale bass. Photo by Walter Carter.

for it, and I still have that one, as well; it was brand new when I got it, and even had the gray case and the cleaning cloth. I got the Hofner and the Vox around the same time.

VG: By that time, did you consider yourself to be a guitar player or a bass player?

AW: I was a guitar player first, but as for the bass players in bands I played in, I really didn't like what they did. I found myself being heavily influenced at the time by Paul McCartney, and a year or so later I was into Jack Bruce and Berry Oakley; I think concentrating on being a bass player probably happened by proxy. I really wasn't a "frustrated guitar player," but I *was* a frustrated bass player, *and I still am.* I like my guitar playing, but my bass playing drives me nuts (laughs)!

I was never a big Fender guy; I own some cool Fender instruments and they're wonderful tools, but back then I was a Beatles nut, and I was into their instruments. By the time I got into playing bass almost exclusively, I got into Chris Squire and John Entwistle in addition to Jack Bruce and Berry Oakley, but because of my "natural progression" as a Beatles freak, the next bass I got was a Rickenbacker 4001 – white with black binding and a black pickguard. I saw Maurice Gibb of the Bee Gees, of all people, on an album cover with a white Rickenbacker and orange Marshalls, and I thought it looked really cool, and that he was finally getting hip! So I bought my 4001 in Nashville in 1974; I still have that bass, too.

VG: What about converting from short-scale on the Hofner to long scale?

AW: Well, I put a set of Roto-Sounds on my Hofner and tried to get the tones that Oakley, Squire and Entwistle were getting, and I realized it wasn't working. I looked at Jazz Basses, but at the time they were 3-bolt style, and the quality wasn't there. The Rickenbacker had a nice neck, looked sexy, and sounded great.

VG: You *do* own some Alembics, and a lot of those instruments are 32" scale, which most people consider to be "medium scale."

AW: Most of mine are 34". I played in a fusion band for several years, so of course I'd gotten into Stanley Clarke, and we did some shows with the Dixie Dregs; Andy West was playing an Alembic, and the sound just jumped out at me. Around Nashville, the music stores wanted the closest thing to

Fender they could get, so any store that dared to get Alembic basses got long-scale ones. I bought mine in early 1977. Alembics bring out all of the characteristics of your playing; you can't "hide behind" an Alembic like you can with some other basses. I've played some medium-scale instruments; it's enjoyable and in some respects it's "the best of both worlds."

VG: Did you play with any notable combos prior to joining the Allman Brothers?

AW: The fusion band I played in was called Montage; we were together for seven years and worked all over the Southeast. I did a lot of studio work, and in some respects I was young and stupid, because I thought I could eschew the usual procedures and play rock and roll my own way in Nashville, and I learned quickly that it couldn't happen (chuckles).

I played with Peter Criss, and I was in Artimus Pyle's band for five or six years; Artimus had a lot to do with me ending up in the Allman Brothers. He introduced me to Warren Haynes around '85, and Warren and I would jam occasionally over the next few years.

Then one time, Warren told me he was going to be in the Allman Brothers, and at the same time we were cutting some tracks for the new Artimus Pyle Band album at Butch Trucks' studio. I'd met Butch earlier; we were friends. He came up to me at his studio and told me his band was going to get back together; I said something to him like "Well, I guess you'll be needing a bass player," almost as a joke, but he said: "Yeah, that's what I want to talk to you about." I thought to myself, "Wow, he's *serious!*"

VG: Did you have to audition?

TOP: *Woody with a Gibson Thunderbird.*

RIGHT: *Onstage with Gov't Mule – playing a Gibson EB-1 reissue.*

AW: Yeah, they went through thirty or forty bass players; there might have been guys that were better bass players than me, but in terms of "better for the band," there weren't. As experienced as the band was, they knew what would be best for them. I played for five minutes, and they told me they were going to take a break and talk; I thought to myself: "I've ****ed up; I've blown it." But Gregg came back a few minutes later and told me I was in the band. We've been married ever since (laughs)!

VG: What studio basses do you use with the Allmans?

AW: You know, that seems to vary a lot from album to album, and I'm really not sure why. I used my long-scale Alembic on the first record I did with the band, and a fretless Jazz-type bass that was custom-made for me by Chandler; it's a powder blue color. I've had an affiliation with Chandler for years, and they've really been able to meet some needs for me. They made a 12-string Korina "V" bass with a Miller High Life logo on the front, with four Chandler lipstick pickups in it; they're set up two-and-two with coil tap. That's a beautiful configuration.

I also used a late model white Fender Jazz bass on the first record, and on "Gambler's Roll" played a fretless Paul Reed Smith; they're not making them anymore. I've got two of them; they're a little unorthodox, but they're killer.

On *Shades of Two Worlds* I used a Washburn AB-20 for the acoustic thing. Most of the other songs had the Alembic again, but for "Kind of Bird" I played a fretless 5-string Steinberger, of all things.

VG: Warren Haynes observed in his own *Vin-*

tage Guitar interview that *Seven Turns* was more of a "songs" album, whereas *Shades of Two Worlds* was more of a "jamming" album.

AW: I agree; the first record was sort of like we were saying "okay, we have to learn how to make a record together," which I think we did very well. The second record was more along the lines of "now we need to do what we do *live*," and by the time we did the third studio album, it was definitely a "jam" situation. *Where It All Begins* was recorded on a sound stage at Burt Reynolds' ranch, and we even had *lighting trusses* rigged up!

VG: How long did the most extended jamming situation you've gotten into with the Allman Brothers Band last?

AW: Probably about four hours.

VG: Performance basses?

AW: There's one bass that crosses over a lot for me, and that's a Warwick. But live, I pretty much go with Thunderbirds; I've been a huge Thunderbird fan for years.

VG: Was that the Washburn AB-20 on the acoustic version of "In Memory of Elizabeth Reed" on the *An Evening with the Allman Brothers Band: Second Set* album?

AW: No, and there's a funny story about the bass I used. I collect Hofner copies; the ****tier the better (chuckles). I was in Japan, and Warren and I had been guitar shopping. In the magazines over there, a store will print pictures of its entire inventory. I saw an Audition violin-shaped bass for sale for $125. Audition was the Woolworth/Woolco house brand. I contacted the store, and an employee brought it to the show. It had a brown vinyl gig bag, and it looked great and sounded great, so I bought it.

Later, we had to do a performance for a record

TOP: *Gov't Mule featuring Allen Woody, Warren Haynes and Matt Abts. Photo by Danny Clinch.*

LEFT: *Woody with a KYDD fretless bass, 30" scale. Photo by Joseph Black.*

association in California. Only four of us were at the meeting; Gregg, Dickie, Warren and me. I had my Washburn AB-20, and I'd brought along the Audition along as a spare and for looks, as well; I thought it would look good for a cozy, intimate acoustic show. I figured I'd better tune it up, so I did, and I started noodling around on it. Our sound man, Bud Snyder, was out in the mobile, and he came in and told me the sound of the Audition was perfect for what we were doing. So the "Liz Reed" acoustic thing on the last live album had a bass that was a $125 Hofner copy.

VG: Were you doing any thumb pops or pull-offs on that song?

AW: No, but I was and still am a *huge* Larry Graham fan. I watched him play with George Clinton at the Rock & Roll Hall of Fame concert, and he had the best bass sound there. I figured out how he got that high-fidelity sound of his; he had the gain way up on his system, and he was barely touching his bass. He got an incredible sound, with a big spongy low end, and a crisp high end. I love Bootsy, too, but Larry Graham's the man; the original is still the greatest.

VG: How does your setup differ when Gov't Mule goes out?

AW: It's a different thing; my amp setup with the Brothers is geared toward a high fidelity sound; lots of power amps, preamps, high-end cabinets, plus one SVT cabinet that we use just for "dirt." Without the SVT, the sound would be *too* clean. But with Gov't Mule, it's all SVTs and Orange amps, and I've also been using the reissue Crossroad stacks; Bud Ross of Kustom fame made them. They're even rolled and pleated.

I used a 1967 EB-3 on the demos for the Gov't Mule record; when I found it, it had been painted flat black but Phil Jones at Gibson's Custom Shop fixed it up for me. Live, I use EB-3s as well; I have three or four EB-3s, five EB-0s, and two EB-1 "Pappalardi" models as well. I've got a '56 and a '71; the '56 is the better bass but the '71 is the one that goes out with me. I used a Hofner on "Temporary Saint" to get that real "Beatle-y" sound.

When we met with Michael Barbiero, the producer, he wanted to know what kind of a sound we wanted, and I said: "I want to sound like Felix Pappalardi." Michael smiled and said that it shouldn't be a problem. You see, Felix was Michael's *cousin*, and Michael was in the control room when Mountain recorded "Mississippi Queen!" If you look at the liner notes, you'll see that I thanked Felix Pappalardi posthumously.

Another thing that affected the Gov't Mule sound was the conversation I had with Tom Dowd, who was on the Brothers' tour bus when we were doing some live recordings. Everybody had gone to bed except Tom and me, and I was thinking: "Here's the man who engineered Cream records and produced Derek & the Dominoes later on." So I sat there and talked with him for hours and played him the Mule demos. Later, when we went to the studio, we elected to do some of the things Dowd told me he'd done in his earlier sessions, like the way the amps had been set up. We knew he was right. He would know, wouldn't he (chuckles)?

VG: Well, do you use medium-scale or long-scale basses at all with Gov't Mule?

AW: At times. The Thunderbird is something that I can always fall back on with either band. A lot of players consider a Fender Precision to be their "Holy Grail;" it seems like the Thunderbird is always my "landing pad." I know where I stand with it, I like the way they look, the way they feel, and the way they hang on me. I

also like the fact that not every Tom, Dick and Harry has one.

I also have a 5-string Les Paul prototype bass Gibson gave me last year. It looks like a big sunburst Les Paul, and it's a fine instrument. I play it all the time in both bands.

VG: I've got the feeling that you've been collecting for a long time.

AW: Yeah, the "bug" got me early; I started hanging out at Gruhn's when I was about 14, around the time George's store first opened. He had Flying Vs, Explorers, Sunbursts, pearly-top Martins; all of the fine stuff. By the time I was 20, he knew that I knew the guitars, and he offered me a job. I worked for him for some time; I'd get mad and quit then come back, then he'd get mad at me and fire me, then call me back. That happened four or five times (chuckles), but George and I are really tight. I worked a lot of guitar shows when I was with Gruhn's.

VG: And currently your collection numbers how many pieces?

AW: About 300 guitars, basses, mandolins and lap steels. I've got a lot of "David Lindley-type" instruments that are really cool. I collect jurangos, which have an armadillo shell for a back.

VG: I'm going to cite a couple of brands and models, and let you comment about each. First, Thunderbirds.

AW: I got my first Thunderbird from my mentor, George Gruhn. It was a non-reverse "IV" with double pickups and was gold. George told me it was the only gold one he'd ever seen. The headstock had been broken and professionally repaired; it was structurally sound for about five years then it came off again, and once again I got Phil Jones at Gibson to repair it; that guy's a wizard. He's made a lot of basses that I've used with the Brothers. I'd met Phil when we both worked at Gruhn's; we were both "pups" there. He repaired that Thunderbird so well that it's stronger than it was *before* it was broken. He's a genius.

I've got a Heather Poly Thunderbird that's somewhat of a hybrid. It seemed to be a '60s bass that had been outfitted with '80s electronics; now it's been modified with nickel Thunderbird pickups that Paul Chandler found for me. Phil Jones found some nickel tuners as well, and we found a nickel bridge somewhere. I've got one of two Korina Thunderbirds that Gibson's Custom Shop made a few years ago, and a Candy Apple Red Thunderbird with a black pickguard that's a prototype. There's two newer Thunderbirds; one black and one sunburst, and Epiphone has been making some new non-reverse Thunderbirds that are cool; I've got three of them.

VG: Alembic.

AW: In addition to the long-scale models I use live, I've got an 8-string model with a 32-inch scale; it used to belong to Rick Nielsen. I have a purple Stanley Clarke model, a long-scale fretless, a long-scale 5-string, a 20th Anniversary, and a John Entwistle-type, which is a Spoiler with an Explorer-shaped body.

VG: Unusual basses?

AW: There's the Modulus 18-string, and a bass that Jaco used to own; it's been authenticated. It's still got two strings on it, and I started to refurbish it, then I thought about how Leo Fender's workshop was sealed when he died, so I left Jaco's bass alone.

I'm using some Epiphone EB-2 copies a bit in the Mule; those things feel like an old Rivoli; they're pretty much "the real thing."

VG: What percentage of the basses in your collection are short-scale?

AW: Maybe 40 percent; the Hofner copies I discussed earlier include Apollos, which, come to think of it, are more like EB-l copies. I've got a Ventura fretless which is the only one I've ever seen, and an Eko.

Other short-scale basses include a Mosrite hollowbody, a Messenger bass like the guitar Mark Farner used to own, a Fender Mustang Bass and a Musicmaster, a Dan Armstrong fretless, a couple of Harmonys and a couple of Kays. I have a weird, short-scale American-made B.C. Rich that was custom-made for me; it's neck-through.

VG: Other than custom-made instruments, what do you think the rarest piece in your collection?

AW: (Pauses) Probably the Messenger bass, even though I've got other instruments that are worth a lot more. I don't know why it's so awe-inspiring, but it never ceases to amaze me how many people have heard of that brand and know about the instrument. It may have been ahead of its time; it had a metal neck that split into a tuning fork inside, but the instrument isn't tuned to the key of the tuning fork! I've got lots of old Gibsons and Fenders that would probably be considered collectible, but the Messenger is probably the one when it comes to just "rare."

VG: In terms of modern innovations, I saw an endorsement ad in *Bass Player* for KYDD basses, which is a stand-up fretless bass with a 30-inch scale.

AW: Those are made in Philadelphia; I needed something that I could consider to be an electric upright. I was never a legitimate upright bass player, and this seemed to be the best tool where someone like me could "cross over;" it's a real "friendly" instrument.

VG: How about the guitars in your collection?

AW: I have a really cool Rick 325 that's in the Tom Wheeler book, and a tulip-shaped Rick. There's a lot of Vox stuff, including a Mark XII and a Phantom. I've got a Gibson Moderne reissue, serial number 007, a cool, white Gibson double-neck, and a Chandler Les Paul-type guitar that has a 25 1/2" scale; it's beautiful. Paul also made me a neat little Firebird-type travel guitar.

There's one custom-made brand that I want to mention, the THCs made by Tom Holmes in Nashville. Billy Gibbons and I are big Bo Diddley fans, and Billy called me one day in the early '80s, wanting some Bo Diddley guitars; he said: "The square ones are easy to copy, but I want me one of them Cadillac-fin guitars!" We both knew one of those was on the cover of *Bo Diddley is a Gunslinger.* So I started looking around, and I found a record shop that had a copy of that album. Tom built some guitars for Billy and me; he also made me a matching bass. I've used those a good bit, and I've been thinking it would be fun if Warren and I used them as a matching set with Gov't Mule sometime in the future, because they're very "thick-sounding," "Cream-sounding" instruments. Tom also made square-shaped travel guitars for Billy and me.

Billy also gave me another guitar that he had custom-made for me; it's called the Coyote.

VG: Other fretted instruments?

AW: A Framus lap steel that's shaped like a rocket ship, and a Morrell 8-string, 9-pedal steel that used to belong to Little Roy Wiggins; I've got some Supro lap steels that I really like. One Silvertone I have looks like it was made by Gibson; it's got Gibson electronics in it.

I also have some electric mandolins, including a Fender electric that my mom and dad bought me in Nashville; it's a last-year-of-production model. I'd been on the road and wasn't home for Christmas; when I got home it was lying on my bed. It looked like a sunburst Strat that had been left out in the rain (laughs)! Remember when Precisions made in the mid-'70s had black pickguards instead of tortoise shell? That mandolin was made the same way; black pickguard, but a brown pickup. I had it in Gruhn's one day, just noodling around, and the store had a blond Fender mandolin that was 20 years older, but the serial numbers were three numbers apart! So I figured mine was one of the last made, and Fender must have run out of pickguards first, so they whipped up some black pickguards to finish things out.

I've got a Vox Mando-Guitar that still has the hang tags on it, a '56 Gibson Florentine electric in mint condition, a Blue Star 5-string Tele-type mandolin, and a Kent electric mandolin shaped like a Hofner Beatle Bass.

I also have a guitar that matches the Kent mandolin; Gov't Mule just did a track for a Hound Dog Taylor tribute album for Alligator Records. We were recording it in Macon, and I was going to play guitar instead of bass. My girlfriend and I were walking to the studio, and we went into a pawn shop to find a guitar for the session; I had Les Pauls down there but I wanted something *crummy*! Lo and behold, there sat a Kent guitar, and I gave $125 for it. I'm looking for a matching bass to complete the set. Actually, those mandolins were called "electric violas;" I think they were marketed like that.

VG: Future recording plans?

AW: We'll do another Mule album later this year, and I'd be surprised if we didn't go back to Bearsville Sound in Woodstock again, and I'd be more surprised if we didn't choose to use Michael Barbiero again.

As for the Allman Brothers, I'd be surprised if Tom Dowd wasn't at the helm for our next record; I'd be nervous if he *wasn't.* I think we'll record the next album live in the studio, as was the case with *Where It All Begins*; probably another sound stage environment.

VG: The last question is sort of a philosophical variant of the "desert island" type. Since you've got a lot of various instruments, what instrument would you like to have on a desert island if you could only have *one*? And if it was a bass, what scale would it be?

AW: (Pauses) Hmmm... you're making this difficult...

VG: Well, then let's fine-tune a bit and assume there wouldn't be any electricity on the island.

AW: (Pauses again) I'd probably want a Gibson B-45-12; they're great guitars. I could sit there, eat coconuts, and play Byrds tunes and songs from *A Hard Day's Night* (chuckles).

Allen Woody has the experience as a player and guitar lover (including his retail days) to have a keen perspective on music and fretted instruments. He's accomplished a lot in both fields, as his recorded work and his instrument collection aver, and he can also be proud of his accomplishments in both areas. Other players and guitar lovers should have it so good, yet most of 'em would readily give credit where credit's due. That Woody purveys a lot of great music is a bonus.

Richard Young

The Ultimate Danelectro Deal and Other Stories

Ask any knowledgeable fan of popular music about the, uh, "cosmetic attributes" of the Kentucky Headhunters, and one of the more polite responses you'll get will probably be along the lines of "They ain't no Duran Duran."

And thank goodness for that. The sideburns of drummer Fred Young are probably the first items cited concerning the 'Heads image, but his brother Richard's long curly, hair and hornrim glasses are also part of the "look."

Richard Young has been a Kentucky Headhunter since the "Itchy Brother days." In conversing with the other two fretted instrument players from the South Central area of the Bluegrass State, we got a great look at a band that's hung in there over the years in a long and arduous climb to success. Lead guitarist Greg Martin's 1992 interview discussed his love of tone and what instruments he uses to acquire his sounds, and bassist Anthony Kenney's interview (conducted prior to a 1994 concert, just as Richard Young's was) was a credible historical conversation with someone who's come full circle with the band. Accordingly, our conversation with Richard Young seemed to concentrate more on guitars, which suited him just fine, 'cause he's had a bunch of 'em:

TOP: *Greg and Richard doing their thing. Greg is playing a '68 Custom and Richard is playing the '63 Tele he got from Steve and Terry Wariner.*

RIGHT: *"A cool 1964 Stratocaster Greg leaves on the runnin' board of Fred's truck, so we can play it while we feed cows."*

VG: Was there any one individual or band that made you want to play in a band yourself?

RY: For me, it was Elvis Presley. I'd never seen anything like that before; of course, nobody else had either (chuckles)! I caught on to not just the music, but the sexual aspect of it as well. By that time I was already infatuated with guitars; I remember getting my grandmother's ukulele and pantomiming to Elvis and Les Paul & Mary Ford records.

I always felt like I had sort of an "insight" about what might be something new in music, and when I saw the Beatles on "Ed Sullivan," I *didn't* want to like them, because I loved Elvis, and I knew Elvis was in serious trouble (laughs)! I was only nine years old then, but I knew what was happening.

The thing that fascinated me about the Beatles, though, was their *instruments*. I know Elvis just had prop guitars, but I thought those Rickenbackers and McCartney's Hofner bass were really cool-looking. This is the twenty-fifth year of the band, and I think the idea of the *look* of guitars and other equipment, right down to the microphones, has been with us all along. We've all owned some good guitars and lost some good guitars.

VG: What was your first instrument?

RY: Some no-name instrument that I bought from a local guy for twenty-five dollars; he liked hot rods better than he liked guitars. It had a lime green pickguard on it; it was hard to play, and my second guitar was a dot inlay 335. Quite a jump up (laughs)! It was a '59; I didn't know what I had; my parents gave three hundred dollars for it. But I'll tell you a sad story: I made the one mistake I've ever made when it comes to trading guitars; I traded that 335 for a Univox hollowbody.

VG: (nonplussed): Good grief...

RY: That's the last time I made a stupid trade like that, but that's how you learn. That Univox didn't last long; I realized real quick I'd screwed up (chuckles). But I've always been constantly trading guitars; to some extent I was trying to find exactly the right kind of guitar for my style of playing. Around 1985 I finally realized it was the Telecaster.

After the Univox, I got a Gretsch with a candy-stripe pickguard. The store where I got the Gretsch was also the local Fender dealer,

and when they went out of business, I got all of their Fender paraphernalia; the leather-bound schematic book, decals, catalogs, wall banners; *anything* that had to do with Fender.

VG: You're primarily the rhythm guitarist for the band. Has that always been the case?

RY: Pretty much. You see, I've always concentrated on songwriting, and the guitar has been a way for me to express myself, and I've been through so many guitars because I've been trying to find one that not only is best for my style of playing, as I said a minute ago, but also that is the best for me to write songs with. After the Gretsch I got an old Goldtop Les Paul with soapbar pickups; that would still be a nice one to have today.

VG: What about the first high-quality, *new* guitar you ever bought?

RY: That would have been a 1980 Gibson Les Paul Heritage with the fancy top. Greg and I knew such guitars were out, and we worried a music store to death trying to get one for each of us. The Gibson rep had told the store the company was only going to make such guitars for players like Charlie Daniels. So we pestered the rep too, whenever we knew he was going to be in the store (laughs)! Somehow we talked both the store and the rep into ordering them for us.

When the guitar arrived, the store owner didn't open them up for us to inspect; he wrote "heads" and "tails" on one box each and flipped a coin.

He didn't want us arguing over the flame tops, so when we opened each one of ours up, Greg's was like a "Jimmy Page" flame top, and mine had a tiger-stripe, "Mick Taylor" top (chuckles). Ultimately I've had some other good pieces, like a '57 Strat and some old Rickenbackers; I've been through a lot of guitars.

VG: So how did your conclusion that the Telecaster is the best performance instrument for you come about?

RY: Around 1985, Steve Wariner's brother Terry was down at our practice house; I told him I wouldn't mind having a nice Telecaster, and it turned out he had one out in his car, which was a '65 Mustang.

I kept it for about six or eight months, and the Headhunters recorded the demos that ended up on *Pickin' On Nashville* during that time. I used that Tele on those sessions; the intro to "Walk Softly on This Heart of Mine" is that guitar. It's a great instrument.

It's a '63 Tele, and I found that Steve and Terry both owned it together. Finally Steve said he'd trade if I'd find him an 1800s Martin with a coffin case. I figured I'd never own that Tele, but the very next day my mom called me from an antique store, telling me she'd found a real old guitar with a weird-looking case. I got her to look inside, and sure enough, it said Martin. *Less than twenty fours after Steve laid down the law about what he wanted, I was on the phone telling him I had it* (laughs)! It was a one in a million thing. Actually, Steve had used the Tele on his first two albums, and if he really hadn't wanted to trade after I wouldn't have forced it.

The other main Telecaster I've used over the last several years is a 1952 one that Kevin Woods sold me for what he had in it; he had been a student of mine when I was teaching guitar, and

TOP LEFT: *A jam session at B.B. King's Club with some friends after playing the Helena Blues Fest. (Left to Right) Greg, James Lewis, Doug Phelps, Fred and Richard.*

TOP RIGT: *Don Everly and Young with Phil's old guitar.*

LEFT: *Richard at three with his first real guitar.*

Kevin was smart; he wanted to concentrate on learning how to play blues.

I've also got a '51 Esquire that I use a lot.

VG: How many instruments do you own these days?

RY: Probably fifteen; Robin guitars gave me a nice Ranger that I've been using a bit. The Roscoe company made me a nice Firebird-style instrument with a custom paint job that included the flag and the seal of the state of Kentucky. I've probably had a hundred and fifty guitars total.

Right now I've got a Gibson "Lucille" that I really like a lot, but I'd really like to have a good old 335 or 345 that resonates real good. I wouldn't even mind having a 330, 'cause the body's lighter; it's sort of the poor man's 335.

VG: Of all the guitars that you've been through, are there any instruments, particularly from the Itchy Brother days, that you have fond memories of?

RY: Yeah; I had a double-cutaway, banana-colored Les Paul Special, and a red double-cutaway Les Paul Jr. Probably my all-time favorite guitar from the Itchy Brother days was a 1959 355 Stereo; man, what I wouldn't give to have that back (chuckles)! Let me back up a minute; when I said earlier I've had over a hundred and fifty guitars, that was about instruments I used in the band; overall I've probably had over four hundred if you include the ones I've collected; when it comes to collecting I've always been trading, buying and selling. Another outstanding guitar I had one time was a black '54 Les Paul Custom.

VG: You've been on a Gibson poster, but you're currently a Fender endorser.

RY: Everybody knows there's enough difference in the brands to where you can like them both. The Gibson on the poster has a 1968 neck but a 1954 body. Since 1985 I've basically been a Fender guy as an individual preference; the Gibson poster was a *band* project.

The Telecaster is simply a better rhythm guitar for me in concert. If I was to use one of my Les Pauls, and Greg was doing his thing on *his* Les Paul, it'd sound almost "too ferocious" (laughs)!

VG: What about amplifiers?

RY: In Itchy Brother I used a Marshall half-stack most of the time. Around 1980 I went to Fender Supers and Pros; I "retired" those to the studio about three years ago and began using '59 Bassman reissues that our tech Steve Wilson modified. He used to work for Stevie Ray Vaughan, and when he gets through working on those Bassman reissues, they're not like anything you've ever heard.

I *have* had some cool old amps; the coolest tweed amp I've had over the years was a three-ten Bandmaster. I found it at an auction one Saturday night; the auctioneer was using it as the P.A. system (chuckles)!

VG: As a player who's primarily a rhythm guitarist instead of a lead guitarist, have you listened to different players compared to who lead players might listen to?

RY: Not really, but there are so many players I've heard over the years that I thought were fantastic players who never got to the level of recognition like Clapton and Page did. Players like Rory Gallagher, for instance; I saw him in Bowling Green, Kentucky playing that beat-up old Strat of his through a small Vox amp sit-ting on a chair. Mel Galley from Trapeze and Tommy Bolin are a couple of other examples.

VG: Other than trading that 335 for a Univox, any other "nightmare" stories?

RY: (chuckles) In 1990, we were on tour with Hank Williams Jr.; he had a guitar that Gibson had made for him that he *worshiped*. Actually, he had *three* of them, but one got stolen and he accidentally broke one. We were opening for him one night, and at the end of our set I was goofing around and accidentally broke the neck on that third guitar. The next day nobody in the band would even get near me, 'cause they knew Hank was going to kill me. That night, we'd already opened for Hank, and he was onstage playing piano by himself; I think this was in Milwaukee in front of maybe 20,000 people. Suddenly he stopped and called me back out onstage; I went out and sat down on the piano stool next to him. He told the audience: "This sumbitch broke my favorite guitar last night; what do y'all think I oughta do about that?" I was afraid the audience would yell "Lynch him!" (laughs), but he told me not to do it no more, like I'd learned my lesson ...of course, he didn't have any of them left anyway (laughs)! Later on in the same performance he demolished some other guitar, and he told me that no guitar was worth what friendship is, and I've always admired him for saying that, because he knew how bad I felt.

VG: Do you do any lead guitar work in performance?

RY: I do a bit on one song, but I realized as early as sixteen that I was going to be a better rhythm player than lead player; I'd broken my thumb and the way it healed meant I couldn't quite get a vibrato off the neck like it needed to be done, so I developed my style as rhythm player in a way that would enhance Greg's work. When I do play lead, I'm strictly a blues-based player; no heavy rock and roll for me. Three strings, nine notes, that's it (chuckles)!

VG: To sum up, what was the best deal you ever got in all of your collecting experience?

RY: This sounds almost too good to be true, but the rest of the band knows it's a fact. One day I was driving into town past a group of older houses called Red Row; they used to be homes but now they're small businesses like washeterias and appliance repair shops. Hanging out in front of a refrigerator repair place was a Danelectro Longhorn six-string bass; I mean, the sun was shining on it and it was "glowing;" it was like some religious experience! I stopped the car and asked the guy what he wanted for it and he said "Ten dollars."

I said "I'll give you five." To this day I feel a bit of regret because he actually took it (chuckles).

When interviewing more than one member of a particular band, sometimes it helps to diversify the line of questioning, in an obvious attempt to avoid potential redundancy. That Richard Young chose to regale *VG* with guitar-collecting anecdotes made his interview all the more fun, and the subject matter was something with which famous and not-so-famous guitar collectors and enthusiasts could identify.

The 'Heads went through more personnel changes; Mark Orr departed, and Doug Phelps returned.

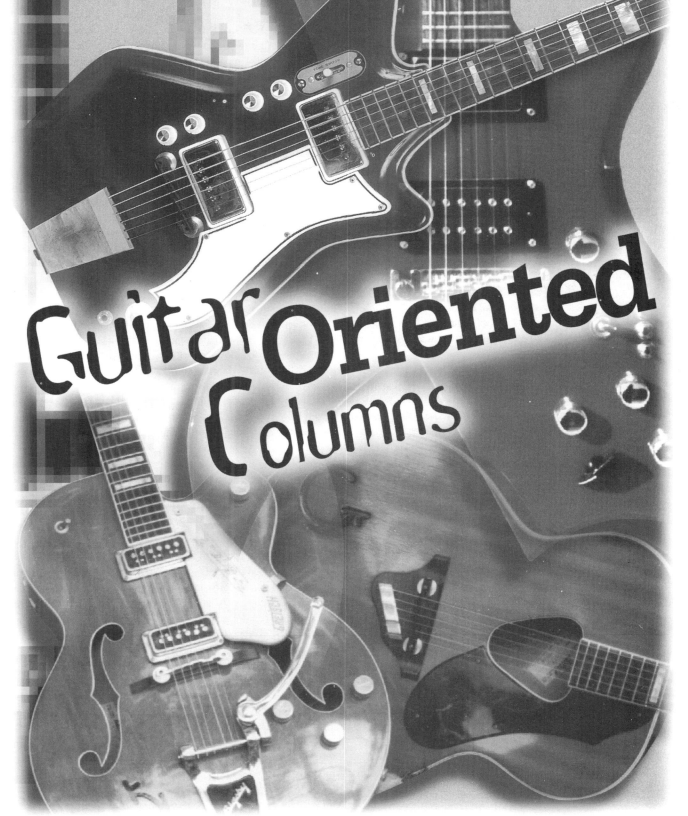

Guitar Oriented Columns

Valco photo by Mike Tamborrino. Fender Percission Bass photo by Ryan Stauffer. B.C. Rich Bich photo by Rick Hogue. Gretsch 6120 and 6022 photo by David J. Walsh.

"I Don't Trust Any Instrument That's Shaped Like A Medieval Weapon"

The title of this essay is in quote marks on accounta I betcha it describes the stereotypical attitude a lot of Boomer collectors might have in

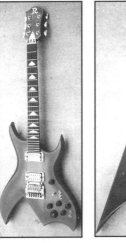

their quest for guitars; such individuals would probably be more interested in a Danelectro-made guitar that was hanging in a vintage store or pawn shop rather than some strange-looking B.C. Rich, Dean or Jackson instrument, even if one of the latter brands was U.S.-made.

Nevertheless, every once in a while I'll encounter U.S.-made, angular-shaped instruments in pawn shops that I go into from time to time. Of course, there are far more *imported* guitars with weird aesthetics in such business establishments than domestic-made ones, and some of 'em have an originally-American brand name on their headstocks (B.C. Rich's "NJ" series is an obvious example). Yet I'll admit that a clean Silvertone "amp-in-the-case" instrument would probably grab my attention more easily than a modernistic style and brand would, so count me in as fitting the stereotype myself.

Younger cynics might sneer: "Oh, yeah? Whaddabout Explorers and Flying Vs?" Those styles are historically important, of course, and I think it's important to note that Gibson met with limited success on such instruments for many, many years; not just the late Fifties originals, but subsequent reissues of such shapes as well ("Medallion" Vs, '76 mahogany Explorers, etc.). My perception is that Gibson really didn't get back into the modernistic guitar-making game until Ibanez copies got a lot of attention (Ibanez's "Rocket Roll," "Destroyer" and whatever the Moderne copy was called were first marketed in the mid-Seventies), followed by the advent of a couple of the aforementioned American manufacturers. Are there really that many *regular production* Gibson Explorers and Flying Vs from the

Seventies out there? I've examined the Gibson shipping total records from that decade in Tom Wheeler's *American Guitars*, and which Explorers and Vs were limited editions isn't designated (custom orders ain't either), but I suspect the majority of the modernistic guitars made by Gibson in the Seventies didn't roll through the factory on regular production runs as frequently as they did in the Eighties, and as they do these days.

At any rate, here's a trio of "medieval weapon" guitars I've encountered recently in area pawn shops. I looked at 'em a bit closer than I might have had there been a Sixties instrument in the same stores, and each one had some unique things going for it.

1989 B.C. RICH "BICH": Actually, I think this one has some extra designation for it like "Custom" or whatever. There's even a bit of controversy concerning whether or not it's domestic or imported; two sources I checked offered opposing opinions. It's got a sort of cherry sunburst finish with iridescent purple edges; seems like somebody told me the name of the finish but I forgot what it's called (B.F.D.). According to one source the gold hardware (Grover Imperial tuners and a Kahler vibrato; the handle was missing) is a plus, as are the "cloud"-shaped fret markers. Obviously, this guitar is a techno-geek's delight, with six knobs (the largest of which is a multi-position rotary gizmo), six toggle switches, and active circuitry that requires *two* 9-volt batteries. That's probably the main reason I wouldn't be interested in such a guitar: Show me some instrument that has more than Volume and Tone controls on it and I'll break out in a cold sweat.

JACKSON RANDY RHOADS: I dunno the year model, but it's a U.S.-made one that has all the desirable features on it that young metalheads want (according to a young metalhead with whom I spoke), including a bound neck, "shark fin" mother-of-pearl inlays, and some of the biggest frets I've seen (and played). A player I know who's in his forties also tried out the instrument, and raved about how comfortable the neck was. It's surprisingly balanced, and was in near-mint condition when I found it in a small pawn shop in southern Alabama.

TOP (Left to right):
1989 B.C. Rich Bich. Jackson Randy Rhoads Circa 1978 B.C. Rico (imported).

CIRCA 1978 B.C. RICO: No, that's not a typo; this guitar does indeed have "B.C. Rico" on its headstock instead of "B.C. Rich." It's based on the "Mockingbird" frame, and according to Michael Wright, who writes *VG*'s "The Different Strummer" column, it's a "pretty rare" instrument that was among the first guitars imported by Bernie Rico; the name difference was an attempt to avoid confusion with B.C. Rich brand instruments. As it's the only one I've ever seen with such a brand name, I did a bit of a double take when I spotted it, and I bet a lot of guitar enthusiasts would have a similar reaction.

Not long ago, an owner of a vintage store I was visiting took me back into his warehouse and got me to try out a now-discontinued Robin "Wedge" guitar. The aesthetics of this model would probably be considered laughable to most observers: Imagine a Flying V body that had been pulled in opposite directions until the angle between the two sides is about ninety degrees. The Wedge body is that shape, and it's been sorta sculpted to where it resembles a "chevron" (for lack of a better term). The guitar's neck pokes out of the right side of the chevron if one is looking at front of the guitar. Ludicrous? Maybe when it comes to looks, but I was astounded at how comfortable the guitar was; my right arm rested on left-side-facing "wing" just exactly the way it does whenever I play an Explorer, and the neck felt great; it was a marvelous instrument, and the dealer's "I told you so" attitude was absolutely on target.

So while many of the more modern-looking guitars are fine pieces when it comes to craftsmanship and playability, their aesthetics simply ain't interesting to this mid-forties casual player. It remains to be seen whether instruments such as these will become collectibles in the future; if some of 'em do, then their designers will have had the last laugh, just as the designers of the original Fifties Explorers and Flying Vs have.

But if I ever see some guy my age onstage with his weekend nostalgia band, and he's whomping out the intro to Sam and Dave's "Soul Man" on a Dean ML, the scenario will be probably strike me as being somewhat silly.

Why I'm a Chump for Valco-made Instruments

"They're definitive examples of classic Americana from the Fifties and Sixties."

Um....well, okay, so that's the first reason, I guess; the reason it's in quote marks is because a dealer said this to me when he was trying to sell me a Valco-made product in late 1991. His pitch worked, as I purchased the instrument a couple of months after I'd seen it at the Arlington show in October, and that particular instrument was the first I bought from a vintage guitar dealer. I called him right after Christmas and he still had the instrument, so we cut a deal that was satisfactory to both of us.

I haven't forgotten the aforementioned "Americana" pitch by the dealer, and that observation really encompasses a lot of different facets concerning Nationals, Supros, and house brands (most of which are Montgomery Ward's Airline brand, from what I've seen) made by the odd duck of Chicago-area budget instrument manufacturers. I've been making a list of reasons why I find Valco-made products so appealing; while several might fit under a "blanket statement" such as that dealer's remark, I think they need to be cited individually, along with some others:

2. AESTHETICS (BODY STYLES): Find another manufacturer from those times that made map-shaped guitars and basses, instruments with two pickguards, angular, asymmetrical body styles, and "Gumby"-shaped headstocks ...and don't forget the "Folkstar" Res-O-Glas resonator guitar (Hyulk!).

3. AESTHETICS (ELECTRONICS): Weird placement of controls, plus the "Silversound" bridge pickup; the exposed wire which runs from the bridge into the body has all the visual appeal of a worm in an apple, but such items are so blatant and unique that they ultimately end up as amenities, in my opinion.

4. CONSTRUCTION: Obviously, I'm referring more to Res-O-Glas instruments instead of wood-bodied Valcos, and other guitar writers have detailed the early Sixties molded fiberglass and resin Valcos elsewhere, so I won't get redundant here. However, even though I'm an advocate of ethics, if a pawn shop had a Res-O-Glas guitar and thought it was a plastic-bodied toy, I'd let him keep thinking such in an effort to get a good deal on the instrument.

5. COMMENDABLE FEATURES: Including a zero fret on most guitars, and pickups that are usually loud as hell. A few years ago I wrote about a wood-bodied Supro Dual-Tone I encountered that had louder and "grungier"-sounding pickups than a white 1963 Gibson SG Special I came across around the same time. Playing other Valco-made guitars since then has bolstered my opinion.

6. ECONOMICS: Valco-made instruments are usually much lower-priced than many other brands from the same era; my perception is they tend to be lumped in with the likes of Harmony and Kay guitars, which is understandable due to the "Chicago budget manufacturer" association, in many folks' opinions.

7. THREE-QUARTER SIZE GUITARS: It seems like a proportionally larger number of 3/4-size electrics made by Valco are around; if someone wanted to experiment with such a scale or start his/her child off on an guitar of that size, a Supro or Airline might be worthy of consideration ...not to mention

easier on the financial investment.

Here's another Valco-made house brand guitar besides Airline that is perhaps a definitive example of their 3/4-scale instruments. This 1959 Oahu looks like a younger sibling of a Super Dual Tone, and it's got gold hardware (including Kluson Deluxe tuners!).

8. JUST WHEN YOU THINK YOU'VE SEEN EVERYTHING THE COMPANY HAD TO OFFER, YOU'LL COME ACROSS AN-OTHER WEIRD GUITAR: I encountered both of the Supros shown here at 1993 guitar shows, and hadn't seen one like either of them up to that point. The white solidbody is a Res-O-Glas instrument (how many were made with a Fender-ish shaped body?) with a small Bigsby plus fancier fretboard inlays that were usually found on upper-end (for the company) National instruments. The thinline has three pickups and a control arrangement that I've not seen on an-other Valco instrument.

To sum up, let me point out a couple of things that I always examine when I plug in a Valco-made electric. First, I always tinker with the tone control on the bridge pickup (if the instru-ment has more than one pickup). It appears that Valco put a capacitor or capacitors on their bridge pickups that may have been too strong (or whatever the electronics term is) or incom-patible with the pickup; the point is, if you're like most players that prefer the tone control

on your bridge pickup at full treble, a Valco pickup will sound very thin. Rolling the tone control almost all the way over to full bass will increase the volume dramatically without re-ally affecting the tone, believe it or not, so be sure to try that procedure before you decide the bridge pickup is shot.

Another point of inspection is an attempt to determine if the instrument was made during the final years of Valco's existence (they went out of business in 1968). Quite frankly, most of the instruments from the company's latter days that I've come across are quite shoddy in their quality and construction; it also appears that some of the instruments had imported parts. In particular, the solidbody guitars from Valco's final days are not appealing at all, due to the almost haphazard workmanship. There are some exceptions, but the stereotype is pretty accurate, based on what I've encoun-tered ...maybe that's why a lot of those gui-tars are priced in the $100-200 range at guitar shows.

In his fine book about National resonator in-struments, Bob Brozman explains in his intro-duction why he opted to end his research with that brand name with the World War II era in-struments; he states that a person who loves post-War Nationals that were made all the way up until the Sixties should write a book about such instruments, and let me add an "Amen" to his challenge. Valco-made guitars have a unique (if cheezy) position in the annals of American guitar history, and I think they're such weird and cool instruments that I'll buy such a book right when it's released; hell, I'll put a "pre-publication" deposit on such a book (which I've never done before).

More than one experienced exhibitor I've talked with at major guitar shows has acknowl-edged that he has a fondness for Valco electrics and has a collection of Res-O-Glas instruments. Moreover, another veteran vintage dealer told me he's noticed prices of Valco-made Nation-als creeping up somewhat due to the name asso-ciation with National resonator instruments from the 1920s and 1930s. About the only thing those guitars and Valcos have in common is the name, so that's an intriguing phenomenon.

And that's all the more reason somebody oughta write a Valco book. Save me a signed copy!

Those Sesational Seventies Instruments!....Uh, Howzat Again???

MTV is still de-programmed from our television, but the cable-ready VCR we own doesn't have a "CHANNEL ADD/DELETE" feature (I don't imagine many VCRs do). Late one night while battling insomnia, I ended up channel surfing through the VCR's tuner, and when I happened to land on MTV, a video by grunge phenoms Nirvana was just beginning.

The tune was called "Lithium;" it was a brutal and brilliant song of the stop-and-start variety, alternating between reflective musings and slash-and-burn power chords. It was basically a performance clip that like all too many videos jumps from image to image in a willy-nilly manner (it would've bothered the Missus's astigmatism *bad*).

Towards the end of the video the band pulled a Who, smashing their instruments. It appeared that the perpetually p.o.'ed Kurt Cobain was trashing some left-handed, no-name Strat clone, while Chris Novoselic was actually shown demolishing more than one bass. Some frames showed him with a Gibson RD-style instrument, while other images offered the silhouette of a Grabber/G-3/Ripper-type bass; Gibson introduced both styles in the 1970s.

Uh-oh.

A general stereotype that seems to be pervasive in the vintage guitar business is that American-made guitars from the Seventies usually aren't all that desirable due to a decline in quality by some of the major manufacturers, and/or that era heralded the advent of some oddball models that bombed back then and *still* aren't all that interesting to many guitar aficionados.

True, the Seventies gave us such oft-maligned instruments as three-bolt/"bullet" truss rod Fenders and Gibson electrics with bolt-on necks, but to what extent such guitars and basses deserve to be excoriated is debatable, in my opinion. The major manufacturers were apparently trying to introduce new innovations and capture a larger portion of the market share, and the marketing philosophy of major *importers* must have changed in the latter part of that decade as well, as many of them begin to introduce their own body styles instead of continuing to produce cheaper copies of classic American guitar styles (I once owned a late-Seventies Ibanez Artist with an ash body and abalone inlay; it was a great instrument).

At any rate, Seventies instruments made by major manufacturers have gotten a nominal amount of press in *VG* (primarily in Michael Wright's "Different Strummer"), and I've had some veterans in the guitar business assert that the construction ideas behind some of the aforementioned models ultimately might have some merit after all. One salesman I know claims that for all the hype about three-bolt Fenders not conducting vibrations through the neck/body joint as well as four-bolt Fenders do, "you can't tell the difference without an oscilloscope." That's an exact quote from him, and he's in a position to know.

There are, however, other Seventies instruments made by less-famous and/or then-fledgling manufacturers that can be had for a pittance these days. "Maybe there's a reason for that," sneered Malc, "Ovation electrics don't fetch **** in the vintage market." Maybe so, but at least the manufacturer (and others like Ovation) were trying to develop and market a desirable product. I submit for your consideration two Seventies electrics that I recently found, which are unusual enough to merit the interest of some budding vintage guitar enthusiasts:

1972 OVATION 1235-5 "ECLIPSE: The only time I've ever heard any vintage dealers even *mention* specific Ovation solidbody guitars was a few years ago when the ergonomically-correct Klein instruments were introduced; more than one dealer noted that the Klein guitars resembled Ovation Deacons and Breadwinners. Can't say that I've seen such Ovations escalate in interest or price, however; almost every Ovation solidbody I see at shows (Deacons, Breadwinners, or otherwise) seems to remain on its stand the entire show despite a price of around $200.

The 1235-5 "Eclipse" thinline model preceded Ovation solidbody models, and it's also the inspiration for Malc's previously-noted sardonic comment. Ovation marketed an entire "Storm" series of thinline electrics with names like "Typhoon," "Thunderhead," etc., and such instruments had German bodies. The "Eclipse" was the last of the original thinline instrument styles; approximately nine hundred were made to use up the remaining bodies. The entire guitar had a black, textured finish; it appears to be a "stealth thinline," for lack of a better term.

However, the Eclipse I found had very potent pickups; they're among the strongest I've heard on production instruments without active circuitry. The frets are tiny and the neck is quite fast (I think the fretboard is ebony); for what my opinion's worth, this would make a fine guitar for playing in some seedier blues joints if someone wanted to leave his/her Gibson ES-335 (or equivalent instrument) at home.

1979 KRAMER MODEL 450 BASS: Is this the model Tim Bogert was referring to in his 1993 interview in *VG*? Could be; almost all of the aluminum-neck Kramer basses I've encountered have been too neck-heavy, but this one had a sorta down-sized P-bass body style like Bogert described. I tried it out with a wide strap, and it does seem to be a bit more balanced than a stereotypical Kramer bass from those times.

The unique feature of that bass, however, was its "sissy lines." It had a lined-fretless Ebonol board, enabling a player to evoke bass trombone licks at will while being able to tell what the hell he/she is doing. Some purists might get uppity about lines on a fretless bass, equating such markings to training wheels on a bicycle, but so what? This instrument represents a relatively economical way to introduce oneself to the wonderful world of Jaco wanna-bees.

So these two instruments are somewhat unique when it comes to their aesthetics as well as their sound, yet they're still quite affordable as used instruments. I already know of one or two collectors who are seeking to acquire various Ovation electrics; I haven't met any collectors whose specialty is aluminum-neck Kramers ...*yet*.

A *VG* research article on Gibson's RD series (which was introduced in 1977) opined that the odd-shaped, short-lived series might ultimately have been Gibson's "Edsel," for lack of a better term.

Accordingly, Ovation electrics and aluminum-neck Kramers from the Seventies might one day be considered by guitar collectors as the stringed instrument equivalents of automobiles such as the Nash, Henry J., or Corvair.

But don't hold yer breath, bubba.

In Memory of the Organization Man

Sometimes a simple business procedure can unintentionally result in some potentially awkward circumstances, and such was the case when Forrest White passed away in late 1994.

Around the first of November my family moved into our new home in the country; we'd been planning this for years, and part of the transition included the acquisition of a local post office box, then letting the appropriate persons know that I could now be contacted directly about the writing I do for *VG*. Several dozen notices were printed on new stationery and mailed to guitar companies, public relations firms, etc. I also mailed a few of them to certain individuals whom I'd interviewed in the past. The mailing was done the first week of December, and one of the form letters in the "previous interviewee" category went to Forrest's address in Banning, California. I had no way of knowing he'd crossed the way in late November.

I don't recall when and where I heard of *The Organization Man*. I don't know if the title is that of a book, play, or movie (or maybe it's more than one of those things). If it's a book, I don't know if it's a novel or a textbook, and for all I know the subject matter could be about either business or anthropology; I simply recall the title.

The point is, I more or less applied that title/phrase/moniker to Forrest White (even before he died) in my own personal opinion as to how he figured into the history of the California guitar manufacturing business.

And Forrest looked the part of an "organization man." He wasn't the tall, dashing figure like many of the musicians he admired during the Golden Days of California guitar-making; in perusing the many historical photos (in his own book and others; more about those later), he looks like a stereotypical accountant from those times.

Forrest wasn't the first "pre-CBS" Fender personality I had the privilege of interviewing. That distinction belongs to Bill Carson, whose interview was subtitled "Chuck Yeager of the Stratocaster" (more about the Edwards AFB connection later as well). Carson's interview was a stroke of luck; less than a year after I'd begun writing for *VG* I happened to be in a town where the local Fender dealer was a vintage guitar buff; he advised that his Fender rep, Bill Carson, was going to be in his store the next day, so l pounced on that opportunity and was rewarded with my initial contact (and interview) with an individual who "was there" during the times that so many vintage guitar lovers want to know about; the quest for history concerning guitars and amplifiers appears to be insatiable, particularly if it involves the recollections of someone with firsthand experience.

Ten months later I flew to California (between a change in "day jobs") to tour some guitar factories, and I also hoped to make some contacts with other historically-important guitar people to arrange more interviews (if not while I was in the Golden State, by telephone at a later date). I'll always be grateful to the redoubtable Ron Middlebrook of Centerstream Publications; with his help I was able to contact Forrest, who agreed to meet me the next day at the residential development where he and his wife resided. Banning, California is about seventy-five miles from the Fullerton area, but it was quite convenient for me; since I was staying with the Lifers out in Moreno Valley I had only a twenty-minute drive east on the freeway to get to the development's clubhouse. So Forrest's interview came off while I was in California — it too was a matter of fortunate timing, as was the case with Bill Carson. Some readers may have noticed that I've been referring to Forrest by his first name; that's because I'd only called him "Mr. White" a couple of times at the outset of our Banning conversation before he told me to call him Forrest.

My perception in this initial face-to-face encounter with Forrest was that he was someone who was intense about business efficiency, regardless of who his employer might have been. His recollections were straightforward; his responses to my questions immediate. Forrest didn't fumble around for an answer; he had one ready for you.

There is one "now-it-can-be-told" anecdote that I need to mention: During my quest to locate historical interviewees, one Fender employee in Brea had told me that Forrest was writing a book about his experiences. I figured this would be an appropriate inquiry for his interview, but when I broached the subject, Forrest grew quite concerned and asked me to keep that bit of information confidential, which I did; nevertheless I knew that the book's title was *Fender: The Inside Story* about three years before it was published in 1994.

A bit of irony that was noted at the conclusion of Forrest's interview deserves to be cited again here: Our conversation took place on May 25, 1991, exactly forty years to the day from when Leo Fender took a photograph of Forrest with his hand-built steel guitar; that photo not only appeared in *Vintage Guitar*, it's in *Fender: The Inside Story* as well.

I'm sure Forrest was delighted to see the growth of interest in vintage instruments over the years, and he was proud of his own involvement. Such pride was evidenced by the fact that he attended all three of the Pomona guitar shows that were staged while he was alive; the Fifties Fender bowling team shirt he wore to the August 1993 show ended up on display in the Leo Fender exhibit at the Fullerton Museum Center. Another bit of irony (albeit sad) is that during our last conversation (when he called to inquire if I'd gotten my signed copy of *Fender: The Inside Story*), he noted that he was looking forward to signing copies of the book at the August 1994 Pomona show. As it turned out, the promoters didn't present California shows in the summer of 1994, opting instead to stage a show on the East Coast, which was the one area of the country where they'd wanted to go but hadn't done so until that opportunity came about.

Some aspects of Forrest's recollections in his book are bound to be controversial. Rather than attempt to ascertain who's right and who's wrong about "how it really happened" in the history of fretted instruments (not just Fender, but other brands as well), I try to keep an open mind, and I read anything and everything I can about such subjects. I make note of the different perspectives, and I remind myself that usually such individuals were part of a corporate whole that had the same goal back then.

The point is, ain't nobody gettin' any younger, and I'm glad Forrest White took the time and effort to publish his memoirs. I suppose if Bill Carson was a "test pilot" for the Stratocaster during the Fifties (the decade that represents the halcyon days of both the California guitar-manufacturing business as well as Edwards AFB), Forrest was a "logistics commander" of sorts. He may not have played guitars for a living, but his efforts in manufacturing for more than one famous brand (not to mention the growth of Fender during his tenure) are an admirable legacy. I'm glad we got to know each other.

Everything You've Always Wanted in a Strat...and More?

Not so long ago, an "Executive Rock" column titled "Those Sensational Seventies Instruments!...Uh, Howzat Again?" cited a couple of bargain-priced instruments from that oft-maligned decade as worthy of consideration by fledgling collectors. The guitars were an Ovation 1235-5 "Eclipse" thinline and a Kramer model 450 fretless bass (with "sissy lines" on its Ebonol board).

I find it somewhat interesting that Music Man guitars from that decade also seem to be available at quite reasonable prices in the vintage market these days; there just doesn't seem to be that much interest in 'em, and that strikes me as odd, for a number of reasons.

Recently I encountered the late Seventies Music Man Sabre I shown here in an area pawn shop, and I took it upon myself to compare it point-by-point with a 1979 four-bolt Fender Stratocaster in a thoroughly non-professional manner (i.e., this ain't no "shoot-out" like what might be found in *Guitar Player*). The "points" listed here (in no particular order, except for the first one) could also be interpreted as reasons that such guitars ought to be more interesting than they seem to be:

1. First and foremost, the Sabre I is indeed a guitar "by Leo Fender," but that's not to say that the '79 Strat *isn't*. The saga of the Stratocaster's development has been well-documented, but CBS had owned Fender for almost a decade and a half when the '79 Stratocaster was manufactured; Leo was long gone. However, Leo's CLF Research company did indeed build this Sabre I for Music Man.

2. An initial reaction by guitar players might favor the four-bolt Strat over the three-bolt Sabre I, but the Sabre I has George Fullerton's patented three-bolt neck joint as discussed in Mr. Fullerton's interview in *Vintage Guitar* in late 1991.

3. The Sabre I has an extra fret.

4. The Stratocaster feels a mite more comfortable to my left arm than the Sabre I. Seems like I'm reaching a bit farther out on the Music Man's neck.

5. Sabre guitars came in two models, the "I" and the "II." The only difference was the neck radius, and a player was made aware of the choice in Music Man catalogs.

6. The pickup configurations are quite different, of course. If you've always wanted a Strat with humbuckers, the Sabre I is a viable alternative; it seems like I'm always hitting the middle pickup on a Strat, so there's a "klutz" factor for me as well...

7. In spite of the Strat having three pickups to the Sabre I's two (and the Strat has a five-position

'78 Music Man Sabre I.

'80 G&L F-100.

toggle switch), this Music Man is more versatile than one might think, since it's got active circuitry. It has two mini-toggles, one of which is a phase switch that works no matter where the pickup switch is set, and the other mini-toggle is a bright boost switch that almost seems to be a volume boost; it fooled me until I read some factory literature.

8. Most Strats have a vibrato arm. Most Sabres don't, from what I can determine.

9. The control knobs on the Sabre I make more sense to me. Like a Strat, the volume knob is the closest to the bridge, but the other two controls are separate bass and treble controls that work for both pickups (instead of a Tone control for each pickup).

10. The Music Man's active circuitry also makes the Sabre I the loudest guitar I've ever heard. If gain/punch is your thing, this guitar is the fretted instrument equivalent of Mike Tyson!

Some weeks after I did the side-by-side comparison between the Strat and the Sabre, I found an early G&L F-100 solidbody that is remarkably similar to the Music Man Sabre guitar. According to *VG* contributor Paul Bechtoldt (who has written some research articles on Music Man and G&L), the Sabre and this F-100 are "practically the same instrument." The main differences with the G&L are adjustable pickup polepieces, no active circuitry (although Bechtoldt asserts that not all CLF-made Sabres had active circuitry), and

a slightly different control system (including a coil tap switch instead of a bright boost switch).

As of this writing I haven't had an opportunity to do a point-by-point comparison between the Sabre and the F-100 (seems like it would be a bit redundant, and the results would probably be a "draw," for lack of a better term), but I have been allowed to pop the neck on both instruments. The F-100's neck and body dates are from the Fall of 1980; curiously, the Sabre's neck date is from 1976, but Sabres weren't introduced until 1978, according to Bechtoldt, who sent me copies of catalogs from that time. So it appears that the earlier Music Man Sting Ray guitars and Sabres had the same neck specs.

I honestly believe the stories that California guitar manufacturing veterans have told me about how Leo Fender was always trying to improve his products; that he was never satisfied. It's my opinion that CLF Research-made Music Man guitars and basses, as well as "pre-Leo" G&L instruments (meaning guitars and basses made prior to Fender's death in 1991) are ample proof of such an effort, even if they don't command top dollar in the vintage market (at least for now). I'm not saying that this Sabre I or this F-100 are superior to a Stratocaster from the same time period; my feeling is that CLF Research-made Music Mans and pre-Leo G&Ls will eventually become much more appreciated than they were during their time, but such an increase in appreciation doesn't seem to have happened yet.

In Praise Of Incongruous Gretsches

Over twenty-five years ago, one of the umpteen high school-age garage bands in my town upgraded their equipment in a big way, trading their "entry level" (although the term probably didn't exist back then) guitars, amps and drums for some quality stuff, and when their lead guitarist showed up onstage with a Gretsch Country Gentleman plugged into a Fender Super Reverb amp, he immediately acquired a level of respect among other players that was higher than it had been before, simply because he now owned some respectable equipment. Whether his talent was improved one iota was irrelevant to other guitarists (I think he'd previously owned a Fender Mustang and a Silvertone Twin Twelve amp, which was still a better rig back then than many folks had); players from other bands would show up at YMCA dances where the Soul Division was playing just to ogle their setup, including the new Gretsch.

Y'see, garage band participants knew that the Gretsch brand signified something different from upgrade models of more popular brands (Fender Stratocasters, Gibson ES-335s, etc.). I'd bet the stereotypical initial reaction someone might have had whenever they heard the Gretsch brand name mentioned was to think of Chet Atkins and then maybe George Harrison. Atkins wasn't whomping out chord-based rock and roll like most garage bands were doing, but most garage band guitarists knew that Chet Atkins was a master of his craft, so maybe the Atkins/Gretsch name association signified a lot of class to teenage players back then, even though most of them didn't play like Atkins and couldn't afford Gretsch guitars.

Jay Scott's long-awaited Gretsch book was an informative read; I never knew Gretsch made "so many weird and wonderful models" (to borrow a line from the redoubtable Randy Bachman, who most likely has the largest Gretsch collection in the world). I'm no literary critic, but one thing I wish Scott had done differently concerns models such as the Beast, Committee, etc. Most guitar enthusiasts will agree with Scott's assertion that such models aren't desirable and are polar opposites from the classic New York styles, but I wish he had listed *and* shown some photos of those types of models, simply to authenticate which models aren't desirable. It would certainly help to have something in print to let some folks such as pawn shop owners know that everything with a Gretsch name on its headstock isn't necessarily a collector's item. Other than that, I think Scott's book is a definitive work, for what my opinion's worth.

Yet every once in a great while I'll happen to encounter one of the older examples of Gretsch guitars in an area pawn shop; most of the time they were models such as the thinline, single-cutaway Clipper (Scott uses the term "cheapo" in his book in describing this model) or the solidbody Corvette (which was also a low-priced model). I can count the number of times I've been made aware of an "above-entry-level" Gretsch guitar that had come out-of-pawn on one hand, and I've been on the road as a traveling salesman for over twenty years.

And two instruments that would count as examples of "above-entry-level" Gretschs for sale in pawn shops are shown here, but before I detail each one, lemme explain what I mean in the title about "incongruous" Gretsch guitars:

I've already noted some of the things that guitar enthusiasts would most likely agree make the Gretsch name interesting; there's the plethora of unique instruments that were made, as well as the "classy" mystique that was associated with the brand. However, there's also the perception by a lot of folks that the quality control in the Gretsch factory wasn't exactly super-efficient at times. There's a photo in Scott's book of a headstock that has "GERTSCH" inlaid on it, and more than one vintage dealer has told me about how Gretsch necks can vary a lot, even on two instruments of the same model made around the same time. So encountering a classic Gretsch might not be a pleasant experience after all if the neck doesn't feel right; it's happened to me and I bet it's happened to a lot of guitar enthusiasts.

Yet another facet of Gretsch incongruities is also applicable to almost any better-grade, professional quality instrument (*particularly* archtop electrics, in my opinion,) and that involves speculating about the circumstances that put such

a fine guitar into a pawn shop, and why it came out for retail. I've commented about such pawn shop experiences before, and won't get redundant here, but let me add that I wouldn't have any collective guilt about purchasing such an instrument for myself. If someone didn't have his/her act together enough to where a classy instrument like the two Gretsches shown here had to be surrendered, I'd give such instruments a good home if I was interested in 'em. I might *speculate* about

the circumstances concerning such instruments being pawned, but I doubt I'd lose any sleep concerning my acquisition of such an instrument. That may sound a bit blunt and/or elitist to some readers, but I betcha most guitar collectors and enthusiasts that have frequented pawn shops feel this way; i.e., egalitarianism probably doesn't count for too much.

The two instruments shown here have their own incongruities (using Scott's book as reference), and they have a few things in common, according to the pawn shops where I saw each one. Both pawn shops said that they were one-owner instruments; according to the individuals that pawned them, each instrument had been purchased new by that person, who ultimately lost the instrument to the pawn shop. Whether the customers' statements were true or not is pretty much irrelevant in the general scheme of things, though, as far as I'm concerned. Both pawn shops also advised that the guitars had each been pawned on numerous occasions before they were surrendered. One pawn shop didn't know the circumstances surrounding the forfeiture of the instrument; the other stated that a business venture went sour for the pawn customer.

As for the aesthetic incongruities of the instruments themselves:

1957 #6190 STREAMLINER: This year model for the one-inch-narrower, single-pickup sibling of the Country Club would have been the last to feature the Melita bridge and the first to feature the orange and gray Gretsch label inside the f-hole. I got to play this guitar before it was sold, and it was as smooth as silk; the DeArmond pickup sounded exquisite.

1965 #6120 CHET ATKINS: Fits the standard profile of 6120s of that time, complete with painted-on f-holes and a padded back. This ex-

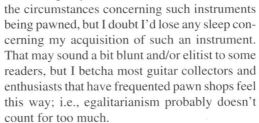

TOP (Left to right): *1957 Gretsch #6190 Streamliner, 1965 #6120 Chet Atkins w/Van Ghent tuners.*

ample has Van Ghent tuners on it, which Scott's book indicates are not often seen. To what extent the value of a 6120 should be raised due to rarer tuners is debatable, of course, and I bet an ad for an instrument like this *would* note Van Ghent tuners. I'd also bet that an ad for this *exact* guitar would note that it has a white case.

I also got to play a 1960 Single Anniversary model (which more or less replaced the Streamliner); in fact, I used to own it, and the action on the Single Anniversary's neck was way too high for me to be comfortable (seems like almost every Single Anniversary I encounter is like that). So there's an example of the quality-control facet, yet the Single Anniversary had its own

(if minor) inconqruity: It had a 1960 serial number but a Hi-Lo 'Tron pickup, which supposedly wasn't introduced until 1961. That's a small bit of hype (which would probably be utilized in marketing such an instrument) in a field that's chock fulla bigger examples of hype.

So on the rare occasions that I'll come across an old Gretsch guitar (or I'm made aware that one has come out of pawn), I'll probably go over it a bit more carefully if I'm able to examine it. Finding extra little incongruities on specific instruments of a brand as diverse as Gretsch is one of the many small bonuses that makes an interest in vintage guitars seem so rewarding at times.

In Search of Mosrite

Jonas Ridge, North Carolina, doesn't even have a stop light, and Semie Moseley's grave doesn't have a headstone.

In 1992, I visited the Mosrite factory in Booneville, Arkansas, some four months after Semie Moseley succumbed to multiple myeloma (bone marrow cancer) at the age of 57. The Booneville facility closed some time later, and since its closure, the survival of the Mosrite guitar brand has once again been the subject of speculation. I spoke with Moseley's widow, Loretta, in 1994 (following the shutdown of the Booneville factory); she advised that she was planning on moving back to Jonas Ridge, and that if anyone asked me about future plans, I should tell them "Mosrite and Loretta Moseley are alive and well." After that conversation, I had no other contact with her.

Some months ago, I was in the Piedmont Triad area of North Carolina (Greensboro, Winston-Salem, and High Point) on business, and when the time came to return to Alabama, I opted to try a different route instead of the usual straight shot down I-85. I knew that Jonas Ridge had been one of the many locations where Mosrite guitars had been made, and I knew that Mosrite's founder, Semie Moseley, was buried there. I figured it would take about three extra hours to navigate the alternate route, find out what I could at Jonas Ridge, then return home via a different interstate until I hooked back up with I-85 around Greenville, South Carolina. Since there were (and still are) many questions about the future of the Mosrite brand, I figured the relative proximity meant the investment in extra time and distance might provide some answers, so I headed west on I-40.

When I visited Booneville, one thing Loretta noted was that Semie had liked that Arkansas community because it reminded him of Jonas Ridge, and I can see why. Both areas are situated in mountainous regions, and the 2-lane roads in the vicinity are winding and inclined, but the slower pace of driving meant that one could observe some natural scenery at a more unhurried pace.

Once I reached Jonas Ridge, I was surprised to discover that it was even smaller than I had imagined. From what I could determine, the main buildings in the community were a general